VIRGINIA BEACH

by

Sally Kirby Hartman

The Insiders' Guide®
An imprint of Falcon® Publishing, Inc.
P.O. Box 1718
Helena, MT 59624
(800) 582-2665
www.insiders.com

•

Sales and Marketing: Falcon Publishing, Inc.
P.O. Box 1718
Helena, MT 59624
(800) 582-2665
www.falcon.com

•

FIRST EDITION
1st printing

•

•

Printed in the United States of America

•

Front cover photo: Virginia Beach aerial, courtesy of Virginia Beach Department of
Convention and Visitors Development; Back photo: Life Saving Museum,
courtesy of Virginia Beach Tourism Corporation;
Banner photos: Olde Towne historic district, courtesy of Portsmouth Convention and
Visitors Bureau; beach umbrellas, courtesy of Virginia Beach Department of Convention and
Visitors Development; fishing boats, courtesy of Eastern Shore Tourism; Inline skaters,
courtesy of Virginia Tourism Corporation; golfers, courtesy of City of Virginia Beach; Spine
photo: Cape Henry lighthouse, courtesy of Virginia Beach Department of
Convention and Visitors Development

•

Publications from *The Insiders' Guide*® series are available at special discounts for
bulk purchases for sales promotions, premiums, or fundraisings. Special editions,
including personalized covers, can be created in large quantities for special needs.
For more information, please contact Falcon Publishing.

ISBN 1-57380-131-3

About the Author

Sally Kirby Hartman

Sally Kirby Hartman first discovered the wonders of Hampton Roads when she moved to Norfolk in 1985. The former mountain dweller from an inland state quickly became a convert to the joys of dining on soft-shell crabs and spending lazy days at the beach.

Sally Kirby Hartman

Photo: Sally Kirby Hartman

She is director of communications for The Norfolk Foundation and a freelance writer who specializes in magazine and public relations work. She formerly was associate editor of *Virginia Business* magazine and editor of *Tidewater Virginian* magazine.

Before becoming a die-hard Virginian, Sally spent most of her life in Arkansas and graduated from the University of Arkansas with a journalism degree. She worked for newspapers in Alabama and Texas before joining the staff of the *Arkansas Gazette* in Little Rock, where for several years she was features editor. Sally, her husband, Ron, and son, Luke, like nothing better than exploring the back roads and historic sites that define the Hampton Roads region. Their favorite family activities include in-line skating along the Virginia Beach boardwalk, going to the beach and playing tennis.

Acknowledgements

There are far too many people involved in this project to thank each one individually. However, you have our gratitude for the information and tips you so eagerly shared. Some of you who have gone the extra mile include photographer Gayle Donovan, Rebecca Cutchins of the Portsmouth Convention and Visitors Bureau, Suzanne Taylor of Virginia's Eastern Shore Tourism Commission, L. Floyd Nock III of Shore Restorations and Designs, Susan Tipton of the Northern Neck Tourism Commission, Mare Carmody of Suffolk, Patricia Rawls of the Business Consortium for Arts Support and Cheryl Cease, co-author of the *Insiders' Guide to Williamsburg*.

Sally would particularly like to thank her husband, Ron, and son, Luke, for their patience, understanding and willingness to explore new places here at home.

Table of Contents

Directory of Maps

GREATER CHESAPEAKE

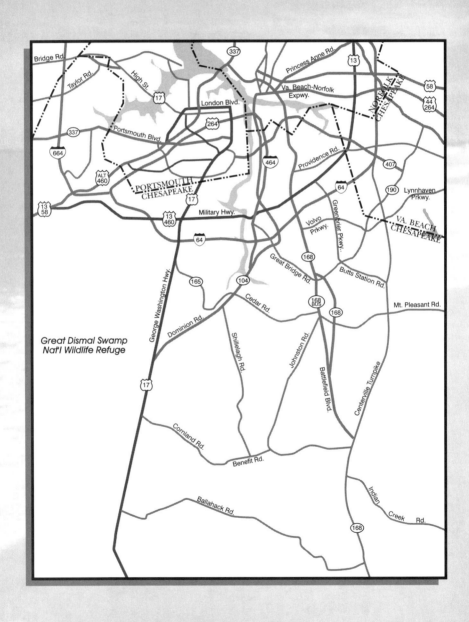

VIRGINIA'S SOUTH HAMPTON ROADS AREA

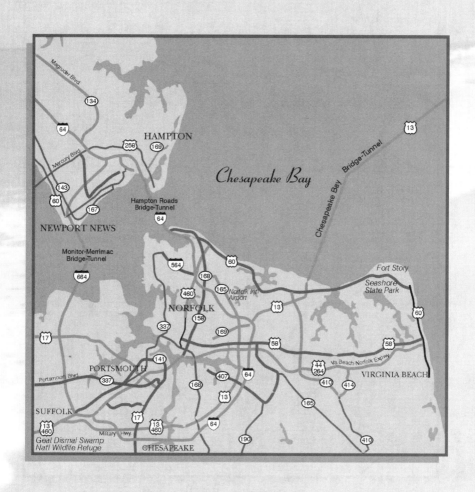

VIRGINIA
BEACH

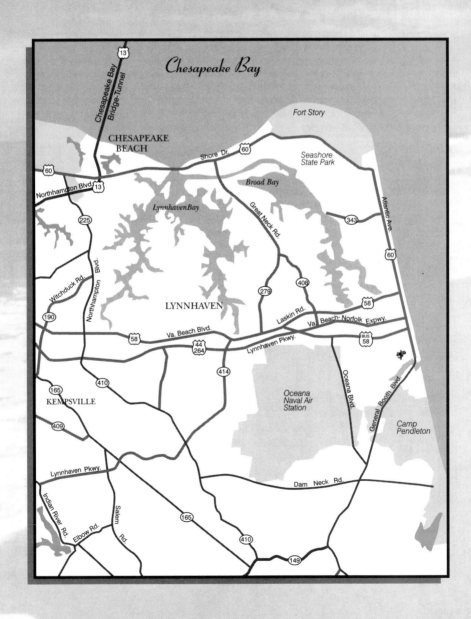

DOWNTOWN NORFOLK

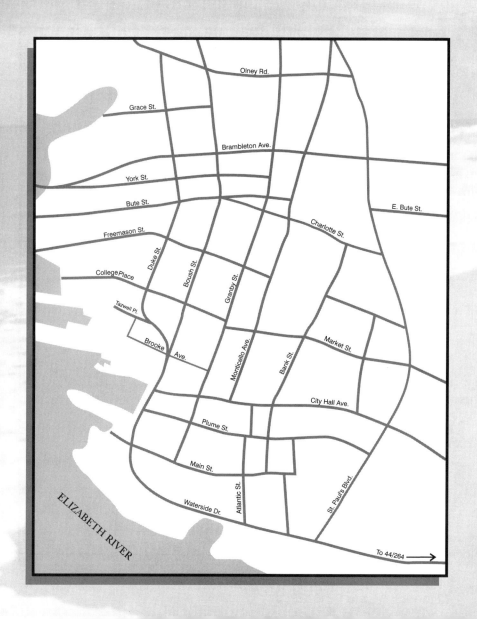

Olney Rd.

Grace St.

Brambleton Ave.

York St.

Bute St.

E. Bute St.

Freemason St.

Charlotte St.

College Place

Duke St.

Boush St.

Granby St.

Tazwell Pl.

Brooke Ave.

Monticello Ave.

Bank St.

Market St.

City Hall Ave.

Plume St.

Main St.

Atlantic St.

Waterside Dr.

St. Paul's Blvd.

ELIZABETH RIVER

To 44/264 →

GREATER
SUFFOLK

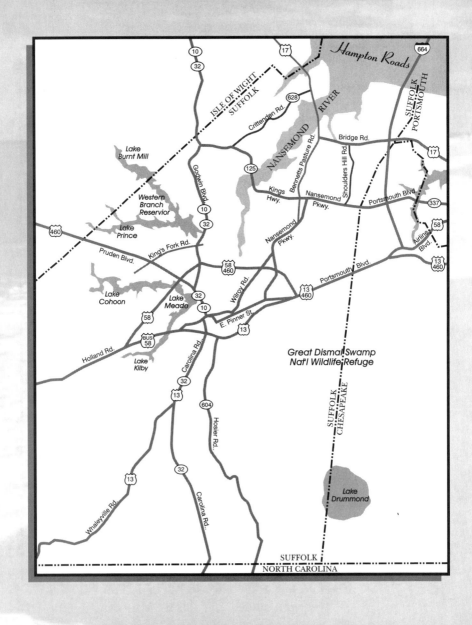

DOWNTOWN
PORTSMOUTH

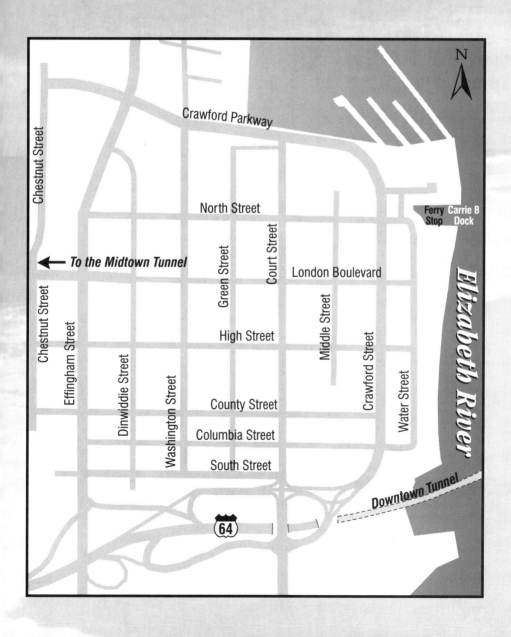

The Cape Henry Lighthouse in Virginia Beach is one example of the fascinating combination of historical and present-day attractions in the Hampton Roads region.

Photo: Courtesy of Virginia Tourism Corporation

Area Overview

Southeastern Virginia surrounds the Chesapeake Bay, one of the country's most ecologically significant resources and one of its most scenic spots. Southeastern Virginia is where the Chesapeake Bay begins its 200-mile journey from the Atlantic Ocean to Havre de Grace, Maryland. From its start near Norfolk and Virginia Beach, the Bay continues a northward journey, providing picturesque shores on both its eastern and western sides and calm waters perfect for boating.

Anchoring the southern end of the Chesapeake Bay is the Hampton Roads region. With both the Bay and the Atlantic Ocean lapping at its shores, this area of beaches and tidal wetlands also happens to be home to more than 1.5 million people.

As a visitor or newcomer to Hampton Roads your mind will be boggled by all the terms you hear to describe this area—Southeastern Virginia, Hampton Roads, Tidewater, Southside, South Hampton Roads and Virginia Peninsula. To add to the confusion, residents often use specific names of the nine cities and six counties that make up this vast region. In recent years a regional tourism marketing campaign has blanketed the East Coast with advertisements for Virginia's Waterfront. That's yet another term for this region.

Ask residents where they're from and you'll get a boatload of answers depending on the circumstances. If they're in Illinois or New York, they'll probably say "southeastern Virginia." If they're visiting Roanoke, Richmond or some other part of Virginia, they might say "Hampton Roads." If the question is asked at the opera, a corporate meeting or elsewhere in the region, the answer is likely to be "Portsmouth," "Virginia Beach" or another specific locality.

All the terminology is accurate. But in today's politically correct times there are some names for this 2,499-square-mile region that are more correct than others.

Geographically, this is southeastern Virginia. Officially, it is the Norfolk-Virginia Beach-Newport News Metropolitan Statistical Area (MSA). This is the 27th most populous MSA in the country and the largest MSA between Washington and Atlanta. Hampton Roads is bigger than San Antonio but smaller than the Milwaukee/Racine metropolitan area. Our population is greater than that of 13 states.

Until 1983 the region was broken into two MSAs—South Hampton Roads and the Virginia Peninsula. The two areas are physically divided by the James River and the body of water known as Hampton Roads. To some extent, residents feel loyalty to one side or the other. However, that is changing as residents live in one city, work in another and shop in a third locality. Although city officials can be pretty territorial about protecting their turf, they are starting to hop on the regionalism bandwagon. In 1996 representatives from 10 area localities formed the Hampton Roads Partnership to plot ways to improve the entire region. Also in 1996, a class of Leadership Hampton Roads, a program that grooms

LOOK FOR:
- Economic Mainstays
- Diverse People
- City Rundown
- Tourist Information

future civic leaders, convinced all area cities to add a new tagline to their city limits signs that proclaims them to be: "A Hampton Roads Community." After initial skepticism, area cities eagerly tacked up the new regional designation.

The politically correct term for this region is Hampton Roads. In the 17th century this name was given to the body of water where the James, Elizabeth and Nansemond Rivers flow into the Chesapeake Bay to form the world's finest deep-water harbor. The name "Hampton" honors Henry Wriothesley, the Earl of Southampton, who supported the colonization of Virginia in the early 17th century.

In past decades, the term "Tidewater" was frequently used for this coastal plain and the adjacent regions that stretch along the York and James Rivers. But in recent years as area cities promoted the region, the name "Tidewater" has been discouraged since it conjures up images of mud flats and brackish water. However, the region's native accent is still called a Tidewater accent. The classic example of this accent is the phrase "out and about the house", in which the first, middle and last words rhyme with boat.

In the 1980s, economic developers began touting "Hampton Roads" as the name for the entire region, which includes Norfolk, Portsmouth, Chesapeake, Suffolk and Virginia Beach on the south side of the Hampton Roads Bridge-Tunnel. To the north are Hampton, Newport News, Poquoson, Williamsburg and the counties of James City, Gloucester and York. In 1993 the MSA expanded to include Isle of Wight County on the south side, Mathews County on the Peninsula, and nearby Currituck County, North Carolina. Since 1990 all the region's mail has been postmarked with "Hampton Roads" rather than the names of individual cities and counties.

For more than a decade, Hampton Roads has ranked second to northern Virginia as the state's fastest growing region. It has six of the state's 10 largest cities, and Virginia Beach is No. 1 in population. Chesapeake in recent years has become one of the country's fastest-growing cities with its array of new neighborhoods, retail centers and industrial parks.

The region, which is crisscrossed by a half-dozen major rivers, feels more unified today than it did 12 years ago. Tunnel crossings link cities separated by rivers, and long-time tolls on roads connecting the cities have been eliminated. The last toll disappeared in 1995. Today it's common for residents to commute to work through a tunnel from Suffolk to Newport News or from Hampton to Virginia Beach. In 1994 another barrier to regionalism fell when long-distance charges were removed between the southside and the Peninsula and Cape Charles on the Eastern Shore. In 1997 the entire region gained its own area code, 757.

To simplify matters for this guide, which concentrates on the five Southside cities, we'll use the names of specific cities if possible. When talking about the region, we'll call it Hampton Roads.

Semantics aside, Hampton Roads is a fascinating, multifaceted area that prides itself on its remarkable history. The earliest recorded mention of the region was in 1607 when the first permanent colonists in the New World landed at Cape Henry in what is now Virginia Beach. Hampton Roads survived occupation during the Revolutionary War and the War Between the States, and it stepped into modern times with quick buildups during World War I and World War II when thousands of military personnel and defense workers came here to work. Many of them liked the area enough to become permanent residents.

INSIDERS' TIP

For quick insight into Norfolk, pick up a copy of "Walking Tours of Historic Norfolk," a brochure produced by the City of Norfolk. Inside is a handy map of significant buildings downtown and in the Freemason and Ghent neighborhoods. The free guide also includes a synopsis of Norfolk's history as well as photos and tidbits about historic structures. Copies are available at the city's Division of Visitor Services, Gen. Douglas MacArthur Memorial, Moses Myers House, Chrysler Museum and d'Art Center.

Economic Mainstays

If there's one thing Hampton Roads is noted for, it is military might. The region's strategic East Coast location has helped it accumulate the world's largest concentration of naval opera-

Mr. Peanut

In 1913 Italian immigrant Amedeo Obici decided to move his fledgling Planters Nut and Chocolate Co. from Pennsylvania to Virginia. He chose Suffolk as a prime location and borrowed $25,000 to finance the relocation.

Obici's new Suffolk processing plant put him in the heart of Virginia peanut country, and Suffolk soon touted itself as "The Peanut Capital of the World."

In 1916 Planters offered a $5 prize to the person submitting the best sketch for a corporate logo. The winner was a 14-year-old Suffolk boy who created a peanut person with arms and crossed legs and labeled it "Mr. Peanut." Later a commercial artist added a monocle, top hat and cane to give the mascot his distinctive look.

Today Planters is owned by RJR Nabisco. The Suffolk plant, whose 500 workers roast and package nuts, is part of the company's Planters Division. Fourteen cast-iron statues of the dapper Mr. Peanut line the fence outside a new plant that opened in 1994. The one built in 1913 was recently demolished. While there is a small museum in the building, it is not open to the public. Mr. Peanut aficionados can check out his memorabilia in a display in the basement of Riddick's Folly, a historic home in downtown Suffolk. It is open 10 AM to 5 PM Tuesday through Friday and 1 to 5 PM on Sunday. Admission is free. There's also a Mr. Peanut statue in the heart of Suffolk at Main and Washington streets.

MR. PEANUT ®

tions. It also has bases representing every branch of the U.S. Armed Forces as well as the Armed Forces Staff College and the headquarters for the North Atlantic Treaty Organization (NATO). The region also has Army, Air Force and Marine bases as well as major Coast Guard operations. Nearly a third of the region's workers earn a paycheck from the Department of Defense or a private defense contractor. It's only been a decade or so since 45 percent of all area paychecks came from the federal government. A more diversified economy has helped bring in new employers.

Mainstays of the economy include shipbuilding and repair, service jobs, tourism and the port. Traditional industries, such as growing peanuts and tonging for oysters, remain the livelihood for some residents. Coal exports are as important to the busy Port of Hampton Roads as they were in the 1890s. These days the area is also a major port for container cargo and products such as grain, tobacco, cocoa beans and rubber.

In recent years new industry has come into the region. There are high-tech Japanese companies in Chesapeake producing industrial gears and copy machine parts. In the past 15 years Hampton Roads has become a hub for the service-oriented fulfillment industry. Various companies use thousands of workers to process credit card transactions, take orders for merchandise and handle insurance claims for some major corporations. The region ranks third in the country in its number of call centers, which handle customer service and sales operations for major companies such as Lillian Vernon, TWA, Avis and Nextel Communications.

Tourism is one of the most important segments of the economy. Each year an estimated 2.5 to 4 million visitors flock here to enjoy the miles of shoreline extending along the Chesapeake Bay and the Atlantic Ocean. Many of them are from other states and Canada. Besides soaking up the sun, visitors can tour a variety of museums and historic homes. They can fish for flounder or sea bass, relax on harbor cruises or exert themselves windsurfing or hiking through nature preserves.

Excellent healthcare is a plus for Hampton Roads. Eastern Virginia Medical School (EVMS) attracts experts in most medical fields, including heart transplants. The medical school has a well-respected in-vitro fertilization program that produced the United States' first test-tube baby in 1981. Researchers at the affiliated Leonard B. Strelitz Diabetes Institutes are hot on the trail of a cure for diabetes. Area physicians, many of whom are on EVMS' faculty, attract patients from around the world for corrective urological surgery, sex-change operations and reconstructive surgery. EVMS is gaining acclaim for its Glennan Center for Geriatrics and the Center for Pediatric Research it operates with Children's Hospital of The King's Daughters.

Diverse People

If you're a newcomer, you'll find plenty of company in Hampton Roads. Most residents have moved here from somewhere else. The region ranks second to Orlando, Florida, in the mobility of its residents. Some of these come-heres are retirees enjoying the good life along the area's waterways. Others are drawn by work at military bases, defense contracting firms or other private employers. During the 1980s the region added nearly 200,000 new jobs, and many workers who came then are still here. Job growth is less manic now but still averages about 1 percent a year.

Interspersed among the newcomers are natives who are fiercely proud of their region and the strides it has made in the past decades to improve itself. Because they're accustomed to the ebb and flow of military personnel, most old-timers quickly accept newcomers.

If you've just moved here, you may be surprised at how readily the Hampton Roads community will welcome your time and talents. The region is filled with tireless volunteers working for everything from the Virginia Opera to Habitat for Humanity. Even before you unpack, you may find yourself recruited to help plan a festival or raise funds for the children's hospital. Getting involved in community work will speed up the process of feeling at home.

Although Hampton Roads doesn't have the ethnic enclaves of Boston or Baltimore, its citizens hail from diverse places, and its military residents have lived all over the world. There are thriving Filipino and Hispanic communities as well as a growing number of residents from India. During the last decade, the region had one of the country's fastest-growing Jewish populations. The 1990 census showed that 68 percent of the region's residents are Caucasian. However, in the last decade the region's African-American population grew slightly faster than that of Caucasians.

Hampton Roads residents are proud of their region and like to tout about what makes it unique. Among the features that give the region bragging rights are that:

Norfolk has the world's largest Navy base.

Portsmouth is home to the world's biggest ship-repair yard.

Suffolk is the Peanut Capital of the world.

The Port of Hampton Roads exports more coal and imports more cocoa beans and rubber than any other United States port.

The United States' first in-vitro baby was born in Norfolk in 1981 with assistance from Eastern Virginia Medical School.

Norfolk is mile zero for the 1,095-mile Atlantic Intracoastal Waterway, which takes boaters on a scenic route to Miami.

With nine underwater tunnels, the region ranks second to Japan as the world leader in traffic tunnels.

City Rundown

Hampton Roads cities pride themselves on their individuality, which sometimes causes them to bicker over issues such as increasing water supplies, developing a light rail system and building a regional sports arena. Although city officials publicly support regional development, they're still looking out for the interests of their individual communities.

Some cities were created centuries ago; others were formed as recently as the 1970s. They run the gamut from urban to suburban and downright rural. Sum up the strengths of the five Southside cities, and you a have a vibrant region with something to offer everyone.

Virginia Beach

With 420,700 residents, Virginia Beach is Virginia's most-populous city. This often surprises visitors focused on the city's resort strip and its 38 miles of Atlantic Ocean and Chesapeake Bay beaches. The city has spent more than $100 million into improving its resort area in recent years and continues to invest in itself to ensure that tourism remains the city's No. 1 industry. However, there's much more to Virginia Beach than waffle houses, T-shirt shops and sunbathers.

Virginia Beach boasts 38 miles of Atlantic Ocean and Chesapeake Bay beaches.

Photo: Courtesy of City of Virginia Beach

Virginia Beach has more office buildings than any other city in the region and also has Lynnhaven Mall, Hampton Roads' largest shopping center. Since this is a city with no traditional downtown, offices and stores have cropped up in suburban office parks. The city has numerous manufacturers and distributors. Stihl chain saws are made here, and Lillian Vernon Corporation ships millions of catalog orders from its mammoth distribution center.

Virginia Beach also maintains its traditional agricultural base. Ride the roads out to Pungo and Sandbridge, and you'll be amazed to learn you're still within the city limits. Stretching for miles are horse farms and fields of soybeans and strawberries. This agricultural heritage dates back centuries before the current city of Virginia Beach was formed in 1963 from the merger of vast Princess Anne County and the tiny resort community of Virginia Beach.

The city is home to The Christian Broadcasting Network (CBN) and its spin-off operations. Rev. M.G. "Pat" Robertson lives on the elegant grounds of CBN, where the "700 Club" show is produced. CBN affiliates include Regent University and a luxury hotel and conference center. Other educational institutions in the city include Tidewater Community College and Virginia Wesleyan College.

Norfolk

The region's oldest city dates back more than 300 years. During the past decade Norfolk has seen decaying waterfront warehouses replaced by The Waterside Festival Marketplace as well as hotels, parks, attractions and new office buildings. In 1991 Norfolk gained a new 23-story Marriott hotel and adjacent convention center. In 1993 Harbor Park baseball stadium opened to much acclaim as the new home of the Triple-A Norfolk Tides. In 1994 the city finished the $52 million National Maritime Center (Nauticus). Three years later it added a branch of Tidewater

Community College to the main downtown street. In 1999 MacArthur center, a gigantic downtown shopping mall, opened with luxury stores Nordstrom's and Dillard's as its anchors. That prompted a slew of new restaurants and shops on streets surrounding the mall. In 2000 the city is bringing the retired battleship Wisconsin to a new home next to Nauticus, where it is expected to be a big tourism draw.

Norfolk, with a population of 221,500 is Virginia's second-largest city. Its downtown is the region's financial hub. Within a two-block radius are regional headquarters for all the major banks in the state. One of the gleaming downtown high-rises is headquarters for Norfolk Southern Corporation, whose rail lines run through much of the United States and Canada. Old Dominion University (ODU), Virginia Wesleyan College, Eastern Virginia Medical School and Norfolk State University (NSU) have their campuses here. Norfolk International Terminals is the state's largest marine terminal.

The city is home to Norfolk Naval Base, the world's largest Navy base. Norfolk is also the region's cultural core and is headquarters for the Virginia Symphony, Virginia Stage Company, Virginia Opera and numerous smaller arts groups. On the weekends, Norfolk is one of the region's most fun places to be with free festivals and other events scheduled on about 100 days of the year. Most are held at Town Point Park, adjacent to The Waterside Festival Marketplace.

Portsmouth

With nearly 100,000 residents, this is one of the region's most charming cities. The Olde Towne Historic District adjacent to downtown has the largest collection of historic homes between Alexandria, Virginia, and Charleston, South Carolina. Portsmouth has more houses on the National Register of Historic Places than any other Virginia city.

Adjacent to the restored 18th-century neighborhood is several museums, including a delightful one for children. A double-decker ferry regularly churns the waters between downtown Portsmouth and The Waterside, across the river in Norfolk. The downtown area is in the midst of a revitalization that includes a new waterfront hotel to open by 2001 and an outdoor performing arts center.

The federal government is the main employer in Portsmouth. The Norfolk Naval Shipyard, the world's largest ship repair yard, is here. Also in the city is the Portsmouth Naval Hospital,

Portsmouth's 85 miles of navigable waterway make it a haven for boaters.

Photo: Courtesy of Portsmouth Convention and Visitors Bureau

the Navy's first hospital. In 1999 the Navy completed a $154 million expansion of what was already the largest Navy hospital on the East Coast. Portsmouth also has a major Coast Guard installation and a branch of Tidewater Community College.

In addition to government operations, Portsmouth has the Portsmouth Marine Terminal and a strong manufacturing base.

Chesapeake

Once the site of the East Coast's largest plant nursery, Chesapeake has been Hampton Roads' boomtown during the past decade and is one of the country's fastest-growing cities. Although Chesapeake maintains a strong agricultural base, in recent years it has sprouted subdivisions, shopping malls, office parks and manufacturing plants. To keep pace with all the new houses going up in family-oriented neighborhoods, Chesapeake has become Virginia's fastest-growing school district.

Like Virginia Beach, the city of 193,900 does not have a traditional downtown. Its business hubs are clustered around exits off Interstate 64. Two manufacturers have their North American headquarters in the city. Sumitomo Machinery Corporation of America, makes industrial drives, while Volvo Penta North America produces marine engines. Sumitomo is one of several Japanese manufacturers with plants in Chesapeake. Japan's giant Mitsubishi Corporation has three operations in the city. Chesapeake has more foreign companies than any other city in the region. The city also has numerous distributors and service companies. Among the largest is Household Finance Corporation, which has its East Coast processing center in Chesapeake.

Chesapeake has two shopping malls—Greenbrier and Chesapeake Square. As a shopping hub, it keeps adding new retail centers and restaurants, primarily along roadways near the malls. The city has a branch campus of Tidewater Community College. Popular recreational areas in Chesapeake include the Great Dismal Swamp National Wildlife Refuge and Northwest River Park.

Old and new lighthouses stand together at Cape Henry.

Photo: Virginia Division of Tourism

Suffolk

With 430 square miles, Suffolk is Virginia's largest city in land mass. The city is renowned for its peanuts, which flourish in its rich soil, and hails itself as "The Peanut Capital of the World." The peanut is the backbone of the city's long-standing agribusiness sector, which includes several shelling companies and some large peanut processors. Planters Peanuts started in the city—as did its mascot Mr. Peanut. Planters, a major employer, makes peanut snacks. The peanuts it roasts gives Suffolk a pleasant aroma.

Besides peanuts, Suffolk manufacturing plants produce Lipton tea and Hills Brothers coffee. One of Suffolk's main employers is a gigantic distribution center that ships merchandise for

QVC, the country's largest TV home shopping channel. Suffolk also has a branch of Paul D. Camp Community College.

Suffolk, which has 61,800 residents, maintains a traditional downtown. It's also a hot spot for residential development in outlying areas near the Monitor-Merrimac Memorial Bridge-Tunnel that opened in early 1992. The tunnel links Suffolk with Newport News, and developers have created a variety of neighborhoods on land near the tunnel. In most years Suffolk leads other cities in percentage increase in residential building permits.

Tourist Information

Various cities in the region run their own convention and tourism bureaus, which are happy to provide you with plenty of brochures. While they focus on their specific localities, most bureaus will also steer you toward attractions in neighboring cities.

For information on Virginia Beach call (800) 822-3224 and order a visitors packet. For hotel reservations, call (800) VABEACH. If you're in the city and want immediate information, stop by the Virginia Beach Visitor Information Center at 2100 Parks Avenue, (757) 437-4888. You can't miss it if you are entering the city on the Virginia Beach-Norfolk Expressway (I-264), since the center sits in the middle of the divided road. The center is operated by the city's Department of Convention and Visitor Development as a gateway to the resort. It is open 9 AM to 5 PM daily with longer hours during the summer. Besides having hundreds of brochures and a staff to answer questions, the center has a short video. It also can help with hotel reservations.

INSIDERS' TIP

The region is blessed with a mild climate that makes a beach stroll a pleasant post-dinner activity even at Thanksgiving and Christmas. There are four distinct seasons but rarely drastic extremes in temperature. The average January temperature is 40 degrees. The August average is 78 degrees.

If you want more specifics on Norfolk, call the Norfolk Convention and Visitors Bureau at (757) 368-3097 or (800) 368-3097. There are three offices run by the Norfolk Convention and Visitors Bureau. Two are in Downtown Norfolk—on the first floor of MacArthur Center mall and in Nauticus, the National Maritime Center. The MacArthur Center bureau is open daily the same hours as the mall, usually 9 AM to 9 PM. The bureau in Nauticus is open the same hours as the science center, usually 10 AM to 5 PM everyday but Sunday when it is open from noon to 5 PM.

There's also a Norfolk visitors center just off Interstate 64 (Exit 273) in the Ocean View area of Norfolk near the Hampton Roads Bridge-Tunnel. It is open from 8:30 AM to 5 PM daily, (757) 441-1852. The center is stocked with brochures and has a helpful staff to answer questions.

For information on Portsmouth call the Portsmouth Convention and Visitors Bureau at (757) 393-5327 or (800) PORTSVA. To pick up brochures stop by the Portsmouth Visitor Information Center on the banks of the Elizabeth River downtown. It is operated by the Convention and Visitors Bureau and is on Crawford Street between North Street and Harbor Court. The North Landing Visitor Center is open from 8:30 AM to 5 PM daily, (757) 393-5111. You'll also find a sampling of brochures available weekdays from 8 AM to 5 PM at the Convention and Visitors Bureau at 505 Crawford Street in Downtown Portsmouth.

In Chesapeake and Suffolk your best bets for information are the local Hampton Roads Chamber of Commerce offices. They are at 1001 W. Washington Street in Suffolk, (757) 539-2111, and 400 Volvo Parkway in Chesapeake, (757) 547-2118.

Getting Around

Welcome to Hampton Roads, where getting from place to place requires going under, over, around or—in the case of a thunderstorm—through water.

During many of these travels, you'll encounter the magic number 64. The Virginia Department of Transportation has given that suffix to all the major highway connectors of the area. Interstate 64 is like a wheel that circles Hampton Roads, and it has many spokes. I-464 is a quick, usually desolate, shot between Norfolk and Chesapeake. I-664 is a connector between I-64 and the Monitor-Merrimac Bridge-Tunnel to the Peninsula—a great alternative when the Hampton Roads Bridge-Tunnel is congested. I-564 zips you from I-64 to the Naval Base, and I-264 takes you from the heart of Downtown Norfolk to I-64, the expressway to the Virginia Beach oceanfront. Once upon a time, you had to shell out a quarter to travel the full length of the expressway. Although the tolls were removed in 1995, some older Insiders still call the expressway "the toll road," so don't let this expression throw you.

While our bridges, tunnels, major arteries and interstates have undergone extensive renovation and expansion in recent years, it is still wise to know the best times to venture out, especially if you're heading for major shopping centers or beaches. Because this is home to the largest military installation in the country, it is common wisdom to avoid base traffic (particularly around Norfolk Naval Base) during rush hours. Heavy traffic rushes to the base from 6 to 8 AM and from the base from 3 to 5 PM. The same congestion periods hold for all tunnels connecting Norfolk to Portsmouth and Hampton and for certain neighborhoods, such as Kempsville, that are home to lots of military and civil service folks.

LOOK FOR:
• Outsmarting The Traffic
• Following The Native Customs and Laws
• Let Someone Else Do The Driving
• The Resort Strip
• Airports
• Train Service
• Travel By Water

INSIDERS' TIP

Witchduck Road in Virginia Beach is named for the city's most infamous former resident—Grace Sherwood. Nicknamed the Witch of Pungo, she was tried in 1706 for witchcraft. After she failed to sink during a dunking in the Lynnhaven River, she was deemed to be a witch and was jailed.

Outsmarting The Traffic

Travelers headed for the base or the Hampton Roads Bridge-Tunnel and points west can avoid some congestion by finding a friend to carpool with and using the HOV-2 lanes. These lanes span the distance from Virginia Beach and Chesapeake to the Norfolk Naval Base and the I-64 entrance to the tunnel and were expanded in 1998 to include downtown Norfolk. The median on I-64 between the I-64/I-264 interchange and

I-564 has been designated for vehicles with two or more persons headed westbound to the Naval Base in the morning, eastbound in the afternoon. Readerboards along the interstate system alert you to the traffic direction of the reversible lanes. One caveat: entries and exits are limited, so unless you're headed to or from the Norfolk Naval Base or the Hampton Roads Bridge-Tunnel, sticking to the regular interstate with the masses might be your best option. All the details of using the HOV-2 lanes are available from the Virginia Department of Transportation, (757) 925-2584.

If you're traveling alone or to a destination other than the base or the tunnel, you'll have to contend with regular traffic woes unless signs say the lanes are open for all traffic. Helpful automated signs along the interstate will alert you to pending backups and direct you to alternate routes.

You can also avoid snarls by listening to the radio. Most local stations are diligent in reporting backup alerts during rush periods; 530 AM, the state-operated station, broadcasts updates all day, though the signal doesn't carry too far beyond the interstate. For information anytime, day or night, you can also call (800) 792-2800. The Hampton Roads Bridge-Tunnel information line can be reached at (757) 640-0055, and is updated frequently. A good rule of thumb is to call just before heading to a tunnel to check on traffic snarls.

Following The Native Customs and Laws

The rules of the road in Hampton Roads are simple and straightforward. Seat belts are required for all vehicle occupants, and children younger than 4 or who weigh less than 40 pounds must be secured in a child-restraint or booster seat. Throughout Virginia, a right turn on a red light after stopping is permitted unless otherwise indicated. It is against Virginia law to cut through a parking lot to avoid a traffic light or stop signal. You'll just have to wait your turn like the rest of us.

Revelers should take note of a new law dealing with drunk driving. Police can take away—on the spot and for seven days—the licenses of any drivers who test drunk or refuse to take the roadside alcohol test. According to Virginia law, that standard applies to anyone who measures .08 or higher on the breath test. More than 4,000 drivers lost their licenses, at least temporarily, during the first year this law was on the books. If you've been drinking, ride with a friend or call a cab.

Finally, newcomers with a fear of merging should know that traveling on Hampton Roads' interstate system can be quite a thrill, due to our diabolically designed entries and exits. Some entrance ramps have pretty short merge lanes. The best way to counter this lack of lane is to wait until you have a decent-size opening and enter the right-hand lane at a fast clip.

INSIDERS' TIP

In an annual write-in poll, the readers of *Port Folio,* a local weekly lifestyle magazine, voted Shore Drive as our worst speed trap. Shore Drive cuts through the tall pine trees of First Landing/Seashore State Park, at the North End of the Virginia Beach resort area. It's a beautiful road, but it has no lights, few guardrails and narrow shoulders. Drivers need to be careful on it, particularly at night. Those little crosses you see at the edge of the trees indicate the sites of fatal accidents.

Let Someone Else Do The Driving

To avoid traffic trauma, you can always put someone else behind the wheel. Our local bus service, Hampton Roads Transit (HRT), can scoot you anywhere in the Southside area for $1.50 cash or a $1 ticket. For interstate-weary military folks, HRT offers an Express Bus service with spanking-new buses to zip you to the Norfolk Naval Base from several convenient Park & Ride locations, including Greenbrier Mall, Indian River Shopping Center and Timberlake Shopping Center. A call to (757) 222-6100 can get you the complete schedule and pickup points.

If charm, not speed, is your fancy, get a ticket to ride on one of HRT's summertime trolleys. You can hop aboard for a trip along five Virginia Beach routes ($.50 to $1.75), take a tour through historic Norfolk or Portsmouth ($3.50) or get an Insiders' look at Naval Station Norfolk ($5). Full information and trolley tokens are available at HRT booths at The Waterside in Norfolk, at the Portsmouth Visitors Information Center in Old Towne, at 24th Street and Atlantic Avenue in Virginia Beach, or at the Naval Station Norfolk Tour and Information Office at 9079 Hampton Boulevard in Norfolk. A $3.50 trolley pass offers up to three days of unlimited rides on HRT's Virginia Beach trolleys.

HRT also operates a pedestrian ferry that travels across the Elizabeth River, from The Waterside in downtown Norfolk to two stops in downtown Portsmouth. It's a wonderful way to get from one city to the other; you can see both waterfronts plus huge ships in dry dock. Ferry fare is $.75 for adults and $.50 for children younger than 12, and you can catch a ride every 30 minutes from either city, seven days a week. Hours are 7 AM to 10 PM Monday through Thursday; 7 AM to midnight Friday; 10 AM to midnight Saturday and 10 AM to 10 PM Sunday. The summer start-up hours are the same with runs ending about 11:30 PM every night. For $9 visitors can buy a three-day HRT pass that allows unlimited use of the ferry, beach trolleys and HRT tours. A $26.50 pass includes all that plus admission to the Children's Museum of Virginia in Portsmouth, The Chrysler Museum and Nauticus in Norfolk and the Virginia Marine Science Museum in Virginia Beach.

In downtown Norfolk hop on the free NET buses that travel through the downtown area. The free electric buses are city owned and operated. They run from early morning to late night.

Finally, if you're headed to someplace a little off the beaten track, a taxi may be the answer. But unless you're at the airport, don't expect to find one waiting at the curb for your fare. In Hampton Roads you have to summon a taxi by telephone, so plan on adding enough time for them to arrive. Companies are listed in the Yellow Pages. Charges average an initial $2.50 plus $1.25 for each mile thereafter.

INSIDERS' TIP

Here's a quick way to tell newcomers from Hampton Roads natives: Just ask them to pronounce the name of area cities. OK, Virginia Beach and Chesapeake are pretty easy, but Norfolk, Portsmouth and Suffolk can trip you up if you're not careful. Norfolk is pronounced naw-fik. If you go calling this city Nor-folk, that's a dead giveaway that you're not from here. Portsmouth is ports-muth. If you hear someone calling it porch-muth, you will have found a bona fide native who's lived here a lifetime. For Suffolk, say suff-ik instead of Suf-folk. Like Norfolk, this is a city whose name should be said quickly.

GETTING AROUND

The Resort Strip

It may not be Rodeo Drive—the retail shops stock mainly T-shirts, suntan lotion and saltwater taffy—but Insiders are pretty proud of the way the Virginia Beach resort strip looks these days. In recent years, the City of Virginia Beach has spent millions of dollars improving Atlantic Avenue. Streets and sidewalks have been widened, power lines are now underground and new landscaping presents an inviting vista to both pedestrians and the auto-bound. For the summer of 2000 beachgoers were greeted with a new, wider boardwalk with a separate path for bikers and inline skaters.

Although some visitors like to drive up and down the resort strip to see what's going on, they should remember that it is illegal to do this. Called "cruising," this activity is a favorite of the young and the dateless, who want to show off their hot wheels and check out their fellow travelers and pedestrians at the same time. The problem was that cruising became such a popular way to see the beach that Atlantic Avenue became a virtual gridlock on many summer nights. Not too safe—emergency vehicles couldn't get through— and definitely not environmentally friendly. So now cruising is a no-no. Traffic cops will be delighted to autograph a ticket for you if you travel past a traffic-control point twice in the same direction within a three-hour period. The cruising law is in effect from 2 PM to 4 AM, April 15 through

INSIDERS' TIP

Get a peek at traffic trouble spots without actually being there by checking out one of two websites that show photos of traffic jams. The Virginia Department of Transportation has 38 cameras working at critical spots along major roadways. The photos are on GoHamptonRoads.com and HamptonRoads.com

September 30, from 1st to 31st streets. Signs are clearly posted along the violation area, lest you forget. If you want to do the strip, walk, hop a trolley bus or rent a bike from one of the many rental stands.

In fact, a bike is a great way to get around the resort area. From 1st to 40th Streets, The Boardwalk offers a special bike path to peddlers. From there, you just need to cross over to Pacific Avenue to pick up a residential bike path that runs north to 50th Street, where the feeder roads begins. This paved street runs parallel to Atlantic Avenue for the latter's entire length.

Airports

Norfolk International Airport
Norview Ave., Norfolk
• (757) 857-3351

Situated right next to our lush, green Norfolk Botanical Garden, Norfolk International Airport provides a beautiful entry to the Norfolk/Virginia Beach area. Norfolk International is just 6 miles from downtown Norfolk and 15 miles from the Virginia Beach oceanfront, so getting from the airport to your destination is quick and relatively painless.

More than 3.4 million passengers passed through electronic surveillance at Norfolk International last year. Most major carriers serve the airport, and you can hop a most affordable nonstop flight to Atlanta, Baltimore, Boston, Charlotte, Chicago, Cincinnati, Dallas-Fort Worth, Detroit, Nashville, New York, Phila-

delphia, Raleigh-Durham, Richmond, St. Louis, Tampa and Washington, D.C.

The airport recently wrapped up a $10 million renovation of its lobby that added branches of local restaurants. Now it is adding a $116 million arrivals terminal and parking garage that should be complete by 2002. Military travelers may want to stop by the Military Welcome Center operated by the Armed Services YMCA. This is a lounge with a television and free coffee and soft drinks. Outside in the main lobby is a military information booth that has a staff person on duty who will also answer questions from civilians.

If you must park at the airport, there are two multilevel, covered parking garages, one open lot for long-term parking and short-term open lots at both arrival and departure sides of the terminal. Overall, there are 4,000 spaces, so the parking nightmare typical of many other large airports just isn't a factor here. Expect to pay $1 an hour up to a maximum of $14 for short-term, $.75 an hour up to a maximum of $5 per day for long-term. If you're lucky enough to find a curbside parking place, meters ask for $.25 for 10 minutes. Cars with handicapped license plates park free for up to four hours.

If you're without personal transportation, taxis circle like vultures at the arrival side of the terminal, so you shouldn't have any trouble hailing one. The cost is about $18 to Down-

The Elizabeth River Ferry is a pedestrian ferry crossing the Elizabeth River between Portsmouth and Norfolk.

Photo: Courtesy of Portsmouth Convention and Visitors Bureau

town Norfolk and about $25 to the oceanfront in Virginia Beach. Taking the Norfolk Airport Shuttle costs about $11.50 to Downtown Norfolk and $15.50 to the oceanfront. To find a shuttle from the airport, check at the glassed-in booth in the median outside the baggage claim area. Some hotels also offer courtesy

It's easy to get around by bicycle in the oceanfront area of Virginia Beach.

Photo: Courtesy of City of Virginia Beach

transportation to and from the airport; you might check on this when you make reservations. If you do need to make specific arrangements, here are a few numbers:

Norfolk Airport Shuttle, (757) 857-1231
Beach Taxi, (757) 486-4304
Norfolk Checker Taxi, (757) 855-3333
Yellow Cab, (757) 460-0605, 622-3232, 399-3077
Black & White, (757) 489-7777
B&W Cabs of Chesapeake, (757) 543-2727
Groome Transportation, (757) 857-1231
Celebrity Limousine Service, (757) 853-5466
Executive Car Service, (757) 622-7441
Atlantic Beach Limousine, (757) 471-0068
Hollywood Limousines, (757) 481-9333

Chesapeake Municipal Airport
1777 West Rd., Chesapeake
• **(757) 421-9000**

Owned and operated by the City of Chesapeake since 1979, this small airport is just south of Great Bridge and is capable of handling small jets on its 4,200-foot runway. The facility is open to the public every day from 8 AM to sun-

down and has 100-octane, low-lead jet fuel. Pilots arriving after hours can call the number above 24 hours a day to make suitable arrangements.

Mid Eastern Airways (FBO) is responsible for the operation of the facility, which offers charter, flight school and major maintenance. Hangar space and rentals are also available, with a small pilot's lounge with all the basic layover amenities. Pilots, take note: the identifier is W36, and there is no landing fee.

Hampton Roads Airport
5192 W. Military Hwy., Chesapeake
• **(757) 488-1687**

With two asphalt runways and four reciprocals, Hampton Roads Airport offers runways from 3,500 to 4,000 feet. Mercury Flight Center is at this general-aviation airport in Chesapeake just past Bowers Hill off South Military Highway. Flight school, maintenance, hangar facilities and tie-downs are available. The airport is attended from 8 AM to 5 PM daily and until 8 PM in the summer; runways are lighted from dusk to dawn. It has 100-octane, low-lead fuel. The identifier is PVG, and no landing fee is required.

Suffolk Municipal Airport
200 Airport Rd., Suffolk
• **(757) 539-8295**

This city-owned airport, which started in 1943, is on the outskirts of Suffolk. Three runways are in operation; two at 5,000 feet and one at 3,600 feet. Hours of operation are 8 AM to 8 PM from April through October and from 8 AM to 5 PM the rest of the year. There are hangars, tie-downs and a maintenance facility as well as 100-octane low-lead and jet-A fuels. The airport's identifier is SFQ. The number above is available 24 hours a day. There is no landing fee.

Train Service

Amtrak
9304 Warwick Blvd., Newport News
• **(800) 872-7245**

Service to Washington, D.C., includes daily departures at 8:45 AM, plus second departures Friday and Sunday at 4:30 PM. Service to Richmond departs every Friday at 10:30 PM.

Amtrak operates shuttle buses to help travelers from Virginia Beach and Norfolk reach the train station in Newport News. Shuttles leave daily from the corner of 19th and Arctic streets in Virginia Beach at 6:50 AM and from 700 Monticello Avenue (the Hotel Norfolk) in Norfolk at 7:20 AM. Shuttle reservations can be made by calling Amtrak.

Travel By Water

The Atlantic Intracoastal Waterway

There's more to Hampton Roads travel than gridlocked interstates and congested tunnels. You can escape it all when you travel on water. It may not be as quick as land or air travel, but it certainly is one of the greatest pleasures of living in this region of river, ocean and bay.

Connecting the area to destinations north and south are the Dismal Swamp Canal and the Albemarle & Chesapeake Canal, which form alternate routes along the Atlantic Intracoastal Waterway between the Chesapeake Bay and Albemarle Sound. The Atlantic Intracoastal Waterway provides pleasure boaters and commercial shippers with a protected inland channel between Norfolk and Miami, Florida.

The Dismal Swamp Canal, the oldest operating artificial waterway in the United States, is on the National Register of Historic Places as a Historic Landmark and is noted as a National Historic Civil Engineering Landmark. It is the primary course for recreational craft making a lazy journey from Deep Creek in Chesapeake down to the Pasquotank River in Elizabeth City, N.C., which in turn spills out to the Albemarle Sound. If you travel this route (along with the Yankee rich and famous steering their boats to warmer climates in fall and the reverse come springtime), be sure to stop at the Mariner's Wharf city docks for a visit with the famous Rose Buddies, Elizabeth City's self-appointed welcoming committee for visiting cruisers. For more information on the Great Dismal Swamp, see our Parks chapter.

The second headwater canal is the Albemarle & Chesapeake, primarily used by commercial vessels. It weaves through the locks at Great Bridge out to the less protected waters of Currituck Sound and on through the locks at Coinjock, North Carolina, to the Albemarle Sound.

Both canals and the rest of the waterway are maintained by the U.S. Army Corps of Engineers. When navigating these waters, you should have both bow and stern lines ready when going though any locks, and reduce speed to eliminate wakes when approaching, motoring through or leaving the locks and bridge structures. You should also stay on the lookout for natural hazards, such as submerged stumps, rocks or logs.

For more information, including charts and available anchorages, contact the U.S. Army Corps of Engineers in Norfolk at (757) 441-7641.

Elizabeth River Ferry

For a quick and fun trip between Portsmouth and Norfolk, ride the Elizabeth River Ferry. The ride takes about five minutes and costs $.75 for adults and $.50 for children. Board at High Street in Portsmouth or The Waterside Festival Marketplace in Norfolk. The passenger ferry runs continuously. It is operated by Tidewater Regional Transit.

Water Taxis

For quick trips around Virginia Beach, call the Virginia Beach Water Taxi at (757) 481-9200. The taxis run during warmer months.

HarborLink Ferry

If you're traveling between Norfolk and Hampton, the HarborLink passenger Ferry offers a scenic way to beat the traffic. The ferry runs numerous times daily between Nauticus in downtown Norfolk and the Hampton Visitor Center in downtown Hampton. During the day it departs each stop about every two hours. It also runs until the wee hours on Friday and Saturday nights. Call (757) 722-9400 for information. The cost is $5 one way for adults, $3 for children. There's also a $20 ticket that gives admission to the Virginia Air and Space Center in Hampton and Nauticus in Norfolk.

> **INSIDERS' TIP**
> For the ultimate taxi ride try one of two water taxis. Ocean Marine Water Taxi transports passengers on demand between Portsmouth and Norfolk. Call (757) 391-3000. Virginia Beach Water Taxi operates along the Virginia Beach waterfront. Call (757) 481-9200.

The Chesapeake Bay Bridge-Tunnel

No discussion of the waterways of Hampton Roads would be complete without a mention of the Chesapeake Bay Bridge-Tunnel, acclaimed one of the Seven Wonders of the Modern World. Considered the world's largest bridge-tunnel complex, it consists of more than 12 miles of trestled roadways, two mile-long tunnels, two sets of bridges, almost 2 miles of causeway, four man-made islands and 5.5 miles of approach roads, totaling an absolutely amazing 23 miles.

The bridge-tunnel connects Southside Hampton Roads to Virginia's Eastern Shore, and those headed north to New York can save 95 miles and one and a half hours by taking a ride across the mighty surge of the Atlantic Ocean and the waters of the Chesapeake Bay. If it is your first trip across the span, you might just want to add those hours back into your itinerary and stop off at the first island for a snack at the Sea Gull Restaurant, a walk down the busy fishing pier, or to snap up a T-shirt at the goodies-packed souvenir and gift shop.

Emergency road service is available, and there are call boxes every half-mile. One-way crossing toll is $10.

A second set of bridges that parallel the first span was completed in 1999. For information about the bridge-tunnel, call (757) 331-2960.

GETTING AROUND

History

Water and war. These two factors are intertwined in the history of Virginia Beach, Norfolk and the neighboring cities of Portsmouth, Chesapeake and Suffolk. Since the 17th century, this region's location on the Chesapeake Bay and the Atlantic Ocean has made it a prime trading partner with the world. However, having one of the world's finest deepwater harbors has pushed Hampton Roads into being a key player in every war from the Revolutionary War to the Persian Gulf conflict of 1990.

Until April 26, 1607, this wooded coastal plain, commonly known as Hampton Roads, was home to about 18,000 Native Americans. The Algonquin, the Nansemond and the Chesapeake tribes thrived on oysters and fish harvested from the ocean, the Bay and its many tributaries as well as on crops sprung from rich soil. On that spring day in 1607 the Indians' world changed when three small ships carrying 104 Englishmen led by Adm. Christopher Newport sailed to what is now Cape Henry in Virginia Beach. Twenty-eight explorers ventured ashore, fell to their knees and thanked God for carrying them safely to land. That night they were attacked by the Chesapeake Indians.

The next day the newcomers hiked for 8 miles, frightening Native Americans tending a smoldering fire. The explorers raked aside coals and sampled their first delicacy in this new land—roasted Lynnhaven oysters. The third day the group ventured about 50 miles to Jamestown Island in search of a protected harbor and fresh water. There they established the first permanent English settlement in America. They later returned to hammer a wooden cross at their landing spot at Cape Henry, where the Chesapeake Bay flows into the Atlantic Ocean.

Capt. George Percy, a member of the expedition, wrote of his first encounter with Virginia, "There we landed and discovered fair meadows and goodly tall trees with such fresh water running through the woods so I was almost ravished at the first sight thereof."

Although illness and the lack of fresh water in Jamestown caused settlers to move to other locations nearby, the British found Virginia's land was so abundant that they eagerly granted colonists 100 acres each to establish plantations. By 1634 Virginia was divided into eight counties, and several settlements had sprung up along the region's riverbanks. Within four years smaller counties were created. Suffolk fell into Upper Norfolk County, which became Nansemond County a few years later. The rest of South Hampton Roads ended up in Lower Norfolk County, which later yielded Princess Anne County, Norfolk County and several cities. By 1703 Virginia had a population of 60,606 living in 25 counties. Norfolk County had 2,279 residents; neighboring Princess Anne County was home to 2,017 people.

Norfolk was chartered in 1682 when 10,000 pounds of tobacco was paid to Nicholas Wise Jr. for 50 acres to lay out a town. Norfolk, which became a borough in 1736, is the region's oldest city. Suffolk was incorporated along the Nansemond River in 1742. Portsmouth, across the Elizabeth River from Norfolk, officially became a town in 1752 when founder Col. William Crawford set aside 65 acres for a community named after the famous English seaport. Virginia Beach, Chesapeake and the modern city of Suffolk are the region's newest municipalities. Virginia

Beach and Chesapeake were created in 1963 by merging large counties with smaller towns. The current city of Suffolk was formed in 1974 by blending a smaller town of Suffolk with vast Nansemond County.

In the 17th and early 18th centuries, tobacco was the mainstay of the local economy. Farmers grew the cash crop along the region's numerous rivers, cured it and shipped it overseas from their private wharves. By 1736, foreign trade had helped make Norfolk the largest town in Virginia, with 1,000 residents. Thirty-three years later its population had swelled to 6,000.

During this time pirates plagued the region by plundering ships coming into the port. The most famous was Blackbeard, who used Virginia Beach as his headquarters as he trolled the waters for treasure. Local legend has it that he was later killed just across the water from Norfolk in Hampton where his skull resided on a pole in public for decades until it was stolen.

In 1763 George Washington surveyed land in what is now Chesapeake and Suffolk for the Dismal Swamp Land Co. He dug the first spade of dirt to create a canal through the Great Dismal Swamp, a 200,000-acre wilderness area.

As the region's prominence as a world port grew, local docks bulged with turpentine, cheese, corn, lumber and other products awaiting export. In addition to Europe, the region had a thriving trade with the West Indies. In 1767 Andrew Sprowle, a merchant and shipbuilder, started Gosport Shipyard near Portsmouth. By the late 1700s three-fourths of Portsmouth's landowners worked in the maritime trade as merchants, shipwrights or other craftsmen.

Revolutionary War

The region's harbor and its proximity to Williamsburg, meeting site of the First Continental Congress in 1774, made it an important player during the Revolutionary War. Since Virginia had the strongest navy of the 13 original colonies, this area's harbor was vital to winning freedom for the colonies.

That fact wasn't lost on the British. In November 1775 Lord Dunmore, the last royal governor of Virginia, captured Portsmouth and boasted that Norfolk was defenseless. Less than a month later, the British were defeated at the Battle of Great Bridge, near the current site of Chesapeake's City Hall. Lord Dunmore's only victory had already come during a battle at Kempsville in 1775, in what is now one of Virginia Beach's most populous neighborhoods.

New Year's Day 1776 was the most fateful day in Norfolk's history. In the afternoon British soldiers opened fire on the city and continued their assault for 11 hours. With the wind whipping flames, two-thirds of the city was destroyed. By the end of February, colonists had torched the rest of Norfolk. The government of Virginia ordered the second burning to prevent sheltering Lord Dunmore and his soldiers. Of more than 1,300 Norfolk buildings only the brick walls of St. Paul's Church remained. Even they were marred by a cannon ball wedged in one side. Norfolk held the dubious distinction of being the most devastated community in the Colonies during the Revolutionary War.

To try and protect the harbor, in early 1776 the Commonwealth of Virginia ordered the construction of Fort Norfolk. Across the Elizabeth River from Fort

At one of the many historical homes in the Olde Towne Historic District in Portsmouth re-enactors take part in a living portrayal. This particular home was built in 1775.

Photo: Courtesy of City of Virginia Beach

Norfolk, the Commonwealth also established Fort Nelson in Portsmouth. In times of likely invasion, soldiers ran a giant chain across the harbor between the forts to snare enemy ships.

During the war the Gosport Shipyard in Portsmouth was one of the busiest places in the colonies. The British burned the yard in 1776 but the colonists quickly built new wharves and scaffolding so they could produce war ships. Although the British were routed from Hampton Roads by the burning of Norfolk in 1776, they returned in 1779 and took over Portsmouth. They promptly proceeded to ransack homes and burn ships anchored in the harbor. Suffolk also was burned in 1779 during a raid that originated in Portsmouth. Traitor Benedict Arnold set up headquarters in Portsmouth in 1781 before moving 50 miles away to Yorktown with Lord Cornwallis, who surrendered there a few months later.

After the war, the region started the arduous task of rebuilding. Former residents were aided by European immigrants, many of them merchants, who saw opportunity in America. Within a few years Norfolk regained its role as a major world port. Suffolk came alive when it was designated as a port of delivery in the Customs District of Norfolk and Portsmouth.

INSIDERS' TIP

American Beer and Ale—a Handbook of Facts and Figures credits this region with having one of the first batches of brew ever made in the New World. A letter that dates from 1587 talks about a member of Sir Walter Raleigh's "lost colony" brewing ale in what is now Virginia Beach.

During this time of reconstruction several major projects were built. The Cape Henry Lighthouse, which had been started before the Revolutionary War, was completed in 1791 under orders from President George Washington. Today the Virginia Beach landmark is the oldest public works project in the country. In 1794 the federal government took over Gosport Shipyard, although it didn't actually buy it until 1801. The yard later was named the Norfolk Naval Shipyard even though it was located in Portsmouth.

In 1795 Congress authorized Washington to build a new fort in Norfolk to protect the harbor, and the government paid 200 pounds of sterling for the dilapidated Fort Norfolk. Permanent brick buildings were constructed around 1810 in anticipation of another war with the British. The region had rebounded from the Revolutionary War when trade restrictions imposed because of the War of 1812 torpedoed foreign trade.

Prosperity began returning to the area. In 1825 there was great fanfare in the region when the Marquis de Lafayette, the French general who had aided the country during the Revolutionary War, visited here as part of his farewell tour of 24 states. By 1851 the Norfolk and Western Railway had laid track in the region and managed to put a roadbed through the Dismal Swamp.

But the good fortune was not to last. In June of 1855, mosquitoes carrying yellow fever and breeding in the hold of a steamer from St. Thomas escaped and wreaked havoc, particularly upon the populations of Portsmouth and Norfolk. Within two months all business in Norfolk stopped. Hotels, homes and warehouses were turned into hospitals as up to 100 residents a day died. Donations flowed in from around the world to help the yellow fever victims. During the plague, only one ship was allowed into the harbor, and its sole cargo was coffins. When those ran out, residents were buried in boxes or blankets sometimes in mass graves. By the end of the plague four months later, 2,000 were dead in Norfolk—one-third of the population. In neighboring Portsmouth yellow fever killed more than 1,000 residents.

At War Again

The region again flexed its military muscle during the War Between the States. On April 12, 1861, it didn't take long for news to arrive that the Confederates had fired on Charleston's Fort Sumter. That day the Confederate flag was raised at the blockhouse on Craney Island near Portsmouth. On April 17, Virginia became the eighth state to secede from the Union. Three days later Union soldiers fled the Navy yard in Portsmouth, burning buildings and 11 warships as they escaped.

One of the first battles was the little-known Battle of Sewell's Point in May 1861. There were no fatalities as local Confederates skirmished with Federal troops stationed across the water at Fort Monroe in what is now Hampton.

By November 1861 more than 20,000 Confederate soldiers were stationed in Portsmouth at the Navy yard, which was at work on eight Confederate vessels. The most famous was the ironclad CSS *Virginia*, which was forged from the partially burned hull of the USS *Merrimac*. The *Merrimac's* historic battle of the ironclads with the USS *Monitor* took place March 9, 1862, in the

Seeing History

It's easy to actually see and experience Hampton Roads' history. By using this book to plan a series of outings and daytrips, you can soak up nearly 400 years of important events. Both the Attractions and Daytrips chapters contain numerous ideas for historic trips. The following are some of our favorite places to visit time after time:

Cape Henry - This is the spot where the region's first settlers landed in 1607 before moving on to settle in Jamestown. A cross and overlook mark the spot. Cape Henry

is on the Fort Story Army base along the Atlantic Ocean and Chesapeake Bay. A driver's license should gain you admission during the daytime. Nearby is the Old Cape Henry Lighthouse, commissioned by President George Washington. The whole base is a vintage World War I post. (See our Attractions chapter for details.)

Jamestown - Take your choice of the federally owned Jamestown Island or the state-run Jamestown Settlement. Children will probably prefer the Jamestown Settlement, with its reproduction of an Indian village and settlers' ships. True history buffs will want to see the actual island where an archeological dig is uncovering parts of the original fort. Both places are well-worth your time. (See our Daytrips chapter for details.)

Colonial Williamsburg - This is where the seat of Virginia's government moved after Jamestown. The 173-acre historic area is devoted to re-creating as accurately as possible Colonial life around 1776. To make the most of Colonial Williamsburg, spring for the year-long Patriot's Pass that allows unlimited admission. Less-extensive tickets—and even a free stroll along the main streets—also help you soak up the ambiance. (See our Daytrips chapter for details.)

St. Paul's Church - This classic 1739 building was the only structure left standing in Norfolk after the Revolutionary War. It still carries a battle scar - a cannonball wedged in one brick wall. This quiet downtown spot with its fascinating burial ground will magically transport you back to the early 19th century. (See our Attractions chapter for details.)

Yorktown - Once again, you can choose between federal and state facilities. Both

The Old Cape Henry Lighthouse (foreground) in Virginia Beach was commissioned by President George Washington and was the country's first federal public works project.

Photo: Courtesy of City of Virginia Beach

do an excellent job of relating this town's critical role as the surrender site at the end of the Revolutionary War. The federal Yorktown Battlefield includes an excellent museum and a drive through battlefields. The state-run Yorktown Victory Center tells the Revolutionary War story through the eyes of ordinary citizens of the time. Outside the museum are a re-created army camp and a typical Virginia farm from the period. (See our Attractions chapter for details.)

Fort Norfolk - This fort along the Elizabeth River near downtown Norfolk was authorized by President George Washington in 1794. Most of its buildings date to 1810, when it was rebuilt. The federally owned fort is home to the Norfolk Historical Society, which usually opens it during warmer months on Sunday afternoons. It's a favorite site for Civil War re-enactors, who invite the public to their weekend events. (See our Attractions chapter for details.)

Military Museums - It's impossible to talk about Hampton Roads' history without emphasizing the role the military has played in the region. To get a sense of the military's importance visit the Hampton Roads Naval Museum inside Nauticus in downtown Norfolk. Operated by the U.S. Navy, this free museum highlights naval history from 1799 to today. In Portsmouth, the Portsmouth Naval Shipyard Museum showcases the work of the Norfolk Naval Shipyard, the country's oldest shipyard. In Newport News the Virginia War Museum will show you Virginians' roles in all wars, starting with the Revolutionary War. The museum includes an outstanding collection of military recruitment posters. Added to the lineup of museums in 1998 was Portsmouth's Museum of Military History. (See our Attractions and Daytrips chapters for details.)

Historic Houses -There's great diversity among the houses typically open for tour. Your choices range from the 1680 Adam Thoroughgood House in Virginia Beach with its simple English cottage style to the ornate Hunter House Victorian Museum in Norfolk built in 1894. In between is the 1787 Moses Myers House, which is the only one in the country to concentrate on Colonial Jewish customs. The Francis Land and Lynnhaven houses in Virginia Beach give a glimpse of daily life in the early 18th century. (See our Attractions chapter for details.)

waters between Norfolk and Hampton. Four hours later the *Monitor* retreated to Fort Monroe, the last Union stronghold in Hampton Roads. Later that year the *Merrimac* ran aground at Craney Island and was blown up by its crew. Fourteen years later its hull was salvaged and hacked up with a few pieces remaining as relics. The *Monitor* sank off the coast of North Carolina a few months after its famous battle. Recently salvagers have brought up parts of the ship and brought them to the Mariners' Museum in Newport News for restoration and display.

In May 1862, the Confederates ordered residents of Portsmouth, Suffolk and Norfolk to evacuate. They burned the Portsmouth Navy Yard to save it from federal troops landing at Ocean View, a Chesapeake Bay community that is now part of Norfolk.

At the start of the war, Suffolk was a training ground for Confederate soldiers from Georgia and South Carolina. But soon the town was occupied by Union soldiers, just like nearby Norfolk and Portsmouth. This was a humiliating time for these three cities. Federal troops ransacked homes and forced ferry passengers to trample on the Confederate flag.

After Confederate Gen. Robert E. Lee surrendered in Appomattox in 1865, the Hampton Roads area began the arduous task of reconstruction. There was no money in Portsmouth's treasury, and the city's Navy yard was in shambles. Norfolk's buildings were once again dilapidated, and the city's foreign trade was nonexistent. There were only 300 residents left in Suffolk, which had boasted a population of 1,395 in 1860.

In the two decades after the end of the war, the region did an about-face. Brick three-story buildings soon lined the streets of downtown Norfolk as carts loaded with oysters, chickens and other provisions rolled toward the city's many hotels and popular farmer's market. Steamships regularly called on the port, and a new rail line linked the city with distant parts of the country.

Although cotton was the main export commodity after the war, that changed in 1883 when the Norfolk and Great Western Railway shipped its first load of coal from western Virginia to Norfolk. To keep pace with demand, the railroad built a new coal pier at Lambert's Point in Norfolk. In 1886 the railroad brought in 504,153 tons of coal. By 1889 trains were hauling more than 1 million tons into Norfolk. At Lambert's Point workers loaded coal on ships bound for overseas or other parts of the United States.

Two other railroads—the Chesapeake & Ohio and the Virginian—also hauled coal into Norfolk and Newport News, making Hampton Roads the world's largest coal port. A constant line of coal trains became a common sight for local residents.

During this period, the town of Virginia Beach also witnessed major changes. In 1880 a wooden clubhouse was built at 17th Street and the oceanfront to entice beachgoers. Three years later a railroad line from Norfolk to Virginia Beach provided an easy way for city dwellers to get to the new Virginia Beach Hotel, which held 75 guests. Soon steamers were transporting vacationers down the Chesapeake Bay from as far away as Washington, D.C., and Baltimore.

In 1887 the hotel was enlarged to hold 400 and renamed the Princess Anne Hotel. The luxury resort boasted electric lights, elevators, saltwater baths and the top bands of the day. Guests included Presidents Benjamin Harrison and Grover Cleveland, inventor Alexander Graham Bell and actor Lionel Barrymore. The hotel burned in 1907, was replaced in 1922 and burned again in 1955.

INSIDERS' TIP

Norfolk's most prized possession is its sterling silver mace that stands 41 inches high. The ceremonial symbol of power was made in England and presented to the Borough of Norfolk in 1754 by Virginia's Lt. Gov. Robert Dinwiddie. During both the Revolutionary War and the Civil War local residents hid the mace to protect it. In the late 1800s it was misplaced and found broken in a back room of the city police station. Today the repaired mace is on permanent display in The Chrysler Museum.

By 1888 leading Norfolk area citizens had begun building large cottages with sweeping verandas along a new boardwalk on the beach. In 1906 Virginia Beach incorporated as a city and continued growing as a resort with the opening of Seaside Park Casino. The resort was renowned for its Peacock Ballroom, which bragged it had the largest dance floor on the East Coast. During the 1920s and '30s the lively resort featured such well-known band leaders as Tommy Dorsey, Duke Ellington and Cab Callaway. Their bands drew big crowds for the ballroom's popular 10 cent dances (or three for $.25).

Jamestown Exposition

One of the biggest national events of the early 20th century was the Jamestown Exposition, held near Norfolk in 1907 to commemorate the 300th anniversary of the settlement of Jamestown. The Exposition site was 340 acres at Sewells Point, 10 miles from downtown Norfolk. Local organizers, who had raised $1 million in stock to help fund the Exposition, spent several years erecting a minicity on marshland and pastures. To celebrate the event, 21 states built replicas of famous buildings such as Independence Hall in Pennsylvania and the Old State House in Massachusetts. Entire halls were devoted to manufacturing, transportation and art.

The Exposition opened April 26, 1907, with a 100-gun salute as President Theodore Roosevelt arrived on the *Mayflower*, the presidential yacht. During a parade 14,000 soldiers saluted Roosevelt, who called the event the greatest military pageant witnessed in the country since the Civil War.

Although foreign dignitaries converged on the Exposition during its seven-month run, the elaborate event was not financially successful. A decade later, just months after the start of World War I, the Exposition site was included in 474 acres purchased by the federal government for $1.2 million. Its destiny was to become Norfolk Naval Base—the world's largest Navy base. Its development started with $1.6 million allocated in 1917 to build piers and buildings. About 20 of the original Jamestown Exposition buildings are still in use on the Navy base.

World War I

In 1914, as the world stood on the brink of war, the Army took over 343 acres of Cape Henry to build Fort Story in what is now Virginia Beach. Fortified with 16-inch howitzers, during

HISTORY

World War I, Fort Story along the Atlantic Ocean was known as the "American Gibraltar." It was considered the Atlantic coast's most strategic heavy artillery fortification. As the Army expanded onto surrounding land, the fort's prominence continued to grow.

The impending world war first touched Portsmouth in 1915 when two German ships were interred in the city. After war was declared in 1917 the Navy yard saw unprecedented growth as three dry docks, four destroyers and a battleship were built. In 1919 shipyard workers converted a collier into the Navy's first airplane carrier. To keep pace, thousands of workers from throughout the country flooded the city. The city's naval hospital, established in 1827 as the Navy's first hospital, quickly expanded into the largest naval hospital on the Atlantic coast. In 1915 Portsmouth had a population of 38,000. By 1918, it was home to about 57,000 residents. At Norfolk Naval Shipyard, employment surged from 2,700 before the war to 11,234 in 1919.

Norfolk also experienced dramatic growth during the war. Within a month in 1917 a training camp for 7,500 soldiers had been completed at the old Jamestown Exposition site. After hastily erecting barracks, warehouses and mess halls, the Navy built a bulkhead, dredged channels and filled in enough areas to add 300 acres to the Navy base. Within a year the base had added a submarine base, landing fields for airplanes and dirigibles, and hundreds of buildings.

Like Portsmouth, Norfolk also had an influx of workers from throughout the country. Besides the military, Norfolk gained numerous private manufacturing plants. In 1910 the city's population was 67,452. By 1920 it had swelled to 115,777.

World War I gave a great boost to the region's port. With northern ports in New York and other large cities unable to handle increased demand, Norfolk and nearby Newport News filled the gap. Their proximity to the Atlantic and eight area rail lines attracted an endless parade of ships from throughout the world. They came primarily for the coal that arrived day and night from West Virginia. Other export commodities included tobacco, cotton and seafood. Norfolk's port also was used heavily by the Naval Overseas Transportation Service, which sent 288,000 soldiers and their provisions to France.

The postwar years were a jolt for the region as it recovered from the days of heady prosperity. To keep solid economic footing, Norfolk residents approved a $5 million bond issue in 1922 that created a grain elevator and terminal. The city built a modern downtown farmers market that cost $500,000. It annexed 27 square miles of adjacent land, including the Navy base and Ocean View resort area.

During the Great Depression, which started in 1929, the region weathered the economic slowdown with help from the Navy. Naval operations gave Norfolk's economy a $20 million a year boost. The port also held its own; when coal exports plummeted, sugar exports picked up the slack. In Portsmouth a drop in employment at the Navy yard after World War I was offset by jobs modernizing 15 Navy ships. The 2,538 workers the yard had on the payroll in 1923 had grown to 7,625 by 1939.

Virginia Beach continued to court the resort trade with the completion in 1927 of The Cavalier, a luxury resort near the oceanfront. Agriculture was the mainstay of what is now Chesapeake, while peanuts and lumber remained the backbone of the economy in Suffolk.

World War II

Once again thousands of workers descended on the region during World War II. The Norfolk Naval Shipyard payroll jumped by more than 36,000 workers from 1939 to 1943 as nearly 1,000 workers a month joined the war effort. Employment reached a record high in 1943 with nearly 43,000 workers. To make room for the construction of the 101 ships and landing craft the yard turned out during the war, it expanded from 352 acres to 746 acres in Portsmouth. During the war, the Navy yard did nearly $1 billion in business—half of it going for workers' wages.

INSIDERS' TIP

Suffolk is the site of 408 significant archeological sites dating back 10,000 years. Most are along the Nansemond River or the edge of the Great Dismal Swamp.

In Virginia Beach and neighboring Princess Anne County, three military bases were added and a fourth was consolidated from smaller operations. The Army leased a Virginia National Guard rifle range to start Camp Pendleton. The Navy built the Oceana air base and the Dam Neck base, which today handles data systems and missile operations. In 1945 the Navy merged four smaller bases into the Little Creek Amphibious Training Command. Off the coast of Virginia Beach, German U-boats patrolled the coast and occasionally sunk Allied ships.

During the war the region benefited greatly from the $12 million the Navy earmarked for construction at the Navy base and the Navy yard. Wooden buildings slapped up during World War I were replaced with solidly built brick and stone structures.

By 1941 apartments and houses were going up faster than they had in the past 20 years. The federal government, the Navy, the Norfolk and Portsmouth housing authorities and private developers all hustled to build new homes. Although Norfolk had two new high schools, they quickly overflowed with military dependents. Some schools had to operate in shifts. City buses, restaurants and hospitals filled to capacity, and Norfolk had to quickly expand its water supply. Norfolk was a prime example of wartime overcrowding.

From 1940 to 1944 Norfolk's population swelled by 44,000. As defense workers searched far and wide for housing, adjacent Norfolk County added more than 40,000 new residents. Portsmouth gained 13,000 residents; Princess Anne County grew by 5,000.

Although shipbuilding and ship repair were the area's claim to fame during the war, the region's fertilizer plants, furniture manufacturers and other industries also were expanding. During the war, the threat of German U-boats off the coast torpedoed much of the area's commercial foreign trade. But the port made up for that by shipping tanks, bombs and other military supplies to Europe and North Africa.

The Moses Myers House was the home of the first Jewish residents to come to this region and is the only museum in the country to feature programs on Jewish life in Colonial times.

Photo: Courtesy of Virginia Department of Tourism

HISTORY

Postwar Years

After World War II—the fifth major war to have an impact on the region—thousands of wartime workers stayed in Hampton Roads. To keep from falling into a postwar slump, city leaders started aggressively modernizing the region. Norfolk initiated a campaign to annex neighboring counties, a move frequently met with opposition by people living near the land-hungry city.

Intercity transportation was a key issue during postwar years. Ferries still connected many parts of the region. To speed car travel, the Elizabeth River Tunnel opened in 1952 between Norfolk and Portsmouth. The success of the region's first underground roadway led to another tunnel between the two cities in 1962. In 1957 Norfolk linked to Hampton via the new Hampton Roads Bridge-Tunnel. At the time its 6,860-foot tunnel was the longest of its type in the world.

As marvelous as those accomplishments were, they paled in comparison to the Chesapeake Bay Bridge-Tunnel. Construction on the 17.6-mile roadway began in 1961. It took three and a half years before Virginia Beach was linked with the isolated Eastern Shore of Virginia. For drivers the bridge-tunnel cut 90 minutes off the drive from Virginia Beach to New York. The feat cost $200 million and required two mile-long tunnels, three bridges, four man-made islands and a causeway. The bridge-tunnel is considered one of the seven wonders of the modern world. Several years of construction added two new bridges to the tunnel complex that were completed in 1999.

Mergers were major news in the early 1960s as large counties and small cities struggled to

24 •

HISTORY

INSIDERS' TIP

Norfolk Public Library's Sargeant Memorial Room is a treasure trove for genealogists and others doing historic research. The room is in Kirn Memorial Library in downtown Norfolk, (757) 664-7323. Among the holdings are census records for six states and the District of Columbia, 20,000 old Norfolk photos, maps, history books and area birth and death records.

combat Norfolk's annexation mania. As a result, in 1963 the resort town of Virginia Beach annexed rural Princess Anne County and instantly became a city of 125,000. The same year South Norfolk merged with agricultural Norfolk County to form Chesapeake. In 1974 Suffolk merged with Nansemond County to create the new larger city of Suffolk. The mergers left south Hampton Roads with five cities and no counties and signaled a new era of growth and prosperity.

In recent years the region's history has been shaped by the rejuvenation of Norfolk and Portsmouth and the coming of age of Virginia Beach, Chesapeake and Suffolk. In the 1960s civic leaders banded together to create Eastern Virginia Medical School. The state's third medical school opened in 1973 in Norfolk and is in the heart of a burgeoning medical center that includes two hospitals and several research institutes affiliated with the medical school.

During the 1970s and early 1980s dilapidated buildings along Norfolk's downtown waterfront were razed to make way for The Waterside Festival Marketplace, Town Point Park, elegant condominiums and Dominion Tower. The National Maritime Center (Nauticus) and Harbor Park baseball stadium now anchor either end of the rejuvenated waterfront, which is slated to gain the retired Navy battleship Wisconsin as a tourist attraction by 2001. A mile away blocks of substandard housing were torn down to create the upscale Ghent Square area. Nearby turn-of-the-century homes in Ghent attracted new residents eager to restore their splendor. Today the city is committed to the revitalization of Park Place, a low-income urban neighborhood, and Ocean View, whose hodgepodge of homes, motels and businesses occupy prime property along the Chesapeake Bay. In 1997 a downtown branch of Tidewater Community College opened along what once was the city's premier retail street. The MacArthur Center, a $300 million downtown shopping mall, was completed in 1999 after three years of construction.

Through the years Portsmouth, which has one of Virginia's largest collection of historic homes, has worked to ensure the preservation of Olde Towne. To complement this historic district, the city has gone through major improvements since the 1970s. In 1998 it turned a former department store into an expanded Children's Museum of Virginia. Recently it has enhanced its downtown

Water is the defining feature of our geography, and our transportation system reflects that.

Photo: Courtesy of Portsmouth Convention and Visitors Bureau

business district with wide brick sidewalks, period lighting and landscaped road dividers. A Renaissance hotel and conference center are slated to open on the waterfront by early 2001 and a new performing arts center should be completed later the same year.

In the late 1980s Virginia Beach joined the revitalization movement with a nearly $100 million face-lift in its resort area. The effort added miniparks, attractive lighting, benches and landscaping along Atlantic Avenue and the 2.9-mile oceanfront boardwalk. The city has continued its efforts within the past year by investing in a new outdoor entertainment amphitheater and by tripling the size of the Virginia Marine Science Museum by widening and improving its oceanfront boardwalk.

A record of the first landing at Cape Henry, "set up a Crosse at Chesupioc Bay, and named Cape Henry, Prince of Wales." is remembered by a monument.

Photo: Courtesy of Virginia Tourism Corporation

In Chesapeake, Virginia Beach and Suffolk, which are blessed with many miles of farmland, the emphasis has been on new development during the past few decades. Agriculture remains important to the cities, whose major commodities include peanuts, soybeans, strawberries and hogs. However, the temptation to sell the family farm has turned many former fields into subdivisions and office parks in the past decade.

The entire region was an economic hotspot during the early 1980s when federal spending was on the upswing. With the military rapidly expanding, eager defense contractors moved in to do business and thousands of workers left tougher economies for the greener pastures of Hampton Roads. As a result neighborhoods, shopping centers and office parks sprung up across the land as the region added 200,000 new jobs during the 1980s.

Development moves at a less manic pace today as the region works to balance its economic prosperity with preservation of its environment. Water still plays a vital role in shaping Hampton Roads' history, as does war. During the Persian Gulf War in 1990 and 1991 more than 40,000 military personnel left the region for the Middle East. In addition, thousands of civil-service workers and employees of area defense contractors also headed to the Persian Gulf. Half the warships in the Gulf were homeported here. When the war ended, the region celebrated with enthusiastic homecomings that harked back to World War II as bands, banners and tearful relatives welcomed home their heroes.

Today Hampton Roads' heritage is still visible despite the area's high-rise office towers, interstate highways and suburban homes. Its economy, although greatly diversified in recent years, remains rooted in the military and the port. Tourism, which started along the Virginia Beach oceanfront in the late 19th century, is a cornerstone of the region's economy. And peanuts still give identity to Suffolk.

Like Hampton Roads' early explorers, many newcomers land here because of the area's proximity to the Atlantic Ocean and Chesapeake Bay. They like what they see and decide to make it their home.

HISTORY

Accommodations

Price Code

Accommodations will be listed in various categories by city, along with a code ranging from one to five dollar signs based on the typical daily rates for a standard room with two double beds. Keep in mind that, come resort or holiday time, these rates may take a considerable hike, so be sure to confirm your price prior to making your reservations.

$	Less than $40
$$	$40 to $60
$$$	$61 to $75
$$$$	$76 to $100
$$$$$	$101 and more

Pull right up—your room's waiting! If you're traveling for pleasure, it's a pretty sure bet that you're headed for one of our oceanfront or bayfront hotels. Travelers with business on their minds are drawn to the hotels circling our major business districts, such as Downtown Norfolk or the Newtown Road corridor in Virginia Beach. And, if you're in town to visit family or friends lacking a guest room, you're likely to unpack in a comfortable, moderately priced suburban motel right around the corner.

If you're pillow counting, there are more than 20,000 hotel and motel rooms in which to rest your weary head in Hampton Roads. More are on the way as Virginia Beach plans for two new luxury hotels on the oceanfront and area cities add hotels to keep up with a booming tourism business. Right now Virginia Beach alone boasts 11,000-plus hotel rooms. The range of accommodations is nearly as great, from econo-boxes to luxury high-rises, mega conference centers to charming bed and breakfast inns. Your particular destination will dictate which of the many brand-name or independent alternatives you target.

Pick your destination and pick your price. Because of the area's ownership of miles of beautiful beaches along the Chesapeake Bay and Atlantic Ocean, demand for beachfront accommodations is heaviest during the summer season, with rates adjusted upward accordingly. On average, however, rates throughout the area take the big swing from a low of about $40 per night all the way to $300 for a drop-dead luxury suite. Your pocketbook, and your need to be pampered, will be your deciding factor, especially if you're planning an extended holiday.

As in any other part of the country, if you are planning a peak resort-time or holiday visit, advance reservations with deposit are definitely a must. On summer weekends and holidays, many hotels require a two- or three-day minimum stay for confirmed reservations, so plan accord-

Downtown Norfolk has several hotels to accommodate the business travelers and tourists who visit the area.

Photo: Courtesy of Norfolk Conventon and Visitors Bureau

ingly. Payment with plastic is the general rule, since it is a rare establishment that will accept a personal check (including restaurants). So pack heavy with credit cards, cash or traveler's checks. Unless otherwise noted, the establishments listed in this chapter accept major credit cards.

If your plans should change, make certain that you are aware of your chosen hotel's cancellation policy. Some require at least a 72-hour notice for a change in reservation dates, and up to seven-day's notice for complete cancellation. Ask about specific rules and refund policies when making your initial reservations.

While it's impossible to list every accommodation in the area in this guide, we'll highlight those hotels and motels that are not only local favorites for out-of-town visitors, but also generally applauded by the business community for both amenities and consistency of guest service.

Also note the weekly rental possibilities in cities where beach properties are available for extended family vacations. These are often privately owned, fully furnished and appointed homes, ready to move into for a week or two of beachy relaxation.

For assistance in selecting the hotel/motel property that best suits your visiting needs in Virginia Beach, call (800) VA-BEACH for advice, availability and specific rate information.

Virginia Beach

Now you're talking hotel rooms. From the ocean to the Bay, central business district to the suburbs, Virginia Beach uses more hotel-issue bed linens than any city in Hampton Roads. To help you decipher between the 122 choices, we'll divide the city into hotel-heavy areas, oceanfront, Chesapeake Bay and out there in the suburbs.

Almost all of these properties offer free in-room cable TV, refrigerators and microwaves, but you should confirm availability early, especially in peak resort or holiday season. Every on-premise restaurant features a pendulum swing of choices, all constantly changing. Most of the properties along the boardwalk area are

within a short stroll of gourmet, casual and convenience dining, with fresh seafood the predominant bill of fare year round. When you're shellfished-out, you'll find excellent alternatives for beef, Italian, Caribbean, Mexican and good old Southern food.

Oceanfront/Resort Area

Angie's Guest Cottage
$$$ winter, $$$$$ summer
• **302 24th St., Virginia Beach**
• **(757) 428-4690**

Whether you opt for the Bed & Breakfast, Lacy Duplex or American Youth Hostel, there's no doubt that Angie's is unique in this sweep of high-rise towers and glitzy motels. Built in the 1900s, the original house was used to accommodate the families of surfmen stationed at the U.S. Coast Guard Station, now the Life-Saving Museum of Virginia. Both Barbara Yates and her mom, Garnette, answer to the name "Angie" and roll out a warm welcome in rooms scented with fresh flowers and breakfasts of breads, fruit and cheeses served on the cozy front porch. The hostel, affiliated with Hostelling International-American Youth Hostels, offers five dormitory rooms. Strict rules on no alcoholic beverages and a "quiet period"—read curfew—apply. Angie's usually closes in the winter.

The Atrium Resort Hotel
$$$ winter, $$$$$ summer
• **315 21st St., Virginia Beach**
• **(757) 491-1400, (800) 96-SUITE**

You'll run right into The Atrium as you shoot down 21st Street off the Norfolk-Virginia Beach Expressway. Every room in the 90-room hotel is a good one because every one is actually a two-room suite with a fully equipped kitchen, perfect for whipping up a hearty breakfast on a family vacation. Someone with a lot of class designed the indoor pool and Jacuzzi, evidenced by the comfy sofas in a true atrium where you can linger to watch the splashing swimmers. What's really great is a tanning room that allows you to go home glowing even if the weather's not cooperative.

INSIDERS' TIP
Be your own tour guide with *Tales of Tidewater, Virginia, and Tour of Virginia Beach, Virginia.* It's a 78-minute audiocassette that takes you on a self-directed driving tour of historic and modern Virginia Beach. Snag one for $8.95, including a map, at the Virginia Beach Visitors Information Center at the foot of the Expressway.

ACCOMMODATIONS

Barclay Cottage Bed and Breakfast
$$$$ • 400 16th St., Virginia Beach
- **(757) 422-1956**

Step back in time at this bed and breakfast a few blocks from the oceanfront. There are only five guest rooms in this restored historic inn. Guests can start their day with a full breakfast. This is not the place to bring the young ones since the cottage caters to grown-ups. It usually closes in winter.

Barclay Towers
$$$$ winter, $$$$$ summer
- **9th St. and Oceanfront, Virginia Beach**
- **(757) 491-2700, (800) 344-4473**

Each of the rooms in this oceanfront hotel is a two-room suite with a kitchen. Feeling like the proverbial 98-pound weakling? Stop by the weight room for a work out and steam bath. Kids younger than 18 stay free here.

Belvedere Motel
$$$$$ • 36th and Oceanfront, Virginia Beach
- **(757) 425-0612, (800) 425-0612**

Here's a hot Insider tip: on Saturday and Sunday mornings, the coffee shop of this hotel is a hangout for hungover North-enders, who don ballcaps and sunglasses to recuperate with pancakes and scrambled eggs. Those less impaired by night-before blues often cycle up the bike path from home. The hotel has 50 units; request an efficiency if you don't want to brave the crowds of the coffee shop at breakfast. It usually closes in winter.

Best Western Beach Quarters
$$$$$ • 3rd St. and Atlantic Ave., Virginia Beach
- **(757) 437-1200, (800) 645-8705**

Situated at the south end of resort area, this hotel is close to lots of good stuff: Rudee Inlet, with its fishing charters, Jet Ski rentals and seafood restaurants; The Virginia Marine Science Museum; Ocean Breeze Fun Park, and of course, the beach! You can get a standard room or an efficiency with a fully-equipped kitchen.

Best Western Oceanfront
$$$$$ • 1101 Atlantic Ave., Virginia Beach
- **(757) 422-5000, (800)631-5000**

You can choose a room or a suite, with a balcony that overlooks the ocean. If you're anticipating a stressful vacation, request a room with a whirlpool tub. Then relax with a cold beer or iced tea under the awning of the out-door cafe and watch the world go by. Believe us, it will.

Super 8 Boardwalk Inn
$$$$ • 2604 Atlantic Ave., Virginia Beach
- **(757) 425-5971, (800) 777-6070**

While not perched over the ocean, the Boardwalk Inn boasts amazingly spacious rooms and efficiencies, with thick, squishy carpet that welcomes bare feet. Each of the 106 rooms is cable-connected and has a balcony so you can check out the sun-worshipers who lounge around the center court pool. There's easy access to on-site washers and dryers and plenty of parking, so you can go about your vacation business without a worry.

The Breakers Resort Inn
$$$$$ • 16th St. and Oceanfront, Virginia Beach
- **(757) 428-1821, (800) 237-7532**

There's not a room in this house that doesn't overlook the blue Atlantic, and every room comes equipped with a coffee maker and a fridge to chill that essential post-beach beverage. If you want to go first class, ask for a deluxe king room with a whirlpool tub, a two-room efficiency or, what the heck, the bridal suite and have a beach blast. You'll have to come out of your room sometime, so if you're weary of the lifeguarded beach with umbrella and chair rentals, request a free bicycle and pedal through the strip.

The Capes Ocean Resort
$$$$$ • 20th St. and Oceanfront, Virginia Beach
- **(757) 428-5451, (800) 456-5421**

Choose from a regular room or an efficiency that sleeps six at this oceanfront gem. You can't go wrong when every room overlooks the ocean. Optional amenities include microwaves and whirlpool tubs, and there's a snack bar for the hungry kiddies at lunchtime. The Capes usually closed in winter.

Carriage Inn Motel
$$$$ winter, $$$$$ summer
- **1500 Atlantic Ave., Virginia Beach**
- **(757) 428-8015, (888) 574-8785**

This is one of the smaller hotels at the beach, but we list it because your pets are welcome here. And you can't say that about every place at the beach. All 38 rooms here are air conditioned. You can swim in the pool if the ocean's rough, and kids younger than 6 stay for free. The motel usually closes in winter.

The Cavalier Hotels
$$$$$ • 42nd St. and Oceanfront and 42nd On The Hill, Virginia Beach
• (757) 425-8555, (800) 446-8199

The Cavalier on the Hill is a landmark in the Beach community and one of the most popular spots in the region for Insider wedding receptions. However, its newer, slicker sister along the oceanfront has the ocean views. Together, these hotels comprise an 18-acre seaside resort with nearly 400 guest rooms and eight suites overlooking the 600-foot private beach along the Atlantic Ocean. The Cavalier has the largest hotel ballroom in the Commonwealth of Virginia, so you can throw an intimate dinner for 1,400 with no problem. There are also three restaurants, two lounges, tennis courts, indoor and outdoor swimming pools and a health club. Other amenities include jogging tracks and facilities for racquetball.

Cerca Del Mar
$$$ winter, $$$$$ summer
• 410 21st St., Virginia Beach
• (757) 428-6511, (800) 442-3722

If you're packing the kiddies, the Cerca Del Mar is a great place to head. Fifty-five two-room efficiencies provide more space for the beach toys than a regular-size hotel room. It's four blocks off the beach, so the rates are perfect for a family budget. There's an outdoor pool plus a kiddie pool, and children younger than 18 can splash and snooze for free.

Clarion Resort
$$$$$ • Fifth St. and Oceanfront, Virginia Beach
• (757) 422-3186, (800) 345-3186

Insiders love this part of Virginia Beach, down near Rudee Inlet where all the city's charter boat fleets congregate. The Clarion has 168 rooms—all with oceanfront views from private balconies—a swimming pool, a whirlpool, a sauna, rooftop tennis courts, a game room and a health club. The hotel was recently renovated.

Colonial Inn
$$$$ winter, $$$$$ summer
• 29th St. and Oceanfront, Virginia Beach
• (757) 428-5370, (800) 344-3342

Go for the king suite with Jacuzzi—it's your vacation after all. Even if you're more practical and opt for a regular double-bed oceanfront room, you'll still get a refrigerator, private balcony over the beach and cable TV. There are 159 guest rooms. The indoor heated pool is kind of nifty, with bright flags hanging from the rafters. But on a glorious sunny day, you'll probably want to go for the outdoor pool and sundeck. If you don't want to venture out to eat, Cary's Restaurant will treat you just fine.

Comfort Inn Oceanfront
$$$ winter, $$$$$ summer
• 2015 Atlantic Ave., Virginia Beach
• (757) 425-8200, (800) 443-4733

All 83 two-room suites in this facility feature private balconies overlooking the ocean, kitchenettes, queen-size bed and queen-size sleep sofa. In town on business? Hold the meeting on your turf, by booking this property's presidential suite, which boasts an executive board room. There's also a honeymoon suite with a king-size bed and wet bar. An indoor heated pool and Jacuzzi and exercise room are open for your comfort all year.

Days Inn Oceanfront
$$$$$ • 32nd St. and Oceanfront, Virginia Beach
• (757) 428-7233, (800) 292-3297

This is a handsome hotel, where every oceanfront room comes equipped with a private balcony. Each of the 120 rooms is surprisingly spacious, and you can zip down the hallway to the laundry when your favorite beach outfit gets pooped. There's an indoor pool for those afternoons when you're not quite in the mood for the beach crunch. And the '50s diner and lounge called Happy Days is a swell place to wind up a sun-filled day.

Diplomat Inn Oceanfront
$$$$ winter, $$$$$ summer
• 3305 Atlantic Ave., Virginia Beach
• (757) 428-8811, (800) 752-1424

From secluded oceanfront balconies to a heated outdoor pool, the Diplomat stands tall along one of the most popular sections of the strip. With spacious guest rooms and oversize efficiencies that are 100 percent oceanfront, this hotel offers the ever-popular (and scarce) free parking and is a quick walk from restaurants and shopping.

The Dolphin Inn
$$$$$ • 1705 Atlantic Ave., Virginia Beach
• (757) 491-1920, (800) 365-3467

No need to suffer the crowded hotel room blues around here. This hotel offers 54 two-room suites, each featuring a private oceanfront balcony, fully-equipped kitchenette and an oversized whirlpool tub, the perfect place to soak your sunburned bod after a day on the

ACCOMMODATIONS

sand. The hotel also features on-site parking and laundry facilities, a rooftop sun deck and a heated rooftop greenhouse swimming pool for those who insist on that resort experience regardless of the temperature outside.

Doubletree Hotel
**$$–$$$$$ • 1900 Pavilion Dr.,
Virginia Beach
• (757) 422-8900, (800) 313-0099**

At the foot of the Norfolk-Virginia Beach Expressway, adjacent to the Pavilion Convention Center, this hotel offers 292 lovely rooms and 6 luxury suites. Banquet facilities for as many as 700 people and 12,000 square feet of meeting space make it a convention favorite. Although it is a few blocks from the oceanfront, it offers shuttle service to the beach. Other amenities include an indoor swimming pool, a jogging track, tennis courts and a restaurant. Pets are welcome.

Dunes Lodge/Dunes Motor Inn
**$$$ winter, $$$$$ summer
• Ninth and 10th Sts. and Oceanfront,
Virginia Beach
• (757) 428-7731, (800) 634-0709**

A lot of sunscreen is squeezed out on the 425 feet of oceanfront that stretch out in front of the Dunes. The two properties have 145 rooms and are right on the boardwalk with a broad-grassed ocean terrace enveloping a super outdoor pool. For more privacy, you can head up to the third and fourth levels of the inn, and plant your body on the tanning deck with whirlpool spa standing by to soothe. When you're burnt to a crisp, rent a bike or head indoors to the oceanfront game room sporting two pool tables, a Ping-Pong table and even more tables for heated games of bridge or gin rummy. For the hungries, there's the Snack Shop or the Pancake House—serving from morning 'til night.

Four Sails Resort
**$$$$$ • 33rd St. and Oceanfront,
Virginia Beach
• (757) 491-8100, 800 227-4213**

The 49 units in this facility are actually time-share vacation homes, but you can rent them just like any hotel room. Located at the north end of the beach, close to the less crowded residential beaches, Four Sails offers "double-wide

---

INSIDERS' TIP

Pet Alert! Your four-legged buddies are not permitted on public beaches, on the boardwalk or in the grassy area between the boardwalk and motel properties in Virginia Beach from May 15 to September 30.

---

whirlpools" in all rooms, plus a health club, indoor pool and sauna for those who prefer to maintain their washboard abs over vacation.

Hilton Inn
**$$$$$ • 8th St. and Atlantic Ave.,
Virginia Beach
• (757) 428-8935, (800) HILTONS**

This place has got it all: a great location on the Boardwalk, indoor and outdoor pools, hot tub, sauna, weight room, restaurant, cafe and snack bar. Even bike rentals for your unnecessary excursions off the premises. There are 120 guest rooms.

Holiday Inn Oceanside
**$$$$$ • 2101 Atlantic Ave., Virginia Beach
• (757) 491-1500, (800) 88BEACH**

This hotel benefits from its easy-to-find location. If you're driving into Virginia Beach from Va. 44, it's straight ahead when the interstate ends. Any further east, and you'd be in the drink, so to speak. One of several first-class Holiday Inns at the Beach, Holiday Inn Oceanside boasts an indoor pool, an oceanfront restaurant and lounge. It has 138 guest rooms.

Holiday Inn Sunspree Resort on the Ocean
**$$$$$ • 39th St. and Oceanfront,
Virginia Beach
• (757) 428-1711, (800) 94BEACH**

This 266-room Holiday Inn has an outdoor pool, an indoor pool complex with two whirlpools, banquet facilities that can serve as many as 400, and more than 9,000 square feet of meeting space on the top floor overlooking the ocean. It's on the boardwalk, so that means if you decide to pass on the excellent restaurant, you've got oodles of dining choices just a short walk away.

Holiday Inn Surfside
**$$$$$ • 2606 Atlantic Ave., Virginia Beach
• (757) 491-6900, (800) 810-2400**

If 25th Street is the epicenter of the Boardwalk, then this 139-room hotel is in the midst of it all. Stay here and walk just one block to lovely oceanfront park that's home to all sorts of entertainment in the summer, from Shakespeare, to puppet shows to rock bands. Of course, you could opt to stay in after that sun, and you'll have your choice of oceanfront dining, lounging in a hot tub or working out in the exercise room.

Howard Johnson Oceanfront North
$$$$ winter, $$$$$ summer
- **3705 Atlantic Ave., Virginia Beach**
- **(757) 428-7220, (800) IGO-HOJO**

This hotel, situated at the north end of the Virginia Beach boardwalk, is a popular choice for families. The 177 guest rooms include singles, doubles and efficiencies. Each room has a private balcony and most have oceanfront views. Special summertime treats include bike rentals and a shop in the lobby that sells gifts, ice cream, pizza and sandwiches. For more serious dining, try the hotel's full-service restaurant, Angelo's, which specializes in seafood, steaks and pasta. You can swim in the ocean or the outdoor pool, or just laze away in one of the deck chairs they set up every morning on a small hill overlooking the beach - just in time for the dolphin runs.

Howard Johnson Oceanfront South
$$$$$ • 18th St. and Oceanfront,
Virginia Beach
- **(757) 437-9100, (800) 258-1878**

You're just one block away from the busiest Dairy Queen in the entire United States here. That's probably because you're also just one block away from an oceanfront park that hosts outdoor concerts, plays, puppet shows and the like all summer long. Each of the 103 rooms at this hotel offers an oceanfront view and private balcony. The hotel also has its own restaurant and parking garage, plus an indoor pool and hot tub.

Idlewhyle
$$–$$$$$ • 2705 Atlantic Ave.,
Virginia Beach
- **(757) 428-9341, (800) 348-7263**

It seems like there are fewer and fewer small hotels and motels left at the beach every summer. This is one of the cozier ones, with a nice Mom and Pop feel, plus all the amenities you'd find at the big chains such as indoor/outdoor pools, a coffee shop, sundecks and an atrium. There are 46 guest rooms.

LaPlaya Motel
$$$$$ • 33rd St. and Oceanfront,
Virginia Beach
- **(757) 428-5933, (800) 458-7674**

You're slightly to the north of the serious hustle and bustle of the boardwalk at this hotel, but it's all within easy reach if you want it.

You're about five blocks from the good shopping of Laskin Road and Pacific Avenue and just a few sandy steps from the ocean. This inn offers 34 rooms, some with balconies, and a heated oceanfront pool, just in case that big body of water is too nippy for you.

Marjac Suites
$$$$$ • 22nd St. and Oceanfront,
Virginia Beach
- **(757) 425-0100, (800) 368-3080**

Life is sweet! Each two-room suite here has a full kitchen and a private oceanfront balcony. There's also a pool and bike rentals for those leisurely rolls down the boardwalk at sunrise. There are 60 suites.

Newcastle Motel
$$$$ winter, $$$$$ summer
- **12th St. and Oceanfront, Virginia Beach**
- **(757) 428-3981, (800) 346-3176**

You know you're going to like this place when you first pull up. Every one of the 83 rooms has an oceanfront vista from a private balcony, along with refrigerator, microwave and whirlpool tub. If you opt for a two-room suite, you'll get a full kitchen as well as a large master bedroom with a king-size bed, a super option for a longer stay. Start out on the ocean view sundeck or indoor heated pool, then warm those lazy muscles with a free bicycle and pedal down the boardwalk to check out the action.

Oceanfront Inn
$$$$$ • 29th St. and Oceanfront,
Virginia Beach
- **(757) 422-0445, (800) 548-3879**

Sprawling along primo beachfront, the Oceanfront Inn is just that—oceanfront. From your private balcony, you can eavesdrop on all the beach activity and then maybe dog-paddle a few lazy laps in the heated indoor or outdoor pools. There's the nifty canopied cafe for a leisurely lunch and a lounge and restaurant too. Sideview and west side rooms are less expensive, but as long as you're on vacation, why not go for a king-size oceanfront job. We would. There are 146 guest rooms.

Ocean Holiday Hotel
$$$$$ • 25th St. and Oceanfront,
Virginia Beach
- **(757) 425-6920, (800) 345-SAND**

Each of the 105 rooms in this hotel has a balcony that hangs over the beach. Ocean Holiday boasts an indoor pool and complimentary morning coffee in the lobby. Don't forget to slide through the gift shop for some tanning lotion before heading to the sundeck to catch those rays. If you want to go all out, call early to reserve one of the specialty rooms that comes with a full-size Jacuzzi and VCR. You can even bring along your favorite pet, who will be as welcome as you are.

Ocean Key Resort
$$$$$ • 424 Atlantic Ave., Virginia Beach
• (757) 425-2200, (800) 955-9300

This is a great place for a longer visit because each of the 150 rooms is actually a two-room suite. Along with 1,500 square feet of meeting space and banquet facilities for 150, the resort has an indoor swimming pool, fitness center, restaurant, lounge and, of course, the beautiful beaches of the Atlantic.

Quality Inn Oceanfront
$$$$$ • 23rd St. and Oceanfront,
Virginia Beach
• (757) 428-5141, (800) 874-8661

You're just a block away from the resort area's hottest nightspots at this 111-room hotel. These all tend to be along 21st and 22nd streets and the block of Atlantic Avenue that stretches between them. Of course, you don't have to go out on the town. There's a restaurant and lounge, indoor heated pool and hot tub on the premises. Or splurge on an in-room fridge and a whirlpool tub to create your very own hot nightspot!

Ramada On The Beach
$$$$$ • 615 Atlantic Ave., Virginia Beach
• (757) 425-7800, (800) 888-4111

On the widest part of the south-end beach, this 168-room hotel offers a private oceanfront balcony with every room. There are four different room styles to choose from here: specialty suites, king-size rooms, standard rooms and efficiencies with kitchenettes. Amenities include a heated indoor pool, Jacuzzi and exercise room and the hotel's full-service restaurant, Mahi Mah's, which lures locals and travelers alike with a first-class selection of seafood and sushi specialties (see our Restaurants chapter).

Ramada Plaza Resort Oceanfront
$$$$$ • 57th St. and Oceanfront,
Virginia Beach
• (757) 428-7025, (800) 365-3032

We'll start just off the boardwalk path with this fine facility that's on Virginia Beach's North End, and that puts you in the midst of the prime residential oceanfront community. The 215 rooms, including three suites, are so nice

they helped the property win a recent title of Best Ramada Inn in the Country. Conference facilities include 12 meeting rooms and banquet facilities for 400. You'll love the swim-up bar in the heated indoor/outdoor swimming pool. There's also an exercise room, a popular neighborhood pub and an excellent seafood restaurant on premises.

The Sandcastle Oceanfront Motel
$$$–$$$$$ • 14th St. and Oceanfront,
Virginia Beach
• (757) 428-2828, (800) 233-0131

If anyone in your family loves to fish, you might want to stay here. The motel is on the same street as the old Virginia Beach fishing pier, a scenic landmark if ever there was one. People fish off the pier all day, and surfers love to catch the waves around the pilings. In need of a cool one? Visit Ocean Eddie's, a popular bar/restaurant situated right on the pier. This motel has standard rooms and suites available and offers those two crucial amenities for families with children: a kiddie pool and a game room.

Sheraton Oceanfront Hotel
$$$$$ • 36th St. and Oceanfront,
Virginia Beach
• (757) 425-9000, (800) 521-5635

Rising above the boardwalk, this 204-room hotel has nine meeting rooms that cover 17,000 square feet, two ballrooms and banquet facilities for 600. Along with glorious ocean views, the Sheraton offers an outdoor swimming pool, an exercise room with an indoor pool, a dining room and lounge.

Turtle Cay Resort
$$$$$ • 600 Atlantic Ave., Virginia Beach
• (757) 437-5565, (888) 989-7788

Just a quick walk across the street will take visitors right to the boardwalk and the ocean. The all-suite resort opened in 1998 with all kinds of amenities. There are 97 suites and villas with oversized baths or whirlpools, fireplaces, kitchens and porches. The resort also has a pool, spa, fitness center and restaurant.

The Viking Motel Apartments
$$–$$$$$ • 2700 Atlantic Ave.,
Virginia Beach
• (757) 428-7116, (800) 828-3063

How much room do you need? At the Viking, you can pick from 82 single or double rooms and one- and two-room efficiencies with separate bedrooms, equipped kitchens and a dining area. Whichever you unpack in, you'll have the second-floor swimming pool with a unique see-through window and great restaurants and shopping just a step away. The beach is just a hop across Atlantic Avenue.

Windjammer Hotel
$$$$$ • 19th St. and Oceanfront, Virginia Beach
• (757) 428-0060, (800) 695-0035
Early morning beach joggers can just roll out of bed into their Nikes and hit the sand running. Choose from 72 regular or deluxe variety accommodations, or maybe go for an efficiency equipped with dishes, utensils and cookware. You'll enjoy great benefits such as private balconies, an L-shaped oceanfront outdoor pool, guest laundry and cable TV with HBO. Since it's on the boardwalk, you can slide out of your room and into the beach's night action with no trouble at all.

Chesapeake Bay

Virginia Beach Resort Hotel and Conference Center
$$$ • 2800 Shore Dr., Virginia Beach
• (757) 481-9000, (800) 468-2722
Rising dramatically over the Chesapeake Bay, this hotel's 295 luxuriously appointed two-room suites all overlook the private beach from their own balconies. Relax in the indoor/outdoor swimming pool, try out the health club, whirlpool and sauna or dine in the two restaurants. Affiliation with the nearby tennis club brings you 30 outdoor and six indoor tennis courts. There are banquet facilities for up to 300, and more than 14,000 square feet of meeting space.

Suburban

The Clarion Hotel Pembroke
$$ • 4453 Bonney Rd., Virginia Beach
• (757) 473-1700, (800) 847-5202
Just off the Norfolk-Virginia Beach Expressway, midway between Norfolk and the Beach in the Pembroke business and shopping corridor, is this popular eight-story hotel with 149 guest rooms, a health club, an indoor pool and a restaurant.

Courtyard by Marriott
$$ • 5700 Greenwich Rd., Virginia Beach
• (757) 490-2002, (800) 321-2211
What appears to be a charming apartment complex is really a 146-room hotel that sprawls across 4 acres. Most of the rooms face a beautifully landscaped courtyard with a swimming pool, garden gazebo, exercise room and a Jacuzzi. Business travelers in town for several days really love the large desks in the rooms. There is a restaurant on the premises, but we hear that taking food back to the room from the pickup counter is a favorite choice for the bone-tired executive.

Extended Stay America
$$ • 4548 Bonney Rd., Virginia Beach
• (757) 473-9200, (888) 398-7829
This motel caters to business travelers, who often need to check in for more than a few nights. Each room is actually a studio efficiency apartment with a queen-size bed, fully equipped kitchen and full bath with shower and linens. Guests can use a 24-hour laundry facility, free voice mail and computer data port for a fax and/or computer. Great weekly rates also make this a smart place to stay if you're moving to town to look for a job and/or permanent place to live.

The Founders Inn
$$$ • 5641 Indian River Rd., Virginia Beach
• (757) 424-5811, (800) 926-4466
This gorgeous facility, tastefully furnished in the Colonial manner, is close to the Christian Broadcasting Network (CBN) and Regent University. Overlooking English gardens surrounding a small lake where swans swim, the inn offers 249 beautifully appointed rooms, with common and sitting areas that have a true resort feeling. Amenities include a fitness center, tennis and racquetball courts, indoor and outdoor swimming pools, bike rentals and a dinner theater. Award-winning chefs serve sumptuous gourmet specialties in the Swan Terrace Restaurant (see our Restaurant chapter.) No alcoholic beverages are served, and smoking is prohibited throughout the complex. There is a free shuttle bus to the oceanfront and Norfolk Harbor.

Holiday Inn Executive Center
$$ • 5655 Greenwich Rd., Virginia Beach
• (757) 499-4400, (800) HOLIDAY
The anchor of the Newtown Road corridor hotel cluster, you can't miss this six-story-high green roof from the Norfolk-Virginia Beach Expressway. It's pretty much green inside, too, with its miles of green carpeting and lavish indoor plantings. The 336 rooms are quite comfortable, and most come with hair dryers in the bathrooms, a nice touch. If you travel heavy,

you'll appreciate the seven parlor/meeting suites, which include two parlor suites with adjoining king bedrooms. You'll also find both indoor and outdoor pools, a whirlpool, a sauna, a health club and the popular Ashley's restaurant that's always busy with local business people for breakfast, lunch and after-work drinks.

Norfolk

Norfolk definitely has a split personality when it comes to accommodations. Downtown is home to hotels, within walking distance of The Waterside Festival Marketplace and MacArthur Center mall, which opened in 1999. Ocean View offers rooms overlooking the Chesapeake Bay, where bathers, anglers and sun-worshippers happily commingle. Undergoing a dramatic but slow rejuvenation, the Ocean View area is regaining popularity that was lost during the 1960s and '70s. Today, with new bayfront parks and lifeguarded beaches, it is once again becoming a favorite for families with small children because of calm, warm waters. Folks headed to the vicinity of Old Dominion University, the airport/Military Circle hub or elsewhere in the city will find suburban motels perfect for their overnight needs.

Downtown

Bed and Breakfast at the Page House Inn
$$$$$ • 323 Fairfax Ave., Norfolk
• 625-5033, (800) 695-1487

This elegant bed and breakfast, in the heart of Norfolk's historic Ghent district, has won accolades from Country Inn Magazine and Southern Living. Less than 10 years ago, the inn was a neighborhood eyesore, but a meticulous restoration has returned it to its original c. 1899 Georgian Revival glory. Owners Stephanie and Ezio DiBelardino offer four rooms and two suites. The daily tariff includes a gourmet continental breakfast and afternoon refreshments.

Rooms are beautifully furnished, with luxurious touches such as fine linens, private baths and private phone lines. Several rooms also feature amenities such as whirlpool baths and fireplaces. A one-night guarantee is required, and there's a seven-day cancellation policy. The inn does not allow smoking, pets or children younger than 12. In 1997 the inn's owners expanded their offerings by opening the Boat Bed and Breakfast. Guests stay on a 43-foot sailboat docked downtown along the downtown Portsmouth waterfront.

Norfolk Waterside Marriott Hotel and Convention Center
$$$$ • 235 E. Main St., Norfolk
• (757) 627-4200, (800) 228-9290

A jewel in the crown of Downtown Norfolk, this glamorous facility welcomes you with the most elegant lobby in the area, just a taste of the good life that awaits you during your stay. A favorite of conventioneers, Norfolk's newest hotel offers 404 guest rooms, including eight suites and three concierge levels plus a parking garage and valet parking. With the health club and rooftop indoor pool, the Dining Room, the Piano Lounge and Stormy's Sports Pub, the Marriott is like a plush mini-city you might never want to leave. There's more than 45,000 square feet of flexible conference space, with a ballroom that can accommodate a sit-down banquet for 1,200. Most of the standard guest rooms are small, however, but you can make up for the size by requesting a room with a view of the Elizabeth River, and The Waterside Festival Marketplace.

Sheraton Norfolk Waterside Hotel International Hotel/Norfolk
$$$$ • 777 Waterside Dr., Norfolk
• (757) 622-6664, (800) 325-3535

The Sheraton has new management committed to pampering you in 446 deluxe rooms including 20 executive suites with spectacular views from balconies overlooking the Elizabeth River. Connected by covered walkways to The

INSIDERS' TIP
The B&B Central: It sounds like railroad, but actually it's a wonderful service for those who prefer the bed and breakfast mode of accommodation to staying in hotels or motels. B&B of Tidewater can help you coordinate a bed and breakfast stay almost anywhere in our area, from the Ghent area of Norfolk, to the Eastern Shore, to Williamsburg to Sandbridge. For information that can make your next visit to our fair region more personal, contact B&B of Tidewater at P.O. Box 6226, Norfolk 23508 or call (804) 627-1983.

Waterside Festival Marketplace, the hotel offers dining in the Riverwalk Restaurant, the outdoor Verandah Cafe and a waterfront bar, Alexander's. Small groups and large conventions can both be accommodated within the hotel's 29,000 square feet of flexible function space. Extra perks are the outdoor pool and access to the YMCA branch located next door in Dominion Tower. In 2000 all hotel rooms were refurbished.

Radisson Hotel Downtown Norfolk
$$$ • 700 Monticello Ave., Norfolk
• (757) 627-5555

A $7 million renovation in 1998 gave new life to this 12-story downtown hotel. The 344 guest rooms are decorated in a soothing green and cream color scheme with watercolor prints of old Norfolk. Desks stocked with office supplies provide a thoughtful touch in the guest rooms. The hotel's attractive lobby lends itself to relaxation with its comfortable seating areas. There is a ballroom and meeting rooms equipped with video-conferencing capabilities. The Chesapeake Room is the hotel's restaurant. Kevin's Pub supplies cocktails and other libations. Plenty of parking is on the hotel site, which is directly across the street from the Scope convention center and Chrysler Hall performing arts center. The hotel is only a few blocks away from MacArthur Center mall.

James Madison Hotel
$$ • Granby and Freemason Sts., Norfolk
• (757) 622-6682, (888) 402-6682

A landmark hotel in the heart of the original Downtown shopping district, the Madison features 124 one- and two-room suites along with Basils, a fine Italian restaurant and an attractive lounge. There are three meeting rooms with more than 5,000 square feet, and the banquet facilities can serve 275 guests. In 1999 the hotel renovated its guest rooms and public areas. Some of Downtown's most popular restaurants are within a few blocks. MacArthur Center mall is about a block away. The Waterside Festival Marketplace is about five blocks to the south.

Hawthorne Hotel & Suites
$$$$$ • 208 E. Plume St., Norfolk
• (757) 623-6200

This 70-room, hotel is a charming boutique property right in the heart of downtown. It was built as an elegant hotel in 1908 but in recent years had fallen on hard times. Until a 2000 restoration, it wasn't the kind of place anyone wanted to stay for long. That image

has been banished with a multi-million makeover that gutted the upstairs floors and restored the elegance of the original lobby down to its elevators with beveled glass doors. The hotel has both rooms and suites. There's a small fitness center and guests can get passes to a nearby fitness center. The hotel is a block away from MacArthur Center and five blocks from The Waterside Festival Marketplace. Guests are treated to a full breakfast.

Suburban Norfolk

Comfort Inn-Naval Base
$$ • 8051 Hampton Blvd., Norfolk
• (757) 451-0000

A few blocks from the Hampton Inn, this 120-room motel welcomes guests of Norfolk Naval Base. An indoor swimming pool, on-site laundry facilities, refrigerators in every room and free local phone calls make this a popular place to stay.

Doubletree Club Hotel
$$ • Military Hwy. and
Virginia Beach Blvd., Norfolk
• (757) 461-9192

If you were born to shop, stash your traveling bags here. An "anchor" of Military Circle Center Mall, this hotel is a neighbor to more than 150 great stores, shops and restaurants. The hotel features 208 recently renovated rooms, a full-service restaurant and lounge, an outdoor pool and a fitness room. Its location is just minutes away from the airport and 10 minutes from Downtown Norfolk.

Hampton Inn
$$ • 1450 N. Military Hwy., Norfolk
• (757) 466-7474, (800) 489-1000

Just a skip from the airport to the north and Military Circle to the south, this is a lifesaver for the budget-conscious traveler who wants a lot for the overnight dollar. There is an outdoor pool and complimentary continental breakfast served each morning. Offered are 129 comfortably sized rooms, with free local phone calls and the obligatory cable TV.

Hampton Inn-Naval Base
$$ • 8501 Hampton Blvd., Norfolk
• (757) 489-1000

Minutes from the main gate at Naval Station Norfolk, the Hampton Inn offers 119 rooms, continental breakfasts and free local phone calls. There's an indoor pool and a whirlpool, and the rooms have kitchenettes plus modem jacks for those who must stay in touch even when they're on vacation.

Norfolk Airport Hilton
$$$ • 1500 Military Hwy., Norfolk
• (757) 466-8000

This deluxe 250-room hotel is as close to the airport as you could possibly want to be and also near the USAA regional headquarters complex. The lobby is impressive with its piano bar accented by polished brass accessories, teak trim and a marble floor. Fine dining (actually one of the area's finest restaurants) is offered at Antiquities. Pasta Grande serves Southern Italian fare and La Promenade is a casual coffee shop (see our Restaurants chapter). The hotel also operates a nightclub, called The Orient Express. A high-tech fitness center with Jacuzzi and sauna plus an outdoor swimming pool and tennis courts round out the amenities. For getting down to business, there are nine salons, parlors and conference rooms, along with the grand ballroom with foyer and a garden. Nice features of the guest rooms are the in-room mini-bars.

Old Dominion Inn
$$ • 4111 Hampton Blvd., Norfolk
• (757) 440-5100

This is a convenient place to stay for visitors to both Old Dominion University and the major medical complex that's a short hop down Hampton Boulevard. Sixty guest rooms, five of which are suites, are surprisingly spacious and well-appointed, and restaurants and shops that serve the University are just across the street.

Quality Inn Lake Wright
$$ • 6280 Northampton Blvd., Norfolk
• (757) 461-6251, (800) 228-5157

A quick zip to the interstate and airport, this 304-room resort and conference center has an easygoing attitude. For specifics, there are eight suites and meeting rooms covering more than 22,000 square feet of flexible space. Opening in 2001 adjacent to the inn is a Quality Suites and a Sleep Inn motel. The inn already boasts a great neighbor—a popular 18-hole golf course and driving range called Lake Wright Golf Course. A swimming pool and tennis courts are also on the premises.

Ocean View

Econo Lodge - West/NAS
$$$ summer, $ winter
• 9601 Fourth View St., Norfolk
• (757) 480-9611

While not directly on the Bay, this motel with 71 rooms and 23 efficiencies offers clean,

Norfolk's Waterside Convention Center and adjacent Marriott Hotel accommodate numerous conventions every year.

comfortable accommodations, worth the easy walk across the street to the beach. Close to the popular Harrison's Boat House and Fishing Pier, the motel offers a laundry room and cable TV.

Quality Inn
$$$ summer, $$ winter
- **1010 W. Ocean View Ave., Norfolk**
- **(757) 587-8761**

You'll find traditional Holiday Inn hospitality in this 118-room oceanfront hotel. It's a comfortable place to hang the family's wet bathing suits in summer and a nice place for business travelers to watch ships and fishing boats any time of year. You have access to swimming and kiddie pools, a cocktail lounge and restaurant and banquet facilities.

Ramada Limited
$$$ • 719 E. Ocean View Ave., Norfolk
- **(757) 583-5211**

Always with a diverse guest list of business people, vacationing families and military guests, this 96-room inn sits directly across from a popular family beach, with next-door tennis courts and the Ocean View Golf Course just a few blocks away. A swimming pool is on site.

Portsmouth

It's not that visitors don't want to stay in Portsmouth, it's just that the competition from neighboring city beaches and business centers preclude many overnight options in this city. However, city planners expect to remedy that within a few years with a new downtown hotel on the waterfront. By spring 2000 the Renaissance Portsmouth Hotel and Conference Center should open. Here's where Insiders would check in if they were to stay overnight in Portsmouth.

Bianca Boat & Breakfast
$$$$ • 10 Crawford Pkwy., Portsmouth
- **(757) 625-5033, (800) 695-1487**

This is the hands-down winner for most unusual bed and breakfast in Hampton Roads. In this case the first "B" stands for boat. When you check into the *Bianca* Boat & Breakfast, you'll be spending the night on a 43-foot sailboat docked at the Tidewater Yacht Agency in downtown Portsmouth. The location gives a great view of downtown Norfolk and is in walking distance of Portsmouth's scenic Olde Towne Historic District. The *Bianca* is owned

by Ezio and Stephanie Di Belardino, who own the Page House Inn in Norfolk. Both had a hand in renovating the yacht to be a floating guest house on the Elizabeth River. There are three cabins and a dining area on board. The gallery is stocked with snacks and fresh fruit. Breakfast is delivered each morning or guests can hop aboard a water taxi and ride over to the Page House Inn to dine. Guests can pay extra if they want to go out on the *Bianca* for a cruise.

Renaissance Portsmouth Hotel and Waterfront Conference Center
$$$$ • 425 Water St., Portsmouth
- **(757) 673-3000, (800) 468-3571**

This eagerly anticipated hotel should open by early 2001 with one of the best views in the region. It is right on the Elizabeth River waterfront in downtown Portsmouth. There are 249 elegant guest rooms, including five suites. Amenities include two-line phones and data ports in all rooms and concierge service. There is an indoor pool, a whirlpool, a fitness center and a deck for sunning. A restaurant seats 144 and offers terrace dining. There is 24,000 square feet of ultra high tech meeting space. The hotel is within walking distance of downtown shops and the Olde Towne Historic District. It's only a quick ferry ride to downtown Norfolk just across the river.

Holiday Inn-Olde Towne Portsmouth
$$ • 8 Crawford Pkwy., Portsmouth
- **(757) 393-2573, (800) 456-2811**

This is a popular place to stay Downtown. The 218 rooms and suites on the waterfront in Olde Towne are just the beginning, because you're not only just across the river from Norfolk's Waterside but also adjacent to Tidewater Yacht Agency marina, one of the area's busiest. The hotel's restaurant and lounge overlook the Elizabeth River and the ferry stop is nearby. Rooms are comfortable and spacious, but be sure to request one that has a view of the river to catch the harbor activity and spectacular sunsets. The hotel has an outdoor swimming pool.

Harbor Tower Corporate Apartments
$$$$$ • One Harbor Court, Portsmouth
- **(757) 393-1600**

If you're planning to stay at least a week and want room to spread out, check into these apartments with the best views in town. The tower is right on the Elizabeth River waterfront downtown and every apartment overlooks the harbor. Amenities include a swimming poll, tennis courts, and concierge and valet services.

Comfort Inn Olde Towne
$ • 347 Effingham St., Portsmouth
• (757) 397-7788, 800-221-2222

This motel is in a terrific location. It's right downtown and within strolling distance of the waterfront. There are 62 rooms on three floors. Amenities include an outdoor pool and an exercise room. A free breakfast is waiting every morning.

Days Inn
$ • 1031 London Blvd., Portsmouth
• (757) 399- 4414, (800) 329-7466

The overnight choice for those with business at the Portsmouth Naval Hospital, the Days Inn is only five minutes by ferry to The Waterside Festival Marketplace in Downtown Norfolk. Sixty-one rooms are offered, with fast food restaurants within walking distance in the local neighborhood.

Best Western
$ • 333 Effingham St., Portsmouth
• (757) 397-5806, (800) 528-1234

Two-room suites and efficiency units provide plenty of space. This motel is near Portsmouth Naval Hospital and two blocks from downtown. It has an outdoor pool and picnic area and offers a free continental breakfast.

Super 8 Motel
$ • 925 London Blvd., Portsmouth
• (757) 398-0612

There are 56 guest rooms and some have refrigerators and microwaves as well as water beds. This motel is conveniently located to everything in Portsmouth. It serves a free continental breakfast.

Hawthorne Inn & Suites
$$$$ • High and Dinwiddie Sts., Portsmouth
• No phone number available yet

Under redevelopment at press time, this boutique hotel was scheduled to open by early 2001. A $3.2 million renovation is transforming the former Governor Dinwiddie Hotel, built in 1946, into 65 studio and one-bedroom suites. Services include a fitness room with sauna, free breakfast and evening social hour. Business travelers will appreciate the inn's data ports, multiple phone lines and facsimile and voice mail services. The inn is in the heart of Olde Towne Portsmouth.

Glen Coe Bed & Breakfast
$$$$ • 222 North St., Portsmouth
• (757) 397-8128

Hostess Ann McGlynn prefers an informal home-away-from-home atmosphere at this small bed and breakfast, and her front porch is a favorite spot for many weary travelers. The home, a Victorian built c. 1890, is just one block from the Portsmouth waterfront in the Olde Towne Historic District. It offers three guest rooms, two with private baths. On weekends and summer mornings, McGlynn offers full breakfasts. Midweek winters it's continental fare.

The Olde Towne Bed & Breakfast Inn
$$$$–$$$$$ • 420 Middle St., Portsmouth
• (757) 397-5462, (800) 353-0278

This grand Italianate home, built during the Victorian era, has had two former lives: first as a women's club and later as a dancing school. Its latest incarnation as a bed and breakfast inn started with a detailed renovation that has returned the old home to it's former days of grandeur. The inn is in the Olde Towne Historic District near the waterfront. Owners Dede and John Braley offer visitors four different room choices, each with its own distinctive flavor. Homey touches, such as fresh flowers, reading lamps, sweets and tea, abound. A full breakfast and afternoon refreshments are served daily.

Port Norfolk Bed & Breakfast
$$$$ • 500 Broad St., Portsmouth
• (757) 397 9134

This 1910 home is in the Port Norfolk Historic District a few miles from downtown. Owners Mark and Jill Cave spent two years restoring the home before opening it as a bed and breakfast in 1999. Guests have their choice of two antique-filled rooms named for the previous owners. Eleanor's Room has a sitting room and a fireplace with a stained-glass cover. Harry's Room overlooks the gardens and swimming pool. Also outside is a hot tub for guests to enjoy. Breakfast includes Belgian waffles and other hearty morning fare.

Chesapeake

In this city that should be suffering from growing pains, there's always a new hub of activity that seems to spring up out of nowhere in the blink of an eye. For most visitors to Chesapeake, however, the Greenbrier corridor seems to be the most logical overnight destination choice since it puts you smack dab in the hustle-bustle for primo shopping, good food and a quick hop to the interstate. And, it seems there's always a new motel under construction.

Comfort Suites of Greenbrier
$$ • 1550 Crossways Blvd., Chesapeake
• (757) 420-1600

One hundred and twenty-three all-suite rooms complete with refrigerators, microwaves, cable TV and VCRs are the offering at this Comfort Suites. An outdoor swimming pool, fitness center with steam room and sauna, and a variety of restaurants, shops and entertainment just around the corner at Greenbrier Mall make it a convenient choice.

Econo Lodge-Chesapeake
$ • 3244 Western Branch Blvd., Chesapeake
• (757) 484-6143

This is our pick for a night somewhere other than in the Greenbrier area. This small and down-home friendly 48-room motel offers you a clean, comfortable room and morning coffee in the lobby but no amenities such as a restaurant or swimming pool. Its big advantage is its location in the city's Western Branch section, an older, established neighborhood with nearby shopping and fast food.

Extended Stay America
$$ 1540 Crossways Blvd., Chesapeake
• (757) 424-8600, (800) 398-7829

This motel caters to business travelers, who often need to stay more than a few nights. Each room is actually a studio efficiency apartment with a queen-sized bed, fully-equipped kitchen and full bath with shower and linens. Guests can use a 24-hour laundry facility, free voice mail and computer data port for a fax and/or computer. Great weekly rates also make this a smart place to stay if you're moving to town to look for a job and/or permanent place to live.

Hampton Inn
$ • 701A Woodlake Dr., Chesapeake
• (757) 420-1550

Just off I-64 and a short distance to restaurants and shops, the Hampton Inn offers 119 rooms with free cable and complimentary continental breakfast. The outdoor swimming pool is open in season.

Holiday Inn Chesapeake
$$ • 725 Woodlake Dr. at Greenbrier Pkwy., Chesapeake
• (757) 523-1500

Here's a real beauty, packed with frills to thrill the overnight guest. There are 230 rooms and suites in seven stories of Holiday Inn at its finest. Our favorite room is the King Executive, with a king-size bed in spread-out comfort, plus a queen-size pullout sofa and nifty wet bar. There's also an indoor swimming pool, whirlpool, sauna and weight room. The Key West Restaurant and Lounge is an especially popular spot with its nightly entertainment. Generous banquet facilities can accommodate up to 700 people with ease. Complimentary airport transportation is available on request, and you're just 15 minutes from the airport, Downtown Norfolk and the Virginia Beach oceanfront.

Red Roof Inn
$$$ • 724 Woodlake Dr., Chesapeake
• (757) 523-0123

Sitting practically on top of the Holiday Inn is the alternative for budget-watching travelers who just want a clean and pleasant place to stay, hold the frills. To eat or shop, you'll have to drive just a few miles down the road, but there is complimentary coffee and a newspaper waiting for you in the lobby each morning.

Wellesley Inn
$$ • 1750 Sara Dr. at Woodlake Dr., Chesapeake
• (757) 366-0100, (800) 444-8880

What we'd call a corporate bed and breakfast, the Wellesley Inn is a favorite of both business people on the road and visiting families. Each of the 106 rooms has a coffee maker. Other amenities include an outdoor heated pool and access to full health club facilities a half-mile down the street. The king and queen suites here are especially plush, with refrigerator, microwave and wet bar. A laundry facility is available to all guests, and a free continental breakfast is served daily.

INSIDERS' TIP

After unpacking your bags in the room, it's always a good idea to discuss an emergency evacuation and meeting plan with the family in the event of fire, earthquake or other disaster. Make sure the kids know where the emergency exits are located.

Suffolk

Holiday Inn Suffolk
$$$ • 2864 Pruden Blvd., Suffolk
• (757) 934-2311, (800) 465-4329

This is the place to stay if you're in town on business with Planters Peanuts, Hills Brothers coffee or Nestle. Dine on old-fashioned coun-

Ocean breezes and sand dunes await the visitors who choose seaside accommodations.

try cooking at the Peanut City Cafe and Lounge, and save time afterward for a swim in the outdoor pool. King-size beds, refrigerators and microwaves are available on a first-come, first-served basis.

Kennedy Suites
$$$–$$$$ (on a daily basis)
• 209 W. Washington St., Suffolk
• (757) 539-9172

This facility caters to relocating homeowners and business people who come for extended stays. The full-size apartments come with all furnishings and kitchens equipped with everything from glassware to grocery staples, and housekeeping services are available. Laundry facilities are on the premises. Although the apartments are normally rented by the week or month, they are sometimes available on a daily basis.

Super 8 Motel
$$ • 633 N. Main St., Suffolk
• (757) 925-0992

This motel gets lots of business in the summer. The motel has 51 standard rooms and offers a complimentary breakfast bar in the

morning. It's within walking distance of a several fast food establishments and a shopping center. Conference facilities available.

Resort Rentals

For a home away from home for a family vacation, it's hard to beat the many condominium and cottage rentals available in Virginia Beach. All are fully furnished and appointed with the right appliances and kitchen gadgets, although some may require packing your own bed linens and towels. For a week or two, even a month, all you need to do is to slide your bathing suits and shorts in a duffle and hit the road.

As with hotel and motel reservations, plan early for a summer or holiday stay, and remember that cash, credit cards and traveler's checks (not personal checks) are the accepted currency. When making reservations, make certain you request the specific cancellation, early/late checkout and refund policies, as they do vary from property to property.

Condominiums

You'll be living high on the hog when you check into one of Virginia Beach's condominium rentals, as most are of the high-rise flavor. As a general rule, you can expect a swimming pool outside, full kitchens inside, balconies and beachfront either at your door or a few short blocks away. Most are two-bedroom/two-bath units that sleep two to 10 adults. Check specifics, especially the availability of linens, when making reservations. Summer rates run from $500 to $1,500 weekly, depending on the amenities, size and location of the property.

Beach Breeze Condos
208 57th St., Virginia Beach
• (757) 422-0579

This complex offers three two-bedroom, two-bath units one block from the ocean.

The Colony
13th St. and Oceanfront, Virginia Beach
• (757) 425-8689

Colony has 38 two-bedroom, two-bath condos right on the ocean.

ACCOMMODATIONS

Dolphin Run Condominium
Third St. and Oceanfront, Virginia Beach
• (757) 425-6166

This large complex features 110 one-, two-
and three-bedroom, two-bath units right on
the ocean.

Edgewater Condominium
37th St. and Oceanfront, Virginia Beach
• (757) 425-6261

Right on the ocean, the aptly named
Edgewater has 35 two-bedroom, two-bath
units.

Mai Kai Resort Condos
56/57th Sts. and Atlantic Ave.,
Virginia Beach
• (757) 428-1096

This complex has 38 one- and two-bedroom,
two-bath units on the ocean.

Oceans II Studio Condominiums
40th St. and Oceanfront, Virginia Beach
• (757) 428-9021, (800) 845-4786

Oceans II has 42 oceanfront studio units
overlooking the Atlantic Ocean.

Seacrest Condominiums
21st St. and Arctic Ave., Virginia Beach
• (757) 428-4441

Seacrest's eight two-bedroom units are two
blocks from the ocean.

Cottage Rentals

For one of the beachiest vacations you'll
ever have, head to the southernmost part of
Virginia Beach and hit land's end at Sandbridge.
You won't find any glitz, glamour or hopping
nightlife in this secluded community, just the
pleasure of rolling dunes, clean beaches and the
saltwater surf of the Atlantic Ocean. If it's a
getaway to total peace and lazy relaxation
you're after, this is the place to come. But not
to worry about those creature comforts you
can't live without. There's a well-stocked grocery (Ben & Jerry's, anyone?), a gas station and
a few great boutiques for that wayward cloudy
day.

Architecture of the Sandbridge rentals varies wildly, from ye olde cottage to high-tech
contemporary, with rental rates that are in sync
with the luxury offered. Most owners have
named their homes, and for natives the moniker is a better handle on location than the actual address. All sleep at least six quite comfortably and come with everything you need

but bed linens and towels. In summer months,
expect to pay from about $900 to $2,500 for a
week of the pleasure of sleeping in a real house
rather than a hotel room.

Should you forget something critical, such
as a cooler, crib or boogie board, there are several reputable "you need it, we got it" rental
places that will even deliver the required goods
to your door. Check with your cottage rental
service for the equipment rental firm they recommend.

Those who know what's available, when
and for how much, are very helpful in matching your particular family and budget to a rental
property in Sandbridge. One quick call will win
you a brochure with photos of all the possibilities and their particulars.

Siebert Realty-Sandbridge Beach, 601
Sandbridge Road, Virginia Beach, (757) 426-
6200, (800) 231-3037

Affordable Properties, 613 21st Street, Virginia Beach, (757) 428-0432, (800) 639-0432

Atkinson Realty, 5307 Atlantic Avenue, Virginia Beach, (757) 428-4441

GSH Real Estate, 3704 Pacific Avenue, Virginia Beach, (757) 428-0201

Hudgins Real Estate, 3701 Pacific Avenue,
Virginia Beach, (757) 422-6741, (800) 553-7089

Long & Foster Real Estate, 205 Laskin Road,
Virginia Beach, (757) 428-4600, (800) 941-3333

Sandbridge Realty, 601 Sandbridge Road,
Virginia Beach, (757) 426-6200, (800) 231-3037

Properties are also available for rent in the
heart of the resort action, with a wide swing in
style, proximity to the ocean and rental rates.
Any of the above real estate companies can
provide detailed information on cottages in the
main resort area.

Campgrounds

For those whose pulses race at the mere
thought of sleeping among the bugs under the
stars, the backwoods and campgrounds of
Hampton Roads have a patch of shaded dirt
ready for the thrill. Since most of the Insiders
we know consider serious camping out an overnight at a Holiday Inn, it's hard to understand
the attraction of any accommodation with a 3-
foot high ceiling and a bathroom decorated with
trees rather than white ceramic tile and fluo-
rescent lights. But, if camping is your thing,
we feel it's our duty to point your canoe in the
right direction.

You'll find overnight camping sites clustered
primarily in rural Virginia Beach, the Hampton Roads city that still has pioneer spaces to

accommodate you L.L. Bean types. Lest you think we're totally primitive, most facilities do offer comfort-zone amenities such as swimming pools, restrooms and showers, playgrounds and camp stores for those basic necessities.

Rates vary with the season and the hookup requested (water, electrical, sewage, etc.), and reservations are recommended to secure your spot. Most also allow pets on leashes, so don't keep Rover away from all the fun.

INSIDERS' TIP

Don't be afraid to ask your hotel or resort for a complimentary ride to your destination. Most offer such a service, though they don't always promote it.

Virginia Beach

First Landing State Park
2500 Shore Dr., Virginia Beach
• **(757) 412-2300, (757) 412-2331**
This is our most popular camping destination, so even with 235 sites, you'd best reserve early through Virginia State Parks (757) 481-2131 or TicketMaster, (757) 671-8100. There's no water or electricity, but there are bathhouses and a store. Best of all, you get to use a secluded Chesapeake Bay beach. Across the road are hiking and biking trails. Check out the new Chesapeake Bay Center in the park. Cabins are available and are open March 30 through November.

Holiday Trav-L-Park
1075 General Booth Blvd., Virginia Beach
• **(757) 425-0249, (800) 548-0223**
Convenient to Croatan Beach, this 700-site park welcomes tents, recreational vehicles and pets on leashes. Pools, laundry facilities, bathhouses, stores and a restaurant are on-site or nearby. Cabins are also available.

KOA Campground
1240 General Booth Blvd., Virginia Beach
• **(757) 428-1444**
This popular spot is open March through November with 402 sites plus cabins. Pools, bathhouses and a store are added attractions.

North Bay Shore Campground
3257 Colechester Rd., Virginia Beach
• **(757) 426-7911**
This Sandbridge campground offers 165 sites with a pool, bathhouse and store. It's open April 15 through October 1.

Outdoor Resorts Virginia Beach
3665 Sandpiper Rd., Virginia Beach
• **(757) 721-2020, (800) 568-7873**
This RV resort is on North Bay, one block from the ocean. There are 175 sites with access to a bathhouse. Tennis courts, a clubhouse, a pool, a hot tub, an exercise room, saunas and a boat ramp are some of the amenities. The resort is open year round.

Seneca Campground
144 S. Princess Anne Rd., Virginia Beach
• **(757) 426-6241**
There are 100 sites at this campground in rural Pungo that's popular with the fishing crowd. You'll find cabins, bathhouses, a boat ramp and a store to add to your good time.

Portsmouth

Sleepy Hole Park
Sleepy Hole Rd., Portsmouth
• **(757) 538-4102**
Overlooking the Nansemond River in Suffolk, this Portsmouth-operated park plays host to 50 campsites with your pick of provided utilities. Also available: bathhouses, laundry facilities, fire rings and a sports fields with recreation equipment checkout.

Chesapeake

Northwest River Park
Indian River Rd., Chesapeake
• **(757) 421-7151**
Nestled in the center of this 763-acre city park are campsites serviced by a camp store and bathhouses. The park itself offers a wealth of goodies for the outdoors person, including extensive hiking trails, boat, canoe and paddleboat rentals, an equestrian center and a gorgeous lake that stretches almost the entire length of the park.

Convention Facilities

Pavilion Convention Center
1000 19th St., Virginia Beach
• **(757) 428-8000**
Virginia Beach's convention center is six

ACCOMMODATIONS

Virginia Beach's Chamberlin Hotel rises majestically above the waterfront.

Photo: Courtesy of Virginia Tourism Corporation

blocks from the ocean and has 57,000 square feet of space.

Scope
Brambleton and City Hall Aves., Norfolk
• **(757) 441-2764**

Owned by the City of Norfolk, Scope has 83,630 square feet of space and is six blocks from the Downtown waterfront. It is where the Ringling Bros. Barnum & Bailey Circus performs, the Hampton Roads Admirals play ice hockey and college basketball teams have their games.

Waterside Convention Center
235 E. Main St., Norfolk
• **(757) 628-6501**

Also owned by the City of Norfolk, Waterside Convention Center opened Downtown in 1991. It is connected to the Marriott Hotel and is across the street from The Waterside Festi-

val Marketplace. It has more than 36,000 square feet of function space.

Waterfront Conference Center
425 Water St., Portsmouth
• **(757) 673-3000**

The region's newest convention center will open in downtown Portsmouth by early 2001. Its 24,000 square feet of meeting space is located along the banks of the Elizabeth River. Adjoining the conference center is a new Renaissance Hotel.

Chesapeake Conference Center
900 Greenbrier Cir., Chesapeake
• **(757) 382-2500**

Opened in 1997, this city-owned center boasts Virginia's largest ballroom. The conference center has 38,000 square feet of space and is in the Greenbrier area within walking distance of 650 motel rooms.

ACCOMMODATIONS

Restaurants

Price Code

Next to each restaurant's name, you'll notice nifty dollar-sign signals, the Insiders' code for what you might expect to pay for entrees for two. This code does not include cocktails, appetizers, dessert, tax or tip. Our codes apply to evening meals, and you can work the math to subtract about one-third for a lunchtime visit.

$	Less than $20
$$	$20 to $35
$$$	$36 to $50
$$$$	$51 and more

Let's face it. Hampton Roads is not the best place on earth to go on a diet. We enjoy a wealth of fresh seafood from the Chesapeake Bay and the Atlantic Ocean, and we've got all kinds of Southern regional specialties to tempt you. You'll discover some great barbecue in our neck of the woods, but you'll also find wonderfully innovative dishes that make good use of our classic local ingredients—delicacies such as Smithfield ham, soft-shell crabs, grits, corn, tomatoes and strawberries.

Our first-class local ingredients do not mean, however, that our chefs are reluctant to find inspiration elsewhere. Hampton Roads is a thriving military community so our restaurants have to satisfy patrons who have dined all over the world. You'll find everything from Thai to Mexican to German on our regional bill of fare. We're also happy to be part of the burgeoning national coffeehouse, bistro and bakery trends.

We have chosen to take you through the wonderful world of caloric intake by category rather than by city. That's because, if you're like us, when you have a taste for mu shu pork, you don't want to have to flip through 18 pages of Cajun-spiced American nouvelle cuisine to locate the best Chinese places in the area. We'll try to give you the decorative flavor of each establishment, along with the most popular menu items, throwing in a few totally subjective opinions along the way.

A word about reservations is in order. If it's Memorial Day weekend and you're in Virginia Beach, don't expect to waltz in unannounced to a waiting table. Ditto that on any holiday or, for that matter, any night during peak summer season. Most restaurants require, or at least recommend, that you make reservations for your dining party, and that (believe us!) has no bearing whatsoever on the time you may actually be seated. This is no way implies that your restaurant of choice does not want to pamper your every culinary desire, it's just that the party of 12 ahead of you may be savoring its umpteenth minicup of espresso. So, wherever your destination for the evening's repast, be prepared to linger at the inevitably well-stocked bar for an aperitif before your name is announced for din-din.

With so many restaurants to sample, we've tried to keep this intro brief, but we must mention the grand finale of every meal—the check. Most places accept plastic as payment, although American Express is not welcome at quite a few establishments. Unless otherwise noted, the establishments listed below accept major credit cards. Personal checks are likewise not a just dessert for many tabs. Be advised to check out each restaurant's specific payment policies when making reservations.

One last note before we're seated. The tour we're about to take is current as of press time, but many of our local chefs seem to have wings under their white smocks. What's pasta today may be pai fan tomorrow. But menu U-turns and restaurant name-changes are all a part of the thrill of the food chase.

INSIDERS' TIP

To check out what's on the menu at a specific restaurant, look in *Port Folio's* weekly dining review. You'll find a weekly restaurant review in the Virginian-Pilot's Sunday food section and in its weekly community tabloids.

American

Norfolk

Charlie's Cafe
$, no credit cards
• **1800-A Granby St., Norfolk**
• **(757) 625-0824**

Hearty breakfasts and comfort food are the hallmarks of this small Ghent eatery that attracts a diversified clientele from police officers to young professionals and the artsy crowd. Omelettes, waffles, pancakes and fluffy biscuits hit the spot at breakfast, which is served all day. For lunch and dinner, burgers, meat loaf and sandwiches share the spotlight with home-cooked specials such as chicken and dumplings and pot roast. The home fries are topnotch.

Do-nut Dinette
$, no credit cards
• **1917 Colley Ave., Norfolk**
• **(757) 625-0061**

If you're a fan of vintage diners, this is the place to go for breakfast or lunch. The dinette opened in the 1940s. Owner Sheila Schneider Mullins took over the diner in 1987 from her parents who ran it for decades. There are only 16 stools, and regular customers occupy most of them. Breakfast and lunch are served daily. The morning meal features eggs, sausage, hash browns and irresistible donuts just pulled from the hot oil and dripping with glaze. There's always a lunch special such as fried chicken or fresh seafood. The dinette has some of the best prices in town.

Doumar's
$, no credit cards
• **20th St. and Monticello Ave., Norfolk**
• **(757) 627-4163**

Doumar's is a Norfolk landmark that shouldn't be missed. It's been at the same location since 1934 and is run by members of its founding family. Some car hops and cooks have worked at Doumar's more than 40 years. When a car hop hangs a tray on your car window loaded with burgers, fries and milk shakes served in real glasses, you'll think the calendar slipped back a few decades. The food is good and cheap. Doumar's opens for breakfast and keeps serving until late night every day but Sunday. Its standouts include pork barbecue and the best limeades in town. Be sure to end your meal with ice cream in a homemade cone—after all, Abe Doumar, the restaurant's founder, invented the ice cream cone in 1904.

The Eaton Gogh Cafe
$ • **806 Harrington Ave., Norfolk**
• **(757) 640-0233**

This unassuming Ghent restaurant has a loyal following, and owner Terry Fraley has a long history of creating great food. Even though it's only been around a few years, the cafe nabbed the title of "Overall Best Restaurant" in a 1999 poll conducted by The Virginia-Pilot. This is mostly a takeout and catering operation with a few seats available for in-house dining. Regulars love the she-crab soup billed on the menu as "positively the best she-crab around." Innovative salads like the Chickaloupe (cantaloupe stuffed with chicken salad) also are popular as are sandwiches rolled in flour tortillas. Desserts include chocolate chess pie and key lime pie. The restaurant serves lunch Monday through Saturday and brunch (known here as the "big breakfast") on Sunday. It stays open until 8 PM on Mondays. The other nights savvy diners know to stop by before the 5 PM closing time to pick up their pre-ordered dinners to take home. If you're doing takeout orders, it's always best to call in ahead of time to avoid a wait.

Freemason Abbey
$$ • **Freemason and Boush Sts., Norfolk**
• **(757) 622-3966**

This aptly named restaurant is in the historic Freemason neighborhood in a former Presbyterian church built in 1873. Before becoming a restaurant in 1988, the building was an Odd Fellows meeting hall. Although the Abbey retains its original exterior, inside it has been remodeled into a modern two-level restaurant. The menu includes seafood, pasta, quiche, sandwiches, chicken and steaks. Perenalli's greens is a notable salad and makes an ideal lunch when accompanied by crab soup or gumbo. Each Wednesday is Lobster Night, with New England lobsters served for a reasonable price. Other nights also have bargain-priced specials such as prime rib or steamed shrimp. Lunch and dinner are served daily, with brunch offered on Sunday. Reservations are accepted.

The Grate Steak
$$ • **235 N. Military Hwy., Norfolk**
• **(757) 461-5501**

Mention beef in this region, and The Grate Steak springs immediately to mind. For years this has been a popular choice for chowing down on cooked-to-perfection steaks. The reason: You charbroil it yourself over a giant grill. This is a fun place to go with a group. Select your cut, plop that baby on the grill and let it sizzle. (Just don't wear a sweater or it will definitely need a trip to the cleaners to get out the smoky smell.) Potatoes, bread and a hefty salad bar make sure you're stuffed when you leave. There's also a regular, cooked-in-the-kitchen menu. The Grate Steak serves lunch on weekdays with dinner available daily.

Kelly's Tavern
$ • 1408 Colley Ave., Norfolk
• (757) 623-3216

Kelly's is one place we go that makes us toss health-consciousness to the wind and go for the hamburger with fries. The grilled chicken sandwich is also a perennial favorite. Kelly's has been in Norfolk's trendy Ghent neighborhood since the late 1970s and has spin-off operations in Virginia Beach at 1936 Laskin Road, (757) 491-8737 and in Pembroke Mall at 4586 Virginia Beach Blvd. (757) 490-7999, and in Chesapeake at Crossways at Greenbrier shopping center at 1412 Greenbrier Parkway, (757) 523-1781. All four restaurants offer sandwiches, salads and appetizers. The newer restaurants also have some full dinners. Kelly's serves lunch and dinner daily, with the Beach locations featuring a Sunday brunch. The Beach establishment also takes reservations.

Lone Star Steakhouse & Saloon
$$ • 450 N. Military Hwy., Norfolk
• (757) 466-0124

The name says it all for this Texas-style chain restaurant that's actually based in Kansas beef country. Lone Star is authentic enough to be a favorite restaurant for some Texas transplants we know. Tossing peanut shells on the floor and line dancing to country music help create the ambiance for the steakhouse. Steaks are huge, and you can pick yours out in the kitchen or trust the staff to find the biggest, juiciest one. Lone Star is open daily for lunch and dinner. The restaurant has a Virginia Beach location at 2712 N. Mall Drive, (757) 463-2879, and a Chesapeake location at 1570 Crossways Boulevard, (757) 424-6917.

Magnolia
$$ • Colley Ave. and Princess Anne Dr., Norfolk
• (757) 625-0400

This attractive Ghent restaurant puts the spotlight on creative cooking. You'll find a good variety on the menu from walnut-encrusted catfish to seafood and some Southern and Southwestern specialties. One of our memorable lunches featured a hefty slab of spicy meat loaf and a wonderful side dish of collards spiced with ginger and curry. The atmosphere is elegant at this restaurant, which serves lunch and dinner daily. It recently garnered acclaim in *Southern Living* magazine.

No Frill Grill
$ • 7452 Tidewater Dr., Norfolk
• (757) 587-0949
806 Spotswood Ave., Norfolk
• (757) 627-4262

The name of this restaurant says it all. Its two locations serve good, basic food at reasonable prices: barbecue ribs, hamburgers, milk shakes, and big salads. The Grills have a '50s feel and are open for lunch and dinner daily. A sister restaurant is Dog-N-Burger, a tiny take-out place at 2001 Manteo Street in the Ghent area, (757) 623-1667.

Open Wide
$ • 124 Granby St., Norfolk
• (757) 533-9153

This downtown Norfolk restaurant consistently earns rave reviews from the downtown Norfolk working crowd. This casual eatery in a row of restored buildings is divided into a restaurant and a bar. Its eclectic menu ranges from comfort food such as meat loaf and chicken pot pie to the more exotic tuna over tortellini. There's a solid lineup of hand-tossed pizzas and sandwiches as well as some killer desserts. Lunch is served on weekdays with dinner offered Monday through Saturday. Open Wide also serves Sunday brunch. On weekend nights you can hear live bluegrass, rock or other music.

The Painted Lady Tea Room
$$ • 112 E. 17th St., Norfolk
• (757) 623-8872

This restaurant took the region by storm when it opened in 1998. It immediately became a favorite of "ladies who lunch." But it also is favored by a variety of people who like good food, interesting ambiance, and antiques. The tea room is in two Victorian houses on the edge of the Ghent area. They are joined together to form one restaurant with lots of nooks and crannies filled with antiques and knick-knacks that are for sale. Our favorite is the seafood quiche served with a flower-bedecked salad and muffins. The she-crab soup is always wonderful. The Painted Lady serves lunch, dinner, and afternoon tea daily. For special occasions you can hire the tea room's limousine to deliver you to a symphony performance, play, or other downtown Norfolk event after having a meal, of course.

Philly Style Steaks & Subs
$, no credit cards
• 7456 Tidewater Dr., Norfolk
• (757) 588-0602

One Philadelphia expatriate we know swears this eatery turns out the most authentic cheese steaks and subs he's had since he left the City of Brotherly Love. Owners Joe and Debbie Hatch opened in 1983 and still import their sandwich rolls from up north. They serve lunch and dinner every day except Sunday.

Rainforest Café
$$ • 300 Monticello Ave., Norfolk
• (757) 627-8440

For a theme restaurant the food here is amazingly good. Kids of all ages are fascinated by the animatronic elephants, birds, and other animals as well as the mock rain storm that rolls through this MacArthur Center mall restaurant. Even without the entertainment, the café's excellent salads and sandwiches are enough to make you want to come back for more. The cafe is open daily for lunch and dinner. Although it doesn't take reservations, you can call ahead to get a seating preference.

The Taphouse Grill
$$ • 931 W. 21st St., Norfolk
• (757) 627-9172

If you're a beer fan, this is the place to go. This relaxing Ghent oasis stocks more varieties of beer than anyone else around, including a slew of microbrews. However, the Taphouse Grill also appeals to those of us who don't even like beer. The menu ranges from casual fare such as nachos to paella, tapas, and homemade desserts. The grill serves lunch on weekdays and dinner every evening. It is open until the wee hours.

The Ten Top
$ • 748 Shirley Ave., Norfolk
• (757) 622-5422

This mostly takeout operation is tucked into a side street in Ghent. There are a few seats for eating in, but takeout is its forte. Specialties include sandwiches—both the vegetarian and the meat-filled variety—and salads. Flatbread pizza also is on the menu as are dinners accompanied by a salad and bread. Delivery is available in Ghent. The restaurant is open daily for lunch and dinner.

Thyme Square
$ • 509 Boutetourt St., Norfolk
• (757) 623-5082

This small gourmet cafe has a constantly changing menu of tempting seafood, meats and side dishes. Seasonal wines highlight the food for the day. You can eat in or carry out your meals. Thyme Square is open for lunch and dinner on weekdays. It is on the edge of the historic Freemason neighborhood.

Wild Monkey
$$ • 1603 Colley Ave., Norfolk
• (757) 627-6462

This currently reigns as one of the most wildly popular restaurants in Ghent. You won't find printed menus or reservations here. Just plan to come and wait for your seat. The good things to eat will be chalked on a 30-foot blackboard on the wall. The menu is eclectic and constantly changing, but you'll usually find all-American meat loaf on the menu along with Indian, European, and Asian dishes. Lunch is served on weekdays with dinner served every day but Sunday.

Uncle Louie's
$$ • 132 E. Little Creek, Norfolk
• (757) 480-1225

This sophisticated restaurant is tucked away in the back of Uncle Louie's gourmet shop. With 275 seats, the restaurant is surprisingly spacious, with an excellent seasonal menu that runs the gamut from seafood to sandwiches. Steaks cut from Angus beef are the house specialty. If you're really starving, get things started with the "mother load," an aptly named dish of potato skins buried under cheese, bacon, and sour cream. Besides homemade desserts, Uncle Louie's has 110 coffees, thanks to its affiliation with First Colony Coffee Co. Stop in during the afternoons for a pot of tea and scones, finger sandwiches and other traditional tea-time fare. Uncle Louie's is open daily for breakfast, lunch and dinner.

Virginia Beach

Aberdeen Barn
$$ • 5805 Northampton Blvd.,
Virginia Beach
• (757) 464-1580

For more than a quarter of a century the

Aberdeen Barn has satisfied the region's hunger for beef. There's nothing trendy about the restaurant, but it does have a solid "we've been here forever" kind of ambiance with a loyal cadre of diners. The prime rib is outstanding and comes in two sizes—jumbo and extra jumbo—so dainty eaters may want to go for the petite tenderloin. Chicken and shrimp also are on the menu. The restaurant serves dinner daily.

Atlas Diner
$$ • 2158 N. Great Neck Rd.,
Virginia Beach
• (757) 496-3839
2135 General Booth Blvd., Virginia Beach
• (757) 430-2839
1432 Greenbrier Parkway, Chesapeake
• (757) 420-6222

Veteran local restaurateurs Corey Beisel and Mike Atkinson hit a winner when they created the first Atlas Diner on Great Neck Road in 1996. They duplicated their success with two other diners that serve the same menu. The restaurants take diners on an All-America road trip and fill them up with comfort food along the way. It's tough to choose between chicken and pork barbecue quesadillas and the New Orleans fried-chicken salad. Desserts are divine, and you'll find a lengthy wine list to please your palate. The Diner serves dinner daily, brunch on Sunday, and lunch every other day of the week. While it doesn't take reservations, if you call as you dash out the door, your name will be put on a seating list so your wait will be shortened.

Baja Restaurant
$$ • 3701 Sandpiper Rd., Virginia Beach
• (757) 426-7748

Despite its Mexican name, this restaurant specializes in homemade pizza and seafood. The Baja has been a casual Sandbridge beach eatery since 1974. It is at the far end of Sandbridge overlooking Back Bay and has a screened dining area. Fresh fish usually includes flounder, tuna, and catfish. The Baja is known for crab cakes. It serves lunch and dinner daily and brunch on Sunday. Hours may vary in the off-season so be sure to call first.

Gus & George's Spaghetti & Steak House
$ • 4312 Virginia Beach Blvd.,
Virginia Beach
• (757) 340-6584

We know liver and onions don't top everyone's favorite-food list, but if you like it, you know it's tough to find liver properly prepared. Well, Gus & George's makes the best liver and onions around according to some liver connoisseurs we know. The restaurant's namesake spaghetti and steak also are outstanding—particularly the marinated Romanian steak. The owners' Greek heritage shows up in the baklava that's on the dessert menu. There's nothing fancy about this restaurant, but it has a loyal following among diners who like good home cooking. Gus & George's is open daily for lunch and dinner.

Hilltop Brewing Co. and Restaurant
$ • 1556 Laskin Rd., Virginia Beach
• (757) 422-5652

The variety of brews is impressive and so is the food at this casual restaurant in the Hilltop East shopping center. Food ranges from basic brew pub sandwiches to lamb, pastas, and fish. There is live music on weekends. The brewing company is open daily for lunch and dinner as well as for libations in the wee hours of the morning.

Hunt Room Grille
$$$ • 42nd St. and Pacific Ave.,
Virginia Beach
• (757) 425-8555

This is a special restaurant known only to true Insiders. The Grille is in the basement of the 1920s-era Cavalier on the Hill hotel. It's open only in winter and is one of the most romantic places we've ever dined. Through the years famous guests of the hotel have eaten here, and the Grille is rumored to have been one of President Richard Nixon's favorite restaurants. The food is sublime, featuring beef, seafood, and pork. Service is impeccable, and the genteel hunt club atmosphere is soothing. Guests are greeted by a fire roaring in the giant fireplaces. Waiting for them are roasting sticks and a bowl of marshmallows to toast. After dinner be sure to wander upstairs to view the hotel's small museum that relates its history. The Grille usually is open from January through April for dinner Wednesday through Saturday. Reservations are recommended.

The Jewish Mother
$ • 3108 Pacific Ave., Virginia Beach
• (757) 422-5430
1 High St., Portsmouth
• (757) 398-3332

The Jewish Mother is a Virginia Beach landmark that's been around since 1975. It's a fun,

New York-deli type place with a big lineup of sandwiches and 90 different types of beer to wash down the food. The same menu is featured at a sister operation in downtown Portsmouth. Lox and cream cheese, latkes, blintzes, and homemade soups are on the menu at both places. The Jewish Mother serves a variety of salads and breakfast items, too. With more than 20 desserts in a showcase up front, it's hard to pass up the sweets. Live entertainment at night brings in some national bands. Breakfast, lunch, and dinner are served daily.

Kitchin's Kitchen
$, no credit cards
• 26th St. and Atlantic Ave., Virginia Beach
• (757) 428-1296

Founded in 1941 as an open-air snack bar along the oceanfront, Kitchin's Kitchen is a local favorite. Hearty breakfasts draw a crowd of regulars. Lunch specialties include fresh-ground hamburgers. Sue Gergen, known as "Sue the Soup Lady," creates a different homemade soup each day as she has done since 1949. Breakfast, lunch, and dinner are served daily in the summer. In the winter, they serve just breakfast and lunch.

Mary's Restaurant
$ • 616 Virginia Beach Blvd.,
Virginia Beach
• (757) 428-1355

Since 1958 Mary's has been dishing out big breakfasts and home-cooked lunches. It's always had the same owners, who specialize in barbecue, meat loaf, and luscious desserts such as German chocolate cake and banana cake.

Outback Steakhouse
$$ • 1757 Laskin Rd., Virginia Beach
• (757) 422-5796
$$ • 1255 Fordham Dr., Virginia Beach
• (757) 523-4832
4312 Portsmouth Blvd., Chesapeake
• (757) 465-1047
333 Waterside Dr., Norfolk
• (757) 622-9101

This steakhouse may aspire to live up to its Australian ambiance, but its menu is pure American with beef, beef, and more beef. From New York strip to prime rib and sirloin, the steaks are big and cooked to perfection. It didn't take long after the Outback's opening in 1993 on Laskin Road for word to spread of its "bloomin' onion" appetizer—a huge batter-fried onion served with spicy remoulade. Meals come with salad, vegetable, and bread. The Outback

serves dinner daily and lunch on Sunday. The Norfolk location is in The Waterside Festival Marketplace.

Pollard's Chicken
$ • 100 London Bridge Blvd.,
Virginia Beach
• (757) 340-2565

Despite the giant plastic chicken out front, there's more than fried hen on the menu at this local chain of family restaurants that's been around since 1967. North Carolina-style barbecue, chicken and dumplings, barbecue, and Brunswick stew are as popular as the chicken. Daily specials feature country-style comfort food such as livers and gizzards. Homemade desserts include five-layer coconut cake and bread pudding. Lunch and dinner are served daily. Other locations are in Chesapeake at 717 S. Battlefield Boulevard, (757) 482-3200, and in Norfolk at 3033 Ballentine Boulevard, (757) 855-7864 and 326 E. Bayview Boulevard, (757) 587-8185.

Pungo Grill
$$ • 1785 Princess Anne Rd.,
Virginia Beach
• (757) 426-6655

This restaurant prides itself on its eclectic menu. On a typical day diners can enjoy crab cakes, pasta, lasagna, catfish, Thai and Jamaican chicken, and 12 different vegetables. The Pungo Grill, which opened in 1988, is in a restored 1919 house in the heart of Pungo in rural Virginia Beach. It works seasonal local produce into the menu when it's available. Homemade desserts include chocolate mousse, hummingbird cake, and lemon meringue pie. Lunch and dinner are served every day except Monday.

The Raven
$ • 1200 Atlantic Ave., Virginia Beach
• (757) 425-9556

Since 1968, The Raven has been a beachfront mainstay. Its offerings include French dip sandwiches and the Raven champignon—a burger dressed up with bacon and sautéed mushrooms. Lunch and dinner are served daily.

Reisner's Delicatessen
$ • Mill Dam and Great Neck Rds.,
Virginia Beach
• (757) 481-3639

This traditional deli has a lengthy history and a new location. It relocated in 1997 to the

Great Neck Village Shopping Center after 32 years in the Janaf Shopping Center in Norfolk. Reisner's was first opened in Norfolk in 1943 by the grandparents of current owner Linda Ausch. You'll find traditional pastrami, corned beef and other deli specialties served with tempting side dishes. Divine desserts are made by Ausch's sister, Jodie Woodward. Reisner's serves lunch and dinner every day but Sunday.

Yukon Steak Co.
$$ • 994 Kempsville Rd., Virginia Beach
• (757) 495-7745

Beef is the star of the menu at this rustic restaurant decorated with an Alaskan theme. Both USDA Choice and Angus beef are featured. You can watch your steak sizzling over an open charcoal hearth. Salmon and crab are available for those who aren't beef lovers. The restaurants serve dinner daily. The restaurant is in Providence Square Shopping Center.

Chesapeake

Cara's
$$ • 123 N. Battlefield Blvd., Chesapeake
• (757) 548-0006

Opened in 1992 along the Atlantic Intracoastal Waterway, this restaurant has expanded Chesapeake's dining options. Its menu is heavy on seafood but also includes chicken, Angus beef, sandwiches, and huge specialty salads. Cara's is in the Island Wharf shops and has a deck overlooking the waterway. Everything is homemade, including breads and desserts such as Mississippi fudge pie and peanut butter pie. Cara's serves lunch and dinner every day but Monday.

Cheer's
$ • 1405 Greenbrier Pkwy., Chesapeake
• (757) 424-4665

Modeled on its Boston namesake, this casual eatery opened in 1990 on the outskirts of Greenbrier Mall. Its big menu includes sandwiches, salads, beef, chicken, and seafood. Popular entrees include barbecued ribs and a Boston chicken and shrimp combo served over fettuccine in cream sauce. There is a fresh fish daily special as well as a cheesecake of the day. An inexpensive express lunch is available for the working crowd. Lunch and dinner are served daily.

Reggie's British Pub
$ • 237 S. Battlefield Blvd.
• (757) 546-2717

It was a happy day in Chesapeake when this traditional British-style pub relocated from Norfolk in 1999 bringing its blend of American and British food as well as array of beers. Cornish pasties and fish and chips share the menu with salads, steaks, and chicken. Desserts are divine. Try the apple dumplings or chocolate mousse pie. There is live music on weekends. The pub serves lunch and dinner daily.

Portsmouth

The Baron's Pub and Restaurant
$ • 500 High St., Portsmouth
• (757) 399-4840

This is a favorite downtown lunch spot. It features daily specials, including meat loaf, chicken and dumplings, and the delicious Baron Burger. The pub is open for lunch and dinner and offers acoustical music in the evenings.

The Café at Pfeiffers
$$ • 606 High St., Portsmouth
• (757) 397-2665

If you love books, wine, and good food then give Pfeiffers a try. This downtown restaurant is housed in an eclectic book and wine shop. Salads, soups, and sandwiches star at lunch with fusion cuisine bursting forth at dinner. Look for Asian, European, and American influences on its ever-changing menu. Dine inside or in the pleasant courtyard. Lunch is served weekdays with brunch offered on Saturdays and dinner Wednesday through Saturday. There is live music to accompany weekend dinners.

Cheshire Grill
$ • 623 High St., Portsmouth
• (757) 399-1990

If you're hankering for a quick Portsmouth history lesson while you dine, then the Cheshire Grill is the place. The restaurant is decorated with objects from now-defunct retail stores

INSIDERS' TIP
While visiting in the region, be sure to try some of our regional cuisine. Soft-shell crabs and crab cakes are two of our favorites. On most menus you'll find crab prepared all kinds of ways. Smithfield ham, Brunswick stew, and peanut pie are other traditional Virginia fare.

Sailing Up For Supper

When Hampton Roads sailors cast off from their docks early in the evening, it's a sure bet that they're setting sail for one of our many restaurants that make a boater welcome. All along the Bay, rivers and creeks, waterfront eateries dot our coastline. While many welcome sailing parties that come unannounced, it's often wise to phone ahead to ensure a berth at your destination.

Starting in Virginia Beach's Long Creek, you can pull into Chick's Oyster Bar, (757) 481-5757, for some delectable steamed seafood in a casual atmosphere. At nearby Lynnhaven Inlet, you have your choice of always-chic The Inlet, (757) 481-7300, or dress down and make a wake to Bubba's, (757) 481-3513.

The ever-popular Rudee Inlet has Rockafeller's, (757) 422-5654 and Rudee's, (757) 425-1777.

Traveling up towards Norfolk, you'll find the waters along Shore Drive quite hospitable to hungry sea travelers. Paddle into the Blue Crab, (757) 362-8000.

You'll find excellent choices port and starboard on the Elizabeth River, which parts Downtown Norfolk and Portsmouth. The premier pull-in would be The Waterside Marina, (757) 627-3300, from which you can take your pick of the many food tastes that await inside The Waterside Festival Marketplace Or head down the promenade to the Riverwalk, (757) 622-6664, at the Sheraton Waterside Hotel.

Across the Elizabeth River in Portsmouth, you can pull into the Holiday Yacht Harbor, (757) 399-0991, and head to Amory's Wharf, an elevated restaurant that offers a panoramic view of Crawford Bay as well as the Elizabeth River. Farther up towards Hampton Roads harbor is our personal favorite, Scale o'de Whale, (757) 483-2772, which sits perched on the end of the pier and welcomes boating patrons on a first-come, first served basis.

In Chesapeake, Lock's Pointe, (757) 547-9618, offers a fine dining room with a casual glassed-in patio. Smithfield Station, (757) 399-2874, welcomes travelers at the confluence of Cypress Creek and the Pagan River in Smithfield. And, lastly, Suffolk offers its own casual boat-up dining at Bennett's Creek Marina, (757) 484-8700, on the body of water with the same name.

After a day of boating, drift up to one of our many waterfront restaurants that welcome boaters to their docks.

Photo: Courtesy of Norfolk Convention and Visitors Bureau

RESTAURANTS

that once lined downtown streets. The menu gives historical tidbits about downtown and names entrees after downtown landmarks. You'll find mostly sandwiches and salads. It may be hard to choose between the Prison Square (a vegetable burger) or St. Paul's (grilled salmon with lettuce). The grill is open daily for lunch and dinner.

Commodore Theatre
$ • 421 High St.,
Portsmouth
• (757) 393-6962

If you like your sandwich or salad with a side order of entertainment, this is the place for you. The Commodore is a restored theater that shows first-run movies while serving light dinners. It's a great place for a date or a relaxing night on the town. You sit in comfy chairs at small tables with your own private phone to call in your dinner order while watching the movie. If you prefer only snacks and drinks, head for the balcony. The Commodore is open for dinner daily. On weekends and when popular movies are showing, you will need to buy tickets ahead of time to get a downstairs seat.

Mom's Best Deli
$ • 340 Broad St., Portsmouth
• (757) 399-1199

One of our favorite stops for a quick sandwich, this small deli in the Port Norfolk neighborhood also turns out some good home cooking. Daily specials include chicken and dumplings and corned beef and cabbage. Homemade salads and desserts also are notable. The deli has gained local fame for its chocolate chip cookies and meringue pies. It serves lunch on weekdays.

New York Delicatessen
$ • 509 Court St., Portsmouth
• (757) 399-3354

The deli has been in downtown Portsmouth since the 1930s and in its current quarters for about 20 years. Kosher foods include Reuben and pastrami sandwiches, lox and bagels and chicken soup. Desserts include homemade

cream puffs. It serves breakfast, lunch and early dinners every day but Sunday.

Suffolk

Bunny's Family Restaurant
$ • 1901 Wilroy Rd., Suffolk
• (757) 538-2325

Bunny's is Suffolk's home-cooking

Take advantage of the fresh seafood that the Chesapeake Bay region has to offer.

Photo: Courtesy of Virginia's Eastern Shore Tourism Commission

standout. It's been dishing up fried chicken, crab cakes and chicken pot pie for 25 years from its location near Wilroy Industrial Park. This is a no-frills place with a big lineup of vegetables such as stewed tomatoes, candied yams, and butter beans. Homemade hush puppies come with meals. Bunny's is open daily for breakfast, lunch, and dinner. Breakfasts feature Belgian waffles, eggs, and pancakes.

Front Street Restaurant
$$ • 434 N. Main St., Suffolk
• (757) 539-5393

Housed in a historic home near downtown Suffolk, Front Street is open for lunch on weekdays and dinner Wednesday through Saturday. Dinner entrees range from steaks and scallops to trout and chicken. Specialty dishes include scalloped oysters and chicken cordon bleu stuffed with Brie and ham. The lunch menu features mainly salads and sandwiches. This is an elegant spot with candlelight and a fireplace in the dining room.

Asian

Norfolk

Bamboo Hut
$ • 2200 Colonial Ave., Norfolk
• (757) 640-1649
6400 E. Virginia Beach Blvd., Norfolk
• (757) 455-6002
7450 Tidewater Dr., Norfolk
• (757) 583-6585
Dependable, fast, and reasonably priced—that's Bamboo Hut. While this restaurant may slide somewhat into the category of international fast food, it's hard to beat the beef and broccoli or the mu shu pork. With both Mandarin and Szechuan menu offerings, Bamboo Hut has spread out to multiple locations throughout the region, which more or less is a clue to its popularity among Insiders. Note: This is strictly a take-out operation, or you can have your order delivered. In Virginia Beach you'll also find Bamboo Huts at 2832 Virginia Beach Boulevard, (757) 340-2820; Larkspur Square, (757) 495-4681; 2407 Pacific Avenue, (757) 422-8230; 1801 Pleasure House Road, (757) 460-6490; and College Park Shopping Center, (757) 424-3388. A Chesapeake location is at 455 N. Battlefield Boulevard, (757) 548-1559. Lunch and dinner are served daily.

China Garden
$$ • 854 N. Military Hwy., Norfolk
• (757) 461-3818
1865 E. Little Creek Rd., Norfolk
• (757) 480-8000
The combination lunches and dinners here are tough to top, but, if you insist, you can order from page after page of an extensive menu, or heap your plate time and again from the lavish lunch buffet spread. Peking duck by Chef Lu is a house specialty, and you'll really enjoy the Chinese brunch tradition of dim sum served here on weekends. You can find other China Gardens at Pembroke Mall in Virginia Beach, (757) 497-3497, and at 303 High Street in Portsmouth, (757) 399-8888. Lunch and dinner are served daily.

Hunan Express
$ • Tidewater Shoppes,
6586-D Tidewater Dr., Norfolk
• (757) 853-8187
When Hunan Express first opened, the only way you could have your Chicken of Four Seasons was to fly it home. Now it's an official full-service eatery, and good eatin' it is. We Insiders will now give you the answer to your question about that gorgeous dish being served at the next table. It's the Four Seasons Bird Nest, made of sliced chicken, thinly sliced strips of beef, jumbo shrimp, sea scallops, baby corn, snow peas, mushrooms and assorted veggies done in a rich brown sauce and spread over a nest formed with crispy fried noodles. Perched on the top of the nest is a bird carved from the rind of a melon! It's almost too pretty to eat. Lunch and dinner are served daily.

Kin's Wok
$ • 222-H W. 21st St., Norfolk
• (757) 623-2933
$ • 7545 Granby St., Norfolk
• (757) 423-2828,
Judging by the sleek imported cars squealing away with their windows fogged from the steam of those little white boxes, you can easily surmise that Kin's Wok has sweet and soured its way into the hearts of nearby Chinese food lovers. With an extensive menu of more than 200 items, you'll have to be prepared to carry it out—there are only a few tables for eating in. Portions are enormous, and chicken or shredded pork with string beans are delish. Kin's Wok 2, on Granby Street, offers the same extensive menu as its original Ghent sister. Kin's Wok serves lunch and dinner daily.

Rom Thai
$ • 7512 Granby St., Norfolk
• (757) 480-7900
This attractive restaurant opened in 1999 in the Ward's Corner area of the city. Its owners stir up traditional Thai dishes fired up with peppers that are tamed with coconut milk. There are several curry dishes and lots of noodle entrees on the menu. Rom Thai serves lunch everyday but Sunday and serves dinner daily.

Szechuan in Ghent
$$ • 1517 Colley Ave., Norfolk
• (757) 625-1551
Ghent has many restaurant choices, and this is a favorite for lunch and dinner. The interior decor is surprisingly elegant for a Chinese eatery, but the extensive menu and cordial service match the best of them. Peking duck for two is a house specialty, but we're partial to the triple seafood delight. A special vegetarian menu is available too. Try the Hunan eggplant. A sister

operation is Szechuan Garden Restaurant at 2720 Mall Dr. in Virginia Beach (757) 463-1680.

Virginia Beach

Bangkok Garden
$$ • 4000 Virginia Beach Blvd., Virginia Beach
• (757) 498-5009

This lovely restaurant introduced Thai cuisine to Hampton Roads several years ago. Since then other Thai restaurants have sprung up but Bangkok Garden has held us as a place for a great meal. Its signature dish is Pad Thai, a noodle dish enhanced with your choice of meats. You can choose the intensity of the peppers in this and all dishes. Stir-fries are another popular menu staple. In 1998, Bangkok Garden opened a sister operation in Norfolk at 339 W. 21st St., (757) 622-5047. Both restaurants serve lunch and dinner every day but Sunday.

Bangkok Street Grill
$ • 4316B Virginia Beach Blvd., Virginia Beach
• (757) 498-2439

This restaurant is easy on the wallet. It specializes in the everyday food of Thailand. Look for lemon grass, lime, ginger, and curry to flavor foods as well as fiery peppers. The menu includes appetizers, entrees and noodles with numerous variations available. Some possibilities include pad Thai with shrimp, beef or chicken; duck noodle soup and stir-fried chicken with curry.

Foon's
$$ • 4365 Shore Dr., Virginia Beach
• (757) 460-1985

One great benefit of the authentic Hunan and Szechuan dishes at Foon's is that they are all prepared without MSG. Outstanding on the menu are Szechuan shredded beef, Peking duck, and soft-shell crab with ginger and scallions. Lunch and dinner are served daily.

Forbidden City
$$$ • 3544 Virginia Beach Blvd., Virginia Beach
• (757) 486-8823

This is one of the priciest Chinese restaurants in town, but once you slide into that "forbidden booth" and close the privacy curtains, you'll understand why. The restaurant recently completed an extensive renovation, adding a bar for patrons awaiting a table or take-out. Try the exceptional General Tso's chicken.

Peking Duck Inn
$$ • 5204 Fairfield Shopping Ctr., Kempsville and Providence Rds., Virginia Beach
• (757) 495-9110

Check the chalkboard when you enter this aroma-filled restaurant to see what delicacies Chef Michael Chou has prepared from fresh local ingredients. And do order the egg rolls for a grand surprise—they're not your usual, run-of-the-mill cabbage crispies. One type, for example, is a soft flour pancake filled with duck, plum sauce, and scallions, just a hint of the light, fresh tastes that await no matter what you order.

Eurasia Intercontinental Cuisine
$$ • Loehman's Plaza, 4000 Virginia Beach Blvd., Virginia Beach
• (757) 463-7146

This restaurant defies categorization, but the rave reviews it has won from both professional and casual diners have made it a place to find. The menu flirts with cuisines from all corners of the globe. Chef/owner Am Reelachart draws on his own Thai heritage in dishes such as spring rolls and fiery curries, but he also shows his years of training at Pasta e Pani, with delectable pastas and rough crusty breads. You'll even find some Provencal influences and few American regional specialties, such as superior crab cakes. Hard to define, hard to resist. Give this one a try.

Vietnam Garden
$ • 2404 Virginia Beach Blvd., Virginia Beach
• (757) 631-8048

This restaurant offers classic Vietnamese dining, such as broken rice platters and rice noodle dishes. Even the beverages are authentic, with an astringent green tea, iced French coffees, and soy milk all offered. Lunch and dinner are served daily.

Chesapeake

Bahn-Thai
$ • 1937 S. Military Hwy., Chesapeake
• (757) 543-9116

Chesapeake Crossings shopping center is the unlikely location for this small Thai restaurant run by a native Thai. A variety of noodle dishes and curry are among the numerous offerings. Divine Massamun is a vegetable-filled curry flavored with coconut milk. Foods here range from four-alarm hot to sweet and sour. The restaurant serves lunch and dinner every day but Sunday.

Bakeries

Norfolk

Bon Apetit
$ • 2708 Granby St., Norfolk
• (757) 625-4777
This tiny Mediterranean bakery turns out an amazing amount of bread, baklava, and specialty pastries. Its products show up in local stores and restaurants, but individuals also can stop by for a coconut macaroon or a bag of croissants. The bakery is part of a small Mediterranean grocery whose wares include phyllo dough, grape leaves, and feta cheese. It is closed on Sunday.

French Bakery & Delicatessen
$ • 4108 Granby St., Norfolk
• (757) 625-4936
This bakery has been run by the Habib family since 1913 and has been in this location since 1942. The Habibs pride themselves on using the same recipes as when the bakery was founded. They produce all types of French pastries, including eclairs and French cigars. The orange doughnuts are popular sellers. The bakery is open Monday through Saturday. For lunch it serves submarine sandwiches on homemade bread.

Naas Bakery
$ • 3527 Tidewater Dr., Norfolk
• (757) 623-3858
Naas has been around for more than 50 years. Its current owners have run the business since the early 1970s and gained a loyal clientele. The bakery is known for its Danish pastries, coffee cakes, and butter cookies. It is open daily, and there are a few tables for dining.

Yorgo's Bageldashery
$, no credit cards
• 2123 Colonial Ave., Norfolk
• (757) 623-6609
Selden Arcade, Plume St., Norfolk
• (757) 623-6609
When it opened in Selden Arcade in 1993,

Yorgo's captured the fancy of the downtown lunch crowd. Several years ago it closed that operation and moved to Colonial Ave. and won over the Ghent crowd. Then in 2000 Yorgo's returned downtown to another Selden Arcade location. The beauty of this place is that no matter how long the line is to order, Yorgo's staff manages to whisk everyone through in record time. About a dozen different New York-style bagels are continually pulled from Yorgo's oven. While they're great slathered with cream cheese, the bagels are even better as a sandwich. Our favorites are smoked turkey with prosciutto on an onion bagel and hummus on a whole-wheat bagel. Yorgo's is open daily for breakfast, lunch, and dinner.

Virginia Beach

Baker's Crust Bread Market
$ • 1080 Laskin Rd., Virginia Beach
• (757) 425-4140
Bread is the name of the game at this trendy bakery/cafe that opened in 1993 in the Hilltop North Shopping Center and in 1995 expanded to Norfolk to 21st Street and Lewellyn Avenue, (757) 635-3600. Choosing from the 18 homemade varieties on hand is a daunting task helped only by eating the generous samples doled out. You'll be tempted to take home crusty French baguettes as well as loaves flavored with pumpernickel, cheese, or figs. There's ample seating to savor a hoagie on fresh bread or a nouvelle turkey with cream cheese and apricot on whole wheat. Salads and soups come in a boule of French bread. Luscious desserts and a variety of coffees round out the menu. The Baker's Crust is open for breakfast, lunch and dinner.

La Bella Italia Bakery and Cafe
$ • 1065 Laskin Rd., Virginia Beach
• (757) 422-8536
This Italian bakery is loved for its breads, particularly the crusty sourdough, and its Italian pastries and desserts. It also has semolina and white bread and rolls. Other products include fresh pasta, ravioli, Italian sauces, cheeses, and cold cuts. The bakery also makes wonderful biscotti. It's open seven days a week.

Sugar Plum Bakery
$ • 1353 Laskin Rd., Virginia Beach
• (757) 422-3913
This nonprofit bakery has a tremendous following in Virginia Beach. It started in 1987 to provide training and jobs for young adults

with mental retardation. It serves that mission well while turning out what one person we know calls "the best cookies I ever ate." There are more than 200 items in the bakery, making it one of the region's largest. Among the best sellers are chocolate mousse cake, six-grain bread, and buttery wedding cookies. There are a few tables so you can savor a sweet roll and coffee. The bakery is open Tuesday through Sunday from early morning to late afternoon.

Portsmouth

Sweet Temptations
$ • 2723 Detroit St., Portsmouth
• (757) 393-0772

Walking into this tiny bakery will take you back in time. The owners are pastry chefs who opened their own business in an old house in the Port Norfolk neighborhood. The aroma of freshly baked pastries, cookies, and cakes is irresistible. Its 6 AM opening time makes this a popular morning stop for many workers. The bakery is open every day except Monday.

Barbecue

Norfolk

Harry's Famous Bar-B-Que
$ • 250 Granby St., Norfolk
• (757) 625-1355

There's no longer a Harry at the helm of this barbecue eatery, but the hickory-smoked que is still just as savory. This big downtown restaurant draws a mix of business types, construction workers, and students at nearby Tidewater Community College. We always order the pork barbecue, but beef also is on the menu, as is shrimp, croaker, and other seafood. The veggie lineup ranges from greens to beans. Harry's serves a traditional breakfast, lunch, and dinner every day but Sunday.

Virginia Beach

The Beach Bully
$ • 601 19th St., Virginia Beach
• (757) 422-4222

Since 1985 this casual tavern-style restaurant has provided a change of pace for beachgoers tired of the resort city's predominant seafood. You'll recognize it right away by the fleet of portable barbecue grills flanking

the building several blocks from the oceanfront. Barbecued beef, pork and chicken are all on the menu. Platters come loaded with two side orders of homemade specialties, including hand-cut French fries. One popular offering is the baby back rib dinner. The restaurant is open daily for lunch and dinner.

Formy's Barbecue
$ • 5785 Northampton Blvd.,
Virginia Beach
• (757) 460-4840

This offshoot of a popular Eastern Shore restaurant opened in 1995. Owner Jim Formyduval specializes in tangy Georgia-style barbecue spiced with his own secret sauce. Pork is the star here with chicken and fish also available. Lunch and dinner are served daily.

Frankie's Place for Ribs
$$ • 408 Laskin Rd., Virginia Beach
• (757) 428-7631
$$ • Kempsville and Providence Rds.,
Virginia Beach
• (757) 495-7427

This Virginia Beach-based chain is known for messy but tasty eating. Beef and pork ribs are the specialty of the house. Frankie's also is famous for its onion loaf—a giant pile of onion rings that is a great way to start the meal. Frankie's corn bread also is delicious. Chicken and steaks round out the menu. The Laskin Road location serves dinner daily. The other Virginia Beach restaurant also serves lunch daily. The Kempsville restaurant is in Fairfield Shopping Center. A Chesapeake location serves lunch and dinner daily at 146 S. Battlefield Road, (757) 546-0030.

North Landing Grocery
$ • 3508 North Landing Rd., Virginia Beach
• (757) 430-2727

There's nothing fancy about this grocery/cafe, but the barbecue is first class. Take your choice of the Carolina-style vinegar sauce or the tangy, red sauce. The Grocery is in the country near the Virginia Beach courthouse complex and is on the way to the beach at Sandbridge. It serves lunch and dinner daily.

Chesapeake

Johnson's Barbecue
$, no credit cards
• 1903 S. Military Hwy., Chesapeake
• (757) 545-6957

Arkansas-style barbecue slathered in a tangy

red sauce is the reason to come here. You'll find your pork minced or served as meaty ribs. Chicken and beef also are treated to Johnson's special touch. Fixings include potato salad, cole slaw and baked beans. Don't miss the homemade fried sweet potato or apple pies. They're so popular they sell out quickly. Lunch and dinner are served every day except Sunday.

Mr. Pig's Bar-B-Q
$ • 445 N. Battlefield Blvd., Chesapeake
• (757) 547-5171

Mr. Pig's has been Chesapeake's main barbecue restaurant since the late 1980s. Vinegar-sauced North Carolina barbecue is the house specialty, but the restaurant also does a brisk business with its fried chicken. Brunswick stew, boiled potatoes, and chicken salad are among the other menu offerings. The restaurant serves lunch and dinner but closes on Sunday.

Portsmouth

Bob's BBQ
$ • 417 County St., Portsmouth
• (757) 399-8060

For a taste of the country in the heart of the city, head to Bob's. This downtown eatery prides itself on its big, country breakfasts and its Carolina-style barbecue. The barbecue comes sliced or chopped. Country cooking also is on the menu. Bob's is open for breakfast and lunch every day but Sunday.

Rodman's Bones & Buddy
$, no credit cards
• 3562 Western Branch Blvd., Portsmouth
• (757) 397-3900

Although this restaurant only opened in the 1980s, it has a rich history. One of the owners was the founder of The Circle, a Portsmouth dining landmark. His partner is renowned for operating Rodman's barbecue. "Buddy & Bones" pays tribute to two deceased Portsmouth restaurant owners who bore those nicknames and served the "square dog," now a staple of Rodman's menu. (Just so you won't be confused, the original Rodman's is in Suffolk and is strictly a catering operation.) Rodman's has loyal customers who lap up the barbecued pork and chicken. Side dishes include Brunswick stew and navy bean soup. Its hush puppies are some of the best around. Featured menu items include sliced Smithfield ham sandwiches and, of course, the square dog. This is a sliced grilled hot dog served with lettuce, tomato and a lump of Smithfield ham just as Bones and Buddy

would have offered it. The restaurant serves both lunch and dinner every day except Sunday. A sister location is Rodman's Bar-B-Que at 5665 Shouldrs Hill Rd., Suffolk (757) 484-1297.

Coffeehouses

Norfolk

Aroma Coffeehouse
$ • 225 Granby St., Norfolk
• (757) 624-1483

Sometimes you want to go where everybody knows your name. If you're looking for place with a friendly neighborhood feeling, this is a great place to try. Maybe it's the fact that the coffee is self-serve or that the owner, Chris Coureas, waits tables when it's busy. Or that we always find familiar faces over the steaming mugs of Rainforest Blend. Try the Middle Eastern inspired specials here—they're home-cooking to Chef Hassan Tambir.

Prince Books and Coffeehouse
$ • 109 E. Main St., Norfolk
• (757) 622-9223

Take an established bookstore, move it to a historic building and add a coffeehouse with an innovative menu. The result is one of the most inviting spots in downtown Norfolk. Housed in the Beaux-Arts Life Building, the coffeehouse always has a coffee of the day brewed and a variety of espressos, cappuccinos, and caffe lattes. The outstanding food prepared Mediterranean style makes even non-coffee drinkers love this place. Our favorite is the grilled panini—Italian-style sandwiches served on seasoned focaccia bread. Salads, muffins and desserts also are on the menu. Seating is limited in the coffeehouse, which is open from morning until evening.

Virginia Beach

Coffease
$ • 321 Little Neck Rd., Virginia Beach
• (757) 857-7182
$ • 1304 Great Neck Rd., Virginia Beach
• (757) 857-7182

These tiny drive-through coffee shops stock an amazing amount of beverages. At these locally owned kiosks, you can have your coffee hot, cold or turned into a fancy concoction such as cappuccino or a latte. Fruit-flavored teas are freshly brewed, and you can have them made into slushy drinks. The shops also offer a variety of fruit slushes and milk shakes. The perfect accompaniments are the Baker's Crust pastries the outlets sell. You can either place your order on foot or from your car. The Great Neck location, which is in Great Neck Shopping Center, has a few outdoor tables. The Little Neck kiosk, which is at the intersection of Virginia Beach Boulevard and Little Neck Road, is strictly a take-out operation. Coffease is open daily from early morning until early evening, except for Sunday when it closes in the late afternoon.

Gloria Jean's Coffee Beans
**$ • Lynnhaven Mall, Lynnhaven Pkwy.,
Virginia Beach**
• (757) 463-5890

Gloria Jean's breaks through the clutter of commonplace mall fare with some outstanding coffee. There are also cookies, pound cakes and coffee-related merchandise to tempt you. Greenbrier Mall on Greenbrier Parkway in Chesapeake also has a Gloria Jean's, (757) 420-6561.

PJ Baggan Java Cafe
$ • 960 Laskin Rd., Virginia Beach
• (757) 491-8900

This gourmet cafe and wine shop also does an excellent job with coffee. It's also known by cigar connoisseurs for its humidor and collection of stogies. PJ's menu offers everything from bagels to sandwiches. And, the restaurant caters to wine lovers with one of the biggest stocks around. The coffee lineup includes basic beans as well as fancy cappuccino and espresso drinks. The cafe is open daily for light lunches and dinners, such as sandwiches and salads. You'll always find urns filled with the brews-of-the-day with plenty of others you can order by the pot. Since PJ's is directly across the road from the Surf'n'Sand Theater, it's a great place for post-movie conversation.

Rumley's
**$ • 32nd St. and Pacific Ave.,
Virginia Beach**
• (757) 422-1260

Coffee lovers may be overwhelmed by the 30 varieties of beans in this tiny shop. Tea lovers will find their niche here too. There's a great stash of books to peruse while enjoying your drinks, and there are a couple of tiny tables for sipping your java. Rumley's is open daily from early morning until early evening except Sundays when it closes about 1 PM.

Seattle Espresso
$ • 301 25th St., Virginia Beach
• (757) 425-7650

Slip into this cozy spot for cappuccino, lattes, and the namesake espresso. You'll find all kinds of unadorned coffees on the menu too. Biscotti, pastries, and bagels are the perfect accompaniments for your drinks. Seattle Espresso is open from morning until early evening seven days a week.

Starbucks
$ • 1860 Laskin Rd., Virginia Beach
• (757) 437-9212

Even though Starbucks coffee has been sold in several locations for years, this was the first Starbucks location in the area. It opened in 1996 in La Promenade shopping center. From here the expansion-minded West Coast coffeehouse chain is continued through the region. In 1997 it opened a Norfolk location in Ghent at 1318 Colley Avenue, (757) 640-8513. A Chesapeake location followed in the Crossways Shopping Center on Greenbrier Parkway, (757) 420-8220. Now there are also outlets in downtown Norfolk at 210 E. Main St., (757) 625-0600, and in Virginia Beach at 3273 Shore Dr., (757) 496-6522. Starbucks typically serves a variety of coffee concoctions—from basic java to fancy cream-laced varieties. The food is limited to muffins, scones, and pastries. Starbucks is open daily from early morning to late evening.

Urban Roasts Coffeehouse and Roastery
$ 1218 Arctic Ave., Virginia Beach
• (757) 437-5116

Here's a place you'll want to linger as long as you can. The aroma of roasting coffee is as irresistible as the homemade pastries. The coffeehouse is in a 50-year-old house furnished with comfortable chairs and couches. It is decorated with funky art. In the winter a fireplace keeps away the chill. There's also a full espresso bar. The coffeehouse is open from early morning to 6 PM daily.

WebCity Cybercafe
$ • 116 Independence Blvd., Virginia Beach
•(757) 490-8690

If you'd like your cappuccino served with a big dose of Internet browsing, slide into a booth and place your order. The Cybercafe opened in 1996 as a hybrid coffeehouse, public access Internet site, and Internet training center. The coffeehouse serves espresso and various coffees as well as sandwiches and pastries. It's open daily for lunch and dinner and stays open to the wee hours on Friday and Saturday. You can buy your Internet time in 30-minute, one-hour, or bigger chunks. The cost starts at $3.95 for a half-hour of online time.

Portsmouth

Brutti's Cafe
$ • 467 Court St., Portsmouth
• (757) 393-1923

Besides the coffee, the "bagelnutz" are the claim to fame here. This Brutti's invention is a mouth-watering nugget of bagel dough stuffed with flavored cream cheese and then cooked. Baguettes baked on site are the basis for sandwiches. Espresso and cappuccino round out the menu. Brutti's is open daily for breakfast through an early dinner.

Contemporary American

Norfolk

219 Restaurant
$$ • 219 Granby St., Norfolk
• (757) 627-2896

This innovative restaurant quickly captured the downtown working crowd's fancy when it opened in 1997. What was once a basic plate-lunch kind of place is now an upscale restaurant that entices discerning diners back downtown for dinner. The decor at 219 is funky— from the vintage wooden ticket booth at the hostess stand to neon signs and an old telephone booth in the back. The food draws from a variety of cultures—pot pies from the U.S.A., pot stickers and wontons from China, to Thai-inspired chicken. Even Caesar salad is served with a snap with a Southwest-inspired blend that includes corn and red pepper. A dessert favorite is a banana pudding made with which chocolate. The 219 serves lunch on weekdays and dinner daily.

Bienville Grille
$$$ • 723 W. 21st St., Norfolk
• (757) 625-5427

The region's lone venue for first-class Cajun cuisine has been going strong for 10 years. Chef/owner Mike Hall, who studied under the great Paul Prudhomme, introduced us to spicy jambalayas, catfish, and crayfish, and we keep coming back for more. The live jazz, rich chicory coffee, and convivial atmosphere also help make this a perennial favorite for lunch and dinner.

Bobbywood
$$$ • 7515 Granby St., Norfolk
• (757) 440-7515

Another chef-owned favorite on the local eating scene, Bobbywood features an ever-changing menu and a friendly atmosphere. Chef Bobby Huber's specialties have included onion-crusted salmon with spinach potato cakes and sage cream, grilled lump crab cakes with garlic grits, grilled summer squash and papaya cocktail sauce, and a signature pizza topped with roasted garlic puree, wild mushrooms, and four cheeses. It's serious food with a casual mood. It serves lunch and dinner.

The Carriage House
$$ • 313 W. Bute St., Norfolk
• (757) 622-4990

This delightful 19th century carriage house is a charming spot to dine. The cuisine is eclectic—from the owner's native Morocco to Chesapeake Bay crabcakes. Pan-fried oysters and Chicken Florentine are always a favorite. Be sure to save room for the bread pudding or other custom-made desserts. The restaurant (formerly Maude's) is in the historic Freemason area, which is perfect for strolling after dining. It serves lunch on weekdays and dinner everyday but Sunday, when it serves brunch.

Kincaid's Fish, Chop and Steak House
$$$ • 300 Monticello Ave., Norfolk
• (757) 622-8000

Some of the finest dining around is at this elegant MacArthur Center restaurant. Seafood and steaks take the starring role here. The salmon always gets rave reviews. The service is excellent, which has helped Kincaid's quickly become the place for movers and shakers to do business. Lunch and dinner are served daily. Reservations are recommended.

Todd Jurich's Bistro!
$$ • 210 York St., Norfolk
• (757) 622-3210

There have been almost as many rave reviews of this eatery in downtown Norfolk as there have been patrons. That said, we too would follow owner/chef Todd Jurich anywhere he chooses to hang his ladle. An upstart and innovator when it comes to combining tastes and textures, Jurich has whipped up some unusual and delightful surprises for lunch and dinner. Try the carpaccio of pastramied lamb or the salmon glazed with molasses, cayenne, and cinnamon. It may sound a bit off the deep end of the griddle, but those and so many other weird menu concoctions that change with seasonal availability are fantastic. Call for reservations to be sure you get a table.

Phantoms at The Chrysler Museum
$ • 245 W. Olney Rd., Norfolk
• (757) 664-6291

Insiders adore this delightful restaurant located on the first floor of The Chrysler Mu-

Our mild climate allows for outdoor dining at least three seasons of the year.

Photo: Courtesy of City of Virginia Beach

seum. With its dark walls and crisp tablecloths, it is an elegant little bistro offering a seasonal variety of salads, such as Cobb salad and a variety of sandwiches. Tempting soups and a few selected entrees are available, too, and it's a wonderfully peaceful oasis for a quiet and intimate lunch. Phantoms is open everyday but Monday and Tuesday for lunch.

Virginia Beach

Coastal Grill
$$ • 1427 N.
Great Neck Rd.,
Virginia Beach
• (757) 496-3348

From the minute you land a table at this intimate bistro, you start right off into the wonderful world of food. A waiting basket of sourdough bread with crocks of unsalted butter may tempt you, but save that appetite for the superb entrees, including beautifully prepared and presented lamb, duck, rabbit and fresh seafood. If you think you'll have room, order the spinach salad, topped with a surpris-

ing garnish of chicken livers. Coastal Grill serves lunch and dinner.

The Bistro & Rotisserie at Le Chambord
$$ • 324 N. Great Neck Rd., Virginia Beach
• (757) 486-3636

This sister restaurant to the more elegant (and more expensive) Le Chambord is no plain Jane. Chef Alvin Williams produces meals that are more casual than the ones he serves next door, but they're just as flavorful. The restaurant serves lunch and dinner, but Insiders says this is the place to go for a special Sunday Brunch.

Five 01 City Grill
$$ • 501 Birdneck Rd., Virginia Beach
• (757) 425-7195

Be advised that this is one of the hottest meal tickets in town for lunch and dinner. It's just smokin' with its cool clientele, casual bar and devastatingly delicious menu. Host Mike Atkinson and chef Corey Beisel have made a winner by serving some of the tastiest treats in town. Veal chop grilled with goat cheese is perfect to follow a starter of charred tuna sashimi with spicy kim chee or the house's signature Michelob shrimp. To top it off, sample the sweet bread pudding drowning in Jack Daniels. What a way to go . . . and you should.

Havana
$$ • 1423 N. Great Neck Rd., Virginia Beach
• (757) 496-3333

This popular restaurant defines itself as an "American cafe with a Cuban twist." You'll find pasta, port, beef, and chicken presented in innovative ways. Try the Casa Havana—grilled filet mignon accented with peppercorns and rum or plantain-encrusted salmon served with mango avocado cream and black beans and rice. Havana serves lunch on weekdays and dinner everyday. A sister operation of Havana opened in downtown Norfolk in 2000 at 255 Granby St., (757) 627-5800.

Lucky Star
**$$$ • 1608 Pleasure House Rd.,
Virginia Beach**
• **(757) 363-8410**

When chef supreme Amy Brandt puts the pedal to the kettle, wonderful things happen. Here in the sparkling white interior, sprinkled with the works of local artists, Amy and partner Butch Butt lay out one magnificent spread after another. Combinations are innovative and seasonal, influenced by the Pacific rim. Crawfish spring rolls, spicy corn cakes, and Thai chicken salad are among our favorites, but when it's apple season, there's no telling what wonderful aromatic delights will greet you at the Lucky Star. Dinner only is served.

Swan Terrace
**$$$ • The Founders' Inn and Conference
Ctr., 5641 Indian River Rd., Virginia Beach**
• **(757) 366-5777**

Putting a spin on Colonial cookery, the Swan Terrace literally sparkles from the beautifully appointed dining room to the individual tables set to Miss Manners' smug satisfaction. Seasonal entrees vary. Swan Terrace serves lunch and dinner.

Timbuktu
**$$$ • 32nd St. and Atlantic Ave.,
Virginia Beach**
• **(757) 491-1800**

Willie Moats is one of our favorite chefs—wherever he happens to be cooking. These days, it's his own place, located on the Boardwalk in the Days Inn Hotel. The menu is creative—how does red pepper pasta with cilantro corn butter sauce sound? Or crab cakes with roasted fennel remoulade? Or cream of artichoke and roasted garlic soup? Heavenly? You betcha. Timbuktu serves breakfast, lunch, and dinner.

Continental/French

Norfolk

Antiquities
**$$$$ • Norfolk Airport Hilton, Military
Hwy. and Northhampton Blvd., Norfolk**
• **(757) 466-8000**

White linen and an attentive wait staff add to the luscious menu featuring continental Euro-American favorites (including wild game) in this elegant, candlelit space inside the Norfolk Airport Hilton. From beginning to end, you'll be enchanted by this old-style dining ex-

perience. Let one of the experienced waiters prepare a delectable Caesar salad, or strawberries Fifi, flambéed tableside in Grand Marnier. This is a place to truly act out the word "dining," as lingering at the table is not only welcome but encouraged. Dinner is served nightly.

Virginia Beach

La Caravelle
$$$ • 1040 Laskin Rd., Virginia Beach
• **(757) 428-2477**

Rich French-Vietnamese offerings in an elegant candlelit setting await you at this much-touted restaurant inside the Seashire Inn. It's decorated in a country French manner. Duckling in Grand Marnier sauce, salmon in champagne sauce and tournedos Caravelle are among our favorite entrees. La Caravelle serves dinner nightly.

Le Chambord
**$$$ • 324 N. Great Neck Rd.,
Virginia Beach**
• **(757) 498-1234**

A wonderful feast for the eyes as well as the stomach, Le Chambord is one of the most charming and consistent restaurants in the area. The crisp decor belies the sensual splendor of the food—entrees such as quail au jus or Chateaubriand Bearnaise with red onion confit. Lunches offer a lighter bill of fare, with some marvelous salads, perfect with a glass of wine for a noontime break. To capitalize on the casual-dining craze, owners Frank and Luisa Spapen have opened The Bistro & Rotisserie next door to Le Chambord, serving American continental cuisine such as pork chops and garlic mashed potatoes. Watching the master chefs at work under the huge, copper-hooded bistro kitchen is a real treat. Lunch and dinner are served daily.

Napolean's Restaurant
**$$$ • 4933 Virginia Beach Blvd.,
Virginia Beach**
• **(757) 497-3400**

It's cozy, romantic, and good enough to earn local dining awards. Situated in a small house on Virginia Beach Boulevard, the restaurant has four separate rooms that seat 50 patrons altogether. The setting is intimate and charming, perfect for a dinner with someone special. Menu choices include the classics of French cuisine, with an emphasis on dishes from Provence. Lunch and dinner are served daily.

Portsmouth

Cafe Europa
$$$ • 319 High St., Portsmouth
• (757) 399-6652

If you ever have a yen for veal cooked to absolute perfection, a trip to Portsmouth's Cafe Europa is almost the only sensible choice. This charming cafe wins the romantic-atmosphere prize hands-down, with lace curtains, exposed brick, warm woods, and flattering candlelight. Long known for its Italian and French cuisine prepared to ultimate perfection by chef and owner Michael Simko, it is a consistent favorite for the quality of food, the beautiful setting, and the impeccable service.

Ethnic

Norfolk

Anthony's
$ • 2502 Colley Ave., Norfolk
• (757) 622-7411

Owner Anthony Chiperas just can't get enough of this location on the outskirts of Ghent. His father and uncle operated a restaurant at the same spot starting in 1943. In 1990, Chiperas revived the restaurant but closed for lack of a liquor license. In 1994 he returned, determined to survive. He's since picked up a loyal following of repeat diners. Mediterranean foods are the stars here, with baby lamb ribs being one of the best sellers. Entrees are creative and range from souvlaki to moussaka and linguine. If you don't see what you want on the menu just, tell the chef, who'll whip up your special request. Anthony's is open for dinner every day except Sunday and Monday and serves lunch Tuesday through Friday.

Crackers Little Bar & Bistro
$$ • 821 W. 21st St., Norfolk
• (757) 640-0200

The Spanish concept of tapas (better known here as appetizers) is the mainstay of this trendy restaurant in the Ghent area. The menu is anchored by 36 different tapas making this the perfect place to be an adventurous diner. The idea here is to order a variety of dishes to share with your dining mate. Most Crackers regulars keep ordering throughout the evening. Multi-cultural dishes range from a spicy tuna sashimi salad to a wild mushroom ragout and herb-crusted lamb. Crackers is also known for its martinis. Crackers is a tiny place with only 12 stools at a bar and 16 seats in the dining room. It is open for dinner daily and stays open until the wee hours.

German Pantry
$ • 5329 Virginia Beach Blvd., Norfolk
• (757) 461-5100

This tiny, authentic German cafe has been in business since the late 1970s. It has a traditional menu that includes a variety of wieners and wursts as well as pork chops with sauerkraut. Daily specials feature such hearty fare as spaetzle with goulash served with an excellent green salad and hard roll. Breads are imported from Canada but most everything else is made on premises, including Black Forest cake. The Pantry has a small store selling German greeting cards, magazines, and cooking supplies. Breakfast, lunch, and dinner are served every day except Sunday and Monday.

Tandoor Indian Restaurant
$ • 5760 Northampton Blvd., Norfolk
• (757) 460-2100

This Indian restaurant opened in 1993 and immediately became one of our favorites. The extensive menu lets you choose from traditional tandoori, curried dishes, and more exotic fare. Besides beef, seafood and lamb dishes, there's a good vegetarian lineup. If you're not sure what to order, try the buffet. The restaurant is open daily for lunch and dinner.

The Monastery
$$ • 443 Granby Mall, Norfolk
• (757) 625-8193

This is one of the city's most venerable ethnic restaurants, and it recently expanded. Chefs Adolf and Anna Jerabek opened it in 1983 after moving from Czechoslovakia via New York. House specialties include roast duck and an excellent goose in the winter. Schnitzel and goulash are also featured on the 38-item menu. Daily specials range from salmon to roast lamb. Guests are welcomed with a plate of cheese, apples, and bread. You'll be tempted to end your meal with

INSIDERS' TIP

The Single Gourmet is a club for unmarried residents who like exploring new restaurants and meeting people. There are usually several organized dinners a month. Call (757) 623-0687 for details.

the Jerabeks' homemade Black Forest cake, strudel, or chocolate fondue. The Monastery is open for lunch Tuesday through Friday. Waiters dressed as monks serve dinner Tuesday through Sunday. Reservations are suggested, particularly if the symphony, opera, or other arts group is performing in downtown Norfolk.

Nawab Indian Cuisine
$$ • 888 N. Military Hwy., Norfolk
• (757) 455-8080

It was a happy day for Norfolk gourmands when this Indian restaurant opened in 1992 on the outskirts of Military Circle Mall—typically a haven for all-American chain restaurants. Nawab was the first regional restaurant to specialize in Indian cuisine. Its vast menu ranges from tandoori dishes cooked in a clay oven to curried chicken or squid. The menu is extensive and includes mulligatawny soup and a good mix of seafood, lamb, beef, vegetarian, and chicken dishes. Nawab's bread is the traditional papadam wafer made from lentil flour. The restaurant is open daily for lunch and dinner. Nawab's lunch buffet is reasonably priced and is a good way to sample Indian cuisine. A second Nawab is at 765 First Colonial Road, Virginia Beach, (757) 491-8600.

Orapax Inn
$, no credit cards
• 1300 Redgate Ave., Norfolk
• (757) 627-8041

This is one of our mainstays. When we can't decide where to go for dinner we usually end up here. The inn opened in 1970 in residential West Ghent and branched out to Virginia Beach in 1994. This casual restaurant is renowned for its Greek specialties, including pastitsio, spanakopita, Greek salads, and a gyro platter. It has some of the best fried calamari around. Meals come with an irresistible homemade bread and melted butter for dipping. Salads are served with a bottle of the tangy house dressing for you to pour. Popular entrees include the spinach pizza and moussaka. There are daily specials. The Orapax is open for lunch and dinner and has delivery to nearby neighborhoods. It closes on Sunday. In September the owners shut down for most of the month for their annual pilgrimage to Greece.

Café Paradise
$ • 4140 Granby St., Norfolk
• (757) 627-1143

Middle Eastern fare is the star of this intimate Norfolk restaurant (formerly Tabouli). The tabouli is some of the best we've ever eaten.

Featured items include kababs, falafel, and salads. You won't find your typical gyros sandwiches here. Adventuresome diners will be enamored with Turkish specialties; more cautious eaters can feel at home with a cheese and herb pizza and sandwiches. There also are sandwiches and seafood on the menu. Café Paradise is open for lunch and dinner every day except Sunday.

Virginia Beach

Azar's Cafe & Market
$ • 108 Prescott Ave., Virginia Beach
• (757) 486-7778

This Mediterranean market moved to a new location in 1995 and added a 40-seat cafe. It still sells spices, vegetables, and other ingredients, but it also serves lunch and dinner daily. Both vegetarian and Mediterranean cuisine are emphasized. If you're a first-time visitor, owner George Azar is likely to let you sample some of the wares in his showcase. Azar's tabouli salad is among the best we've ever eaten. Also on the menu are pizzas, hummus, vegetarian sandwiches, and the Nada Burger made of falafel beans and vegetables. Azar's is off Bonney Road but may be difficult to find. Call for directions.

Bangkok Garden
$$ • Loehmann's Plaza, Virginia Beach Blvd., Virginia Beach
• (757) 498-5009

The region finally gained a full-fledged Thai restaurant when Bangkok Garden opened in 1993. It is owned by a Thai native who's run a Hampton restaurant for several years. Fiery food will whip your palate into shape. You'll find the seafood stir-fried or bathed in a lemongrass broth. One top choice is the pork seasoned with mint, lime, and a potent chili powder. The staff dons Thai costumes at night and occasionally treats customers to traditional Thai dancing. The restaurant is open daily for lunch and dinner.

The Street Cook
$$ • Lynnhaven Pkwy. and Princess Anne Rd., Virginia Beach
• (757) 471-7810

This Mediterranean restaurant has a cuisine its owner describes as "a little Greek, a little Italian, and a little Virginia Beach." It turns out great seafood crepes, veal Erica, and poulet Florentine among other entrees. Homemade desserts include a chocolate torte and baklava. The Street Cook is open for lunch Tuesday through Friday and for dinner Tuesday through Sunday. Reservations are accepted.

Portsmouth

Bier Garden
$$ • 434 High St., Portsmouth
• (757) 393-6022

This relaxing spot in the heart of downtown Portsmouth in the place for sauerbraten, goulash, spatzel, and other German favorites. It also is the place for beer connoisseurs since it has more than 100 international beers in stock. The Bier Garden is open for lunch and dinner everyday but Monday.

Italian

Norfolk

Cafe Rosso
$$ • 123 W. 21st St., Norfolk
• (757) 627-2078

This European bistro/trattoria offers diners a cozy and casual atmosphere built around warm woods, red brick, and wrought-iron details. The restaurant's wood-burning oven turns out smoky-flavored pizzas. But there are also wonderful pastas—try the spicy seafood puttanesca—and an extensive, welcome list of wines by the glass. Lunch and dinner are served daily.

Castaldi's Market & Grill
$$ • 300 Monticello Ave., Norfolk
• (757) 627-8700

Don't be surprised when your server suddenly bursts into song after delivering your salad. Everyone who waits on you is a singer waiting for a big break. The music is as much a part of an evening at Castaldi's as the food. You'll find excellent Italian cuisine here. Our favorite is linguine with white clam sauce. The warm bread that is continually delivered to your table is a treat. This is a great place to celebrate a birthday. Lunch and dinner are served daily.

Fellini's
$$ • 40th St. and Colley Ave., Norfolk
• (757) 625-3000

This popular restaurant introduced "California pizza" to the palates of Hampton Roads residents and visitors. So cancel that chain restaurant pizza and order one of Fellini's Thai Chicken, BLT (the "L" is spinach), or Cajun pizzas. There's more than pizza, though. Fellini's pasta dishes are phenomenal. The staff prepares one of the best and biggest Caesar salads in town, and they even offer gourmet burgers. You can get the same Fellini's taste at the Beach, too, via its speedy home-delivery service. Place your order by calling 422-3500. Fellini's serves lunch and dinner.

Franco's Italian Restaurant
$ • 6200 N. Military Hwy., Norfolk
• (757) 853-0177

There aren't many restaurants like this any more, which makes Franco's a special place to dine. It's a traditional family-owned Italian restaurant that's been around for decades and has many loyal customers. Don't be taken aback that everyone eating here seems to know everyone else. Just order the pizza bread, which isn't on the menu, and you'll look like a regular. Chicken marsala is a standout entrée. Franco's is open for lunch and dinner everyday but Monday. Franco's is in the Bromley Square Shopping Center near Norfolk International Airport.

La Galleria Ristorante
$$$ • 120 College Pl., Norfolk
• (757) 623-3939

Valet parking outside, mahogany, veined marble, and hammered copper inside . . . a tiny hint of the spectacular evening you'll have dining at La Galleria in downtown Norfolk. This place can only be classified as an "event," and has to its credit awards for its wonderful food as well as its decor. Recognized as one of the 10 most beautiful restaurants in the country by two national trade magazines, La Galleria serves northern Italian specialties. Get your taste buds activated with a white pizza from the wood-burning oven, then move on to Polla alla Sorentina (chicken stuffed with spinach, zucchini and mozzarella in wine sauce) or Vittello La Galleria (veal with fresh tomato sauce). The bar that floats off-center in the restaurant is gorgeous, and it's a popular spot for gathering after work or dinner. Lunch is also served daily.

Spaghetti Warehouse
$ • 1900 Monticello Ave., Norfolk
• (757) 622-0151

We're talking volume here—both in terms of the food of your plate and the number of plates they serve. The food literally hangs off the platter no matter what you order, and the number of patrons lined up to take their turn at the vast menu, especially on weekend nights, is amazing. The Spaghetti Warehouse is a great family place housed in a rehabbed warehouse on the outskirts of Ghent. It's a bit noisy for sharing a romantic bottle of Chianti, but a super place if you have teenagers who never seem to be filled up. The Spaghetti Warehouse serves lunch and dinner daily.

Virginia Beach

Aldo's Ristorante
$$ • 1860 Laskin Rd., Virginia Beach • (757) 491-1111

Not only will you eat well here, but you'll also look good doing it. At first glance Aldo's might strike you as one of those flavor-of-the-month type restaurants, populated by the herd that always tries any place that's new. But Aldo's has been popular for years. It never goes out of style because the food, service and ambiance are consistently enjoyable. The homemade pastas are graced by light and tasty sauces, each one better than the next. Aldo's fantastic pizzas, baked in a wood-burning pizza oven, are likewise yummy. Popular for lunch and dinner, it's a fun place when you're in the mood for a taste of Italy.

Bella Monte
$$ • 1201 Laskin Rd., Virginia Beach • (757) 425-6290

This is one of our favorite places, a combination Italian/gourmet grocery (where you can buy real proscuitto by the pound), upscale take-out and full-service cafe. You can enjoy a first-rate meal, before or after a browse, that's sure to awaken your hunger. The atmosphere is casual and fun. Bella Monte serves lunch and dinner everyday but Sunday.

Ciola's
$$ • 1889 Virginia Beach Blvd., Virginia Beach • (757) 428-9601

What masquerades as a good-old roadside diner is actually the laboratory for Italian chemists who whip up some of the most tummy-pleasing dishes this side of Italy. From pasta to lasagna, the portions are generous, and the flavors excellent. A longtime family-owned-and-operated Virginia Beach landmark, Ciola's (that's Alice and Dominick to Insiders) has changed neither its I Dream of Jeannie interior decor nor the quality of its delicious food in many a year, for which its loyal fans are quite

grateful. For something deliciously different, try the steak Margeurite. Dinner is served nightly.

Dough Boy's California Pizza
$ • 19th St. and Atlantic Ave., Virginia Beach • (757) 422-3211
$ • 25th St. and Atlantic Ave., Virginia Beach • (757) 425-7108

This is the everybody's favorite pizza place at the Beach, hands down. Dough Boy's does a Hawaiian pizza with pineapple chunks, a Santa Fe pizza, and even a Philly cheese-steak pizza as well as delicious renditions of more expected combinations that your school-age children will love. If you're not in the mood for pizza, try one the pasta specials or a calzone; there aren't many places that serve those around here. Lunch and dinner are served daily.

Il Giardino Ristorante
$$$ • 910 Atlantic Ave., Virginia Beach • (757) 422-6464

While dressing up isn't required when you eat here, you'll want to look your best to impress all the beautiful people you'll bump into. There's no doubt you'll be tempted by the dazzling array of appetizers, but do share one. You'll want to save room for the entrée—a little veal, perhaps? A supper here may be the very best meal you have in Virginia Beach, both for divinely prepared dishes and superb service. We suggest you also meander into the European-style outdoor cafe, where you'll certainly want to linger over espresso. Afterwards, there's a happening piano bar, and the lounge stays open until 2 AM. It all adds up to a first-class dining experience with considerable social cachet. The restaurant serves dinner only.

Isle of Capri
$$$ • 39th St. and Atlantic Ave., Virginia Beach • (757) 428-1711

For four decades the Isle of Capri was a fixture on the beach's main retail drag, Laskin Road. Today, the restaurant has been reborn, and the Isle of Capri has a new, heavenly setting: six floors above the boardwalk, overlooking the Atlantic Ocean in the Holiday Inn Sunspree Resort. If you're after a dining room with a view, this is a great spot to try. The restaurant is still in the capable hands of the Arcese family and still features classics such as pizzas, linguine with clam sauce, fettuccine

Alfredo, and veal dishes. Don't shy away from the creative seafood preparations or house specials, however. Dinner is served nightly.

Pasta e Pani
$$ • 1069 Laskin Rd., Virginia Beach
• (757) 428-2299

The running battle here is which is more delicious—the homemade pasta or the pani (bread). Simplicity is the key, whether it's a pizza from the wood-burning stove or delicately flavored pasta entrees. Owner Andrew Serpe moved his popular restaurant to a larger location in 1996, but the parking lot is still packed. Its present setting features a large open kitchen and enough room for the hungry hordes who make this restaurant a perennial favorite. Lunch and dinner are served daily.

Zia Marie
4497 Lookout Rd., Virginia Beach
• (757) 460-0715

The co-owners of this restaurant have established a winning formula with a combination of Italian classics (eggplant Parmesan, Tony Bennett on the sound system) and a Chick's Beach location. Next time you're on the north side of Virginia Beach and you're in the mood for some unfussy Italian food, give Zia's a try. It's open for dinner everyday.

Portsmouth

Henrico's International Pizzeria
$ • 600 Frederick Blvd., Portsmouth
• (757) 393-2680

Not just another pizza place, Henrico's also offers a wide selection of pastas, subs, chicken, ribs, and salads. Since there are only a few tables you should plan to get everything to go or have it delivered. A local favorite is the pasta feast, featuring such delectables as baked spaghetti, veal, eggplant Parmigiana, and baked lasagna with broccoli. The restaurant also offers free delivery within 2 miles. Lunch and dinner are served daily.

Mario's Italian Restaurant
$$ • 611 Airline Blvd., Portsmouth
• (757) 399-8970

A Portsmouth tradition since 1955, Mario's offers authentic Italian cuisine in a traditional Venetian-style setting. Pasta, pizza, and fine wine are offered under the direction of owner Nick Arcese. Lunch and dinner are served.

Japanese

Norfolk

Kotobuki
$$ • 721 W. 21st St., Norfolk
• (757) 628-1025

This Ghent restaurant is at the top of our list of places to go for Japanese food. The sushi is prepared to order and the sukiyaki and udon dishes are divine. Our favorite is the dinner for two that includes a sampling of sushi, tempura, and an array of other traditional dishes. Lunch and dinner are served daily.

Virginia Beach

Ginza Japanese Restaurant
$$ • 3972 Holland Rd., Virginia Beach
• (757) 431-8000

The decor is traditional Japanese, with paper-lined windows, floor cushions, and screens. The menu centers on traditional delicacies such as fried dumplings, tempura and, of course, sushi. Miso soup and a nice selection of innovative salads round out the meals. Ginza serves lunch and dinner daily.

Kyushu
$$ • 400 Newtown Rd., Virginia Beach
• (757) 499-6292

Fresh, beautifully presented sushi and sashimi platters are the standard at this newly renovated sushi bar. Watching chef Ebigasko deftly layer a touch of wasabi and a slender slice of yellowtail on an oval of rice is true culinary theater. Of note here is the shabu-shabu, a popular dish the diners cook for themselves at the table. Kyushu serves lunch and dinner daily.

Mizuno Japanese Restaurant
$$ • 1860 Laskin Rd., Virginia Beach
• (757) 422-1200

One aficionado of all things Japanese we know declares this to be her "ichiban" Japanese restaurant. There's quiet elegance here along with excellent, traditional Japanese cuisine. Hint: The food is so good it's a regular dining spot for some of the region's best-known chefs. Mizuno is in the La Promenade shopping center. It is open for lunch Tuesday through Friday and for dinner everyday but Monday.

Osaka Japanese Restaurant
**$$ • 1807 Mediterranean Ave.,
Virginia Beach**
• (757) 428-8699

This 36-seat sushi bar and restaurant is a friendly place perfect to pop into during a day at the oceanfront. Look for sushi, sashimi, tempura, and other Japanese favorites. Combination dinners are available. Sushi is available to please newcomers to this delicacy as well as those who love all forms of the rice, seaweed, fish, and vegetable rolls. Osaka serves lunch Monday through Saturday and dinner everyday but Wednesday.

Shogun
**$$ • 313 Hilltop Shopping Ctr., Laskin Rd.,
Virginia Beach**
• (757) 422-5150

You just know you're in for something extraordinary when you first spot the chefs wearing tall, brilliant red chef's hats and neck scarves and bearing mega-sized knives sharp enough to split a human hair. You have entered the Shogun zone, and you are going to have the most entertaining meal of the year—a full seven courses prepared with the speed of lightning right before your very eyes. The food, especially the tempura, is excellent, and watching the skilled preparation is an event. Don't miss it. Shogun serves lunch and dinner daily.

This Old House
$$ • 309 Aragona Blvd., Virginia Beach
• (757) 518-8888

The name conjures having a home-improvement dinner with Bob Villa, but this is a traditional Japanese restaurant that serves tempura, teriyaki, yakitori, tonkasu, and hot pots, washed down with either a Sapporo, the well-known Japanese beer, or sake. If you do happen to be a sushi fanatic, don't miss the Saturday night all-you-dare-to-eat sushi buffet. Lunch and dinner are served daily.

Daruma
$$ • 608 N. Birdneck Rd., Virginia Beach
• (757) 437-8511

This is a small place, tucked next to a 7-11 and a Laundromat on the corner of Laskin and Birdneck roads. But it's a venerable location that was once home to La Caravelle, then La Brocca. It must be something ethnic in the air. At any rate, a sushi restaurant that serves lunch and dinner is a welcome addition to this part of the beach, which is now home to a half-

dozen good restaurants. The sushi is beautiful and available at lunchtime, too, when you're in the mood for something different.

Chesapeake

Nagoya Japanese Restuarant
$ • 1400 N. Battlefield Blvd., Chesapeake
• (757) 382-7788

Sushi, sukiyaki, and other Japanese favorites star at this restaurant in the Battlefield Marketplace. Choose from the five-seat sushi bar or the small dining area. For lunch try a "bento box," a compartmentalized lunch box stocked with Japanese delicacies. Sukiyaki is a delicious one-pot meal. Nagoya is open for lunch on weekdays and dinner everyday but Sunday.

Mexican

Norfolk

Colley Cantina
$ • 1316 Colley Ave., Norfolk
• (757) 622-0033

We can't quite figure out whether it's the food or the fun that keeps this place in Ghent jammed every night. As Mexican food goes, it has all your favorite basics—lots of it for a reasonable price. But toss in a phenomenal Margarita and perhaps you've unlocked the secret to this popular place's success. It's especially nice in spring through fall, with outdoor seating where you and your taco can watch the Colley Avenue cruising. The Cantina serves lunch and dinner.

El Rodeo
**$ • Janaf Shopping Ctr.,
5834 Virginia Beach Blvd., Norfolk**
• (757) 466-9077

Direct from Guadalajara in the state of Jalisco, Mexico, comes the Lopez clan, opening their 14th restaurant in the mid-Atlantic region. El Rodeo at Janaf joined its sister at 6209 Providence Road in Virginia Beach, 474-2698, in serving dishes that represent the various sections of Mexico, from the hot and spicy beef steak ... la Tampiquena to combo dinners such as a pair of tacos, enchiladas, and chile con queso. Whether you like your Mexican spicy or mild, there's a dish to please the palate and the pocketbook. El Rodeo serves lunch and dinner.

Luna Maya Cantina
$ • 2000 Colonial Ave., Norfolk
• (757) 622-6986

Don't look for Tex-Mex food at Luna Maya. The Bolivian sisters who own this restaurant serve spicy Mexican food with a twist. They pride themselves on the freshness of their ingredients and preparation. Tamales are among customer's favorites along with beef strips marinated in beer and spices. Luna Maya serves lunch and dinner Tuesday through Saturday. In 2000 it relocated from its original Virginia Beach location to the Ghent neighborhood and instantly gained new fans of its excellent cuisine.

Mi Hogar
$ • 4201 Granby St., Norfolk
• (757) 640-7705

This is one of the most popular Mexican restaurants in town. When redevelopment of its building forced a move in 1999 from its location near Old Dominion University, Mi Hogar fans flocked to the new restaurant in Riverview. Good quality, low prices and friendly service are the hallmark of Mi Hogar. The menu features dozens of daily specials and more than 20 combination dinners. The owners prefer not to cook food "too spicy." For those who want a little extra heat, they serve a dish of hot sauce with the entree. Mi Hogar serves lunch and dinner.

Virginia Beach

Coyote Café and Cantina
$$ • 972 Laskin Rd., Virginia Beach
• (757) 425-8705

At peak hours you can hardly get in the door of this popular beach restaurant. The food is American regional, from the Tex-Mex/Southwest region, and the decor is up-to-the-minute L.A. The combined effect is upscale, fun, and spicy. No wonder it gets so crowded. Come here for lunch any day but Sunday or for dinner daily.

INSIDERS' TIP
To create your own flavor of Virginia's Chesapeake Bay region, sample some of these excellent local cookbooks: *Tidewater on the Half Shell, Gourmet by the Bay, Virginia Hospitality*, and *Very Virginia*. All were produced by the excellent cooks in area Junior League or other civic organizations. Virginia Waterfront Cuisine showcases recipes from local chefs. All are available in area bookstores.

El Azteca
$ • First Colonial and Laskin Rds., Virginia Beach
• (757) 437-1890

If you're longing for a Mexican feast that's more like authentic Mexican than Tex-Mex, here's the place. Sit inside or out under the umbrella-covered tables on the walled patio and enjoy our favorite—a chicken enchilada topped with sauce mole. The salsa is fresh and spicy, and the chips are great. Bring amigos and give it a try for lunch or dinner. A second location is now open in Norfolk at 1552 Little Creek Road. A sister operation is at 314 Constititon Dr., Virginia Beach, (757) 473-1746.

Ensenada Mexican Restaurant
$ • 2824 Virginia Beach Blvd., Virginia Beach
• (757) 631-1090

Just what the doctor ordered: a huge menu of authentic Mexican dishes, most priced at less than $7. Combination dinners and specialty platters take center stage. Lunch and dinner are served daily.

Mi Casita
$ • Rosemont and Bonney Rds., Virginia Beach
• (757) 463-3819

Arguably the area's most authentic Mexican eatery, this place is so packed with piñatas dangling from the ceiling and draped on shelves that you have to blink to make sure you haven't been whisked to a side street in Tijuana. All your favorites are here as well as some superb homemade guacamole and chips to wash down with a bottle of Tecate, but we'd advise staying clear of the cactus that's stir-fried with tomatoes and onions. The bartender makes a mean Margarita. The huevos rancheros served only at lunchtime are muy bueno.

San Antonio Sam's
$ • 604 Norfolk Ave., Virginia Beach
• (757) 491-0263

It's Tex-Mex and more in this jumping place packed with Lone Star memorabilia and roadhouse-style tunes on tape. A hint to the creative touches is its wonderful way with enchiladas. Try the crab and avocado or enchiladas del mar, stuffed with crab, scallops and shrimp. Find San Antonio Sam's the sequel at 1501 Colley Avenue in Ghent in Norfolk, (757) 623-0233, with a casually Western showplace atmosphere. Sway to the classic '60s and '70s tunes on the house soundtrack while you chomp on state-of-the-art Tex-Mex revisionist cuisine for lunch or dinner. You can even take home Sam's signature salsa and barbecue sauces.

Portsmouth

La Tolteca Mexican Restaurant
$ • 6031 High St., Portsmouth
• (757) 484-8043

If you can pronounce camarones al mojo de ajo, order it. It's shrimp sautéed in garlic and butter and it's to die for. Or be dull and go for the familiar fajitas or tacos—they're exceptionally good here, too. If you're watching your fat intake, you'll be glad to know Chef Jose Baragas uses a more healthful vegetable oil rather than the standard lard for frying. So go ahead and indulge at lunch or dinner.

Chesapeake

El Loro
$ • 801 Volvo Pkwy., Chesapeake
• (757) 436-3415

El Loro has an extensive menu of authentic Mexican specialties, including many combination platters. It's open for lunch and dinner daily.

Three Amigos
$ • 200 N. Battlefield Blvd., Chesapeake
• (757) 548-4105

The menu is so extensive at Three Amigos you may have trouble deciding what to order. You'll find all the classics you'd expect plus children's platters and vegetarian specialties. Three Amigos serves lunch and dinner daily.

Seafood

Norfolk

Blue Crab Bar & Grille
$$ • 4521 Pretty Lake Ave., Norfolk
• (757) 362-8000

With its location overlooking the waters of

Little Creek, this is a scenic spot to dine—complete with boats tied up at a neighboring marina. Blue Crab opened in 1989 with a menu that features a lot of seafood prepared in Caribbean and Cajun styles. Salmon, tuna, catfish, and crabs are menu staples, with seasonal fish offered when available. Blue Crab closes on Monday but serves dinner the other days. Brunch is offered on Sunday. Reservations are recommended on the weekend.

Lockhart's Seafood Restaurant
$$ • 8440 Tidewater Dr., Norfolk
• (757) 588-0405

Since 1959 the Lockhart family has prided itself on its seafood. Don't expect anything trendy here. Instead, you'll find excellent renditions of old favorites such as crab Norfolk, deviled crab, and fried fish. Lockhart's is open for lunch and dinner and is closed on Monday.

O'Sullivan's Wharf
$$ • 4300 Colley Ave., Norfolk
• (757) 423-3753

This is a perennial favorite for dining or relaxing with a beer. The Wharf is near Old Dominion University and sits on scenic Knitting Mill Creek with boats anchored outside. In warm weather O'Sullivan's deck is a popular gathering spot, and on weekends the restaurant presents live acoustic music. Menu offerings include crab cakes and seafood combinations. There also is a variety of sandwiches, soups and salads. The restaurant is open for lunch and dinner daily and frequently has live entertainment. Reservations are accepted. A sister restaurant is in Virginia Beach at 2701 N. Mall Drive outside Lynnhaven Mall, (757) 431-8948.

Ships Cabin
$$$ • 4110 E. Ocean View Ave., Norfolk
• (757) 362-4659

A Norfolk dining landmark since 1967, the Ships Cabin has new owners and a menu that blends old favorites with innovative cuisine. This lovely restaurant has a terrific view of the Chesapeake Bay and a seafood menu to go with it.

Servers continually make the rounds with a variety of tasty bread, including blueberry and raisin. Oysters Bingo (named after a local attorney) is oysters sautéed with shallots, butter, and wine. Crab soup and crab cakes are other menu mainstays. Other offerings include a variety of shrimp, crab, and fresh fish as well as steaks. It is open for dinner every day but Monday.

Virginia Beach

Alexander's on the Bay
**$$$ • 4536 Oceanview Ave.,
Virginia Beach
• (757) 464-4999**

This elegant restaurant is a standout for its terrific view and fine dining. It's a romantic restaurant where diners can eat on an open deck overlooking the Chesapeake Bay. Since Alexander's originally opened in 1985, one of its signature appetizers has been Oysters Alexander—sautéed herb-coated oysters served with a white wine and shallot sauce. Entrees

A hot day at the beach works up an appetite for nearby tempting snacks.

Photo: Courtesyof Virginia Beach Convention and Visitor Development

range from seafood to steak and veal. Popular entrees are seafood Madagascar—shrimp, scallops, and lobster cooked in a creamy peppercorn sauce—and a Mariner's Platter loaded with five types of seafood. Favorite desserts are the homemade cheesecakes. Dinner is served daily, and reservations are recommended. Be sure to ask for directions when you call. Alexander's is off the beaten path near the Chesapeake Bay Bridge-Tunnel.

Anchor Inn
**$$ • 2100 Marina Shores, Virginia Beach
• (757) 481-2151**

This has long been a locals-only place highly recommended by seafood lovers. The fish is fresh, and menu offerings include a three-fish platter and crab cakes. For appetizers try fried calamari or crab-stuffed mushrooms. Home-

made desserts include chocolate mousse pie and Key lime pie. The inn has been in business since 1983 and is open for dinner daily and lunch every day except Saturday.

Angelo's
**$$ • 37th St. and Oceanfront,
Virginia Beach
• (757) 425-0347**

Right next to Howard Johnson's sits a jewel of a restaurant, a Beach favorite for more than 20 years. While Angelo and brother George will be pleased to put a 16-ounce Black Angus New York strip in front of you, we have to suggest the wonderful seafood pastas, such as shrimp over a steaming bed of linguine or our favorite pasta dish with lobster, scallops, mussels, and shrimp. If you can't decide between the two, order the famous Land and Sea Platter with a fork-tender filet and delightfully seasoned New England lobster tail. Don't let the homemade desserts overwhelm you, especially the chocolate Chambord cake. Angelo's is open daily for all three meals but is best known for its dinners.

Blue Pete's
**$$ • 1400 N. Muddy Creek Rd.,
Virginia Beach
• (757) 426-2005**

This is the ultimate off-the-beaten-path restaurant, but once diners find Blue Pete's, they're glad they made the trek. This rustic restaurant, founded in 1973, is known for its variety of fresh seafood. It recently expanded its menu to include all-natural Colorado beef. The house specialty is sweet potato biscuits, and the restaurant cheerfully hands out the recipe for this treat. Blue Pete's typically closes during the winter, but from spring through fall it is open for dinner Monday through Saturday. Call for directions and reservations. Driving to Blue Pete's will take you on a jaunt through rural Virginia Beach.

Blue Heaven Cafe
**$$ • 33rd St. and Atlantic Ave.,
Virginia Beach
• (757) 491-0188**

This innovative restaurant has some of the best food at the Beach. Its location in the Four Sails Hotel also gives it a front-row view of the ocean, which makes for a pleasant outing. Expect the unexpected here, such as salmon with wild mushrooms baked in parchment. Be sure to save room for homemade Key lime pie, rum cake, and other divine desserts. During summer the outdoor dining area is a wonderful place to while away an evening. The Blue Water serves breakfast, lunch and dinner daily. Reservations are recommended in the evenings.

Capt. George's
$$$ • 1956 Laskin Rd., Virginia Beach
• (757) 428-3494
$$$ • 2272 Pungo Ferry Rd., Virginia Beach
• (757) 721-3463

These restaurants originated the gorge-till-you-burst concept in the region. They offer an amazing variety of seafood, salads, side dishes, soups, and desserts for one price. For landlubbers, there is a good selection of other foods. The steamed crab legs and shrimp are irresistible to most diners, especially since they can fill their plates as often as they like. The restaurants do a big volume of business, so fresh batches of food are continually being hauled out from the kitchen. Captain George's opens daily for dinner.

Captain John's Seafood Company
$$$ • 4616 Virginia Beach Blvd.,
Virginia Beach
• (757) 499-7755

If you're really starved, head for this all-you-can-chow-down seafood buffet. It seems to stretch for a mile with a gargantuan array of crabs, clams, fish, and shrimp prepared in endless ways. You'll also enjoy all kinds of other entrees, salads, side dishes and scrumptious desserts. You'll find Captain John's anchored next to Pembroke Mall and serving dinner daily and lunch on weekends.

Charlie's Seafood Restaurant
$$ • 3139 Shore Dr., Virginia Beach
• (757) 481-9863

Charlie's is a homey seafood place near the Chesapeake Bay with a 1950s aura. It was started in 1946. Little has changed since then in this utilitarian restaurant. It remains in the Rehpelz family, with the founder's grandsons now at the helm. The menu of flounder, fried oysters, steamed clams, and seafood platters is still intact. Home-cooked side dishes include squash, collards, and black-eyed peas. One standout is the she-crab soup. It's so good we've

even heard well-traveled strangers in Pennsylvania describing how sublime it is. Desserts usually feature Key lime, lemon meringue, and chocolate-banana pies. On most nights there is an all-you-can-eat steamed shrimp special. Charlie's is open for dinner daily and serves lunch every day except Monday. Reservations are accepted.

Chick's Beach Cafe
$ • 4600 Lookout Rd., Virginia Beach
• (757) 460-2580

This casual eatery near the Chesapeake Bay has a loyal band of followers. It's tucked into the Chick's Beach neighborhood off Pleasure House Road and Shore Drive. The menu leans toward the sea with blackened tuna with tropical salsa, jambalaya, and seafood fettuccine. You'll also find such esoteric fare as lamb fajitas and smoked chicken quesadillas. The menu changes seasonally so be prepared for some surprises. The cafe is open for lunch and dinner daily and serves a Sunday brunch. If it's your first visit, call for directions.

Chick's Oyster Bar
$$ • 2143 Vista Cir., Virginia Beach
• (757) 481-5757

We love to go to this laid-back restaurant on the Lynnhaven River for the scenery and the excellent seafood. This is a local hangout with a deck overlooking the Lynnhaven Inlet. Fresh fish is the backbone of the menu that features the best of what is currently available. Chick's is one of the few restaurants that serves deviled crab. Steamed mussels and shrimp also are big sellers. You can dine inside or eat outside on the deck and watch the fishing boats coming to and from a neighboring marina. You're forewarned that in the summer the wait for dinner can stretch to an hour or more. Chick's is open for lunch and dinner daily.

Dockside Inn
$$ • 3311 Shore Dr., Virginia Beach
• (757) 481-4545

This is another local hideaway we almost hate to divulge for fear it will get too crowded to enjoy. But if you're looking for casual fun and fresh seafood, this is the place to come. The inn is an outgrowth of Lynnhaven Sea-

INSIDERS' TIP
If you're in Virginia Beach and longing for a great meal to come to you, call Takeout Taxi, (757) 456-5678. The delivery service will rush over with meals from about 20 different restaurants. It also delivers to some parts of Norfolk.

food Market and opened in 1994. It's got a dynamite view of boats at the adjacent marina and the Lynnhaven River. You eat on a wooden deck that is enclosed during the winter. Feel free to order steamed crabs and crack them to your heart's content. Or get your clams and oysters ready to eat. The menu ranges from basic steamed or fried seafood to dishes that are creatively prepared. The inn is open for lunch and dinner daily.

Duck-In & Gazebo
$$ • 3324 Shore Dr., Virginia Beach
• (757) 481-0201

The Duck-In has an ideal location right on the Chesapeake Bay with a beach and gazebo in its backyard. Diners can eat inside or on a deck under a striped canopy overlooking the Bay. The restaurant is renowned for its crab cakes, hush puppies and fisherman's chowder. It's been in business since 1952 when it was converted from a bait shop into a restaurant. Although its regular menu of seafood platters, crab, and shrimp is good, the Duck-In has gained a following for its buffets. The all-you-can-eat buffet is offered nightly during the summer and on Friday and Saturday during off-season. The buffet usually is loaded with snow crab legs, shrimp Creole, and other seafood

dishes. Popular desserts include bread pudding with pecan glaze and the Volcano—a brownie and ice cream with all the fixings. The Duck-In serves lunch and dinner daily and has a Sunday brunch buffet. Reservations are accepted.

Gus' Mariner Restaurant
$$$ • 57th St. and Atlantic Ave.,
Virginia Beach
• (757) 425-5699

With its ocean view and excellent cooking, Gus' has earned a permanent positive reputation with area diners. It has been in the Ramada Plaza Resort Oceanfront since 1981. There are usually at least five types of fresh fish on the menu. Hush puppies are hard to resist. Specialty desserts include Belgian whiskey pudding made with pound cake and raspberry sauce. Gus' serves breakfast, lunch and dinner daily with a brunch on Sundays.

The Happy Crab
Restaurant and Raw Bar
$$ • 550 Laskin Rd., Virginia Beach
• (757) 437-9200

This place offers the authentic crab-pickin' experience. If you're in the mood for a messy pile of crabs, we recommend it wholeheartedly. There are two choices for seating. Inside

For the full experience of Virginia Beach diners should try one of the many beach-side restaurants with terrace dining.

Photo: Courtesy of Virginia Beach Convention and Visitor Development

RESTAURANTS

are long picnic tables, where you'll rub elbows with a family from Ohio or a couple from the down the street. Outside are a handful of tables on an elevated deck, where you can toast the sunset with long-necked beers (they bring them to you in a tin bucket full of ice) and fantasize about how nice it would be to own one of those boats docked nearby. Guess where we always sit?

Harpoon Larry's Oyster Bar
$$ • 216 24th St., Virginia Beach
• (757) 422-6000

Fresh seafood served in a casual atmosphere is the draw at Harpoon Larry's. The restaurant opened near the beachfront in 1990 as a spin-off of a Hampton restaurant. The menu is heavy on shrimp, crab legs and seafood platters. There are lots of appetizers, including chicken wings. Harpoon Larry's also has a raw bar. It is open for dinner daily. Lunch is served daily during spring and summer and on weekends the rest of the year.

The Inlet Restaurant
$$ • 3319 Shore Dr., Virginia Beach
• (757) 481-7300

Located on the Lynnhaven River near the

You'll find tasty things to eat at many of our annual festivals and events.

Photo: Courtesy of City of Virginia Beach

Chesapeake Bay, The Inlet (formerly Henry's Raw Bar & Sea Grille) is a big, busy restaurant. One claim to fame is having one of the world's largest cylindrical aquariums in its lobby. There are typically six seafood entrees with a few daily specials. If you're really hungry go for the Fisherman's Platter with its shrimp, crab cake, flounder, oysters, and scallops. The restaurant is open daily for dinner and for a Sunday buffet brunch. During weekends there is usually evening entertainment on the deck overlook-

ing the river. Reservations are needed during the summer, especially on weekends. There is free valet parking on weekends.

Hot Tuna Bar and Grill
$$ • 2817 Shore Dr., Virginia Beach
• (757) 481-2888

As Hot Tuna's name suggests, you'll find fresh tuna fixed in some adventuresome ways —Oriental style, blackened, and in fajitas. The menu is much broader than that, however. Hot Tuna also serves barbecue ribs, crab cakes, steaks, and pasta. Although this lively restaurant leans toward heart-healthy cooking, it also prides itself on its fried calamari. Hot Tuna is open for dinner daily. Reservations are accepted.

King of the Sea
$$ • 27th St. and Atlantic Ave.,
Virginia Beach
• (757) 428-7983

This venerable seafood restaurant has been at the same location since 1965 and was re-modeled in 1993. It draws crowds with its nightly all-you-can-eat crab leg and shrimp specials. The family-run restaurant is known for broiled seafood platters and blackened fish as well as steaks. King of the Sea is open for dinner daily and lunch on weekends. Reservations are accepted.

Laverne's Seafood Restaurant and Chix Cafe
$$ • Seventh St. and Oceanfront, Virginia Beach
• (757) 428-6836

There are lots of early bird specials to tempt diners at Laverne's and sister restaurant, Chix Cafe. Both are adjoined to the Hilton Inn in Virginia Beach. The restaurants have been cooking fresh seafood since 1981 and have identical menus. Specialties include build-your-own-seafood platters as well as a prime rib and seafood combination. The restaurants are open daily for breakfast, lunch and dinner.

The Lighthouse Oceanfront
$$$ • First St. and Atlantic Ave., Virginia Beach
• (757) 428-7974

Located on the Atlantic Ocean at Rudee Inlet, this airy restaurant has a terrific view. To make it even better, outdoor seating lets you enjoy your meal with cool breezes in summer.

The Lighthouse is a special-occasion restaurant that has been in business since 1963. House specialties are she-crab soup, steamed shrimp and crabs and a variety of broiled fish. Lobster tails are flown in from New England, while shellfish come from the Eastern Shore. Steaks brought from the Midwest and trimmed on site also are popular menu items. Lunch and dinner are served daily, with brunch featured on weekends. There usually are early-bird specials for dinner. Reservations are accepted.

Lynnhaven Fish House
$$$ • 2350 Starfish Rd., Virginia Beach
• (757) 481-0003
This popular restaurant is on the Lynnhaven Fishing Pier right on the Chesapeake Bay and just off Shore Drive. Since 1979 it has prided itself on having an atmosphere similar to San Francisco's Fisherman's Wharf. Noted menu items include she-crab soup, Mediterranean salad and at least five types of fresh fish. Crab cakes, oysters on the half shell and surf-and-turf-platters are menu staples. Dessert features Belgian whiskey pudding and a variety of cakes. The Fish House is open for lunch and dinner daily. The adjoining Pier Cafe, (757) 481-5950, is a casual eatery that has both indoor and outdoor seating for lunch and dinner.

Mahi Mah's Seafood Restaurant and Sushi Saloon
$$ • 615 Atlantic Ave., Virginia Beach
• (757) 437-8030
Mahi Mah's isn't your typical seafood-platter type of place. There's an intriguing mix of seafood and sushi at this oceanfront restaurant. Look for seafood prepared with Thai and Vietnamese influences thanks to chef Thomas Cramer and food director Chuck Sass. Both are veterans of other well-known restaurants. The sushi bar adds another dimension for gourmands. Mahi Mah's is adjacent the Ramada Inn. It serves a traditional breakfast, lunch and dinner daily.

Nick's Hospitality Restaurant
$$ • 508 Laskin Rd., Virginia Beach
• (757) 428-7891
Founded in 1952, this is a locals' restaurant, partly because Nick's location next to a laundry doesn't seem too exciting. But step inside, where the menu is another story. Nick's serves fresh seafood in a comfortable atmosphere that's changed little since the '50s. The menu features whatever is in season with bargain prices and all-you-can-eat specials. This is one of the few places where you can get crack-'em-and-eat-'em steamed crabs. They're usually in season May through October. The menu sometimes has surprises, such as blackened alligator and other Cajun dishes. Nick's serves breakfast, lunch and dinner daily. One best-seller at breakfast is the crab omelette. Maybe it's just as well that we locals keep this one secret.

One Fish Two Fish
$$ • 2109 W. Great Neck Rd., Virginia Beach
• (757) 496-4350
This may be the hottest restaurant in the city right now. Its location at Long Bay Pointe Boating Resort overlooks Long Creek. The restaurant's forte is serving sophisticated food in a casual environment. Try the pan-seared halibut and potato-crusted grouper but be sure to save room for the homemade desserts. Our vote is for the Godiva chocolate crème brûlée.

Rockafeller's
$$ • 308 Mediterranean Ave., Virginia Beach
• (757) 422-5654
This restaurant and raw bar opened in 1990 on the scenic Rudee Inlet. Its specialties include oysters Rockefeller and clams casino. While seafood is a big part of the menu, Rockafeller's entrees also include pasta, chicken, and seafood. It's gained a following for its Caesar salad. Lunch and dinner are served daily, with brunch offered on Sunday.

Rudee's Restaurant & Raw Bar
$$ • 227 Mediterranean Ave., Virginia Beach
• (757) 425-1777
This casual Rudee Inlet restaurant that's very popular with the locals is known for its raw bar and steamed-shrimp specials. Steaks, crab, scallops, and lobster round out the menu, which also includes sandwiches. There is a wide variety of seafood appetizers. Desserts range from Key lime pie to carrot cake. Rudee's, which was started in 1983, serves dinner daily and is open for lunch Monday through Saturday, with brunch served on Sunday. Reservations are accepted.

Sandbridge Restaurant & Raw Bar
$$ • 205 Sandbridge Rd., Virginia Beach
• (757) 426-2193
The Sandbridge Restaurant has been around since the early '60s and is in the Sandbridge beach area. Fresh seafood and prime rib are the

house specialties. Baby-back ribs also are big sellers. Dinner is served nightly during late spring and summer with breakfast and lunch available on weekends. During winter the restaurant closes some days so be sure to call first for exact hours and days.

Seacrest Restaurant
$$ • 1776 Princess Anne Rd.,
Virginia Beach
• (757) 426-7804

Located in Pungo, the Sea Crest prides itself on its she-crab soup, broiled seafood platter, and prime rib. Its noted dessert is rice pudding. The Sea Crest is open daily for dinner with a varying schedule in winter.

Steinhilber's Thalia Acres Inn
$$$ • 653 Thalia Rd., Virginia Beach
• (757) 340-1156

Steinhilber's is one of Virginia Beach's oldest restaurants, and you can count on it for good food served in an elegant environment. It's our first choice for special occasions. One Pennsylvanian we know who travels the East Coast for a living calls Steinhilber's his all-time favorite restaurant. His top pick: the delicate tempura-fried shrimp. Steaks are a close runner-up. Fresh seafood grilled over a mesquite fire is also a delicacy. Brothers Robert and Herman Steinhilber opened the restaurant in 1935 as part of a country resort, and it still retains its hunt club atmosphere despite a recent expansion. The site once was a Prohibition-era private club. During World War II the military took over Steinhilber's for an officers club. Nearby was a German prisoner of war camp. The restaurant was returned to the owners after the war. Today it is run by Robert Steinhilber's children. During their father's tenure, Steinhilber's was a locals-only restaurant that closed during the summer to avoid tourists. The restaurant is now open year round Tuesday through Saturday for dinner. If it's your first visit, ask for directions since the restaurant is off the beaten path.

Surf Rider
$$ • Wesleyan Dr. and
Diamond Springs Rd., Virginia Beach
• (757) 497-3534

Started in 1979, the Surf Rider has had various locations. However, its loyal following keeps coming for the crab cakes and other fresh seafood. Everything is homemade, including cream of broccoli and crabmeat soup, clam chowder, and a variety of pies. The Surf Rider

is in Cypress Point Shopping Center. A Norfolk location is at 723 Newtown Road, (757) 461-6488. The restaurants serve lunch and dinner every day but Sunday.

Tautog's
$$ • 205 23rd St., Virginia Beach
• (757) 442-0081

For fresh fish in a neat atmosphere step into Tautog's and step back in time. The restaurant is housed in an old beach cottage two blocks from the oceanfront and prides itself on its fresh salmon, tuna, and snapper served in a variety of ways. Dinner is available nightly.

Worrell Bros.
$ • 1910 Atlantic Ave., Virginia Beach
• (757) 422-6382

Steamed shrimp is the star at this restaurant named for the brothers who established it in 1968. This is a casual spot that features nightly all-you-can-eat specials of crab, shrimp, and steak. The seafood is fresh, and most of it is home grown in the Chesapeake Bay.

Chesapeake

The Lock's Pointe Restaurant at Great Bridge
$$ • 136 S. Battlefield Blvd., Chesapeake
• (757) 547-9618

Overlooking the Atlantic Intracoastal Waterway, Lock's Pointe gives diners a great view of boats plying the waters. The restaurant opened in 1984 and has never wavered from its emphasis on seafood. Specialties include baked salmon stuffed with prosciutto and Gouda and topped with a crab sauce. A veal, crab, and artichoke pasta dish also is a crowd pleaser. Meals often start with Oysters Rockefeller or she-crab soup. There are at least six homemade desserts on the menu. Lunch and dinner are served Tuesday through Sunday. Lock's Point also features a Sunday brunch. Reservations are recommended. In back of the restaurant is Hodad's Bar & Grill, a sister eatery that is more casual, (757) 547-9619.

The Oysterette Restaurant & Raw Bar
$$ • 3916 Portsmouth Blvd., Chesapeake
• (757) 465-2156

The Oysterette opened in 1992 to give some dining diversity to the Western Branch area of Chesapeake. This small, casual raw bar is in Stonebridge Center at the foot of the Hodges Ferry Bridge. Its menu includes crab cakes,

RESTAURANTS

stuffed flounder, and a variety of other fresh seafood. There is a large assortment of appetizers, and each weekday night a different entree is highlighted with a bargain price. The Oysterette serves lunch and dinner daily. It stays open late for night owls.

Portsmouth

Amory's Seafood
$$ • 5909 High St., Portsmouth
• (757) 483-1518

If anyone knows fresh seafood it's George Amory, owner of Amory's Seafood. His family has been in the seafood business for more than 100 years and at one time was the East Coast's largest seafood distributor. Amory opened his restaurant in 1976 in the Churchland area of Portsmouth. The menu offers many shrimp, scallop, crab, and fish dinners. Some are made from old family recipes, including Crab Maryland and Flounder Supreme. Popular items include she-crab soup, a New England clambake and homemade marinara sauce for pasta. For a real regional taste try the crabmeat topped with Smithfield ham. There is a raw bar, and Amory's oysters come from the family's oyster beds. On weekday nights there are bargain-priced specials on the menu. Dinner is served daily with lunch available every day but Saturday. Reservations are accepted.

Amory's Wharf
$$ • 10 Crawford Pkwy., Portsmouth
• (757) 399-0991

An Amory's Seafood spin-off, this waterfront restaurant opened in 1992. Its owner is David Amory, a Culinary Institute of America graduate whose father runs the other Amory's. Both restaurants share many of the same seafood dishes. However, the Wharf puts its own spin on the menu with some upscale, trendy dishes such as a mozzarella appetizer wrapped in romaine and prosciutto, grilled with garlic, and served with a fresh tomato vinaigrette. Besides seafood, there are pastas, steaks, sandwiches, and salads on the menu. The Wharf is in downtown Portsmouth at the end of a marina. It is a compact second-story restaurant overlooking the Elizabeth River and Downtown Norfolk across the water. It has a small parking lot inside the marina fence. In December this is one of the best spots for viewing the holiday lights in downtown Norfolk.

Circle Seafood Restaurant
$$ • 3010 High St., Portsmouth
• (757) 397-8196

Since its opening in 1947, The Circle has been a Portsmouth dining landmark. It retains the same round, diner look it had back in the days when it had car hops and was a Chicken in the Rough franchise. On one wall are caricatures of Hollywood celebrities whose heydays have long passed. Ambiance aside, The Circle is known for its seafood and steaks. Menu standouts include crab cakes, lobster tails and seafood platters. There also is a raw bar and a solid list of reasonably priced entrees such as ribs, ham steak and a broiled chicken breast. Side dishes include cabbage, yams, black-eyed peas and collards. The Circle is open for three meals a day, including a big breakfast buffet. On Sunday there is a popular buffet that includes all-you-can-eat crab and prime rib at night. Reservations are accepted and definitely needed on weekends. Children who clean their plates are rewarded with free ice cream.

The Flagship Restaurant
$$ • 103 Constitution Ave., Portsmouth
• (757) 399-2233

Hidden off Va. Route 17 on the banks of Scotts Creek is Portsmouth's oldest restaurant. The Flagship has been serving fresh seafood since the early 1940s. New owners in 1999 have kept the traditional look of a vintage ship's

INSIDERS' TIP

Several annual events let you sample the fare from a variety of restaurants for the price of a single ticket. All are heavily publicized events. Each March the Taste of Hampton Roads benefits the Foodbank of Southeastern Virginia. It is usually held at the Sheraton Waterside Hotel in Norfolk and features food from 35 area restaurants. Call (757) 624-1333. A Taste of Portsmouth, a February event, showcases about a dozen Portsmouth restaurants and is held at the Holiday Inn-Portsmouth Waterfront. The sponsor is Ports Events. Call (757) 393-9933. Zoo To Do is a September bash at the Norfolk Zoo that benefits the zoological park in Norfolk. About 25 area chefs try to outdo each other with their cuisine. Call (757) 624-9937.

cabin while modernizing the menu. Owner/ chef Peter Pittman is a Portsmouth native renowned regionally for starting some innovative restaurants. The Flagship now boasts such entrees as roasted sea scallops, shrimp jambalaya, and rockfish on balsamic greens. The Flagship is open for dinner daily. Reservations are recommended.

Lobscouser Restaurant
$$ • 337 High St., Portsmouth
• (757) 397-2728

This downtown restaurant bears the nickname for the chef on a ship. Its menu leans toward fresh seafood with some beef and chicken included for balance. There are usually four soups on the menu, and homemade desserts often include bread pudding and strawberry shortcake. Lobscouser is open for lunch and dinner daily. Reservations are accepted.

Scale O' De Whale
$$$ • 3515 Shipwright St., Portsmouth
• (757) 483-2772

Since the opening of the Western Freeway in 1992, this obscure seafood restaurant on the Western Branch of the Elizabeth River has been a little more accessible. It is in a ship perma-nently moored in a marina and has a varied menu that features seafood, beef and chicken. Noted entrees are the Neptune Feast—a dinner for two that includes lobsters, filet mignon, and stuffed shrimp—and kebabs laced with shrimp, scallops, and filet mignon. The she-crab soup is excellent. Homemade desserts include apple cobbler and bread pudding with lemon custard. Dinner is served daily with lunch offered on weekdays. Reservations are accepted. Be sure to call for directions to the restaurant.

Suffolk

Bennett's Creek Marina & Seafood Restaurant
$$ • 3305 Ferry Rd., Suffolk
• (757) 484-8700

This is a real Insider find: a small rustic seafood place out on pilings above the water at Bennett's Creek. It's the kind of place you feel real smart just to know about. The seafood is fresh, the preparations simple and the portions always ample. Bennett's Creek is an excellent choice when you're hankering for high-quality fare in a no-nonsense atmosphere. It's open for dinner daily plus Sunday lunch.

Nightlife

There must be something in our water that gives us the stamina to stay up all night and boogie. And, judging from the sheer numbers of hot places where you can exercise your right to pop, rock, bluegrass and jazz yourself into a wee-hours frenzy, we must be drinking from that well every night of the week.

Which brings us to a word on drinking. The legal age to enjoy alcoholic beverages in the Commonwealth of Virginia is 21—no ifs, ands, buts, or fake IDs about it. Patrons who are at least 18 years old may be allowed into most nightspots, but they are usually burdened with a hand stamp that indicates their money's no good at the bar. Bouncers and bartenders alike find no joke in any underage shenanigans. After all, their jobs and reputations are at stake. So, while taking teenagers to dinner in our region is encouraged and appreciated, please park them in a safe place before taking off for a night of festivities at any local night spot.

Now that we have the attention of all you adults in the audience, let's take a trip to some of the area's most lively late-night spots. Most of the venues we include revolve around the music du jour, so when possible we separate your destination choices by the type of music you'll find. This isn't always the case however. Lots of places book a mellow acoustic guitarist one night and a jazz ensemble the next. About the only places that stick to one type of music are—you guessed it—the clubs that cater to the country-music lovers. Further complicating the matter, many of our "clubs" lead dual lives as restaurants. This is especially true for popular eateries at the Beach such as Hot Tuna, Five 01 City Grill and The Jewish Mother, where a pre-planned linger after dessert can mean entry into a late-night wave of music. So if you're just out for a delectable dinner, hang around. You never know what's going to happen when the 10 o'clock curtain rises. Of course, there are also plenty of nightspots that can draw a crowd without ever booking a live band, and we cover the hottest bars for you too.

Since it's not humanly possible for your Insiders' hosts to have frequented every nightspot in town, we'll give you our best shot at those we know are the places to see—and be seen—on tips from wired friends and associates who require minimal sleep.

Rock, Acoustic and New-music Venues

Virginia Beach

Ocean Eddie's
15th St. and Oceanfront, Virginia Beach
• **(757) 425-7742**
This is a great place to take your visiting cousin from Iowa because it's literally plopped out on the boardwalk fishing pier. It's loud, crowded and absolutely fun. A generally more mature crowd—say thirtysomething plus—squeezes into Ocean Eddie's every night of the week. It's blistering hot in the summer, and that's both in popularity and sheer physical heat from the crowd. If you can find the elbow room to eat, try the superb crab cakes. There is a cover charge,

but it varies from night to night and is worth every penny.

Abbey Road Pub & Restaurant
203 22nd St., Virginia Beach
• **(757) 425-6330**

Celebrating more than 10 years in the entertainment game, Abbey Road has been the magnet for some of the finest acoustic action in town. The resort-strip nightclub has built a reputation on its excellent menu too. Usually packed tight with happy patrons, there's live entertainment seven nights a week in the summer, six in the off-season. Along with a kitchen that's open from lunch until 2 AM, you can drink your way around the world from an impressive selection of imported beers. There's ample on-site parking too—a real benefit for the seasonal gridlock we've come to expect during summer evenings at the Beach.

The Abyss/Nocturnal Cafe
1065 19th St., Virginia Beach
• **(757) 422-0480**

You've got to have the strength of youth to make it at The Abyss, a techno club with DJ music on Wednesday nights and weekends. Folks 18 and older spill onto (and into) the sunken-pit dance floor, and the bravest of them make it up to the rear gangway that doubles as a dance stage, as they mosh to the techno and alternative rock music. If you hit it on the right night, you'll have first peek at up-and-coming college rock bands who perform on a national basis. This place can get really, really crowded, even at the pool tables. But, if you're into blinding strobes, synchronized Intellibeam lights and a booming sound system, go for it. The Nocturnal Cafe is an addition with a full stage, kinder, gentler sounds and a more laid-back coffeehouse atmosphere.

Crocs
620 19th St., Virginia Beach
• **(757) 428-5444**

Are you noticing a trend with these addresses here? Lots of our hot nightspots occur in colonies, and one of the most popular clusters extends along 19th Street from the Radisson Hotel east. This is a slightly smaller venue, but it's still popular with beach locals. The music is progressive rock.

Five 01 City Grill
501 N. Birdneck Rd., Virginia Beach
• **(757) 425-7195**

If you travel west from the Pavilion Convention Center and take a right onto Birdneck Road, you'll find a great place to spend an evening just a few blocks up on your right. Five 01 City Grill has some of the best food in the area and a separate bar area that rocks into the wee hours with hot tunes from popular local bands. The combination attracts a hip, local clientele of all ages. It's locally renowned as a place to see and be seen.

Hot Tuna
**2817 Shore Dr.,
Virginia Beach**
• **(757) 481-2888**

Another hot area for bar hopping is at the extreme north end of Virginia Beach along Shore Drive. This seafood restaurant/nightclub is the doyenne of Shore Drive nightlife. Some say the prettiest bar crowd in town is to be found at Hot Tuna, but we'll leave the superlatives to your own judgement.

Beach Grill
3152 Shore Dr., Virginia Beach
• **(757) 496-2755**

Not so big, not so fancy, this seafood restaurant and raw bar reflects the traditional Shore Drive values of beach casual. It features live music almost every night of the week from popular local blues, rock and acoustic bands.

Smackwater Jack's
3333 Virginia Beach Blvd., Virginia Beach
• **(757) 340-6638**

This rock and acoustic venue wins the longevity prize. It's been going strong every since we started keeping up with the club scene—and don't even ask how long that's been. This one appeals to a slightly older, less la-de-dah crowd. It's a place to kick back, have a beer and listen to music.

South Beach Grill
**Norfolk Ave. and Birdneck Rd.,
Virginia Beach**
• **(757) 428-0820**

If you've graduated from alternative rock, head to South Beach Grill for some bluesy, classic good-time rock from popular local bands. South Beach attracts an older locals crowd, and very casual is the standard attire.

INSIDERS' TIP

For a taste treat, sample some of Norfolk's own Steamship Brewing Co. products. At many restaurants and bars, you'll find either Steamship's Captain's Lager or its Raspberry Ale.

Worrell Brothers
19th St. and Atlantic Ave., Virginia Beach
• (757) 422-6382

Chill out on the deck at this resort-strip landmark. There's a DJ most nights and occasionally a classic rock cover band to compete with your conversations. A little older crowd hangs out here, which means that the decibel level is bearable.

Peabody's
21st St. and Pacific Ave., Virginia Beach
• (757) 422-6212

This venue is a beach tradition. It has booked the same kind of music for decades—the hottest local bands and national acts on their way up. As always, it attracts a young crowd, and it's smack-dab in the middle of the resort area nightlife too. Summer nights here can be downright sultry.

Norfolk

The Waterside Festival Marketplace, Norfolk
333 Waterside Dr., Norfolk
• (757) 627-3300

This is the ultimate place to go for late-night fun. Since 1999 this downtown waterfront mall has repositioned itself as an entertainment center. The fun starts around 10 AM daily and rolls on until the wee hours. There are so many night clubs, restaurants and other places to go that if you don't like the crowd or the music in one, you can merely slide down the hall to a totally different venue. Your choices include BAR Norfolk with music from the '50s through the '90s (757) 627-2899, Dixie's Tavern with its Cajun flair (757) 624-9422, Have a Nice Day Café Bar & Restaurant with its hip '70s theme (757) 627-2270 and Crocodile Rocks Dueling Pianos (757) 625-7625. Upstairs in Waterside is Jillian's with more than 150 arcade games and virtual bowling. Jillian's (757) 624-9100 also includes a café and bar with 18 huge TVs.

The NorVa
317 Monticello Ave., Norfolk
• (757) 627-4500

It didn't take long for this classy concert venue to catch on when it opened in 2000. It's been years since the NorVa was a theater but after years as a fitness center, it is back with a vengeance. James Brown was the opening act for the NorVa's debut, and a variety of national artists of all types have hit the stage. When there's no one playing live on stage you can wind down at the Backstage Café. Just look for the life-sized mannequins of the Blue Brothers outside the door and you will have found the right place.

The Boathouse
119 Bessie's Pl., behind Harbor Park, Norfolk
• (757) 622-6395

Believe it or not, this old cement-floored warehouse has been the No. 1 live-music venue in the area for eons. This is where the up-and-coming bands play right before they hit the concert arena stages, but many big-name artists also include a stop at the Boathouse because it's just fun to play this smaller, more intimate venue. You'll probably need to purchase tickets in advance (they range from $5 to $18), and the beer garden is strictly off limits to anyone younger than 21. Word of mouth and local concert listings are the best way to hear who's playing next.

O'Sullivan's Wharf
43rd St. and Colley Ave., Norfolk
• (757) 423-3753

What first appears to be a couple of weather-worn shacks tossed together by a sarcastic hurricane is actually home to some of the tastiest food and entertainment on Norfolk's west side. After a fantastic meal of crab cakes, Alaskan crab legs or tempura shrimp, you can settle in for the nightly acoustic entertainment. Open when weather permits is a great deck that juts out over a branch of the Elizabeth River, which always seems to catch a great breeze. The crowd's a mix of ODU students, professors and just plain locals—you'll fit right in.

Cogans Instant Art Bar
1901 Colonial Ave., Norfolk
• (757) 627-6428

Is it open? Is it closed? If a cat has nine lives, then this Norfolk institution must be a reincarnated cat. It's a dive, to be sure, but this tiny, dark nightspot in the Ghent section of the city has been giving local bands a stage for years and years.

The Tap House Grill at Ghent
931 W. 21st St., Norfolk
• (757) 627-9172

This Ghent restaurant and bar offers a good selection of beers, a comfortable atmosphere and frequent live music. It appeals to young, hip crowd and has what one Insider calls "that West Coast/Seattle" kind of feeling.

Open Wide
122 Granby St., Norfolk
• (757) 533-9153
This is the kind of place its hard to be sure about: is it a bar with food or a restaurant with music? This smoky hangout draws a young crowd and features both a Foosball table and gourmet meat loaf. Go figure.

Portsmouth

Towne Point Pub
3558 Towne Point Rd., Portsmouth
• (757) 483-2500
This is a Western Branch destination for hordes of regulars who pop in for one of the Pub's enormous club sandwiches. Live bands grab the mikes on Wednesday, Friday and Saturday nights, and the rock 'n' roll gets even the shyest guests out on the dance floor. This is a real friendly neighborhood place where there's not a stranger in the crowd.

Chesapeake

Winston's Cafe
1412 Greenbrier Pkwy., Chesapeake
• (757) 420-1751
It's got that Jewish Mother kind of atmosphere, what with all the local lounge lizards that stream in to Winston's, especially on Friday and Saturday nights when they roll back the carpets for the crowds of pasta-hungry patrons. There's live entertainment on occasional Thursdays and every Friday and Saturday night, but the casual come-as-you-are (or want-to-be) feeling prevails all week long, from 11 AM until 2 AM every day except Sunday.

Jazz and Blues

Virginia Beach

The Jewish Mother
3108 Pacific Ave., Virginia Beach
• (757) 422-5430
Self-billed as the premier blues club in town, The Jewish Mother tops its corned beef with a blues jam every Wednesday night and live blues performers every other night of the week. It's

also a popular stopover on an all-night Beach hop, especially if you get the hungries. The excellent food and generous portions are legendary, and you can even slide into Mom's Deli Section and brown bag a sinful dessert. Also known as "The Jew Mo" and "The Blue-ish Mother" for its blues bookings, this place is more than a restaurant and more than a nightclub—it's a Virginia Beach institution! There's also a sister operation in Portsmouth at 1 High Street, (757) 398-3332.

Norfolk

Alexander's Sheraton Norfolk Waterside Hotel
Waterside Dr., Norfolk
• (757) 622-6664
Several years ago, the hotel underwent a $4 million renovation, and Alexander's was its crowning glory. It has a scenic waterfront view, a menu of bistro-type light snacks and entrees, a nice wine list and the area's only vodka bar. Alexander's is a great place to unwind, and some evenings it features live jazz music.

Bienville Grill
723 W. 21st St., Norfolk
• (757) 625-5427
Late night at the Grill has some wicked tunes coming your way, thanks to live jazz every Friday and Saturday night from 9 PM until 12:30 AM. For more about this divine gem of a restaurant, see the Restaurants chapter.

Blues Alley
455 Granby St., Norfolk
• (757) 622-0081
The name says it all for lovers of blues and jazz music. This bistro and café opened in 2000 as part of downtown Norfolk's renaissance of Granby St. Look for live jazz on Friday and Saturday nights and at Sunday during the champagne brunch.

Country/Bluegrass

Virginia Beach

Desperado's Restaurant & Bar
315 17th St., Virginia Beach
• (757) 425-5566
"We're not snooty . . . we're rooty tooty." That's their motto, so we guess that's what

they mean. Home to the only mechanical bull in the area, perhaps the state, Desperado's rocks Thursday through Saturday nights with house band Thunder Creek. The food's pretty good too—Tex-Mex style with some mean jumbo nachos, a taco plate that will set you on fire on Saturday nights and 10 cent shrimp on Thursday night.

Norfolk

The Banque
1849 E. Little Creek Rd., Norfolk
• **(757) 480-3600**

If we're in a Garth Brooks kind of mood, take us to The Banque for the cure. We're talkin' country—real country—and you'd better know your stuff before you put your boots on the dance floor. Proclaimed Club of the Year several times by the Virginia Country Music Association, The Banque seats 500 people (most of whom are on the huge dance floor). The Banque has live toe-tapping music, super food and free dance lessons five nights a week. If you get country fever, you can do a little late-night shopping at Belle's Dry Goods inside. The Banque is open Tuesday through Sunday from 6 PM until 2 AM.

The Lido Inn
839 E. Little Creek Rd., Norfolk
• **(757) 480-1953**

A lot of people we know go to The Lido just for the steamed shrimp—some of the best in the region. Many of these people are the same folks who don't admit to hanging around to get into the country-rhythm frenzy that picks up when the live entertainment begins. But, plenty of patrons are known to leave half-finished plates to hit the dance floor. It's really a fun place, with a broad range of guests from old to young. Everyone is truly kind in teaching you how to line dance around the dance floor without looking too much like city folk. There's no cover charge, so give it a try for a real good time.

Chesapeake

Blakelys
414 S. Battlefield Blvd., Chesapeake
• **(757) 482-2121**

Self-billed as the only one of its kind on the East Coast, Blakelys is becoming Chesapeake's

INSIDERS' TIP

If you know you'll be out partying late and will need a ride home, check with the front desk of your hotel to find out if they offer shuttle services. Many of the area's hotels will be happy to bring you back in for the night.

The Commodore Theatre is a luxuriously restored 1945 art deco-style motion picture theater that shows first-run movies while serving light dinners.

Locals think nothing of making the short drive to Hampton's Coliseum for big name concerts.

Photo: Courtesy of Virginia Division of Tourism

premier nightclub and, in fact, was nominated for the Country Music Club of the Year award. Two-step through two floors of fun and slap your boots on the dance floor for a free line-dancing lesson every Wednesday through Saturday from 7:30 to 8:30 PM. DJ's and live bands take the stage each night, and if hunger should hit, you can order some of their world-famous barbecue, steak or seafood. They're open Wednesday through Saturday only, from 6 PM until 2 AM.

There's More ???

Two categories of after-sundown entertainment that we haven't covered are comedy clubs and movies. And we have both.

Comedy Clubs

Virginia Beach

Thoroughgood Inn Comedy Club
4801 Shore Dr.,
Virginia Beach
• **(757) 460-8399**
Comedy clubs have come and gone around here, but this one in the

Bayside Shopping Center stays alive and stays open. We caught a rising star named Jay Leno here years ago, and this is still a great place to see national talent on the rise. Wednesday and Thursday nights are improv workshops. National acts come in on Friday and Saturday nights. Admission charges vary according to the notoriety of the act.

Distinctive Movie Theaters

When it comes to movie theaters, we've got them playing first-run flicks from one end of the region to the other. In recent years there has been an influx of mega-plexes with stadium seats, which make for great viewing of first-run flicks. As Insiders, however, we feel it's our duty to point out three of the many theaters that have as much personality as the reels they run up in the projector room.

Virginia Beach

Cinema Cafe
758 Independence Blvd.,
Virginia Beach
• **(757) 499-6165**
In this movie theater,

A thousand sparkling lights reflect the excitement of the evening's entertainment at the Pavilion Convention Center.

Photo: Courtesy of Virginia Tourism Corporation

you can enjoy dinner or snacks as you watch a feature film. And you can go straight from the office (or the beach) because the menu includes heftier fare, such as a pretty good chicken sandwich, fries and an ice-cold beer.

Norfolk

The Naro Expanded Cinema
1507 Colley Ave.,
Norfolk
• (757) 625-6276

The Naro is an old-fashioned, big 70mm screen armed with Dolby stereo sound and comfy seats, with the added benefit of baklava and Quibel for sale in the lobby. Along with current hits, you'll likely find those Academy Award winners you missed during the first run, along with some arty, off-thewall offerings. If the movie is a dud, pop out to

INSIDERS' TIP

Virginia Beach helped lead the beach music craze back in the late '60s with hometown boys Bill Deal and the Rhondels. Country singer Juice Newton graduated from high school in Virginia Beach. Mr. Las Vegas himself, Wayne Newton, hails from Portsmouth as does rhythm and blues great Ruth Brown. But just ask any Insider who our favorite hometown musician is. There's no contest. It has to be Williamsburg native Bruce Hornsby.

the concession counter for brownies or a giant cookie. Call for current listings.

Portsmouth

The Commodore Theatre
421 High St.,
Portsmouth
• (757) 393-6962

This is what a movie theater experience is all about. In the grand artdeco theater with a huge 42-foot screen, squishy carpet, murals and chandeliers, you plop in a stuffed chair at your own private table. Got a twinge of hunger? Just pick up the phone on your table and order some carrot cake or hot chocolate with tiny floating marshmallows. Even with the super THX sound system, the homey atmosphere gives you that kick-your-shoes-offand-enjoy-the-movie feeling.

Shopping

The demographers and social pundits who say that conspicuous consumption is out of style probably haven't tried to find a parking spot close to the mall recently. Some people were simply born to shop, and if you're one of them, you'll find plenty to interest you in our local malls, boutiques and specialty stores. And just think—your closet, your pantry, your living room and your country will all benefit every time your lace up your Air Nikes and spend, spend, spend.

We'd give almost anything to go along with each and every one of you on a personally guided shopping tour, but we know we'd be the first to succumb to the world of temptation that lies just behind those glass double-doors. Therefore, we accept the responsibility, and the duty, to point you in the direction of our favorite shopping haunts, and hope you leave the really marked-down goodies behind for us.

Believe us, there has never been a better time to shop in this region. In 1999 Norfolk debuted it downtown crown jewel-the $300-plus million MacArthur Center mall. Just knowing the giant 1 million-square-foot retailing mecca was coming put other retailers in high gear. By the time MacArthur Center opened, existing shopping malls had begun making $160 million in improvements. These changes come on top of expansions and renovations already done in the past few years. And, various cities are turning what once were downtrodden, vacant urban storefronts into quaint antique and gift shops and sidewalk cafes perfect for a day of strolling and shopping.

So grab your credit cards and let us steer you in the direction of where you can shop to your heart's content.

LOOK FOR:
- **Malls and Shopping Areas**
- **Specialty Shops**
  —**Antiques**
  —**Bookstores**
  —**Used Bookstores**
  —**Health Foods**
  —**Consignment Stores**
  —**Collectibles Shops**
  —**Quilt Shops**
  —**Virginia Shops**

Malls and Shopping Areas

Virginia Beach

Pembroke Mall
Virginia Beach Blvd. at Independence Blvd., Virginia Beach
- **(757) 497-6255**

Right in the hub of what is officially Virginia Beach's central business district, Pembroke Mall has sprawled larger and larger to accommodate both new stores and stalwart shoppers. Dillard's and Sears are the main anchors. Stein Mart is our very favorite upscale discount store in the area. S&K Menswear, a clothing discounter is also here, plus mall favorites such as Waldenbooks and Athlete's Foot. If you're hungry stop by Kelly's Tavern for one of the best burgers around. Those who need a break can cruise over to the Regal Cinema to catch a new release. Across from the movies, there's Coney Island Family Arcade, boasting an indoor miniature golf course, plus all the popular arcade games.

Columbus Village
4485 Independence Blvd., Virginia Beach
- **(757) 490-8181**

Just when you get comfortable with a broad expanse of emptiness, along comes a very sharp developer who knows just what you've been missing. Columbus Village, across Virginia Beach Boulevard from Pembroke Mall, has risen out of no-

where to a hub of activity where parking spaces are scarce. There's an enormous Barnes & Noble Booksellers complete with an oh-so-chic coffeehouse and overstuffed chairs for perusing books. You'll also find a Bed, Bath and Beyond store with everything imaginable for the home and Columbus Movies with 12 screens of the newest releases.

And nearby . . .

Music-lover alert! Planet Music has been sighted! No ordinary extraterrestrial music store, Planet Music has a population of 100,000 CDs and tapes spread over 30,000 square feet of space. To make contact with the music, just stop at one of the 100 listening stations to check out unknown titles before you buy. And, if the name of that song or artist is lost in cyberspace, four touchscreen database kiosks called Muze systems need only a key word to investigate. To ensure a safe return to earth, you can sign up for The Star Club and save 20 percent on anything, anytime you buy.

Lynnhaven Mall
Lynnhaven Pkwy., Virginia Beach
• **(757) 340-9340**

Many of us go to Lynnhaven just to take a "trip out of town." While it isn't very far in miles, once inside, you can leave your worries in the parking lot or garage and drift aimlessly inside all day long. In 1999 the mall debuted the region's first Lord & Taylor store as part of a $100 million makeover. Coming on line in 2000 is a 24-screen movie theater and more stores and restaurants.

Two major book stores, endless women's and men's apparel (including the Gap, Anne Taylor Loft, Abercrombie & Fitch, Lerner's, The Limited and Express), jewelry stores and an out-of-this world Disney Store await. On the upper level is a food court to soothe whatever taste you have, from burgers to Chinese to pizza. A giant Hecht's is among the anchors. Others include JCPenney, Montgomery Ward, and Dillard's are the other big anchors, but some of our favorite shops are of the smallish variety, such as The Bombay Company, Bath and Body Works and Victoria's Secret.

Countryside Shops
1985 Landstown Rd., Virginia Beach
• **(757) 427-9009, (757) 430-0903**

This unique shopping experience is just 10 minutes from the oceanfront and right next door to the Farmer's Market. The Countryside Shops are weathered and purposely worn-looking on the outside, but inside is a hallway of boutiques with many one-of-a-kind collectibles.

Heart & Hand Gallery offers antiques, pottery and jewelry; The Wedding Shoppe has everything for a memorable wedding. We especially like Just Imagine, with its doll houses and miniatures, and Randales of Humingwood, which sells Native American arts and crafts. Need to find a perfect teddy bear? Try Me and Grannies. For hand-carved decoys visit Feathers & Wood. If you're in the neighborhood around lunchtime, duck into the Countryside Tea Room for homemade soups and desserts, overstuffed sandwiches and great barbecue.

Birchwood Consumer Center
3750 Virginia Beach Blvd., Virginia Beach
• **(757) 463-8665**

What was formerly the Great American Outlet Mall has created a new identity in the past few year. It is now an off-price shopping center with an interesting mix of store. The biggest one is BJ's Wholesale Club, which sells a staggering array of merchandise. A Burlington Coat Factory is a large store specializing in clothing and baby paraphernalia. Bugle Boy, and Dress Barn are geared toward fashion.

Hilltop
Laskin and First Colonial Rds., Virginia Beach
• **(757) 627-8611**

Once upon a time, Virginia Beach residents had to travel to the big city (i.e., Norfolk) to go shopping. But with the continued development of this retail area, we've pretty much got everything you could ask for right at home.

The Hilltop area is actually a collection of strip centers whose tenants run the economic gamut from Kmart, Target and Big Lots to sophisticated gift and clothing stores. We'll give you a quick rundown of the major centers and send you out with a warning: If someone tells you a store is at Hilltop, find out where at Hilltop before you set out on your journey. Some of our favorite stores, and the centers you'll find them in, follow.

Hilltop North: Try Dan Ryan's for Men and Blue Ridge Mountain Sports, a great place for rugged outdoor wear. Eateries range from the urbane Baker's Crust to the middle-American Shoney's.

Hilltop West: Taste Unlimited was our first gourmet grocery and we still love its sandwiches, gourmet goodies and wines. Culinary delights await you at El Azteca Mexican restaurant and The Barbecue Grill. You can shop for the perfect cut of meat at the Village Butcher.

Hilltop East: This center is home to the

wonderfully aromatic First Colony Coffee-house, a Birkenstock store, and The Quality Shoppe, which sells menswear. Other tenants include the Maternity Boutique, Ethan Allen, The Entertainers and Posh Kids. An addition to this center has made room for Chesapeake Bagel Bakery and Decorum (fine furnishings).

La Promenade
1860 Laskin Rd., Virginia Beach
• (757) 422-8839

This center, also in the Hilltop area of Virginia Beach, is one where the shoppers look as rich as the merchandise offered. You'll find unusual gifts at Simply Selma's, designer fashions at NYFO Boutique and K. Lilly Evening & Formal, and gifts to wow your significant other at Facets Jewelry. This center is also home to Talbots, Jos. A. Bank clothiers and Williams-Sonoma with its eclectic kitchen wares. Girls Play Too! is the region's only store devoted to women's sports gear. Nearby is Work Out Wear to complete any athletic ensemble. For sophisticated dining that matches the upscale taste of the center, slip into Aldo's Ristorante for designer pasta or Starbucks for some of that famous coffee.

Regency Hilltop
1900 Laskin Rd., Virginia Beach
• (757) 627-8611

If you have any pennies left over from La Promenade, take a short hop down Laskin Road to the bargains at Regency Hilltop. Here's off-price heaven, with Michael's Arts and Crafts, Dollar Tree, Phar-Mor and Wherehouse Music. Satisfy the hungries in the popular Old Country Buffet or at Sal's Pizza & Italian Restaurant. Also here is Plaza Bakery, which has been making birthday cakes for Virginia Beach kids for more than 20 years.

Loehmann's Plaza
4000 Virginia Beach Blvd., Virginia Beach
• (757) 627-8611

Although the shopping center's namesake store, Loehmann's, is no longer here, you'll find plenty of other shops to tempt you. For starters try the Lillian Vernon Outlet Store, Marc Lance Menswear, Off Broadway Shoes and Babies R Us.Home decorators will go zonkers in Calico Corners with a huge selection of decora-

tor fabrics and trims. Also here is QVC Outlet, A&N sporting goods and an Advanced Nutrition Center juice bar/health food store.

Norfolk

MacArthur Center
300 Monticello Ave., Norfolk
• (757) 627-6000

Where do we begin to talk about what true Insiders' consider the shopping coup of a lifetime—landing a big, ritzy mall right in the heart of downtown? Suddenly, downtown Norfolk where you couldn't buy a pair of pantyhose in recent years, is now filled with high fashion.

For starters there are the anchors-Nordstrom with its vast shoe selection and noted customer service and Dillard's with one of the largest stores it has opened anywhere. Then there are specialty retailers like Pottery Barn, Bebe, and Restoration Hardware that had would-be shoppers hitting the floor running the day the mall opened. Most of the 100-plus stores are new to the region with many of them new to Virginia. The mall draws not only local shoppers but people throughout Virginia and North Carolina as well as vacationers.

For sheer fun, try Jeepers, a 20,000-square-foot indoor amusement park or the 18-screen movie theater. For food and entertainment head to the Rainforest Cafe with its animated animals or Johnny Rockets with its '50s ambiance. Beside a fully stocked food court, there are upscale restaurants such as Kincaid's Fish, Chop & Steakhouse, and Max & Erma's Restaurant, Bar & Gathering Place. Both have indoor and outside sidewalk seating.

There are two parking garages that lead right to the mall, and parking prices are reasonable. If you don't find what you want inside MacArthur Center, stroll a few blocks over to Granby Street. This once was Norfolk's main shopping hub. It is in the middle of a renaissance that is lining it with cafes and small shops that provide an alternative to the enclosed mall.

The Waterside Festival Marketplace
333 Waterside Dr., Norfolk
• (757) 627-3300

This waterfront mall is Norfolk's fun spot. Built in the early 1980s as a retail center,

> ## INSIDERS' TIP
> This is a great area for high-quality second-hand shopping. To get the bargains, you need to frequent the shops, be open-minded about what you're looking for, and have an eye for quality.

Waterside has a revamped identity. If you haven't stopped by in a while, you'll be amazed at the changes. Gone are many of traditional Watersides stores and restaurants. In their place are new restaurants, night clubs and a huge entertainment center.

The dozen or so retailers that remain here have a definite niche. You'll find the Christmas Attic with its year-round holiday spirit, Dollar Tree with an assortment of handy, $1 merchandise and The Virginia Company with its peanuts and other goods produced right here in the Old Dominion.

Waterside is definitely a destination for those with an appetite. Restaurants include Joe's Crab Shack, Outback Steakhouse, and King's Chinese Restaurant and Sushi Bar. There's also a food court with a variety of vendors. You'll find food and late-night fun on the menu at the Have a Nice Day Café with its '70s theme, the Southern style Dixie's Tavern and Hooters with its fiery chicken wings and scantily clad waitresses. BAR Norfolk provides late-night entertainment as does Crocodile Rocks Dueling Pianos and many of the restaurants.

Upstairs is Jillian's, a 50,000 square foot entertainment arcade. It has a game room with more than 150 electronic games, a café and bar. While Jillian's welcomes all ages until early evening hours for late nights it becomes and adult-only place.

There's the huge city parking garage directly across the street that allows access to The Waterside by a pedestrian bridge over Waterside Drive.

Ghent
Colley Ave. and 21st St., Norfolk

While not really a mall, the time you can spend sauntering in and out of the many shops and restaurants in this Norfolk neighborhood puts it in the park-and-shop category. The neighborhood landmark is the Naro theater, which shows first-run and revival pics and still boasts one of the only lighted movie marquees we know about.

If you're a parallel-parking pro, you can whip into one of the spaces along the Colley Avenue storefronts. Bouillabaisse is the ultimate chef's shop for kitchen goodies. Gale Goss Country French Antiques sells divine furnishings, china and accessories, and you'll find a great selection of cards—both naughty and nice—at The Entertainers.

Just around the corner, on W. 21st Street between Colonial and Lewellyn avenues are The Palace Shops. Highlights here include Decorum, for exquisitely affordable home furnishings; and Lili's of Ghent with wonderful women's wear. One popular store is The White Rabbit, a consignment and gift shop.

In addition to these wonderful places, there are restaurants galore, antiques shops and art

Portside is the scene of much of Portsmouth's action.

Photo: Courtesy of Virginia Department of Tourism

galleries. Among the eclectic mix of Ghent shops and eateries are The Baker's Crust, Luna Maya, Starbucks Coffee, The Ten Top restaurant and a '50s-style Dairy Queen.

Military Circle
Military Hwy. at Virginia Beach Blvd., Norfolk
• **(757) 461-1940**
Military Circle has undergone some major renovations in recent years. In 1999 a $20 million makeover added a Sears store and 20-screen theater. Department-store anchors include Hecht's and JC Penney. You'll also find those popular mall favorites such as Victoria's Secret and Bath and Body Works. For the younger crowd, Legends is a favorite, with all the right name-brand sports shoes and gear.

Janaf Shopping Center
Military Hwy. at Virginia Beach Blvd., Norfolk
• **(757) 461-4954**
This huge strip center is the place to shop for a bargain in Norfolk. You can pop into TJ Maxx or Marshalls for clothes and home decor or swoon over the latest audio-video gadgetry at Circuit City. (For the Circuit City of flea collars, check out PETSmart, with more than 7,000 pet supplies we're sure Rover's been asking for.) Teenagers find A&N a magnet for sweats and tennies and love the clothes at Old Navy Clothing, an affiliate of The Gap. The Sports Authority offers more sports stuff than humankind could ever play with in a lifetime, and for playthings that float, try the new Boater's World. Track your expenses with supplies from Office Max.

Floating out on the perimeter of Janaf is Montgomery Ward near Hooters, a restaurant known for great Buffalo wings and barely dressed waitresses. There's a post office and a city library in this shopping center, and Comp USA, the computer superstore, is right across the street just in case you need your daily computer-game fix.

Restaurants include the Olive Garden, El Rodeo, Applebee's, Friendly's, and Pizzeria Uno.

Portsmouth

Olde Towne
This is one of the most charming shopping districts in the region, and it's getting better all the time. It borders Portsmouth's Olde Towne Historic District, which is lined with vintage homes. In years past, High Street, downtown

Portsmouth's traditional shopping street, declined as department stores closed or moved to the suburbs. But all that has changed in recent years.

Anchored by the popular Children's Museum of Virginia, High Street has been spruced up and gained a good variety of new tenants, most of them small stores. There are at least a half dozen antique shops as well as boutiques and gift shops and art galleries. Smithfield Rare Books, 429 High Street, is stocked with vintage tomes. The Kitchen Koop, 638 High Street, has a huge array of kitchen gadgetry. Pfeiffer's Books, Cards & Fine Wines, 606 High Street, is everything its name says plus a cafe. Smithfield Gourmet Shop & Deli, 331 High Street, is stocked with Virginia food products. The King's Domain, 425 High St., is stocked with all kinds of accessories for home and garden. There also are various restaurants along High Street, which has a ferry stop where it ends at the Elizabeth River.

Chesapeake

Greenbrier Mall
Greenbrier Pkwy., Chesapeake
• **(757) 424-7100**
Rising like a modern monument on a huge berm is Greenbrier Mall, where Chesapeake shoppers travel to spend their paychecks. Run amuck through two levels of temptation, including the popular anchors Sears, Hecht's, and Dillard's. Other popular draws include Casual Corner, Victoria's Secret and The Disney Store. On the top level of the mall is a particularly inviting food court, with your choice of pizza, chicken or good old American hamburgers. The mall is also home to Mozzarella's Cafe, which serves Italian specialties, and Piccadilly Cafeteria.

Crossways Shopping Center
Greenbrier Pkwy., Chesapeake
• **(757) 627-0661**
Right across the street is Crossways Shopping Center, bursting at the sidewalks with great places to shop. Along with a plethora of specialty boutiques, there's Marshall's, S&K Menswear, Rack Room Shoes and Dress Barn waiting to spiff up your wardrobe, Best and Montgomery Ward for household stuff and a huge Circuit City for all your electronic needs. In the good eats department, Old Country Buffet, Pargos, Lone Star Steakhouse, Cheer's and Kelly's Tavern are all in the general vicinity. Also here is an entertainment district with ice

skating and roller skating rinks, and video arcades.

Chesapeake Square
Portsmouth Blvd. and Taylor Rd., Chesapeake
• (757) 488-9636

Built in 1989, Chesapeake Square grew out of a faraway pasture, and suddenly traffic was ferocious. Sparkling new, modern and spit-polished, it's a replay of your favorite places, such as anchors Hecht's, Sears, Montgomery Ward and JCPenney. Inside are the bookstores you expect to find, plus some special places like Gymboree kids clothes and the Disney Store, American Eagle Outfitters, Sea Dream Leather and Ingle's Nook (super kitchen stuff). If you're feeling a little frisky, there's a Frederick's of Hollywood. Sister stores Limited and Express cover a zillion square feet. There's little way you won't find everything you like here, but if not, pop across the street to The Crossroads and run amuck in TJ Maxx, Circuit City and Wal-Mart.

Suffolk

Suffolk maintains a traditional downtown whose ongoing Main Street revitalization program is giving a face-lift to the city's storefronts. There are several upscale clothing and shoe stores downtown and a few specialty businesses.

There are no malls in Suffolk, but there are several shopping centers with grocery stores, discount stores and smaller businesses. You'll find them on Holland Road, Constance Road and on N. Main Street. Anchoring the downtown area are several special stores.

From socks to hats, Hobbs Clothiers., 126 N. Main Street keeps men in fashion. It carries a big variety of suits, shirts, casual clothes and accessories. Although it's not a snobbish shop, Hobbs' owners like to say they provide quality that's higher than basic department stores.

No trip to Suffolk is complete without picking up some peanuts fresh from the antique roaster at the Planters Peanut Center, 308 W. Washington Street. The aroma is irresistible. You'll also find canned peanuts packaged a few blocks away in Suffolk's Planters factory. Other Planters' treats also fill the shelves, such as chocolate-covered cashews, sugarcoated almonds and candy bars.

The Shoetique, 147 N. Main Street, is where fashionable women shop for shoes in Suffolk. The Shoetique has been in business for more than a decade and stocks footwear for all occasions in various prices.

Specialty Shops

While you'll find a good variety in the region's malls and shopping centers, there are plenty of other jewels waiting to be discovered on side streets and specialty shops. We love to wander through antiques stores, used book shops and out-of-the-way spots when we visit other cities. We've included some tidbits about some of our favorite places here at home. Have fun exploring them.

Antiques

There are numerous small shops to tempt you if you're interested in antique furniture, glassware and bric-a-brac. In fact, there are more than 125 dealers in the region and several flea

You'll find fun and distinctive gifts at the Chrysler Museum gift shop.

Photo: Courtesy of The Chrysler Museum

markets or antiques malls with multiple vendors.

Shops range from those filled with rare antiques to the ones selling the Mrs. Butterworth bottle you unloaded at your last garage sale. The thrill of antiquing is in the hunt for that perfect oak filing cabinet or piece of Depression glass, so grab your cash and credit cards and start prowling.

Since we can't cover all the shops, we'll steer

you in the direction of areas that have a concentration of stores. That way you can hit a bunch of shops on the same trip. In the cities that don't have an antique row, we've mentioned a few of our favorite haunts. For other suggestions check the Yellow Pages. The Virginian-Pilot's classified section is the place to watch if you are interested in auctions and estate sales. For household goods, baby furniture, antiques and just about anything else you want, buy a copy of the Trading Post. The shopper is published each week and is filled with merchandise for sale by private owners. It's sold in most convenience and grocery stores.

Virginia Beach

In Virginia Beach, the antiquing isn't in one easy location. There's no great concentration of dealers, but you'll find a few quality shops scattered throughout the city.

Barrett Street Antique Center
2645 Dean Dr., Virginia Beach
• **(757) 463-8600**
This huge warehouse operation, formerly British-European Antique Importers Ltd., is near Lynnhaven Mall. Its specialty is European country antique pine furniture. There are 130 dealers in this 28,000 square foot center that is just off Lynnhaven Parkway.

Colonial Cottage Antiques Mall
3900 Bonney Rd., Virginia Beach
• **(757) 498-0600**
This 9,000-square-foot store is in the Grande Junquetion Center just off Virginia Beach Boulevard. It is filled with 18th- and 19th-century furniture, jewelry, porcelain, glassware and collectibles. Several dealers share space in the mall.

Echoes of Time
700 Norfolk Ave., Virginia Beach
• **(757) 428-2332**
We seldom go to the resort area without stopping by this neat store just a few blocks from the oceanfront. This is a vintage-clothing paradise with garments and jewelry from the 1800s to the 1950s. It's a fun place to browse. Books and collectibles also are for sale.

Eddie's Antique Mall
4080-A Virginia Beach Blvd., Virginia Beach
• **(757) 497-0537**
Eddie's is one of the oldest and largest antiques dealers in the region. Its building is crammed full of china cabinets, bedroom suites, tables, chairs and any other kind of antique furniture you can imagine. Lamps, china and bric-a-brac round out the merchandise.

Norfolk

In Norfolk, the must-see area for antiques is along 21st Street between Manteo and Granby streets and in the 2600 and 2900 blocks of Granby Street. There are about 25 antiques shops in Norfolk, and the bulk of them are along these two streets. You'll need to drive from 21st Street to Granby Street since its main antique shop district is across the railroad tracks. You can park in both areas and then stroll from one shop to the other.

There also is a cluster of antique shops in the 1900 block of Granby street as well as others scattered around this part of town. Most of the shops are in the Ghent area of town and its outskirts. The merchants have produced a brochure and map featuring Norfolk antiques shops so pick up a copy in one of the stores to guide you to the others.

Carriage House Antiques
110 W. 21st St., Norfolk
• **(757) 625-4504**
This shop has supplied several of our favorite pieces of furniture. It has 12 dealers who run it - each with their own special niche. Look for turn-of-the-century furniture and housewares, linens and textiles, art pottery, toys and one of the largest selections of Depression glass in the area.

Futures Antiques
3824 Granby St., Norfolk
• **(757) 624-2050**
For 20th-century kitsch, this is the place. Even the aqua, silver and black trim on the building shouts art deco. This fun shop specializes in furniture and decorative items from the 1920s through the 1970s. There's everything here from high-end investment pieces to low-cost '50s and '60s kitschy items your mother unloaded at a yard sale decades ago.

Ghent Market and Antique Centre
1400 Granby St., Norfolk
• **(757) 625-2897**
This giant antique mall opened in 1996 in two connecting warehouse buildings that sprawl along a city block. With 42,000 square feet, this is the largest antique center in the area. It has 120 dealers with permanent booths but also features monthly auctions. Merchandise runs the gamut from huge architectural

pieces to furniture and glassware. Also in the center are a cafe, frame shop and gallery. Outdoors a farmer's market sells local produce in warmer months. The best parts for us are the room with old arcade games and the not-for-sale display of antique toys owned by a local collector.

Morgan House Antiques Gallery
242 W. 21st St., Norfolk
• (757) 627-2486

This gallery features antiques designed to give your home an elegant flair. You'll find 18th- and 19th-century American furniture supplemented by pieces from Europe and the Orient. Shipments routinely arrive from England. Also for sale are antique and estate jewelry, sterling flatware, chandeliers and a large array of decorative accessories.

Nero's Antiques & Appraisals
1101 Colonial Ave., Norfolk
• (757) 627-1111

Long before antiquing became trendy and there was a proliferation of shops, Nero's was helping home owners give their abodes a classic, timeworn feel. It specializes in 18th- and 19th-century American and European furniture. Wares typically feature Oriental rugs, clocks, silver, china, paintings and glassware.

Palace Antiques Gallery
21st and Llewellyn Sts., Norfolk
• (757) 622-2733

This is an upscale shop that appeals to interior designers and collectors with a sense of style. There are several dealers operating out of this 4,500-square-foot building. They sell 18th- and 19th-century American and European furniture, rugs, crystal, accessories and silver pieces.

Portsmouth

There's a nice enclave of antique shops in downtown Portsmouth between the 300 and 600 blocks of High Street. This area is near the Olde Towne Portsmouth Historic District. The Port Norfolk neighborhood also has several shops along Broad Street and Mount Vernon Avenue.

Anderson-Wright Rooms & Gardens
622 High St., Portsmouth
• (757) 398-0990

This pleasant shop is known for its furniture, which ranges from wardrobes to bedroom suites. Interspersed with the bigger pieces are glassware, silver and other decorative items. Garden furniture is a specialty of the shop.

Antique Adventures Ltd.
432 High St., Portsmouth
• (757) 398-8763

This well-stocked shop features general merchandise from days gone by.

Deja Vu Antiques
327 High St., Portsmouth
• (757) 393-4804

Two floors are filled with furniture, glassware, and just about anything else you can imagine.

Grandma's Attic
359 Broad St., Portsmouth
• (757) 393-1644

Take a trip back in time to this shop stuffed with things you'd be likely to find in your own grandmother's attic.

Grape Arbor Antiques
353 Broad St., Portsmouth
• (757) 397-6438

Furniture, glassware, and other odds and ends are among the wares offered in this shop.

The Ship's Store
624 High St., Portsmouth
• (757) 399-7447

Military and nautical antiques and memorabilia are the mainstay of this shop.

Treasures of Yesterday
628 High St., Portsmouth
• (757) 397-1666

There's a little bit of everything in this shop-from decorative items to useful household gadgets.

Way Back Yonder Antiques
620 High St., Portsmouth
• (757) 398-2700

This is a general line shop with furniture, linens, pottery, and glassware. There's a big collection of flow blue glassware.

Chesapeake

In Chesapeake, you'll want to hit the shops along S. Military Highway at Canal Drive, which has been an antiquing hotspot for more than 40 years. There's a concentration of about 20 shops, mostly in converted houses that make it easy to while away an afternoon.

If you're not familiar with this area, you should call for directions. Basically you head down Military Highway south from Norfolk and keep going long past the time you're convinced you're hopelessly lost. Cross over the Gilmerton Bridge, a huge drawbridge, and keep going. Your reward are small shops filled with all kinds of bric-a-brac and furniture. For many of them you can park at one place and walk from shop to shop.

Maria's Antiques and Collectibles
3021 S. Military Hwy., Chesapeake
• (757) 485-1799

Primitive country collectibles are the star of this 4,000-square-foot shop, which features room after room of furniture, Victorian art glass, pottery and other collectible items. Don't miss the two small buildings outside.

Suffolk

Suffolk has several antiques shops in various parts of town. Since they are off the beaten path, you might find the unexpected at reasonable prices.

Village Auction Barn
101 Philhower Dr., Suffolk
• (757) 539-6296

This is our favorite place to buy antiques—one we like so much we hesitate to tell you about it. The auction barn is on the outskirts of Suffolk as you drive into town, but it's easy to miss, so call for directions. The barn holds an auction every Saturday at 7:30 PM that draws dealers as well as regular folks like us. On the third and fourth Saturdays of each month, the barn features estate sales. But on the first two Saturdays of each month veteran auctioneer Dewey Howell hauls in a load of furniture and goods from England. These English nights are the prime time to be at the auction barn, especially if you're in the market for oak or mahogany furniture. Check the classifieds in the newspaper for specifics. In May of 1997 the barn suffered a devastating fire that forced Mr. Howell to rebuild. The barn re-opened in October, and plans are being made for daughter, Lynn Howell Sheckler, to take over the business in August 1998.

The Attic Trunk
167 S. Main St., Suffolk
• (757) 934-0882

The owner of this shop can't resist snatching up beautiful pieces of vintage furniture.

You'll also find an abundance of glassware and sterling silver in this well-stocked shop that is near downtown Suffolk.

Nansemond Antique Shop
3537 Pruden Blvd., Suffolk
• (757) 539-6269

If it's variety you crave, then stop by this antique shop that's 1 mile from the U.S. Highway 58 bypass on Route 460. This 3,750-square-foot shop is filled with furniture and all types of glassware—from Depression to crystal, plus frames, clocks and lamps. You may want to call for directions.

Bookstores

Echo Audio Books
525 N. Birdneck Rd., Virginia Beach
• (757) 425-2365

This shop provides a nice variation on the book business: you can rent or buy audio books. It has the largest selection of books on tape we've seen. We wouldn't even think of going on a long road trip anymore without a good book to listen to. Try it! You'll be at your destination before you know it.

Barnes & Noble Booksellers
4485 Virgina Beach Blvd., Virginia Beach
• (757) 671-2331
1212 Greenbrier Pkwy., Chesapeake
• (757) 382-0220

These national chain stores have an incredible selection of books in every category imaginable. The Chesapeake store sells music too. Allow yourself extra time to browse around among the titles or even to plop down on a sofa and do a little decision-making. Cafes in the stores sell a variety of coffees, teas and treats.

Once Upon a Time Children's Books
4206 Virginia Beach Blvd., Virginia Beach
• (757) 498-4111

If it's children's books your after, this is the ultimate place to go. This shop, in the Willis Wayside Shopping Center, is filled with books and some toys for children of all ages. This is one of our preferred places to buy kids' birthday gifts.

Prince Books and Coffeehouse
109 Main St., Norfolk
• (757) 622-9223

This is a wonderful place to browse and

buy. It's in downtown Norfolk and carries a diverse stock that's strong in children's, regional and cooking books. The friendly staff is always happy to assist you and eagerly places special orders and gift wraps your purchases. Prince Books also has a small coffeehouse that's one of the best places to eat lunch downtown.

Riverbend Books
1248 N. Great Neck Rd., Virginia Beach
• (757) 496-2758

This small shop's eclectic selection appeals to public radio fans as well as children and other readers. The shop is tucked in the Great Neck Village Shopping Center. We never travel in this part of the city without stopping in to browse. You'll find the coffee pot on, and a plate of cookies waiting for you.

Used-Book Stores

Part of the joy in shopping in these stores is never knowing what you'll find—a cherished book from your childhood, a rare volume of poetry or a spellbinding novel for the beach. Here are some of the used bookstores we frequent.

Bargain Books
7524 Granby St., Norfolk
• (757) 587-3303

This discount bookstore sells a variety of new and used books. It also operates a trade-in service on paperbacks only. Special orders are not a problem. The staff is knowledgeable on a wide range of subjects, from science fiction to romance, and they'll help you find what you're looking for.

Beacon Books of Ghent
2410 Granby St., Norfolk
• (757) 623-5641

This cozy shop has all kinds of used books crammed inside. If you've got time to browse, you'll probably find what you're looking for.

Bibliophile Bookshop
251 W. Bute St., Norfolk
• (757) 622-2665

This is our all-time favorite local bookstore.

It's in the historic Freemason area near downtown. Owners Susan Lendvay and Uwe Wilken maintain one of the region's best-stocked stores. Their inventory runs from the classics to military history and paperback Westerns.

Bazemore's Friendly Market
6412 Hampton Blvd., Norfolk
• (757) 489-1002

This well-stocked grocery store is in the Larchmont neighborhood. In addition to basic staples and gourmet items, it has a bakery, deli, and seafood department. Its wine selection is superb. But what Bazemore's regulars love are its daily dinners for two that are reasonably priced and different each day. To be sure you don't go hungry, you may want to call ahead and order a dinner. Children's dinners are also available as is a monthly calendar detailing the daily entrees.

Pfeiffer's Books, Cards & Wine
606 High St., Portsmouth
• (757) 397-2665

This charming store is in the heart of downtown. It offers a variety of used books as well as some new ones. The store has a sideline of selling candles, wine and gift baskets.

Smithfield Rare Books
429 High St., Portsmouth
• (757) 393-1941

This venerable bookstore carries a big variety of all kinds of used books.

INSIDERS' TIP
If you're looking for a special souvenir to take home, check our Annual Events chapter for arts and crafts fairs scheduled during your visit. These events offer visitors a wide array of unique, made-in-Virginia creations and often come with a bonus: food, music, and other entertainment.

Gourmet and Wine Shops

All-purpose gourmet shops let you pick up unusual spices, grab a sandwich and select a special wine. The following are some of our favorite places to pamper our palates.

Bella Monte Gourmet Italian Marketplace & Cafe
1201 Laskin Rd., Virginia Beach
• (757) 425-6290

This Italian market carries a tempting array of imported cheeses, pastas and olive oils. Wonderful Italian bread and desserts are created in the kitchen. If you can't wait to take your food home, you can enjoy soups, salads, sandwiches and pastas at the cafe.

P.J. Baggan Cafe
960 Laskin Rd., Virginia Beach
• (757) 491-8900

This cafe stocks one of the region's biggest selections of wines—from those created from Virginia grapes to more exotic varieties. Also for sale are a good selection of beers and coffees as well as cigars.

Taste Unlimited
638 Hilltop West Shopping Ctr.,
Virginia Beach • (757) 425-1858
36th St. and Pacific Ave., Virginia Beach
• (757) 422-3399
4097 Shore Dr., Virginia Beach
• (757) 464-1566
1619 Colley Ave., Norfolk
• (757) 623-7770
237 S. Battlefield Blvd., Chesapeake
• (757) 546-9000

Taste Unlimited stores have been pleasing discriminating palates for more than a decade. All the shops are packed with excellent wines, innovative food and tempting treats. The staff prepares great box lunches for diners on the go. The best-seller is The Picnic, which comes with a turkey and Swiss cheese sandwich, potato salad and a brownie. The Hilltop West store is in the shopping center at the intersection of Laskin and First Colonial roads.

West Side Wine Shop
4702 Hampton Blvd., Norfolk
• (757) 440-7600

There's a lot more than an excellent selection of the fruit of the vine in this shop. The shelves are jammed with an intriguing variety of gourmet products. In the dairy case is Bergey's bottled milk fresh from the farm. Bergey's, which produces its products in Chesapeake, also sells its scrumptious ice cream here. Sandwiches and deli fare are another brisk sideline for this shop, which is across the street from Old Dominion University.

Health Foods

If you long for organic tomatoes, basmati rice and fresh cilantro, you'll find several health-food stores designed just for you. Through the years these down-to-earth shops have broadened their wares to serve gourmet cooks as well as health-food enthusiasts and vegetarians.

Azar's Natural Foods Market & Cafe
108 Prescott Ave., Virginia Beach
• (757) 486-7778

For health foods with an ethnic flair, Azar's is the place to go. It is stocked with olive oils, cheeses, organic rice and barley. You may be tempted to stay for lunch or dinner at Azar's cafe. Be sure to sample some of the tabouli; it's the best in the area.

Heritage Health Food Store
314 Laskin Rd., Virginia Beach
• (757) 428-0500

This 22,000-square-foot store has been in business since the late '70s. It is the largest health-food store around and has a huge selection. The store has the region's only organic deli, which features all wheat-free and sugar-free products. Affiliated businesses include a bookstore and holistic health services. Next door is the Heritage Cafe, where you can chow down on meat-free foods.

The Kosher Place Meats & More
738 W. 22nd St., Norfolk
• (757) 623-1770

This is the only store in the region to specialize in kosher products. There's a variety of frozen kosher foods as well as a butcher, deli and a small cafe. During Passover the store carries a full supply of unleavened foods.

Whole Foods Co-op
119 W. 21st St., Norfolk
• (757) 626-1051

This food co-op in the Ghent shopping district is a neat place to find specialty food items. It has more than 500 members and was started in 1973. You don't have to be a member to shop here, but you'll get a 10 percent discount if you pay the $12 annual fee. There is a good selection of bulk grains, nuts and seeds. You'll also find olive oil and tahini for Mediterranean cooking. There are about 200 fresh spices and herbs in big glass jars, and you can buy as much or as little as you like. Also in stock are foods for diabetics and others on special diets.

Consignment Stores

Since we became parents, used-clothing stores have become our favorite haunt. Besides snaring some terrific duds for our fast-growing children, we've also picked up some designer labels for ourselves. To get the bargains, you need to frequent the shops, be open-minded about what you're looking for and have an eye for quality. There are plenty of wealthy people in the region with expensive cast-offs that have hardly been worn. These shops are the perfect places to snare special-occasion clothes. Here are some of our best shopping spots.

INSIDERS' TIP
It is a good idea to carry Traveler's Checks to secure your vacation funds.

Act II
816-A 21st St., Norfolk
• **(757) 622-1533**
This stylish store is run by the Organization Through Rehabilitation and Training (ORT). Act II specializes in women's clothes, has a big selection of party clothes and often sells new clothes donated by local stores.

Consignment City
4805 Shore Dr., Virginia Beach
• **(757) 363-7176**
There's something for everyone in this big store that opened in 1998. Look for jewelry, tools, clothing, and just about any other item you can imagine. There also are plenty of books here for the bibliophile.

Discovery Shop
1556 Laskin Rd., Virginia Beach
• **(757) 425-7014**
This shop is staffed by volunteers, and all proceeds benefit the American Cancer Society. The shop has a reputation for selling some wonderful women's clothing and accessories as well as housewares. It is in the Hilltop East Shopping Center.

Elephants Galore
3900 Bonney Rd., Virginia Beach
• **(757) 463-2823**
In this two-story store you'll encounter a little bit of everything - baby items, furniture and lots of clothes for the entire family. You also will find antiques, art and collectibles mingling with more basic merchandise.

Encore
3636 Virginia Beach Blvd., Virginia Beach
• **(757) 431-6941**
This is one of the largest consignment shops in the area. Proceeds benefit Helping Hands of Virginia. Encore features men's and women's clothes, jewelry, furniture, books and household goods. It also has a large baby department filled with gently used clothes and furniture.

Sand Bucket
3006 Arctic Ave., Virginia Beach
• **(757) 425-6016**
This tidy shop draws its merchandise from some ritzy nearby neighborhoods. You'll find clothes for boys and girls ranging from items for infants to size 16.

2nd Time Around
3772 Virginia Beach Blvd., Virginia Beach
• **(757) 498-3927**
This store's motto is that "you can dress like a million without spending it." The racks are filled with clothes for women and children. There's usually a big variety of party clothes. Also in the store is The Diamond Jewelry exchange, which sells a stunning array of jewelry.

That Baby Place
2354 E. Little Creek Rd., Norfolk
• **(757) 583-8294**
This hybrid store has half its merchandise that is gently used. The other half is all new. You'll find clothes for preemies through size 8 as well as cribs, high chairs and other paraphernalia for babies and toddlers.

Things Unlimited
501 Virginia Beach Blvd., Virginia Beach
• **(7570 428-7841**
This big store is filled with all kinds of clothes and household goods. We always try to stop here when we're in the neighborhood. Things also has a good selection of jewelry and a wonderful costume department that is a mainstay for Halloween. Proceeds benefit the Virginia Beach Friends School.

The Velveteen Rabbit
3115 Western Branch Blvd., Portsmouth
• **(757) 483-0750**
This shop is in the Churchland Place Shopping Center. It has a mix of both new and used children's clothes. You'll find clothes for babies as well as those for children wearing as large as a size 14.

The White Rabbitt
334 W. 21st St., Norfolk
• **(757) 627-4169**
This is our favorite place to spend our cash. The store is stuffed with all kinds of children's clothes. Most are pristine consignment clothes

but some are new. There are delightful smocked dresses here as well as children's birthday and baby gifts. Around the corner is a sister operation, The Wild Hare, which is devoted to women's clothes, and also sells handmade gifts and decorative items.

Collectibles Shops

We have friends always on the prowl for that special baseball card, comic book or old record. Baseball card and comic book collectors will find dozens of shops listed in the Yellow Pages. Some places to check out include the following.

Comics & Things
4406 Holland Rd.,
Virginia Beach
• (757) 486-5870
This store features new and collectible comics, collector cards, Star Trek and Star Wars items and related paraphernalia. The Holland Road store is in Holland Plaza Shopping Center. There's also a kiosk in Pembroke Mall on Virginia Beach Blvd. in Virginia Beach.

D&D Sports Cards
5622 Portsmouth Blvd., Portsmouth
• (757) 488-4961
No matter what your sport is, you'll find new and used cards that celebrate its stars—from baseball, soccer and hockey to car racing.

B&B Cards & Collectibles
Holland Road and South Plaza Trail,
Virginia Beach
• (757) 495-5523
NASCAR and baseball fans will have a heyday here hunting for the right collectible card to complete their collections. All other sports are well represented, too, at this store in Timberlake Shopping Center.

Skinnies Records
814 W. 21st St., Norfolk
• (757) 622-2241
Record collectors will love rummaging through the oldies but goodies at Skinnies, which is in Norfolk's Ghent area. Rock music is the great love here. In addition to records and tapes, you'll find a great selection of used CDs.

Trilogy Comics
857 Lynnhaven Rd., Virginia Beach
• (757) 468-0412
5773 Princess Anne Rd., Virginia Beach
• (757) 490-2205
700 E. Little Creek Dr., Norfolk
• (757) 587-2540
Besides current and vintage comic books, these well-stocked stores also draw loyal fans who come to buy baseball cards, games and science fiction merchandise.

Quilt Shops

This is a big interest of ours, and we love to search these shops for the perfect fabric to add to our stash at home. There are some well-respected shops here. All are well-stocked, offer excellent classes and have helpful staffs.

INSIDERS' TIP
Check out the Sugar Plum Bakery for goodies that support a good cause. This bakery and café hires and trains people with developmental disabilities.

Sis 'n Me
3361 Western Branch Blvd., Portsmouth
• (757) 686-2050
This store will tempt you with its big line of colorful fabrics and all types of supplies. The shop is in the Farm Fresh Plaza on Route 17.

What's Your Stitch 'n Stuff
5350 Kempsville Dr., Virginia Beach
• (757) 523-2711
This is where we like to stock up on fabric, books and gadgets. The selection of fabrics is mind-boggling. The shop is behind Kempsriver Crossing Shopping Center just off Indian River Road near CBN.

Virginia Shops

If you want to take home a Virginia souvenir that everyone will adore, try some of the Commonwealth's highly acclaimed food products. Peanuts, wine, jams, pound cakes and hams are the logical choices. In many shops you'll also find tempting local cookbooks and the Blue Crab Bay Co. line of seafood-related products from the Eastern Shore.

Old Virginia Ham Shop
217 E. Little Creek Rd., Norfolk
• (757) 583-0014
This shop, which looks like a red barn, is in

SHOPPING

the Wards Corner area. It sells all kinds of Virginia hams—country, sugar-cured, spiral sliced, Smithfield—the list goes on and on. If you can't decide what to buy ask for a free sample. The shop also stocks Virginia turkeys, cheese and bacon. It will ship its products for you.

The Planters Peanut Center
308 W. Washington St., Suffolk
• **(757) 539-4411**
This is the place to buy Planters peanut products made right in the city.

Pruden Packing Co.
1201 N. Main St., Suffolk
• **(757) 539-6261**
This longtime meat packer has a retail shop to sells hams that were cured in the plant. Other items available for retail sale include bacon and a variety of Virginia jams, jellies, pickles and peanuts.

Rowena's
758 W. 22nd St., Norfolk
• **(757) 627-8699**
This Ghent business has gained international acclaim for its homemade pound cakes—especially when topped with Rowena's heavenly lemon-curd sauce. Rowena's sells an innovative line of jams, sauces and other tasty food products. The business is run by its founder Rowena Fullinwider, and her products are made right here. For many locals Rowena's is the first stop for out-of-town holiday presents.

Smithfield Gourmet Shop & Deli
331 High St., Portsmouth
• **(757) 397-9530**
Step in for a taste of the cuisine Virginia is famous for. You'll find salty Smithfield ham, traditional ham and irresistible peanuts. There also is a delicatessen serving a variety of sandwiches.

Sugar Plum Bakery
1353 Laskin Rd., Virginia Beach
• **(757) 422-3913**
This nonprofit bakery trains and hires workers with developmental disabilities. The products they turn out are outstanding. Sugar Plum has a loyal following of people who won't buy bakery items anywhere else. Our favorites include the nutty Chesapeake cookies and the carrot-laced Morning Glory Muffins. A perfect gift is a loaf of bread or an assortment of cookies or pastries plucked from the tempting display case. The bakery includes a small cafe if you want to have lunch or eat your goodies on premises.

The Virginia Company
333 Waterside Dr., Norfolk
• **(757) 623-4547**
This store in The Waterside Festival Marketplace has one of the biggest selections of all kinds of Virginia products. It's got peanuts, barbecue sauce, jams, and gourmet items as well as cookbooks, regional travel books, T-shirts, and other Virginia paraphernalia.

Attractions

There is so much to do in Hampton Roads you can live here for years and never get to everything. But there are three surefire ways to get motivated to see the sites:

Be a tourist determined to make the most of your visit.

Be a new resident eager to explore your adopted environs.

Welcome out-of-town visitors and play tour guide while they're here.

We're long past relying on the first two excuses, so we're always grateful to have guests come and get us out of our rut. When that happens, you'll find this chapter will guide you in planning perfect outings to entertain visitors while showing off the best parts of our region. For detailed maps and brochures for specific attractions stop by the tourism bureaus mentioned in our Area Overview chapter.

When you're talking about attractions the biggie, of course, is the beach. You'll find 38 miles of it stretching along the Atlantic Ocean and Chesapeake Bay in Virginia Beach. Norfolk also has its stretch of Chesapeake Bay sand. For specifics on the best ways to see the beaches check out our Beaches chapter.

Even if it's not raining or the off-season, the region's other attractions are worth working into anyone's vacation agenda. They run the gamut from history and nautical to educational and just plain fun. Hampton Roads has played host to some of the country's most important military events, such as the Revolutionary War and the battle of the Monitor and the Merrimac during the Civil War. Therefore, this area excels in military history. Taking in the nearby Virginia Peninsula area, no other region in the country can boast as big a collection of military bases, museums and other military-related attractions. At least some of these should be on your to-do list of attractions.

Over the years we've found that even visitors who aren't military buffs are fascinated by a tour through Navy bases and a visit to a Navy ship. They can put what they see into historical perspective with companion visits to Norfolk's Hampton Roads Naval Museum, the Douglas MacArthur Memorial or some of the excellent military museums on the Peninsula (See our Daytrips chapter for ideas).

Besides military history, you'll find gracious old homes of various vintages open for tours throughout the region. For a concentrated dose of historic homes, head to Olde Towne, the neighborhood surrounding downtown Portsmouth. It contains the largest assortment of restored historic houses between Alexandria and Charleston.

Old salts will feel at home exploring the National Maritime Center (Nauticus) in Norfolk or the Virginia Marine Science Museum or Old Coast Guard Station in Virginia Beach. For those who just like a good time, the Children's Museum of Virginia, the Virginia Zoo and Ocean Breeze Water Park bring out the kid in everyone.

To get a real feel for this region where bays and rivers run into the Atlantic Ocean, put on your deck shoes and book a seat on a cruise boat (see the sidebar in this chapter for details). You'll get a new perspective from the water and have a few hours of relaxing fun before plunging into your next activity.

LOOK FOR:
- **Museums**
- **Historic Houses and Sites**
- **Military Bases**
- **Miscellaneous Attractions**

Museums

Virginia Beach

Atlantic Wildfowl Heritage Museum
113 Atlantic Ave., Virginia Beach
• **(757) 437-8432**

This museum spotlights all kinds of wildfowl from ducks and geese to songbirds. It is run by the Back Bay Wildfowl Guild and opened in 1995. Five galleries feature artwork and decoy carvings, including some from the turn of the century. Outside are occasional demonstrations by decoy carvers and boat builders.

The museum overlooks the ocean and is in one of our favorite houses—the 1895 Dewitt Cottage. This is the last remaining oceanfront cottage from the late-19th century and features a sweeping porch overlooking the beach. The clapboard house was built by Virginia Beach's first mayor, B.P. Holland. It is named for Cornelius Dewitt, whose family owned it from around 1900 until just a few years ago. Hours are Tuesday through Saturday from 10 AM until 5 PM and Sunday noon to 5 PM. Admission is free but a donation is requested.

Old Coast Guard Station
24th St. and Oceanfront, Virginia Beach
• **(757) 422-1587**

This museum is housed in a former U.S. Life-Saving/Coast Guard Station built in 1903. The simple wooden structure along the Virginia Beach boardwalk gives a hint of simpler pre-condo days at the oceanfront. Two galleries highlight the history and tools of those who risked their lives to save others during shipwrecks. A permanent display focuses on the impact of World Wars I and II on Virginia Beach. If you have time, take a docent-led tour; you'll be amazed how much you'll learn. Hours are Tuesday through Saturday from 10 AM to 5 PM and Sunday noon to 5 PM. The museum is also open Mondays from Memorial Day to October 1. Admission is $2.50, $1 for children older than 5.

Virginia Marine Science Museum
717 General Booth Blvd., Virginia Beach
• **(757) 437-4949, (757) 425-FISH**
(recorded information)

This is one of the most-visited museums in Virginia. In 1996 it completed a major expansion that tripled its size, and in 2000 the museum is gearing up for yet another expansion.

Even before the last $35 million was pumped into improvements, this popular museum, which opened in the mid-1980s, kept both tourists and locals coming back to enjoy its exhibits. Since its expansion the museum began welcoming as many as 700,000 visitors a year. Crowds can get overwhelming in summer so watch out for rainy days and go early in the day when possible. Locals prefer to visit in spring, fall and winter when the tourists have gone home.

Old favorites include a 50,000-gallon Chesapeake Bay aquarium and 60 hands-on exhibits that explore Virginia marine life by letting visitors tong for oysters or create waves. Children especially like the touch-tank where they can get their hands on crabs, turtles and starfish with the help of museum docents. The museum frequently features a decoy carver and other demonstrations. Outside, a boardwalk takes you on a peaceful walk through the Owls Creek salt marsh.

Be sure to visit the 20,000-square-foot Owls Creek Marsh Pavilion, which opened in 1996 just across the marsh from the main museum. You can enjoy a six-minute stroll to the new building or hop on a red tourist trolley for a less scenic but quick ride via the main road outside. Inside the new pavilion are exhibits that bring to life the marsh outside. An excellent film gives an overview of the crabs, rabbits, frogs and other critters that call the marsh home. In one favorite exhibit, powerful cameras let even tiny hands zoom in on fiddler crabs and spiders living in special micro marshes. Next door you can get a bug's-eye view of the marsh. Here, you pretend to shrink as you are surrounded by giant grass, huge snakes and other creatures. Other exhibits keep visitors busy seeing, touching and even sniffing the marsh.

The museum's 3-D IMAX theater is one of only a handful in the country using three-dimensional technology. The expansion also introduced a 300,000-gallon ocean aquarium, an aviary and viewing tanks with river otters, harbor seals and sea turtles. All these additions help make this museum one of the top-10 marine facilities in the country.

The Virginia Marine Science Museum is known for its educational boat trips. Each year it takes thousands of nature lovers on outings off the coast to view whales and dolphins. Whales swim the waters during the winter while playful dolphins make their appearances in the summer. During the trips docents and staff members are on hand to provide lively commentary about the marine life you're seeing. Call in advance to book a trip since they fill up fast.

Admission for the museum is $8.95, $5.95 for children ages 4 through 12 and $6.50 for seniors. The IMAX theater costs $6.95 for adults and $5.95 for children. A combination ticket for both is $12.95, $9.95 for children and $10.50 for seniors. Hours are 9 AM to 5 PM daily with longer hours during summer.

Norfolk

The Chrysler Museum of Art
245 W. Olney Rd., Norfolk
• **(757) 664-6200**

This is the region's premier art museum. It is in the historic Ghent district overlooking The Hague, a scenic canal lined with turn-of-the-century homes. With more than 30,000 pieces from every time period, this massive museum is considered one of the best art museums in the country. The Chrysler's 8,000-piece glass collection is one of the world's largest. Holdings include works by Renoir, Matisse and Gauguin. The museum's diverse collections include contemporary art, photographs and Egyptian artifacts. The bulk of the collection came from the late Walter P. Chrysler Jr., a son of the auto magnate. He was an eclectic collector who decided to place his art in Norfolk since it was his wife Jean's girlhood hometown. To hear a recorded rundown on current exhibitions call 622-ARTS. (For detailed information see our Arts chapter.) Hours are Wednesday through Saturday 10 AM to 4 PM and Sunday 1 to 5 PM. Admission is $7; $5 for students and senior citizens and free for children younger than 6. Admission is free on Wednesdays.

Hampton Roads Naval Museum
Inside the National Maritime Center (Nauticus), One Waterside Dr., Norfolk
• **(757) 444-8971**

This fascinating museum is on the second floor of Nauticus and appeals to visitors of all ages—even those with no military ties. The Navy-owned museum relocated here in 1994 after many years on the Norfolk Naval Base. Even though there is a charge to see the rest of Nauticus, you can wander through the naval museum for free.

Exhibits include naval artifacts and a collection of nautical prints and artwork. Displays focus on regional warship construction from the frigate *Chesapeake* in 1799 to today's

airaircraft carriers. The museum also highlights major naval actions and events, including the duel between the *Monitor* and the CSS *Virginia* (*Merrimac*) during the Civil War, the departure of the great White Fleet and the first flight from a ship.

The naval museum is open daily—even on Mondays during off-season when the rest of Nauticus is closed. To see just the naval museum, enter through Nauticus' guest relations door and let the attendant know you want to see only the Navy museum. You'll be steered upstairs to the museum. (For more details see the Nauticus entry in this section.) Hours in summer are 10 AM to 7 PM daily; other times the museum is open 10 AM to 5 PM daily. Admission is free.

The Douglas MacArthur Memorial
City Hall and Bank Sts., Norfolk
• **(757) 441-2965**

The rotunda of the memorial is the burial spot for Gen. and Mrs. Douglas MacArthur. Their main link with Norfolk is that the city was his mother's childhood home. Since 1964 this museum's extensive holdings have detailed the life of the famous general. The museum is in downtown Norfolk in MacArthur Square right across from MacArthur Center mall. You can park in the mall's parking garage. Be sure to bring your parking ticket for validation at the museum. This will get you three free hours of parking.

The main building, a Virginia Historic Landmark, was built in 1850 as Norfolk's courthouse. Exhibits are revamped every few years and new ones are added. In recent years the museum has gained displays on female war prisoners during World War II and segregated military forces. A 1999 renovation made the Memorial more interactive. There are three other buildings on the grounds, including a library, gift shop and theater.

To begin your visit, stop by the theater building for a 24-minute film on MacArthur that features newsreel footage. Inside the main building, the first thing you will see is MacArthur's final resting spot in the rotunda. There are nine galleries on two floors that take MacArthur's life from boyhood to his glory years as General of the Army. One favorite display includes his desk, uniform, medals and signature corncob pipe. Don't miss the gift shop outside; that's where MacArthur's gleaming 1950 Chrysler Imperial limousine is displayed. Out front of the memorial is a bronze statue of the general that is a popular photo spot. Hours

ATTRACTIONS

are 10 AM to 5 PM Monday through Saturday and 11 AM to 5 PM on Sunday. Admission is free.

The National Maritime Center (Nauticus)
One Waterside Dr., Norfolk
• **(757) 664-1000, (800) 664-1080**

This $52 million attraction opened in 1994 as a tribute to maritime technology. In 2000 it is gaining an expanded focus in anticipation of the arrival of its new neighbor—the retired Navy battleship *Wisconsin*. The *Wisconsin* is scheduled to permanently dock next to Nauticus by the end of this year and to open to visitors in 2001. Nauticus is adding interactive exhibits that explain the importance of the mighty battleship

The 120,000-square-foot hybrid museum/science center/attraction anchors the western edge of the Downtown Norfolk waterfront. With its location adjacent to Town Point Park and near The Waterside Festival Marketplace, Nauticus helps make the Norfolk waterfront as lively as Baltimore's Inner Harbor.

Plan to spend about four hours in Nauticus. Paid parking is available in city garages across Waterside Drive. Once you've ditched the car, follow the wooden gangplank to the Nauticus entrance. Look up to see the A-4 Navy jet parked on the roof and painted like a Blue Angels flying machine. Three gangways lead to the main lobby where you can quiz the staff at the guest relations desk. Also on this floor are a well-stocked gift shop and a restaurant.

Then step on the world's longest inclined people mover, with a design that ripples like waves. In 90 seconds you're on the third floor ready to start your tour. For the less adventurous, old-fashioned stairs and elevators also will whisk you skyward. Once on the third floor, you can use telescopes to check out the view. Among the highlights are the world's largest floating dry dock, historic Portsmouth and the buoy that marks Mile 0 on the Atlantic Intracoastal Waterway.

The third floor houses Nauticus' 350-seat wide-screen theater. *The Living Sea* is an underwater adventure created just for Nauticus. It's a spectacular film with a great soundtrack and was nominated for an Academy Award in 1996 for best documentary film. This must-see film has a soundtrack by Sting. Since the theater exits onto the second floor, be sure to check out all the third-floor attractions before watching the film. The third floor houses the bulk of Nauticus' major displays in more than a dozen themed areas. Among the best are a ship's bridge complete with captain's chair and all kinds of mind-boggling instruments, a working submarine periscope that goes right through the roof and a hands-on marine exploration area for younger children. There's also a play area for young children.

Also on the third floor are interactive exhibits where you can hunt for submarines with Sonar, design a ship, land a fighter jet on an aircraft carrier and navigate a tanker. There are also small theaters devoted to shipbuilding and the Port of Hampton Roads. Another video wall shows the Blue Angels flying team in action. One major attraction is the Aegis Theater. In a Universal Studios' twist, actors, film and computers meld together for a 15-minute adventure. As many as 40 visitors enter what looks exactly like the command center of a Navy destroyer. They pretend to be part of a routine briefing and even have computer monitors to use. Then all hell breaks lose as the ship comes under attack. Alarms blare forcing you to make quick decisions to avoid missile attacks, and the thrill is on.

For the environmentally inclined, both Old Dominion University and Norfolk State University operate working labs on this floor. ODU monitors water quality in the Chesapeake Bay while NSU runs a cell biology lab. There is an aquarium nearby as well as a touch tank with crabs and other hardy creatures in it. The National Oceanic and Atmospheric Administration (NOAA) has an exhibit on weather. Next door is a TV studio where you can do your best Willard Scott impression and watch yourself on camera giving a weather report.

Be sure to stop on the second floor to visit the Hampton Roads Naval Museum, which is operated by the U.S. Navy. The museum's ship models, uniforms and treasure trove of other artifacts chronicle 200 years of Navy history. With its move to Nauticus, the museum doubled its space and brought many artifacts out of storage. You can easily spend an hour wandering through here. The naval museum jazzed up its displays to correspond with Nauticus' high-tech touch but still gives a solid historical perspective on the Navy.

Hint: If you only want to see the naval museum, you can be admitted to this part for free, since it is operated by the U.S. Navy. It is open daily even on Monday when Nauticus closes in the off-season. Enter through the guest relations door. For information call (757) 444-8971. (See entry above for more details.)

If you're weary after all the action, take a

break in Nauticus' first-floor restaurant. Outside is the relaxing Celebration Pavilion, a 40,000-square-foot covered deck with comfortable seating. Adjacent to it is a pier on the Elizabeth River where there frequently is a Navy ship or other ship to tour. In 1996 a vintage tugboat became a permanent fixture alongside the Nauticus dock. Tours cost $2. (See description below.)

The first floor of Nauticus includes a gift shop and restaurant, which are open to the public. You'll also find a Norfolk Convention and Visitors Bureau booth ready to arm you with information about the entire region. Hours are 10 AM to 7 PM daily from Memorial Day through Labor Day and 10 AM to 5 PM everyday except Monday the rest of the year. Admission is $7.50 for adults, $5 for children older than six, and $6.50 for seniors, military personnel and AAA members.

Tugboat Museum
One Waterside Dr., Norfolk
• **(757) 627-4TUG**

This floating museum opened adjacent to Nauticus, where it is permanently docked. The tug *Huntington*, which was built in 1933 by apprentices at nearby Newport News Shipbuilding, teaches visitors about one of Hampton Roads' working ships. The sturdy tugboat plied area waterways for more than 50 years before its retirement in 1992. Visitors can wander through the ship where they'll see the engine room, crew's quarters, galley, captain's quarters and the wheelhouse. Photos and videos recall the *Huntington's* working years. Hours are 11 AM to 5 PM daily in summer and 11 AM to 5 PM Tuesday through Sunday off season. The tug is closed from January through March. Admission is $2, and $1 for children younger than 12.

Portsmouth

Children's Museum of Virginia
221 High St., Portsmouth
• **(757) 393-8393**

This is the liveliest place in the region and is a must-see for anyone with children. The city-owned museum is fun for all ages—from toddlers, who can safely roam the "quiet room"

stocked with simple toys, to even the most jaded teenager.

For nearly 15 years the downtown museum thrived in Portsmouth's historic 1846 Courthouse on High Street. With its move in 1994 to a revamped former department store, the museum has mushroomed into the largest children's museum in Virginia with more than 100,000 people visiting annually.

If time is critical, go early or late in the day on a weekend or on a weekday when all you're likely to face are school or summer camp groups.

Even with heavy attendance, the 64,000-square-foot museum has plenty of room to spread out. Children love to roam through the room full of bubbles, the thousands of Legos and the city room with its grocery store and mail-carrier's equipment.

The museum's displays range from a crane that hoists white foam beams to activities that focus in a fun way on flexibility, balance and reflexes. All exhibits allow hands-on entertainment. Our favorites are:

• The rock-climbing wall strong enough to support even adventuresome adults.

• Art Moves, a darkened alcove where colored laser lights project your image on screen as you dance to music.

• The city room with its 1960 Mack fire engine and real police motorcycle.

• The Science Circus where you can race rolling hockey pucks and pound a rubber air cannon all in the name of testing scientific principles.

• The art room lined with old Frigidaire doors where kids can post their favorite masterpieces with magnets.

The museum includes a 64-seat planetarium with frequent shows. Admission is included in your museum fee. Be sure to ask for a ticket at the museum entrance to hold you a seat for a specific show. Get there early to make sure your family can sit together.

Plan on spending several hours in the museum. There is a large gift shop but no food or drink available other than water. Be sure to feed the kids before you come and have drinks in the car for when your tired, thirsty bunch leaves. Immediately behind the museum on County Street is a large, city-owned parking garage where you can park for free on nights, weekends and holidays.

New in 1998 was a $3.4 million, second-

ATTRACTIONS

Holiday Lights

Hampton Roads is dazzling in December. It's not that our fair region isn't attractive the rest of the year, but at holiday time we knock ourselves out stringing miles and miles of festive holiday lights for your enjoyment. This is a spectacular time of year to fly in at night and gaze down at a twinkling fairyland just before your plane dips down at Norfolk International Airport. Since most of us are earthbound, however, our own vehicles also give a good vantage point.

It was 1985 when the first wave of light mania hit Hampton Roads. That year the Downtown Norfolk Council challenged the city's downtown building owners to outline their skyscrapers in white lights. The tradition continues each year from the week before Thanksgiving through New Years Day when owners of downtown buildings string more than 10 miles of white lights along their property. In 1997 Portsmouth also joined the festivities by lighting up its downtown buildings, which are just across the river from Norfolk. The lighting of the cities kicks off in November on the Saturday night before Thanksgiving with a lighted holiday parade through downtown Norfolk. It is followed by a whole roster of Holidays in the Cities events. Call the Downtown Council at (757) 623-1757 for a schedule or watch local publications for details.

There are two formal December light festivals in Norfolk and Virginia Beach. In 1994 the Norfolk Botanical Garden got the bright idea of planting lighted displays throughout its vast acreage. A year later, the City of Virginia Beach began celebrating the holiday season by lighting the boardwalk along the ocean. Both are spectacular events that already have become part of family holiday traditions. To

The Virginia Beach Boardwalk is ablaze with lights during the winter holidays.

Photo: Courtesy of City of Virginia Beach

beat the crowds either go just after sundown or schedule a visit for a weekday when you're less likely to sit in a line of idling cars.

The Norfolk Botanical Garden is at Azalea Garden and Airport roads adjacent to Norfolk International Airport. Visitors are dazzled by more than 200,000 colorful lights during a half-hour drive through the garden. Lighted displays are stationed along two miles of winding roadway and have a four-season theme. They include a giant windmill surrounded by tulips, a gingerbread house, a pumpkin patch, falling leaves and dancing snowflakes. This magical drive along the garden's roads yields surprises around every bend. It's exciting to see lights twinkling in the distance and then to view them in their full glory when you pass by. The switch is flipped on at Thanksgiving, and the show continues each evening through early January from 5:30 to 10 PM. Admission costs $9 a carload Sunday through Thursday and $10 Friday and Saturday. Call (757) 441-5830 for details.

For a different view, head to Virginia Beach for its Holiday Lights at the Beach extravaganza. We'll confess that for us the real thrill is getting to drive our car down what is otherwise a pedestrian-only boardwalk. During the 2-mile trip from the Eighth Street entrance off Atlantic Avenue to the 33rd Street exit, you're surrounded by more than 150 displays, including animated sea creatures, mermaids and even a fishing Santa. You don't get the perspective of distance that comes with driving through the botanical garden, but it's neat to be surrounded by 250,000 colorful lights. The Virginia Beach display goes up around Thanksgiving and comes down in early January. During that time, cars have the right-of-way on the boardwalk at night, and pedestrians are barred from walking there after dark. The lights go on at 5:30 PM and stay on until 10 PM Sunday through Thursday and until 11 PM otherwise. Admission is $7 a carload Sunday through Thursday and $9 on Friday and Saturday. Call 491-7866 for details.

If a road trip appeals to you, head to Newport News for a drive through Newport News Park. It's about a 30-minute trip from Norfolk. Since 1993 the park has sponsored its annual Celebrations in Lights. During a 2-mile drive through the park you'll be enchanted by 350,000 lights. The display goes up around Thanksgiving and runs through New Years Day starting at 5:30 PM nightly. It ends at 10 PM Sunday through Thursday and 11 PM on Friday and Saturday. Admission costs $6 a car Sunday through Thursday and $7 on Friday and Saturday. Call (757) 247-8451 for information.

Also all lit up in December is the Founder's Inn and Conference Center in Virginia Beach. It strings lights along its 26 acres of grounds along the Christian Broadcasting Network complex. Call (757) 424-5511 or (800) 926-4466.

Our family's traditional way to get in the holiday mood is to drive through the Commodore Park neighborhood in Norfolk. It's just off the 8700 block of Granby Street across from Northside Middle School. Each year owners of these modest homes go all out with fabulous lighted displays. The result is a splendid showing of reindeer, Santas and other illuminated holiday symbols. Streets are narrow in the neighborhood so go early or on weekdays to avoid the crush of traffic.

floor expansion that includes many hands-on science exhibits as well as trains from the Lancaster Train and Toy Museum. The toy train display is one of the largest on the East Coast and is valued at nearly $1 million. It was donated to the museum by a local resident and longtime train collector.

Hours are 9 AM to 5 PM Monday through Saturday and 11 AM to 5 PM on Sunday. Admission is $5 and free for children younger than 2. A $6 Museum Key pass allows you to also visit three other nearby Portsmouth museums—the Lightship Museum, the Portsmouth Naval Shipyard Museum and the Courthouse Galleries. You must visit all the museums on two consecutive days to take advantage of the pass.

Lightship Museum
Water St. and London St., Portsmouth
• **(757) 393-8741**

This is a restored lightship that was commissioned in 1915 to help mariners navigate through treacherous waters. Until 1964 it was anchored at strategic East Coast locations to guide ships. In 1976 the ship became a permanent tourist attraction on the banks of the Elizabeth River. Thirteen years later the lightship was designated a National Historic Landmark. The bright red ship has been restored to its early 20th-century appearance and includes the captain's quarters, officer's head and officer's mess. Children and nautical buffs particularly like exploring the ship. Hours are 10 AM to 5 PM Tuesday through Saturday and 1 to 5 PM on Sunday. Admission is $1 and a $6 Museum Key pass includes admission to three other city museums. Pass holders also can visit the Portsmouth Naval Shipyard Museum, the Courthouse Galleries, and the Children's Museum of Virginia during two consecutive days at no extra charge.

The Museum of Military History
701 Court St., Portsmouth
• (757) 393-2773

This private museum opened in 1998 in a former downtown bus station. It is owned by two area collectors of military memorabilia. Exhibits are housed on two levels. They span the time from the Civil War to World War I. Hours are 10 AM to 5 PM every day and noon to 5 PM on Sunday. Admission is $5, $3 for children, and $4 for seniors and military personnel.

Portsmouth Naval Shipyard Museum
2 High St., Portsmouth
• (757) 393-8591

Housed in an old machine shop for the Portsmouth-Norfolk ferry, the museum pays tribute to the nearby Norfolk Naval Shipyard. The government-owned shipyard, which is in Portsmouth, is the oldest shipyard in the country and was building ships before the Revolutionary War. The museum, which was founded in 1949, displays models of ships constructed at the yard as well as uniforms, swords, cannon balls and other memorabilia. The museum also has a piece of the CSS *Virginia* (the *Merrimac*), which was built at the yard and had its historic battle with the *Monitor* in nearby waters. Hours

are 10 AM to 5 PM Tuesday through Saturday and 1 to 5 PM on Sunday. Admission is $1 and a $6 Museum Key pass includes three other museums—the Children's Museum of Virginia, the Lightship Museum and the Courthouse Galleries.

Chesapeake

Chesapeake Museum
381 S. Bainbridge Blvd., Chesapeake
• (757) 494-0577

Chesapeake's first museum opened in 1999 in a 1908 schoolhouse. It has changing exhibits that emphasize the past in Chesapeake and surrounding communities. Exhibits in the four galleries change frequently. Admission is free. Hours are 10 AM to 4 PM Tuesday through Saturday.

Suffolk

The Suffolk Museum
118 Bosley Ave., Suffolk
• (757) 925-6311

The city-owned museum is housed in a former library near downtown. It opened in 1986 to emphasize art and features changing exhibits. Regional artists create some of the exhibits while others are traveling exhibits from the Virginia Museum of Fine Arts in Richmond. The museum also has periodic arts and crafts, theatrical and children's programs. It is home to the Suffolk Art League. Hours are 10 AM to 5 PM Tuesday through Saturday and 1 to 5 PM on Sunday. Admission is free.

Historic Houses and Sites

Virginia Beach

Adam Thoroughgood House
1636 Parish Rd., Virginia Beach
• (757) 664-6283

Operated by The Chrysler Museum, this home bears the name of Adam Thoroughgood

INSIDERS' TIP
Take a peek at the normally off-limits Norfolk Naval Shipyard in Portsmouth. Trolley tours are available three times a day during summer. The shipyard is the oldest in the country and was founded in 1767. Also on the tour are the Portsmouth Naval Hospital, the oldest naval hospital in America, as well as the Olde Towne Historic District. Tours leave at 11 AM and 12:30, 2 and 3 PM from Portside along Portsmouth's downtown waterfront. They last about an hour and cost $3.50, $1.75 for seniors and children. Call (757) 393-5111 for ticket information.

who came to Virginia in 1621 as an indentured servant. He performed the first survey of the region and started the first ferry service across the Elizabeth River. King Charles I rewarded Thoroughgood with 5,350 acres. The home was built by a Thoroughgood descendant around 1680. About three acres of the original grounds remain with the home, one of the oldest brick houses in the country. Its style resembles an English cottage. Outside are herb and flower gardens. Hours are 10 AM to 5 PM Tuesday through Saturday and 1 to 5 PM on Sunday. It's closed from January through March Admission is $4, $2.50 for children older than 6 and free for active-duty military. An $8 pass also provides admission to the Moses Myers House and the Willoughby-Baylor House, both in Norfolk.

Battle Off the Capes Monument
Fort Story, Virginia Beach
• **no phone**

A monument, overlook and plaques help visitors understand the important Revolutionary War battle that took place near this spot. In 1781 the French victory over the British here helped pave the way for the British surrender at Yorktown. This site is in Fort Story, an Army base. It is near the Old Cape Henry Lighthouse and First Landing Cross. You can drive right on the base armed with nothing more than a driver's license and current car registration any day during daytime hours.

First Landing Cross
Fort Story, Virginia Beach
• **no phone**

This large cross marks the spot where it's believed some of America's early English settlers landed upon arriving in the New World in 1607. They spent the night here before moving on to Jamestown Island where they settled. They later returned to hammer a wooden cross in the spot where they originally landed. Today's replica of the cross is in Fort Story, an Army base. It is near Old Cape Henry Lighthouse and an overlook where the Battle off the Capes took place. You'll need only a driver's license and car registration to drive onto the base during daytime hours.

Francis Land House
3131 Virginia Beach Blvd., Virginia Beach
• **(757) 431-4000**

This home was built c. 1732 for one of the first settlers in Princess Anne County. It was home to four generations of the Land family and later was an exclusive dress shop. Today the house is sandwiched among a busy strip of

stopping centers. The City of Virginia Beach saved the house from demolition by buying it and the surrounding 35 acres of land in 1975. The house features a Dutch gambrel roof and period furnishings. Docents in period costumes lead tours that usually start whenever you arrive with the last tour at 4:30 PM. Outside the grounds include authentic plantings, such as flax. Hours are 9 AM to 5 PM Tuesday through Saturday and noon to 5 PM on Sunday. Admission is $3, $2.50 for senior citizens and military personnel, $1.50 for students and $1 for children younger than 6.

Lynnhaven House
4405 Wishart Rd., Virginia Beach
• **(757) 460-1688**

Built around 1725 by the Thellaball family, this is one of the best-preserved 18th-century buildings in the country. It is owned by the Association for the Preservation of Virginia Antiquities. The brick house features period furnishing and frequently has cooking and crafts programs that showcase the lifestyle of 18th-century residents. Costumed docents lead tours that start when you arrive. The last one begins at 3:30 PM. You'll find the house just off Independence Boulevard where it intersects with Haygood Road. Hours are noon to 4 PM Tuesday through Sunday from June to September and weekends in May and October, and it's closed otherwise. Admission is $3 for adults and $1 for children.

Old Cape Henry Lighthouse
Fort Story, Virginia Beach
• **(757) 422-9421**

Completed in 1791, the lighthouse guided mariners until it was replaced in 1881. Its construction was authorized by President George Washington and Congress, making the lighthouse the first federal public works project. The stone used in the structure came from the same Virginia quarry that supplied the White House, Capitol and Mount Vernon. Construction of the lighthouse cost $17,500.

Since 1930 the lighthouse has been owned by the Association for the Preservation of Virginia Antiquities. Kids particularly like climbing to the top of the 75-foot tower and peering out the windows. The lighthouse is the official symbol of Virginia Beach.

Even when the lighthouse isn't open, you can drive onto the Fort Story Army base and look at it from outside. Nearby is the newer lighthouse as well as the First Landing Cross and the site of the Battle Off the Capes. Hours are 10 AM to 5 PM daily mid-March through

ATTRACTIONS

October. Admission is $2, $1 for students and senior citizens and free for ages 6 and younger.

Norfolk

Fort Norfolk
810 Front St., Norfolk
• (757) 625-1720

You may have trouble finding Fort Norfolk, but it's worth the hunt. This jewel of a historic site is one of our favorite spots for a family outing. The fort along the Elizabeth River near downtown was authorized by President George Washington and Congress in 1794 to protect the Norfolk harbor. Most of the buildings date from 1810. Since then the fort has hardly changed. Its arched gateway, double oak doors, gunpowder magazine, guardhouse and other buildings remain intact. Surrounding the fort are a wall and ramparts built to protect against British invasion. Among the fort's distinctions is having some of the oldest-existing graffiti in the country. It was scribbled on the walls of the Officer's Quarters by Confederate blockade runners held there during the Civil War.

Today the fort is owned by the U.S. Army Corps of Engineers, whose glassy regional headquarters dwarfs this historic site. After being closed to the public for years, the fort is gradually being renovated with the help of the Norfolk Historical Society, which has its headquarters in the fort. To get there, take Brambleton Avenue to Colley Avenue and head south. Go a few blocks until the road dead ends at Front Street. You will think you've made a mistake since you appear to be in an old warehouse district. But, go right on Front Street, and the road will end at the fort. For an extra treat, visit the fort during one of its special events when local military re-enactment troupes are camped there. Watch local media for details of dates and times or call the historic society. Hours are Sundays from 1 to 4 PM. Admission is free.

Hermitage Foundation Museum
7637 North Shore Rd., Norfolk
• (757) 423-2052

This English Tudor-style home is in Lochaven, one of Norfolk's loveliest neighborhoods. It was built in 1908 on 12 acres along the Lafayette River as a summer home for the late art patrons William and Florence Sloane. They established the Hermitage Foundation in 1937 to promote the arts. The Hermitage grounds are a terrific spot for picnics or strolling. There is no charge to enter the yard, which has picnic tables. In front of the house is a large, shady playground. Today the house, its contents and the grounds are a treat to see. The house features intricate woodcarving, while its holdings range from paintings, glass and textiles to carvings and other art works. Tours start when you arrive. Hours are 10 AM to 5 PM Monday through Saturday and 1 to 5 PM on Sunday. Admission is $4, $1 for ages 6 to 18 and free for active-duty military.

Hunter House Victorian Museum
240 W. Freemason St., Norfolk
• (757) 623-9814

Built in 1894, this is a Victorian jewel that showcases the furnishings and household goods of the James Wilson Hunter family—whose children never married and appear to have never thrown anything away. The house is in Norfolk's oldest neighborhood, the cobblestoned Freemason district near downtown.

The three-story brick home is in the Richardsonian Romanesque style and has gorgeous stained-glass windows. Inside are a nursery filled with delightful toys, a bed covered with a crazy quilt and all kinds of Victorian bric-a-brac and furniture. One room preserves the medical office of one son who was a physician. Tours begin on the hour and half-hour. The last one starts at 3:30 PM. The museum often has special events such as teas and storytelling that make it even more interesting to tour. There is a nifty gift shop upstairs with delightful reproduction Victorian items.

Although this is a narrow house filled with breakable items, the museum welcomes children and has a children's membership for ages 4 to 12. On some Saturdays the museum sponsors a Victorian children's hour with crafts, games and other activities. Hours are Wednesday through Saturday from 10 AM to 3:30 PM and Sunday noon to 3:30 PM. The museum is closed January through March. Admission is $3, $1 for children and $2 for senior citizens.

Moses Myers House
323 E. Bank St., Norfolk
• (757) 664-6283, (757) 664-6200

This is one of three historic homes operated by The Chrysler Museum. It was the home of the Moses Myers family, the region's first Jewish residents. Myers was a merchant who moved to Norfolk in 1787, ran a successful import-export business and served on the city council. During his lifetime, he was one of the wealthiest men in the country. He also was known as the last man in Norfolk to continue wearing a Colonial-style ponytail. The Myers family raised nine children in the brick Georgian house built in 1792. The home stayed in the family for six generations, therefore 75 percent of its current furnishings and artifacts belonged to the Myers' family.

The historic house is in Downtown Norfolk and is the only one in the country to feature programs on Jewish practices in Colonial times. It's worth a visit just to see the home's massive dining room and its elegant furnishings. Hours are 10 to 5 PM Tuesday through Saturday and 1 to 5 PM on Sunday. The house is closed on Sunday and Monday from January through March and opens at noon on Tuesday through Saturday during the winter. Admission is $4, $2.50 for children older than 6 and free for active-duty military. An $8 combination ticket also provides admission to the Adam Thoroughgood House in Virginia Beach and the Willoughby-Baylor House in Norfolk.

St. Paul's Church
201 St. Paul's Blvd., Norfolk
• **(757) 627-4353**

This is Norfolk's oldest building and was the only structure to survive the burning of Norfolk that was started on New Year's Day 1776 by the British. The church's war wounds include a British cannonball still stuck in its southeastern wall. The building dates to 1739 and features a Tiffany window and original box pews. Outside under live oak trees is a traditional burial ground with some fascinating tombstones to study. The sanctuary is open to the public, and there is a small museum on the second floor of the adjacent 1906 parish house. Its most notable holding is the chair John Hancock sat in to sign the Declaration of Independence. A detailed brochure makes it easy to tour the church, its grounds and the museum. Hours are 10 AM to 4 PM Tuesday through Friday. Visitors are welcome to attend Sunday worship services. Admission is free with a requested donation.

Willoughby-Baylor House
601 E. Freemason St., Norfolk
• **(757) 664-6283**

This 18th-century home is one of three operated by The Chrysler Museum, which is transforming it into an educational center that focuses on 18th-century Norfolk life. Guests must arrange in advance to see the house although it is occasionally open for special events.

The house was built in 1794 by Capt. William Willoughby, and its style is a blend of Georgian and Federal. Period furnishings reflect the household inventory made in 1800 when Willoughby died. The grounds of this Downtown Norfolk home include a lovely garden that usually welcomes guests during May to come for lunch on Wednesdays. You can bring your own picnic or buy a box lunch there. The museum is open for tours on Sunday from 1 to 5 PM and by appointment between 10 AM and 5 PM on Tuesday through Saturday. Admission is $4, $2.50 for children older than 6 and free for active-duty military. An $8 pass also provides tours of the Moses Myers House in Norfolk and the Adam Thoroughgood House in Virginia Beach.

Portsmouth

Hill House
221 North St., Portsmouth
• **(757) 393-0241**

This c. 1825 home is headquarters for the Portsmouth Historical Association. It is in the heart of the Olde Towne Historic District and is the only residence there open to the public. The home was given to the association in 1961 by the last of the six Hill children, none of whom ever married. The four-story English basement home is furnished entirely with Hill family belongings.

While in the neighborhood be sure to allow time to stroll through Olde Towne, which has the largest collection of Virginia homes on the National Historic Register. Hours are 12:30 to 4:30 PM Wednesday and 1 to 5 PM Saturday and Sunday from April through December. Admission is $2.50 and free for children.

Suffolk

Riddick's Folly
510 N. Main St., Suffolk
• **(757) 934-1390**

This is a massive Greek Revival home with 21 rooms, 16 fireplaces and four floors. It was built in 1837 by Mills Riddick, who had 14 children. The house is dubbed his folly because it is so big. In 1967 the city of Suffolk purchased the home to save it from demolition. It had a major restoration in 1988. There is only one original piece of Riddick furniture, a butler's desk, but other period furnishings show off the graceful lines of the house, which has elaborate

ATTRACTIONS

Cruising

The best way to get a feel for this coastal region is to take a look at it from the water. While you're here, try a leisurely sightseeing cruise so you can check out the largest natural harbor in the world. You have a variety of ways to set sail.

Spirit Cruises operates the *Spirit of Norfolk*, which has lunch, brunch, dinner and moonlight cruises. Spirit Cruises is a Norfolk-based company that initiated the idea of local dinner cruises and now operates in Boston, New York and other major

cities. The *Spirit*, which was completed in 1992 and resembles a cruise ship, has room for 450 guests and runs year round. The ship leaves from The Waterside Festival Marketplace and cruises along the Elizabeth River from Downtown Norfolk to the Norfolk Naval Base. Cruises last two to three hours and cost from $25.95 at lunch to $41.95 at dinner Tuesday through Thursday, with weekend rates slightly higher. The price includes a buffet, band music and a musical revue. Discounts are available for children, retired people, military personnel and groups. A smaller sister ship The Elite takes 75 people out on $69 dinner cruises on Saturday night.Call (757) 627-7771.

The *Carrie B* is a replica of a 19th-century riverboat that has been plying the Hampton Roads harbor since 1959. The *Carrie B* offers 90-minute cruises and takes in the downtown harbor and Norfolk Naval Shipyard. The boat holds 275 people and runs from April through October, with up to three trips a day during summer. There are also 2 ½-hour cruises that take visitors to the Norfolk Naval Base and site of the *Monitor* and *Merrimac* battle during the War Between the States. The *Carrie B* picks up passengers both at The Waterside Festival Marketplace in Norfolk and Portside in Portsmouth. Reservations aren't necessary. The cost is $12 for the shorter cruise, $14 for the longer one, with children ages 6 to 12 riding for half-price. Children younger than age 6 can tag along for free. Group rates are available. Hamburgers, hot dogs and drinks are sold on board. Call (757) 393-4735.

The *American Rover* bills itself as the "largest three-masted topsail passenger schooner under U.S. Flag." The 135-foot ship was designed and built by a local

See us by sea—on any number of local cruises

Photo: Courtesy of the City of Norfolk

naval architect in the 1980s and resembles a 19th-century tall ship. When the Rover's massive sails are at full mast, it is a breathtaking sight. The Rover sails through the Hampton Roads harbor from late April through October up to four times a day. Cruises last two or three hours and leave from The Waterside Festival Marketplace in Downtown Norfolk. Costs range from $14 for the shorter trips to $20. Children younger than 12 sail for $7 or $10. Group rates are available. Snacks, sandwiches and drinks are sold on board. Call (757) 627-7245.

The Elizabeth River Ferry offers the quickest and cheapest way to take in the downtown harbor. It is a paddlewheel boat that regularly runs from The Waterside Festival Marketplace in Norfolk to High Street Landing in Portsmouth The ride lasts about five minutes and costs 75› each way; 50› for children and 35› for seniors and passengers with disabilities. When the Norfolk Tides are playing at Harbor Park, the ferry makes a special trip to drop baseball fans off at the park and picks them up when the game is over. The ferry is operated by Hampton Roads Transit, the area bus company and is the world's first natural gas-powered pedestrian ferry. Call (757) 222-6100 for information..

Blue Moon Cruises offers a different water view. Its yacht takes passengers through the secluded bays and inlets of Virginia Beach. The sights include luxury homes costing up to several million dollars as well as marinas for both pleasure craft and commercial fishing boats. Both lunch and dinner cruises are available from May through October. Lunch lasts about 2 hours; dinner cruises last for 2« hours. The cost starts at $23.95 for lunch and $36.95 for dinner and rises on weekends. The yacht, which seats 64, leaves from Long Bay Point Marina at 2109 W. Great Neck Rd. in Virginia Beach. Call (757) 422-2900 for information..

To get a different perspective on the water take the short drive over the Hampton Roads Bridge-Tunnel to Hampton. There you can board the Miss Hampton II docked outside the Hampton Visitor Center and cruise through the Hampton Roads harbor and part of the Chesapeake Bay. The double-decker boat runs daily at 10 AM from mid-April through May and from September through October. In the summer it adds a second trip at 2 PM. Miss Hampton's three-hour harbor cruise takes visitors past the spot where Blackbeard the Pirate's skull was impaled on a pole after his death. You'll motor past the Norfolk Naval Base for a good look at mighty Navy ships. If the weather permits, the boat will dock at Fort Wool, where visitors can wander through the abandoned 18th-century military post that's in the waters along the bridge-tunnel. Tickets cost $14.50, $8 for children ages 6 through 11 and $12.50 for seniors. Make reservations by calling (757) 722-9102 or (800) 800-2202. The boat dock is at 710 Settlers Landing Road. Free parking is available in a city-owned parking deck that is in the block before the visitor center.

For outings that let you observe marine life, check with the Virginia Marine Science Museum, (757) 473-4949, to see if it is running boat tours. The museum frequently sponsors seasonal programs that take participants out on the water. Popular outings include whale-watching trips in winter and dolphin-watching trips that run from summer through fall. Trips last about two hours. Advance reservations are a must. They depart from the Virginia Beach Fishing Center at the end of Atlantic Avenue on Rudee Inlet. For its outings, the museum charters the fishing center's boat, the Miss Virginia Beach. The fishing center also offers its own dolphin- and whale-watching trips when the museum hasn't booked the boat. Call (757) 422-5700 for times and details. Across the bridge-tunnel in Hampton, Venture Inn II Whale Watching Cruises sponsors winter outings from the downtown pier at 710 Settlers Landing Road. For details call (757) 850-8960 or (800) 320-2055. These trips last five hours and go into the Atlantic Ocean.

ATTRACTIONS

plaster moldings and ceiling medallions. On the third floor are penciled messages from the family who fled the Union occupation during the Civil War. Riddick's Folly was used as a hospital during the war, and the walls also bear messages from recuperating Union soldiers.

The house features a gallery with changing exhibits. Permanent exhibits are on the manufacturing of Planters peanuts, which started in Suffolk, and native son the late Gov. Mills Godwin. Hours are 10 AM to 5 PM Tuesday through Friday and 1 to 5 PM on Sunday. Admission is free.

Military Bases

Military bases are open to the public from 5:30 AM to 9 PM daily. There are no charges to get in unless you take a guided tour.

Virginia Beach

Fort Story
Shore Dr. and Atlantic Ave.,
Virginia Beach
• **(757) 422-7755**

This World War I-era Army base is at the extreme north end of Atlantic Avenue. There also is an entrance off Shore Drive to the Fort, which is affiliated with Newport News' Fort Eustis, a major Army transportation center. Fort Story's whitewashed buildings give it an appealing look, and it has a great Atlantic Ocean beach that is open to the public on weekends during late spring and summer. There are also several historical sites on the base—First Landing Cross, the Old Cape Henry Lighthouse and the Revolutionary War site of the Battle Off the Capes (see previous entries). You can drive right on the base, but make sure you have driver's license and current car registration in case you're asked. Hours are 5:30 AM to 9 PM daily. Admission is free.

Little Creek
Naval Amphibious Base
Shore Dr., Virginia Beach
• **(757) 462-7923**

This is the Navy's major amphibious base. It's where the elite Navy SEALS do their train-ing. This base, which sprawls through Virginia Beach and Norfolk, is closed to the public. If you happen to know someone who works there, they can bring you on base for a personal tour.

Oceana Naval Air Station
Oceana Blvd., Virginia Beach
• **(757) 433-3131**

This is one of the Navy's four master jet bases, and you can see traces of it as F-14 Tomcats, A-6 Intruders or F/A-18 Hornets streak across the sky. It's one of the busiest airfields in the world, with a plane landing or taking off every few seconds. Oceana is home to about 30

The 300,000-gallon Norfolk Canyon Aquarium is just one of the many fascinating sights at the Virginia Marine Science Museum, recently named one of the top-ten aquariums in the nation.

Photo: City of Virginia Beach

aviation squadrons. To get on base you can take a tour bus from 24th St. and Atlantic Ave. along the oceanfront. Tours run at various times Saturday through Tuesday and cost $3.50 for adults, $1.75 for children and seniors. Call HRT at (757) 222-6100.

Norfolk

Norfolk Naval Base
Hampton Blvd. at Taussig Blvd., Norfolk
• **(757) 444-7955**

The world's largest Navy base is a big draw for area visitors. Even people not normally interested in military affairs are intrigued by the sight of mammoth aircraft carriers, stealthy submarines and squadrons of airplanes. This busy base encompasses thousands of acres and

ATTRACTIONS

includes some charming buildings from the 1907 Jamestown Exposition.

The main way for visitors to get on the base is through a guided tour unless you know someone who is in the Navy or works on the base. If you are in the military, reserves or are retired from services you can drive on base in a personal vehicle with a pass from the pass office. You can obtain a pass from the pass office located outside the main gate on Hampton Boulevard. For maps and detailed information stop by the Naval Base Tour Office just outside the gate at the end of Hampton Boulevard.

Unless you're with a real Navy Insider, you'll learn the most by taking the guided tour offered through Hampton Roads Transit (HRT). Tickets and transportation are available at the Naval Base Tour Office at 9079 Hampton Boulevard and The Waterside Festival Marketplace in downtown Norfolk. Tours cost $5, $2.50 for children. Note: in January and February tours originate only at the Naval Base Tour Office.

During the summer, naval base tours depart at 10 AM, 11 AM, 12:30 PM and 1:30 PM from The Waterside and every half-hour from 9 AM to 2:30 PM from the Naval Base Tour Office. Schedules vary during other times of the year with six daily tours offered in September, four a day in early winter, one a day in January and February and six a day in spring. Tours last about an hour. For times and details consult an HRT trolley and tours brochure. To be sure you don't miss the bus, verify departure times by calling the Naval Base Tour Office, (757) 444-7955, or HRT, (757) 222-6100.

Naval base tours take passengers past the piers where they can see ships and submarines, the Naval Air Station and the historic homes of the Jamestown Exposition. A guide boards the bus at the Tour and Information Center and conducts the entire tour from the bus.

On Saturdays and Sundays from 1 to 4:30 PM, except Christmas Day and New Year's Day, there is at least one Navy ship open for visitation on the base. Unless you have a pass or are riding on base with someone who works there, you'll need to take a tour to see the ships. Children

especially like to clamber up and down ship ladders and check out the captain's bridge. You'll find the sailors on board eager to answer your questions and explain their work. In the summer, arm yourself with hats, sunscreen and snacks for children. The wait to get on board usually isn't long, but you'll swelter standing on the ships' hot tarmac. Touring the ships is free and a lot of fun - especially for children.

If you're in the area during December, it's worth driving onto the base at night to see the lighted ships. Hours are 5:30 AM to 9 PM daily. Admission is free except for guided tours.

Miscellaneous Attractions

Some of the region's major attractions defy easy categorization, but they are definitely worth seeing while you're in town. If you live here and haven't made it out to see these attractions, put them on your must-do list.

Virginia Beach

The Artists Gallery
2407 Pacific Ave., Virginia Beach
• (757) 425-6671
This cooperative of 30 area artists opened in 1991. About 10 artists have their studios here while the rest rent walls to display their works. All art is for sale. Artists working on site include marble sculptors as well as painters and weavers. Hours are 10 AM to 5 PM Tuesday through Friday and 10 AM to 4 PM on Saturday. Admission is free.

Association for Research and Enlightenment (A.R.E.)
67th St. and Atlantic Ave., Virginia Beach
• (757) 428-3588
The A.R.E. is one of Virginia Beach's more intriguing attractions. This organization is dedicated to Edgar Cayce, a psychic who resided in Virginia Beach and was known worldwide for falling into a trance and being able to diagnose and prescribe treatment for medical ailments. Cayce, who died in 1945, built

> ## INSIDERS' TIP
> The Taiwan Observation Tower is an unusual site along Norfolk's Freemason Harbor waterfront. The ornate red and green Asian-style tower was a gift from the Republic of China that commemorates the 1983 start of trade between Virginia and the Republic. The tower was built on a defunct 500,000-gallon molasses tank from materials manufactured in China. It was dedicated in 1989. The surrounding land is known as Friendship Park.

the Edgar Cayce Hospital in Virginia Beach in the late 1920s. The hospital, which focused on holistic healing, failed to survive the Great Depression and closed in 1931.

Today the white frame former hospital is headquarters for A.R.E., whose conferences draw participants from around the world. Adjacent to it are the A.R.E. Visitor and Conference Center. Stop by and you can view a film about Cayce's life, hear free lectures and see exhibits on Cayce's work. You can also enjoy a meditation room overlooking the ocean and a well-stocked bookstore. Outside is a serene Japanese-style garden. In the summer there are occasional guided tours of the Cayce headquarters.

Try to sit in on the group ESP testing if you can. Visiting relatives of ours who attended a session proclaimed it to be one of the most fun things they did on their vacation. During the testing, a leader asks volunteers to send messages to each other by using an electric box that flashes shapes at one person. Another volunteer and the audience try to pick up on the vibes from the sender. The leader also administers other ESP tests and answers questions about psychic phenomenon. Hours are 9 AM to 8 PM Monday through Saturday and 11 AM to 8 PM on Sunday. Admission is free.

The Christian Broadcasting Network
1000 Centerville Tnpk., Virginia Beach
• (757) 226-2745

Virginia Beach is headquarters for The Christian Broadcasting Network CBN's 685-acre complex features attractive Georgian-style buildings, including the home of founder Rev. M.G. "Pat" Robertson. Also on the grounds are Regent University and a hotel and conference center.

Studio tours are available Monday through Friday at 11:30 AM, 2 PM and 3 PM. Groups need reservations for tours. But if there are only a few of you, just show up a few minutes ahead

INSIDERS' TIP

You can save money on admissions by purchasing a joint ticket to four Norfolk attractions. For $15 the Big Ticket gets you get into Nauticus, The Chrysler Museum of Art, Norfolk Botanical Garden and the Virginia Zoo. Children's tickets cost $7.50. Call (757) 441-1852 for details. Portsmouth has a similar program. For $21, the Olde Towne Portsmouth Pass gets you admission to six museums, including the Children's Museum of Virginia. You also get a sightseeing cruise on the Carrie B, a trolley tour of the downtown historic district and discounts at restaurants and shops. The pass is $14 for children 4 to 11. Call (757) 393-5111 for details.

of the tour time and you'll be led behind the scenes of this international TV network and its ministry. If you want to be in the audience for the "700 Club" taping, call ahead and get reservations, (757) 579-2745. The "700 Club" is CBN's flagship program featuring Robertson as host. It is usually produced five mornings a week from 10 AM to 11:30 AM. Try to call at least a day or two in advance to make sure you have seats. CBN also has a chapel service for visitors at 8:45 AM on weekdays. Hours are 9 AM to 4:30 PM Monday through Friday. Admission is free.

Contemporary Art Center of Virginia
2200 Parks Ave.,
Virginia Beach
• (757) 425-0000

Formerly known as the Virginia Beach Center for the Arts, this is the only arts center in the region to focus on 20th-century art. It was formed in 1952, and in 1989 completed a new 32,000-square-foot building whose highly acclaimed architecture touches on Oriental and Southern styles. The center is near Virginia Beach's Visitor Center and is one of the most attractive buildings in the city. Featured are changing exhibits as well as classes and programs for all ages. The center sponsors the popular Boardwalk Art Show each June. Hours are 10 AM to 5 PM Tuesday through Friday, 10 AM to 4 PM on Saturday and noon to 4 PM on Sunday. The center stays open until 8 PM on the first Thursday of each month. Admission costs $3, $2 for students, senior citizens and those in the military.

Haunted Mansion
2008 Atlantic Ave., Virginia Beach
• (757) 428-3327

Take a terrifying walk through a scary building and watch out for ghouls jumping out at you, and get ready to scream. The mansion stays open as long as it has visitors. The mansion opens daily at noon from June 1 through Labor Day. In the off-season hours vary so call first. Admission is $4 for all ages.

Ocean Breeze Water Park
849 General Booth Blvd., Virginia Beach
• (757) 422-0718, (757) 422-4444

This amusement park is less than 2 miles from the oceanfront and is a spot where kids and their families are guaranteed to have a blast.

This is the only water park in south Hampton Roads. Its 6 acres include eight slides, a half-acre wave pool and a big children's activity pool. In 2000 the park gained a new Caribbean look and theme. Young children can ride down slides and get in the pools with their parents. Once you've paid the WildWater admission, you are issued a wrist band, which gets you discounts at the other attractions. Be sure to hustle in and stake your family's claim on the deck chairs that will be your home base for the day. You probably will want to rent a big innertube for floating in the giant wave pool. The tubes you use for the slipping and sliding are provided at the entrance to each slide.

Next door is Motor World, which has 9 acres of miniature race tracks. The most popular is the Grand Prix track with 3/4 size race cars. There are rides here for all ages of children as well as adults.

Hours are 10 AM until 8 PM daily June 1 through Labor Day. For Ocean Breeze Water Park admission is $16.95 plus tax or $12.95 plus tax for children less than 42 inches tall, and there are discount rates in the evenings. Admission is free for ages 2 and younger. At Motor World individual ride tickets are $2.50 with adult rides requiring two tickets and children's rides one ticket. There is a joint ticket available for both parks.

Rockin' Rosie's Fun House and Mirror Maze
1910 and 1910-B Atlantic Ave., Virginia Beach
• (757) 425-5233

Rockin' Rosie's resembles a carnival fun house with a maze and tricky places to walk through. Strobe and black lights make maneuvering through here a challenge. The adjacent Mirror Maze will fool your eyes with its room full of mirrors. Seeing multiple images of yourself makes it easy to get lost. These sister attractions stay open as long as they have visitors with no set closing times. They open daily at noon from June 1 through Labor Day with variable off-season hours. Admission is $4 to each attraction.

Tidewater Veterans Memorial
1000 19th St., Virginia Beach
• no phone

Unveiled in 1988, this memorial is dedicated to military veterans from the area who served in all wars from the Revolutionary War to more

ATTRACTIONS

Explore the world's largest natural harbor, see the nation's first naval shipyard and cruise the site of the battle between the Monitor and the Merrimac aboard a replica of a 19th century Mississippi riverboat, the Carrie B.

current ones. The memorial's concept came from area students and was carried out by a local architect. The symbolic structure includes a waterfall, flags and a series of split spheres. The project was built with both city and private support. You can stop by any time of day or night, and there is no admission fee.

Norfolk

d'Art Center
125 College Pl., Norfolk
• (757) 625-4211

This is a fun place to wander because you never know what you'll find. It's a cooperative center for about 30 area artists who have their studios here. You'll see sculptors, jewelry makers and painters at work. If you find something to your liking, the artist will be happy to sell it to you. The center opened in 1986 in Downtown Norfolk. Hours are Tuesday through Saturday from 10 AM to 6 PM and Sunday from 1 to 5 PM. Admission is free.

Norfolk Armed Forces Memorial
Town Point Park, Norfolk

This moving memorial on the banks of the Elizabeth River was completed in 1998. It is in downtown Norfolk off Waterside Drive at the western end of Town Point Park near Nauticus. The memorial features 20 bronzed letters from men and women killed while doing military service. Letters date from the Revolutionary War to Operation Desert Storm. They are moving to read. Admission is free, and the memorial is always open.

Norfolk Botanical Garden
Azalea Garden and Airport Rds., Norfolk
• (757) 441-5830

This 155-acre garden has more than 12 miles of pathways and is a wonderful oasis in the middle of Norfolk. With its location adjacent to Norfolk International Airport, it gives airport arrivals an impressive first look at the city.

The botanical garden was started in 1938 as a Works Project Administration endeavor

and is composed of 20 theme gardens. Through the years it has gained status as one of the country's top botanical gardens and is renowned for its All-American Rose Garden. It's also one of the region's most popular spots for weddings. The botanical garden is midway through a $10 million improvement plan and already has finished the new Baker Hall visitors center. This is where you should start your visit and buy tickets for tram and boat tours.

Although the peak time to see the garden is spring when thousands of azaleas are in bloom, it's a treat any time of year. Among the highlights are the Renaissance Garden, the Kitakyushu Park Japanese garden and a pathway lined with marble statues of famous artists. If it's spring don't miss the Bunny Morgan Wildflower Garden, which stretches as far as you can see with a colorful palette of flowers. An overlook near Baker Hall is a favorite of children who love to watch planes take off and land at the neighboring airport. Despite all the aviation activity, the botanical garden remains a secluded spot.

To get a better view and make sure you don't miss far-flung parts like the wildflower garden, take either a relaxing tram or boat ride

Festivals and concerts are held oceanside at Virginia Beach's 24th Street Stage.

(available only in warm-weather months). Drivers provide a lively narration that explains the plants you see. Each tour lasts about 30 minutes and costs $2.50 for adults and $1.50 for youths. Children younger than 6 ride for free. If you have time, enjoy a picnic overlooking

Lake Whitehurst or bring along a pole (and the appropriate license) for fishing. Be ready to share your crumbs with friendly ducks and geese that are eager for handouts. You also can take a break in the Garden House Cafe, which serves lunch and a variety of snacks. From late November through early January the garden hosts a gigantic drive-through holiday light display. There is an additional admission charge for the Garden of Lights event. (See the close-up in this chapter.) The garden also is the site of the Vietnam Veterans Haunted Forest put on by local veterans. This sell-out event is on the two weekends preceding Halloween and requires advance tickets.

Hours are 9 AM to 5 PM every day. Admis-sion is $4, $2 for ages 6 through 18 and $3 for senior citizens.

The Virginia Zoo
3500 Granby St., Norfolk
• (757) 441-2706

The 53-acre zoo is a favorite spot for all ages, but children particularly get a kick out of it. Although you won't find any giant pandas, lions or gorillas, the zoo has a charm of its own. In recent years it has reduced the number of animals to ensure that it has the proper environment for those in its care. One popular exhibit features two elephants who amuse visitors by getting baths from zookeepers or splashing each other with water. Next door

ATTRACTIONS

Portsmouth offers twilight walking tours of Olde Towne, called Lantern Tours, which are led by knowledgeable guides dressed in period attire.

Photo: Courtesy of Portsmouth Convention and Visitors Bureau

are rare white rhinoceroses. Other zoo favorites are the llamas, ostriches and primates. Be sure to look for Lefty the friendly black gibbon with only one hand.

The zoo's most famous inhabitants are two Siberian tigers who were confiscated as cubs in 1992 from a private owner who illegally owned them. They were housed temporarily in the zoo and won the hearts of local residents who started a fund-raising campaign to build an area for them. In 1995 the sisters, Shere Khan and Shaka Khan, moved into a new 8,000-square-foot habitat designed just for them. Their new abode is designed so visitors can get great close-up views of the tigers.

While in the zoo be sure to take a walk through the barn yard, the reptile and small mammal house, the gazebo where injured birds recuperate, and the turn-of-the-century botanical conservatory. Kids love getting a handful of food from a dispenser to feed ducks in the pond. They also like stopping by The Beastro restaurant and eating a reasonably priced lunch that comes in a bag decorated with animals. Outside the zoo grounds are a playground and picnic area in Lafayette Park.

In 1997 the zoo started construction on an ambitious $15 million improvement plan created by the designer of the renowned Audubon Zoo in New Orleans. In 1999 it debuted and African plains exhibit with a variety of animals co-existing in the same environment. Still to come are a Dismal Swamp walkway and butterfly house. Hours are 10 AM to 5 PM daily. Admission is $2 and $1 for children ages 2 through 11 and for senior citizens. Admission is free from 4 to 5 PM on Sunday and Monday.

The Waterside Festival Marketplace
333 Waterside Dr., Norfolk
• (757) 627-3300

This is Norfolk's festival marketplace—the city's version of Boston's Fanueil Hall. It has a lively mix of restaurants, night-

clubs, entertainment centers and shops. The Waterside opened in the mid-1980s to revital-

Visit the restored Lightship Museum in Portsmouth and see how sailors worked on this floating lighthouse during their many months at sea.

Photo: Portsmouth Convention and Visitors Bureau

ize the Downtown Norfolk waterfront along the Elizabeth River. Although it originally had a focus on shopping, Waterside was revamped in 1999 to have a new emphasis on food and entertainment.

The top outdoor attraction is the never-ending parade of tugs, sailboats and Navy ships moving along the Elizabeth River. A boardwalk takes visitors past some huge yachts anchored at an adjacent marina. There are numerous benches for relaxing. Neighboring Town Point Park is the site of festivals on most weekends.

The Waterside is also the place to catch the ferry to Portsmouth, embark on a harbor tour or take a trolley tour of the city or the Norfolk Naval Base. Inside is a visitors center with tourism brochures and an interesting movie about Norfolk history. There is a city-

INSIDERS' TIP

Since this is a flat, coastal area, you may be amazed to see a giant 68-foot mountain looming along the Virginia Beach-Norfolk Expressway (I-264). This man-made peak is aptly named Mount Trashmore after the 650,000 tons of garbage buried in it. Mount Trashmore was created nearly 25 years ago as a Virginia Beach city park, complete with playgrounds, a lake and picnic tables. Its pinnacle is a preferred spot for kite flying and winter sledding. Mount Trashmore also is home to Kids Cove—a huge playground that was built by 3,000 volunteers. (See our Parks chapter.)

owned parking deck across the street. Hours are Monday through Saturday from 10 AM to 9 PM and Sunday noon to 6 PM. There are longer hours during the summer. Waterside's bars keep later hours, particularly on weekends. Admission is free.

Portsmouth

Virginia Sports Hall of Fame and Museum
420 High St.,
Portsmouth
• **(757) 393-8031**

Organized in 1966, the Hall of Fame honors Virginia sports heroes, including golfer Sam Snead and tennis star Arthur Ashe. Inductees include well-known names in football, basketball, golf, baseball, auto racing, horseback riding, speedboat racing, wrestling, bowling, swimming, sail boat racing, track, tennis and coaching. Displays include uniforms, photos and other memorabilia. Hours are 10 AM to 5 PM

INSIDERS' TIP

The Norwegian Lady Statue at 26th Street and the Boardwalk in Virginia Beach was a gift to the city from the people of Moss, Norway. It commemorates the wreck of a Norwegian ship off the city's shore in 1891. The statue's predecessor was the wooden figurehead that washed ashore from the sunken ship.

Tuesday through Saturday and 1 to 5 PM on Sunday. Admission is free.

Chesapeake

Chesapeake Planetarium
300 Cedar Rd.,
Chesapeake
• **(757) 547-0153**

The planetarium opened in 1963 and was the first in Virginia to be built by a school district. The Chesapeake School District continues to operate the planetarium, which attracts about 40,000 visitors a year. Program topics change monthly and include the summer sky, falling stars and lunar eclipses. Reservations are a must since most programs fill up quickly. Shows last about an hour with a telescope available afterward for stargazing on clear nights. The planetarium is in a freestanding building near Chesapeake City Hall. You'll recognize it by its 30-foot dome. Shows are at 8 PM each Thursday. Admission is free.

ATTRACTIONS

Kidstuff

LOOK FOR:
• 30 Suggestions
  For Fun Things
  To Do

While thumbing through this book you'll find dozens of ideas for entertaining your children. But just in case you missed them, here are 30 suggestions to keep kids of all ages on the go. The following are places our entire family is happy to visit over and over again.

1. If you do nothing else, go to the **Children's Museum of Virginia** in downtown Portsmouth, (757) 393-8393. This 90,000-square-foot wonderland is in a former department store in the heart of downtown. A $3 million expansion and renovation in 1994 made the museum the coolest place to be for kids of all ages and for adults too. The museum added to that image in 1998 when a second-floor addition brought in new exhibits and one of the East Coast's largest antique toy train displays.

The Museum's 90 displays range from a room filled with soap-bubble experiments to a real fire truck in the city section. There are dozens of computer activities and hands-on games to challenge both the mind and body. The museum also includes a planetarium with daily shows. Our family favorites are the rock-climbing wall and Art Moves, a laser-light room where images of your body in motion are projected on a colored screen.

Admission is a bargain at $5, free for those younger than 2. Be forewarned, kids never want to leave this fun place. Be sure to bring drinks and snacks for after the fun as there is no food service at the museum. There are a few restaurants nearby, however. Museum hours are 10 AM to 5 PM Tuesday through Friday; 10 AM to 9 PM Saturday and 1 to 5 PM on Sunday.

2. Make the kids think they've been to sea by taking a jaunt on the **Elizabeth River Ferry**, which links the downtowns of Norfolk and Portsmouth. The trip lasts only about five minutes, but it's neat to breeze across the river on a paddlewheeler. The cost each way is $.75 for adults, $.50 for children 12 and younger. Hitch a ride at The Waterside Festival Marketplace in Norfolk or at Portsmouth's High Street Landing, which puts you within walking distance of the Children's Museum of Virginia. The ferry arrives every 30 minutes.

3. Check out **Nauticus**, the National Maritime Center, (757) 664-1000. This $52 million museum/attraction can be found on the downtown Norfolk waterfront. While geared toward adults and older children, even preschoolers will find plenty to amuse them inside. Nauticus takes a high-tech, energetic look at the Navy and maritime industry. It's a hands-on place with lots of computer-interaction exhibits. Favorites include the tank full of nurse sharks to pet and lively science demonstrations given by staff members. In 2000 Nauticus is getting a new look in preparation for the docking of its neighbor, the **USS *Wisconsin*** battleship. The ship will open to the public in 2001, and Nauticus will have new interactive displays about the historic Navy ship. Touring Nauticus costs $7.50, $5 for children ages 6 to 16. The excellent Hampton Roads Naval Museum, which is owned by the U.S. Navy, has free admission if you only want to see that part of Nauticus. Hours are 10 AM to 7 PM daily Memorial Day through Labor Day, 10 AM

to 5 PM otherwise but closed on Monday in the off-season. There is a cafeteria in Nauticus in case children get an attack of the hungries during the several hours it takes to fully enjoy this museum.

4. Go to the **Virginia Marine Science Museum**, 717 General Booth Boulevard in Virginia Beach, (757) 437-4949. A $35 million expansion, provides extra incentive to head to this fascinating museum. A new 300,000 gallon aquarium, a 3-D IMAX theater and a salt-marsh pavilion help make this one of the country's top-10 marine museums. Highlights of the new area are exhibits of frisky river otters and seals, and a bug's-eye view of the marsh á la *Honey, I Shrunk The Kids*. Be sure to wear walking shoes since there is about a six-minute walk between the museum's two buildings. There is a shuttle to ride, but most children prefer to walk along the walkway through the marsh.

One Virginia Beach grandfather marvels that his visiting grandkids never tired of this museum even before it expanded. This is a hands-on place that lets kids touch turtles and crabs, create real waves, tong for oysters and meander along a walkway that cuts through a saltwater marsh. Kids can also watch a woodcarver create duck decoys. Admission costs $6.95 for adults, $5.95 for children 4 and older. Children younger than 4 are admitted free. The IMAX theater costs an additional $6.95, $5.95 for kids. A combination ticket that includes admission and the IMAX theater costs $10.95, $9.95 for kids. Hours are 9 AM to 5 PM daily with longer hours in the summer. The expanded museum includes a cafeteria that helps fortify kids for a few hours of exploring the museum.

5. Visit **The Virginia Zoo**, 3500 Granby Street, Norfolk, (757) 441-2706 or (757) 441-5240. The zoo has many of children's favorite animals and wide-open spaces for kids to run around. The hands-down favorite of most visitors is the Siberian tiger exhibit. The sister tigers have been zoo residents since they were tiny cubs. The community pitched in to raise funds for a fitting habitat for the tigers. Improvements at the zoo continue with an African plains exhibit that opened in 1999 and a planned butterfly house and Great Dismal Swamp exhibit.

To get to know the zoo better, sign up preschoolers for the Zoo Tot or Early Bloomers programs. These are held on Saturday mornings to give children and parents a behind-the-scenes look at the zoo. They meet animals up close or work with plants. Sessions include crafts, games and songs. Students who have finished kindergarten can participate in summer zoo camps. There also are occasional weekend camp-outs in the zoo for kids and parents.

Admission costs $3.50 for adults, $1 for children ages 2 to 11. You can enter for free from 4 to 5 PM on Sundays and Mondays. Hours are 10 AM to 5 PM daily. There is an outdoor cafe in the zoo that has huge sandwiches for adults and box lunches that kids adore. You can share your crumbs with visiting pigeons.

6. Go camping at **Northwest River Park** in Chesapeake—or at least spend the day there. This terrific park is nearby but makes you feel like you've truly escaped city life. The 763-acre park has a 29-acre lake, numerous trails and 72 well-maintained campsites. It also features Charlie, the resident peacock, and hungry ducks and geese to feed. There are canoes and paddleboats for rent and a miniature golf course. Friendly park rangers are ready to answer questions or lead programs on snakes or other woodland creatures. The park is at 1733 Indian Creek Road. Call (757) 421-3145 or (757) 421-7151 for directions and camping reservations.

Another great camping spot is **First Landing State Park** in Virginia Beach with campsites near a pristine beach along the Chesapeake Bay. Call (757) 481-2131 for reservations.

7. Visit **Bergey's Dairy Farm** at 2221 Mount Pleasant Road in Chesapeake. It's a pleasant country drive to this working dairy farm, known for its residential milk deliveries and scrumptious homemade ice cream. Be sure to call for directions, (757) 482-4711. The kids can see cows and horses and pet some Guernsey calves. Best of all, you can go in Bergey's store for an ice cream cone or a quick lunch. During one spring weekend, the farm sponsors back-to-the-farm days with hayrides and other entertainment. Otherwise you can visit any day except Sunday. Hours are 9:30 AM to 7 PM Monday through Saturday.

8. Head to **Pungo** to pick whatever's in season in this rural section of Virginia Beach. If it's summer you'll find strawberries, blueberries and blackberries. If it's fall you can pull a pumpkin

The Children's Museum of Virginia, the state's largest children's museum, offers more than 80 hands-on exhibits, temporary rotating exhibits, a 64-seat planetarium and a $1 million antique toy and train collection.

KIDSTUFF

out of the patch. To keep up with what's in season look in *The Virginian-Pilot* classifieds under the section called "Good Things to Eat." Be sure to call and get directions. Once you're in Pungo, you may want to keep going a few miles to **Knotts Island**, North Carolina. If it's late summer there is a peach orchard with fruit just ripe for the picking.

9. Plan an outing to one of the region's three terrific community-built playgrounds. The original is **Kids Cove** at Mount Trashmore Park in Virginia Beach just off the Route 44 express-way. It was built by 3,000 volunteers in 1993 and paid for with everything from school kids' pennies to corporate donations.

Norfolk's contribution to kid fun, **Imagination Island**, can be found at Northside Park off Tidewater Drive. Chesapeake offers its own super playground, **Fun Forest** at Chesapeake City Park off Greenbrier Parkway. All three parks are giant wonderlands with lots of nooks and crannies to explore as well as slides, swings, swaying bridges and much more. The parks are fun for all ages with comfortable spots for parents to rest and watch. The playgrounds are usually crowded but are so big that it doesn't matter. Be sure to pack snacks and drinks so the children will take a cool-down break now and then.

10. Take a daytrip and go to **Fort Fun** in Newport News. This terrific playground was built by volunteers in Huntington Park off Warwick Boulevard (near Mercury Boulevard). Children can play in the fort for hours, and there are comfortable benches overlooking the James River for weary parents. The playground has lookout towers, mazes and traditional swings and slides. There are also picnic tables, a crabbing pier and a slew of friendly ducks. Remember to bring along some breadcrumbs to feed the hungry quackers.

11. For indoor fun check out **Jillian's** entertainment center in Waterside Festival Market-place on the waterfront in downtown Norfolk, (757) 624-9100. There's something here to entertain kids of all ages. This 50,000-square-foot entertainment complex takes up most of the second floor of Waterside. It has more than 150 electronic games, including virtual bowling. Jillian's is open daily starting at 11 AM. Children are allowed to play games until 7 PM when Jillian's becomes adults only. Also in downtown Norfolk is **Jeepers**, a game center on the third floor of MacArthur Center mall. Besides the video games you'd expect, there is a small roller coaster young children enjoy as well as bumper cars, (757) 622-8700.

Another sure-to-please place for the whole family is **FunScape** in Chesapeake, just off Greenbrier Parkway on Jarman Road, (757) 523-0582. You'll definitely need plenty of money because you'll have trouble choosing between the seven main attractions, including two indoor miniature golf courses, bumper cars, virtual-reality games and a giant indoor play area. There also are several snack bars for when you're ready for a break. Adjacent to this glorified arcade is a movie theater.

12. Ride the **Pokey Smokey** in Portsmouth's City Park. This is a real coal-fired miniature train that puffs through a lovely 93-acre park along the Elizabeth River from April through October. Rides are daily during the summer and on the weekends otherwise. The cost is $1; a book of 10 tickets costs $7. Nearby is a nifty playground and a picnic area. Call (757) 465-2937.

13. Explore the **Norfolk Botanical Garden**, (757) 640-6879 or (757) 441-5830, and examine whatever is in bloom. If it's spring, summer or fall be sure to leave time for either a tram ride or a boat ride. Either ride costs $2.50, with young children going along for free. Kids love the rides, and parents get to see parts of the gardens they didn't know were there. Pack a picnic lunch because there is a playground with tables on the shores of Lake Whitehurst. Kids also enjoy the overlook that lets them watch planes take off from neighboring Norfolk International Airport. On most Sunday afternoons at 2 PM there often are free, themed nature walks geared for the whole family. The garden also offers some children's classes. Admission costs $4, $3 for children over age 6. Hours are 8:30 AM until sunset daily.

14. If you have kids age 6 and older, get a group together for fun at **Ultrazone** at 2682 Dean Drive in Virginia Beach, (757) 463-6300. All ages love to play laser tag here. Games cost $6.75 for each person.

Kids and Eating Out

If you're dining with children, you'll find your family is welcome almost anywhere. Although there are many familiar fast-food restaurants here, branch out and try some local spots. Even if your children detest seafood, they'll usually find chicken fingers or hamburgers on the menu. The only restaurants where you

might hesitate to take the young ones are to some of the romantic continental or French restaurants and the trendy nouvelle American or new Southern bistros.

Once the lack of a babysitter forced us to take a 3-year-old on our anniversary dinner to a candlelit restaurant by the Chesapeake Bay. We went early and were treated graciously by the staff. Recently we took the same child, now a more sophisticated 8 years old, to a

fine-dining restaurant. We went early and fortified him with pizza before we arrived. The staff treated him kindly and surprised him with a palate-cleansing sorbet and a flower-bedecked plate bearing a warm cloth for his hands. In cases where you aren't sure whether a restaurant will be this accommodating for children, be sure to call ahead and ask.

At most restaurants you'll find children's menus, booster seats and a staff quick to supply a basket of crackers while you peruse the menu. At places where there is no children's menu (like most Chinese restaurants), we find an appetizer that will work or just share our dinners if portions are large enough. No one seems to mind.

There are numerous restaurants that dole out crayons and coloring sheets. The following eateries are some that go the extra mile to make young customers feel welcome.

Chuck E Cheese, 1528 Sam's Circle, Chesapeake, (757) 549-2775, is the ultimate place for kids. Besides serving pizza and soft drinks it has what seems like hundreds of arcade games, a crawl-through maze and an animated show. The new restaurant is just off the busy Battlefield Boulevard shopping corridor.

Doumar's, 20th Street and Monticello Avenue in Norfolk, (757) 627-4163, has carhops as well as burgers, shakes and

An entertainer amuses children at a local restaurant.

Photo: Courtesy of Fuddruckers

other kid-friendly fare. Each day the owners make ice cream cones on a vintage machine and are happy to show off their skills for youngsters.

Fuddruckers Restaurant, 4625 Virginia Beach Boulevard in Virginia Beach, (757) 456-1118, lets children eat free Monday through Thursday evenings and for 99 cents on weekends. Be sure to ask for one of the paper Fuddruckers hats like the ones the workers wear. Other amusements include video games and an outdoor playground. Recently joining the chain's lineup are two Chesapeake Fuddruckers with the same meal arrangement for kids. The one near Greenbrier Mall is at 1105 Merchants Way, (757) 549-1670. The Fuddruckers near Chesapeake Square mall is at 2400 Ring Road, (757) 465-4165.

Huckleberry's, 440 High Street in Portsmouth, (757) 397-3752, is a casual eatery with sandwiches, soups, and ice cream. It serves breakfast, too. It's near the Children's Museum of Virginia.

The Jewish Mother, 3108 Pacific Avenue in Virginia Beach, (757) 422-5430, serves a variety of sandwiches and tops off each child's meal with a free dish of ice cream. There's a second Jewish Mother in Portsmouth at 1 High Street, (757) 398-3332.

The Lighthouse, First Street and Atlantic Avenue in Virginia Beach, (757) 428-7974, provides a relaxing upscale outing for parents in a kid-friendly atmosphere. Children can chow down on shrimp, all-you-can-eat crab legs or sandwiches. Popular items include kids' cocktails and junior-sized sundaes.

Lynnhaven Fish House, 2350 Starfish Road in Virginia Beach, (757) 481-0003, is a treat for parents and perfect for kids. They can peek at lobster tanks and the fish-cutting rooms. Half-price entrees are available for children.

Spaghetti Warehouse, 1900 Monticello Avenue in Norfolk, (757) 622-0151, offers dining in a trolley or brass bed. The kids' menu is packed with activities. Picky eaters can choose from 12 pasta sauces and usually leave with a free balloon.

Uncle Al's Hotdogs, 29th and Pacific streets in Virginia Beach, (757) 425-9224, has chairs pushed up to pinball machines so half-pints can reach the buttons and see the action. This establishment also stocks Power Ranger ice cream bars.

Whistle Stop, 509 Middle Street in Portsmouth, (757) 393-3747, has a menu children love, including ice cream, cookies, hot dogs, barbecue and pizza. Even better, it's close to the Children's Museum of Virginia.

15. Attend a Family Fun Day activity at **The Chrysler Museum**, 245 W. Olney Road, Norfolk, (757) 664-6200, ext. 268. These are usually held twice a month on Sunday afternoons. The events are designed to get families into the art museum, and they truly are fun. Most events have a theme, sometimes tying in with an exhibition or a holiday. The series has included storytellers, bands, crafts, scavenger hunts, plays and even a family circus. You can attend Family Fun activities for the cost of the museum admission—$7 for adults, $5 for students and free for members and children younger than 6.

16. Head to **the beach** for a day. It's hard for out-of-town friends to imagine living this close to the beach and not going there all the time, but that's what tends to happen. So drag out all the paraphernalia, pack a picnic lunch and head on down for some fun. Insiders are particularly fond of the beach during the spring and fall when it's less crowded. In the summer, going in early morning or late afternoon will help you avoid throngs of people. One of our favorite family excursions is to go in-line skating on the Boardwalk early in the morning before it's crowded. Then we skate back to the car and put away the gear. We pull out the beach umbrella, cooler and boogie board and head down for a few hours of beach fun. We pay about $5 for the privilege or parking close to the Boardwalk in the summer, but we feel like we get our money's worth. You'll usually find free parking in fall and early spring.

17. When the little ones need a place to run around, head to one of the free play areas at area malls. MacArthur Center's playground has a picnic theme. It's on the third floor next to the food court and is perfect for toddlers through preschoolers with its giant plastic hotdogs and cupcakes to climb. There are comfortable seats for parents, and many a mom has met new friends at the play area. Military Circle mall opened a nautical theme play area in 2000 right next to its food court. In 2000 Lynnhaven Mall in Virginia Beach was planning to add a similar play area. In Hampton, Coliseum Mall has a NASA-themed play area.

18. If it's warm weather, spend an afternoon at **Ocean Breeze Water Park**, 700 S. Birdneck Road, (757) 422-4444. This amusement park has eight giant water slides and a wave pool. Motor World with its race tracks for mini-cars, Shipwreck Golf for miniature golf and the Strike Zone with nine batting cages, (757) 422-6419. All the attractions are open weekends in spring and fall

KIDSTUFF

and open daily during the summer. There is an admission fee for the waterpark, and the other attractions sell tickets for each activity you want to do; call for current prices. Hours are 10 AM until 10 PM daily June 1 through Labor Day.

19. Take your children to some spectator sports. Both **Old Dominion University** and **Norfolk State University** field some fine teams. Kids love **Norfolk Tides** baseball games in the summer and **Hampton Roads Admirals** hockey games in the winter. The region also boasts a professional soccer team, the **Mariners** and an arena football team, the **Nighthawks**. See our Spectator Sports chapter for more information.

20. Go see some performances geared toward children. The **Hurrah Players** troupe features talented children in its musical productions, (757) 627-5437. Willett Hall sponsors the **Portsmouth Storybook Theater Children's Series**, which brings traveling productions to town, (757) 393-5144 or (757) 393-5327. The **Virginia Symphony** performs a fun family concert series, (757) 623-2310 or (757) 623-8590. There are several puppet troupes that regularly perform in the area, including **Wappadoodle Puppets**, (757) 481-5599; **Spectrum Puppets**, (757) 491-2873; and **Fuzz & Stuffing Puppets**, (757) 480-2991. The **Generic Theater** has a Saturday ChildsPlay program to produce family productions, (757) 441-2160.

21. Enjoy some of the free weekly **story hours** sponsored by area libraries. Besides reading stories, innovative librarians often have seasonal crafts and other activities to keep little hands busy. Summer library programs are a great way to inspire young readers. Look for magicians and storytellers to help the librarians keep the kids motivated. Virginia Beach libraries have a newsletter available at each branch that lists story hours. Check with your particular branch library for a schedule of events.

INSIDERS' TIP

Homemade ice cream is a treat for all ages. The best is at Uncle Harry's Cones & Cream and Bergey's Dairy Stores. You'll find Uncle Harry's at two Virginia Beach locations—Loehman's Plaza at 4000 Virginia Beach Boulevard and 3623 Pacific Avenue. Call (757) 431-3636 or (757) 425-8195. Bergey's stores are in Chesapeake on the Bergey Dairy Farm at 2221 Mount Pleasant Road and at 1128 N. Battlefield Boulevard. Call (757) 482-4711 or (757) 547-7360.

22. If it's December, go one night to see the **holiday lights** in Norfolk. The city strings its downtown office buildings with thousands of white lights. With more than 10 miles of lights, from a distance downtown Norfolk looks like a giant gingerbread village. For a different perspective, drive to the downtown Portsmouth waterfront and gaze across the river or take a ride on the Elizabeth River Ferry. To kick off the season, the city of Norfolk sponsors a wonderful lighted Christmas parade, usually on the Saturday evening before Thanksgiving. There is a whole roster of Holidays in the City activities that goes along with the lights.

The ships at the Norfolk Naval Base and the Naval Amphibious Base in Virginia Beach also are lighted at this time of the year. For one of the best displays of gaudy but great Christmas lights, head to Commodore Park in Norfolk. This neighborhood is just off Granby Street across from Northside Middle School. Just follow the line of cars, and you'll be amazed at how each neighbor tries to outdo the other with elaborate Christmas scenes and lights.

There are three excellent drive-through lighted displays that pull out all the stops to wow the whole family. The **Norfolk Botanical Garden** transforms itself into a magical wonderland of butterflies and flowers with its Garden of Lights. Drivers follow a winding road with surprises around every bend. Be sure and stop at the cider and cookies stand on the way in. It's a straight shot down the **Virginia Beach boardwalk** for the city's lighted extravaganza. This display of fishing Santas, leaping fish and mermaids is for anyone who's ever wanted to drive a car on the boardwalk. **Newport News City Park** also strings an impressive array of lights for its December display. All three charge a price per carload for admission. To beat the crowds go early in the evening and plan to drive through on a weeknight. The light displays start around Thanksgiving and run through New Year's Day.

23. Another December must is a trip to **Coleman Nursery** at 4934 High Street in Portsmouth, (757) 484-3426. The plant nursery plays Christmas to the hilt with its Christmas

KIDSTUFF

Crabbing

For sheer relaxation and low-budget fun there's no better pastime than crabbing, and kids love it. For a true Insider, crabbing is one of the best things to do in warm weather. With the constant need to check to see if a crab has latched onto the bait, this is a perfect activity for children who may not be patient enough for fishing. Crabbing is easy to do in the Chesapeake Bay region, which is blessed with an abundance of blue crabs plus access to tidal waters where the crabs like to hide.

To get started all you need is a sturdy piece of twine, a bony chicken part and a sinker. A five-foot or longer crab net also is helpful for hauling in the catch. Another must is a small cooler to hold the crabs. Just tie a chicken neck or wing onto a long piece of twine and add some kind of a weight. Even an old bolt will work. It's best if you can get the string long enough to reach the bottom of the river. Lower the string, hold on and wait for a gentle tug that means a crab is nibbling. Haul up the rig and scoop up the crab in your net. Be sure to watch out for the crab's powerful pinchers.

For a more sophisticated system you can buy a $2 ready-made, twine-and-weight crabbing rig that includes a string, a weight and a clip for holding the bait. Our preference is for a collapsible cotton net that costs less than $5. It has a hook for attaching the bait. All you need to do is attach a long twine. This gear makes it easier for kids to not drop a crab feeding on the chicken. If you really get into crabbing, you can advance to metal collapsible crab pots or a commercial pot that you leave in place for awhile. Most area hardware and sporting goods stores carry crabbing paraphernalia.

The best places to crab are calm tidal waters where the water is salty. If you're lucky enough to have access to a private pier on a river or creek, you can crab to your heart's content. When that's not possible look for public areas where you don't see any "No Crabbing" signs. If the sign isn't there, then it's probably okay to drop your line into the water and see what happens.

Only a few simple tools are needed for crabbing.

Photo: Sally Kirby Hartman

Some potential public crabbing spots to check out are:

The Narrows along 64th Street in Virginia Beach in First Landing/Seashore State Park.

Back Bay in Virginia Beach's Sandbridge area. Try the shore there across from the Little Island Fishing Pier.

Beside the Lynnhaven Inlet Bridge on Shore Drive in Virginia Beach as well as on the nearby giant mound of sand on the Norfolk side of the bridge.

The shore near the boat ramp on the Lafayette River in Norfolk. This is behind The Virginia Zoo.

(Continued on next page)

The foot of any bridge in the area that's on the Elizabeth River, Lafayette River, Broad Creek or Western Branch of the Elizabeth River.

The bridge at Little Creek in Norfolk, which is on Shore Drive just north of Little Creek Road.

The public boat ramp at City Park in Portsmouth, which is off Portsmouth Boulevard and City Park Avenue.

Commercial fishing piers charge about $5 to let you crab or fish there. But paying for the privilege is a surefire way of knowing it's okay to drop your line. Choices include Harrison's Pier, (757) 587-9630, and Willoughby Bay Marina, (757) 588-2663, in Norfolk's Ocean View area and the Lynnhaven Inlet Fishing Pier east of Lynnhaven Inlet in Virginia Beach, (757) 428-2333. As a recreational crabber you can use up to two crab pots for each person. There's no limit on the number of baited strings you drop in the water. Each crabber can keep one bushel of crabs a day. We tend to toss back our entire catch since we usually snare small crabs. By law, you can only keep hard crabs measuring at least 5 inches across the top shell.

Wonderland. Two buildings showcase dozens of animated Christmas scenes of animals, Santa and elves and even a circus. For many area families, visiting Coleman's is a holiday ritual. Admission costs $.25 for children and $.50 for adults. Arm your kids with handfuls of pennies to toss at the elaborate displays. All donations go to charity. There also is a carousel as well as well-stocked shops to tempt you with candy, Christmas decorations, plants and Virginia food products.

24. To try scaling some new heights, sign yourself and your child up for a session at the **Rock Gym** at 5049 Southern Boulevard in Virginia Beach. In a $10 introductory class you'll learn to use the right equipment as well as basic techniques needed to scale the gym's bumpy walls. Call (757) 499-8347 for times and details.

25. Buy your child a membership to the **Hunter House Victorian Museum**, 240 W. Freemason Street, Norfolk, (757) 623-9814. It is for ages 4 through 12. The membership entitles

Young climbers try out one of the hands-on exhibits at the Children's Museum of Virginia.

Photo: Courtesy of Portsmouth Convention and Visitors Bureau

KIDSTUFF

them to a newsletter that includes games and stories, and they also get invited to monthly programs scheduled for April through December. These range from croquet and tea parties on the lawn to turn-of-the-century crafts programs.

26. Plan some day trips to **Williamsburg, Yorktown, Jamestown, Hampton and Newport News** to soak up history that spans from the settling of the country right to the Space Age (see our Daytrips chapter.)

While on the Peninsula, see some of its other attractions that children love, such as the **Virginia Air and Space Center** and the restored carousel next door in Hampton or the **Virginia Living Museum** and **Mariners Museum** in Newport News. Anyone enamored with the Civil War will like **Fort Monroe** in Hampton. Another possibility is the petting zoo and menagerie of exotic animals maintained by the Newport News SPCA. Scenic Newport News Park is one of the largest city parks in the country. See our Daytrips chapter for more information.

Kids love the several miniparks along the boardwalk in Virginia Beach.

Photo: Courtesy of the City of Virginia Beach

27. Satisfy your sweet tooth with a free tour of **Rowena's** cake, jelly and jam factory. The aroma of Rowena's pound cakes alone is worth the visit. This Norfolk business delights in showing young visitors the ropes - from cake and jam-making to the packing and labeling process. Call ahead at (757) 627-8699 to book a tour.

28. On the weekend before Halloween take the annual **Ghost Walk** in Portsmouth to learn about the spooky legends of historic Olde Towne and its houses. Advance tickets are a must for this sellout event. For information call the Portsmouth Convention and Visitors Bureau at (757) 393-5327 or (757) 393-5111. Another holiday event to check out is a ghostly re-enactment at **Fort Norfolk**. Typically held on the weekend before Halloween, this tour of the early 19th-century Norfolk fort teaches history in a fun way. Call (757) 625-1720 for details. If you're not faint of heart, board the "tram of terror" for the **Vietnam Veterans Haunted Forest** ride at the Norfolk Botanical Garden. It's held on the two weekends before Halloween and always sells out. Get tickets early. Note: the scary ride will probably terrify young children. Call (757) 498-2541.

29. Attend some of the many weekend festivals that go on throughout the year. Children love the music and funnel cakes and other festival food. Some favorites include **Virginia Beach's Neptune Festival**, **Norfolk's Harborfest** and **Portsmouth's Seawall Festival**. For a festival calendar call Virginia Beach's BeachEvents at 800-VA-BEACH, Norfolk's FestEvents at (757) 441-2345, and Portsmouth's Ports Events at (757) 393-9933 for details.

30. To keep up with children's activities pick up a copy of *Tidewater Parent*, which is published monthly and distributed for free at grocery stores, child-care facilities, fitness centers and many other locations. Each issue of this tabloid newspaper features a comprehensive calendar of events with many ideas to entertain the family, (757) 363-7085. Reading the weekly *Port Folio* and *The Virginian-Pilot's* Friday "Daily Break" section also help keep you on top of fun family events.

Annual Events

LOOK FOR:
• Monthly Annual
Event Schedule

Just about 25 years ago, the city of Norfolk threw a party called Harborfest. Organizers arranged for a fleet of majestic tall ships to visit the city's downtown waterfront. They put up tents and filled them with music, beer and food. A handful of people came, these authors among them, and had a blast. The next year, that handful returned and brought lots of friends—and those revelers returned with more friends the next year. Eventually, Harborfest grew to become one of the largest summer festivals on the East Coast, and the prototype for many, many more local celebrations.

While few parties match Harborfest for volume and intensity, we have festivals to celebrate everything from the local strawberry harvest to the king of rock and roll himself, Mr. Elvis Presley. Throw in the regular celebrations of our many ethnic heritages, music festivals, al fresco art shows, big sporting events and the traditional holidays, and you can have a very full social calendar.

Spring and summer are festival season in Hampton Roads. That's when groups such as Virginia Beach's Beachevents, Norfolk Festevents, and Portsmouth's Ports Events kick into high gear. Their missions are to help the public utilize the refurbished areas of their respective cities. At the Beach, we're talking about the Boardwalk. In Norfolk, that's the Town Point Park/Waterside and Ocean View Beach areas. In Portsmouth the action is along the downtown riverfront. All the sites benefit from waterfront locations with their cooling breezes during the hot summer months, and both have proved to be popular spots for concerts, festivals and other family activities.

Those are the hot spots for festival-type activities, but they are by no means the only places to find a party. The Virginia Waterfront International Arts Festival takes place at venues throughout Hampton Roads in the tourism shoulder season of early spring. Norfolk's Azalea Festival is a weeklong celebration that takes place at sites throughout the city. The cities of Chesapeake and Suffolk have big annual parties on their turf too. And in addition to the annual events and festivals listed here, there are also hundreds of smaller community-generated events, including chamber of commerce outings and fund-raising galas for area museums and nonprofit agencies.

Before you become a card-carrying Hampton Roads party-goer, you should know the rules. First, come hungry. Food vendors literally come out of the woodwork with delicacies for every taste. The prices may be a bit higher than the local fast food drive-through, but what could match the thrill of eating a steaming pit-cooked barbecue sandwich while juggling an ice-cold beer and admiring a summer sunset?

Second, if you want peace and quiet, stay home. With few exceptions, the events listed here feature live entertainment broadcast nice and loud.

Finally, know that the big events have instituted transportation systems to help ease traffic congestion. Don't even think about driving to the heart of Harborfest, the Chesapeake Jubilee or the Neptune Festival at the Beach. Park at one of the designated pickup locations, and you can be zipped to partyland for a very reasonable charge and with very little gridlock. Check *The Virginian-Pilot* or other local papers for details close to party time.

One special note for newcomers to our great region. Volunteers put together most of the events listed here. If you're new to the area and want to meet some fine people, jump on the party-making bandwagon. Not only will you gain hands-on experience (and a VIP parking pass!), but you'll also get the chance to work with business people and community leaders you might not otherwise have the good fortune to meet.

For information on some of the major events contact one of the following organizations and get their calendars: the Beach Events, 2100 Parks Avenue, Virginia Beach 23451, (757) 491-7866; Norfolk Festevents, 120 W. Main Street, Norfolk 23510, (757) 441-2345; and Ports Events, 355 Crawford Street, Portsmouth 23704, 393-9933.

Unless otherwise noted, all events listed are free and open to the public. So get the spirit. Get involved and go have some fun!

January

Whale-Watching Trips
Rudee Inlet
• (757) 437-4949

One of our most spectacular annual events happens in the late-winter/early spring, when the whales migrate through the offshore waters of Virginia Beach. Every year, the Virginia Marine Science Museum sponsors boat trips to watch the gentle giants of the ocean at play. Trips run every day until early March, except Tuesday and Thursday and tickets are less than $15. For more information, call the museum at (757) 437-4949. Trips leave from the Virginia Beach Fishing Center, 200 Winston-Salem Avenue.

February

A Taste of Portsmouth
Holiday Inn-Olde Towne, Portsmouth
• (757) 393-9933

Experience the best that Portsmouth's restaurants have to offer at this annual one-day food extravaganza.

March

St. Patrick's Day Parade
Granby St. and Ocean View Ave., Norfolk
• (757) 597-3548

A family favorite in Ocean View, the area's largest Irish stronghold, this annual parade is

The Seawall Festival is one of the city's most popular festivals.

Photo: Courtesy of Portsmouth Convention and Visitors Bureau

ANNUAL EVENTS

produced by the local Knights of Columbus and features floats, marching units and all sorts of shamrock shenanigans. It's a real treat for leprechauns of all ages. It is held on the Saturday before St. Patrick's Day and is one of the biggest St. Patrick's Day parades on the East Coast.

Shamrock Marathon and Sports Fest
Atlantic Ave., Virginia Beach
• (757) 481-5090

Not all sporting events count as festivals, but this one always draws a big crowd of enthusiastic supporters who line up along the race course (Atlantic Avenue) for a marathon cheering and clapping session. An annual March event since 1972, the marathon is held on a Saturday near St. Paddy's Day. The Shamrock Marathon is one of Virginia's most popular marathons, averaging 2,000 runners. There's the Open 8K Run, Masters 8K Run, 5K Fitness Walk, Children's Marathon and Sports Trade Show. The race takes place along the boardwalk, through Fort Story and along the entire oceanfront and ends at the Pavilion.

The Greening of Ghent and the Wearin' o' the Green on Granby St.
20th St. and Manteo Ave. and
100 block of Granby St., Norfolk
• (757) 441-2345

Everybody's Irish at St. Patrick's Day celebrations in Ghent and downtown. No matter which location you choose, there is guaranteed to be dancing in the street to live music and lots of refreshments. These annual evening parties held on St. Patrick's Day.

Crawford Bay Crew Classic
Portsmouth City Park, Portsmouth
• (757) 393-9933

Rowing teams from waterworthy colleges and universities converge on the Elizabeth River in Portsmouth to row to victory. One of our classier sporting events, this is one to pack a tailgate lunch for. You'll think you're on the shores of the Thames.

April

Easter Sunrise Services and Celebrations
Various locations
• (757) 441-2345

Various denominations of Norfolk churches sponsor an annual outdoor Easter Sunrise Service in Town Point Park on the Downtown

Norfolk waterfront. There's one at the Beach, too, at the Cape Henry Cross on the Fort Story Army Base. Virginia Beach hosts an egg-cellent party for the little ones on Easter weekend. It is usually scheduled for the Saturday afternoon before Easter, at the 24th Street park at the Beach. Check newspaper listings for details.

International Azalea Festival
Various locations, Norfolk
• (757) 622-2312

This weeklong celebration is the granddaddy of area festivals, the oldest in the region and a favorite of the military community it honors. The Azalea Festival started in 1953 to acknowledge Norfolk's role as headquarters for the North Atlantic Treaty Organization's (NATO) Supreme Allied Command Atlantic (SACLANT). NATO countries from all over the world select one young woman to represent their country in the Festival's court, with the candidate of the Most Honored Nation serving as Queen. Packed with pomp and circumstance, the festival's highlights include the flag raising at SACLANT headquarters, Saturday's Grand Parade through Downtown Norfolk, coronation of the Queen and her court in Norfolk's beautiful botanical garden and the City of Norfolk Azalea Ball on Saturday evening. Complementing these events is a weekend of entertainment at Town Point Park and a super air show held Saturday and Sunday at the Naval Air Station Norfolk. The City of Norfolk and Hampton Roads Chamber of Commerce cosponsor the event.

Virginia Waterfront International Arts Festival
Various locations
• (757) 664-6492

This 25-day arts festival started in 1997 to lure visitors to the area during the most glorious off-season weeks of the year; namely, the last part of April and the first part of May. Savvy locals know to buy their arts festival tickets early since performances usually sell out. The festival hosts dozens of internationally renowned artists on stages throughout the entire region. Performances by the Virginia Opera, the Virginia Symphony, the Virginia Stage Company, and other local arts groups are also incorporated into the festival.

Historic Garden Week
Various locations
• (804) 644-7776

Peek into the lifestyles of the rich and tasteful during the last week in April when both historic homes and exquisite private residences are open for touring. Initiated in 1929, this annual event attracts thousands of visitors to the meticulously maintained homes and gardens that reach their peak beauty during this spring month. Proceeds from the event provide for the restoration of gardens throughout Virginia. To receive a guidebook for all homes included in the Garden Tour, contact the Historic Garden Week Headquarters at the number above or write them at 12 E. Franklin Street, Richmond 23219.

Spring Wine Fest
24th Street Park,
Virginia Beach
• (757) 491-7866
Sample a variety of new wines during this oceanfront festival that includes musical entertainment.

Suffolk Spring Spectacular
Suffolk Municipal Airport, Rt. 13 , Suffolk
• (757) 539-2111
New in 1997, this three-day festival features more than 40 hot-air balloons, skydiving exhibits and live music. It is sponsored by city-run Suffolk Festivals Inc.

May

Elizabeth River Run
Hampton and Terminal Blvds., Norfolk
• (757) 421-2602
Virginia's largest road race is held every May in Norfolk. The 10K course stretches from the Armed Forces Staff College near the Naval Base to Town Point Park in downtown Norfolk so find your spot to cheer on the thousands of runners flooding the streets.

Ocean View Beach Festival
Ocean View Beach, Norfolk
• (757) 583-0000
This beach-front festival provides pure family fun, and it's been doing that since 1978. During a three-day weekend there's a full-blown carnival along with music, food and fireworks. Sponsored by the Kiwanis Club of Ocean View Beach and Ocean View Events LTD, this event benefits various charities.

TGIF Concerts
Town Point Park, Norfolk
• (757) 441-2345
May signals the annual kickoff for the TGIF

concerts in Downtown Norfolk's Town Point Park. Wind down the week listening to national pop-alternative performers in concert on selected Friday evenings from 5 to 9 PM. Each event, with hot music and cold beer, benefits a local charity. Admission costs $3 after 6 PM but is free for those 12 and younger. Beer sales benefit local charities.

The Greek Festival
Greek Orthodox Church Annunciation, 7220 Granby St., Norfolk
• (757) 440-0500
Talk about good things to eat! Every year this annual celebration of the rich heritage of our Greek community draws throngs of locals who set aside their diet-for-summer plans to sample the divine dishes prepared by some of our community's best cooks. After you're full, roll out to see works of Greek artists and many handmade arts and crafts. It lasts four days, starts at noon each day and ends later in the evening.

Art Explosure
Town Point Park, Norfolk
• (757) 441-2345
Contemporary oils to photographs, ceramics to watercolors—if it's art, it's at this annual arts festival that started in 1971. More than 200 visual, performing and literary artists are on hand for the event that also features food vendors, music and a children's area. The festival is held Friday through Sunday on Mother's Day weekend.

AFR'AM Fest
Town Point Park, Norfolk
• (757) 456-1743
This weekend-long festival is held annually during Memorial Day weekend in Norfolk's Town Point Park. It celebrates the accomplishments of African-Americans through music, dance, theater, art and educational displays, and it always draws a huge crowd.

Beach Music Weekend
Virginia Beach Boardwalk
• (757) 491-7866
Shag til you drop—it's the Beach Music Festival at Virginia Beach! Crowd in to hear national beach music stars take the stage for this annual three-day event held on the boardwalk. This event started in 1994 and has just gained momentum.

INSIDERS' TIP
Outdoor entertainment is exhilirating but don't forget your suncscreen.

ANNUAL EVENTS

The Cock Island Race is the biggest and best sailing event on the East Coast with over 300 sailboats.

Photo: Portsmouth Convention and Visitors Bureau

Pungo Strawberry Festival
Virginia Beach
• (757) 721-6001

Be tickled pink with the variety of strawberry cuisine offered in this rural Virginia Beach harvest celebration held near the intersection of Indian River and Princess Anne roads. Live entertainment is always on hand so you can dance away the calories, but don't miss the arts and craft show, petting zoo, military display area or the pig races! This favorite family event has been the high point of Pungo's strawberry season since 1983.

Worrell 1000
Oceanfront, Virginia Beach
• (757) 422-1000

This one-of-a-kind sailboat race was reborn in 1997 after being inactive for eight years. The grueling catamaran race starts in Ft. Lauderdale, Fla., and finishes in Virginia Beach 12 days later. There is great fanfare at the finish line.

The Chesapeake Jubilee
Chesapeake Park
• (757) 547-2118

Not to be outdone by neighboring cities, Chesapeake pulls out all the stops for this annual free-for-all in Chesapeake Park. Top-name entertainment, carnival rides, food of every description and more is the order of the week-

end. This is one event to check into shuttle service to the festival site, which doesn't have lots of good, paved parking. Check the newspaper listings for park-and-ride locations. The Jubilee is sponsored by The City of Chesapeake and Hampton Roads Chamber of Commerce.

Big Bands on the Bay Concert and Dance Series
Ocean View Beach Park, Norfolk
• (757) 441-2345

Slip on your dancing shoes each Sunday from May through September. Various big bands are ensconced under a gazebo along the Chesapeake Bay. There's a great dance floor. Bring a lawn chair for resting between favorite numbers. Admission is free.

June

Harborfest
Norfolk
• (757) 627-5330

If most of Hampton Roads' festivals are whirlwinds of activity, Harborfest is a tornado. More than 250,000 people attend this annual waterfront celebration, which began in 1976. The star of the East Coast annual waterfront spectaculars, Harborfest is a nonstop flurry of live entertainment, sailing ships, water and air shows, more food than you could possibly sample in a weekend, and the most singular display of fireworks you'll witness all year. The crowds can be overwhelming, so use the efficient shuttle service available from a multitude of convenient locations. It's held on the first weekend in June.

Cock Island Race
Portsmouth Seawall
• (757) 393-9933

This is the largest sailboat race on the East Coast, featuring a total of 300 boats in various classes and assorted festivities throughout the weekend. Spectators can watch from the Portsmouth Seawall or from The Waterside in Norfolk. A festival atmosphere prevails, especially during the evenings, when the sails are down.

Seawall Festival
Portsmouth Waterfront
• (757) 393-9933

To mirror the activity on Norfolk's waterfront during Harborfest, Portsmouth answers with its own festival on the first weekend in June. It is geared toward children and their families. Live entertainment and food galore compete for your attention just across the Elizabeth River.

Beach Street USA
Virginia Beach Boardwalk
• (757) 491-7866

This family festival takes place each evening until September along the Virginia Beach boardwalk. It started in 1998 as a collaboration between the City of Virginia Beach and Busch Gardens. Featured are all kinds of musicians, jugglers, and other entertainers doing impromptu performances.

Dolphin Watching Boat Trips
Rudee Inlet, Virginia Beach
• (757) 437-2628

Two-hour boat trips run daily until October. They are sponsored by the Virginia Marine Science Museum, which sends along informed docents or employees to talk about the playful dolphins leaping beside the boat.

Viva Elvis Festival
Virginia Beach Boardwalk
• (757) 491-7866

Almost everybody's heard of the Skydiving Elvises, but how about Black Elvis, the African-American Elvis impersonator? Or El Viz, the Hispanic Elvis impersonator? You'll find all kinds of hound dogs, plus karaoke opportuni-

ties at this truly innovative festival, which takes place at the 17th and 24th Street stages on the Virginia Beach Boardwalk. The Elvis festival started on a whim in 1994 and has become an annual phenomenon. We wonder if vendors sell Elvis' favorite fried peanut butter and banana sandwiches at this one?

North American Sand Soccer Championships
Virginia Beach Oceanfront
• (757) 456-0578

It's hard enough to walk in the sand. Imagine running up and down a sand soccer field for four quarters! That's what the athletes in this international tournament do every year. It's held on the beach, from 2nd to 7th streets.

Boardwalk Art Show and Festival
Virginia Beach Boardwalk
• (757) 425-0000

This juried art show sponsored by Contemporary Art Center of Virginia, draws artists of every medium from all over the country, who set up their masterpieces on the boardwalk in Virginia Beach along the Atlantic Ocean. The show has been going on since 1955. You'll see everything from paintings to photography to ceramics to outlandishly underclad spectators as you stroll through the area's largest outdoor art gallery. If you tire of the art check out the musical performances, food vendors and adult libations for sale.

July

Great American Independence Day Celebration
Town Point Park, Norfolk
• (757) 441-2345

Celebrate the Fourth of July with children's activities, live patriotic music, down-home food, fireworks and old-fashioned family fun. The fireworks start just after dark, about 9 PM. If you don't want to venture downtown, try spreading a blanket on the banks of the Hague in Ghent and watching from there.

July 4 Celebration
Mt. Trashmore, 300 Edwin Dr., Virginia Beach
• (757) 471-5884

The City of Virginia Beach throws its annual Independence Day celebration at Mt. Trashmore featuring fireworks, music, carnival rides, food and fun for everyone. There is also a fireworks display at the oceanfront.

Bayou Boogaloo and Cajun Food Festival
Town Point Park, Norfolk
• (757) 441-2345

This one is hot . . . literally! You'll find spicy foods and equally spicy music by nationally known entertainers. If zydeco music and New Orleans fare get you swaying, you'll love the seafood gumbo, steamed crawfish and crawfish etouffe. Since 1989 this festival has featured Cajun dance lessons, armadillo races and performances by nationally known artists such as the Neville Brothers. For $5 you can buy a pass that lets you attend all the concerts. If you bring $5 in Dollar Store receipts, four people get in free. Those 12 and under are always admitted for free.

Princess Anne Park Art & Craft Festival
Princess Anne Park, Virginia Beach
• (757) 471-5884

More than 100 artisans from across the country show their wares under the trees at the park. Live bands, food vendors, and children's entertainment add to the fun.

Blues on the Boardwalk
17th Street State, Virginia Beach
• (757) 491-7866

Bring your lawn chair and settle back for free Tuesday evening concerts featuring local blues musicians. There are usually two headliners starting at 7:30 p.m. This weekly showcase is co-sponsored by the Natchel Blues Network and Beachevents. The concerts run through the end of August.

TGOV Celebration
Ocean View Beach Park, Norfolk
• (757) 441-2345

Wind down the week with free Friday concerts along the Chesapeake Bay at this Thank Goodness It's Ocean View gathering. The fun runs from 6 to 10 PM each Friday with a variety of local bands performing. Activities center around the park's gazebo.

August

A Faire for the Arts
High Street Landing, Portsmouth
• (757) 393-8481

Here's the perfect weekend to snap up an original piece of art while enjoying a variety of performing artists. Every year, more professional and amateur artists join the respected list of artists on hand to discuss their work with show visitors. This event is always on the last week of August.

Gospelrama
Olde Towne Waterfront, Portsmouth
• (757) 393-0318

This music festival promotes unity through gospel music, and related family entertainment.

Low Rent Regatta
Chick's Beach
• (757) 460-2238

This competition for boardsails and catamarans got its tongue-in-cheek name from its snootier neighbors, who have traditionally called the Chick's Beach location "low rent." The Chick's Beach locals decided to turn that stigma to their advantage and now host one of the summer's most popular sailing events. The Low Rent Regatta is held every Labor Day weekend on the Bay at Chick's Beach. If you're heading from the resort area, follow Shore Drive over the Lesner Bridge and take a right on any street. Eventually, you'll find the Bay.

Virginia Beach East Coast Surfing Championships
1st to 9th streets, Virginia Beach
• (757) 499-8822

This is a serious Beach tradition started in 1962. Any local surf shop will be abuzz with the news about this August tournament. Even if you don't know the first thing about the boards, it's a great excuse to get a lot of sun while watching the competition—or the scantily clad spectators.

Chesapeake Bay Art Show
Ocean View Beach Park, Norfolk
• (757) 588-4805

Since 1962 local and regional artists have showcased their talents at this summer show along the Chesapeake Bay. You'll also find live music and food at this free event sponsored by the Chesapeake Bay Art Foundation.

September

Pontiac-GMC American Music Festival
Various locations, Virginia Beach
• (757) 491-7866

National acts perform at the oceanfront parks as well as on an enormous stage set up on the sand. Performers in recent years have included The Beach Boys (naturally), Blood Sweat & Tears, The Temptations, The Four Tops, Wilson Pickett, America, Billy Ray Cyrus, and Kool & The Gang. Ticket prices range from free for some concerts to around $10 for headliners. This four-day event started in 1993 during Labor Day weekend as a way to wind down the summer.

Reggae On The River
Town Point Park, Norfolk
• (757) 441-2345

Transport yourself to an exotic locale at this two-day island musical festival. In addition to the music, you can enjoy flavorful island cuisine, cool beverages and a retail shopping area specializing in Caribbean arts and crafts. A $5 festival pass buys admission to all concerts. If you bring a $5 or more Dollar Store receipt four people get in free. Children younger than 12 are always free.

Town Point Jazz and Blues Festival
Town Point Park, Norfolk
• (757) 441-2345

You get to see the hottest jazz artists around for free! It's a hot, jazzy weekend on Norfolk's

downtown Waterfront. At last count, more than 60,000 jazz lovers traveled to Norfolk to get in tune with world-class jazz acts. A $5 festival pass lets you attend all concerts or bring a $5 or more Dollar Store receipt and four people get in free. Children 12 and younger always attend for free.

The Neptune Festival
Various locations, Virginia Beach
• (757) 498-0215

Virginia Beach's premier festival, this five-day family affair includes activities that range from the Sand Castle Classic to a spectacular air show, not to mention tons of fresh seafood and top-billed entertainment. King Neptune, chosen from the city's business and civic leaders, leads his court of young outstanding women through the festivities, right up to the royal fireworks display. King Neptune's Ball, a formal affair, is one of the highlights of the Beach's social season.

World Championship Rodeo
Princess Anne Park, Virginia Beach
• (757) 721-7786

More than 250 of the best bronco and bull

> **INSIDERS' TIP**
> The nearby Eastern Shore area is the scene for two very popular annual events—the Chincoteague Seafood Festival in May and the Eastern Shore Harvest Fest in October. See our Eastern Shore chapter for details.

King Neptune is the official symbol for the Neptune Festival. A real-life King Neptune is chosen from the city's civic and business leaders for the festival.

Photo:Courtesy of Virginia Departmen of Tourism

ANNUAL EVENTS

The Umoja Festival celebrates African-American culture along the Portsmouth waterfront.

Photo: Courtesy of Virginia Department of Tourism

riders in the country compete during this International professional Rodeo Association event.

Umoja Festival
Portsmouth Waterfront, Portsmouth
• (757) 393-8481

Umoja means "Unity" in Swahili, and that's what this weekend festival symbolizes. It celebrates African-American art, cuisine and culture. In addition to music and entertainment, special tours of historic Portsmouth emphasize African-American history.

October

Virginia Town Point Wine Festival
Town Point Park, Norfolk
• (757) 441-2345

Step aside Joe Bob. Sometimes we can be downright sophisticated. Whether you fancy a Cabernet Sauvignon blanc from the heart of the Shenandoah or a rich Burgundy from Williamsburg, this palate-pleasing event is for you. Sample products from more than 25 premium wineries throughout the Commonwealth along with gourmet Virginia foods. This started in 1997 and has become one of the largest outdoor wine festivals in the state. General admission is $5. Expect to pay $15 in advance ($20 at the gate) for a ticket that lets you sample

everything. You also can reserve a table. Be sure to call ahead for details on pricing.

Virginia Children's Festival and Halloween Spooktacular
Town Point Park, Norfolk
• (757) 441-2345

If anyone less than 4 feet tall lives in your home, get them to Town Point Park in Norfolk for this magical day! Kids on Parade, costumed characters, nationally known children's entertainers, giant puppets and more attract kids of all ages for this all-day event. Everything is free and geared for those 10 and under. This magical event started in 1988 and has become a family tradition.

Olde Towne Ghost Walk
Portsmouth Historic District
• (757) 397-2796 or 399-2497

Be spooked out of your trick or treat as actors dressed for the ghoulish occasion tell tales of ghosts and goblins while you tour through the historic district in Portsmouth. The tour is held on the Friday right before Halloween. Advance tickets are a must and cost $5.

Peanut Fest
Suffolk Municipal Airport, Rt. 13, Suffolk
• (757) 539-2111

It's really worth the drive (about 20 minutes from Norfolk) to the area's "nuttiest" festival, held at Suffolk's Municipal Airport. There's entertainment, a parade, a phenomenal Shrimp Feast and so much more—all to celebrate the area's top crop.

Blues and Brews
24th Street Park, Virginia Beach
• **(757) 491-7866**

Blues music and microbrews from some of the country's best small breweries star in this two-day festival.

November

Holidays in the City
Various locations,
Norfolk and
Portsmouth
• **(757) 627-1757 and**
(757) 393-5394

This celebration begins in November with a Grand Illumination of the downtown Norfolk and Portsmouth skylines. As miles of tiny white lights spring to life along downtown buildings, a parade on the Saturday before Thanksgiving sets off to signify that the holiday season has begun. The celebration continues throughout December, with a Lighted Boat Parade, trolley tours, strolling carolers and the like.

INSIDERS' TIP
If you're new in town and looking for ways to fill up your social calendar, volunteer to help a local charity put on its annual fundraiser. You'll make new friends and have a terrific party to attend in the end.

December

Holly Festival
Various locations, Norfolk
• **(757) 668-7098**

This annual event to benefit The Children's Hospital of The King's Daughters brings out the very best of the season. The Holly Festival of Trees is a three-day event featuring a gala auction of decorated trees and a day of family fun. For an Insider's look at very special private residences, there's the Holly Homes Tour of historic homes or newer custom-built homes in Virginia Beach and Norfolk; for all-out glitz and glamour, there's the Holly Ball. Ticket prices run the gamut. Some events are free, some run in the $20 range, and tickets for the Holly Ball cost $275 per couple.

Holiday Festivities
Throughout Hampton Roads

Grand illuminations, yuletide carols and good cheer can be found in every city in Hampton Roads. Yule logs are stoked to the max by

The Olde Towne Holiday Music Festival includes musical performances ranging from barbershop harmony and jazz to steel drums and brass ensemble tunes.

Photo: Courtesy of Portsmouth Convention and Visitors Bureau

ANNUAL EVENTS

Outdoor art shows on the Boardwalk are popular with locals and tourists.

Photo: Courtesy of Virginia Tourism Corporation

the spirit of the season. For those who prefer their holiday with 18th-century ambiance, Colonial Williamsburg's Grand Illumination is really a spectacular, and humbling, experience. Watch local papers for specific dates and times for all these special events.

First Night Norfolk
Various locations, Norfolk
• **(757) 441-2345**
This community-wide New Year's Eve celebration features visual and performing arts shows at more throughout downtown Norfolk. It includes a bonfire for burning regrets and fireworks. A family alternative to the typical New Year's revelry, First Night Norfolk attracted almost 30,000 participants its first year in 1996.

Garden of Lights
Norfolk Botanical Garden, Norfolk
• **(757) 441-5830**
More than 200,000 lighted displays give a new perspective to the garden. Load up the car and take a half-hour evening drive through the garden for a magical treat. The lights go on Thanksgiving weekend and stay on until New Year's Day.

Holiday Lights at the Beach
The Boardwalk, Virginia Beach
• **(757) 491-7866**
This is the only time of year you can drive

down the usually pedestrian-only boardwalk. This special trip is guaranteed to get you in the holiday spirit. You'll be surrounded by whimsical lighted holiday displays. They are lit Thanksgiving weekend and stay that way each night until after New Year's.

Olde Towne Holiday Music Festival
High Street, Portsmouth
• **(757) 393-9933**
There is definitely music in the air at this one-day festival. Carolers, jazz bands, church choirs, barbershop quartets, and every other group you can imagine line seven blocks of High Street starting at the waterfront. The event ends with fireworks at High Street Landing.

Olde Towne Historic Holiday Trolley Tours
Olde Towne, Portsmouth
• **(757) 393-3332**
Sit back and relax on a guided tour of Portsmouth's decked out Olde Towne Historic District. Tours run throughout most of the month. Stops include Trinity Episcopal Church and the Hill House. Refreshments are served along the way, and there's an option to include dinner before the tour at a selected Olde Towne restaurant.

The Arts

If you're from New York, Boston or some other metropolis, you may not expect Hampton Roads to have much to offer in the way of the arts. But open your eyes, ears and mind, and you will be pleasantly surprised.

Arts aficionados will find their calendars crammed from October through May with a full season of operas, plays, ballets, concerts, lectures and art exhibitions. The region keeps its residents and visitors culturally minded through the spring, with the 25-day Virginia Waterfront International Arts Festival. It has gained national acclaim since its inaugural year in 1997 as it has continued to bring in international musicians and dancers and is now the biggest annual arts event in Virginia.

Aside from this world-class event, south Hampton Roads offers about 100 arts groups that regularly perform and exhibit here. Since this region is a major metropolitan area only three hours from Washington, D.C., it's a regular stop on the traveling circuit that buses in talent ranging from the Bolshoi Ballet to the Sesame Street characters.

Local arts groups include large, professional organizations and shoe-string operations glued together by enthusiastic volunteers. Norfolk has traditionally been the region's cultural hub, but in recent years arts groups have sprung up in other area cities. To keep audiences happy, the symphony and other performing artists alternate performances between Norfolk and Virginia Beach.

For performing arts, the main stages in Norfolk are at Chrysler Hall, the Wells Theatre, the Harrison Opera House and the L. Douglas Wilder Performing Arts Center at Norfolk State University. Chrysler Hall, with 2,043 seats, is adjacent to the Scope arena at Brambleton and Monticello Avenues. It is Norfolk's all-purpose hall used for everything from the symphony to ballets and lectures. The Wells Theatre, with 677 seats, is home to the Virginia Stage Company but also welcomes other groups. It is at 110 E. Tazewell Street. The Harrison Opera House at 160 Virginia Beach Boulevard is home base for the Virginia Opera but shares its stage with other organizations. The city-owned theater has 1,680 seats. Norfolk also has a 300-seat auditorium in The Chrysler Museum at Olney Road and Mowbray Arch. The Wilder Performing Arts Center, the city's newest venue, is located on the NSU campus and seats 1,900. All these theaters are in or near downtown.

Concerts in Portsmouth frequently are at 2,000-seat Willett Hall, which sponsors a season of traveling Broadway shows and children's plays. The theater is at 3701 Willett Drive just off High Street. By 2001 Portsmouth will have another venue—a $10 million, 7,000-seat outdoor amphitheater it is building along its downtown waterfront. Virginia Beach has the 1,000-seat Pavilion Theater in the Pavilion Convention Center at 1000 19th Street. Across the street at 2200 Parks Avenue, the Contemporary Arts Center of Virginia, has a 262-seat auditorium. Performing groups also frequent stages at area colleges and schools throughout the region.

The hottest venue around may be the 20,000-seat outdoor GTE Virginia Beach Amphitheater. The $17.5 million amphitheater is located on Princess Anne Road adjacent to Princess Anne Park. Since its debut in 1996, the amphitheater has proved a smashing success, hosting such popular performers as Jimmy Buffett and Elton John. It has 7,500 covered seats and room for another 12,500 people to relax on blankets on the lawn.

Keeping tabs on all the arts groups can be a tough job. Each September *The Virginian-Pilot* and *Port Folio* weekly magazine publish annual arts calendars. These comprehensive listings are worth saving since they detail the entire season for most arts groups. To stay current on arts events, check *The Virginian-Pilot's* Friday and Sunday "Daily Break" sections and the weekly *Port Folio*. The publications do a good job of profiling arts groups and upcoming performances. The Cultural Alliance of Greater Hampton Roads, an umbrella organization that keeps an arts calendar, publishes an annual resource directory called Sketches that gives details on most arts groups. It costs $10 but is available in most area libraries. To obtain a copy of the directory call (757) 440-6628 or write the Cultural Alliance at 5200 Hampton Boulevard, Norfolk 23508.

Once you get a feel for the arts, you may want to hook up with one or more organizations. Since volunteers are the lifeblood of these groups, they'll be happy to see you. Most of the larger groups sell memberships or season tickets. These usually entitle you to newsletters, invitations to special events and gift-shop discounts. Many groups have guilds that let you do hands-on work.

INSIDERS' TIP

A few months before you move to a new community, subscribe to its local paper to get a clear picture of the cost of living, cultural events, and issues of local importance.

If you're between the ages of 22 and 45 you can join an affiliated organization for young adults. Membership fees are very reasonable, and this can be a great way to meet people and learn more about the arts. The Virginia Beach Center for the Arts sponsors Art & Co. The Chrysler Museum has For Art's Sake. The Virginia Symphony has Bravo. The Virginia Opera sponsors Phantoms of the Opera. These popular groups give an inside look at arts and culture. They serve educational, fund-raising and social functions and get members invited to posh members-only previews and parties. To join them call the sponsoring organization and talk to the membership department.

While all performing arts groups sell season tickets, feel free to sample their offerings by purchasing tickets to single performances. Most groups have two-for-one tickets in the annual Entertainment coupon books that are sold each December by various charities.

The Big Four

There are four dominant arts organizations in the region: The Chrysler Museum, the Virginia Opera, the Virginia Stage Company and the Virginia Symphony. All are large professional organizations with long histories and reputations that extend far beyond the region.

The Chrysler Museum
245 W. Olney Rd., Norfolk
• (757) 664-6200,

This is one of our favorite spots. There is so much to see that you can go time after time and not feel like you're peering at the same works. Founded in 1933 as the Norfolk Museum of Arts and Sciences, the museum changed its name in 1971 to honor the late Walter P. Chrysler Jr. Chrysler, the automobile heir and avid art collector, married a Norfolk native and made his home in the city. Many of the 30,000 pieces in the museum are from Chrysler's vast personal collection.

The museum has one of the largest art collections south of Washington, D.C., and is considered one of the best art museums in the

country. Its art library is the largest in the southeastern United States. The museum overlooks The Hague in the historic Ghent area. In 1998 it added 8,700 square feet to its gallery and education space.

The permanent collection is an eclectic one, with pieces dating from 2700 B.C. to the present. The museum is renowned for its 8,000-piece glass collection including the works of Tiffany, Lalique and other masters. The Chrysler has the second-largest collection of Tiffany glass and a special room to house it. The museum is known for its French and Italian paintings as well as its photography collection. Among the museum's most famous holdings are works by Bernini, Renoir, Gauguin, Cassatt and Matisse.

The Chrysler Museum is the permanent home of the Norfolk Mace, the silver symbol of the city created in 1753 (see the close-up in our History chapter). Besides the permanent collection, there are always special exhibitions that stay for several months. An elegant cafe, Phantoms, is inside the museum and serves lunch and Sunday brunch.

With its solemn guards and subdued lighting, the museum seems like an adults-only place. However, it does welcome children, and on many Sunday afternoons it goes all out with family activities that range from scavenger hunts to crafts and storytellers. The museum also operates three historic houses: the Adam Thoroughgood House in Virginia Beach and the Moses Myers House and Willoughby-Baylor House in Norfolk. (See our Attractions chapter).

The museum is open from 10 AM until 4 PM Wednesday through Saturday, 1 to 5 PM on Sunday and is closed on Monday. On the first Thursday of each month the museum is open until 9 PM. Admission costs $7, $5 for senior citizens and students 6 and older. On Wednesdays admission is free for everyone.

The Virginia Opera
Harrison Opera House,
160 E. Virginia Beach Blvd., Norfolk
• (757) 627-9545, (757) 623-1223

This professional opera company has earned national acclaim and has taken some of its performances on the road to South America. The Norfolk-based company was formed in 1975 and performs regular series in Norfolk, Richmond and northern Virginia. It is led by founding general and artistic director Peter Mark, who also is the opera's conductor. During a typical season it produces four major operas that star professional national and international singers. In the past, the opera has premiered several works by Thea Musgrave, wife of Peter Mark. Among the premieres generating international acclaim were *Harriet, The Woman Called Moses*; *A Christmas Carol*; *Mary Queen of Scots*; and *Simon Bolivar*.

The opera house is named after two local residents—the late Stanley Harrison and his wife Edythe, the opera's founding board president.

Virginia Stage Company
Wells Theatre,
Monticello and Tazewell Sts., Norfolk
• (757) 627-6988, (757) 627-1234

Founded in 1978, this is a professional, non-profit regional theater company. It puts on a dynamite season with the help of actors drawn primarily from New York and Los Angeles.

It's worth a trip to the theater just to see its home, the venerable Wells Theatre. This elaborate Beaux Arts structure was built in 1912 and is a National Historic Landmark.

Virginia Symphony
P.O. Box 26, Norfolk
• (757) 466-3060, (757) 623-2310

This is one of the busiest performing arts

The d'Art Center in Norfolk, a cooperative center for about 30 local artists, is a fun place to wander and witness the creation of art.

Photo: Courtesy of Norfolk Convention and Visitors Bureau

groups around with more than 100 concerts a year. The symphony, which was founded in 1919, has a core group of 50 professional musicians and about 40 others who play as needed. It is led by JoAnn Falletta, one of America's most promising young conductors. The orchestra performs at Chrysler Hall, the Pavilion Theatre in Virginia Beach, Ogdon Hall in Hampton and Phi Beta Kappa Hall in Williamsburg.

Besides its classical series, the symphony produces pops, dance, Mozart and family concert series. You can also catch its players at free outdoor concerts at some area festivals. One of our favorite events is the occasional outdoor pops concert the symphony performs at the Norfolk Botanical Garden.

Both the classical and pops series feature prominent guest artists.

Other Arts Organizations

Other arts groups may not be as large as the four listed above, but they have plenty to offer in the way of talent and diversity. The following is a sampling of area arts organizations.

Dance

Virginia Beach Ballet
4718 Larkspur Sq.
Shopping Ctr.,
Virginia Beach
• **(757) 495-0989**
This amateur ballet organization offers productions featuring classical ballet and modern dance. Classes are held at the Virginia Beach studio at Larkspur Square Shopping Center. Performance sites vary.

Virginia Ballet Theater
134 W. Olney Rd., Norfolk
• **(757) 622-4822**
This is a professional company that performs regularly and offers a variety of classes at its studio on W. Olney Road in Norfolk. Performance sites vary.

Lectures

Virginia Beach Forum
Pavilion Theater, Virginia Beach
• **(757) 490-3585**
This series began with a bang in 1996 with

talk show host Larry King. Other interesting speakers, such as satirist P.J. O'Rourke, followed. Lectures are held in Virginia Beach at the Pavilion Theater. Each talk costs about $25.

Virginia Wesleyan College Series
Various on-campus buildings,
Virginia Wesleyan College, Virginia Beach
• **(757) 455-3200**
This free campus series covers a variety of topics from story telling to poetry to current events. Recent speakers included Dr. Jeanne J. Kilpatrick, former United Nations representative.

The Norfolk Forum
Chrysler Hall, Norfolk
• **(757) 627-8672**
This thought-provoking series always sells out early and has recently brought such notable speakers as journalist Dan Rather. Call in the summer to get information about series tickets, which cost $70.

Old Dominion University President's Lecture Series
Mills Godwin Building Auditorium, Old Dominion University, Norfolk
• **(757) 683-3115**
This free series started in 1992 with the goal of bringing diverse speakers to campus. Civil rights attorney Morris Dees and civil rights leader Julian Bond have lectured here.

Second Tuesday Lecture Series
Commodore Theater, 421 High St., Portsmouth
• **(757) 393-8501**
This free series features eclectic area speakers talking about their areas of expertise. Recent speakers have hailed from area colleges, The Virginian-Pilot and the NASA Langley Research Center. The series is sponsored in part by the City of Portsmouth and the Portsmouth Museum and Fine Arts Commission. Talks are at noon on the second Tuesday of each month.

Tidewater Jewish Forum
Locations vary
• **(757) 489-1371**
The Jewish Community Center sponsors this series that brings a variety of interesting

INSIDERS' TIP
Many theaters and event organizers seek volunteers to help conduct various productions. Get your name on the volunteer list and see the show from an Insider point of view—for no admission fee.

speakers. Recent speakers have included singer/dancer Joel Grey and actor Edward Asner. Locations of lectures vary. Open-seating season tickets cost $75.

Music

Virginia Beach Chorale
Pavilion Theater, Virginia Beach
• **(757) 486-1464**
These vocalists present a variety of music during two concerts a year and at benefit performances throughout the year.

Virginia Beach Symphony Orchestra
Pavilion Theater, Virginia Beach
• **(757) 671-8611**
This community group has a September through May series of five to six concerts with featured soloists.

Virginia Wesleyan College Concert Series
Hofheimer Theater,
Virginia Wesleyan College, Virginia Beach
• **(757) 455-3200**
The college's "familiar-faces" series sponsors performances by local professional musicians.

Cantata Chorus
Christ and St. Luke's Episcopal Church,
Olney Rd. and Stockley Gardens, Norfolk
• **(757) 627-5665**
This amateur chorus specializes in sacred works during five to six annual concerts at Christ and St. Luke's Episcopal Church in Norfolk.

Feldman Chamber Music Society
Chrysler Museum Theater, Norfolk
• **(757) 498-9396**
The society sponsors five concerts between October and May, usually at the Chrysler Museum Theater.

First Presbyterian Music Series
First Presbyterian Church,
820 Colonial Ave., Norfolk
• **(757) 627-8375**
The organ and other instruments are featured in three classical concerts a year. Tickets cost $10 each, and season tickets are available.

Hampton Roads Early Music Society
Chandler Recital Hall,
Old Dominion University, Norfolk
• **(757) 421-0341**
This concert series features early music and

The Chrysler Museum is a first-class resource for the Hampton Roads community.

Photo: Courtesy of The Chrysler Museum

instruments such as the baroque violin and recorder.

Norfolk Chamber Consort
Chandler Recital Hall,
Old Dominion University, Norfolk
• (757) 440-1803, (757) 622-4542
   This chamber-music group features winds, strings, keyboard instruments and vocalists.

Old Dominion University Concert Series
Chandler Recital Hall, Old Dominion University, Norfolk
• (757) 683-4061
   Free concerts feature up-and-coming national musicians as well as performances by local artists.

Bay Youth Orchestra of Virginia
Locations vary
• (757) 461-8834
   This organization sponsors 8 to 10 concerts a year throughout the region. The orchestra features youth in grades 7 through 12 and also has a string group. Kids can set up auditions by calling the number above.

Capriole
Locations vary
• (757) 220-1248
   This professional Williamsburg-based group performs throughout Hampton Roads. It is a vocal and instrumental ensemble specializing in 17th-century music.

Chesapeake Civic Chorus
Locations vary
• (757) 421-9784
   This is an amateur chorus that presents a variety of music during annual concerts.

Governor's School for the Arts
Locations vary
• (757) 683-5549
   Concerts feature talented high-school musicians who are attending the regional arts school.

Hardwick Chamber Ensemble
Locations vary
• (757) 424-4277
   The Hardwick Chamber Ensemble's concert series runs September through May and focuses on chamber music.

I. Sherman Greene Chorale
Locations vary
• (757) 467-8971
   This African-American community chorus performs traditional music as well as the works of contemporary composers.

Virginia Chorale
Locations vary
• (757) 627-8375
   This 23-member chorus presents a broad repertoire of chorus music ranging from Renaissance to 20th-century songs. It is Virginia's only professional chorale ensemble.

Tidewater Classical Guitar Society
Locations vary
• (757) 625-2411
   The society brings internationally known and regional guitarists to the area for concerts and workshops.

Virginia Children's Chorus
Locations vary
• (757) 397-0779
   The chorus features talented youths ages 6 to 16 and performs throughout the area.

Virginia Choral Society
Locations vary
• (800) 400-4VCS
   This polished amateur organization performs throughout the region. Its repertoire ranges from religious songs to Christmas tunes.

INSIDERS' TIP
If you are a student, make sure to travel with your student ID. Many venues offer a student discount when you show your card.

Theater

The Actor's Theatre
Pembroke Mall, Virginia Beach and Independence Blvds., Virginia Beach
• (757) 557-0397
   This amateur company performs in a theater at Pembroke Mall in Virginia Beach. This regional company presents a variety of productions.

Little Theatre of Virginia Beach
24th St. and Barberton Dr., Virginia Beach
• (757) 428-9233
   This amateur theater company produces a variety of plays. Recent performances included *Broadway Bound* and *Threads*. Performances are held at the theater at the above address.

Virginia Musical Theatre
Pavilion Theater, Virginia Beach
• (757) 340-5446

This professional theater company uses regional talent to produce musicals such as *Fiddler on the Roof* and *Pajama Game*. All performances are at the Pavilion Theater in Virginia Beach.

Virginia Wesleyan College
**Various on-campus theaters,
Virginia Beach**
• (757) 455-3200

Productions star Virginia Wesleyan students. Recent ones included *Camino Real* and *The Merry Wives of Windsor*.

Broadway at Chrysler Hall
Chrysler Hall, Norfolk
• (757) 622-0288

This professional series brings elaborate traveling Broadway productions of popular musicals such as *Phantom of the Opera*, *Miss Saigon* and *Les Miserables* to the stage at Norfolk's Chrysler Hall.

Encore Players
Little Creek Naval Amphibious Base Theater, Norfolk
• (757) 460-5152, (757) 436-9512

The Encore Players feature actors who are in the military performing in musicals such as *Nunsense* and *Footloose*. Performances are at the Little Creek Naval Amphibious Base Theater in Virginia Beach.

Generic Theater
912 W. 21st St., Norfolk
• (757) 441-2160

The innovative theater specializes in new works not previously seen in the region. It also presents a weekend children's series called Child's Play. Performances are at the theater at the address above.

Little Theatre of Norfolk
**801 Claremont Ave.,
Norfolk**
• (757) 627-8551

Founded in 1926, this is the country's oldest continuously active little theater. The group specializes in light comedies and musicals, all mounted at its theater on Claremont Avenue in Norfolk. Recent performances included *Bell, Book and Candle* and *A Little Night Music*.

Norfolk State University Players
Brown Theater or Wilder Performing Arts Center, Norfolk State University, Norfolk
• (757) 683-8341

These productions showcase talent from the university and are held on campus in either the

INSIDERS' TIP

If you enjoy a particular artist's work be sure to ask the gallery manager for information about that artist. They usually provide valuable insights that add to the enjoyment of the piece.

The Edythe C. and Stanley L. Harrison Opera House is a restored USO Hall.

Photo: Courtesy of Virginia Opera

Brown Theater or the Wilder Performing Arts Center. Recent ones included *Little Red Riding Hood* and *Bubblin' Brown Sugar*.

Old Dominion University Players
Various on-campus theaters,
Old Dominion University, Norfolk
• (757) 683-5305

Productions feature ODU students in such works as *A Raisin in the Sun* and *Angels in America*. Plays are presented in various campus theaters.

Little Theatre of Portsmouth
Wilson High School, 1404 Elmhurst Ln.,
Portsmouth
• (757) 488-7866

Five to six performances a season feature such works as *Chapter Two* and *Pippin*, held at Wilson High School in Portsmouth.

The Hurrah Players
Locations vary
• (757) 623-7418 or (757) 627-KIDS

The elaborate musicals performed by this group feature highly trained local children in productions geared toward families. Recent productions included *Charlotte's Web* and *The Wizard of Oz*. Performance locations vary.

Norfolk Musical Theater
Locations vary
• (757) 588-1072

This is an amateur company that specializes in light musicals. Recent productions included *Rose of the Danube* and *The Gift of Song*.

Norfolk Savoyards
Locations vary
• (757) 484-6920

This group specializes in the works of Gilbert and Sullivan and presents several musicals a year.

Mixed Series

Portsmouth Community Concerts
Willet Hall, 3701 Willet Dr., Portsmouth
• (757) 393-5144

Subscription-only concerts and performances at Willett Hall draw professional artists to the region. Recent performers included

the Black Mountain Male Chorus of Wales and Epic Brass.

Tidewater Performing Arts Society
Locations vary
• (757) 627-2314

The society provides some of the most innovative programs in the region by bringing in nationally known dance groups, singers and other artists. Recent performers included the dance troupe Pilobolus, juggler Michael Moschen, the Alvin Ailey Repertory Ensemble and Diva, an all-female Big Band.

Virginia International Waterfront Arts Festival
Locations vary
• (757) 664-6492

This eclectic celebration of the arts started in 1997 with an 18-day spring festival designed to attract arts-oriented travelers to the region. It has served that mission while satisfying area residents, who look forward to the festival each year. The festival has since expanded to 25 days.

Performances are staged daily throughout the region from Virginia Beach to Williamsburg and feature renowned musicians, singers and dancers from around the globe. Special visual arts displays also are part of the festival. One popular mainstay is the Virginia International Tattoo, which features fife and drum corps, bagpipe brigades, and other groups in a military-type spectacle of music. Local arts groups also showcase their talents with performances and displays held as part of a spring festival called the Waterfront Wave.

Call for a detailed brochure. Tickets usually go on sale in January and frequently sell out before festival time.

Art Centers and Museums

Atlantic Wildfowl Heritage Center
Atlantic Ave. and 12th St., Virginia Beach
• (757) 437-8432

The five galleries at this center feature carved decoys and paintings related to birds. The center opened in late 1995 in the historic DeWitt Cottage, the only remaining late 19th-century oceanfront home. (See our Attractions chapter.) Hours are 10 AM to 5 PM Tuesday through Saturday and noon to 5 PM on Sunday. The center is open until 6 PM in summer. Admission is free, but a donation is suggested.

Contemporary Art Center of Virginia
2200 Parks Ave., Virginia Beach
• (757) 425-0000

This regional arts center fosters the exploration, appreciation and understanding of significant contemporary art through changing exhibitions, a studio school and innovative educational programs for adults and children. This is also the sponsoring organization of The Boardwalk Art Show and Festival one of the region's most popular summer events. (See our Annual Events chapter.) Hours are 10 AM until 4 PM Tuesday through Saturday and noon to 4 PM Sunday. Admission costs $3.

The Old Coast Guard Station
24th St. and Oceanfront, Virginia Beach
• (757) 422-1587

This Virginia Beach museum's two galleries feature traveling displays of maritime art. A permanent display focuses on the impact of World Wars I and II on Virginia Beach. The museum is in a former U.S. Lifesaving/Coast Guard Station built in 1903. (See our Attractions chapter.) Hours are Tuesday through Saturday 10 AM until 5 PM and Sunday from noon until 5 PM. In summer, the museum is open Mondays and has longer daily hours. Admission is $2.50, $1 for children older than 5 and $2 for active-duty military and senior citizens.

Hermitage Foundation Museum
7637 North Shore Rd., Norfolk
• (757) 423-2052

This museum features changing exhibits by local artists and a permanent display of art housed in a 1908 Tudor-style home. (See our Attractions chapter.) Hours are 10 AM to 5 PM Monday through Saturday and 1 to 5 PM on Sunday. Admission is $4, $1 for ages 6 to 18 and free for active-duty military

Courthouse Galleries
420 High St., Portsmouth
• (757) 393-8543

The visual arts center is one of three city-operated museums. It is housed in the historic 1846 Courthouse and displays a variety of exhibits ranging from traveling shows to retrospectives of renowned local artists. Hours are Tuesday through Saturday from 10 AM to 5 PM, Sunday 1 to 5 PM, and it is closed on Monday. Admission is $1.

Riddick's Folly
510 Main St., Suffolk
• (757) 934-1390

This Suffolk museum features changing exhibits and permanent displays related to local history. The late Governor Mills Godwin and the history of Planters peanuts are the topics of the permanent displays. The museum is housed in an 1837 Gothic Revival home. (See our Attractions chapter.) The museum is open 10 AM until 5 PM Tuesday through Friday, 1 to 5 PM Sunday and is closed Monday and Saturday. Admission is free.

The Suffolk Museum
118 Bosley Ave., Suffolk
• (757) 925-6311

A city-run arts center, the Suffolk Museum presents a variety of art exhibits. Some exhibits are produced by local artists, others travel from the Virginia Museum of Fine Arts in Richmond. (See our Attractions chapter.) The museum is open 10 AM until 5 PM Tuesday through Friday, 1 to 5 PM Sunday and is closed Monday and Saturday. Admission is free.

Retail Art Galleries

The Artists Gallery
2407 Pacific Ave., Virginia Beach
• (757) 425-6671

This gallery is in the resort area of Virginia Beach so it may be a little hard to get to in the summertime. Here's an Insider tip: Park in the municipal lot just a block away at 25th and Pacific. You can see (and purchase) works by local artists here, Tuesday through Friday from 10 AM until 5 PM and from 10 AM until 4 PM Saturday.

Artifax
Hilltop North Shopping Ctr.,
Virginia Beach
• (757) 425-8224
1511 Colley Ave., Norfolk
• (757) 623-8840

This is a hip place to shop for a one-of-a-kind gifts and a visually inspiring spot to browse. Hours are Monday through Friday from 10 AM to 7 PM, Saturday from 10 AM to 6 PM and Sunday from noon to 5 PM.

d'Art Center
125 College Pl., Norfolk
• **(757) 625-4211**

The d'Art center is a combination working studio, gallery and art center situated in downtown Norfolk. If you like to know the artist you're buying from, this is the place to shop. Hours are 10 AM until 6 PM Monday through Saturday and noon to 5 PM on Sunday.

Art Works Gallery
321 Bute St., Norfolk
• **(757) 625-3004**

This sprawling space is chock-full of wonderful works. The gallery is in the Freemason area of downtown Norfolk, a little cobblestone haven that features lots of interesting architecture as well as a few retail gems such as this one. Hours are 9:30 AM until 5:30 PM Monday through Friday and 9:30 AM until 3 PM on Saturday.

Harbor Gallery
1508 Colley Ave., Norfolk
• **(757) 627-2787**

Fine art, prints, jewelry and an array of other art objects are among the diverse works featured in this Ghent gallery. Hours are Monday through Saturday 10 AM to 6 PM.

Pantera Glass Studio Gallery
409 W. York St., Norfolk
• **(757) 622-2680**

Stop by and watch artisans transform molten glass into amazing works of art. This studio is in the historic Freemason area. Hours vary so call ahead.

Art Atrium II Gallery
629 High St., Portsmouth
• **(757) 393-1215**

This privately owned downtown gallery specializes in original and contemporary African-American art. It is open from 11 AM to 5:30 PM weekdays and until 6 PM on Saturdays. It also opens the first Sunday of each month from 11 AM to 5 PM.

Riverview Gallery
1 High St., Portsmouth
• **(757) 397-3207**

This shop in the Jewish Mother restaurant features distinctive work from local and national artists. It is open from 11 AM to 8:30 PM every day but Sunday when it closes at 6 PM. Look for longer hours in the summer.

Show Galleries

The following locations often feature artwork by local and regional artists. Hours vary according to businesses so a call ahead is suggested.

Cape Henry Collegiate School, 1320 Mill Dam Road, Virginia Beach, (757) 481-2446

Commons Gallery, Church of the Ascension, 4853 Princess Anne Road, Virginia Beach, (757) 495-1886

Regent University Library Lobby, Regent University, 1000 Regent University Drive, Virginia Beach, (757) 579-4180

Virginia Wesleyan College Hofheimer Library, 1584 Wesleyan Drive, Virginia Beach, (757) 455-3200

Eastern Virginia Medical School Galleries, Lewis Hall, 700 Olney Road, Norfolk, (757) 446-6050

Jewish Community Center's Lobby Art Gallery, 7300 Newport Avenue, Norfolk, (757) 489-1371

Norfolk Academy Grandy Gallery, 1585 Wesleyan Dr., Norfolk, (757) 461-6236

Norfolk State University Wise Art Gallery in the Fine Arts Building, 2041 Corprew Avenue, Norfolk, (757) 683-8844

Old Dominion University Gallery, 100 Granby Street, Norfolk, (757) 683-6227.

SunTrust Bank Gallery, 500 Main Street, Norfolk, (757) 583-3586

Virginia Natural Gas Gallery, 5100 E. Virginia Beach Boulevard, Norfolk, (757) 466-5439

Wachovia Bank Gallery, 100 World Trade Center, Main Street and Waterside Drive, Norfolk, (757) 539-7411

WHRO Fine Arts Gallery, 5200 Hampton Boulevard, Norfolk, (757) 489-9476, (757) 425-6671

Tidewater Community College's Visual Arts Center, 340 High Street, Portsmouth, (757) 822-6999

Parks

These are the kinds of places we Insiders hesitate to talk about. Everybody knows about the beach—you really can't keep that a secret—but what about our secluded hiking trails and picnic spots? Do we really want to put the word out on the places we go to escape the crowds?

It's a tough call, but we've decided to share. In this chapter you'll find information on our favorite parks, both city and state. Some of these are civilized and suburbanized places to lug children, coolers and Frisbees on the first day of spring. Others require a backpack, hiking boots and an effective mosquito repellent. In the most spectacular spots, our parks take you back three centuries, to the age when pirates smuggled their loot onto our raggedy shoreline. The trees drip with Spanish moss, and swamp creatures croak in the mud. Our parks can be downright spooky in spots and incredibly beautiful in others. When you visit them, please treat them with the respect they deserve.

LOOK FOR:
• Virginia Beach
• Norfolk
• Portsmouth
• Chesapeake
• Suffolk

Virginia Beach

First Landing State Park
Shore Dr., Virginia Beach
• **(757) 481-4836**

Designated a Registered National Landmark in 1965, this state park is an environmental magnet for visitors and residents. In 1999 it added the Chesapeake Bay Center to help explain all the wonders that visitors see in the park and along the bay (757) 412-2331. Entering this 2,770-acre sanctuary is like stepping out of the hustle-bustle of civilization into a faraway world. Much of the park is preserved as a natural area, with sights that run the gamut from semitropical forest to giant sand dunes. In just one day's visit, you're sure to catch a glimpse of a number of the 336 species of trees and plants, ranging from cypress draped with Spanish moss to hardy yuccas.

Daytime visitors will find a picnic area, hiking trails, a self-guided nature trail and a visitors center with exhibits and book sales. Nine trails, including one for handicapped visitors, cover 17 miles and are part of the National Scenic Trails System. Bikers will enjoy a

A day at the park is the perfect way to make a youngster happy.

5-mile bike trail that connects to the city's bike trails.

The Shore Drive side of the park borders on the Chesapeake Bay where you'll find an overnight camping section with 215 sites and 20 group sites, along with a camp store, a mile-long beach reserved for campers, restrooms, showers and an amphitheater for interpretive programs. Twenty cabins are also available in this area, but you must reserve early. Call the park office, (757) 481-2131, for more information. You can reserve cabins or campsites by calling the Virginia State Parks Reservation Center at (800) 933-PARK. Reservations are a must during warmer months.

From 64th Street, you can access the east end of the park, where there's a boat ramp that slides you into Broad Bay leading to Lynnhaven Inlet and then out to the Chesapeake Bay. Great hiking and biking trails veer off to the right and left just opposite a small ranger station near the 64th Street entrance. For more information, stop in at the Visitors Center off Shore Drive. Admission to the park is free, but there is a nominal parking fee.

Back Bay National Wildlife Refuge
4005 Sandpiper Rd., Virginia Beach
• (757) 721-2412

If you follow the thousands of migrating geese, ducks and swans, you'll find yourself in the natural habitat of the marshy islands of shallow Back Bay. Here, on 5,000 acres of virtually untouched natural beauty, you can be witness to the splendor of beach, dunes, marsh and woodlands along with resident waterfowl, deer and other animals.

To preserve the integrity of the park, strict rules are enforced. First, the park is only open during daylight hours, from sunrise to sunset. Parking is permitted only in designated areas during open hours, and only those with special permits are allowed motorized-vehicle access to beaches and unpaved dirt roads. Other no-no's: unleashed pets, guns, horses or open fires. Likewise, the fragile dunes are off-limits to visitors, but that still leaves the beach shore and nature trails for hiking.

The Seaside Trail and Dune Trail guides you from the parking lot to the stunning beach. The north mile of the beach is closed to protect shore birds there; the south beach is open, although swimming, sunbathing and surfing are prohibited. Just consider Back Bay to be the perfect place to bring your binoculars, a canteen of water, a camera, a picnic lunch and a big can of bug spray.

False Cape State Park
4001 Sandpiper Rd., Virginia Beach
• (757) 426-7128

Five miles south of the Back Bay Refuge sits Virginia's most remote park. Home to migratory waterfowl, deer, wild horses, wild pigs and protected marshlands, False Cape got its name because sailors used to mistake it for Cape Henry. The park is a 6-mile stretch of undisturbed beach along a barrier spit that divides the ocean from Back Bay and was accessible until recently by foot, bicycle or boat only. Park rangers help visitors get to False Cape by an electric tram that departs from the Back Bay National Wildlife Refuge. The tram runs from April through October. It departs daily at 9 AM and returns at 12:45 PM. From November through March access is provided on a limited basis by a smaller beach vehicle. The cost is $6 for adults, $4 for children under 12 and senior citizens. Call (757) 721-7666 or (757) 498-BIRD for details.

If you're interested in learning about the park's diverse ecosystem, the Wash Woods Environmental Education Center, housed in a converted hunting lodge near the southern end of the park, is the place to turn. For small groups, comfortable overnight accommodations can be arranged to allow time for more intensive study of the area's natural resources.

For a day visit during peak visiting periods, any questions can be answered at the park's ranger station just about a mile south of the northern entrance.

Mount Trashmore
Edwin Dr., Virginia Beach
• (757) 473-5237

Boasting one of the city's highest elevations—all of 68 feet!—Mount Trashmore comes by its name honestly. A brilliantly conceived solid waste management project, what was once a huge hill of 750,000 tons of trash was transformed in 1973 into what is now a beautifully landscaped hub of activity, and one of Virginia Beach's most popular parks.

When you're finished flying kites or model airplanes from its peak just lie back and toss bread crumbs to the resident ducks, geese and coots that have no problem marching right over to you for a handout. Also part of the complex are several playgrounds, picnic shelters, basketball courts and volleyball nets where pickup games are the norm.

In the shadow of the Mount is one of the region's largest, most ambitious and innovative playgrounds, a 25,000-square-foot park designed by children called Kids Cove. This colossal wooden playground, which incorporates slides, mazes, ramps and bridges all built around a nautical theme, was constructed and funded through an all-volunteer effort that equally matched its project in magnitude. A five-day "barn-raising" in 1993 made this children's fantasyland a reality. At peak times, Kids Cove can be terribly crowded; try it first on a Tuesday morning.

Princess Anne Park
Princess Anne Rd., Virginia Beach
• **(757) 427-6020**

Almost 300 acres of sports-lover's paradise sit right off Princess Anne Road. Along with plenty of wide-open space, Princess Anne Park is proud of its outstanding facilities, including four playgrounds, a number of baseball and softball fields, plus equipment for basketball, volleyball, croquet and horseshoes. Really special is the horse arena for horse shows and rodeos. A children's garden and wooded picnic area are also popular. Next door is the city's soccer complex where hundreds of soccer playing youths spend their weekends. Also in the neighborhood are the GTE Virginia Beach Amphitheater and the Sportsplex, where the Mariners soccer team plays.

Bayville Park
First Court Rd., Virginia Beach
• **(757) 460-7569**

Bayville has the city's only disc course for Frisbee golf players, an 18-hole challenge that is considered by experts to be one of the toughest in the nation. The tree-shaded 66-acre park has features designed for the handicapped and facilities for basketball, shuffleboard, softball, volleyball, handball, badminton and horseshoes alongside a comfortable picnic area. For kids, Bayville is a veritable Garden of Eden with one of the neatest playgrounds in town. Just watch their smiles as they come face to face with giant futuristic structures, wood and metal towers, swinging tires and rocking metal disks.

Red Wing Park
1398 General Booth Blvd., Virginia Beach
• **(757) 437-4847**

Because of its proximity to some of the Beach's favorite attractions—Croatan Beach, Ocean Breeze Water Park and the Virginia Marine Science Museum—Red Wing Park is a super stopoff for a picnic lunch. Once here, you can't leave until you've strolled through the lovely Japanese garden and aromatic fragrance garden and had a look at the prisoner of war memorial.

Red Wing has a fitness course, a playground, three ball fields and facilities for tennis, volleyball, badminton, basketball and horseshoes. And, like most Virginia Beach parks, all you need is a valid I.D. to borrow any sports equipment you left at home.

Little Island Park
Sandpiper Rd., Virginia Beach
• **(757) 426-7200**

Almost a secret treasure, Little Island takes full advantage of its location on Sandbridge Beach and Back Bay, and its fishing pier makes it especially attractive for anglers. The broad beach is lifeguarded during summer months from 9:30 AM to 6 PM, and after a swim you can move on to the playground, tennis courts, basketball or volleyball courts. A snack bar and shaded picnic area are also at Little Island.

Munden Point Park
Munden Point Rd. off Princess Anne Rd., Virginia Beach
• **(757) 426-5296**

Getting to Munden Park is an excursion in itself—a long ride through the rural areas of Virginia Beach to the North Landing River. Once here, the 100 scenic acres offer a multitude of choices for boaters and landlubbers alike. Since the North Landing River is a link to the Intracoastal Waterway system, you can either watch fancy vessels powering out, rent a canoe or paddleboat or launch your own boat from the boat ramp for a small usage fee.

Landside, there are facilities for softball, basketball, volleyball and horseshoes and a playground and picnic area. Also noteworthy is a Parcourse Fitness Circuit.

Beach Garden Park
Holly Rd. at 29th St., Virginia Beach
• **(757) 471-4884**

A quiet retreat from the busy oceanfront scene, this delightful park features a playground, fitness trail and picnic tables.

Norfolk

Lafayette Park
25th and Granby Sts., Norfolk
• **(757) 441-2149**

One of Norfolk's oldest parks, Lafayette Park boasts two outdoor basketball courts, four tennis courts, an amphitheater, picnic shelters,

PARKS

The Great Dismal Swamp

One of the most asked-about attractions in Hampton Roads is also one of its most inaccessible. At area convention and visitors bureaus, the world-renowned Great Dismal Swamp draws frequent inquiries. But unlike many attractions, the area has

few campgrounds and hiking trails, and many parts of it are accessible only by small boats. Despite its remote location, the swamp manages to attract more than 10,000 visitors a year.

The 200,000-acre wilderness is much more than pure swamp and is one of the largest natural areas on the East Coast. It is considered one of the most scenic spots in Virginia and North Carolina with lush greenery, cypress trees, calm waters and an incredible variety of wildlife. Among its residents are bears, bobcats, river otters, weasels, frogs, 23 fish species, bats and butterflies. More than 200 different kinds of birds have been sighted in the swamp, which is also a haven for swarms of mosquitoes and 21 varieties of snakes. The swamp also has about 1,000 square miles of primeval forest.

Col. William Byrd gave the swamp its gloomy name in 1728. Thirty-five years later George Washington surveyed the swamp and dreamed of draining it and cutting the timber on the 40,000 acres he and several other businessmen owned in the swamp. In 1793 slaves started digging at both ends of a 22-mile canal, which took 12 years to complete. It is still in use today, making it the oldest operating artificial waterway in the United States. The swamp's canal, which has two sets of locks, is an alternate route for the Atlantic Intracoastal Waterway and during spring and fall it's lined with yachts headed to and from Florida. It connects the Deep Creek area of Chesapeake with Elizabeth City, North Carolina. The Dismal Swamp Canal is on the National Register of Historic Places and is a National Civil Engineering

The Great Dismal Swamp is one of the region's most scenic and remote attractions.

Photo: Courtesy Portsmouth Convention and Visitors Bureau

Landmark. A second waterway, the Albemarle and Chesapeake Canal was dug through the swamp between 1855 and 1859. It runs from the Great Bridge area of Chesapeake to the Albemarle Sound in North Carolina.

There are several ways to take in the beauty of the swamp, which spreads through Chesapeake and Suffolk and northeastern North Carolina:

In Suffolk there is the Great Dismal Swamp Wildlife Refuge operated by the U.S. Fish and Wildlife Service, (757) 986-3705. The office there is staffed from 7 AM to 3 PM Monday through Friday, and the refuge is open from a half-hour before sunrise to a half-hour after sunset. From the refuge you can hike or bike along a 4.5-mile road beside the Washington Ditch, named for George Washington who dug the first spade of dirt to create the canal. The Washington Ditch ends up at Lake Drummond, the largest natural lake in Virginia.

There also is a 7-mile road along the Jericho Ditch that leads to the lake, but it is not maintained as well as the shorter route. For the less hardy or those with small children, there is a half-mile boardwalk. Meandering along it will give you a feel for the swamp.

To get to the refuge take Route 58 to Suffolk, turn left on E. Washington Street (Route 337) and go left on White Marsh Road (Route 642). Look for the refuge signs and turn into the Washington Ditch entrance, which has a parking lot.

In Chesapeake you can enter a 3.5-mile feeder ditch if you have a small boat or canoe. It is across the Dismal Swamp Canal on Route 17 (George Washington Highway), about 3 miles north of the North Carolina border. There is a city-owned boat ramp and parking lot on Route 17 a mile north of the feeder ditch entrance. You can rent a canoe from the Chesapeake KOA Campground on Route 17, 485-5686. It is about 8 miles north of the feeder ditch entrance. Canoe rental costs $2 an hour or $15 a day.

If you're handy with a paddle, it will take about two hours to maneuver down the ditch to Lake Drummond, where the Corps of Engineers maintains a rustic campground. Bathrooms with toilets and sinks are on site but there are no showers or running water. You will find grills, picnic tables, places for campfires and two screened dining areas. No reservations are required, and camping is free. For information call (757) 421-7401. Remember that access to Lake Drummond is only by foot, bicycle or boats weighing less than 1,000 pounds.

To see the swamp, you can also drive to North Carolina down Route 17 S., also known as George Washington Highway, and look at dense woods that border the road. There are several picnic areas along the way.

Just 3 miles over the state line in South Mills, North Carolina, is the Dismal Swamp Canal Visitor Welcome Center run by the state of North Carolina. It prides itself on being the only visitors center in the country whose clients come by both boat and car. The center provides brochures and maps, has a helpful staff to answer questions and maintains a picnic area. There is a 150-foot dock at the center. Each year about 2,000 boaters tie up there for the night. The center is open Tuesday through Saturday.

a boat ramp, well-maintained fields for softball and rugby and a grand playground, including special play equipment for the disabled. The scenic pathways that wind through the mature flora and fauna are especially appealing, and you can stop for a soft drink or snack at the nearby concession stand. We call it City Park, and it sits next to the 55-acre Virginia Zoo, so plan a full day to take in all this park has to offer.

Town Point Park
Waterside Dr. at Boush St., Norfolk
• (757) 441-2149

Those of us who were raised in Hampton Roads find it simply amazing that this wonderful park sits in the very location that we were never allowed to enter after dark while we were growing up. But just look at it today! Only a footstep from Norfolk's primary downtown business district, adjacent to The Waterside Festival Marketplace, Town Point Park is indeed the visible tribute to Downtown Norfolk's revitalization spirit. With its meandering walkways, gay nineties street lamps, London plane trees and comfy benches set between large expanses of incredibly lush green lawn, it is a wonderful place for a quiet stroll or to sit and watch ships gliding down the Elizabeth River.

Come almost any warm-weather weekend, however, and this sleeping giant really roars. Festevents, Norfolk's premier party-thrower, engineers events and festivals that fill even the most insatiable desire for activity, from after-work concerts on selected Friday afternoons to festivals in honor of countries, kids and cultures of every kind. Town Point Park is also home to Norfolk's biggest party, Harborfest, held every June.

To accommodate all this fun, the city has added parking at nearby lots and ramps, and you can even take a short ferry ride across the Elizabeth River to Portsmouth for a nominal fee. The Waterside Marina is adjacent to the park, and a favorite Sunday excursion is to walk up and down the docks checking out the visiting vessels and their ports of call. There are also frequent visits from foreign ships that dock at Otter Berth, homeport to *The Spirit of Norfolk*, and the public is often invited to come aboard for tours.

Ocean View Beach Park
Ocean View, Norfolk
• (757) 441-2149

The jewel of Ocean View and a landmark in this close-knit community's rejuvenation efforts, this 6.5-acre park is Norfolk's newest addition to its park portfolio. On the site of the old Ocean View Amusement Park, it features a large gazebo for presentations and dancing, a beach that's lifeguarded during summer months, a boardwalk, a beach access ramp for the handicapped and lovely lawns. It plays host to the summer season's free Big Bands on the Bay series, held Sunday nights from 7 until 9 PM.

Norfolk Botanical Garden
Airport Rd. off Azalea Garden Rd., Norfolk
• (757) 441-5830

Botanical splendor along 12 miles of lush pathways awaits viewing every day of the year

in this 155 acre floral wonderland. (See our Attractions chapter.)

Northside Park
8400 Tidewater Dr., Norfolk
• (757) 441-2149

Here's where many softball and tennis champs meet to defend their titles. With two lighted softball diamonds, seven tennis courts, an outdoor basketball court plus playground and picnic shelters, this place is always hopping with activity of one sort or another. Especially popular is the year-round indoor pool and sun patio, staffed by certified lifeguards who offer aquatic games and classes for all ages. Seasonal tennis instruction by a part-time tennis pro is also available. The community-built Imagination Island is a mega-playground for kids. There's no direct phone, so to get more information contact the Recreation Department at the number above.

INSIDERS' TIP
January is the best month to spot humpback whales off the Virginia Beach shoreline. For a closer look, jump aboard a charter sponsored by the Virginia Marine Science Museum.

Lakewood Park
1612 Willow Wood Dr., Norfolk
• (757) 441-5833

Headquarters to the Bureau of Recreation's Athletic and Dance/Music divisions, Lakewood Park sits in the heart of Lakewood, a lovely residential neighborhood. It features nine tennis courts, picnic shelters, two lighted multipurpose ball fields, a playground, restrooms and plenty of free parking. Moms who drop off their kids for league play have been known to slip right across the street to the Lafayette Library for a little peace and quiet.

Barraud Park
Off Tidewater Dr. on Vista Dr., Norfolk
• (757) 441-2149

From June to September, this large community park is staffed to organize activities and sign out equipment. You'll find lighted softball and football/soccer fields, six tennis courts, a playground, a picnic shelter, an amphitheater and ample free parking. Summer months bring organized playground games for ages 6 to 12 as well as a free-lunch program for children from low-income families.

Tarralton Park
Tarralton Dr. and Millard St., Norfolk
• (757) 441-1765

The most recent addition to the network of parks maintained by the Recreation Bureau,

Tarralton features more than 70 acres with three family-size picnic shelters, a colorful play area and tot lot, lighted tennis courts, a lighted basketball court, three soccer fields and a BMX bicycle trail. There's also a little-league complex and softball field. Tarralton is also home to the region's only fenced-in, lighted in-line skating facility.

Neighborhood Parks and School Grounds

Throughout the city of Norfolk, you'll find mini-parks, beautiful little pockets of well-manicured common grounds and land-scaping. In addition to the 112 such areas maintained by the Norfolk Department of Parks and Recreation (often on school grounds), there are many other neighborhood quiet spots, such as Stockley Gardens in Ghent. Take a look around—there's more than likely a playground or park right around the corner from where you are!

Portsmouth

City Park
City Park Ave., Portsmouth
• (757) 456-2937

Tucked behind the tombstones of the Olive Branch Cemetery are 93 gorgeous acres with a recently renovated golf course, six lighted tennis courts, boat docks, duck ponds, gardens and playgrounds. Once voted best park in the state in 1989 by the Virginia Parks and Recreation Association, City Park borders the western branch of the Elizabeth River and Baines Creek. The highlight for little ones is the mini-train, a coal-fired engine called Pokey Smokey with open seating that whistles its way through a tunnel and around a pond—a real treat of an attraction. This is an absolutely delightful place to spend a lazy day—with or without children.

Hoffler Creek Wildlife Preserve
4510 Twin Pines Rd., Portsmouth
• (757) 398-9151

Wetlands, a dense forest and a saltwater lake make this a thriving habitat for native plants and animals. The 142-acre site was recently declared a nature preserve. It is on the shores of Hoffler Creek and is the last wilderness area in Portsmouth. This is a secluded spot for hiking or bird watching.

Sleepy Hole Park
Sleepy Hole Rd., Portsmouth
• (757) 538-4102

Once the plantation of Amadeo Obici, the Italian immigrant who founded the Planters Peanut Company, Sleepy Hole Park overlooks the Nansemond River. Purchased by the city of Portsmouth in 1972, the park is actually in Suffolk. It has since developed into a premier playground for area residents. Along with the popular Sleepy Hole Golf Course, the park boasts a well-stocked lake for fishing, nature trails through the tidal marsh that surrounds the park (including one trail especially constructed for the handicapped), picnic shelters and playgrounds. This is a great spot for campers since there are 50 camping sites available under tall oaks—28 tent sites with water, tables and grills and another 22 with electric and water hookups. Campers also have access to modern restroom facilities with hot showers and a laundry area.

INSIDERS' TIP
Vacationing for a while? Your local post office will hold your mail for up to six weeks at a time.

PARKS

High Street Landing
at the foot of High St., Portsmouth
• (757) 393-8481

This delightful little park is located where the Elizabeth River Ferry docks. It's a wonderful place to relax and just watch the ships glide by or to begin a sightseeing tour of Portsmouth attractions. Nearby, you'll find the Children's Museum of Virginia, the Lightship Museum and Naval Shipyard Museum.

Chesapeake

Chesapeake City Park
500 Greenbrier Pkwy., Chesapeake
• (757) 382-6411

This 75-acre site features rows of reforested pine trees bordering 45 acres of open space. The open space is divided by roadways into segments that can be rented for corporate or private events according to the space needed. A network of electricity and water services are in place. For regular daytime visitors, there's a fitness trail, play equipment, basketball courts, a skateboarding area and a picnic shelter. Fun Forest playground, an imagination center and family adventure area, can be found on three acres in the southern corner of the park. Skateboard ramps can be found next to a comfort station and concession building.

Northwest River Park
1733 Indian Creek Rd., Chesapeake
• **(757) 421-7151**

This 763-acre park in the southeastern section of Chesapeake has been developed as a natural, heavily wooded recreation area incorporating camping, an extensive trail system, picnic shelters, play areas, an equestrian area, miniature golf and plenty of open spaces. Water abounds, including the lake that stretches almost to the southern activity area that runs along the banks of the Northwest River where canoes and boats can be rented. Of special note is the fragrance trail created for the visually handicapped, a ropes and initiative course, 103 campsites, a camp store, two modern bathhouses, a laundry room, picnic tables and fire rings. It's also a favorite place for horseback riding and hikes along the 8-mile nature trail system.

Deep Creek Lock Park
300 Luray St., Chesapeake
• **(757) 382-6411**

This is a 25-acre site named for the Corps of Engineers' lock that separates the salt water of Deep Creek from the fresh water of the historic Dismal Swamp Canal. The heavily wooded park includes several overlook towers, picnic shelters, play areas, a fitness trail, indoor restrooms and a combination pedestrian bridge and elevated walkway system to traverse a tidal inlet and marsh area. Diverse foot trails wind through the woods, and canoeing, fishing and crabbing are favorite Deep Creek activities.

Great Bridge Lock Park
Lock Rd. off Battlefield Blvd., Chesapeake
• **(757) 382-6411**

At the transition from the Southern Branch of the Elizabeth River to the Albemarle and Chesapeake Canal along the Intracoastal Waterway, this 19-acre park features a two-lane boat ramp, picnic shelters and a foot trail along the northern shoreline and through the western portion of the park. There's also a large play area and extensive fishing and crabbing areas at the bulkheaded banks. Because one of the area's favorite activities is boat-watching, bleachers have been erected for glimpsing the

many yachts that transit the lock southbound in the fall and northbound in the spring.

Indian River Park
Military Hwy., Chesapeake
• **(757) 382-6411**

While the City of Norfolk actually owns the 100-acre tract known as Indian River Park,

Canoeing is a popular pastime in the Chesapeake Bay and its tributaries.

Photo: Courtesy of City of Virginia Beach

the City of Chesapeake uses 35 acres of the northern section for activities including basketball, baseball and picnicking. There's also a playground. Discussions on joint development of the southern section, such as undeveloped trail opportunities, are still under way.

PARKS

Western Branch Park and Sports Park
4437 Portsmouth Blvd., Chesapeake
• **(757) 382-6411**

This 80-acre park, where volunteers planted thousands of wildflowers and scouts marked a rudimentary nature trail, features a community center, two playgrounds and a picnic shelter. The Sports Park area has an access road leading to five lighted softball (multi-use) fields, a concession stand and comfort station, two volleyball courts and two half-court basketball courts.

Lakeside Park
Byrd and Holey Aves., South Norfolk
• **(757) 382-6411**

Large lawn areas, a wooded section, picnic shelters with grills, play areas and walkways highlight this 6.5-acre park. Fishing along the bulkheaded lake is popular.

Greenbrier Sports Park
Greenbrier Pkwy. Chesapeake
• **(757) 382-6411**

When you come here, get ready to play! A 15-acre site, this sports park lives up to its name with eight tournament-quality lighted tennis courts and two tournament-quality softball fields. For spectators, there's also a picnic shelter and play equipment.

Oak Grove Lake Park
Great Bridge Bypass, Chesapeake
• **(757) 382-6411**

Chesapeake's newest park opened in 2000

with the lake as its centerpiece. With 130 acres and a one-plus mile trail around the lake, this is already becoming a favorite spot for runners and bikers.

Suffolk

Lone Star Lakes Park
Pembroke Ln., Suffolk
• **(757) 255-4308**

Lone Star Lakes Park is a 1,063-acre wilderness park in the Chuckatuck section of the city. It offers 11 lakes for freshwater fishing, plus nature trails, a picnic area with tables and grills, a playground, a 4.5-mile horse trail, an archery range, a model airplane flying field, a fishing and crabbing pier and shoreline fishing areas. The park is open seven days a week, with daily hours varying roughly from dawn to dusk. Daily fees range from $1 to $3 according to activity. There are no boat rentals, and gas motors are not permitted.

Bennetts Creek Park
Rt. 659 Shoulders Hill Rd., Suffolk
• **(757) 925-6325**

The main attractions at this 50-acre park are two free boat ramps that access the Nansemond River. You'll also find a playground, tennis courts, picnic shelters, a nature trail, open fields, a handicapped accessible fishing and crabbing pier and plenty of fresh air and sunshine. Park hours are sunrise to sunset, seven days a week.

PARKS

The Beaches

Just as the eyes are the mirror to the soul, so is the vanity license plate a window to the passions. And around Hampton Roads, our vanity plates spell out a love of surf and sand, with messages such as 2D-SEA, SEA4ME, SURFER, SUNFUN, SUNBUM, BCHBUM, WAVES and H20-CAR.

As you can see, we aren't shy about loving the beach. On a nice Saturday morning in summer, thousands of us pack up our gear and head for the oceanfront or bayfront to soak up the rays, frolic in the waves, take a walk or build a castle, depending on the age group of our party. There's just nothing like it for relaxation.

But maybe relaxing isn't your style. Maybe you want a high-powered beach experience with a colorful crowd to look at and an outdoor patio for lunch. We have that too. We even have beaches without people - but please don't tell anybody.

In this chapter, we'll give you the lowdown on the region's favorite pastime of hitting the beach. You may be surprised to learn how many different beaches we have to choose from—a whopping 38 miles in Virginia Beach—and that each has its own distinct personality. We have several on the Atlantic Ocean and several on the Chesapeake Bay. Our beautiful state parks also have beaches, although these are more for roaming than swimming.

While swimming is only one of the reasons to visit the beach, it is the most dangerous seaside recreation and requires the most precaution. In general, the more crowded the beach, the more likely it is to have a lifeguard. Lifeguards are on duty from 9:30 AM to 6 PM daily from mid-May to mid-September between 1st and 41st Streets and at Camp Pendleton, Croatan, Sandbridge and Fort Story beaches in Virginia Beach. These physically fit individuals will keep you out of the water when it's too dangerous to swim. Since many smaller beaches in the region are not guarded at all, common sense is one of the most important things you can take with you to the beach. If the waves look big or if the lifeguards are flying "dangerous currents" flags, don't risk it.

You also need to use common sense with the sun. Many vacations have been ruined for people who didn't think they needed sunscreen when they discovered later, in the emergency room, that protection would have been a good idea. That large body of water you sit beside at the beach reflects the sun's rays like a mirror. So even if you normally forgo sunscreen, use it at the beach.

Finally, if you want to blend in easily with our native flora and fauna, here are a few beachgoing tips. Guys, leave the Speedos for sunbathing at home and doing laps at the Y. We don't wear them on the beach. Cut-off jeans will also mark you instantly as a tourist. Local males wear baggy surf shorts that drip-dry quickly, so they can throw on a T-shirt and pair of shoes for a quick lunch or run to the store. Teva or Birkenstock sandals and tiny sunglasses will give teenagers a head-to-toe "I-was-born-here" look. If you're too mature or too preppy for that look, try a pair of Land's End or Patagonia trunks with an old polo shirt, boat shoes and a pair of Ray Bans.

Women need only look to the latest swimwear fashions in Vogue or any publication like it. Local women buy lots of swimsuits and they're usually right on top of whatever the trend of the moment happens to be. In recent years, we've seen neon, gingham and push-up bra tops all over the place. Black is always correct and so is showing off a great body, if you have one. We don't go in much for elaborate cover-ups. A husband's button-down shirt or a pair of shorts usually does the trick.

Of course, one of the easiest ways to look local is to shop local. The surf shops always have the most current styles. One of the biggest shops is Wave Riding Vehicles on 19th Street and Cypress Avenue. Another popular store for beachwear is 17th Street Surf Shop. Its flagship location is at 307 Virginia Beach Boulevard with offshoots in various shopping centers throughout the region. Women who find surf shop suits a little skimpy can find high fashion that they feel comfortable in at Megs or Hobies, both of which are on Laskin Road. Ready to dive in? Here's the nitty gritty on our beaches.

The Virginia Beach Resort Oceanfront

This is the first area most visitors and newcomers think of when you mention the beach. The resort area, also called The Strip stretches roughly from 1st to 38th Streets in Virginia Beach. If you want an action-packed beach experience, this is the spot for you. You can rent a bike or a pair of in-line skates on the boardwalk, eat lunch at an outdoor cafe, fish from the pier at 14th Street, watch a city-sponsored concert or play at either the 24th Street or 17th Street stages and buy outrageously tacky souvenirs at one of the many shops on Atlantic Avenue—it's all happening here.

The city posts lifeguards on every block along the resort strip. In addition to looking out for your safety, the lifeguards also rent chairs, umbrellas and rafts, so you don't have to lug all that stuff with you. To avoid parking problems, the city now has big public lots at Fourth Street under the Rudee Inlet Bridge and on 25th and Pacific, 19th and Pacific and 1st and Atlantic. Fees are charged at all of them. Free parking is available at the Virginia Beach Pavilion on 19th Street, but it's a long walk to the beach. There also are 25 private lots and metered street parking that costs $.75 an hour. Don't park too long at a meter—it costs $12 per violation. Public restrooms without changing facilities are at 2nd, 17th, 24th and 31st Streets. A public restroom with changing facilities is at 1st Street.

Although the resort strip is home to most of the beach's hotel rooms and visitors, it isn't just a tourist area. In recent years the boardwalk has been widened and refurbished with wonderful sculptures, native landscaping and benches that beckon anyone with a few extra minutes and an ice cream cone. Locals who work in the resort area in the summertime commute to their jobs via the boardwalk's bike path. The boardwalk is also a popular hangout spot for area hardbodies who want to show off their hard-won muscles and teenagers with outlandish haircuts. It's prime people-watching territory. A few hours amidst the varied crowd here and you'll begin to understand the saying, "Life's A Beach."

The North End Beach

North of 40th Street is where most of the local families get their feet wet. The beach widens the further north you go and by the 70th and 80th blocks of Atlantic Avenue, it's downright huge, with sea oats, dunes and little sun-browned children in addition to the waves and sand. Visitors pay a price for this added beauty, however. There are no public restrooms or public parking lots near this area of the beach. There are also no lifeguards. To enjoy the North End beach, you need to get there early to find one of the few hard-won parking spots available on the street or park by an understanding friend's house. Pack a lunch or snacks. Lifeguards are not on duty here.

Croatan

This beach flanks the resort area on the south. It's popular with locals because it has an all-day surfing area while most of the Virginia Beach oceanfront is off-limits to surfers from 10 AM to 6 PM. There's a lifeguard at the surf area as well as a public restroom and pay phone. The south end of Croatan is not guarded and mainly attracts the well-heeled crowd that can afford to live along its shores. To reach Croatan, take Atlantic Avenue south to General Booth Boulevard and make a left onto Croatan Road.

The Narrows

A small beach for fishing, crabbing and boating is tucked away at the end of 64th Street on a body of water called Broad Bay. This is also a favorite spot for area Jet Ski enthusiasts to practice their sport. Just follow Atlantic Avenue north from the resort area to 64th Street and turn left. You'll see the entrance to First Landing State Park at the end of the street. A park ranger will probably stop your car just inside the park to gather your fees (they are nominal) and give you directions to the boat ramp/fishing area. If you visit in the off-season, just follow the directions on the signs. The trails on either side of the ranger station are unsurpassed for hiking and jogging. Public restrooms are near both the boat ramp and the ranger station.

Fort Story

This best-kept secret beach is at the extreme North End of the numbered streets in the Virginia Beach resort area. To find it, simply travel along Atlantic Avenue as far north as you can go. Between 82nd and 83rd Streets, Atlantic Avenue will curve into Shore Drive. There's a light there, and you need to take a hard right to stay on Atlantic Avenue. After five more blocks, you'll see the entrance to Fort Story Army Base. Be prepared to show a picture ID at the guard station and tell the guard you want to use the beach—it's open to the public on Friday through Monday. Free parking, plus a portable toilet, will be immediately to your right after the guard station. Like the rest of the North End, the beach here is wide and beautiful, but it offers out-of-towners the advantages of easy parking, a lifeguard in the summer and a bathroom, albeit a primitive one. Another bonus is that the area behind the beach is largely undeveloped, making this a particularly pretty spot to soak up some sun.

INSIDERS' TIP
Although common wisdom might suggest that dolphins would prefer quiet waters, researchers have found just the opposite to be true. Dolphins, just like people, seem to gravitate toward the beach in the summer. In fact, so many of these marine mammals visit the beach in the summertime that researchers have dubbed the Cape Henry area, at the north end of the resort city, "Dolphin Disneyland." You can spot these frolicsome creatures anywhere along the beach, between 1st and 88th streets, jumping joyfully up out of the water and diving back in again. They travel in groups, so if you spot one, keep looking at the same area and more will soon appear.

INSIDERS' TIP
If you've got a burning desire to get out on—or above—the ocean, rent a jet ski or go parasailing. Jet skis are available in Virginia Beach at Enticer Water Sports, 308 Mediterranean Avenue (757) 422-2277, and Rudee Inlet Jet Ski Rentals, 300 Winston Salem Avenue (757) 428-4614. To soar above the ocean, hook up with Air America Parasail at 227 Mediterannean Avenue (757) 428-1240.

Dam Neck

Once open only to military personnel, Dam Neck's beaches started welcoming the public in 1998. The Fleet Combat Training Center Atlantic Dam Neck has wide, secluded beaches right along the Atlantic Ocean. The Shifting Sands and Sea Breeze beaches are open daily from 10 AM to 6 PM during warmer months. Lifeguards are on duty.

There is plenty of parking nearby. A $2 per carload fee is charged on weekends and holidays. Also available are barbecue and picnic areas as well as a snack bar, showers and equipment rentals. The beach is at General Booth Boulevard and Dam Neck Road. Call (757) 433-62264 for more details.

THE BEACHES

Chick's Beach

This is one of two popular Chesapeake Bay beaches. To find it from the resort area, take Atlantic Avenue to 82nd Street and bear left onto Shore Drive. This beautiful road will first take you through the densely wooded areas of First Landing/Seashore State Park. When you begin to emerge from the woods, you'll be in the region of the good Bay beaches.

The first beach you'll pass is actually part of Seashore State Park. (To reach it use the turn-in on the right-hand side of the road if you're traveling away from the resort area.) Here you'll find a ranger station with a restroom and one of those unpopulated beaches we mentioned in the introduction. We refer to it only in passing so as not to draw a crowd.

If you continue on Shore Drive, you'll come to the Lesner Bridge, which spans the junction of Broad Bay and Chesapeake Bay. The Duck-In, a landmark seafood restaurant by the base of this bridge, signifies that you're in Chick's Beach territory. The restaurant has a spectacular view and serves as popular meeting places for Chick's Beach visitors. With its outdoor bar housed in a pier/gazebo combination, The Duck-In hosts popular beach parties that draw throngs of revelers in the summertime. To find the beach, go over the bridge and turn right onto any street. Parking is catch as catch can, and there are no public restrooms.

The Bay tends to be a lot calmer than the ocean so you'll see lots of sailboats, board sails and kayaks around here. Chick's Beach Sailing Center, on the northwest end of the bridge, is the place to go for more information on watersports and Chick's Beach events.

With 38 miles of varied coastlines, we have beaches to suit every mood.

Photo: Courtesy of City of Virginia Beach

Back Bay National Wildlife Refuge

A pristine Atlantic Ocean beach for nature lovers is found within this home to thousands of migrating geese, ducks and swans. To find it from the resort area, take General Booth Boulevard to Princess Anne Road to Sandbridge Road and follow the signs. To preserve the integrity of the park, strict rules are enforced. First, the park is only open during daylight hours. Parking is permitted only in designated areas during open hours, and only those with special permits are allowed motorized vehicle access to beaches and unpaved dirt roads. Other no-nos: unleashed pets, guns, horses or open fires. Likewise, the fragile dunes are off-limits to visitors, but that still leaves the beach shore and nature trails for hiking.

The Seaside Dune Trail guides you from the parking lot to the stunning beach. The north mile of the beach is closed to protect shore birds. The south beach is open, although swimming, sunbathing and surfing are prohibited. Just consider Back Bay to be the perfect place to bring your binoculars and camera, a canteen of water, a picnic lunch and a big can of bug spray.

False Cape State Park

Five miles south of the Back Bay Refuge sits Virginia's most remote beach. Home to migratory waterfowl, deer, wild horses, wild pigs and protected marshlands, False Cape got it's name because sailors used to mistake it for Cape Henry. The park is a 6-mile stretch of undisturbed beach along a barrier spit that divides the ocean from Back Bay and, until recently was accessible only by foot, bicycle or boat. Now, rangers are shuttling visitors in via trams, from the Back Bay Refuge (see Parks chapter for details). Despite the additional access, the beach remains pristine and undeveloped. Other than pit toilets, there are absolutely no amenities.

Sandbridge/Little Island Park

Ah, Sandbridge. This beachy neighborhood is best appreciated as a small city-within-a-city. It's a private, residential community, with its own stores, restaurants and churches, but locals are always happy to have visitors around. To find Sandbridge, take General Booth Boulevard away from the resort area. At Nimmo United Methodist Church (a very Insider landmark) make a left on Princess Anne Road. Follow that to Sandbridge Road and make another left. When you see Sandfiddler Road and the silver-blue water tower, you're in Sandbridge.

Twenty years ago, Sandbridge was a wide gorgeous beach. Unfortunately, the area has taken the brunt of almost every significant storm to pass our way since then, and the beach is narrower than it used to be. You'll want to time your visit for low tide (call (757) 640-5555 for tide information) or try Sandbridge's other beach, Little Island Park. This beach takes full advantage of its location on Sandbridge Beach as well as Back Bay, and its fishing pier makes it especially attractive for anglers. The broad beach is lifeguarded during summer months from 9:30 AM to 6 PM, and after a swim you can move on to the playground, tennis courts, basketball or volleyball courts. A snack bar, restrooms and shady picnic area are here at Little Island. You'll probably have to pay for parking in a nearby lot. On-street parking is very limited and once yielded us a parking ticket.

INSIDERS' TIP

It's illegal in Virginia Beach to do the following on the beach during the summer: play ball, toss a Frisbee, walk a dog, sleep there at night and drink alcoholic beverages. It's also illegal to change clothes in public restrooms. Fines average $43.

Ocean View

At the end of Shore Drive or at the foot of Granby Street, depending on where you're coming from, is Norfolk's Chesapeake Bay beach. Popular with families who don't want to make the jaunt all the way to oceanfront, Ocean View has a nice beach, calm waters and public restrooms. The beach is near upscale homes going up in an area that is being rejuvenated.

Ocean View Park is a 6.5-acre plot that features a large gazebo for presentations and dancing, a beach that's lifeguarded during summer months, public restrooms, a short boardwalk, a beach handicap access ramp and lovely lawns. It plays host to the summer season's free Big Bands on the Bay series, held Sunday nights from 7 until 9 PM.

Golf

From the sting of Honey Bee to the agony of Hell's Point, Hampton Roads has the makings of a duffer's paradise. You could play 700 holes of golf between Virginia Beach and Williamsburg, and our average daily temperature of 60 degrees will keep your bag parked at the front door almost every day of the year. You can even watch the pros at work: in October the $1.1 million Michelob Golf Classic is held at the Kingsmill in Williamsburg, where two-time U.S. Open Champion and native son Curtis Strange is the resident celeb/pro.

According to the National Golf Association, there are 518,000 golfers age 12 and older in Virginia, a quarter of whom call Hampton Roads home. That's nearly 10 percent of our population. A word to the wise: this area proudly features some of the state's toughest advanced courses that gained their reputation for good reason. The options on where to play have picked up with the opening of new courses in the past few years and the complete refurbishing of several older courses. There are even more courses under construction as the region strives to make itself a golf destination.

If the 20 or so courses in southside Hampton Roads aren't enough to satisfy the golf urge, then hop in the car and head to the Williamsburg area or Hampton, Newport News and other nearby cities. There golfers will find even more courses. Several of those in the Williamsburg area have won Golf Digest's coveted best new course awards in recent years.

For those who prefer golf packages, there are two options. The Virginia Beach Golf Association packages six area courses with rooms at an area hotels. Call 757-422-5115. Golf Williamsburg provides a similar plan for the Williamsburg area. Call 1-888-246-5392.

If you're long on ambition but short on temper, you may want to wait until you can consistently break 100 before you consider shelling

LOOK FOR:
- **Basic Beautiful Courses**
- **Intermediate Play**
- **Killer Courses**

With an aggressive marketing campaign of its top courses, Virginia Beach hopes to become a golfing destination.

Photo: Courtesy of City of Virginia Beach

out greens and cart fees for the most difficult courses. Unless, of course, you have stock in the golf ball industry and room on your score card to fill in those triple figures. If your clubs still have their initial shine, wide fairways, few sand traps and little or no water hazards will make your 18 a lot more pleasurable. To that end, we'll list all the public play possibilities not only by city but also by degree of difficulty. We've also included the toughest holes as defined by some of the area's leading pros.

This area has some gorgeous private courses, but to play on one of these, you'll need an invitation from someone other than us. Fees for play vary as wildly as the complexity of the courses. You can whack at the ball on most of our local basic courses for an average of $10, intermediates for about $20 and killers for around $60 and up. Guess it's a quirk of nature that the more pain you want to inflict on yourself, the more you'll pay. So step up to the white tees, or blue if you dare, and ping your way into one of the most popular sports in Hampton Roads.

The Basic, Beautiful Courses

Virginia Beach

Bow Creek Municipal Golf Course
3425 Club House Rd., Virginia Beach
• **(757) 431-3763**
Thank goodness. Here you'll find wide, forgiving fairways and few man-made hazards and trees. This par 70, 5917-yard course does have small greens and sharp doglegs along some fairly ominous wooded roughs, so we're not exactly talking a cakewalk. Even so, it's quite a reasonable course, with greens fees to match. Greens fees are around $25. Ask about seniors and juniors special discounts, and if you plan to get a snack here, bring lots of quarters—it's vending machines only, folks.

Kempsville Greens Municipal Golf Course
4840 Princess Anne Rd.
• **(757) 474-8441**
A Russ Breeden-designed 6013-yard, par 70 course, Kempsville Greens has the devilish habit of confiscating your ball in one of its three lakes or thick woods. There are some fine greens, an excellent driving range and super senior discounts at this city-owned facility. There's also

a practice green, pro shop and snack bar to further eliminate the possibility of yard work on Saturday. Greens fees are $16 weekdays and $18 on weekends. Carts are $9 per player.

Norfolk

Lake Wright Golf Course
6280 Northampton Blvd., Norfolk
• **(757)-461-6251**
It appears easy enough, but it plays far tougher than its par 70. You'll find trees, water and nasty prevailing winds. No. 5, a testy par 3, is a 190-yard nightmare over Lake Wright that was judged the fourth toughest hole to play in the area. If you make it over the lake, you're up against a trap to the left and bunker to the right of the green. Just pray the wind's going in your direction. For extra practice, however, there is one of the best driving ranges around. You'll also find a putting/chipping area, a pro shop and a snack bar. Greens fees are $18 weekdays and $20 weekends; carts are $10 and mandatory until noon on weekends.

Ocean View Golf Course
9610 Norfolk Ave., Norfolk
• **(757)-480-2094**
Voted Norfolk's best golf course in 1994-95, Ocean View is getting a complete makeover in 2000. The original course featured straight, if narrow, fairways, a few sharp doglegs and trap-lined greens. The renovated course promises to be even more challenging. There's also a practice area, pro shop and snack bar. Greens fees for this 5900-yard course range from $22 to $27. Carts are mandatory until 10 AM on weekends and holidays from March through November.

Portsmouth

The Links at City Park
Portsmouth City Park, Portsmouth
• **(757) 465-2935**
Let's start simple. This nine-hole executive course is really the easiest place in the area to test your clubs. It's the perfect place for juniors and others just getting their first taste of the golf bug. Matching the ease of the course are the truly affordable fees for both unlimited weekday and 36-hole weekend play.

In 1998 the course had a $1.9 million upgrade that made it even better to play. One thing that couldn't be improved upon is the course's scenic location along the Elizabeth

River. In addition to its nine holes, The Links has a 30-station lighted driving range and a challenging 18-hole putting course. Golf fees are $12 for Portsmouth residents for 18 holes and $8 for nine holes. Golfers from outside the city pay slightly more.

Intermediate Play

Virginia Beach

Honey Bee Golf Course
5016 S. Independence Blvd., Virginia Beach
• (757) 471-2768

Designed by Rees Jones, Honey Bee is a 6005-yard challenge, what with its 80 monstrous sand traps, elevated tees and water on 10 holes. Honey Bee is privately owned but open to the public and is home to the Virginia Beach Golf Academy, an assemblage of four of the finest teaching professionals in the area. Get there early or hang around late to practice on the driving range and putting and chipping greens. There's also a full-service restaurant for that much-needed refreshment after play. Carts are required at peak time on weekends. Greens fees range from $32 to $42.

Owl's Creek Golf Center
415 S. Birdneck Rd., Virginia Beach
• (757) 428-2800

Designed by Brook Parker, this is a great course for the golfer who wants to pack 18 holes into three hours or less. Dubbed "The Little Monster," this executive 4155-yard, par 62 course, all par 3s and 4s, does offer the opportunity for extra practice on its lighted driving range and super practice putting greens. Greens fees are $16 to walk and $24 to ride. There's also a twilight special of $18 for 18 holes with a cart. Check out the pro shop, snack bar and all-grass putting course, which costs $5 for adults and $3 for kids.

Red Wing Lake Golf Course
1080 Prosperity Rd., Virginia Beach
• (757) 437-4845

The greens are large and the fairways wide, but you'll still have to face water hazards on 10 holes and 84 traps along the fairways and long sloping greens. If you're adept at short-iron shots, have at the par 5 No. 18, the ninth-tough-

est hole in the area. It not only challenges your birdie with the lake in front of the heavily trapped green, but also tests your accuracy just getting there through a narrowing fairway. The city owns and operates this 7080-yard course, which has a driving range and small snack bar. In 1999 it added another 18 holes. Greens fees are reduced for Virginia Beach residents. For others they range from $29 to $31.

Stumpy Lake Golf Course
4797 Indian River Rd., Virginia Beach
• (757) 467-6119

This is one to write home about. A Robert Trent Jones-designed 6846-yard course, Stumpy Lake is surrounded by water on four sides and entered via a bridge. Amateurs and professionals alike fear the 400-yard, par 4 No. 5, the 10th-toughest hole in the region. The dogleg right to an elevated, gently trapped green presents a hint of the difficulty that awaits. Your choice at the tee is directly over the trees or a long fade or slice to hold the fairway. And don't count on the green to hold a flat approach shot. At least you can enjoy the quiet tranquility of the secluded location and get plenty of practice on the driving range and two practice putting/chipping areas. Greens fees are $29.75 to ride and $20.75 to walk. Afterwards, console yourself in the pro shop or the snack bar.

Portsmouth

Bide-A-Wee Golf Club
83 Bide-A Wee Ln., Portsmouth
• (757) 393-5269

This par 72, 6800-yard beauty is a pretty rough trip for even a fairly good shotmaker, and it also boasts the toughest hole in our area—the 405-yard Hole 8. If you've got a booming tee shot, you're looking at a narrow, critical landing area flanked by sentinel oaks. Ahead there's more to outsmart you on this, one of the longer dogleg par 4s in the area—an elevated green with water hazard to the left and woods that flank the entire right side of the hole. Just try and break 73, the course record that stood for many years. The course closed for a $9 million renovation in 1997 and reopened in spring of 1999. U.S. Open champion and homegrown hero Curtis Strange served as design consultant on the renovation, which in-

INSIDERS' TIP
Call ahead for tee times. When you are visiting for a short time or have other activities, calling ahead will give you a chance to schedule your golf game in too.

GOLF

cludes a clubhouse and restaurant and driving range. Greens fees range from $25 to 30 weekdays and $30 to 35 on weekends, including carts.

Chesapeake

Chesapeake Golf Club
1201 Club House Dr.,
Chesapeake
• (757) 547-1122

You've got to hit the ball straight to beat this 6100-yard, par 3 course. It's a tight, challenging course that winds through the Las Gaviotas neighborhood. This 18-hole course, formerly the Seven Springs Golf Club, recently became an American Golf property and is open to the public as well as members. A few years ago the course had $500,000 in renovations. Greens fees range from $23 to $35 with a cart. Carts are optional, and walking the course costs $11.

Suffolk

Harbour View Golf Course
5801 Harbour View Blvd., Suffolk
• (757) 484-7172

Opened in 1999, this course takes golfers

on a scenic jaunt through the wetlands and marshes that border the Nansemond River. The course is part of the Harbour View upscale housing community that is under construction. Its 18 holes stretch along 6800 yards and have fast greens. The course was designed by Tom Doak and is a nominee for Golf Digest's "best new course" award. Greens fees were still being determined at press time.

Sleepy Hole Golf Course
4700 Sleepy Hole Rd., Suffolk
• (757) 538-4100

Even though it's long and surrounded by water, the secluded Suffolk location of this City of Portsmouth-owned course offers little distraction or excuses. The past home of the Crestar LPGA Classic, this 6853-yard course boasts the second-toughest hole in the area, the par 4, 423-yard No. 18. It requires a long, slight draw off the tee to clear the rolling hill and carry down the open fairway to within 180 yards of the green. Don't even think about the marshes of the Nansemond River on the left and the Obici House and trap on the right as you land on the green. Just lob your second shot short, chip and pray. Greens fees range

Golfing is a year-round passion in Hampton Roads' mild climate.

Photo: Courtesy of Virginia Fairways

from $32 to $38. Carts are mandatory until noon on weekends, and the grill room here is a full-service restaurant, worthy of consoling your wounded pride.

Suffolk Golf Course
1227 Holland Rd., Suffolk
• **(757) 539-6298**

With wide fairways on the front nine and narrow ones on the back, Suffolk claims a birdie killer with its par 5450-yard No. 18, the 18th-toughest hole in the area. A gambler's hole, it's dominated by a lake that begins on the left side of the fairway and lingers to about 20 yards short of the narrow green. If you make it through the 15-yard-wide fairway, look out for the traps to the right, left and rear of the green. The course has all the extras to distract you: driving range, putting and chipping green, pro shop and snack bar. Residents play only $9 to walk 18 during the week and just $10 on weekends. Nonresident fees are around $23.

Killer Courses

Virginia Beach

Hell's Point Golf Club
2700 Atwoodtown Rd., Virginia Beach
• **(757) 721-3400**

Designed by Rees Jones, the 6900-yard Hell's Point has been rated one of the top-130 courses in the country by the Golf Architects of America. If you survive the three large lakes and 61 sand traps, you'll still have great stories to tell about the snake that fought you for your ball in the dangerous rough. Watch out for the 389-yard No. 2, judged the 11th-toughest hole in the region. It's a long par 4 with a narrow fairway and double-trapped green. For the thrill of defeat, reserve a tee time a week in advance. Carts are required for play, and greens fees are $60. There's a snack bar, driving range and putting/chipping area too.

Heron Ridge Golf Club
Seaboard Rd., Virginia Beach
• **(757) 426-3800**

This 7012-yard, 18-hole Fred Couples course was completed in 1999 in the Virginia Beach countryside. It is only the third Couples signa-

ture course built in this country. For this one he teamed up with noted golf designer Gene Bates. Their handiwork brought a new dimension to the region's golf options. This tricky course meanders around lakes and wetlands making it a perfect home for its namesake heron. Greens fees at this semi-private course are about $60, which includes a cart.

Tournament Plays Club of Virginia Beach
1801 Princess Anne Rd., Virginia Beach
• **(757) 563-9440**

This much-awaited $15 million, 18-hole golf course opened in 1999 with the promise of taking the region's golfing to a new level. It is a contender for Golf Digest magazine's "best new courses" award for the year. The club's setting among rolling meadows and hardwood forests is just a few minutes drive from the beach. TPC, as it is known, was designed by architect Pete Dye and U.S. Open champion Curtis Strange, who grew up nearby and is a pro at Kingsmill near Williamsburg. The 7500-yard-long course is expected to host the Nike Tour. But any other time the public is invited to meet the challenge of this killer course. Greens fees range from $65 to $110 with discounts available for Virginia Beach residents, the military, youth players, and retired golfers.

Chesapeake

Cahoon Plantation
1501 Cedar Rd., Chesapeake
• **(757) 436-2775**

This semi-private club opened in 1999 to give a new challenge to golfers. Maryland-based Aulton & Clark Associates did the honors as course designers. Cahoon Plantation's goal is to rival the Williamsburg-area Kingsmill Resort courses, which had the same designer. This is the only complete bent grass course in the area, making the entire course smooth and green year-round. This is a 45-hole course, giving plenty of options for which holes to play. Each 18-hole, par 3 course is over 7000 yards long. Daily greens fees range from $50 to $65, which includes a cart. Carts are required for the 18-hole courses with walking option on the nine-hole course.

Fishing

Oh, to be an angler when spring hits Hampton Roads. You can tell the season is starting because all those funny, fuzzy little lures, and rods and reels start taking over shelf space where footballs used to be. Fishing frenzy hits, and the throngs head to the seas—each angler looking for the one that got away last season.

The beauty of it all is that you don't need a lot of talent or a lot of money to enjoy this sport. The basic prerequisites are patience and a lift to the nearest pier or head boat. Whether you're inshore or offshore, the biting's grand from March through December, thanks in great part to the Chesapeake Bay, considered by some marine biologists to be the country's most productive spawning ground for saltwater fish. Each spring many fish, such as striped bass, herring, shad and sturgeon, migrate to the Bay's tributaries to spawn. Others—speckled trout, flounder, spot, croaker and gray trout—call the Bay home for the first stages of their lives.

Beyond the Bay, the big bluefish, bluefin and yellowfin tuna, marlin, dolphin and wahoo are a hook away in the Atlantic Ocean. Likewise, there's some of the hottest angling action when the big billfish, amberjack, cobia and black drum start their summer runs. To find out the fishing hot spots of the week, call the guy who makes it his business to know what's biting: Bob Hutchinson, who writes about the open-air pursuits of hunting and fishing for *The Virginian-Pilot.* Bob has a weekly fishing report that you can access by calling (757) 640-5555 and pressing category number 3474. There's no cost for the call.

Whether you cast a line on one of hundreds of freshwater lakes, head off to a quiet cove, drag your tackle to the nearest pier or trawl for big ones on the open ocean, your chances of a big catch are better here than almost anywhere on earth. That may or may not be a fish story depending on your results on any given day.

No fishing license is required to fish in salt water from Cape Henry in Virginia Beach south to the North Carolina line; a license is required for

Fishing is a great way to spend a day together.

Photo: Courtesy of Northern Neck Travel Council

all anglers age 16 and older to fish in the Chesapeake Bay. In fact, a license is needed for resident anglers 16 and older for all freshwater fishing. Licenses are valid for the calendar year January 1 through December 31 and cost $12.50 for fresh water, $7.50 for salt water. Nonresidents can purchase a five-day license for $6 fresh water and $5.50 salt water. Most bait and tackle shops, marinas and department store sporting goods counters sell fishing licenses.

Avid anglers should take note of the Annual Virginia Saltwater Fishing Tournament held April through November. It is a Commonwealth of Virginia program that maintains state records and honors certain catches with a citation—a laminated certificate that displays the angler's name, the species caught, the date, etc. The tournament is open to anyone, and 22 species are eligible for citations. If you're interested, call the tournament's headquarters at (757) 491-5160.

If you're a clubby kind of angler, there are a few local organizations that would love to lure you in. Get the angle from the following:

Tidewater's Angler's Club, Virginia Beach, (757) 496-3664
Virginia Beach Angler's Club, Virginia Beach, (757) 481-5719
Little Creek Bassmasters, Chesapeake, (757) 548-3784

Places To Fish

Virginia Beach

Virginia Beach Fishing Pier
15th St. and Oceanfront, Virginia Beach
• **(757) 428-2333**

Fish, or just watch those who try, 24 hours a day all summer long. You can even rent a rod to try your own luck. Crabbing is also popular from this Atlantic Ocean pier, where crab cages and bait are available. Open April through October, there's a small fee to fish and an even smaller fee just to watch.

Lynnhaven Fishing Pier
2350 Starfish Rd. off Shore Dr., Virginia Beach
• **(757) 481-7071**

Twenty-four-hour fish-a-thons happen here along the Chesapeake Bay all summer. Look for spot and croaker early in the season, then cast for flounder, speckled trout and puppy drum. There's a small fee to fish or watch, and equipment is available for rent.

Sea Gull Fishing Pier
Chesapeake Bay Bridge-Tunnel, South Island
• **(757) 464-4641**

Perhaps one of the country's most unusual

INSIDERS' TIP
Winter is the only time to catch striped bass, a.k.a rockfish. A longtime ban on rockfish was lifted several years ago, and there's now alimited season in which it can be caught legally.

fishing piers, Sea Gull pier is rooted from a man-made island that's part of the Chesapeake Bay Bridge-Tunnel and extends 600 feet into the middle of the Bay. Beginning in mid-June, you might reel in a cobia of 40 pounds or more. It's also the best time to catch the biggest gray trout. There's no fee to fish here, but you will have to pay the regular $10 one-way fare to cross the bridge-tunnel.

Little Island Fishing Pier
Sandbridge, Virginia Beach
• **(757) 426-7200**

From this pier it's possible to snag a big bluefish, along with a plethora of other choppers that come close to the Atlantic Ocean shoreline. A favorite summer hangout for Sandbridge visitors, there's a small fee to park as well as to fish from April through October.

Norfolk

Harrison Boat House and Pier
414 W. Ocean View Ave., Norfolk
• **(757) 587-9630**

A Chesapeake Bay landmark on the fishing scene, this is the place to count on the biggest spot and croaker hauls. Granted, these are little-league fish, most less than 12 ounces, but their numbers are incredible. Harrison's is the perfect place to be when Virginia's most popular inshore fishing season begins in late July or

FISHING

Fishing, like agriculture, is a traditional way to make a living in this area.

Photo: Courtesy of Eastern Shore Tourism Commission

early August. The season lasts well into September and even into October if mild weather continues.

Willoughby Bay Marina
1651 Bayville St., Norfolk
• (757) 588-2663

Even if you're not an angler, this is a great place to wander on a summer's day, taking in the sights of sailboats and boaters in the Chesapeake Bay. Count on bringing in more spot and croaker here than you can catch all summer long.

Lake Smith
5381 Shell Rd., Norfolk
• (757) 460-2487

One of the largest freshwater lakes in the area, Lake Smith boasts an ample supply of largemouth bass, bluegill, crappie, catfish, stripped bass and carp. Eighty boats are available for rent, but you can also just cast from the shore. A fully stocked bait and tackle shop is available for anything an angler might need for a day of promising fishing.

Portsmouth/Suffolk

Sleepy Hole Park
Sleepy Hole Rd., Suffolk
• (757) 393-5056

This gorgeous park is located in Suffolk, but owned and operated by the city of Portsmouth. It's home to immense mature oak trees that shelter a lake well-stocked with panfish, catfish and large mouth bass. Charge is only $1 for a full day of possible frustration.

Deep-Sea Fishing and Marinas

How about a 1,000-pound blue marlin? Or a 50-pound white marlin? Not to mention bluefin tuna, dolphin, wahoo, false albacore, amberjack and the possibility of a wicked sunburn. They're all out in the blue waters of the Atlantic, and there are many charter boats waiting to cruise out to where they can be found.

Offshore fishing does have its price, however. Fleets sail from several sites in both Virginia Beach and Norfolk, and you and five of your buddies can be aboard for a price of $500 for a day of bottom-fishing to as much as $1,000 for a jaunt out to the marlin grounds. A less expensive alternative is an outing on a head boat, so named because they charge by the person, or by the head. Head boats, which depart from Virginia Beach and Norfolk, concentrate mainly closer to shore, and rates run from as little as $20 for a four-hour spot fishing trip to $40 for an all-day adventure.

Charter and head boats are very popular, especially when local fishing forecasters raise the checkered flag for a big score. The following marinas, fishing centers and charter services can put you in touch with boats if you want to go out. Call well in advance to confirm availability, amenities and fees.

Virginia Beach

Bubba's Marina, 3323 Shore Drive, Lynnhaven Inlet, (757) 481-3513

Fisherman's Wharf Marina, 524 Winston-Salem Avenue, Rudee Inlet, (757) 428-2111

Jeannie Lee Charters, 3323 Shore Drive, (757) 496-9192

Lynnhaven Seafood Marina, 3311 Shore Drive, Lynnhaven Inlet, (757) 481-4545

Rudee Inlet Station Marina, Foot of Mediterranean Avenue, (757) 422-2999

Undersea Adventures/Eco-adventure Charters, 1294 Katch Point, (757) 481-3688

Virginia Beach Fishing Center, 200 Winston-Salem Avenue, Rudee Inlet, (757) 422-5700, (757) 491-8000, (800) 725-0509

Norfolk

Capt. Alex Charters, 1227 Little Bay Avenue, (757) 588-2733

Harrison Boat House, 414 W. Ocean View Avenue, (757) 587-9630

Ocean View Watersports, 1000 E. Ocean View Ave., (757) 583-8888

Taylor's Landing, 8172 Shore Dr., (757) 587-3480

> ## INSIDERS' TIP
> Waterside Marina at The Waterside Festival Marketplace in Downtown Norfolk, along with Portsmouth's Tidewater Yacht Agency directly across the Elizabeth River, is mile mark zero on the Atlantic Intracoastal Waterway.

Avid fisherman enjoy varied fishing in Virginia Beach's many different types of waterways.

Photo: Courtesy of City of Virginia Beach Tourist Development Division

Willoughby Bay Marina, 1651 Bayville Street, (757) 588-2663

Bait and Tackle Shops

Most of the piers and fishing centers listed above can help you with bait. If you're looking for bait and tackle, try one of the following stores.

Virginia Beach

Bait Barn, 5785 Northampton Boulevard, (757) 464-6544

Bubba's Marina, 3323 Shore Drive, (757) 481-3513

Oceans East Tackle Shop, 309 Aragona Boulevard, (757) 499-2277

Norfolk

Cobb's Marina, 4524 Dunning Rd., (757) 588-5401

C-Tackle, 1821 E. Little Creek Road, (757) 587-1003

Taylor's Landing Tackle Shop, 8180 Shore Dr., (757) 587-5595

Portsmouth

Portsmouth City Park Bait and Tackle, 5660-E Portsmouth Boulevard, (757) 465-5399

Chesapeake

Chesapeake Bait and Tackle, 123 S. Battlefield Boulevard, (757) 482-0627

Suffolk

Lake Meade & Cohoon Bait & Tackle, 1805 Pitch Kettle Rd., (757) 539-6216

Lakeside Bait & Tackle, 3717 Lake Prince Dr., (757) 923-0842

FISHING

Tennis

You've got the gear, you've got the serve, you've even got the backhand. But do you have a court to call your own? Yes! There are literally hundreds of free courts throughout Hampton Roads, and one of them is sure to be lit at night for an after-work workout.

Virginia Beach alone has more than 188 public tennis courts and Norfolk has 150, most of which are lighted and may be played at no charge. The majority of these public courts are in the parks and schools maintained by each individual city. In this chapter we'll give you the locations of the most popular courts in each locale and highlight the specific ones where lessons are offered. Also note the private, indoor facilities listed for each city.

Virginia Beach

Virginia Beach Tennis and Country Club
1950 Thomas Bishop Ln.,
Virginia Beach
• (757) 481-7545

If you see a car packed with tennis players during a cold snap, chances are they're headed here. Of course, you'll have to be a member, but if you're a got-to-play fanatic, this is the place to join. Six indoor courts plus 30 outdoor courts are just an appetizer for what's available, including both group and private lessons from some of the most patient, encouraging pros in the area. The vibes from all the tennis mavericks who wander around only make the experience all the more invigorating—or intimidating—depending on your skill level. Check out the excellent junior academy in the summer, as well as the swimming pool, exercise room, sauna, Jacuzzi and pro shop.

Indoor and outdoor courts provide recreational and competitive tennis enthusiasts with year-round activity.

Owl Creek Municipal Tennis Center
928 S. Birdneck Rd., Virginia Beach
• (757) 437-4804

Secluded, shady, well-lit, and that's just for starters. Named one of the 50 best municipal tennis centers in the country by Tennis Magazine, Owl Creek offers grand-slam wannabes expert instruction from U.S.P.T.A. and U.S.P.T.R. instructors who conduct private and group lessons and various clinics. On hand at this city-owned public facility are 12 hard-surface and two tournament courts, all lit for night play until 10 PM, and there's seating for 1,300 spectators. Fees vary, as do reservation requirements, so call ahead.

Lynnhaven Middle School
1250 Bayne Dr., Virginia Beach

This is a super-popular place to test the reaction to your new tennis outfit. There are 12 courts here that stay lit until 11 PM. There's no fee to play and no reservations are taken. If courts are full, you can always get in a practice session at the backboard.

INSIDERS' TIP
At Tidewater Tennis Center in Norfolk, not only can you play indoors and outdoors, but you can also be videotaped to reveal every single flaw in your game.

Find other lighted courts in Virginia Beach at the locations listed below. For more information, call the Virginia Beach Department of Parks and Recreation at (757) 563-1100.

Bayside High School, 4960 Haygood Road, Virginia Beach

Bayville Farm Park, First Court Road, Virginia Beach

Creeds Athletic Park, Morris Neck and Campbell Landing Road, Virginia Beach

First Colonial High School, 1271 Mill Dam Road, Virginia Beach

Great Neck Middle School, 1840 North Great Neck Road, Virginia Beach

Green Run High School, 1700 Dahlia Drive, Virginia Beach

Kellam High School, 574 Kempsville Road, Virginia Beach

Kempsville High School, 574 Kempsville Road, Virginia Beach

Lynnhaven Park, Bayne Drive, Virginia Beach

Plaza Middle School, 3080 S. Lynnhaven Drive, Virginia Beach

Princess Anne Park, Princess Anne Road, Virginia Beach

Princess Anne High School, 4400 Virginia Beach Boulevard, Virginia Beach

Norfolk

Tidewater Tennis Center
1159 Lance Rd., Norfolk
• (757) 461-3015

Not only can you play indoors and outdoors, but you can also be videotaped to reveal every single flaw in your game. Instructors are forgiving and encouraging, however, so it's a great place to winter your game in preparation for the big time. There are four indoor courts.

Northside Park
8400 Tidewater Dr., Norfolk
• (757) 441-2149

Headquarters for Norfolk Parks and Recreation tennis activity is Northside Park, where classes for all levels are offered seasonally by resident pros. Many of the city's tournaments are held here. The facility offers lighted courts to soothe night-owl lobs. Reservations are not required, and there is a $1 court fee.

Find other lighted courts in Norfolk at the locations listed below. For more information on tennis in Norfolk, call (757) 441-2149.

Azalea Garden Jr. High School, 7721 Azalea Garden Road, Norfolk

Barraud Park, Barraud Avenue, Norfolk

Booker T. Washington High School, 1300 Virginia Beach Boulevard, Norfolk

Granby High School, 7101 Granby Street, Norfolk

Lafayette City Park, 3500 Granby Street, Norfolk

Lake Taylor High School, 1380 Kempsville Road, Norfolk

Larchmont Park, 5210 Hampton Boulevard, Norfolk

Little Creek Elementary School, Tarpin and Little Creek roads, Norfolk

Maury High School, 322 Shirley Avenue, Norfolk

Norview High School, Middleton Place, Norfolk

Ocean View Elementary School, 9501 Mason Creek Road, Norfolk

Ocean View Recreation Center, 600 Ocean View Avenue, Norfolk

St. Helena Elementary School, 903 S. Main Street, Norfolk

Portsmouth

Classes for all skill levels and ages are offered during the summer through the Portsmouth Parks and Recreation Department at both Churchland Park and City Park, along with annual Junior and Senior Tournaments. For more information on class schedules and fees call (757) 393-8481.

Find other lighted courts in Portsmouth at the following locations.

Cavalier Manor, 404 Viking Street, Portsmouth

Churchland Park, 4300 Cedar Lane, Portsmouth

City Park, City Park Avenue, Portsmouth

Hunt-Mapp Middle School, 3701 Willett Drive, Portsmouth

I. C. Norcom High School, 2900 Turnpike Road, Portsmouth

Park View Athletic Complex, 1401 Crawford Parkway, Portsmouth

Tidewater Community College, Frederick Campus, Portsmouth

Woodrow Wilson High School, 1401 Elmhurst Lane, Portsmouth

Chesapeake

The City of Chesapeake sponsors men's and women's team tennis for ages 18 and older for both spring and fall seasons. For more information on team tennis sign-up call (757) 547-6642.

Greenbrier Sports Park
112 A Mann Dr., Chesapeake
• (757) 382-6400

Take center court on any of eight tournament-quality lighted courts—this is the big time in Chesapeake. Novices bored with ball-chasing can always sneak away to the softball fields or picnic areas. This area is operated by the city's Department of Parks and Recreation.

Find other courts in Chesapeake at the locations listed below. For more information call (757) 382-6400.

Crestwood Junior High School, 1420 Great Bridge Road, Chesapeake

Deep Creek Junior High School, 2901 Margaret Booker Drive, Chesapeake

Deep Creek High School, 1955 Deal Drive, Chesapeake

Great Bridge Junior High School, 301 W. Hanbury Road, Chesapeake

Hickory Elementary School, 2701 S. Battlefield Boulevard, Chesapeake

Indian River High School, 2301 Dunbarton Drive, Chesapeake

Oscar Smith High School (lighted), 2500 Rodgers Street, Chesapeake

Western Branch High School, 4222 Terry Drive, Chesapeake

Suffolk

Tennis is a big sport in Suffolk, mainly due to the influence of Suffolk resident Howard Mast, who's known throughout the state as "Mr. Tennis." You can get into the swing by contacting the Suffolk Department of Parks and Recreation at (757)923-2360. Or check out one of the following public courts.

Lake Meade Landing, North Main Street, Suffolk

Lakeland High School, 215 Kenyon Road, Suffolk

Booker T. Washington High School, 204 Walnut Street, Suffolk

Forest Glen Middle School, 200 Forest Glen Drive, Suffolk

INSIDERS' TIP

The Chesapeake Tennis Association, (757) 543-3347, and the Norfolk Tennis Patrons, (757) 543-9555, are a couple of local tennis organizations that would love to take a swing at signing you up.

Other Participatory Sports

Maybe it's because we're so focused on the beach where it's customary to wear a bathing suit, but we tend to exercise a lot here in Hampton Roads. Call it vanity, the quest for eternal youth or just plain blowing off steam, but many of us get out there and run, walk, cycle, surf, swim and sail as much as we possibly can. Fortunately, we have an obliging climate and lots of resources to support us in our collective obsession.

In this chapter we'll give you a brief rundown of the area's most popular participatory sports and places to practice them.

For more in-depth information about each city, the parks and recreation departments furnish detailed brochures and newsletters listing facilities, classes and athletic programs for all ages.

Virginia Beach Department of Parks and Recreation, (757) 471-5884
Norfolk Parks and Recreation Department, (757) 441-2149
Portsmouth Department of Parks and Recreation, (757) 393-8481
Chesapeake Parks and Recreation Department, (757) 547-641
Suffolk Department of Parks and Recreation, (757) 923-2360

Baseball/Softball

All the cities organize highly competitive teams for both adults and kids. Registration normally is in the winter and early spring, with the season running from May through the heat and humidity of late July. Teams for males, females and coeds are here for the joining. Call your city's parks and recreation department for exact registration times and locations. In Norfolk call Naval Base and Wards Corner little league at (757) 451-1050. In Suffolk, contact the Suffolk Youth Athletic League at (757) 539-0102 or (757) 539-2323.

Hampton Roads is home to the Amateur Softball Association (ASA), the largest amateur association in the world. The ASA operates in each Hampton Roads city and provides playing opportunities for children and adults. In any given year, you can count as many as 150 different teams in the association, and they can play as many as 200 games on a weekend. Junior Olympic leagues are for girls ages 12 to 18, with play in the fall. Adult leagues, for ages 18 and older, are grouped according to ability, with a season that runs from April to November. For more information call (757) 427-5219 or (757) 428-0784.

Baseball players 18 years and older can check into the Virginia Adult Baseball League, (757) 487-0824 or (800) 435-3588.

LOOK FOR:
- Baseball/Softball
- Basketball
- Boxing
- Bowling
- Canoeing and Kayaking
- Cycling
- Crew
- Fencing
- Football
- Horseback Riding
- Ice Skating/Hockey
- Jet-Skiing
- Racquetball
- Rugby
- Running and Walking
- Sailing
- Scuba Diving
- Skatboarding and In-line Skating
- Skydiving
- Soccer
- Surfing
- Swimming
- Swimming (indoor)
- Volleyball
- Windsurfing
- Danger Zone Sports
- Who Ya Gonna Call ?

To get your swing whipped into shape head to two places that are favorite haunts of area ballplayers. Grand Slam USA Indoor Batting at 2682 Dean Drive in Virginia Beach has batting cages and experienced instructors. In addition, there is a fully stocked baseball and softball store. Call (757) 431-0505. Sports Zone at 7542 Granby St. in Norfolk is a sporting goods store that has several batting cages. Call (757) 588-7700.

Basketball

Each of the Hampton Roads' city recreation departments sponsors both adult and youth basketball leagues, with registration beginning in November and play continuing through mid-March. Youth leagues begin at age 10, and you must be 18 before you join the adult ranks. For complete information, contact your city's recreation department. Other contacts for avid slam-dunkers are The Sharks in Virginia Beach, (757) 436-6037, and Virginia Beach Future All-Stars, (757) 468-1820. In Suffolk, contact the Suffolk Youth Athletic League at (757) 539-0102 or (757) 539-2323. Two excellent youth basketball programs in Norfolk are at the Downtown YMCA, 312 W. Bute Street, (757) 622-9622, and the Jewish Community Center, 7300 Newport Avenue, (757) 489-1371.

For casual players, scads of indoor and outdoor courts are scattered throughout the region at schools and parks and recreation facilities. You shouldn't have far to go for a quick game of one-on-one.

Boxing

Would-be boxers have it made in Hampton Roads. For starters, Norfolk's recreation department teaches boxing at Barraud Park, on Vista Avenue and Tidewater Drive in Norfolk, (757) 441-2149. Sweet Pea Whittaker, a former Lightweight Champion of the World, was a student here. In Virginia Beach, Wareing's Gym, 700 19th Street, (757) 491-0770, is the hot spot for training—you might even see Sweet Pea working out there.

Bowling

There are bowling centers through the region that range from those with high-tech gadgets that automatically keep score to retro places with a '60s orange-and-avocado-colored ambiance. The dominate name in 10-pin bowling is AMF, which has centers in Virginia Beach, Norfolk, and Chesapeake. For duckpin bowling head to Bowlarama in Norfolk at 7641 Sewells Point Road, (757) 587-5261. It's the only place around where duckpins are the stars of the alleys.

To check out league action call the Norfolk Bowling Association at (757) 420-2278 or the Tidewater Women's Bowling Association, (757) 467-6648.

INSIDERS' TIP

Bicycle riders age 14 and younger must wear a helmet in Virginia Beach. This law became effective several years ago, thanks to a group of seventh graders from Kempsville Middle School, who worked on getting the law passed as a class project. Violators face a $25 fine, although the fine may be suspended for first-time offenders who purchase helmets before the due dates of their fines. The law applies to bike rentals and riders along the oceanfront too. If your child rents a bike from a boardwalk stand, the bike stand should supply a helmet.

Canoeing and Kayaking

Virginia Beach and Chesapeake both offer lots of quiet waterways to paddle around, and in recent years kayaking has become a popular way to take in the scenery and get some exercise. Some of the most scenic spots are found in the southern part of Virginia Beach, along the tributaries of the North Landing River. To find kayaks, tour guides or lessons call: Wild River Outfitters, (757) 431-8566 or (877) 431-8566. This retail store at 4646 Virginia Beach Boulevard was the first to promote paddling as an ideal way to tour the region's waterways. These days there are lots of people willing to rent boats, lead tours and teach lessons. Kayak and canoe experts include: Chesapean Kayak Tours, (757) 425-0990, Tidewater Kayak Adventures, (757) 480-1999 or (888) 669-8368, Sandbridge Ecosports, (757) 721-6210 or (800) 695-4212 or The Nature Team, (877) 483-3246. You can also rent an ocean kayak at Rudee Inlet Jet Ski, (757) 428-4614. For paddling tours of various Virginia waterways call the Virginia Professional Paddlesports Association, (888) 42-FLOAT.

If you'd like to rent a canoe for the day, head to Northwest River Park in Chesapeake (see our Parks chapter) or Munden Point Park in Virginia Beach (call (757) 426-5269 first). Looking to purchase some equipment for enjoying the great outdoors? Any of the following businesses can set you up, and/or give you tips on where to use your new equipment locally. In Virginia Beach visit Blue Ridge Mountain Sports, Hilltop North Shopping Center, (757) 422-2201 or Wild River Outfitters, Virginia Beach Boulevard and Rosemont Road, (757) 431-8566. In Norfolk go to M & G Sales, 2609 Granby Street, (757) 622-9065.

Cycling

Have bike, will travel. And travel Hampton Roads cyclers do. Weekend leisure riders will find bike paths throughout Hampton Roads and special trails reserved for bikers in most of our area's parks. Minibikers, mountain bikers and BMX aficionados will find their own tracks too. (See the Parks chapter for specifics.) Serious peddlers won't long for companionship with several clubs active in planning special events, competitions and field trips. To get the full scoop, contact the Tidewater Bicycle Association (touring and racing), (757) 523-2596; L'team Junque (touring and training), (757) 486-1948; or Colley Off-Road Club (touring and training), (757) 622-0006. To rent a bike on your visit to Virginia Beach, check out Northend Bikes, (757) 425-5120, or Oceanfront Bikes, (757) 428-4235, both along the Boardwalk.

Crew

Rowing is an up-and-coming sport in this region blessed with quiet waters. The most-established group is the Hampton Roads Rowing Club. Novices and experienced rowers are welcome to join the club for both recreational and competitive thrills. Call (757) 451-8488. Another club is the Olde Towne Rowing Club in Portsmouth, which in 2000 spearheaded getting a boat launching ramp at City Park in Portsmouth. Call (757) 397-3481.

Fencing

Yes, fencing. The Tidewater Fencing Club is always looking for new targets to sign up for membership in this very active organization. Annual membership is $80, which includes instruction and equipment. Call (757) 460-2975.

Football

Knock 'em, pop 'em, sock 'em. Pack your kids into the pads and get them off to sign up for your city's youth community football league. Registration is in August, with power play for city titles running from September through November. Volunteer coaches are widely respected and known for teaching more than just the principles of the game. Sportsmanship, leadership and team spirit messages prevail, even if you're on the bench. Contact your city's recreation department for exact registration times and locations.

Horseback Riding

Virginia Beach, Suffolk and Chesapeake are the area leaders when it comes to riding rings and stables. In the still-rural areas of Virginia Beach, many people board their own horses, while several private stables rent mounts by the hour. In Chesapeake, Northwest River Park, 1733 Indian Creek Road, (757) 421-7151, offers the city's only designated horse trails, with 3 miles of interconnected loops. Private stables and farms also offer lessons and rentals. Stables in Suffolk offer boarding, training and lessons, but no rentals are available. Excellent sources for information to steer you in the right direction are: Acredale Saddlery, (757) 467-3183; Pleasant Ridge Stables, (757) 721-3819; Sterling Meadows Feed & Tack, (757) 471-2133; and Hunter's Run Stables, (757) 465-5530.

Ice-skating/Hockey

Even in a region of moderate temperatures, ice-skating is popular—for Olympic hopefuls or just for one heck of a party idea. The center for the activity is Iceland Skating Center at Virginia Beach, 4915 Broad Street, (757) 490-3907, where excellent instruction is available. The most promising students are part of a figure-skating team that has traveled as far as Chicago to compete in United States Figure Skating Association events. Iceland also sponsors hockey teams. The newest cool place in the region is ARC Ice Sports, which opened in 1998 in Chesapeake's Greenbrier area. The ice skating center features two junior Olympic rinks, lessons, and hockey teams. It is at 1416 Stephanie Way, phone (757) 420-4488. Also worth checking out is the Tidewater Figure Skating Club, (757) 423-5411, which welcomes skaters of all abilities.

If you've got a hankering for the game of ice hockey, check out the Virginia Beach Open Hockey League, (757) 490-3999.

Jet-Skiing

If it's a sport, there's a club for it with folks who share your passion. If you're into Jet-Skiing, find out about the Tidewater Personal Watercraft Club that meets monthly at Marina Shores in Virginia Beach, (757) 496-2325. To rent a Jet-Ski for a trial run, call the pros at Rudee Inlet Jet Ski Rentals, 300 Winston Salem Avenue, Virginia Beach, (757) 428-4614, or Ocean View Watersports, 100 E. Ocean View Avenue, Norfolk, (757) 583-8888.

In-line skating has become another favorite Boardwalk activity.

Photo: Courtesy of Virginia Tourism Corporation

Racquetball

It's a most civilized racquet sport, but you won't find many public facilities to satiate the habit, other than the courts at the Virginia Beach recreation centers. There are, however, two membership facilities where you can happily box yourself in: in Virginia Beach at Gymstrada, 4444 Expressway Drive, (757) 499-9667 or in Norfolk at the YMCA, 312 W. Bute Street, (757) 622-6328.

Rugby

You may see bumper stickers around town that say, " Love an Animal . . . Kiss a Rugby Player." Well, maybe before one of the games sponsored by the Virginia Beach Rugby Club, which fights it out at Princess Anne Park in Virginia Beach. Right now, they're looking for new players (makes you wonder what happened to the old ones!). Go ahead give them a call at (757) 497-2208. You can reach the Norfolk rugby hotline by calling (757) 490-6735.

Running and Walking

Whatever your speed, you can be in a crowd—or all alone—when you put one foot in front of the other for recreation. Every park in every Hampton Roads city has well-marked, well-shaded paths for walking and jogging, and you'll see people of all ages out in neighborhoods. Some of the most popular places to jog include the Boardwalk in Virginia Beach, the feeder road and First Landing State Park at the Beach, and around the Ghent/Hague and Town Point Park areas of Norfolk. For those who prefer their walking indoors, several area malls have walking clubs whose members are mostly older adults.

If you're serious about running or walking, you might check out some of the clubs in the area. Tidewater Striders, (757) 627-RACE; Gator Volksmarching Club, (757) 486-0664; Mount Trashmore Walking Club, (757) 474-0460; Suffolk Field Trail Club, (757) 986-4585; and From Start to Finish, (757) 482-5932, all sponsor a multitude of competitive and recreational events for athletes of all ages and abilities.

INSIDERS' TIP

MacArthur Center has the most comprehensive mall walking program in the region. A certified Walk Reebok instructor is on duty from 8 to 9 AM on weekdays to lead warm-up and cool-down sessions and answer questions. Registered walkers earn gifts for walking 100 or more miles. There are free monthly educational programs and screenings. Parking is free with ticket validation. Walkers can enter the mall from 7:30 to 9 AM on weekdays and Saturday and from 10 to 11 AM on Sundays.

Sailing

If you don't know the difference between a boom and a spinnaker, you're missing out on one of the most popular addictions in the area—sailing. From baby Sunfish to beamy Morgans, there's a vessel just waiting to launch you out into the calm waters of the Chesapeake Bay. One great place to chart your sailing adventure is the Chesapeake Sailing Association at Willoughby Harbor in Norfolk. CSA offers ASA-certified sail training, along with super five-day "Learn to Sail" vacation packages and SPAR charters. Call them at (757) 588-2022. At the Beach, Chick's Beach Sailing Center, 3716 Shore Drive, Virginia Beach (757) 460-2238, is a beehive of sailing, sailboarding—even skateboarding and snowboarding activity—and a great place to take a lesson. They're situated at the foot of the Lesner Bridge on Shore Drive, the unofficial portal to the Chick's Beach area of Virginia Beach. Yet another sailing center is Ocean View Watersports, 1000 E. Ocean View Avenue, Norfolk (757) 583-8888.

Scuba Diving

With all the water around here, it's no surprise that diving is a popular sport for the people of

Hampton Roads. In fact, it's a popular job here for folks such as Navy Seals and underwater construction specialists. Recreational diving usually is done around the underwater wrecks that lie just offshore. If you're interested in learning how to dive, joining scheduled group dives or just updating your equipment before your next trip to the Caribbean, check out one of the popular local dive shops listed below. For other class options, call your local parks and recreation department or YMCA. They sponsor classes from time to time as well.

In Virginia Beach try Lynnhaven Dive Center, 1413 Great Neck Road, (757) 481-7949; or Mid-Atlantic Dive Center, 5350 Kempsriver Drive, 420-6179. In Portsmouth check out the Chesapeake Bay Diving Center, 653 Mt. Vernon Avenue, 397-0422

Skateboarding and In-line Skating

For those few who haven't traded in their skateboards for in-line skates, you can head to the last remaining bowls and ramps at the beach at Mount Trashmore Park in Virginia Beach, (757) 473-5237, and at Chesapeake City Park in Chesapeake (757) 547-6411. An indoor option is Virginia Beach Skate Park at 2682 Dean Drive, Virginia Beach, (757) 498-3436. At all these facilities, proper safety equipment is required, as well it should be. In-line and roller skaters can wheel with the pack by joining the Beach Skater Club, (757) 422-6105. The place to skate in your bikini? Where else but the Virginia Beach Boardwalk.

Skydiving

Beam me up, Scottie! If leaping into thin air is your kind of thing, head out to Suffolk Municipal Airport. Skydive Suffolk Inc., (757) 539-3531, offers lessons on Saturday mornings by appointment, and you can make your first jump that same day. For the experienced skydiver, an accelerated free-fall program is offered. Or contact Chesapeake Sky Dive Adventures (is that name redundant?) at (757) 421-9245. Call for fees and details.

Bicycling on the Boardwalk and the many bike paths around Virginia Beach is an enjoyable family activity.

Photo: Douglas Peebles, courtesy of Virginia Tourism Corporation

Soccer

Soccer's hot here, so sign your kids up quick. Every city and practically every neighborhood has its own team, so have your child talk to classmates about the best place to put on the cleats.

Youth soccer leagues sprout up so quickly that they can't be counted. Boys and girls are encouraged to join. Kids have a great time wearing their uniforms after the games in fact, no kid worth his salt would show up at McDonald's on a spring or fall Saturday without knee socks and cleats. Contact your city's recreation department for full details on spring and fall registration times and locations. At the beach, contact the Virginia Beach Soccer Club, (757) 424-8800, or the Neighborhood Youth Soccer League, (757) 340-1800. In Norfolk, call either the Norfolk Youth Soccer League, (757) 588-3294 or the Norfolk Soccer League (757) 552-1748. In Suffolk, contact the Suffolk Youth Athletic League at (757) 539-0102 or (757) 539-2323.

Adults don't have to miss out, either. Several soccer clubs are active and alive in Hampton Roads. Tidewater Soccer Association, (757) 489-2724, is a men's league and member of the USSF. It's for those experienced enough to play at collegiate level or better. Southeastern Virginia Women's Soccer Association, (757) 625-2414, is a regional league that's busy all year, with teams divided according to age and play ability. Southside Soccer League, (757) 423-3147, is for men who play well but not quite at championship speed. Virginia Beach Soccer Club, (757) 424-8800, (mailing address listed above) has more than 7,000 members. This club for youths and adults has leagues for both neighborhood play and advanced teams. Both spring and fall seasons are packed with play.

Surfing

OK, maybe it's not Hawaii, but when a nor'easter blows, we can get some pretty decent waves. Needless to say, Virginia Beach lays claim to all surfing rights in the area, but there are certain places you can and cannot take your board. Restricted surfing areas are established to protect your average lazy backstrokers and waders, as well as surfers themselves. Leashes are required, and you'll have to pay a $50 fine if caught untethered from your board. If you get the urge to catch a wave, call Wave Riding Vehicles at (757) 422-8823 for the local surf report. For surfing lessons call The Surf School, (757) 491-0747 or (757) 463-0980. Then head to one of the following surf zones.

Area A: Little Island Park. Stick to the north side of the pier from Memorial Day to Labor Day, 9 AM until 5 PM.

Area B: South of Little Island Park. You are allowed to surf off False Cape's beach, but restricted within the boundaries of the Back Bay National Wildlife Refuge.

Area C: Between the southern line of the U.S. Naval Reservation/Dam Neck and the northern line of Little Island Park. Between Memorial Day and Labor Day you can only surf

Surfing is the rage at the less populated areas of Virginia Beach.

Photo: City of Virginia Beach

here before 10 AM and after 5 PM. Otherwise, surf's up between sunrise and sunset.

Area D: North of Camp Pendleton to 42nd Street, except for the area 300 feet north and south of the pier. Again, you're beached between 10 AM and 5 PM, May 15th through September 30th. Other times, have at it from sunrise to sunset.

Area E: Fort Story to 42nd Street. No surfing between 10 AM and 5 PM, Memorial Day through Labor Day. Allowed sunrise to sunset at all other times.

Area F: South end of Croatan Beach (600 feet). Except for occasional military maneuvers, you can maneuver on your board from 9:30 AM until 6 PM from Memorial Day through Labor Day.

Area G: Croatan Beach for 800 feet below the southern jetty of Rudee Inlet. Open and waiting for you from sunrise to sunset.

Area H: North of Rudee Inlet's northern jetty (500 feet). Hang 10 sunrise to sunset.

Swimming

We're surrounded by water in Hampton Roads, so learning to swim is as much a safety issue as it is a recreational one. Please don't wade into any water unless you have fundamental swimming skills and a basic knowledge of ocean safety. Strong currents and rip tides (dangerous currents that can draw even experienced swimmers out to sea) can be difficult to spot and very dangerous. Be particularly careful with rafts and swimming aides that lull you into feeling safe. While experienced lifeguards are on duty at several locations, lives are still lost every summer. If you are a newcomer from dry terrain, we urge you to check into the swimming courses offered at nominal fees through your new city's recreation department and to take extreme safety precautions when you visit any of our wonderful beaches. See our Beaches chapter for a rundown on all the beaches in the area. Lifeguards are on duty daily from Memorial Day to Labor Day at the following beaches:

Virginia Beach
Croatan Beach, General Booth Boulevard
Fort Story, 89th Street
Little Island Park, Sandbridge
The Ocean Front, Atlantic Avenue Resort Strip, 1st through 40th streets
Sandbridge Beach Park, Sandbridge

Norfolk
City Beach, East End of Ocean View
Community Beach, 601 E. Ocean View Avenue
Ocean View Beach Park, E. Ocean View Avenue and Granby Streets
Sarah Constant Shrine, E. Ocean View Avenue and Tidewater Drive.

Swimming (Indoor)

Whether you want to learn how to do the backstroke, or dive into the wet world of competitive freestyle, there are several options for water babies and adults alike. Most city parks and recreation departments, neighborhood pools and YMCAs offer the basic Red Cross-sanctioned swimming courses plus times for lap swimming. The Tidewater Swim Team, (757) 496-3979, is a great connection for young swimmers, and the team travels to competitions along the East Coast. To perfect your stroke, call the Old Dominion Aquatic Club, (757) 683-3403. It offers an excellent development program for novice and intermediate swimmers with an emphasis on stroke mechanics. There's also the Springboard Diving Team, (757) 683-5569, for those not afraid of heights, and the Virginia Community Swim League, 441-1547, for fun competition.

For lessons or laps, here are the pools to check out when it gets a little too brisk for a bikini at the beach.

Virginia Beach
Bayside Recreation Center, 4500 First Court Road, (757) 460-7569
Bow Creek Recreation Center, 3427 Clubhouse Road, (757) 431-3765
Great Neck Recreation Center, 2521 Shorehaven Drive, (757) 496-6766
Kempsville Recreation Center, 800 Monmouth Lane, (757) 474-8492

Princess Anne Recreation Center, 1400 Ferrell Parkway, (757) 426-0022
Seatack Recreation Center, 141 S. Birdneck Road, (757) 437-4858

Norfolk

Berkley, 145 Liberty Street, (757) 441-1969
Huntersville Pool, 830 Goff Street, (757) 664-7430
Northside Pool, 8400 Tidewater Drive, (757) 441-1760

Chesapeake

YMCA, 1033 Greenbrier Parkway, (757) 547-9622

Suffolk

Cypress Park Pool, Arizona Avenue, (757) 539-9793
Suffolk Family YMCA, 2769 Godwin Boulevard, (757) 934-9622

There are designated volleyball areas at the beach so players won't kick sand on tanners.

Photo: Courtesy of City of Virginia Beach

Volleyball

When you're hot, you're hot. This is one old sport that's enjoying a major renewal across Hampton Roads—as evidenced by the nets strung out along the beaches and parks throughout the area. There are city leagues wherever you live, just waiting for a great spiker like you. When you get the action down pat, why not call the Tidewater Volleyball Association, (757) 498-5052, to get the low-down on any upcoming tournaments.

Windsurfing

It looks easy, but it's not. If you want to put that upper body strength and miracle balance to the test, this is the sport to do it. You can start easy, with a smooth glide over one of the area's many lakes, then graduate to the more wicked waters of the Chesapeake Bay or Atlantic Ocean. Why not let the experts at Chick's Beach Sailing Center, 3716 Shore Drive, Virginia Beach, (757) 460-2238, give you a lesson or two before you rush out to invest in a board of your own. Other great guidance counselors can be found at Wave Riding Vehicles, 1900 Cypress Avenue , (757) 422-8823, and Ocean View Watersports, 1000 E. Ocean View Avenue, (757) 583-8888.

Off-beat Sports

If the mainstream isn't to your liking, get your blood pumping with some alternative sports. To scale new heights head to the Rock Gym where you can don harness, crawl up a 30-foot wall, and leap off a repelling tower. You'll be secured all the while with a rope. A few introductory lessons don't hurt either. The gym is at 5049 Southern Boulevard in Virginia Beach, (757) 499-8347.

A favorite with teens and the you-at-heart is Ultrazone at 2682 Dean Drive in Virginia Beach, (757) 671-8399. This is the local laser tag headquarters. Players are divided into teams that wear battery-powered vests accented with flashing colored lights. The challenge is to enter a darkened arena armed only with a laser gun and your wits. The goal is to sneak around and zap members of opposing teams before they wipe out your team's score.

Paintball is an outdoor hide-and-seek activity gaining in popularity. Action Town paintball at 1528 Holland Road in Suffolk provides acres of bunkers and hideaways. You can also purchase supplies and arrange to play elsewhere at Ka-Splat at 4015 Cedar Road in Portsmouth, (757) 482-5870.

Who Ya Gonna Call?

For up-to-the-minute info on all sporting activities offered for children and adults through city parks and recreation departments, contact: Virginia Beach Athletics, (757) 471-5884; Norfolk Athletics, (757) 441-5834; Portsmouth Athletics, (757) 393-8481; Chesapeake Athletics, (757) 547-6400; or Suffolk Athletics, (757) 925-6235.

Other local sports-minded organizations you may want to call are Virginia Beach Special Olympics, (757) 422-4423, and Sun Wheelers (a wheelchair sports club), (757) 471-5884.

Recreation Centers

Got an urge to learn to tap dance? Weave an Appalachian basket? Strum a guitar? Improve your swimming skills? Hampton Roads not only has the talented teachers but also has easy-to-get-to facilities where you can take classes on the cheap—and have a fantastic time while you're at it!

Special programs, classes and activities are scheduled year round in each of the area cities, and held at their respective recreation facilities. Because programs change seasonally, we won't be able to be more specific than to say that whatever you've got the urge to do, you'll likely find it coming up in the next class session. In most cases, the following centers are open daily from 10 AM until 6 PM, with some offering various nighttime hours that change from winter to summer. You usually have to pay a small fee to get a membership card. A call to check on your nearest center's hours is recommended.

Virginia Beach

Since you can't always go play on the beach, Virginia Beach operates excellent recreation facilities that seem to be jammed with activity almost every day of the year. In fact, these facilities are one of the nicest things about living at the beach. Most facilities have pools, weight/cardio rooms, dance studios, tennis and racquetball courts, gymnasiums, game rooms and classrooms. The program offerings suit practically every taste, from arts and crafts, dance, music, drama and, of course, SPORTS! If you're a newcomer, one of the best ways to meet people is to take a class or work out at a recreation center. If you're visiting, it's great to have the opportunity to continue your favorite sport while you're away from home.

You'll need a Facility Use Card to use any of the Virginia Beach Rec facilities. For children 6 to 17, the yearly fee is $12; adults 18 to 64, $30. Seniors older than age 65 can snag a lifetime membership, the Golden Age Card, for $55. Want to check out the facilities for a day? A guest pass is just $3.

City-Run Recreation Centers

Bow Creek Recreation Center, 3427 Clubhouse Road, Virginia Beach, (757) 431-3765
Bayside Recreation Center, First Court Road, Virginia Beach, (757) 460-7540
Great Neck Recreation Center, 2521 Shorehaven Drive, Virginia Beach, (757) 496-6766

The Kempsville Recreation Center, 800 Monmouth Lane, Virginia Beach, (757) 474-8492

Princess Anne Recreation Center, Ferrell Parkway at General Booth Boulevard, (757) 426-0022

Seatack Community Center, 141 South Birdneck Road, (757) 437-4858

Therapeutic Recreation Centers

A number of programs, many at no fee, are offered for children and adults who are physically, mentally or emotionally disabled. These include instructional classes and recreational programs to promote independence and are found at the locations listed below. For more information, call (757) 471-5884.

Bow Creek Recreation Center, 3427 Clubhouse Road, Virginia Beach

Center for Effective Learning, 233 N. Witchduck Road, Virginia Beach

City-Wide Programs Office, 2289 Lynnhaven Parkway, Virginia Beach

Kempsville Recreation Center, 800 Monmouth Lane, Virginia Beach

Community Centers With A Membership Fee

The YMCA Mount Trashmore is at 4441 South Boulevard, (757) 499-2311. If you're traveling on the Norfolk-Virginia Beach Expressway (I-264) by Mount Trashmore, you'll spot its sprawling brick building with a parking lot jammed with cars. How that many people can pack this Y every day of the year amazes us all, but perhaps it's because the facilities and programs offered are some of the finest in the city. You can swim in the heated pool, balance on a beam, play tennis or work out in the fitness center. In summer families love the outdoor swimming pool. Housed here are a number of charitable organizations, including the The Boy's and Girl's Clubs of Virginia Beach, Family Services and the Retired Senior Volunteer Program. Newcomers should put this topnotch center on one of their first-to-check-out lists.

Hilltop Family YMCA, 1536 Laskin Road, (757) 422-3805, opened in 1995 in the Hilltop area, is the newest Y in Virginia Beach. Amenities include a 25-yard, five-lane lap pool, a weight room, cardiovascular workout equipment and classes in aerobics, aqua fitness and aqua aerobics. Like most Y's, the facility also offers before and after-school care, a preschool enrichment program, babysitting while parents work out and spring and summer camps for kids.

The Indian River Family YMCA, 5660 Indian River Road, (757) 366-0448, which looks more like an expensive spa-place, takes center stage at the University Shoppes across from CBN University. Along with family fitness programs for every level, you'll find a large free-weight selection and preschool and before- and after-school care programs.

Norfolk

To use any of Norfolk's 25 recreation centers, you must obtain a facility use card. Cost of the card is $5 for youths ages 5 to 17 and $10 for adults ages 18 to 64. The cards are available at two sites: Lakewood Athletic Office, 1612 Willow Wood Drive, 441-5834, and Northside Pool, 8400 Tidewater Drive, (757) 441-1760. You will not need a card if you attend a fee-based class or attend a special event or meeting at any of the facilities, and both "good grade" and family discounts are available. You can also get a temporary three-day pass to give you an opportunity to check out the facility before you purchase a card.

City-Run Recreation Centers

Bayview, 1434 Bayview Boulevard, Norfolk, (757) 441-1768

Berkley, 89 Liberty Street, Norfolk, (757) 543-1230

Bowling Green, 1319 Godfrey Avenue, Norfolk, (757) 441-2746

Crossroads, 8044 Tidewater Drive, Norfolk, (757) 441-1769

Diggs Town, 1401 Melon Street, Norfolk, (757) 441-1975

East Ocean View, 9520 20th Bay Street, Norfolk, (757) 441-1785

Fairlawn, 1132 Wade Street, Norfolk, (757) 441-5670

Grandy Village, 3017 Kimball Terrace, Norfolk, (757) 441-2856

Huntersville, 830 Goff Street, Norfolk, 664-7430
Ingleside, 940 Ingleside Road, Norfolk, (757) 441-5675
Lakewood (Dance/Music), 1612 Willow Wood Drive, Norfolk, (757) 441-5833
Larchmont, 1167 Bolling Avenue, Norfolk, (757) 441-5411
Merrimack, 8809 Monitor Way, Norfolk, (757) 441-1783
Northside Pool, 8400 Tidewater Drive, Norfolk, (757) 441-1760
Norview, 6800 Sewells Point Road, Norfolk, (757) 441-5836
Ocean View (Seniors), 600 E. Ocean View Avenue, Norfolk, (757) 441-1767
Park Place, 620 W. 29th Street, Norfolk, (757) 664-7531
Sherwood Forest, 4537 Little John Drive, Norfolk, (757) 441-5824
Southside (Seniors), 925 S. Main Street, Norfolk, (757) 664-6484
Tarrallton, 2100 Tarrallton Drive, Norfolk, (757) 441-1765
Therapeutic Recreation, 180 E. Evans Street, Norfolk, (757) 441-1764
Titustown Center for Arts and Recreation, 7545 Diven Street, Norfolk, (757) 441-2245
Young Terrace, 804 Whitaker Lane, Norfolk, (757) 441-2754
Call for information concerning specific activities: Athletics, (757) 441-2149; Senior Citizens, (757) 441-2109; Special Events, (757) 441-2140.

Therapeutic Recreation Centers

The City of Norfolk sponsors a complete year-round program for children and adults with disabilities, from clinics and workshops, sports classes (swimming, golf, tennis, horseback riding and more) to field trips. The Therapeutic Recreation Unit at 180 E. Evans Street in Bayview Park boasts a kitchen with low countertops and work areas that are wheelchair accessible, plus a fresh new look throughout workshops and game rooms. Special events are free and open to the public; class fees range from $6 to $25. For a full schedule and details, call (757) 441-1764 (V/TDD). Note: If you are hearing impaired, press your space bar so that the staff will know you are calling on TDD.

Community Centers With A Membership Fee

At the Jewish Community Center, 7300 Newport Avenue, (757) 489-1371, you can backstroke any day of the year, thanks to an indoor heated pool protected by a huge domed skylight roof and a terrific outdoor pool. The gymnasium is almost always a noisy place, thanks to the pickup basketball games you'll find on almost any given day. Ditto for the well-equipped exercise room. The center offers a variety of programs for all ages, including special programs for retired people. Membership fees are very reasonable for the beautiful facilities. An outdoor family park is part of the complex too. You need not be Jewish to join.

Boys & Girls Clubs of South Hampton Roads W. W. Houston Memorial Club, 3401 Azalea Garden Road, (757) 855-8908, offers swimming, cheerleading, football, wrestling, cooking, crafts and more for kids 6 to 17 years. The large pool is the central focus year round, from lifeguard training to classes designed for babies. Annual membership is $15, with additional fees for special classes and training.

The main YMCA in Norfolk, the Downtown Norfolk YMCA, is at 312 Bute Street, (757) 622-9622. It's definitely "the thing" to belong to this outstanding facility in the heart of Downtown Norfolk in the historic Freemason district. Businessmen and women trade in their suits for jogging shorts and hit the newly expanded cardio-fitness room or one of a zillion aerobics classes before work, at lunch or at the end of the day. Swim laps in the indoor aquatic center, play racquetball, basketball or volleyball—it's all here, and there's always someone to play and strain with. Through the years this has become more of a family YMCA with a variety of children's activities and sports. Extra perks are babysitting services available for some classes, along with a super summer camp program and fitness evaluations. Corporate memberships are available.

INSIDERS' TIP

Always take time to stop at visitors centers or chamber of commerce offices when you're new in town or just visiting. The staff can point you in the direction of fun and may know of special events or have coupons for you to use.

The stated purpose of the special William A. Hunton YMCA, 1139 E. Charlotte Street, (757) 622-7271, is to "nurture positive self image, develop leadership skills and assist in fostering positive values in our youth." Established to help children and youths who might otherwise be just hanging out or a number in the juvenile justice system, the center gears its programs and activities to meet the special needs of these kids, many of whom are from single-parent or low-income families. After school and day care, team sports, youth employment, summer camps and a number of other activities are scheduled year round.

Portsmouth

The game's the same, only the place and people have changed. Any activity, class, workshop or program you can find in other Hampton Roads cities, you can find here at any one of the eight recreation centers operated by the City of Portsmouth. Arts and crafts, games, field trips and the very popular adult softball, basketball and volleyball leagues are par for the frantic pace. As in other cities, the facilities vary from neighborhood to neighborhood, but all feature gymnasiums and lockers, exercise equipment and activity rooms.

City-Run Recreation Centers

Cavalier Manor Recreation Center, 404 Viking Street, Portsmouth, (757) 393-8757
Craddock Recreation Center, 45 Afton Parkway, Portsmouth, (757) 393-8757
Hi-Landers Recreation Center, 409 McLean Street, Portsmouth, (757) 393-8441
Joseph E. Parker Recreation Center, 2430 Turnpike Road, Portsmouth, (757) 393-8340
Kingman Heights Recreation Center, 105 Utah Street, Portsmouth, (757) 393-8839
Neighborhood Facility, 900 Elm Street, Portsmouth, (757) 393-8595
Port Norfolk Recreation Center, 432 Broad Street, Portsmouth, (757) 393-8709

Therapeutic Recreation

A packed calendar of activities is available for children and adults, each geared to accommodate a specific disability. For full information concerning class offerings, schedules and fees, call (757) 393-8481.

Community Centers With Membership Fees

One of the most popular features of the Portsmouth YMCA, 4900 High Street, (757) 483-9622, is the indoor running track, so you can deliver your laps through wind, rain or snow. Also aboard: a pool, a gymnasium, basketball, handball and volleyball courts, exercise/weight-lifting rooms, a sauna, steam room and whirlpool. A variety of classes and fitness evaluations is offered to both regular and corporate members.

The Effingham Street YMCA is at 1013 Effingham Street, (757) 399-5511. You know you're seeing pride and practice in motion when you spot the award-winning special drill team from the Effingham Y march in a local parade! This is but one of the outstanding results of the leadership at this Y, which offers a family-night program, youth Bible class and a Golden Age club. Activities include everything from judo and karate to crocheting and ballet, all in a facility that houses a gymnasium, basketball court, pool tables and meeting rooms. A new outdoor pool has been added for cooling off in the summer heat.

Chesapeake

It's soccer, basketball and ballet! It's volleyball, quilting and karate! It's more activities, classes, daytrips and workshops than one person can squeeze into a lifetime. But, come on, give it a try. Hook up with the City of Chesapeake's Parks and Recreation facilities and it's bye-bye spare time.

Chesapeake operates six community centers that each feature a full plate of activities and classes. You'll find squeaky-clean gyms and lockers at all of the centers, along with weight rooms, kitchens and outdoor sports facilities. Membership and I.D. cards for residents are $5 per year for adults, $2 for kids 9 through 17, free for seniors. One-day guest passes are available for $3.

City-Run Recreation Centers

Deep Creek Community Center, 2901 Margaret Booker Drive, Chesapeake, (757) 487-8841
Great Bridge Community Center, 212 Holt Drive, Chesapeake, (757) 547-6292
Indian River Community Center, 2250 Old Greenbrier Road, Chesapeake, (757) 547-6292
River Crest Community Center, 1001 Riverwalk Parkway, Chesapeake, (757) 436-3100
South Norfolk Community Center, 1217 Godwin Avenue, Chesapeake, (757) 543-5721
Western Branch Community Center, 4437 Portsmouth Boulevard, Chesapeake, (757) 465-0211

Therapeutic Recreation

Chesapeake extends a particular welcome for children and adults with disabilities. A full schedule of programs, classes and trips is on the agenda, and many are free. Preschool and after-school programs are also offered. Volunteers are always needed to assist during activities, so if you've got some spare time, this would be a rewarding way to pass an afternoon. For information and assistance, call (757) 547-6639. If you require a TDD, call Chesapeake's main library at (757) 436-8300 to serve as a relay station.

Community Centers With Membership Fees

The Chesapeake Family YMCA, 1033 Greenbrier Parkway, (757) 547-9622, adjacent to the city's sports complex, is a beautiful, modern facility complete with all the sports trappings: a large swimming pool, a complete Nautilus center, saunas, showers, locker rooms and a large activity room. Take your pick of classes, from scuba diving and gymnastics to aerobics and martial arts. Working moms are particularly fond of the center's Before and After School Fun Club, available for elementary school children and a wonderful, activity-packed program for latchkey kids. The Y's summer day camp called Y.E.S. (Youth Experience Summer Program) is especially popular with Chesapeake children.

INSIDERS' TIP
Visit Insiders.com or Falcon.com for more great books to help guide your travels.

The Greenbrier North Family YMCA is at 2100 Old Greenbrier Road, (757) 366-9622. Bring the family to sweat together on this Y's racquetball courts or in the gym. They've just added a new kindergarten program to their excellent before- and after-school programs.

Suffolk

City-Run Recreation Centers

Birdsong Recreation Center, 301 N. Main Street, Suffolk, (757) 925-6325
Cypress Park Swimming Pool, Arizona Avenue, Suffolk, (757) 539-9793
Suffolk Senior Center, 350 N. Main Street, Suffolk, (757) 925-6388
Whaleyville Community Center, Va. Route 13, Suffolk, (757) 986-3556

Community Center with Membership Fees

The Suffolk YMCA at 2769 Godwin Boulevard, (757) 934-9622, is a popular family athletic center. It offers a four-lane heated indoor pool, a six-lane outdoor pool, a whirlpool, a sauna, an aerobics studio, a basketball court, two racquetball courts, an outdoor sand volleyball court, free weights, cardiovascular equipment and babysitting for family members.

Spectator Sports

The Hampton Road sports scene is a good news/bad news kind of thing. The bad news first: we're still the largest metropolitan region in the country without a major-league sports team. The good news? We're working hard to get one.

In the meantime, we do a good job supporting the teams we have: the Norfolk Tides, a AAA farm team for the New York Mets; and the Hampton Roads Admirals, three-time champions of the East Coast Hockey League. In 2000 the team will move to the American Hockey League as an affiliate of the Chicago Blackhawks. We cheer the runners of the Shamrock Marathon and various road races and triathlons throughout the year. We admire fall foliage while watching the play at the annual Michelob PGA tournament every October. We follow the careers of hometown heroes such as boxer Sweet Pea Whittaker and golfer Curtis Strange wherever fate may lead them. And of course, we'll turn out in droves to watch any machine that speeds across the water—from a sailboat to a surfboard. So even if we don't yet have all the spectator sports we'd like, we're loyal and enthusiastic about supporting the teams we have.

LOOK FOR:
- **Professional Teams**
- **Hockey**
- **Soccer**
- **Professional Wrestling**
- **Football**
- **Rugby**
- **Basketball**
- **Annual Sporting Competitions**

Professional Teams

Baseball

The Norfolk Tides
Harbor Park,
Downtown Norfolk
- **(757) 622-2222**

The Class AAA farm team of the New York Mets, the Tides are the biggest success story of local professional sports. They can also boast about some of the players who've filled out their roster: pitcher Dwight Gooden and tough-guy Lew Dystra all started with the Tides before moving up to the Mets.

The Tides got their start in 1962, competing in the old Sally League at Frank D. Lawrence Stadium. In 1969, they leapfrogged to AAA status, and the following year took up residency at the then-brand-new Met Park in Norfolk. In 1993, The Tides moved to another brand new, state-of-the-art facility along the waterfront in Downtown Norfolk. Harbor Park, which has gained a reputation as one of the best minor-league ballparks in the country, features plush skyboxes for corporate sponsors, seating for 12,000, a restaurant and a unique walkway constructed from paver stones embedded with the names of fans who paid $30 to be a part of history.

A visit to see the Tides, or the many high school football teams that compete here during baseball off-season, is a blast. You can get a great chili dog or a plate of mean ribs, and the park and surrounding parking lots are well-patrolled by Norfolk's finest, giving you the real sense of safety throughout the evening. Tickets cost $5 and $7. All this fun for less than $10? It's great to be American!

Hockey

The Norfolk Admirals
**Scope, St. Paul's Blvd. and
Brambleton Ave., Norfolk**
• **(757) 640-1212**

You want winners? Hey, we got 'em. The Admirals have come out on top of the East Coast Hockey League at least three times, drawing sellout crowds to home games in Norfolk's Scope. Now the Admirals are moving up to the big leagues. Starting in October 2000 the Admirals moved up to the American Hockey League as an affiliate of the Chicago Blackhawks.

The Admirals' season starts in October, and face-offs continue through March with more than 40 home games.

Soccer

Hampton Roads Mariners
**Virginia Beach Sportsplex, Landstown Rd.,
Virginia Beach**
• **(757) 464-6257**

Need to put a little kick in your life? Check out the Hampton Roads Mariners. The franchise competes in the South Atlantic Division of the 72-team United States Interregional Soccer League (USISL), sanctioned under the U.S. Soccer Federation. The league plays a 28-game schedule, April through September. The Mariners are part of the DC United club and play hardball soccer that is fun for fans to watch. Soccer-playing kids particularly love to come to the games. In 1998 the Mariners moved into the new Sportsplex designed just for soccer. Children will like the Fan Zone play area adjacent to the playing field. Tickets cost between $6 and $15 and are available at the stadium.

Professional Wrestling

**Scope
St. Paul's Blvd. and Brambleton Ave.,
Norfolk**
• **(757) 664-6464**

Boy, we really debated whether to include

this under "sports" or "theater." Mid-Atlantic Wrestling is a big-time spectator sport for Hampton Roads kids of all ages who are just hankering to see that big throw across the turnbuckle. It all happens every year at Norfolk Scope (you can tell when a bout is upcoming from all the screaming TV commercials hawking tickets), and the crowds of seemingly timid, well-dressed patrons turn into vicious, make-him-suffer lunatics. It's not for everyone, but our job here is not to judge—just to let you know what's available. Tickets cost between $15 and $25.

Football

Lack of a pro team doesn't deter locals with football fever. They'll wrap up and pack off to a local high school football game, or better yet fill the car with cronies and light out for D.C., Philly or Pittsburgh to cheer their football teams on. The same enthusiasm prevails for college ball, and following the stats for Norfolk State University and Hampton University is a local pastime.

New to the area in 2000 are the Norfolk Nighthawks, an Arena II pro team that play at Scope, St. Paul's Blvd. and Brambleton Ave., (757) 626-0500. The Nighthawks quickly gained a loyal following with their high-scoring games. The team takes on contenders from North and South Carolina, Tennessee and Florida as well as other Virginia cities. Pre-game parties and halftime hoopla add to the fun for fans. The season runs from April through July. Tickets cost from $11-$24 and are available through TicketMaster.

Rugby

The Norfolk Blues
Lafayette Park, 3500 Granby St., Norfolk
• **(757) 455-9037**

For another twist on football, take in a game of rugby. While the sport is still somewhat misunderstood and unappreciated in the region, the sheer ferocity and stamina of this winning team has brought attention, if not small fame, to its stars. Call to find out all about season

INSIDERS' TIP

For more information about sports in Hampton Roads, contact one of these local organizations:
Norfolk Sports Club, Norfolk, (757) 497-9583
Southside Athletic Association, Suffolk, (757) 539-9657
Virginia Beach Sports Club, Virginia Beach, (757) 428-1470

play at Lafayette Park. The games are free to anyone who comes to watch.

Basketball

Some of us can remember the old Virginia Squires, with Charlie Scott, George Gervin and Julius "Dr. J" Erving taking center court back in the olden days of the 1970s. The Squires were the first major-league sporting franchise in Hampton Roads and died a slow, painful death due to lack of spectator support just before the NBA-ABA merger.

Support is not the problem for the Monarchs of Old Dominion—both the men's and women's teams. Each year the women's team is a contender in the NCAA tournament. Buy your tickets early (or better yet, buy season tickets) for games played at Norfolk's Scope or the ODU's fieldhouse. Across town, the Spartans and Lady Spartans of Norfolk State University are always crowd pleasers. For schedules and ticket info, call ODU sports at (757) 683-3372 and NSU sports at (757) 455-3303.

Hoop fever hits at the high school level too. Fans pack gymnasiums all over town to cheer on their favorites. We grow them good, too, like alumni-turned-pro Joe Smith of Maury High School, J. R. Reid from Kempsville High School and Alonzo Morning, straight from Chesapeake's Indian River High.

Annual Sporting Competitions

There are competitions for nearly every sport in Hampton Roads, and many bring out scores of spectators. Here's a list of the big ones.

Shamrock Sportsfest
Virginia Beach
• **(757) 481-5090**

An annual March event, held on a Saturday near St. Paddy's Day, the Shamrock Marathon is one of Virginia's most popular marathons, averaging 2,000 runners. There's the Open 8K Run, Masters 8K Run, 5K Fitness Walk, Children's Marathon and Sports Trade Show. The race takes place along the boardwalk, through Fort Story and along the entire oceanfront and ends at the Pavilion, where there's always a party atmosphere.

Crawford Bay Crew Classic
Portsmouth City Park
• **(757) 393-9933**

One of our classier sporting events, the Crawford Bay Crew Classic gathers rowing teams from several East Coast colleges (the roster varies every year) in Portsmouth every March to race on the Elizabeth River. Watch from the park's waterfront.

SPECTATOR SPORTS

Harbor Park on the downtown Norfolk waterfront is the home of the Norfolk Tides.

Photo: Norfolk Convention and Visitors Bureau

Portsmouth Invitational Basketball Tournament
Portsmouth
• (757) 393-8481

This tournament is an annual showcase of basketball talent from across the country, with players competing for NBA recruitment. This tournament is held every spring, usually in April, at Churchland High School.

Elizabeth River Run
Norfolk
• (757) 421-2602

Virginia's largest road race is held every April in Norfolk. The 10K course stretches from the Armed Forces Staff College near the Naval Base to Town Point Park in downtown.

North American Sand Soccer Championships
Virginia Beach
• (757) 456-0578

This on-the-beach soccer tournament is held every June at the oceanfront from 3rd to 16th streets. It attracts teams from around the globe as well as locally.

Cock Island Race
Portsmouth Seawall
• (757) 393-9933

This is the largest sailboat race on the East Coast, featuring a total of 300 boats and assorted festivities. Spectators can watch from the Portsmouth seawall or from Norfolk Waterside. The race is held every year in June.

Budweiser Pro-Am Volleyball Tournament
Virginia Beach
• (757) 437-4800

These guys really know how to spike the ball. This annual tournament takes place every August at the Virginia Beach oceanfront.

East Coast Surfing Championships
Virginia Beach
• (757) 499-8822

This is a serious Beach tradition. Any local surf shop will be abuzz with the news about this August tournament that attracts the big-gest names in surfing. Even if you don't know the first thing about the boards, it's a great excuse to get some sun while watching the competition—or the scantily-clad spectators. The tournament is held at the oceanfront from 1st to 9th streets.

World Championship Rodeo
Virginia Beach
• (757) 721-7786

For the horsey set, this annual September competition at Princess Anne Park gets big scores for the high level of showmanship.

Sandman Triathlon
Virginia Beach
• (757) 437-4700

Held annually in September as part of the Neptune Festival, this race draws the toughest

The Hampton Roads Admirals draw loyal fans to Norfolk Scope.

Photo: Norfolk Convention and Visitors Bureau

competitors who go neck-to-neck in a 2K swim, 20-mile bike race and 10K run.

The Michelob Golf Classic
Williamsburg
• (757) 253-3906

The PGA comes to the Kingsmill Golf Course in Williamsburg every October. Players vie for $1.1 million in winnings.

The Chesapeake Bay

LOOK FOR:
• Watershed
• Environmental Concerns
• Seeing The Bay
• Up the Western Shore
• For More Information

When you're in Hampton Roads it's impossible to ignore the Chesapeake Bay, one of the region's most important geographical features. Even when you're not in direct view of the Bay, you're near one of the many rivers and creeks that flow into it.

Besides creating some breathtaking scenery, the Chesapeake Bay influences countless aspects of daily life:

It is the main reason Hampton Roads excels as a port and a popular tourism destination. It is the engine that drives much of the region's industry—from shipbuilding and ship repair to manufacturing and distribution.

It provides the livelihood for hundreds of hardy watermen whose families have plied the waters for generations. The crabs and finfish they harvest make Virginia the third-largest seafood-producing state.

The species of fish and shellfish pulled from the Bay has a direct impact on what's on the menu when you go out to eat. If rockfish or soft-shell crabs are in season, they'll be hot items at area restaurants.

The Bay and the deep Hampton Roads harbor were the main reasons the Navy built its largest installation here.

The Bay enticed the first permanent English settlers in the New World to stay in the area after they landed here in 1607. One of the Bay's tributaries led them to Jamestown where they began colonizing this country. The region surrounding the Bay gave birth to the New World's first permanent towns and plantations and its initial crops of tobacco and wheat. Today you can see traces of this rich past in a treasure trove of historical sites.

Because of the Bay and its tributaries, getting from here to there can be tricky in this coastal region. Bridges and underwater tunnels are vital links between cities divided by the Bay and other waterways.

With its 200-mile length, the Chesapeake Bay is the United States' largest estuary, and Hampton Roads is where it starts its journey northward from the Atlantic Ocean to Havre de Grace, Maryland.

Watershed

Although the Chesapeake Bay is physically surrounded by only Virginia and Maryland, its watershed stretches as far as Cooperstown, New York, and Pendletown County, West Virginia. In this drainage area nearly 50 rivers and thousands of streams, creeks and ditches empty into the Bay, making it vulnerable to any pollutants they carry. The largest tributary is the Susquehanna River in Pennsylvania, which is why that inland state is a key player in keeping the Bay healthy. Because of the Bay's sprawling watershed, rain that falls on the 64,000 square miles between North Carolina and Vermont always ends up in the Bay.

For most people, the Bay's special meaning comes from watching a glorious sunrise, spending the day pulling flounder or drum from its waters or strolling along one of its many beaches. Every city in south Hampton Roads is situated on hundreds of miles of coastline along the Bay and its tributaries. Portsmouth alone has 185 miles of shoreline, and Norfolk stretches along 140 miles of waterfront.

Environmentally, the Bay is revered as one of the most productive places on Earth. Its waters, marshes and wetlands shelter an incredible variety of life—from clams and flounder to egrets and whistling swans. More than 2,700 species of plants and animals depend on the Bay for life— including the succulent crabs the Bay is renowned for producing.

The Chesapeake Bay is where salt water from the ocean meets and mingles with fresh river water. Geologists believe it was created at the end of the last Ice Age approximately 12,000 to 18,000 years ago when melting glaciers and rising seas flooded the Susquehanna River.

One theory supported by recent U.S. Geological Survey research is that a falling meteorite carved out the Bay 35 million years ago. The theory holds that the meteorite crashed into a shallow sea near what is now Cape Charles on the Eastern Shore. As a result, 1,600-foot tidal waves ripped through the shoreline and created the Bay.

No matter how the Bay got here, the Native Americans who were Virginia's first inhabitants recognized its majesty and honored it with various names that meant "Great Waters," "Mother of Waters" and "Great Shellfish Bay." In the 1600s British colonists named the Bay "Chesapeake" from the Indian word "Tschiswapeki."

Environmental Concerns

The Chesapeake Bay has long been famous for its oysters, crabs and finfish, but their populations have dropped drastically in the past 100 years. Pollution, overharvesting and stress from development have reduced the oyster population to only one percent of what it was in the late-19th century. Rockfish, once one of the Bay's most prolific fish, nearly disappeared until a multistate ban on catching them was implemented in 1986. The ban's success helped the rockfish rebound, and now anglers harvest regulated quantities of one of the Bay's tastiest fish. Fishing for rockfish has become a popular fall and winter hobby for many anglers.

A 1983 Environmental Protection Agency study showed the Bay was ailing from too many nutrients, toxic substances and sediment. That assessment led Virginia, Maryland and Pennsylvania to voluntarily unite to save the Chesapeake Bay. Their efforts helped create public awareness that the Bay is a fragile resource and it must be protected. A ban on phosphate detergents, restrictions on wetland destruction and other coordinated efforts are helping turn the tide for the Bay.

You'll still spot blue-and-white "Save the Bay" bumper stickers on cars, but there are hopeful signs that the Bay's health is on the mend. One improvement is the growth of underwater grasses, which are vital to filtering pollutants and are one of the best indicators of the Bay's health. Underwater grass fields have increased from a low of 35,000 acres in 1984 to more than 75,000 acres today. This is nowhere near the historic high of 600,000 acres, but it is a step in the right direction.

To get involved in improving the Bay, join the **Chesapeake Bay Foundation.** Since its founding in 1966 it has grown to include more than 87,000 members. The foundation is headquartered in Annapolis, Maryland, but it has a field office in Norfolk at 100 W. Plume Street, (757) 622-1964. The foundation is the country's largest regional environmental organization and a powerful voice for the Bay. You can join one of the foundation's local BaySavers groups whose members dedicate themselves to environmental endeavors such as cleaning streams and planting trees.

Other organizations with an interest in the Bay and related areas include the **Center for Marine Conservation**, (757) 496-0920; **Virginia Ecotourism Association** (757) 471-5884 and the **Back Bay Restoration Foundation**, (757) 412-0563 or (757) 426-3643. There is a local chapter of the **Sierra Club**, (757) 467-2775, and two **Audubon Society** chapters, (757) 464-9437 or (757) 588-8410. There also are numerous clubs for anglers. In 1992 the nonprofit

Elizabeth River Project was created to restore the Elizabeth River, a tributary of the Bay, to health. Four years later the organization created an ambitious plan to revive the waterway by 2010. The plan is supported by state government officials, the Navy, civic leaders and corporations. To help with the Elizabeth River Project call (757) 625-3648. On the first Saturday of every month local environmental enthusiasts congregate for the **Environmental Green Breakfast of Hampton Roads** at the Golden Corral restaurant at 470 Newtown Road in Virginia Beach. The informative breakfast meeting starts at 8 AM and often draws more than 100 people. For information call (757) 427-6606.

Another event that attracts a huge response is the annual **Clean the Bay Day** on the second Saturday in June. The effort started in this region in 1989 when volunteers joined forces for three hours to clean 52 miles of local waterways. Their reward was the satisfaction of hauling away 30 tons of trash. Since 1989, Clean the Bay Day's momentum has swelled to include more than 4,000 volunteers combing 200 miles of shoreline and collecting about several hundred tons of aluminum cans, old tires, cigarette butts and other junk each year.

As Clean the Bay Day approaches each spring you'll see and hear a barrage of publicity that brings out families (including ours), Scout troops and individuals. But in case you miss the media messages, call (757) 427-6606 or (800) SAVEBAY for information. If you miss Clean the Bay Day, you can get out your work gloves for the **International Coastal Cleanup** usually held on the third Saturday in September. The local media carries details on this cleanup effort.

Another big local environmental event is **Earth Day**, usually celebrated with lots of displays and activities on the first Sunday in May. The site rotates between Mount Trashmore Park in Virginia Beach and Town Point Park in Norfolk.

Seeing the Bay

With only two percent of the Chesapeake Bay's shoreline accessible to the public, it is sometimes difficult to gaze upon this national treasure.

To truly appreciate the majesty of the Chesapeake Bay, you must get out on the water. There are many fishing boats and tour boats that take groups out daily in Hampton Roads as well as elsewhere along the Bay. For ideas see our chapter on Fishing, the close-up on Cruising in our Attractions chapter, the Smith Island information in Daytrips, and the Tangier Island section in the Eastern Shore chapter. If you're part of a group, you can schedule field trips coordinated by the Chesapeake Bay Foundation. These range from canoeing on creeks to spending a few hours on the foundation's *Baywatcher* boat exploring the Elizabeth and James Rivers. Groups can also plan several-day environmental meetings at the foundation's facilities at Port Isobel Island or Fox Island near the Eastern Shore. Both are pristine, uninhabited islands with lodging facilities operated by the Chesapeake Bay Foundation. For information call (804) 622-1964 or (410) 268-8816.

To soak up the beauty of the Bay there are several places to go in Hampton Roads. The **Cape Henry** area inside Fort Story in Virginia Beach has a good stretch of undeveloped beaches open to the public on weekends. Along Shore Drive in Virginia Beach you can dine at several bayfront restaurants, including the **Duck-In**, a transformed bait house with a screened gazebo and a private beach. The **Virginia Beach Resort and Conference Center** also has its own beach as well as a restaurant and rooms that overlook the Bay. **Alexander's on the Bay**, a restaurant in the Chick's Beach area, is an elegant dinner spot with a front-row view of the Bay. **First Landing State Park** on Shore Drive has a wonderful beach that can only be used by people spending the night in the park. Getting one of the 215 campsites and 20 cabins can be a difficult feat in summer, but it's definitely worth the effort. Call (757) 481-2131 for reservations. In 1999 the park opened the Chesapeake Bay Center, an environmentally focused visitor center.

You can admire the Bay from the Chesapeake Bay Bridge-Tunnel, which connects Virginia Beach with the Eastern Shore and has an overlook on a man-made island. Once on the Eastern Shore, **Kiptopeke State Park i**s probably your best choice for experiencing the Bay (see our Eastern Shore chapter for details). Near the park's beach, the waters are shallow, making this a great spot for families with children. There also is a public beach in downtown Cape Charles. One fun option is to catch a boat to either **Tangier Island** or Smith Island, where you'll find yourself surrounded by the Bay (see our Eastern Shore and Daytrips chapters for details).

In Norfolk, the **Ocean View** beaches stretch for miles along the Bay's calm waters. You'll find a boardwalk, a gazebo, picnic shelters and restrooms at some parts of the Ocean View beach. The **Ship's Cabin**, one of Norfolk's oldest and best restaurants, fronts the Bay in Ocean View and is a romantic spot for twilight dining.

Across the Hampton Roads Bridge-Tunnel in **Hampton**, you can view the Bay from historic **Fort Monroe** and the adjacent recently renovated Chamberlin Hotel and its restaurant. Within the fort there is a fishing pier that juts out into the Bay and is perfect for dropping a fishing line or a crab pot. Or travel through Hampton's quaint Phoebus area to **Buckroe Beach**. There you will find a paved boardwalk along the Bay. Buckroe is a nice family beach with gentle waters perfect for children. An outdoor pavilion usually has Wednesday and Sunday night entertainment in the summer. Picnic shelters and restrooms make it easy to settle in for a day. Beyond the beach is the 600-acre **Grandview Nature Preserve**, which fronts the Bay. The preserve truly is a wilderness, and hikers are directed to a beach that is perfect for finding shells and fossils. Without lifeguards, this really isn't a beach for swimming. However, it is a great place for exploring. For details on seeing the Bay in Hampton, call the **Hampton Convention and Tourism Bureau** at (757) 487-8778.

Up The Bay's Western Shore: The Middle Peninsula and The Northern Neck

When the thought of another day of the regular grind gives you palpitations and you start to develop a migraine after just the first paragraph of the business page, the only remedy is a journey to The Land That Time Forgot.

Enveloped by scenic rivers that feed into the nearby Chesapeake Bay, Virginia's Middle Peninsula/Northern Neck region is a million miles away in attitude. Known by natives and weekend residents as "the rivah," this area sprawls just north of the Virginia Peninsula. It mirrors its sister Eastern Shore, likewise trapped in history by the Chesapeake Bay and its tributaries. The Industrial Revolution took a lunch break when it came to Gloucester and Mathews counties, Urbanna and the Northern Neck. This remains to this day a lazy, tranquil network of minitowns that retain the charm of yesterday, with little visible intrusion by the scatter-and-panic environment of nearby urban hubs.

Unlike Williamsburg, which has purposely and for a profit re-created the look and feel of the early days, the Middle Peninsula and Northern Neck come by it naturally—with picturesque little wharfs where watermen embark to make their livings, with restaurants serving the same delicious cholesterol-laden suppers they have for generations, with charming antiques shops and galleries—all with little regard for the pressures of time.

One day is just not enough to absorb the rejuvenating forces of this lovely part of Virginia so plan on staying at least overnight. Your choices include warm and welcoming bed and breakfasts and elegant resorts as well as waterfront marinas and motels. If you own a boat, feel free to use it as your main mode of transportation since many accommodations come complete with a marina or a dock. A car works equally well and lets you explore more territory.

The basic rule when heading this way is to take time to linger, a pastime we bet you've almost forgotten. We guarantee that once you've kicked off your shoes, chatted with a few locals and polished off a dinner of jumbo lump crab cakes, you'll agree—it's like taking a Valium the size of a watermelon.

Gloucester County

This is a picture-book county tucked into a finger of land bounded by the Piankatank River on the north, Mobjack Bay and the Ware River on the east and the York River on the south. Lush green farmlands, yellow carpets of daffodil fields and sparkling blue waters paint just the right palette for a lazy-day outing.

Named for Henry, Duke of Gloucester, the area proudly claims a rich history that dates back

Chesapeake Bay Facts

The Chesapeake Bay is the largest and most biologically productive estuary in North America. More seafood is harvested from the Bay than from any of the 840 other estuaries in the United States.

The bay is 200 miles long and averages 15 miles in width. Its depth averages a shallow 21 feet. At its deepest point it is 150 feet.

If you reduced the Chesapeake Bay to the scale of a football field, its average depth would equal that of three dimes. The Bay's shallowness makes it vulnerable to pollution because there is not ample water to absorb toxins, nutrients and sediment.

Flowing into the Bay are 49 rivers with 102 branches and tributaries. They are navigable for 1,750 miles.

There are more than 15 million people living in the Bay's watershed, which includes Virginia, Maryland, West Virginia, Pennsylvania, Delaware and New York.

The Bay is home to more than 2,700 species of plants and animals. The Bay's shallow edges help make it one of the most biologically productive places on earth.

The Bay's blue-crab harvest annually represents more than half the country's total catch.

The Bay is the winter home for about 500,000 Canada geese and 40,000 whistling swans.

The Bay is the nesting area of choice for 1,600 pairs of ospreys —the largest population in the United States. It also is the nesting area for about 125 pairs of bald eagles—one of the largest populations in the lower 48 states.

The Bay has more than 8,000 miles of shoreline, but only 2 percent of it is accessible to the public. The rest is privately owned.

—Source: The Chesapeake Bay Foundation

The Bay's blue crab harvest represents more than half of the country's total catch.

Photo: Courtesy of Eastern Shore Tourism Commission

to the early 1600s. Legend holds that it was here that Indian princess Pocahontas saved the gallant Captain John Smith from a tragic death at the hands of her tribe. It was the same Captain Smith who proclaimed, perhaps in gratitude, "Heaven and earth never framed a better place for man's habitation."

This was a tobacco-producing area in the 1600s and 1700s, and many original plantation homes and magnificent private residences remain in remarkable condition. Gloucester County is home to about 33,000 residents, many of whom leave daily from seafood wharves to take their livings from surrounding deep tidal waters. The county is at heart an agricultural community of crops and pasture lands. While dubbed the "land of the life worth living" by its residents, visiting cityfolk call it "the land that time forgot." And that's exactly what gives it the charm and the hypnotic personality that draws us to visit time after time.

Gloucester County is one of our favorite spots for daytripping. Its main town, Gloucester Court House, has a traditional Main Street with historic buildings surrounding a village green. There are antiques and gift shops to explore, historic sites to see and excellent restaurants with tables waiting for when you need a break.

Getting There

Arriving by boat would be our first choice, pulling into any of the numerous marinas that dot the 100-plus miles of shoreline. If you're like most of us who don't own a boat, you'll get here by car. The most direct route is north on Interstate 64. Then take Route 17 and cross the Coleman Memorial Bridge over the York River. You'll pay a $2 toll on the way over but nothing on your return trip. At the end sprawls Gloucester County, about 45 miles from Norfolk. Getting here requires a leisurely drive, and the only real gridlock might be at the Coleman drawbridge if it's time to raise the bridge for boat traffic below. Most of the time road traffic moves smoothly thanks to a recent bridge-widening project.

Commercial crabbers are a common sight on the Chesapeake Bay.

Photo: Courtesy of Northern Neck Travel Council

Landlubbers will probably want to stick to Route 17 and take the business route to check out the town of Gloucester Court House with its historic district. Old salts will love pulling off the main drag and winding down lesser county roads to reach the picturesque sights on the Severn or Ware rivers. Lots of small towns and villages are scattered through Gloucester County, and a stop at any one should reap accurate directions to your chosen destination.

Events and Attractions

Let's start with the best. **The Daffodil Festival**, held the first Saturday in April, coincides with the time when daffodils are in full glory. We're talking mega-fields of yellow here since Gloucester County is one of the world's largest suppliers of daffodil bulbs. Sponsored by the Daffodil Festival Committee and the Gloucester Parks and Recreation Department, the festival salutes the annual daffodil harvest with a parade, arts and crafts show, 5K and 1-mile runs, historical exhibits, live entertainment, regional food, children's games and rides. To check out the festival agenda, contact the Gloucester County Chamber of Commerce, (804) 693-2425. It's open Monday, Wednesday and Friday.

Other annual events to mark on your calendar are **Historic Garden Week**, held Friday and Saturday of the last full week in April; the **Abingdon Ruritan Seafood Festival** on the third Wednesday evenings in May and October (advance tickets required); and the **Annual Christmas Parade and Open House** at Gloucester Court House the first Saturday in December. The Gloucester Chamber can fill you in on specifics.

The **Gloucester Courthouse Square Historic District** on Main Street is like a time-warped version of a movie set. You'll see an immaculately restored Colonial courthouse, (open weekdays 9 AM to 4 PM), Debtors Prison (now a visitors center open Wednesday and Friday 10 AM to 2 PM), the old jail and many other preserved buildings. They are enveloped by a charming walled courtyard with a village green. One landmark is a Confederate monument unveiled in 1889 to honor the 132 Gloucester men who lost their lives during the War Between the States.

South of Gloucester Court House, close to Carter's Creek off Route 614, is **Rosewell**. This once was one of America's finest colonial houses. Although the house was gutted by fire in 1916, you can explore its ruins: magnificent brick walls, massive chimneys and elaborate doorways framed by superb brickwork survive. If you're lucky you'll catch archaeologists at work at the site.

A new visitor center provides insight into this grand home's history. There is a great view of the ruins from the second floor. Rosewell is open every day but Saturday from 10 AM to 5 PM.

There are guided tours of the Rosewell ruins on Sundays from April through October from 2 to 5 PM. For details call (804) 693-2585. Donations for the site's preservation are welcome.

For history buffs, a visit to the **Warner Hall Graveyard** is in order. Off Route 629 south of Gloucester Court House, you'll see a roadside marker on the right indicating the site of a Colonial family cemetery where ancestors of George Washington, Robert E. Lee and Queen Elizabeth II are buried. At the intersections of routes 616 and 614, is the birthplace of Dr. Walter Reed, the conqueror of yellow fever. This is a small mid-19th-century building, authentically furnished. However, it's open only in April during Historic Garden Club Week and the Daffodil Festival.

Two historic churches of note are **Abingdon Episcopal Church** on Route 17 and **Ware Episcopal Church** on Route 14. Abingdon Episcopal is a rare cruciform Colonial church completed in 1755. Its surrounding cemetery dates from the mid-1600s. It is open for weekly Sunday services, in April during the Daffodil Festival and Garden Club Week and by appointment. Ware Episcopal is an early 18th-century example of rectangular Colonial churches. It is open for weekly Sunday services, the April Garden Club Week and by appointment.

Of interest to young and old is the **Gloucester Point Archeological District**, just off Route 17 at Gloucester Point. Here you can check out portions of Tyndall's Point Park, remnants of Confederate and Union fortifications and the site of Colonial Gloucestertown, which is now home to the Virginia Institute of Marine Science of the College of William and Mary. Interesting to tour is Waterman's Hall, with its exhibits of Colonial artifacts and an aquarium featuring 50 varieties of marine animals. Waterman's Hall is open to the public 8:30 AM to 4:30 PM Monday through Friday. Call (804) 642-8176.

If you need a little exercise after all that sightseeing, pack the family off to **Beaverdam Park**, which you can enter from either route 616 or 606. Here you'll find boat ramps, canoe rentals, picnic shelters and hiking trails around the Gloucester County Reservoir. Or you can hit **Gloucester Point Beach Park** on Route 17. This is a 5-acre park right on the York River next to the Coleman Bridge, complete with a fishing pier, a beach, a horseshoe pit, a volleyball court, a concession stand and restrooms.

Shopping

You wouldn't call Gloucester County the mall capital of the world since there aren't any. But when it comes to antiquing, here are a few places we suggest. The **Stagecoach Markets and Antique Village**, on Route 17 a mile south of Gloucester Court House, is an emporium of more than 35 shops selling you-name-it. It's open only on Saturday and Sunday, and it's worth a look-see. Also check out Plantation Antique Mall along Route 17. Downtown in Gloucester Court House is **Lord Botetourt Antiques**, which is crammed with all kinds of furniture and books.

We never visit Gloucester Court House without popping into our favorite clothing consignment shop. Gloucester County may be rural, but there are a lot of wealthy people living here and the quality of the clothes in **Deja Vu** reflects that. The shop also is an outlet for new J. Crew clothing for women and men. Also perfect for browsing are the upscale **Village Clothes Tree** for women, **The Gift Garden** and the well-stocked **Twice Told Tales** bookstore. While in town pop into **Peace Frogs**. This company is known internationally for its whimsical T-shirt and other clothing designs. Gloucester is its corporate headquarters, and Peace Frogs has a retail shop downtown.

Accommodations

There are two bed and breakfast inns in Gloucester County, and both are real beauties. The **Willows Bed and Breakfast**, on Route 3, just 5 miles from Gloucester Court House,

(804) 693-4066, rests on an acre of daffodil fields. It's a large white farmhouse with a shady porch filled with ferns and wicker. Ted and Angela Kristensen have restored the old house, and renovated the former church and general store that dates back to the 1880s. The rooms are comfortably furnished with old family pieces and other pieces collected during their travels. Danish-born Ted and English-born Angela give Southern hospitality an injection of continental spirit, from the chef 's Danish country omelette called Aegekage to afternoon tea on the porch. Each bedroom offers a queen-size bed, a private bath and a TV. Reservations are highly recommended. Credit cards are not accepted, but personal or traveler's checks and cash will guarantee you a delightful, totally pampered stay.

Also in Gloucester County is **Airville Plantation** at 6423 T.C. Walker Road, 1.5 miles outside Gloucester Court House, (804) 694-0287. This 1756 plantation home is on the National Historic Register and is owned by Kathie and Larry Cohen. Guests can stay in either one of two rooms in the main house or a cozy overseer's cottage. The cottage dates from the 1700s and comes with an inviting downstairs woodstove and an upstairs fireplace. Guests in the house and the cottage are offered a full breakfast. Bicycles are available for exploring the surrounding 50 acres. On the property two miles away is Mobjack Bay. If you want to arrive by water, you can dock your boat there.

Another option is **North River Inn**, a bed and breakfast at the 17th century estate called Toddsbury. Guests stay in cottages and other dependencies on the grounds, which are on Route 17 about four miles outside Gloucester Courthouse. The inn has two guest rooms and three suites. Each has private bathrooms and air conditioning. Outside are 100 acres of gardens to explore as well as the North River and a creek. Guests can arrive by boat or car. Call (804) 694-0216.

New in 2000 is a **Comfort Inn** on Route 17, (804) 695-1900.

Restaurants

Standing out for those who love a serving of history along with their dinner is **Seawell's Ordinary** in Ordinary on Route 17 just across the York River. Reservations are suggested; call (804) 642-3635. While visiting this historic treasure, which was built as a residence in 1712, you may glimpse your former life as you dine by flickering candlelight in the authentic Colonial atmosphere of the five dining rooms. Restored by Eleanor and John Evans in 1989, the restaurant's French-American regional menu, excellent wine list and gracious service have earned raves from the most critical of Insiders.

Goodfellas on Route 17 in White Marsh, (804) 693-5950, is another favorite for locals and travelers. You can be certain of an excellent choice if you order an Italian pasta or beef entree.

One of our favorite lunch places is **Sutton's**, (804) 693-9565, on Mary Sutton Road just off Route 17 where it connects with Route 17 Business. This homey spot specializes in plate lunches that make you want to eat all your veggies because they are so good. We've been known to drive from Norfolk to Sutton's just to eat the outstanding crab cakes. Even though the restaurant's namesake and former owner is deceased, the food quality remains high.

INSIDERS' TIP
Pick up a free copy of *The Rivah*, a quarterly visitor's guide, when visiting the Middle Peninsula or Northern Neck region. The tabloid newspaper is available in shops, museums and restaurants throughout the area. It highlights events and activities and steers visitors toward the best fishing spots.

You can't go wrong if you wait to dine until you've explored downtown Gloucester Court House. There are several excellent restaurants along Main Street. **Kelsick Gardens**, (804) 693-6500, is known for its gourmet salads and soups and sandwiches served on homemade bread. **Victoria's**, (804) 693-0111, is where the locals enjoy pizza. **The Blue Fin**, (804) 693-9390, specializes in seafood. **Stillwater's** is known for its upscale cuisine, (804) 694-5618. Outside town off Route 17 is a restaurant that has wowed locals and visitors alike since its 1996 opening. **River's Inn**, (804) 642-9942, overlooks the York River at the York River Yacht Haven near Gloucester Point. Seafood is the cuisine of choice here. Also outside town is **Chesapeake Bay Prime Rib and Seafood**, (804) 642-2222.

Mathews County

As you continue your journey up Route 17, you'll come to the smallest of Virginia's counties, Mathews. Mathews is a hot ticket right now, as many Hampton Roads residents have discovered that it's the perfect place to buy a second home. In fact, many of the same people with whom we Insiders used to share a patch of beach in summer or football game in fall now streak out of town to their getaway homes even before the weekend begins.

Separated from Gloucester County by the North River and Mobjack Bay, Mathews County was formed in 1791 and named for Major Thomas Mathews, Speaker of the Virginia House of Delegates who enacted the legislation for its formation. With more than 200 miles of shoreline along the tributaries and the Chesapeake Bay, it's no wonder that the people of Mathews have a deep-seated appreciation for the water, marshlands and forests that comprise the natural environment. Indeed, the water and rich agricultural lands are the mainstay of the economy, with commercial fishing, boat building, field crops and livestock production heading the employment scene. This is an early-to-bed, early-to-rise sort of place, with water sports and taking time to smell the flowers heading the recreation and relaxation list.

Events and Attractions

Mathews Market Days is the highlight of the year in the county. The event takes place in Mathews, the county seat, the weekend after Labor Day. On Friday and Saturday the event fills the historic Courthouse Green with wares from local craftspeople and artists, steaming seafood, music and other entertainment. For something special sign up for boat tours to the North River and Mobjack Bay. You can register in advance by calling the Mathews County Chamber of Commerce, (804) 725-9029. A street dance winds up Market Days on Saturday night. In December the Courthouse is the site of the annual **Holiday Parade** and **Candlelight Open House**, complete with Santa Claus. This is always on the first weekend in December. The Mathews County Chamber of Commerce can provide details.

On either the fourth weekend in June or the first weekend in July, it's Gwynn's Island's time to shine. The **Gwynn's Island Festival** is a nonstop celebration of food, music, games, balloon rides and an antiques show that begins Friday night and ends on Saturday afternoon. While you're on the island, which is reached by a bridge, stop by the **Gwynn's Island Museum** housed in a former school on Route 633 to see its displays on Mathews County life from pre-Colonial to modern times. The museum is open May through October from 1 to 4 PM on Friday through Sunday. For information call (804) 725-7949 or 725-7941. Museum admission is free, but contributions are welcome.

If you're around the county in May, you may catch the Mathews High School crew team competing in the East River against some of Virginia's top high-school rowing teams. This popular competition brings out many family members to cheer on their student athletes.

Believe it or not, Mathews is home to the region's capital of country music. **Donk's Theater**, at the intersection of routes 198 and 223, is called Virginia's "Li'l Ole Opry." Hometown and big-name stars alike show up on the stage every other Saturday night. To get in rhythm call (804) 725-7760.

For the history buff, your expedition should start at the county's splendid **Courthouse on the Village Green**, a nationally registered landmark in continuous service since it was built in 1792. While you're there, stop into the restored **Tomkins Cottage** (c. 1818) and pick up more information from the **Mathews County Historical Society**, which is headquartered there. It's open on Fridays from 11 AM to 2 PM and by appointment at other times, (804) 725-9508. A map of historic Mathews sites is available for $1 by calling the Chamber of Commerce in advance or stopping by its office on Main Street.

There are many Colonial and Civil War sites to explore, especially **Cricket Hill** overlooking Gwynn's Island. It was here in July 1776 that Lord Dunsmore, the last of Virginia's Royal Governors, was driven from American shores by continental sharpshooters. You might also want to visit the nonfunctioning **New Point Comfort Lighthouse**, guarding the entrance to Mobjack Bay and restored by the county in the 1970s as a National Historic Landmark.

Shopping

Like Gloucester County, Mathews County is a good place to come for shopping-addiction withdrawal. But if you do get the urge to splurge, head to downtown Mathews and visit **Country Casuals**, which has clothing for men and women, and **Sibley's General Store**, where you'll find things you never knew you wanted or needed. Both are along Mathews' Main Street.

Accommodations

If you want to stay in town, try the **Inn at Tabb's Creek Landing**, which is on Tabb's Creek (804) 725-5136. Innkeeper Catherine Venable opened the inn in 1994 and welcome you to their 1820s farmhouse and its six guestrooms. The house is nestled amid magnolias and is near the creek. There is a private dock for canoeing and crabbing. A swimming pool, bicycles to borrow and a full Southern breakfast complete the hospitality.

New in 2000 is **Buckley Hall Inn**, a bed and breakfast inn. Owner Barry Thompson welcomes guests to his restored vintage home. It's right in town on Buckley Hall Road, (804) 725-1900

On Gwynn's Island, you'll find the appropriately named **Islander Motel** nestled just off the Bay in a sheltered harbor, (804) 725-2151. There are 40 waterfront rooms, a swimming pool, sandy beach and tennis courts.

For outdoorsy funseekers there's the **New Point Campground**, just 7 miles south of the Courthouse on Route 14 E. Open April through October, it's right on the Bay, with a beach, boat rentals, a marina, fishing access, a swimming pool and a mini-golf course. The nearby lighthouse has a real light that shines at night. For reservations for one of the 300 hookup sites, call (804) 725-5120.

Restaurants

When hunger strikes there are several options in Mathews County. **Lynne's Family Restaurant**, in the country on Highway 14, (804) 725-9996, also will fill you with familiar comfort food. **Andy's Barbecue & Ribs**, in downtown Mathews on Main Street, (804) 725-9320, has the pork you'd expect plus seafood on the menu. For more elegant offerings head to S**andpiper Reef** off Route 626 in Hallieford, (804) 725-3331. If hunger strikes while you're on Gwynn's Island, try **Seabreeze Restaurant**, (804) 725-4000. It's right on the water next to The Islander motel and features crab and shrimp. Boats can dock right at the restaurant.

Newcomers to the dining scene include **Dolls and Deli** in downtown Mathews, which has sandwiches and soups as well as luscious desserts, (804) 725-2766. Daffodils offers fine dining in a renovated Victorian-style home on Main Street, (804) 725-0725. For casual fare try the Irish Pub on Main Street, (804) 725-7900.

INSIDERS' TIP
If you're curious about all the ships plying the waters, get a copy of *What Ship Is That?* by Bob Basnight. The book, published in 1996, identifies in words and drawings all kinds of military and civilian vessels likely to pass through the Chesapeake Bay region.

Urbanna

Across the Piankatank River from both Gloucester and Mathews counties is scenic Middlesex County. Its best-known locale is Urbanna—a picture-perfect location surrounded by Urbanna Creek, the Rappahannock River and Sprout Spring Cove. To get there stay on Route 17 N. to Saluda. Turn right on Route 33 and you'll see signs steering you toward Urbanna.

Urbanna is one of four remaining Virginia towns created in 1680 by an Act of the Assembly. It was laid out in 1681 and named in honor of Britain's Queen Anne. Urbanna's early life centered around its wharves where tobacco was shipped overseas. Today Urbanna is a hub for recreational boating and still has working watermen who dock their boats here just as their forbears did generations ago. Urbanna retains its small-town charm and pride in its history.

The center part of town is listed on the National Register of Historic Places and the Virginia Landmarks Register. When you come to Urbanna it will be obvious why it earned these designations. There are numerous homes, commercial buildings and churches dating as far back as the early 1700s.

Events and Attractions

The town's traditional crowd pleaser is the **Urbanna Oyster Festival**, proudly hailed as the Official Oyster Festival of the Commonwealth. You're forewarned that recent festivals have drawn as many as 80,000 funseekers to this small town so be prepared to park outside town and ride the shuttles provided for the festival.

For nearly 40 years the festival has been the place to see and be seen, not to mention get caught up in the spirit of the parade, carnival, arts and crafts, tall ships and entertainment galore. Held the first full weekend in November, the festival's main attraction is, of course, oysters served in what seems a hundred different ways—raw, roasted, stewed, fried or frittered. If you don't like the salty bivalves, then perhaps piping-hot clam chowder, clam fritters, crab cakes or steamed crabs will surely satisfy. The confirmed landlubber will find vendors hawking burgers, hotdogs and ham biscuits. For a schedule of events, call the Urbanna Oyster Festival Foundation, (804) 758-0368, or the Urbanna Merchants Association, (800) 523-4711.

During the first week in May the town goes all out with tours of historic buildings as part of **Virginia Heritage Week**. On **July 4**, Urbanna celebrates with a pet parade, free watermelon and other traditional small-town events.

The merchants association has brochures that help you enjoy the Urbanna experience at any time of the year. Historic sites abound in the town, which is transforming a 1763 tobacco warehouse in the heart of downtown into an information center that will open by 1998. Take either a walking or driving tour to see such sites as **Lansdowne**, built in 1740 and today one of Virginia's examples of the Georgian architectural style; the **Old Custom House**, which dates from 1755, and **Fort Nonsense**, a whimsically named Civil War fortification.

Classic plantation homes anchor Urbanna on two sides. To the south across Urbanna Creek is **Rosegill Plantation**, built in the early 18th century by Ralph Wormeley IV and used as a summer home for the Colonial governor. To the north of town is **Hewick Plantation**, a 17th-century Colonial Virginia landmark that is on the National Register of Historic Places. Hewick is just north of Urbanna off Route 227 and is open for tours. The house also has two guest rooms for rent offering visitors the opportunity to sleep in one of the Commonwealth's oldest homes. Breakfast is continental plus. Call (804) 758-4214.

Hewick was built c. 1678 in the Colonial-Federal style for Christopher Robinson, a burgess, a member of the King's Council and an original Trustee of the College of William and Mary. Current residents Ed and Helen Battleson are 10th-generation descendants of Hewick's builder. The house is open for tours from 10 AM to 4 PM. The admission fee also lets you see the site of the College of William and Mary's archaeological dig.

Shopping

Downtown Urbanna, which is only a few blocks long, is perfect for strolling and checking out an eclectic mix of retail stores. **Urbanna Antique Mall** is open seven days a week with 30 dealers who spread their wares throughout 6,000 square feet. Thursday through Sunday the mall expands with the help of numerous flea market vendors. Nearby is not-to-miss retailer **R.S. Bristow**, a classic general store stocked with clothing, notions and gifts. **Nimcock Gallery** has a changing display of art. **Papeterie** is a gift shop that seeks out the unusual. **Cyndy's Bynn** specializes in clothing and gifts. **The Antique Shop** on Virginia Street is filled with the vintage items you'd expect, while nearby **Make Thyme** specializes in crafts. **Colonial Brass**, **Rappahannock Jewelry Co**. and **Taylor Hardware** also add to the downtown ambiance. Near the bridge that leads into town is **Haywood General Store**, which sells antiques and collectibles.

Accommodations

In addition to the Hewick estate, there are two other excellent bed and breakfast homes. In the heart of Urbanna is **Atherston Hall Bed & Breakfast**, (804) 758-2809. This former sea captain's home dates from 1880. It is tastefully decorated with Virginia and Southern antiques. Host Phyllis Hall will lend bicycles for pedaling through the tree-lined streets of this delightful town. In the morning, she'll whip up a full breakfast.

Also right in town is **The Inn**, a 13-room motel decorated in the style of a country inn (804) 758-4852. The Inn, which is at 250 Virginia Street, is in a former Coca-Cola bottling plant and includes a restaurant.

If camping is more your style, check into **Bethpage Camp Resort** on Route 602, (804) 758-4349. With a swimming pool, lake, beach, a restaurant, tennis and basketball courts plus two recreation buildings, you'll never be bored. The owners are happy to outfit you for crabbing, fishing or cruising on the Rappahannock. The campground is also the place to board the *Bethpager*, a traditional Chesapeake Bay deadrise vessel, beautifully restored for today's passengers. Catering and fishing charters are available.

Restaurants

Of course, you'd never go to Urbanna without planning at least one meal of fresh seafood or Virginia country cooking. Highly recommended is the **Virginia Street Cafe**, **Virginia and Cross streets**, (804) 758-3798. The cafe is a locals' favorite known for traditional Virginia fare. The **Inn at 250 Virginia Street**, (804) 758-4852, serves the oysters and seafood you'd expect as well as beef, chicken and veal dishes. Also in town is **Colonial Pizza**, on Route 227, (804) 758-4079, noted for its Italian and Greek dishes as well as its namesake pizza. For a quick lunch and an infusion of nostalgia, pull up to the lunch counter at **Marshall's Drug Store**, 50 Cross Street, (804) 758-5344, and order your favorite sandwich or fountain drink.

The Northern Neck

The next skinny finger of land that points directly to the Chesapeake Bay is the Northern Neck, which has held tightly to its own identity for more than 400 years. Bounded by the Chesapeake Bay to the east, the Potomac River to the north and the Rappahannock River to the south, the Northern Neck region stretches through five rural counties: Lancaster, Richmond, Northumberland, Westmoreland and King George.

Called the "Athens of America" during the early 18th century, the Northern Neck boasts great plantations and reigns as the birthplace of three presidents - George Washington, James Madison and James Monroe. Remaining true to its agricultural heritage, the region appears suspended in time. Look closely at the picture-perfect towns, however, and you'll find a few gas stations and wine-and-cheese shops ready to cater to modern needs. There are only 10 stoplights in the whole region, and many highways trace old Indian trails and Colonial roads. Laced with small rivers and long tidal creeks, the Northern Neck is one of Mother Nature's finest backgrounds for a boater's paradise. Many Hampton Roads anglers prefer to park their boats at one of the region's marinas. In fact there are 12,000 boats registered in the Northern Neck.

INSIDERS' TIP

Fishing in the Chesapeake Bay is likely to yield plenty of rockfish, spot, perch, hardhead, drum, croaker, whiting and gray trout.

In our brief visit, we'll hopscotch across the Northern Neck, pointing out special places of interest along the way. We won't break everything down town by town, because in this unique community, if you blink, you're in the next town anyway. If, for example, you're planning a peaceful day exploring the rivers and the Chesapeake Bay, you might pop into the Tri-Star "Social" Grocery in Kilmarnock, swing over to White Stone to snag a bottle of Chablis from the White Stone Wine & Cheese Shop, then coast back to Irvington to board your boat. You can do this all in less than 30 minutes.

During a recent long weekend getaway, the Northern Neck was our destination. For us the main goal was relaxing. We whiled away our time crabbing, taking leisurely drives to check out attractions and eating some of the freshest seafood around. At the end of three days our relaxation mission was accomplished. Although we'd hit many of the Northern Neck's high points, there were still plenty of attractions we didn't have time to see. So it won't be long before you'll find us back in this bit of Virginia paradise.

The Northern Neck is a place that's as intertwined by geography as it is history. And, as you launch over the Rappahannock River Bridge and coast down to its shore, you'll know immediately that it's a place you might never want to leave. For a visitors' guide to get you started, call the **Northern Neck Tourism Council** at (800) 453-6167 or (804) 333-1919.

Attractions

You'll definitely need a map and a car to explore all the sites in this five-county region. As you could probably guess, the main attraction around these parts is the water. That means boats, and if you don't have one, you can catch a ride on a boat operated by **Smith Island & Chesapeake Bay Cruises out of Reedville**, (804) 453-3430. You'll cruise from the KOA Campground and dock 13 miles off the Virginia shore at Smith Island, Maryland. You're welcome to pack your own picnic lunch or eat at one of several Smith Island restaurants (see our Daytrips chapter for details). You'll need to make reservations for the Smith Island trip, which takes up most of a day.

From Reedville you also can cruise to Virginia's Tangier Island (see our Eastern Shore chapter). **Tangier Island & Rappahannock River Cruises** makes regular runs to the island. It also takes visitors on tours of the Rappahannock River from its dock in Tappahannock. For details call (804) 453-BOAT.

If you've got a bit of angler's blood, you can satisfy it by calling a charter service to arrange a day on the water. Choices in Reedville include **Bayfish Charters**, (804) 453-9069, the *Jeannie C*, (804) 453-4021 or **Pittman's charters**, (804) 453-3643.

Just up the road a piece in Wicomico Church, there are a few other fishing boat possibilities. Sailing out of Ingram Bay is **Captain Billy's Liquid Assets**, a 40-footer designed for fishing parties and sightseeing. Call (804) 580-7292. In Ophelia is **Capt. Danny Crabbe's Kit II**. Call (804) 453-3251. In Lottsburg **Capt. Chuck O'Bier** has two charter boats, (804) 529-6450.

While in Reedville, take time to linger at the **Reedville Fishermen's Museum**, (804) 453-6529. It is open daily May through October from 10:30 AM to 4:30 PM, and Friday and Sunday during the same hours in March, April, November and December. The museum features artifacts of the fishing industry, especially menhaden, which is the lifeblood of Reedville's economy. The museum also includes the Walker House, a restored waterman's home that dates from 1875 and is Reedville's oldest house. You'll probably drive to the museum, but go around back and look for visitors who come via Cockrell's Creek, rowing or motoring in by dinghy to the museum dock. Behind the museum you'll find a historic boat collection that includes a 1922 buy-boat and a 1911 skipjack undergoing restoration.

Reedville's **Main Street Historic District** is worth driving to its end, which fronts on Cockrell's Creek that leads to the Chesapeake Bay. Or you can get a walking tour map at the Fisherman's Museum and walk the length of what is dubbed **Millionaire's Row** to see its elaborate turn-of-the-century houses. At that time this town of sea captains and industrialists boasted one of the highest per-capita incomes of any American community. The fruits of their labor have been lovingly restored today, and several homes are operated as bed and breakfast establishments.

While in Reedville occasionally you'll notice the slightly fishy odor that permeates the air. This comes from a plant that processes menhaden, the small fish whose oil extracts are in demand for food products and cosmetics.

Scattered throughout the Northern Neck are fascinating historic sites. Near Montross is **Stratford Hall Plantation**, birthplace of Gen. Robert E. Lee. Besides having a grand house to tour, the 1738 plantation is a working farm with 1,600 of its original acres. Nature trails lead you along a 3-mile hike to see wildflowers and wildlife. Stratford Hall is open daily from 9 AM to 4:30 PM. Lunch and dinner are served during warmer months in a log-cabin dining room. Call (804) 493-8038.

Read All About It

There are many excellent books that focus on the splendor and bounty of the Chesapeake Bay. The following are favorites of Mike Kensler, who runs the regional Chesapeake Bay Foundation office in Norfolk. You'll find most titles in area bookstores and libraries. Booksellers will be happy to order a copy for you. One excellent resource is the Chesapeake Bay Foundation in Annapolis, Maryland. Call (800) 728-5229 and your order will be shipped to you pronto.

An Island Out of Time: A Memoir of Smith Island in the Chesapeake by Tom Horton focuses on the island and its hardy inhabitants. The author spent three years living on the island while doing research for this new book.

Awesome Chesapeake: A Kid's Guide to the Bay by David Owen Bell is a great book for children elementary age and up.

Bay Country, with stories by Tom Horton about oysters, sea nettles, barrier islands and other nature topics.

Beautiful Swimmers, a Pulitzer Prize winner by William Warner, focuses on the blue crab.

Chesapeake Almanac: Following the Bay Through the Seasons by John Page Williams is a series of natural history sketches.

Chesapeake Legacy: Tools and Traditions by Larry Chowning focuses on the lives of the people who make a living on the water.

Exploring the Chesapeake in Small Boats by John Page Williams gives a close-up look at the Bay.

Harvesting the Chesapeake: Tools and Traditions by Larry Chowning highlights working watermen and their way of life.

Preserving the Chesapeake Bay is a new book on the Bay's health by former Virginia Gov. Gerald Baliles.

Turning the Tide: Saving the Chesapeake Bay by Tom Horton and William Eichbaum analyzes the Bay's environmental status.

Waters Way by Tom Horton is a pictorial essay perfect for the coffee table.

George Washington's Birthplace National Monument is in Oak Grove, 8 miles west of Montross on Route 204. A reconstructed house and farm manned by costumed interpreters depict Washington's boyhood lifestyle. There are easy walking trails and picnic tables. The historic site is open daily from 9 AM to 5 PM except Christmas and New Year's Day. Call (804) 224-1732. Off Route 3 in Lancaster County, you can see the **Mary Ball Washington Museum,** which honors its former resident who was the mother of the first president. Museum exhibits highlight several centuries of life in Lancaster County. The museum is open 10 AM to 5 PM Wednesday through Friday and from 10 AM to 3 PM on Saturday. Call (804) 462-7280. Included in the museum complex are the **1797 Old Clerk's Office** and the **1820 Old Jail**. Self-guided walking tours are a good way to see the **Lancaster Courthouse Historic District**.

In Irvington, **Historic Christ Church** dates from 1735 and is considered the country's best example of an unchanged Colonial church. The church, a National Historic Landmark built in the shape of a cross, is open year round Monday through Saturday from 10 AM to 4 PM and on Sunday from 2 to 5 PM. Call (804) 438-6855. Tours are offered from April through November, and there is also a museum.

Four other small but well-done museums to put on your itinerary if you have time are the

Westmoreland County Museum and Visitor Center in Westmoreland, (804) 493-8440; the **Kilmarnock Museum** in Kilmarnock, (804) 435-0874; the **Richmond County Museum** in Warsaw, (804) 333-3609 or (804) 394-4901; and the **Kinsale Museum** in Westmoreland County, (804) 472-3001. Another historic site is **Menokin**, just outside Warsaw. This plantation home was built in 1769 and was the residence of Lightfoot Lee, a signer of the Declaration of Independence. After years of decay, the house is being restored. Tours are available by appointment, (804) 580-8581.

Also in Heathsville is the **Northumberland County Historical Society**, whose library has extensive genealogical records. Nearby is the town's **1851 Courthouse** and **1844 Jail**. Both are part of the **Heathsville Historic District** walking tour. A map is available at the historical society behind the county courthouse. The society is staffed Tuesday and Thursday from 9 AM to 4 PM. Call (804) 580-8581.

If you happen to be in Kilmarnock looking for entertainment, check for the schedule at the **Center for the Arts**, (804) 435-2400. Annual events include children's plays, operas, musicals and concerts featuring professional and community musicians.

Something different to explore on the Northern Neck is **Ingleside Plantation Vineyards** near Oak Grove, (804) 224-8687. The plantation dates to 1834 and has been in the current owner's family since the late 19th century. It's been growing grapes since the 1960s and became a winery in 1980. Besides touring one of Virginia's largest wineries and sampling its wares, you can visit a museum and gift shop and take a break at an outdoor picnic area. The museum features mostly Native American artifacts and stuffed native animals such as fox and deer. Allow plenty of time for a winery visit since you may arrive to find a tour in progress and have a short wait. Of course, there's always the time you need to properly taste the fruits of the vineyard at the end of your tour. The winery is open from noon to 5 PM Sundays and from 10 AM to 5 PM on other days.

One fun family place is **Westmoreland Berry Farm & Orchard**, three miles south of Route 3 on Route 637, (804) 224-9171. It is open May through November every day except Sundays. The farm grows about 20 different fruits and, depending on when you're there, you will find luscious blueberries, blackberries, cherries, raspberries, peaches or apricots ripe for eating. This is a pick-your-own operation, but you'll also find a shop filled with produce as well as jellies and other Virginia products.

If you're dying to put on your hiking boots and take in some stunning scenery, the Northern Neck has numerous natural areas designed with you in mind. Keep a sharp eye out for the eagles' nests tucked high in tall trees along some waterways. Many trails are comfortable for the novice or those taking children along, while some challenge the more advanced hiker. You'll find the easiest trails at **Belle Isle State Park** in Lancaster County, (804) 462-5030; the **George Washington Birthplace National Monument** in Oak Grove, (804) 224-1732; **Totuskey Creek Park** off Route 3 near Warsaw (no phone); **Rappahannock River National Wildlife Refuge** near Warsaw, (804) 333-5189, and **Westmoreland State Park** in Montross, (804) 493-8821. Moderately difficult trails are at the **Caledon Natural Area** in King George, (804) 663-3861; **Voorhees Nature Preserve** at Westmoreland Berry Farm in Oak Grove, 224-9171; **Bushmill Stream Nature Preserve** near Heathsville, (804) 462-5030, and **Hughlett's Point Nature Preserve** along the Chesapeake Bay, (804) 462-5030. **The Hickory Hollow Nature Trail** on Route 3 in Lancaster has moderate to difficult trails, while **Stratford Hall Plantation** in Montross has trails that range from easy to difficult, (804) 493-8038.

Some fun ways to explore the great outdoors in the **Northern Neck** are by kayak or canoe. **Belle Isle** and **Westmoreland** state parks both have programs for this. **Heritage Park Resort** in Warsaw rents small boats and canoes for exploring Cat Point Creek, Menokin Bay and other waterways, (804) 333-4038. **River Rats** in Ophelia has kayaks for rent and leads tours of the Little Wicomico River, (804) 453-3064. Horseback riders will be in their element at **Breezewood Farms** in Irvington, which has guided rides along trails and Western riding lessons. Appointments are necessary, (804) 438-5141.

Shopping

As in the rest of the locales we've encountered in our Bay exploration, shopping in the Northern Neck leans toward antiques and gifts. Many shops mix the old with the new to create an intriguing shopping experience. Stores to browse include either the **Country House**, **The General Store** in Burgess; **The Corner Store** near Montross; **Potomac Accents** in Colonial Beach, and **Josiane's Collection** in Montross. Antiques lovers will have a heyday exploring the **Kilmarnock Antique Gallery** with over 100 dealers or the shops in nearby Tappahannock (see our Daytrips chapter). Another possibility is **Commonwealth Antiques** in Wicomico Church. Art connoisseurs should visit **Horn Harbor Studio** in Wicomico Church, which features the works of artist May Lou Hann. Her area of expertise is Chesapeake Bay watercolors. **Left Bank Gallery** in Hague has Bay and wildlife limited-edition prints. Those hunting for regional books will enjoy **Twice Told Tales** in Kilmarnock.

While driving around the Northern Neck's country roads you'll notice signs by some farm-houses that advertise "Woodcarvings for Sale" or some other craft item. Feel free to pull up and knock on the door. Inside you may find some real treasures. **J.H. (Herb) Lewis** of Fleeton, near Reedville, is one artisan who uses this marketing technique to sell his wooden duck decoys, (804) 453-3320. He is descended from generations of carvers and menhaden fishermen.

Accommodations

We must start with *the* place to stay, known worldwide for its elegant yet casual-in-a-genteel-sort-of-way atmosphere and unbeatable Southern hospitality. This is **The Tides in Irvington**, (800) 843-3746. Until Recently, The Tides was two separate family-owned resorts, The Tides Inn and The Tides Lodge Resort & Country Club. Now they share a common name and unified ownership.

The Tides Inn has long been the more elegant sister, with the Tides Lodge being less formal. Both have always been owned by members of the Stephens family. Both specialize in pampering, excellent cuisine, and outstanding golf. The inn closes in winter and reopens in March, but the lodge welcomes guests year round.

Guests can choose from two golf courses, cruises on the resident yacht, swimming, and tennis. In the summer, there's a full roster of children's activities. Expect to dress somewhat formally for dinner at the Inn. And, if you see soft-shelled crabs on the menu in any of The Tides restaurants, be sure to sample this regional delicacy.

For a super casual and relaxing stay, we recommend **Windmill Point Resort and Conference Center**, (804) 435-1166. The resort is perched at the end of Route 695 at the tip of the Northern Neck peninsula where the Rappahannock River flows into the Bay. Wrapped around a 150-slip marina, the 62-room resort literally spills onto a mile-long sandy beach. If you must get some exercise, you'll find two swimming pools, a nine-hole golf course, tennis courts, nature trails for hiking and, of course, plenty of boating. Although the resort is open year-round, its main restaurant, **The Hearth**, closes in winter and reopens in March. For a taste of native seafood try either the oyster stew or bay scallops.

If it's a bed and breakfast experience you long for, you'll find the greatest concentration of inns in Reedville. Many gracious Victorian homes dating from the late 1800s have been converted into bed and breakfasts.

Get acquainted with other visitors over a glass of wine during cocktail hour at the **Morris House** at the foot of Main Street in Reedville, (804) 453-7016. The inn is an exceptional restoration of a sea captain's home built in 1835 and has just been renovated. You can borrow the house skiff for a water tour or just stretch out on the dock watching the sailboats glide by. If you elect to stay here, request the top-floor suite that has its own wet-bar refrigerator and Jacuzzi.

The Gables is another Reedville sea captain's home updated for spoiled guests of the '90s. You can arrive at The Gables, (804) 453-5209, by boat to be pampered with a lavish breakfast spread and a long soak in a Victorian footed bathtub with original brass fixtures. (A modern shower is available, too, if you must hurry.) Only two rooms are offered in this 1800s home of Dr. and Mrs. Norman Clark. The house rests just off the Bay on Cockrell's Creek.

The Bailey-Cockrell House bed and breakfast inn, (804) 453-5900, is a Victorian house with a relaxing front porch and a back yard that overlooks Cockrell's Creek in Reedville. Innkeeper Alf Braxton will be glad to lend you a paddleboat or bikes for touring. Janet's Bed & Breakfast, (804) 453-5222, has three guest rooms in a restored Victorian home. Guests can look forward to a grand country breakfast in the morning. Just three miles from Reedville at the edge of the charming hamlet of Fleeton is **Fleeton Fields B&B**. The owner is a landscape designer and noted flower arranger. Guests rave about sitting in the garden and watching the nesting ospreys on Fleet's Pond, (804) 453-5014.

Outside Reedville, there are other bed and breakfasts scattered throughout the Northern Neck. In Lancaster you'll find **The Inn at Levelfields**, (804) 435-6887 or (800) 238-5578. Inside this antebellum house (c. 1857) are lush accommodations, including a private bath and fireplace in every guest room and a swimming pool. You'll wake up to a full breakfast.

The **Hope & Glory Inn**, (804) 438-6053 or (800) 497-8228, in Irvington puts you within shouting distance of the fine restaurants and golf courses of The Tides. It is on King Carter Drive and is a renovated 1890s school house right in town. Its seven guest rooms and three cottages are perfect for romantic weekends. Guests are greeted by a full breakfast.

One of the oldest bed and breakfasts on the Northern Neck is the **Mt. Holly Steamboat Inn** overlooking Nomini Creek just northeast of Montross, (804) 472-3336. It is just off Route 3. The inn has welcomed guests since steamboats delivered them to its dock in the last century. It has six guest rooms. In addition to serving breakfast, the inn's dining room is open to the public for dinner Tuesday through Sunday and for Sunday brunch.

Other bed and breakfast options include: **Flowering Fields Bed and Breakfast** in Kilmarnock, (804) 435-6238; **Waverly House** in Kilmarnock, (804) 435-0458; **Heathsville Ordinary** in Heathsville, (804) 580-2157; **Porterville Bed & Breakfast** in Montross, (804) 493-9394; **Greenwood Bed & Breakfast** in Warsaw, (804) 333-4353; **River's Rise Bed & Breakfast** in Deltaville, (804) 776-7521; **Linden House Bed & Breakfast** near Tappahannock, (804) 443-1170 or (800) 622-1202; and **Little Greenway Bed and Breakfast** in Tappahannock, (804) 443-5747.

Fairly new to the bed and breakfast scene are '**Tween Rivers** in Montross, (804) 493-0692; **Up the Creek B&B** in Deltaville, (804) 776-9621; **Skipjack Inn** at the Port Kinsale Marine in Kinsale, (804) 472-2044; **Bushfield Manor** in Mt. Holly, (804) 472-4171; **The Little Inn** at Lottsburg, (804) 529-5938 and **Dove Cottage** in Wicomico Church, (804) 580-3683. Returning to the B&B lineup in Montross is the refurbished **Inn at Montross**, (804) 493-0573.

If it's privacy you crave, you may want to consider a private guest cottage overlooking a scenic waterway. Choices include the **Guest House at Greenvale** near Mollusk, which fronts

Anglers find the catch to their liking in the Chesapeake Bay's tributaries.

Photo: Northern Neck Travel Council

THE CHESAPEAKE BAY

on the Rappahannock River, (804) 462-5995, or **Cats Cove Cottage** in Northumberland County on Mundy Point near the Potomac River, (804) 453-5171.

Those who long only for basic comforts will feel at home at one of several motels scattered throughout the Northern Neck. Your choices include a **Best Western** at Warsaw on Route 360, (804) 333-1700; **Days Inn** at Colonial Beach, (804) 224-0404 or (800) 325-2525; a **Comfort Inn** in Dahlgren on Route 301 near the Potomac River, (800) 228-5150; **Reedville's Bay Motel**, (804) 453-5171; and the **Whispering Pines Motel** on Route 3 just north of White Stone, (804) 435-1101.

Campers have several options on the Northern Neck. We've had a good experience with **Reedville's KOA Campground**, (804) 453-3430. It is right on the Bay and puts you within walking distance for the Smith Island cruise boat, which the campground owners operate. Besides camping sites you'll find 10 miniature sleeping cabins for rent. A crabbing pier is a big hit with kids as are hayrides and other events such as nighttime lollypop hunts using flashlights. Another campsite with boat ramps and numerous amenities is near **Warsaw at Heritage Park Resort**, (804) 333-4038. Besides having campsites, **Coles Point Plantation** in Coles Point, (804) 472-3955, has a 115-slip marina and restaurant.

Restaurants

All this relaxation has a way of making you ravenous. Here are a few of the places we've been advised to visit to soothe the hungries and have a good time while we're at it. For the most elegant dining, make reservations for the resorts we've mentioned above, particularly **The Tides**. For a relaxing repast on a screened porch try dinner at the **Mt. Holly Steamboat Inn**.

You'll by no means be roughing it, however, if you venture into other Northern Neck restaurants. For seafood head to **Wilkerson's Seafood Restaurant** in Colonial Beach, (804) 224-7117; or **The Pilot's Wharf** at Coles Point Plantation, (804) 472-4761. In **White Stone** try the **Sandpiper Restaurant**, (804) 435-6176. Local diners often split a crabcake dinner here since the two huge lump cakes are too much for most appetites. The stuffed flounder is excellent in Kilmarnock at **The Northside Grill** on Highway 3, (804) 435-3100.

You can pick your own fresh fruit at Westmoreland Berry Farm and Orchard.

Photo: Courtesy of Northern Neck Travel Council

To make sure you have a great view as well as satisfying seafood, go to the **Dockside Restaurant** in the Colonial Beach Yacht Center, (804) 224-8726 or the **Mooring Restaurant** at Yeocomico Marina in Kinsale, (804) 472-2971. The **Crab Shack** outside Kilmarnock on Indian Creek at Route 672, (804) 435-2700, is a delightful choice with some of the best crab cakes around. You can enjoy your seafood inside the restaurant or al fresco on the deck outside. Burgess is home to **Horn Harbor House Restaurant**, which overlooks the Great Wicomico River, (804) 453-3351. Seafood, steaks and chicken anchor the menu. A 1999 addition to Reedville's culinary scene is The **Crazy Crab Restaurant** at Reedville Marina. It has great views of Cockrell's Creek from either inside or the deck that hangs over the water. Seafood is the cuisine of choice here, (804) 453-6789.

A locals-only place is **L. W. Bogart's** near Kinsale at the intersections of Routes 202 and 203,

(804) 472-2331. Bogart's has great hamburgers. Just across the road is the Good Eats Cafe, which features seasonal and vegetarian specialties using the owners' organically grown herbs and veggies, (804) 472-4385. Despite its homey-sounding name, this restaurant produces sophisti- cated food in a casual atmosphere. Husband and wife chefs Sally Rumsey and Steve Andersen are earning a reputation for the big-city experience they bring to this rural setting.

INSIDERS' TIP

When you get too much sun, one of the best cures is to wrap the crispy areas in cold, wet towels. Any product with aloe listed in the ingredients is also a great soother.

For elegant dining, you'll find Insiders heading to **Bambery's** in Heathsville, (804) 529-5200. The restaurant has a prime view of the Village Green Golf Course. Locals also recommend **Chesapeake Cafe** and **Angler's Cove Lounge** in Kilmarnock for casual dining, (804) 435-3250. For elegant Italian cuisine, try **DeMedici** on School Street in Kilmarnock. Veal and pastas are the stars at this sophisticated restaurant, (804) 435-4006.

Despite its Irish name, **McPatty's** in Kilmarnock, (804) 435-2290, also dishes out local seafood. With its location on Cralle Court across from the bowling alley, the locals have dubbed McPatty's "the galley in the alley." The walls are plastered with old pictures, and the owners serve up a great time in a neat atmosphere, along with some pretty tasty menu offerings. On Main Street in Kilmarnock, **Lee's**, (804) 435-1255, is a mainstay with its hard-to-beat home cooking. For a quick lunch, try the soda fountain at **Peoples Drug Store** of Montross, (804) 493-9505.

A mainstay of Reedville's culinary scene is **Elijah's Restaurant**, (804) 453-3621, which is in an elaborately restored 1885 mercantile store downtown overlooking Cockrell's Creek. Seafood and beef are the standouts here. If the fisherman's penne pasta is on the menu, give it a try. It's delicious.

For some family-style fare, **Lancaster Tavern** comes highly recommended, (804) 462-5941. This restaurant has the locals' stamp of approval. It is on Route 3 in downtown Lancaster Court House. The menu features typical Southern foods such as fried chicken and ham served with a slew of side dishes and scrumptious homemade bread. Guests are served family style. The tavern dates to at least 1790 and has been serving food since that time. The restaurant is open for lunch Thursday through Sunday and for dinner Thursday through Saturday.

For More Information

INSIDERS' TIP

Be sure to dial the 804 area code when calling the Middle Peninsula or Northern Neck. When Hampton Roads switched to the 757 area code in 1997, these areas retained the 804 code.

You'll find a wealth of good information about the Middle Peninsula and the Northern Neck by calling the following sources: the **Gloucester County Chamber of Commerce**, (804) 693-2425; the **Mathews County Visitors Council**, (804) 725-4229; the **Urbanna Merchants Association**, (800) 523-4711, or the Northern Neck Tourism Council, (800) 453-6167. Ask plenty of questions and request brochures ahead of time. Be sure to study the maps and bring them along so you'll know where you're headed.

For those determined to explore this region by water, the best source of information on publicly owned landings throughout the system is *Virginia's Chesapeake Bay Boating and Fishing Guide*. It has a good map of all public boat landings and marinas as well as listings of charter fishing captains and canoe and kayak outfitters. To order a free copy call toll free (877) 285-4593.

For tips on some of the best restaurants along the Chesapeake Bay, check out the *Chesapeake Bay Restaurant Guide & Recipe Book* by Susan and Charles Eanes. The book, published by Espichel Enterprises, covers 99 restaurants in Maryland and Virginia.

Daytrips

No matter how stimulating our great region is, there comes a time when you just want to get the heck out of Dodge. That's when it's time to pack a suitcase or a picnic basket and hit the road in search of a new perspective on life. We call these excursions adventures, and whether they last an afternoon, a day or a weekend, they always give us a mental boost.

Thanks to our great location, you can reach lots of exciting destinations within the comfort of your own sedan and within a few hours traveling time. From southside Hampton Roads, you can steer yourself toward a big dose of history, a wild and wonderful shopping excursion, an out-of-this-city dining experience, or an empty plot of sand along some rolling surf—"BYO pulp fiction". You might opt to cross the Chesapeake Bay Bridge-Tunnel to the bucolic Eastern Shore, don your walking shoes and a tri-cornered hat for a stroll through Colonial Williamsburg, or pack up your sand chair and sunscreen for the broad beaches of the Outer Banks. Whatever your mood, you can be in a faraway place in no time, all on one tank of gas.

So fasten your seat belt. Come with us on a whirlwind tour of the cities and sights that are right around the corner, but miles away in spirit, from home. For other get-away ideas, check out the chapters on the Chesapeake Bay and the Eastern Shore.

Hampton/Newport News

You've noticed, we're sure, that we constantly refer to our own fair community as "southside Hampton Roads." Where, you ask, is the northside? Well, it's right up there on the other side of the James River and Hampton Roads. We call it "the Peninsula," but it mainly consists of the cities of Hampton and Newport News.

Although we are separated by a large body of water, statisticians regard the Peninsula and the Southside as a single metropolitan region. The Peninsula does, however, have its own newspaper, the *Daily Press*; its own convention dome, the Hampton Coliseum; its own beaches, like the refurbished Buckroe; and even its own superstar attractions. It is home to one of the state's largest private employers, Newport News Shipbuilding.

In the next section, we'll combine topics for the entire Peninsula, since the cities blend geographically from one to the other. You can choose which places to visit based on your personal preferences.

First, a quick history lesson. Hampton was born in 1610 when the first settlers landed on the beach, probably to the utter amazement of the native Kecoughtan Indians. The city lays claim to the beginnings of free education, the downfall of Blackbeard the pirate (though there is a competing claim of the same from Ocracoke Island, North Carolina), and the training of America's first astronauts. If that's not enough, it also has a rich military history tracing back to the Civil War.

Newport News got its start in 1607 when the Virginia Company of London gave Captain Christopher Newport the assignment of finding a site for a new settlement on the James River. Newport, and his crew from the ships **Susan Constant**, **Godspeed** and **Discovery**, liked the looks of the sandy point at the mouth of the river. So they set up camp and called their settlement Jamestown. Legend has it that the city got its name because everyone would rush out to the point whenever Captain "Newport" came in with "news" from home. By 1619, the name Newportes Newes had stuck, and today it is believed to be the oldest English place-name of any city in the New World.

The places to go and see in Hampton and Newport News will whisk you from the long-ago past to the space-age future. We'll give you phone numbers for the attractions you might want to visit.

Getting There

Getting to the Peninsula is a snap, unless you see the flashing light on I-64 indicating traffic congestion at the Hampton Roads Bridge-Tunnel. If the lights are on hold and you get the all-clear signal, just zip down I-64 W., and in less than 30 minutes you can be inside a museum. An alternate route, an especially wise choice is you're coming from Chesapeake, Portsmouth or Suffolk, is the Monitor-Merrimac Bridge-Tunnel (locally referred to as the M&M), accessed through I-664 in Suffolk.

Attractions

Peninsula museums are a visual and rich experience for all ages. Starting in Newport News, you'll want to visit the world-renowned **Mariner's Museum** on J. Clyde Morris Boulevard, (757) 595-0368, which explores our relationship with the sea. You'll love the exquisite miniature ship models, carved figureheads, unbelievable scrimshaw, working steam engines and the antique boats gallery. Alongside the museum is the 550-acre **Mariner's Museum Park** with nature and bike trails as well as boat rentals for fishing on Lake Maury. Open Monday through Saturday from 9 AM to 5 PM and Sundays from noon to 5 PM, there is an admission charge to enter the museum.

Just across the street from the Mariner's Museum is the **Peninsula Fine Arts Center**, (757) 596-8175, which has tripled its size in the last few years. Changing exhibits by living artists along with contemporary art from museum

INSIDERS' TIP

Before setting out on a Virginia daytrip adventure, arm yourself with "A Map of Scenic Roads in Virginia." The free map is produced by the Virginia Department of Transportation and is available at area tourism bureaus or by calling (800) VA-LOVE. It covers more than 2,000 miles of scenic byways throughout the Commonwealth.

collections and private sources are on display. The gift shop is a treasure house of gifts, books, cards and unique decorative objects, so while admission to the museum is free, plan on spending a few dollars anyway. The art center is closed Monday, but visit Tuesday through Saturday from 10 AM to 5 PM and Sundays from noon to 5 PM.

Also on J. Clyde Morris Boulevard is the museum created for kids of all ages, The **Virginia Living Museum**, (757) 595-1900. Part zoo, part botanical garden, part observatory and planetarium, you'll also find an aviary and massive aquarium. Especially popular is the touch tank for hands-on learning. Here you can reach out and touch something fishy. Outside there are animals, skunks and even a bald eagle that you can observe in their natural wooded habitats. There are nominal admission fees that vary with the parts of the museum you want to explore. As experienced parents, we say go for it all.

Next head for downtown Hampton and the $30 million **Virginia Air and Space Center**, (757) 727-0800, designated the official NASA Langley Visitor Center. On Settlers Landing Road and open every day of the week, the center features aircraft and spacecraft suspended from a 94-foot ceiling, a 3 billion-year-old moon rock, a flying machine tested before the Wright Brothers' flyer aircraft and the Apollo 12 Command Module. Plus, there's the **Hampton Roads History Center** and an **IMAX** theater. There's an admission charge for the center and the theater. Right next door on the downtown waterfront is the **Hampton Carousel**, built in 1920 and completely restored to its original beauty. For just 50 cents from April through October you can climb aboard history and take a twirl on an original steed or chariot.

Other sightseeing possibilities include The **War Memorial Museum** in Newport News and **Casemate Museum**, **Air Power Park**, **Bluebird Gap Farm** (the ultimate petting zoo for kids of all ages) and **Fort Wool/Fort Monroe** in Hampton.

Restaurants

On the Peninsula, you can take your pick of brand-name burger and fast-food places, but here are a few culinary gems that we favor. For the freshest seafood around head to **Harpooon Larry's** at 2000 N. Armistead in Hampton, (757) 827-0600. Locals love the steamed shrimp. If it's Italian food you crave, then **Carmela's** is the place to go at 2123 Coliseum Dr. in the Coliseum Crossing shopping center, (757) 825-5375. The linguine with white clam sauce and bruschetta get rave reviews. In Newport News **Port Arthur** near the Mariner's Museum, 11137

Pocahontas

One of Virginia's most famous residents of all time was Pocahontas, the daughter of the powerful Chief Powhatan, who once ruled 30 tribes in coastal Virginia.

Pocahontas was born about 1596 in what is now Virginia's Peninsula area and has been immortalized for centuries in paintings, stories and songs. The most recent tribute to her was the almost pure-fantasy version of her life in the Disney animated movie, "Pocahontas." Besides giving this flat coastal region some stunning mountain scenery, Disney also provided Pocahontas with a fictionalized romance with British colonist Capt. John Smith.

Pocahontas, whose formal names were Amonute and Matoaka, was Powhatan's "most deare and wel-beloved daughter," according to Smith's writings. She met the colonist in 1607 and was credited, in a story that may be fact or fiction, with saving Smith's life by flinging her body over him when her father was ready to beat Smith to death with stones. In 1613 Pocahontas was kidnapped by the British and held for ransom. An agreement was not worked out, and she never returned to her people. In 1614 she was baptized and given the name of Rebecca. She married British tobacco planter John Rolfe and traveled with him and their young son, Thomas, to England. She died there in 1617 of an illness as she was preparing to set sail for Virginia. Her husband returned to become secretary of the colony but left his won in England. Thomas Rolfe returned to his mother's homeland in the 1630s after his father died.

Children like posing with the Pocahontas statue at Jamestown Island.

Photo: Kathy Jublou

Today you'll see statues of Pocohantas and John Smith on the federally run Jamestown Island. Both are favorite photo spots for visitors. Both the visitor center on the island and the nearby Jamestown Settlement museum include copies of artwork featuring Pocahontas and Smith.

Warwick Boulevard, (757) 599-6474, is a popular Chinese restaurant with an elegant decor. Down the road, **Das Waldcafe**, 12529 Warwick Boulevard, (757) 930-1781, dishes up authentic German food, including sauerbraten, spaetzle and the most divine hazelnut cake.

A sweetheart of a place is under the green awning at the **Grey Goose**, (757) 723-7978, in Old Hampton across from the Air and Space Museum, with its intimate country ambiance and wonderful homemade soups, Brunswick stew and ham biscuits.

One of the hotspots on the Peninsula is **Bobby's Americana** in downtown Hampton at 17 E. Queen's Way, (757) 727-0545. This is an offshoot of **Bobbywood**, a popular Norfolk eatery. Expect innovative nouvelle cuisine with a frequently changing menu.

Shopping

Your main choices are two malls in Hampton and Newport News and the power centers in Newport News' Denbigh area. Hampton's indoor shopping arena is **Coliseum Mall** on Mercury Boulevard, (757) 838-1505. **Hechts**, **Dillards**, **Wards** and **JC Penney** are the main anchors. There are several large strip shopping centers near the mall.

In Newport News, the recently expanded **Patrick Henry Mall** on Jefferson Avenue is the place to shop, (757) 249-4305. Anchor stores include **Dillard's** and **Hecht**s. The Denbigh area, where the mall is located, has emerged in recent years as the Peninsula's shopping mecca. Lots of large retailers such as **Barnes & Noble**, **Home Depot**, and **Costco** have moved into power centers and freestanding stores.

Phoebus

Phoebus is cute. This small pocket of cuteness is actually a tightly-knit Hampton community you can find when you take the Mallory Street Exit off I-64 W. (the first exit you come to after the tunnel) and head towards Fort Monroe. Along Mallory Street are some of the best eats and most unique shopping experiences just waiting to happen, and a stopover there is similar to being whisked back in history to a time when people were friendlier, life was slower and love was always in the air.

See what we mean with a browse through the incredible **Benders Books** and **Card**s with its array of comic books and the **Electric Glass Company**, where you'll find hand-blown goblets, Tiffany glass and etched glass for your front door. Locals are hard-pressed to reveal the secret that **Paul's**, (757) 723-9063, serves the coldest beer and best burger this side of Kansas. **Victorian Station**, (757) 723-5663, in a charming Victorian home, not only offers a silky smooth quiche or chunky chicken salad but also is one of the last remaining places on the face of the earth where you can linger over afternoon tea enjoyed with jam-lathered scones, tea cakes and open-faced sandwiches. Even hard-nosed Insiders know that an afternoon in Phoebus is better than a month with a therapist. Don't even think about leaving town until you've been h**ere.**

For More Information

As in all Hampton Roads cities, an army of knowledgeable patriots stands ready to swamp you with information about their respective cities. In Hampton, you can reach the **Visitors Center** at 710 Settlers Landing Road, (757) 727-1102 or (800) 800-2202. The Newport News **Visitor Information Center** is at 13560 Jefferson Avenue, (757) 886-2737 or (888) 4WE-R-FUN. You can also pick up information at the Newport News **Tourism Development Office** downtown at 2400 Washington St. (757) 926-3561 or (88) 493-7386.

Smithfield

Smithfield may be best known for its distinctive, salty-flavored hams. But it's also the perfect destination for an afternoon drive in the country. We particularly like to motor over in our 1947 Chrysler sedan. Riding in a vintage car puts you in the proper mood for this traditional

Virginia town that proudly preserves its historic past. Feel free, however, to arrive in a more modern vehicle or by boat.

The Warascoyak Indians were the first residents of this lush land along the Pagan River. British colonists arrived in the mid-1600s and turned the area into a prosperous seaport that became home to sea captains and merchants. Smithfield was incorporated as a town in 1752 and named for Arthur Smith, who in 1637 became the first person to officially own land here. For more than 20 years Smithfield remained a British colony.

The Isle of Wight County town has produced its world-famous hams since 1779 when Bermuda native Capt. Mallory Todd established a pork curing and shipping business here. By that time Smithfield was a bustling port for the tobacco and peanuts that flourished in its rich soil. The secret to Smithfield hams hasn't changed since Capt. Todd's time. Hogs are still fattened on native peanuts, and their meat is cured over slow hickory fires. To get a Smithfield pedigree, a ham must hail from Smithfield and nowhere else.

Getting There

From Virginia Beach, Norfolk, Chesapeake and Portsmouth, get on Route 17 N. in Portsmouth (High Street) and stay on it until it intersects Route 10. Turn left and follow the signs to downtown Smithfield. The trip should take no more than an hour. From Suffolk, take Route 258 N. and you'll be in Smithfield in about 30 minutes.

Attractions

The town itself is charming and is designated a National Historic District. Restored homes, many of them large, ornate Victorians, line its Main Street. The whole downtown is perfect for strolling and, in recent years, has gained a reputation as a treasure trove for antique lovers. There are 15 pre-Revolutionary War homes to delight those who love historic architecture. Many of the backyards of these homes run right down to the Pagan River. Recent improvements to part of Main Street hid utility wires underground, bricked the sidewalks and added benches, whimsical bronze sculptures of people and vintage street lights.

To get oriented to Smithfield, stop by the **Old Courthouse of 1750** that houses the county tourism bureau and chamber of commerce, and pick up brochures and a walking-tour map. The courthouse is at Main and Mason streets and is open daily from 9 AM to 5 PM. For information call (757) 357-5182 or (800) 365-9339.

On your way into town, you'll see a sign for Saint Luke's Church on Route 10. This is a not-to-miss historic spot. Built in 1632, St. Luke's is the country's only original Gothic church and the oldest church of English foundation in America. This Episcopal church, nicknamed "Old Brick," is still in use and has lovely wooded grounds. Architectural historian Thomas E. Tallmadge has called St. Luke's, "in many respects the most precious building in America." St. Luke's Jacobean interior features gables, buttresses and traceried windows. The church's silver baptismal basin and handcrafted communion table date from the 17th century. Church members donated the stained-glass windows in 1890. One of them was dedicated in memory of Pocahontas, honoring her as "the first convert of Virginia to the gospel."

St. Luke's, a National Shrine, is open from 9:30 AM to 4 PM Tuesday through Saturday and from 1 to 4 PM on Sunday. It closes during January. The shrine sits back from the parking lot, so plan on a short, pleasant walk. There are benches along the way to accommodate those who like to rest now and then. Admission is free. The church is about 2 miles from downtown Smithfield. Call (757) 357-3367 for information.

Once you're downtown you can park and stroll to several historic sites. **The Isle of Wight County Museum** at Main and Church streets, 357-7459, is housed in a former bank built in 1913. It has archeological displays highlighting county history, including a country store and Civil War artifacts. The building itself is worth seeing for its imported marble and tile and impressive Tiffany-style dome skylight. Admission is free. The museum is open 10 AM to 4 PM Tuesday through Thursday; 10 AM to 2 PM on Friday; 10 AM to 4 PM on Saturday; and 1 to 5 PM on Sunday.

The **Old Isle of Wight Courthouse** dates from 1750 and was used as a courthouse until

1800. Its clerk's office and county jail are restored. The courthouse, which houses the tourism bureau, is owned by the Association for the Preservation of Virginia Antiquities. It is open 9 AM to 5 PM daily. Call (757) 357-5182.

While at the courthouse pick up a copy of a walking-tour map. It will lead you past 65 of Smithfield's historic homes and buildings, including **Oak Grove Academy** at 204 Grace Street that was built in 1836 as a school for young women. The **Keitz-Mannion House** at 344 S. Church Street was constructed in 1876 as a Methodist parsonage and was originally located across the street. For the full tour, allow about an hour plus an extra 15 minutes for a brisk walk to **Windsor Castle** on Jericho Road. This stucco-covered brick home was built in 1750 by Arthur Smith IV, who in 1750 had Smithfield surveyed and laid out as a town.

For a peek inside one of Smithfield's stately houses visit The Collage and Gallery Studios, (757) 357-7707, a gallery and working studio in a Victorian home built around the turn of the century. It is at 346 Main Street and also houses the Isle of Wight Arts League. Hours are from 10 AM to 3 PM Tuesday to Saturday and 1 to 5 PM Sunday. Many handcrafted items are for sale.

You'll get a real treat if you time your visit for Smithfield's popular **Olden Days Festival**. It usually is held the last weekend in May and starts on a Friday. Crowds have been known to top 7,000. Free events include an antique car show, street bazaar, fire engine rides, a children's buggy parade and raft races. You can chow down at an all-you-can-eat pancake breakfast or spaghetti dinner or attend an old-fashioned ice cream social. Another fun event is Christmas in Smithfield, held throughout December. It includes an antique show, trolley tours of the historic district and visits to some of the oldest houses in town. The county tourism bureau can provide details on all three events.

Out in the country on Route 673 is **Fort Boykins State Park**, (757) 357-2291, with a fort created in 1623 to protect settlers from Native Americans and raiding Spaniards. This fort on the banks of the James River still has its Civil War-era earthworks and has been involved in every military campaign fought on American soil. There is a gazebo overlooking the river and a picnic area. From the river banks you can see the Navy's "mothball fleet" of retired warships anchored in the James River. The grounds are open daily from 8 AM to dusk. Admission is free. Walk around and you'll see the second-largest black walnut tree in the state and a variety of blooms in the fort's gardens. To guide you through the fort, pick up a brochure and map at the tourism bureau in town before you visit.

About 20 minutes outside of town is **Chippokes Plantation State Park** on the James River. The park is on Route 634 and is open daily from 8 AM to dusk. From Smithfield take Route 10 W. and follow the brown signs. Farming started here in 1619, making this the oldest continually farmed property in the country. The property includes an antebellum mansion, visitors center, and a farm and forestry museum. There are picnic spots near a beach where fossils poke through the sand. While there's no swimming allowed in the river, a swimming pool is open in warmer months. Admission is free, but parking costs $1 in the off-season on weekdays; $2 in summer and on weekends year-round. Call (757) 294-3625 or (757) 294-3439. One fun annual event at the park is the Pork, Peanut and Pine Festival in July, which features all kinds of Virginia foods and music. On the last weekend of October visit the park for its Plantation Christmas celebration. At this annual event all kinds of artisans and craftsmen showcase their talents and their wares. There also is entertainment and interesting food available. This is a good place to find unique holiday gifts in a relaxed setting.

Restaurants

For a small town, Smithfield has some excellent dining choices offering everything from down-home cooking to refined cuisine. If truth be told, eating is one of the main reasons we like to venture to Smithfield.

Smithfield Station at 415 S. Church Street, (757) 357-7700 or (800) 399-2874, on the banks of the Pagan River, has a regional reputation that draws diners from throughout Hampton Roads. The restaurant serves seafood, pork, pasta and other local favorites during lunch and dinner daily. On Sundays a breakfast buffet includes an omelet bar. Dinner reservations are recommended.

After dining at Smithfield Station, be sure to stroll along the boardwalk that links the restaurant to its marina. In warmer months an outdoor raw bar serves crabs and other seafood

DAYTRIPS

for casual dining. During summer weekends you may find musicians entertaining here. If you want to pass more than an hour or two here, you can spend the night in one of Smithfield Station's rooms or suites. (See our Accommodations section below.)

One charming place to dine is the **Smithfield Inn** at 112 Main Street, (757) 357-1752, a town mainstay since 1752. The inn fell on hard times in the early 1990s and closed for several years. It reopened in 1995 with a fresh face and culinary style that attracts food lovers from various Hampton Roads cities. The restaurant carries the reputation as one of the most romantic dining spots in the entire region. Smithfield Foods, the meat packer and corporate giant, owns the inn and footed the bill for its opulent restoration. Today's inn is decked out in Victorian finery and is open for lunch and dinner every day except Monday and Tuesday. The inn serves Sunday brunch with a menu that ranges from breakfast fare to prime rib. In one of two elegant dining rooms you can sample regional cuisine, including fried chicken and crab cakes. Of course, you'll find Smithfield ham starring on the menu in a

Downtown Edenton, North Carolina, is built around Edenton Bay and features many historic homes.

Photo: Chowan County Tourist Development Authority

multitude of ways. You'll need reservations for dinner. If you're tempted to linger, the inn has a tavern where you can pass the time. It also has five suites available if you want to spend the night.

Other Smithfield dining options include **Angelo's Seafood and Steak House**, 1804 S. Church Street, (757) 357-3104, which serves mainly steak and seafood for lunch and dinner. **Smithfield Confectionery and Ice Cream Parlor**, 208 Main Street, (757) 357-6166, has a menu of sandwiches and ice cream. Its classic soda fountain will take you back in time. Also available to satisfy your sweet tooth is **Smithfield Gourmet Bakery** at 218 Main Street, (757) 357-0045. The 25-seat cafe will tempt you with a variety of breads, cakes and pastries, including salt-rising loaves. The bakery takes orders for dietetic desserts. Lunch features sandwiches, and in the summer you'll find fresh lemonade on the menu.

We're fond of the **Twins Old Town Inn** at 220 Main Street, (757) 357-3031, a cafe frequented mostly by locals. It is run by twin sisters who whip up good country cooking for breakfast and lunch. The restaurant closes on Sunday and serves only breakfast on Saturday. Another possibility is **Ken's Bar-B-Q Place** on Highway 258, (757) 357-5601. Fans of North Carolina-style barbecue will find the barbecue to their liking. Ribs, pit-cooked steaks and homemade desserts are on the menu during both lunch and dinner. You'll find a varied menu at **Cowling's** in Smithfield Shopping Center on Route 10, (757) 357-0044. Among the standouts are cheese-broccoli soup and clam chowder. Just outside town, the new **Battery Park Grill** features upscale dinner cuisine. It is at 201 Battery Park Rd. (757) 357-1747.

Accommodations

The Isle of Wight Inn, 1607 S. Church Street, (757) 357-3176, has 12 guest rooms, including honeymoon suites with hot tubs and fireplaces. Although it is in a newer building on the outskirts of downtown, the inn has a charming historic feel.

Besides being a restaurant (see description above), Smithfield Station has 15 guest rooms, most of which overlook the inn's 61-slip marina. Smithfield Station, which is just outside downtown, includes a lighthouse-shaped building that houses elegant suites with panoramic views of the river. Call (757) 357-7700 or (800) 399-2874.

The **Smithfield Inn** at 112 Main Street, (757) 357-1752, (see description above) also has a dual personality as a restaurant and a place to check in for overnight pampering. The inn's five suites are decked out in antiques. The inn is in the heart of Smithfield's downtown, which means you can park your car and remain on foot for your entire stay.

If you prefer to wake up in the country, check into **Four Square Plantation** west of Smithfield on Route 620, (757) 365-0749. This bed and breakfast inn is in an 1807 home surrounded by four landscaped acres that sit in the midst of farm crops. The antique-filled house is on the National Historic Register. It has three guest rooms and serves a full breakfast topped off with Smithfield ham, of course. Another country inn made for relaxing is **Porches on the James** at 6347 Old Stage Hwy., which is near Chippokes Plantation State Park (757) 356-0602. This home on the James River was built in 1998 with modern amenities but in a classic style. Unwind on the screened porch or wander along the river banks. The full breakfast includes homemade bread.

Shopping

Antique collectors will have a heyday in Smithfield. The largest selections are at the **Smithfield Antiques Center** and the **Antiques Emporia** of Smithfield. Each store has about 25 dealers. You'll find these antique centers a few paces apart at 131 Main Street and 108 Main Street. Also downtown are **Victoria's Legacy** at 235 Main Street and **Wharf Hill Antiques**, 218 Main Street. Both are general antiques stores carrying a variety of merchandise. Just outside town is the **Isle of Wight Inn** at 1607 Church Street. Its gift shop has some unusual vintage pieces and is where we go to buy restored antique clocks.

Downtown has lots of charming shops. Kids of all ages like **Grampy's Lucky Penny** and its array of candy and other treats. The **Christmas Store** has a big variety of ornaments for sale all year. If you want a Smithfield souvenir, try **Simpson's Pharmacy**, 221 Main Street. Or for the ultimate Smithfield gift, go to the **Joyner of Smithfield Ham Shop** at 315 Main Street. There you'll find Smithfield and country hams as well as peanuts and gift baskets. **Basse's Choice,** a local mail-order company that features Virginia food products, operates a retail store at 224 Main Street that has similar gift items. For a catalog call (800) 292-2773.

On the way to Smithfield along Highway 10 is the small community of Carrolton, where there are several stores specializing in antiques and reproduction furniture.

Recreation

If someone in your group would rather golf than shop or eat, drop them off at the **Smithfield Downs Golf Course.** This 18-hole course is open daily to the public. It is on Highway 258 just outside town. Although it is only 5,200 yards long, this course is a challenging one for all golfers. You can book a tee time by calling (757) 357-3101. For a top-notch course head to Cypress Creek. This 18-hole course opened several years ago and has become a favorite of area golfers, (757) 365-4774.

Williamsburg

If you're seeking the perfect hodgepodge of Colonial ambiance tossed with a little contemporary bargain shopping, set your cruise control towards mecca—to Williamsburg. In fact, you can work up into a full-blown sightseeing/shopping frenzy in the mere 45 minutes it will take you to get there from Hampton Roads.

Because this is intended to be a daytrip guide, we won't even begin to tell you about all the teeth-gritting rides, fabulous architecture and wonderful food that you'll find at **Busch Gardens** theme park on the fringes of Williamsburg. That alone is a daytrip unto itself. If you're so inclined to stretch your Williamsburg visit into more than one day, there are numerous motels

DAYTRIPS

and hotels with open registers, ranging from the lovely Williamsburg Inn—which offers the finest lodgings you'll find in these parts—to brand-name sleep-places such as Econo Lodge, Ramada Inn and Holiday Inn. If you plan to stay over during peak summer season or on a holiday, definitely make reservations in advance.

A few notes about conduct in the **Historic Area**. While touring any restored building, even thinking about fondling the priceless furnishings and accessories is prohibited, as is smoking, drinking or eating. No pets, strollers or baby carriages are allowed either. You may bring a camera or camcorder into the buildings and shops, but you will be asked to put them away in their cases during any program or tour lecture. Cranky children will have to be likewise stowed, preferably beyond earshot of your fellow visitors.

Getting There

From southside Hampton Roads, Williamsburg is a fairly quick shot north on Interstate 64 W. (Yes, the road is the western leg of I-64, but you're actually heading north—go figure.) The only congestion you're likely to encounter is at the Hampton Roads Bridge-Tunnel that connects Norfolk to Hampton. Once you've made it through the tube, it's a pleasant 45-minute drive. Interstate exit signs are clearly marked. Take the Busch Gardens Exit for that destination, or follow the signs a few more miles north pointing you to the College of William & Mary to reach the Historic Area.

Attractions

Wherever do we begin? Colonial Williamsburg's 173 acres occupied by **Williamsburg's Historic Area** is chocka-block with 18th-century public buildings, homes, crafts shops and more than 90 acres of gardens and greens. This historic site is in a continual improvement mode, most recently with a $100 million renovation of its Visitor Center and hotels. If you're a true history buff, we suggest you first go to the **Visitors Center**, which is on Route 132Y off the Colonial Parkway. Keep in mind that it costs $5 to park here if you buy an admission ticket. It you don't buy one, parking costs a whopping $20. A ticket to all exhibits costs $30, $18 for children over age 6. An annual pass is available for $65 for adults and $22.50 for children. If you just want to soak up the ambiance without actually touring anything, park in the Merchants Square parking lot for a nominal amount and stroll through the Historic Area for free.

While in the Visitor Center be sure to watch the film **Williamsburg—The Story of a Patriot**, which is shown continuously throughout the day. Then hitch a ride on one of the shuttle buses that leave every few minutes from the lower level. They take you directly to the Historic Area, so you'll not have any parking headaches.

We'll start at the **Governor's Palace**, the place where everyone wants to have their picture taken. The residence of seven royal governors and the first two governors of the Commonwealth of Virginia, the restored interiors and formal gardens are simply gorgeous. Walking down Palace Green will take you to **Duke of Gloucester Street** (Dog Street in local language), where Colonial milliners, silversmiths, wigmakers, bakers, blacksmiths and more set up shop 300 years ago. All are staffed by contemporary craftspeople, donning authentic wardrobes, who will be pleased to answer any of your questions and sell you a few wares priced at today's dollar.

The trail down Duke of Gloucester ends at the front steps of the **Capitol**, where the principles of self-government, individual liberty and responsible leadership were developed by Virginia's patriots. If you hike across the green on the pedestrian pathway, you'll come to a popular photo opportunity . . . the **Public Gaol** on Nicholson Street. Here you can fling your arms into the wooden shackles while your partner snaps away.

Two fine museums are also a part of Colonial Williamsburg. The **DeWitt Wallace Decorative Arts Gallery** houses more than 8,000 objects from Colonial Williamsburg's permanent collection of 18th-century ceramics, furniture, metals, maps, prints and textiles. The **Abby Aldrich Rockefeller Folk Art Center** offers changing exhibits of American Folk art. Both museums require a separate ticket for admission.

On the opposite end of Duke of Gloucester from the Capitol, you'll be able to stroll through

Merchant's Square and then onto the campus of the **College of William & Mary**. You'll feel smarter just touching the weathered brick walls of these truly handsome buildings, home to the second-oldest college in the country.

If you've had enough of history, take your choice of **Busch Gardens** or **Water Country USA**. Either one promises a full day of fun for the entire family. Both attractions are just outside Williamsburg in nearby counties and are owned by Anheuser-Busch, which has a brewery next to Busch Gardens.

Busch Gardens is on U.S. Rt. 60 just three miles west of Williamsburg. Here you'll find heart-thumping roller coasters and dozens of tamer rides all contained in a mini version of Europe. Busch Gardens is open daily from mid-May through early September and on weekends for a few extra weeks at the start and end of the season. Admission is $35 for adults, $28 for children. Parking costs $6 a car.

Sister attraction **Water Country USA** is in York County three miles in the other direction from Williamsburg. It is just off Interstate 64 and has all kinds of water rides scattered around its 40 acres. Some are for daring fun seekers while others are tame enough for even young children. A favorite attraction is Surfers' Bay, Virginia's largest wave pool. Water Country is open daily from Memorial Day through Labor Day and on weekends just before and after these holidays. Admission costs $27, $19.50 for children age 3 to 6. There also is a combination ticket for Busch Gardens and Water Country that costs $55 and lets you go to both attractions on different days.

Restaurants

You can dine in or eat-on-the-run. The choice is yours. We prefer the Colonial taverns for their warm, fuzzy feeling and consistently excellent menus. There are three in the Historic Area. **Christiana Campbell's Tavern**, one of George Washington's favorites, offers skillet fried chicken, pecan waffles and Southern spoon bread. **Josiah Chownings Tavern**, adjacent to the Courthouse, is a typical Colonial alehouse, favored for its sandwiches, Brunswick stew and Welsh rabbit. At night take in the Gambols for Colonial games, entertainment and diversions. Lastly, there's **King's Arms Tavern** on Duke of Gloucester Street, where peanut soup with Sally Lunn bread is a must to start, followed by Virginia ham or prime rib. To make reservations at any of the taverns, call (757) 229-2141 or (800) TAVERNS.

For contemporary dining with all the graciousness of Southern hospitality, our unanimous vote goes to a tie. First, we highly recommend **The Regency Room** at the Williamsburg Inn. Divine breads, prime rib, seafood and veal match beautifully with the extensive wine list. Sunday brunch here is one you'll talk about for weeks. Reservations are definitely required for dinner, (757) 229-2141 or (800) TAVERNS. Next is the **Trellis**, in Merchant's Square and the creation of renowned Executive Chef Marcel Desaulniers, host of his own TV show, *Death by Chocolate*, which should give you a clue as to what to order as your feast finale. The mesquite-grilled fare and regional specialties—Chesapeake Bay seafood and Smithfield ham laced with divinely delicate sauces—cannot be imitated. The prix fixe seasonal supper is always a superb choice, but a limited number of à la carte main dishes are available. Whether you opt for a table in the intimate Vault Room, Grill Room or Garden Room, or linger in the Cafe or outdoor bistro, your meal will be a delight. Call early to reserve the room of your choice, (757) 229-8610.

We hardly every venture near Williamsburg without stopping at **Pierce's Pitt Barb-B-Que** just off Interstate 64 near Lightfoot. (757) 565-2955. The pulled-pork barbecue is excellent as are all the side dishes. Another favorite restaurant is **Old Chickahominy House** at 1211 Jamestown Rd. (757) 229-4689. It features classic Virginia cooking for breakfast and lunch. Bestsellers are ham biscuits, Brunswick stew and homemade pies.

Shopping

Now we're getting warm. Williamsburg is host to some of the finest discount shopping this side of the recession. Comfy shoes are the basic entry requirement at the world-famous **Williamsburg Pottery Factory**, (757) 564-3326, located 5 miles west of Williamsburg in Lightfoot. From its origins as a roadside shed on a half-acre lot, the Pottery has sprawled to more than 200 acres, with more than 30 structures including a massive solar building the size of eight football fields. This book isn't long enough for a laundry list of what goodies you can snap up for tiny prices. China, glassware and stemware, furniture, lamps, wicker and, of course, pottery is just the beginning. It also has a wonderful gourmet food section, and the largest wine selection in the state of Virginia.

Stuff those newspaper-wrapped goodies from the Pottery in your trunk and drive back towards town to the **Williamsburg Outlet Mall**, (757) 565-3378. The one-story bargain mecca is so popular that it expanded to its full-blown size of more than 60 factory outlet shops, all arranged in a cross pattern with the food court in the middle of the "X." For ladies, there's the **Dress Barn**, **Hit or Miss** and **Bruce Alan Bags, Etc.** For men, head to **Bugle Boy, Casual Male Big & Tall**, and **S&K Menswear**. Join forces to browse **Linen Barn, The Paper Factory, Book Hutch** and **Solid Brass of Williamsburg**. Grab a sugar hit from the **Fudge Factory**, jump in the car and head on to more shopping.

Prime Outlets (757) 565-0702, is just a hop down Richmond Road towards town. We are now talking top-of-the-line, bottom-of-the-wallet-type shopping mania. **J. Crew, Jones New York, Coach, Anne Kline, Liz Claiborne, Geoffrey Beene, Brooks Bros., Nike** and **Seiko** . . . need we say more? The outlet center, which has expanded in recent years, is charming and especially attractive with its savings to 70 percent off the original hefty price tags that designer wear demands. There are several eateries here for when you need to refuel for more shopping.

All along Richmond Road are other small centers with wonderful crafts and gift shops. Back in town adjacent to the historic area, there's **Merchant's Square i**n the city's center. Here are some exquisite shops offering fine apparel for women (**Binn's** and **Laura Ashley**). For kids, don't pass up the **Toymaker of Williamsburg**, and everyone will enjoy relaxing in the wonderful **Rizzoli Bookstore**. Nancy Thomas Gallery for folk art and Quilts Unlimited are also on the must-see list.

Antique lovers can browse for hours in the 45,000 square foot **Williamsburg Antique Mall** in Lightfoot, (757) 565-3422. It's just off I-64 at exit 234.

On your way back to Hampton Roads, there are two other stops you should make . . . Yorktown and Jamestown, which, along with Williamsburg, define the Historic Triangle. See our next section for details.

INSIDERS' TIP

Civil War buffs could spend years studying Virginia's role in the War Between the States. There are more than 200 battlefields and other significant Civil War sites in the state. To find them all get a free copy of the Virginia Civil War Trails map at area tourism bureaus or by calling 1-888-CIVILWAR. A separate map on the 1862 Peninsula Campaign focuses in greater detail on war sites in Hampton Roads.

Christmas in Williamsburg

Christmas in Williamsburg is Christmas in another era, stepping back from the modern shopping lists, wrapping paper and glitzy tinsel into a time more than 200 years past.

For a day or a weekend, nothing will instill the holiday spirit like a visit to Colonial Williamsburg during the holiday season. From the **Grand Illumination** in early December through Christmas week itself, there are programs, events and exhibitions galore. Not to mention the decorations, handmade from fruits, greens, berries and candles, one more exquisite than the next. Sing along with the strolling carolers and musicians, delight at the flaming cressets (iron baskets hung from iron poles that burn fat wood) that line the streets for warmth and light, try to count the more than 1,200 candles lit throughout the historic district and simply enjoy the old-fashioned Christmas cheer that's impossible to duplicate anywhere else.

If you do plan to make an overnight stay, reservations should be made as early as possible. For a free Christmas brochure that includes all the programs and events of the holiday season in Colonial Williamsburg, call (800) HISTORY.

For More Information

For more than you'd even really want to know about Colonial Williamsburg and beyond, call

(800) HISTORY or (800) 246-2099. The free call will earn you a complimentary copy of the **Vacation Planner**, with all the details for full enjoyment of this special place. Another resource is the **Williamsburg Area Convention and Visitors Bureau**, (757) 253-0192 or (800) 368-6511. You should also pick up a copy of the *Insiders' Guide to Williamsburg*, which, as you should already know from this book, will give you the true inside scoop on the area.

Jamestown/Yorktown

Two of the most historic sites in the country are within an easy hour's drive from the Virginia Beach/Norfolk area. If you're already planning a trip to Williamsburg, they are definitely worth working into your itinerary. However, it is feasible to zip up for a fast-paced day and tour both Jamestown and Yorktown.

Jamestown, founded in 1607, is the site of the country's first permanent English-speaking settlement. The early years were tough on the settlers as humid summers, cold winters, hungry mosquitoes, stagnant water and unfriendly Indians thwarted their settlement efforts. Jamestown endured, however, and became Virginia's first capital. After the Colonial capital moved to Williamsburg in 1699, Jamestown ceased to exist as a community. Today it is the site of a painstaking, ongoing restoration.

Nearby **Yorktown** is a scenic town on the banks of the York River. Its claim to fame is as the place where the British threw up the white flag in 1781 and ended the Revolutionary War. Yorktown was established in 1661 and is filled with history.

Getting There

Take Interstate 64 and head west. Go through the Hampton Roads Bridge-Tunnel and keep going. If you're not familiar with the area, it's easiest to head for Yorktown first and start your tour there. Take Va. Route 17 N. (J. Clyde Morris Boulevard) in Newport News. Look for signs steering you toward the Yorktown Visitor Center run by the National Park Service.

When you finish at Yorktown, take the scenic Colonial National Parkway to Jamestown. This 23-mile wooded stretch directly links the Yorktown Visitor Center with Jamestown Island. Along the way you'll see historic markers, picnic areas and magnificent views of the James and York rivers. In spring and fall the scenery is spectacular. Keep a light foot on the gas pedal. The parkway is part of a federal park, and the speed limit is only 45 mph.

If you're returning to the Virginia Beach/Norfolk area from Jamestown, get on Va. Route 5 and take it to I-64 E. Or for fun, ride the free Jamestown ferry to Surry County and take a roundabout way home that leads through Suffolk along Va. Route 10 where you can catch Va. Route 460 and head towards I-64.

Attractions

Both the Yorktown Battlefield and Jamestown Island are part of Colonial National Historical Park, which includes the scenic parkway that connects them.

In Yorktown, start your tour at the **Yorktown Visitor Center**, (757) 898-3400. Admission to this National Park Service site costs $4. Get oriented with a 15-minute film, pick up maps and check out the exhibits. Our favorites are George Washington's canvas battle tent preserved behind glass and a replica of a British warship. Children love prowling through the ship. Older kids will enjoy dioramas depicting the Revolutionary War through a boy's eyes.

Be sure to take a drive through the battlefields where you'll see earthworks, a historic house and the surrender site. There are markers along the way and free maps to guide you. To help interpret what you're seeing, rent a narrated audiotape. The tape comes with its own cassette player. There are numerous places to get out of the car and inspect the battlefields. The visitor center is open daily from 8:30 AM to 5 PM.

The **Yorktown Victory Center** is on Old Va. Route 238, (757) 887-1776. It was built by the Commonwealth of Virginia and is operated by the state-run Jamestown-Yorktown Foundation. Outside is a re-creation of a Continental Army camp. Interpreters also bring to life an 18th-century farm as they garden, dip candles and prepare wool and flax. Inside the center are exhibits pertaining to the Revolutionary War and the events leading up to it. There also is a 28-minute film that focuses on the people who lived during the Revolution. If you haven't been here in a few years, grab your family and go. A $4 million makeover completed in 1995 has transformed this from a ho-hum attraction into an amazing historic site the entire family will enjoy. Today the center shows off more than 500 original Revolutionary War artifacts. Our favorites include the 1700s ship extracted from the York River and the room where children can try on Colonial garb and play period games.

The best ticket deal is a $15.50 combination ticket ($7.25 for those ages 6 to 12) to the center and Jamestown Settlement in Jamestown. An individual $7.75 ticket also is sold at the Yorktown center ($3.75 for children 6 and older). Visit the Victory Center from 9 AM to 5 PM on any day but Christmas and New Year's Day.

Another interesting site in Yorktown is the **victory statue**, which was ordered by the Continental Congress in 1781 but not started until 1881. The statue is downtown. Note the inscriptions on the base and the lightning rod on top.

To get completely away from the Revolutionary War stop by the **Watermen's Museum** on Water Street, (757) 887-2641. It pays tribute to the crabbers, fishermen and oystermen who work the Chesapeake Bay and its tributaries. The museum is housed in a 1935 Colonial Revival wooden house floated across the York River in 1987 to its present site. It features an excellent collection of artifacts, photographs and literature about watermen. Outside are work boats and other traditional tools of the trade. There is a small admission fee. The museum generally closes in winter. It opens in April and welcomes tourists until December 15. Hours are 10 AM to 4 PM Tuesday through Saturday and 1 to 4 PM Sunday.

From a dock outside the Watermen's Museum, you can board the *Miss Yorktown*, a Chesapeake Bay deadrise, for a day-long fishing trip. The traditional waterman's boat requires a minimal number of passengers and runs from Memorial Day through October. Call ahead for times and prices, (757) 879-8276 or (804) 693-8276. If you're more into pleasure cruising try an excursion on the *Yorktown Lady*, which has lunch, dinner and moonlight cruises. The boat leaves from the museum's dock. For a schedule call (757) 229-6244.

While in Yorktown you may want to check out the York River beach in downtown Yorktown and also drive past some of the town's historic homes, businesses and churches. The town celebrated its 300th anniversary in 1991. Its oldest remaining building is the Sessions House, built in 1692.

In Jamestown there are two main places to see. The Jamestown-Yorktown Foundation runs Jamestown Settlement. Jamestown Island is part of the Colonial National Historical Park. Start your tour at either place.

At the **Jamestown Settlement**, which is just off Va. Route 31, you'll see costumed participants pretending to be settlers living in a re-created fort. There you can talk with a blacksmith, hear a soldier explaining the intricacies of his musket or try on armor for size.

Docked along the James River are full-size replicas of the three ships that brought the first settlers in 1607. There is also an extensive museum with displays on English colonization, the Powhatan Indians and the settlement's early years. A 20-minute film gives a good overview. There is a charge to visit the settlement, which is open daily; call (757) 229-1607. The best deal is to buy a $15.50 joint ticket that also admits you to the Yorktown Victory Center. Children younger than 6 get in free. Older ones pay $7.25. You also can purchase a $10.25 ticket just to Jamestown Settlement ($5 for ages 6 and up). The Settlement is open from 9 AM to 5 PM daily except Christmas and New Year's Day.

There is a $5 per-person fee to visit **Jamestown Island**, which is a National Park Service site, 229-1733. Paying the fee also lets you visit the **Yorktown Battlefield**. Once on the island you can see a 15-minute film in the visitors center and look at displays of 17th-century artifacts. Outside are 3- and 5-mile drives that loop through the island. Jamestown Island is open daily from 9 AM to 5 PM.

To explore the area around the visitors center you can either take a guided walking tour or do your own tour with the help of a brochure. Our favorite tact is to move at our own pace and eavesdrop on nearby tours. In this area you'll see the Old Church Tower, the only 17th-century structure left on the island. It is attached to a small brick church built in 1907 on the site of a former church that dated from 1617. Statues of Pocahontas and Capt. John Smith salute two of

Jamestown's most famous former residents. A memorial cross marks the spot where 300 colonists were buried in shallow graves during the harsh winter of 1609–10.

One of the most fascinating sites outside the visitors center is an archeological dig that is part of a 10-year mission that has unearthed the original fort built by settlers. Here you can peer over ropes to see archaeologists doing their delicate work. If they're not too busy, they'll take time to talk about some of their finds. You'll also see a display showing some of the artifacts they've found.

When leaving the island be sure to stop near the exit and walk down to the glassblowing area where costumed glassblowers demonstrate the island's first industry established in 1608. Everyone is intrigued by seeing a glob of molten glass hanging from the end of a long pipe. As a glassblower gently puffs air into the glass, the object suddenly becomes a pitcher or other household object. You may be tempted to pick up some delicate handmade items for souvenirs.

Restaurants

If you want to eat in Jamestown your only options are the cafe at Jamestown Settlement or the picnic lunch you brought along. There is no food available on Jamestown Island, but drinks are sold in a machine outside the glassblowing area. There are numerous restaurants in Williamsburg, a few miles down Va. Route 31.

For a real culinary treat, ride the ferry from Jamestown to Surry County and eat at the **Surrey House Restaurant** on Va. Route 10, (757) 294-3389 or (800) 200-4977, which is renowned for its country cooking and has been pleasing families since 1954 by dishing up traditional breakfast, lunch and dinner. Local ham and seafood anchor the menu, and peanut soup is a must-try dish. Be sure to save room for peanut-raisin pie, fruit cobbler or other delicacies. The 20-minute trip across the James River to Surry County on the state-owned ferry is great fun and provides a terrific view of the three replica ships docked at Jamestown. There are frequent departures, and the free ferry runs around the clock. A big billboard in Jamestown gives departure times so note them before starting your visit. For information call (757) 823-3779 or (800) VA-FERRY.

There are several restaurants in Yorktown. The most famous is **Nick's Seafood Pavilion** on Water Street, (757) 887-5269. Founded in 1940, the restaurant has elaborate decor and excellent seafood. More informal restaurants include the **Yorktown Pub** at 540 Water Street, (757) 886-9964, **Sammy & Nick's Family Steak House**, 11806 George Washington Boulevard, (757) 898-3070, and **The River Room of the Duke of York Motor Hotel** at 508 Water Street, (757) 898-5270.

Shopping

There are gift shops at the various historic sites. For art try the **On the Hill Creative Arts Center** in Yorktown at 121 Alexander Hamilton Boulevard. This is a cooperative gallery of local artists. Nationally known folk artist Nancy Thomas also maintains a Yorktown gallery, the **Nancy Thomas Gallery**, 145 Ballard Street, that features many of the angels that have gained her acclaim. The **Yorktown Shoppe** at 402 Main Street has a variety of gift items.

The **Galleria Antique Mall** on Va. Route 17 in Yorktown is the place to shop for collectibles and vintage furniture. This 40,000-square-foot antiques mall has 130 dealers selling everything from art nouveau to precious European antiques. The mall also runs several weekly auctions. It is at 7628 George Washington Highway in Yorktown and is open daily. Another possibility is **Swan Tavern Antiques** at 300 Main Street.

Accommodations

You can choose from the more than 85 motels and hotels in or near Williamsburg (see our section on Williamsburg in this chapter). Most are just a few miles from Yorktown. If you want to stay right in Yorktown try the **Yorktown Motor Lodge** on Route 17, (757) 898-5451 or the

DAYTRIPS

Duke of York Motor Hotel overlooking the York River, (757) 898-3232. The **Marl Inn** at 220 Church St. is a two-room inn that is right in town (757) 898-3859. For information on area accommodations call the **Williamsburg Hotel/Motel Association** at (800) 446-9244.

For More Information

Write the **Williamsburg Area Convention and Visitors Bureau** at P.O. Box 3585, Williamsburg 23187 or call (757) 253-0192 or (800) 368-6511. For a detailed guide, our sister book, *the Insiders' Guide to Williamsburg* is the way to go.

The James River Plantations

This is one of our favorite daytrips because the journey is every bit as pleasant as the destination. Between Williamsburg and Richmond, in historic Charles City County, you can visit a handful of graceful old Virginia plantations, dotted along a beautiful road called The John Tyler Memorial Highway (more

A variety of vintage airplanes fascinate visitors to Hampton's Virginia Air and Space Center.

Photo: Courtesy of Hampton Convention and Tourism Bureau

prosaically known as Va. Route 5). The signs for Route 5 are clearly marked on I-64 from both directions. On a fine spring or fall day, there isn't a prettier drive around than this one—even if you never get out of the car.

Be sure to pack along a picnic lunch or plan to eat at the **Shirley Plantation** snack bar. For another option try the **Coach House Tavern** in a restored building on **Berkeley Plantation**. You can just stop by for lunch, but plan to make a reservation if you intend to have dinner. Call (804) 829-6003. For an elegant restful lunch, try **Indian Fields Tavern** along Va. 5 in Charles City County, (804) 829-5004. We heartily recommend visiting at least one of the following historic homes or grounds. Since these are all private homes, you may want to call ahead to verify tour times.

If you long to spend the night in historic surroundings there are three options in Charles City County. **Edgewood Plantation** on Route 5 is a Gothic Revival home built in 1849, (804) 829-2962. **North Bend Plantation** is an 1819 Greek Revival Federal Period home built for the sister of former President William Henry Harrison. It is on Weyanoke Road. Call (804) 829-5176. **Piney Grove** at Southall's Plantation is an early 1800s log home on Southall Plantation Lane. Call (804) 829-2480. All three homes promise lots of pampering, antique-filled rooms, excellent breakfasts, and swimming pools.

For more information on the James River Plantations in general call (800) 704-5423.

Shirley Plantation

This National Historic Landmark was founded in 1613. The present mansion was built between 1723 and 1738 and has remained largely unchanged—and in the hands of the Carter family—since that time. The elegant brick mansion features a famous carved-walnut staircase that rises for three stories without any visible means of support, an incredible boxwood garden and many exquisite antiques. Distinguished visitors included George Washington, Thomas Jefferson, Teddy Roosevelt and John Rockefeller. Civil war history buffs will want to step into the parlor, where Robert E. Lee's mother, Anne Hill Carter, was married to "Light Horse" Harry Lee. The house and grounds are open daily except Christmas day. Indoor tours are offered from 9 AM to 4:30 PM The grounds stay open until 6 PM. Admission fees are $9 for adults, $6 for people ages 13 through 21 and $5 for children ages 6 through 12. Call (804) 829-5121 or (800) 232-1613.

Berkeley Plantation

Berkeley Plantation is the birthplace of Benjamin Harrison, who signed the Declaration of Independence, and his son, William Henry Harrison, who was ninth president of the United States. It is also the site of the first official Thanksgiving in North America, celebrated in 1619. The three-story home was built in 1726 of brick that was fired on site. It is in the Georgian style, with a gently sloping roof and three dormer windows. The home's wide hall features a pilastered arch. Decorative woodwork is elaborate throughout the interior and a second-floor landing has a musician's balcony. Berkeley is open for touring every day except Christmas. The fee is $8.50 for adults, $4 for children 6 to 12 and $6.50 for children 13 to 16. The grounds open at 8 AM and close at 5 PM. Tours begin at 9 AM. Since the turn of the century, Berkeley has been owned by the Jamieson family. Call (804) 829-6018.

Westover Plantation

This palatial estate was once the home of Virginia's famous Byrd family and is considered by many to be one of the finest examples of Georgian architecture in the United States. Highlights include a magnificent marble doorway, Rocaille ceilings, paneled walls and a staircase with spirally turned balusters and steps that are 5 feet wide. Unfortunately, you can't tour it very often. The home is only open once a year, for Historic Garden Week in April. Groups can arrange to tour the first floor by calling for an appointment. On any day but Sunday, however, you can see the exterior and the garden, which has a yew tree planted by George Washington. The grounds tour costs $2, $.50 for children. The home has been owned by the Fischer family for several generations. For more information call (804) 829-2882.

Evelynton Plantation

This plantation was part of the original 1619 grant of Westover Plantation. Since 1847 Evelynton has been home to the Ruffin family. Edmund Ruffin is known for firing the first shot of the Civil War. The Georgian Revival manor house was built in 1935 to replace an earlier dwelling. It is part of a 2,500-acre farm along Herring Creek, which feeds into the James River. The home is filled with period antiques. Outside are lovely gardens and a gift shop. Evelynton is open daily for tours from 9 to 5 PM. Admission costs $8.50, $5.50 for children 6 and older. Call (804) 829-5075 or (800) 473-5075.

Sherwood Forest

President John Tyler purchased Sherwood Forest as a retreat from Washington while he was living in the White House. Eventually, he retired here. The house is made of framed timbers and stands in a beautiful 10-acre grove of original growth oaks. It was built c.1730 and renovated by President Tyler in 1844. Highlights of the interior include a large ballroom and a library containing President Tyler's books. The home is still owned by Tyler's grandson. It is open for tours every day except Thanksgiving, Christmas and New Year's Day from 9 AM to 5 PM. Admission is $8.50 for adults and $5.50 for students in kindergarten through college. For more information call (804) 829-5377.

Carter's Grove Plantation

Although it isn't on the same stretch of road as the other plantations, this beautiful home owned by the Colonial Williamsburg Foundation is a real treasure. It is off Rt. 60 in James City County along the banks of the James River. This Georgian mansion was built in 1755 and is furnished with antiques from the 17th through 20th centuries. In addition to seeing the house, visitors can tour Wolstenholme Towne, an archeological site of an English settlement established in 1619. Tickets cost $18, $11 for children. If you bought a general admission or annual pass to Colonial Williamsburg, you will be admitted for no extra charge. For information call (757) 220-7453.

Richmond

There is so much to do in Richmond and surrounding counties that you could spend days here. It's one of our favorite cities to visit. With nearly 20 museums and 30 other interesting places to visit, we still haven't seen all of it yet so we keep going back.

While Richmond is a shrine to anyone who revels in Civil War history, there's a lot more here than Confederate heritage. Richmond boasts historic neighborhoods, a variety of excellent museums, intriguing shops and fine restaurants. In fact, during one budget-watching summer Richmond was our main vacation destination. After spending four days here, we still had plenty on our to-do list that we hadn't had time to hit. We'll save that for another excursion.

Getting There

Head straight up Interstate 64 W. and keep going for about 90 minutes. To get downtown take the Fifth Street Exit to Broad Street and maneuver through the city from there.

Attractions

If you're fascinated by history of the War Between the States, start at either the **Richmond National Battlefield Park Visitor Center** or the **Museum** and **White House of the Confederacy**. The visitor center at 3215 Broad Street, (804) 226-1981, has exhibits, a film and employees to guide you toward the city's numerous battlefields. It is open daily and admission is free.

The Museum and White House of the Confederacy (former home of Confederate President Jefferson Davis) own the world's largest collection of Confederate memorabilia. Both are fascinating to tour, so plan on spending several hours. While you'll find the collection of uniforms, pistols and swords you'd expect, you'll also see displays dealing with soldiers' families, the lives of slaves and other related topics. The restored **Davis house** will please those who adore either history or antiques. The house and museum are at 12th and E. Clay streets, (804) 649-1861, and are open daily. There is an admission fee.

If you have children one must-see is the **Children's Museum of Richmond** at 2626 W. Broad Street (804) 474-2667. In 2000 the hands-on museum moved into a new building five times bigger than the old one. It is one of the East Coast's biggest children's museums. Next door is **The Science Museum of Virginia** at 2500 W. Broad Street, (804) 367-6552. Both are hands-on places designed with children and families in mind. The children's museum charges $5 admission. The science museum charges $5 for adults, $4 for children and seniors. There is an extra charge for IMAX theater shows. The **Virginia Museum of Fine Arts** at 2800 Grove Avenue, (804) 367-0844, has a vast art collection from all periods. Admission is free with a suggested $4 donation. The science museum is open daily. The other two museums close on Monday.

Two other museums that are favorites of ours are the **Edgar Allan Poe Museum** at 1914 E. Main Street, (804) 648-5523, and **The Valentine Museum** at 1015 E. Clay Street, (804) 649-0711. The Poe museum pays tribute to Richmond's native son. It is housed in Richmond's oldest building, a stone house built in 1737. Tours are given on the hour and cost $6 for adults, $5 for students. The Valentine Museum focuses on the life and times of old Richmond and has one of the country's best costume collections. A visit to the museum includes a guided tour of the adjacent **Wickham House**, which was built in 1812. Admission costs $5 for adults, $3 for children age 7 to 12. Both museums are open daily.

For a peek at Richmond life in the 18th century, sit in on a docent tour of **St. John's Church**. This is where Patrick Henry made his "Give me liberty, or give me death" speech, and the tour

Revolutionary War re-enactments are realistic at Yorktown Victory Center.

Photo: Courtesy of Yorktown Victory Center

guides give just about as rousing an oratory. The church is at 2401 E. Broad Street in Church Hill, (804) 648-5015, and is Richmond's oldest church. Admission costs $3 for adults, $1 for children. Tours are offered from 10 AM to 3:30 PM Monday through Saturday and on Sunday from 1 to 3:30 PM. Outside is the burial spot for Edgar Allan Poe's mother, colonist George Wythe and several Virginia governors.

You also might want to check out the **State Capitol** at Ninth and Grace streets, (804) 786-4344. The building was designed by Thomas Jefferson and built in 1788. The grounds include fountains and statues of famous Virginians, including a revered likeness of George Washington. The Capitol is open daily. You can tour on your own or take a free 20-minute tour that starts frequently.

For outdoor activities wander along the James River downtown along **Tredegar Street** or along **Monument Avenue**, named for its many historic statues. This is one of the country's longest streets. This avenue's lineup of statues features mostly Confederate generals. Also among the honored is native son and tennis great Arthur Ashe.

During our last Richmond excursion we spent a delightful Sunday afternoon at **Maymont**. This is a 100-acre Victorian estate with a mansion, elaborate gardens and petting zoo. The paths along its grounds attract wildlife lovers, joggers, parents strolling babies and all kinds of other people. Maymont is at 1700 Hampton Street, (804) 358-7166. It is open daily with guided tours of the house and gardens available. In 1999 Maymont opened a new nature and visitor center. Admission is free with a $3 suggested donation.

While in Richmond try to wander through some of the historic neighborhoods such as **The Fan**, **Church Hill** and **Jackson Ward**. You'll see some eclectic architecture that reflects the city's gracious lifestyle.

One fun event to attend in Richmond is the **Bizarre Bazaar** held in December at the Virginia Fairgrounds' Strawberry Hill. The show features 30 juried exhibitors. Call (804) 288-3200.

Another event we'll drive to Richmond for is the giant **flea market** held the first weekend of every month at the Virginia Fairgrounds, (804) 228-3200. The **state fair**, held every September, is another reason to drive to the capital city. You'll see and hear lots of ads for the fair about the time school starts. A visit there one year pleased our entire family, including one boy who called the fair "just as good as Disney World." Parents will like the fact that the admission fee covers the cost of all rides, so kids can hurl themselves on as many rides as their stomachs can stand. While at the fair be sure to stop by the Virginia Tech booth for some homemade ice cream. It's delicious.

About 20 miles outside Richmond is one of our favorite family places—**Paramount's Kings Dominion**, (804) 876-5000. This 400-acre theme park is open daily from Memorial Day through Labor Day with more than 40 fun rides. It usually is open weekends in spring and fall. The theme park is at I-95 N. and Route 30. We like to arrive before the 10 AM opening time to study a park map and plot our strategy for the day. Plan to stay a whole day, and be sure to bring your bathing suits and towels for the nifty water park that's included in the admission price of $28.95 for anyone older than 6 and $19.95 for those who are younger. We always save the water park for late in the day when we're hot, tired and ready for a break. There are comfortable lounge chairs for those who just want to watch all the activity. The water park has areas geared for toddlers as well as high-speed slides that start at dizzying heights. The park usually closes around 10 PM so you may want to get a room at a nearby motel.

Restaurants

You'll find lots of choices in the Shockoe Bottom and Shockoe Slip areas, Carytown, the Fan District and around Virginia Commonwealth University (VCU). Also, suburban Chesterfield and Henrico counties have many good places to eat. The showplace of Richmond is undoubtedly **The Tobacco Company Restaurant** at 1201 E. Cary Street in Shockoe Slip, (804) 782-9555. This three-story restaurant is in an old warehouse and is decorated with scads of antiques, including a brass elevator from New York's Con Edison building. The gigantic menu ranges from seafood to ham, and the prime rib is a house specialty. For some of the best food in town try **The Frog** and the **Redneck** at 1423 E. Cary Street. Numerous culinary awards have been bestowed on this restaurant that fuses regional cuisine with classic French food, (757) 648-FROG.

Recommendations from Richmond residents include ethnic dinners at **Havana '59**, a trendy spot at 16 N. 17th Street in Shockoe Bottom, (804) 649-2822. This tropical oasis hearkens back to Cuba's carefree pre-Castro days right down to the deck of cards on each table. The food has a Cuban salsa flair. Another local favorite is **Bottoms Up Pizza** at 17th and Dock streets, (804) 644-4400, whose gourmet pies have won honors as Richmond's best pizza. The restaurant is in Shockoe Bottom along part of an old canal under railroad trestles. Local Insiders rave about **Skilligalee Seafood Restaurant** at 5416 Glenside. Drive just off I-64, (804) 672-6200, noted for its outstanding seafood. They also like to hang out at **Millie's Diner**, 2603 E. Main Street in Church Hill, (804) 643-5512, where they get a jukebox at every table. Although Millie's looks like a diner, it serves upscale fusion cuisine drawn from around the world.

Another good choice is the **River City Diner** at 1712 E. Main Street in Shockoe Bottom, which has the timeless ambiance of a neighborhood diner (804) 644-9418. Burgers, shakes and meat loaf headline the menu.

For fine dining there are some excellent choices. **The Frog** and the **Redneck** at 1423 Cary Street in Shockoe Slip, (804) 648-FROG, blends regional French and American specialties. Reservations are recommended, particularly on weekends. For outstanding cuisine reserve a table at **Lemaire**. Lemaire is in the Jefferson Hotel near downtown at Franklin and Adams streets, (804) 344-6366. You'll definitely need reservations.

Accommodations

There are many downtown and suburban hotels and motels in all price ranges as well as bed and breakfasts. If you're looking for something elegant try the **Jefferson Hotel**, built in 1895 and splendidly restored in the 1980s. This top-rated hotel is on Franklin and Adam streets, (804) 788-8000, (800) 424-8014. It has a grand staircase that resembles the one in *Gone With the Wind*. **Linden Row Inn** at 100 E. Franklin Street, (804) 783-7000, (800) 348-7424, was created from seven restored antebellum townhouses and is a lovely choice for lodging. The **Berkeley Hotel** at 12th and Cary streets, (804) 780-1300, is a European-style hotel. It is right in historic

Shockoe Slip and is two blocks from the State Capitol. By calling a central reservation hotline at 1-888-RICHMOND, you can get information on all accommodations in the city.

If your prefer a bed and breakfast call the **Bensonhouse** reservation service at (804) 353-6900. This service keeps tabs on what's available at area bed and breakfasts. Two magnificent bed and breakfasts you might want to consider are the **Emmanuel Hutzler House** at 2036 Monument Ave., (804) 355-4885 and **Summerhouse** on Monument Ave., (804) 353-6900. Both are in the historic Fan District.

Shopping

For fine boutiques and specialty shops, park your car and stroll through **Shockoe Slip**, **Carytown**, **Sycamore Square** or the **Shops of Libbie and Grove**. In these areas it's fun to set out on foot for a few hours of exploring small interesting shops. There also are several malls in suburban areas.

For More Information

Write or visit the **Metropolitan Richmond Convention and Visitors Bureau**, 550 E. Marshall Street in the Sixth Street Marketplace, Richmond 23219, (804) 782-2777 or (800) 370-9004. You can pick up brochures there, at the **Richmond Visitors Center** at Robin Hood Road and the Boulevard, (804) 358-5511, or at a visitor center in Richmond International Airport, (804) 236-3260. For more extensive information, check out *The Insiders' Guide to Richmond*.

Tappahannock

In the mood for a day of antiquing and filling up on home cooking? Tappahannock is the place to go. With about 9,000 residents in the town and surrounding Essex County, this is a small but charming community on the banks of the Rappahannock River. The town has existed since the mid-17th century but was officially founded in 1705. Its Native American name means "on the rise and fall of water."

Getting There

Jump onto Interstate 64 headed west. Go through the Hampton Roads Bridge-Tunnel and turn north on Route 17 through Yorktown. It takes just over two hours to get to Tappahannock from Virginia Beach or Norfolk.

Attractions

Eating and antique hunting are always at the top of our list. However, there are other things to do while you're in town.

To soak up the small-town atmosphere, start with a walking tour of the **Tappahannock Historic Landmark District** with about 15 notable buildings. Maps are available at the Tappahannock-Essex County Chamber of Commerce on the courthouse square. It is open from 8:30 AM to 4:30 PM on weekdays. To get the map in advance call (804) 443-5241 or write the Chamber at Box 481, Tappahannock 22560.

Your walk will take you past an 1800s customs house; the Scots Arms Tavern, built around 1680; an 18th-century debtor's prison and several historic houses and churches. Most are on four main streets that dead end at the river. Genealogy buffs can have a heyday in the historic county courthouse, which contains the oldest records in Virginia. The **Essex County Library** is another treasure trove of research material.

If you're yearning to get on the water, **Rappahannock River Cruises**, (804) 453-2628 or

DAYTRIPS

(804) 333-4856, runs all-day excursions from May through October. The **Captain Thomas** leaves Hoskins Creek in Tappahannock at 10 AM and returns at 4 PM every day except Monday. Be sure to bring the binoculars for some spectacular glimpses of bald eagles, which nest in the cliffs along the Rappahannock.

During your boat trip you'll stop at **Ingleside Plantation Winery** in the Northern Neck. This is Virginia's third-largest winery. You can purchase an excellent buffet lunch or bring your own to enjoy. Either way, you'll get a tour and a chance to sample the fruits of the winery's labors.

The 150-passenger boat is enclosed and runs rain or shine. Tickets for the trip cost $20 with children younger than 14 going along for half-price. Lunch costs extra. Reservations are a must.

If you enjoy a ride in the country you may want to cross the river and enjoy an afternoon in the Northern Neck (see our Chesapeake Bay chapter for ideas). If you aren't taking the boat trip, you can drive to the **Ingleside Winery** near Oak Grove off Route 3. It is open daily and offers tours, (804) 224-8687. Admission is free. Another possibility is the 45-minute trip to **Stratford Hall**, the birthplace of Robert E. Lee and other members of his famous family. This lovely manor house was built about 1730 and is open for tours. It is on Route 214 off Route 3 and is open daily, (804) 493-8038. There is an admission fee.

Restaurants

Now we get to the real reason we like to visit Tappahannock—**Lowery's Seafood Restaurant**, (804) 443-2800. We've been known to time trips up this way so we hit Lowery's at a mealtime. Even if it's in between we stop for a meal anyway. Since 1938 the Lowery family has dished up some of the best seafood and home cooking around. Today's restaurant is run by the sons of founders Wesley and Lorelle Lowery. From the homemade vegetable soup to the coconut cream pie, everything tastes like Mom's cooking if she'd known how to do it this good. The menu is huge and reasonably priced, and the restaurant is large enough to require a staff of 80. Entrees run the gamut from seafood platters to steaks and sandwiches. Be sure to try the softshell crabs if they're in season and save room for homemade desserts.

The back of Lowery's is a minimuseum that houses a 1910 Cadillac, a 1926 Chrysler and miscellaneous memorabilia. There's also Jake the myna bird. Kids love this place because after eating they get to fish in a wishing well and trade their catch for a prize. Lowery's is at the intersection of Routes 17 and 360. It serves breakfast, lunch and dinner daily.

Locals recommend the **Hobbs' Hole** dinner with its fried quail, oysters, frog legs and ham. The restaurant is on Hobbs Hole Drive in the midst of a golf course, (804) 443-4451.

Another dining option is **Ferebee's at Church Lane** and **Price Street**, which is gaining a reputation for its huge servings and excellent food. It is open for lunch and dinner, (804) 443-5715. If you're in the mood for Italian cuisine, locals recommend **Roma Italian Restaurant** on Route 17 in the Rappahannock Shopping Center, (804) 443-5240. It serves pasta, pizzas and sandwiches for lunch and dinner.

Accommodations

There are a few budget motels in the area, but your best options are the two bed and breakfasts. The oldest is the **Linden House Bed & Breakfast**. This restored planter's home is 8 miles outside town. Built in 1760, it is on the National Historical Register and features five porches for relaxing. Beautifully appointed rooms are in both the main house and a two-story coach house. The 200-acre grounds include an English garden. Call (804) 443-1170 or (800) 622-1202.

Little Greenway Bed and Breakfast at 431 Prince Street, (804) 443-5747 is run by two teachers. This Victorian home has two guest rooms. Staying here puts you right on the Tappahannock walking tour and gets you near the river cruise departure site.

Shopping

Shopping is an adventure in Tappahannock, and some of our favorite pieces of antique furniture hail from here. There are about a half-dozen antique shops in the area. Most are right on Route 17—the main drag—or on Queen Street.

One of the best is the **Nadji Nook** on Queen Street. This place is overwhelming. Its two floors are stuffed with everything from fine furniture to vintage clothing, cooking utensils and glass doorknobs.

Another must-see shop is **A to Z Surplus** on Route 17 near Lowery's. Furniture is the name of the game here with other collectibles thrown in for good measure. Other shops to check out are **Hodge-Podge** on Route 17, and **Queen Street Ltd.** and **Tappahannock Antique Mall**, both on Queen Street.

Smith Island

Smith Island in the Chesapeake Bay is Maryland's only inhabited offshore island. It actually is a chain of marshy islands with a fascinating history. A sliver of the uninhabited southern tip of the island is actually in Virginia. Centuries ago, pirates hid their boats in the tricky waters surrounding this archipelago while waiting to raid passing ships.

Jamestown's Capt. John Smith explored the island in 1608 and wrote: "Heaven and earth seemed never to have agreed better for man's commodious and delightful habitation."

Dissenters from the Jamestown colony settled here in the 17th century, eventually forming the three villages of Ewell, Rhodes Point and Tylerton.

Today, Ewell, the island's largest town, is sometimes referred to as its capital. Here, anglers catch hard and soft-shell crabs and send them to the mainland to serve markets throughout the world. The lives of these 500 island inhabitants is often harsh but is guided by a strong religious faith. Joshua Thomas established the Methodist church here and on several other Chesapeake Bay islands during the late 1800s. It continues to be the only organized religion on the island today.

Most of Smith Island's residents are watermen continuing the traditions their families have had for generations. You'll hear a distinctive speech pattern among residents that is reminiscent of their British ancestors' Elizabethan/Cornwall dialect.

Getting There

Depending on where you're starting from you can cruise to Smith Island from Reedville, Virginia, or Crisfield, Maryland, just past Virginia's Eastern Shore.

In Reedville boats to Smith Island leave from the Chesapeake Bay/Smith Island KOA Campground in the Smith's Point area of Reedville. To get there take Route 17 N. to Tappahannock. Get on Route 360 and take it to Highway 652. Go east on Highway 652 until it becomes Highway 644, then turn northeast on Highway 650. This sounds complicated, but signs for the **Smith Island Cruise** provide adequate direction. The drive takes about two and a half hours from Hampton Roads but allow plenty of time to get there.

Once you've made it to the boat dock, you'll board the **Captain Evans**, which leaves at 10 AM and pulls in at Ewell around 11:30. You'll have several hours to roam at will before the 2 PM departure. Current round-trip rates are $20 for adults and half price for children 13 and younger. Children younger than 3 ride free. Groups of 25 or more can get a group rate that includes the cruise, luncheon and island bus tour. During warmer months trips are made every day except Monday. For information about the cruise or camping at Smith Point KOA call (804) 453-3430.

If Crisfield is your departure site, you have several options. To get there take Route 13 N. over the Chesapeake Bay Bridge-Tunnel. This will set you back $10 for the toll. Stay on Route 13 into Maryland. You'll see signs for Crisfield just before you turn off on Route 413, 4 miles south of Princess Anne. Crisfield is just 12 miles west of Smith Island. Allow at least 2½ hours to get to Crisfield from Norfolk or Virginia Beach. Before boarding stop by the **Historic Heritage Foundation** along the dock and pick up information from the Smith Island information booth.

The ***Capt. Tyler II*** leaves from Somers Cove Marina at 12:30 PM daily in warmer months and arrives back at the dock at 5:15 PM. Current prices are $20, half-price for children through age 12 and free for children younger than 6. There are packages available that include the cruise, island tour, lunch and a stay at a Crisfield motel. Group rates also are available. For reservations call (410) 425-2771.

Also leaving from Crisfield is the ***Chelsea Lane Tyler***. It leaves from the City Dock May through October at 12:30 PM and returns at 5 PM. Cruises cost $20. Children 6 through 12 ride for half price. Those younger than 6 tag along for free. For reservations call (410) 425-2771.

You also can cruise to Smith Island year-round from the City Dock aboard the **Capt. Jason**. The boat departs from Crisfield daily at 12:30 PM and returns at 4:40 PM. The cost is $10 roundtrip, free for those younger than 12. One-way trips are $7. For reservations call (410) 425-4471.

If you're not a group-tour person and are interested in seeing the island without boatloads of tourists, talk to the boat operators. Some of them live on the island and head to the mainland early in the morning and are happy to give you a ride back after you spend a restful night on the island.

Attractions

The main attraction, of course, is the island. The leisurely pace of life on Maryland's only inhabited island is a welcome change from the hustle and bustle of mainland existence. This is a place where you can put your feet up on a back porch railing and enjoy the soft breezes off the Chesapeake Bay. If it's spring, you might catch the fragrance of the blossoming fig, pear, mimosa and pomegranate trees that grow in all of the island's towns.

Once you're rested, there is enough to see to keep you occupied until your boat departs. You're forewarned that tour boats tend to dock about the same time so you may want to grab lunch before sightseeing. Or you could look around first and wait for the crowds to thin out before ordering your meal.

To see the island you can walk around, rent bikes at Ruke's Seafood Restaurant or take a $2 bus tour operated by the owners of the ***Capt. Evans*** boat. Actually you probably have time to do all three things before your boat departs. A short walking tour of Ewell will take you past clapboard homes, a rustic country store and the sunken remains of the ***Island Bell I***, one of the earliest island ferries. **Goat Island**, across Levering Creek, is home to a herd of about 20 formerly domestic goats. Natives rely on the goats' movements toward the water's edge to obtain salt from the marsh grasses as a sign that rain or snow is imminent. Other attractions include **Pitchcroft**, the island's first settlement, and the wooden keel remains of the 60-foot bugeye ***C.S. Tyler***, built for islander Willie A. Evans. The Evans and Tyler names are among the most common surnames on this island where many residents are related.

On foot or bicycle, you can tour Rhodes Point, the island's center for boat repair. This small town originally was called Rogue's Point because of the pirates who frequented the area. Here, you can watch boats being made and repaired and see the ruins of some of the earlier vessels that plied their trade on the Bay. In 1996 the Smith Island Center, the island's first visitor center and heritage museum, opened just past where the boats dock. The center has an interesting collection of artifacts highlighting not only the watermen's life, but the contributions of women on the island as well as the role of the Methodist church.

During your visit, you may notice how friendly everyone is. Islanders in cars and trucks honk their horns and wave to greet every vehicle and pedestrian they meet. The hospitality is extended to a hefty population of healthy stray cats that seem to be everywhere.

Restaurants

The island has two dining choices. Both are in Ewell and cook up the seafood you'd expect on the island. If soft-shell crabs are in season, they are excellent as are crab cakes and any finfish likely to be on the menu. **Bayside Inn Restaurant** is at the island's dock, (410) 425-2771 and offers moderately priced, hearty family-style meals. The charming **Ruke's Seafood Restaurant** and **Store on Caleb Jones Road**, (410) 425-2311, sells inexpensive seafood platters along

The Chicamacomico Life Saving Station is restored to the glory it enjoyed back when it guarded the northern coast of Hatteras for 70 years.

Photo: Courtesy of Virginia Beach Tourism Corporation

with burgers and sandwiches. Even if you don't eat there, spend a few minutes looking around Ruke's gift shop.

Accommodations

If you want to spend the night on the island, reserve one of the three guest rooms at the **Ewell Tide Inn**, 4063 Tyler Road, (410) 425-2141. Rates are reasonable, and the menu features herbal teas, homemade yeast and fruit breads. Visitors love the English muffins layered with ham, egg, cheese sauce and local crab meat all baked together in the oven. The inn also offers two sitting rooms and a large screened back porch for some true R and R.

Another pleasing bed and breakfast is the **Inn of Silent Music** in the tiny island community of Tylerton. It's at 2955 Tylerton Road and overlooks the water. All four guest rooms have waterfront view. Guests can enjoy a full breakfast and optional seafood dinner. Call (410) 425-2541.

The island's single motel, **Smith Island Motel**, on Smith Island Road, (410) 425-3321, offers eight air-conditioned rooms with TVs. The motel also rents bicycles.

Visitors who prefer to sleep on the Virginia mainland can reserve cabins or tent or camper spots at the **KOA campground** near Reedville. There also are several bed and breakfast inns in Reedville, which has some gorgeous turn-of-the-century mansions (see our Chesapeake Bay chapter). Three to keep in mind are **Morris House**, at the end of Route 360 on Reedville's main street, (804) 453-7016; **Bailey-Cockrell House**, along Cockrell Creek (804) 453-5900; and **The Gables**, also at the end of Route 360 on Reedville's main street, (804) 453-5209.

If you want to stay overnight in Crisfield, you'll find three motel choices: **The Paddlewheel Motel** at 701 W. Main Street, (410) 968-2220; **The Pines Motel** on N. Somerset Avenue, (410) 968-0900; and **Somers Cove Motel** on Norris Drive, (410) 968-1900 or (800) 827-6637.

For More Information

Call the **Somerset County Tourism Office** and ask for a brochure about the island, (800) 521-9189. It includes a self-guided walking tour of Ewell along with maps, historical information and important tips on island etiquette. For example, the island is dry, and islanders don't appreciate public consumption of alcohol.

Northeastern North Carolina

One of our favorite getaway destinations is a trio of nearby North Carolina cities—Elizabeth City, Hertford and Edenton. They're part of the historic Albemarle region of North Carolina. All are within an easy hour's drive but are so different from Hampton Roads they make you think you've been on a long trip.

History is the main reason for journeying to this part of North Carolina, which once was a seat of Colonial government. You'll find one of the oldest house in the state here as well as many other historic structures. Since this part of North Carolina is unofficially dubbed the "barbecue belt," eating also is an excellent reason to get in the car and hit the road.

Getting There

The most direct route is to take Route 17 S. out of Chesapeake. One road leading to this is Route 104, which is at the end of Interstate 464 in Chesapeake. If you get on I-464 in downtown Norfolk and head toward Chesapeake, just follow the Elizabeth City sign at the end.

Along the way you'll be surrounded by the **Great Dismal Swamp**. For miles you'll parallel the Dismal Swamp Canal, which was dug in 1793. Along the way are several picnic areas where you can gaze at this natural wonder. One of them has a boat ramp where you could put in a canoe or small boat. Be sure to stop at the Dismal Swamp Canal Visitor Center outside South

Mills, (919) 771-8333. You'll find a friendly staff, all kinds of North Carolina brochures and the coffee pot filled. This state-run center has a 150-foot dock on the canal and picnic tables. In the warmer months dozens of pleasure craft tie up here as they take a break from traveling the Atlantic Intracoastal Waterway. The center is open Tuesday through Saturday from 9 AM to 5 PM in the off-season and daily from Memorial Day through October.

Elizabeth City will be the first city you'll hit, followed by Hertford about 15 miles later and Edenton another 12 miles away. Your total distance traveled will have been no more than 75 miles. To really see these lovely towns, be sure to take the business exits off Route 17 S.

Attractions

History and scenic beauty are the big draws in this region, which was one of the first parts of North Carolina to be settled in the 17th century. Each city has its own charm, so try to visit all three.

Elizabeth City is on the Pasquotank River where the Dismal Swamp Canal ends. It was an Indian town until British colonists moved in during the early 1600s. The town was established in 1793 and has a population of about 14,000.

Downtown, which runs along the river, you'll find two National Historic Districts with 32 historic homes and sites. Walking tour maps and other brochures are available at the **Elizabeth City Area Chamber of Commerce**. It's on your way downtown at 502 E. Ehringhaus Street, (252) 335-4365 and is open weekdays from 9 AM to 5 PM. One unique aspect of Elizabeth City that's gained international fame is the Rose Buddies, a local welcoming committee that provides free refreshments, roses and information for boaters docking downtown.

Be sure to visit the **Museum of the Albemarle** on Route 17. This free museum provides an ideal overview for your visit to this region near the Albemarle Sound. Its displays range from Indian artifacts to those used by early settlers and watermen. Two treasures are beautifully restored city fire trucks dating from 1890 and 1917. The museum is a division of the North Carolina Museum of History and is open every day except Monday. Hours are 9 AM to 5 PM except Sunday, when they are open from 2 until 5 PM, (252) 335-1453.

Hertford may be the best-kept secret in this part of North Carolina. While its sister cities draw the most tourism traffic, Hertford is a real jewel waiting to be discovered.

You'll sense its charm when you drive onto Business Route 17 and find the roadway surrounded on both sides by the broad Perquimans River. Spanish moss is draped over broad-bottomed cypress trees, and the only S-shaped drawbridge in the country leads you right to the heart of this town with 2,000 residents. There you'll find an all-American downtown complete with a dry goods store and a soda fountain in the local drugstore.

Established in 1758, Hertford has about 50 19th-century buildings, including an 1825 Federal-style courthouse containing North Carolina's oldest deed. A walking-tour map is available from the **Perquimans County Chamber of Commerce**, (252) 426-5657. It is on Punch Alley right by the downtown waterfront and is open from 10 AM to 3 PM on weekdays. Downtown you'll find a plaque honoring native son Jimmy "Catfish" Hunter, who retired from the New York Yankees and returned home to run the family farm before his death in 1999.

Just a mile outside town in Perquimans County is the **Newbold-White House**. Built in the early 18th century, this two-story brick home is a well-preserved example of residential architecture. It is one of the oldest houses in North Carolina. The house is open March through November, Monday through Saturday from 10 AM to 4:30 PM, (252) 426-7567. There is a $3 admission fee for adults, $1 for children. During the off-season groups can call ahead and arrange for tours.

Edenton is built around Edenton Bay and the head of the Albemarle Sound. It's often touted as one of the prettiest towns in the South and was the center of Colonial government in North Carolina. This town of 5,000 has a wonderful historic district that's perfect for strolling. You'll find street after street of homes dating from the 18th and 19th centuries. For one couple we know, Edenton is their all-time favorite place to go for a romantic weekend away from the kids.

Before you get to Edenton, arm yourself with information from the Chowan County Tourism Development Authority, (800) 775-0111.

Once you're in town, start your tour at the **Historic Edenton Visitor Center**, housed in a pink Victorian house at 108 N. Broad Street, (252) 482-2637. It's open every day except Monday from 9 AM to 5 PM. You can watch a slide show, pick up maps and brochures or sign up for a guided tour of five 18th-century buildings. Included are **St. Paul's Episcopal Church**, begun in 1736; the courthouse; the **Cupola House**, a Jacobean-style residence dating from 1758; the **Barker House**, built in 1782; and the **James Iredell House**, built in 1773 and the home of the former U.S. Supreme Court Justice it's named for. While downtown be sure to stop by the **Chowan County Courthouse**, built in 1767, if for no other reason than to gaze at its green lawn that extends right to the bay. It's a gorgeous spot.

Restaurants

Barbecue is the food of choice for many visitors in this region. While you'll find other types of cuisine, be sure to work in at least one authentic North Carolina-style pork sandwich complete with a traditional vinegar sauce.

For some local flavor in Elizabeth City try **Tuck's Barbecue and Seafood Oyster Bar** on Route 17, (919) 335-1509. For some shoreline scenery with your meal, head to **Mulligan's Waterfront Grille** at 400 Water Street for sandwiches, soups and salads, (919) 331-2431. Seafood and other sandwiches are on the menu at the **Marina Restaurant** overlooking the river at the Camden Causeway, (919) 335-7307. **Thumper's Bar & Grill** at 200 N. Poindexter Street, (919) 333-1775, seasons food with a Southwestern and Cajun flair. A newcomer is **Cypress Creek Grill** at 218 N. Poindexter, (919) 334-9915. Seafood, pasta and Mexican food headline the menu.

In Hertford, Carolina-style barbecue is the local standout. Take your choice of longtime favorite **Captain Bob's BBQ & Seafood Restaurant** or **Tommy's Family Restaurant**. You'll find **Captain Bob's** on the Route 17 bypass, (919) 426-1811. **Tommy's** is on Edenton Highway, which is the same as Route 17 Business, (919) 426-5020. Both places also dish up a variety of other food in addition to their signature barbecue. In downtown Hertford, you can get a grilled sandwich at the fountain in **Woodard's Pharmacy**, 101 N. Church Street, (919) 426-5527. Top it off with a limeade or milk shake. Even if it's not lunchtime stop in for a dip of Ben & Jerry's ice cream at a bargain price. For homecooking try **Frankie's Hertford Cafe**, 127 N. Church Street (919) 426-5593. Outside town on **Snug Harbor Road**, **Anglers Cove Seafood Restaurant**, (919) 426-7294, specializes in seafood and is decorated entirely in nautical memorabilia. The most elegant restaurant around is the **Soundside Grill at Albemarle Plantation** outside town off Route 17 (919) 426-2252. The restaurant is in the golf course clubhouse and overlooks the Albemarle Sound.

In Edenton barbecue fans should check out **Lane's Family Barbecue** and its secret sauce at 421 E. Church Street a few blocks from downtown, (919) 482-4008. At **Waterman's Grill** on Broad Street you'll find a variety of sandwiches and salads as well as a great view of the bay, (919) 482-7733.

Another scenic spot is the **Creekside Restaurant** at 406 Queen Street. It overlooks Pembroke Creek and features eclectic dinners as well as lighter lunch fare. Call (252) 482-0118.

Accommodations

Bed and breakfast homes are a wonderful way to soak up the local flavor. In Elizabeth City you'll find The **Culpepper Inn**, a 1935 Colonial Revival house with a swimming pool. It has 11 guest rooms and is at 609 W. Main Street, (919) 335-1993. **Elizabeth City Bed & Breakfast** has two historic buildings, one a home built around 1898 and the other a fraternal lodge that dates from 1847. The buildings are at 108 E. Fearing Street in the midst of the historic district walking tour, (919) 338-2177. **The Church Street B&B** has two rooms right along a historic street. It is at 1108 W. Church St., (919) 335-1441.

Hertford has two delightful choices that can give you a blissful night in the country. At the **Beechtree Inn**, outside town just off Snug Harbor Road, guests can stay in either the 18th-century main house or a cozy cabin built around the early 19th century. Both are filled with period reproduction furniture made by the owners. The property includes a collection of 19th-century smokehouses, dairies and other outbuildings, (919) 426-7815.

Fans of plantation houses will feel right at home at 1812 on the **Perquimans**. This home with wonderful double verandas is outside town off Route 17 on a working farm on the Perquimans River. The owners have had their early 19th-century home in the family for generations and still cook in a kitchen connected to the main house only by a screened porch. Guests can borrow bicycles, a sailboat or a canoe, (919) 426-1812.

There also are two bed and breakfasts in vintage homes located right in Hertford. Staying in either of these puts you within strolling distance of downtown. The **Eagle and Anchor Bed and Breakfast** is at 215 W. Market Street, (252) 426-8382. **Covent Garden Inn** is on Covent Garden Lane, (252) 426-5945.

Edenton is renowned for its wonderful bed and breakfasts that specialize in pampering their guests. **The Lords Proprietors' Inn** at 300 N. Broad Street, (919) 482-3641 or (800) 348-8933, has three restored homes right in the historic district. There are 20 guest rooms in the homes that feature parlors and gracious front porches. The inn serves both breakfast and dinner.

Granville Queen Inn also is in the historic district at 108 S. Granville Street, (919) 482-5296. Furnishings from around the world provide the theme for nine guest rooms ranging from the Queen's Cottage to the exotic Egyptian Queen bedroom. Wake up to a five-course breakfast served on the porch in warmer months.

The **Captain's Quarters Inn**, 202 W. Queen Street, (919) 482-8945, puts a new twist on the bed and breakfast idea by offering two-night "sail and snooze" specials that include a three-hour sail on the Albemarle Sound. For a real adventure ask for Blackbeard the Pirate's Room. In addition to a three-course breakfast, you can opt for dinner at this 1907 home in the historic district.

INSIDERS' TIP

When driving on the Outer Banks, remember that the center lane of U.S. Highway 158 is for turning, not passing.

Governor Eden Inn at 304 N. Broad Street, (919) 482-2072, is a neoclassical-style home in the historic district. The **Trestle House Inn** is on a private estate on Soundside Road outside Edenton, (919) 482-2282. Built in 1972 it features exposed redwood beams milled from old railroad trestle timbers. Guests can fish in the inn's private lake or wander its extensive grounds.

Edenton's newest bed and breakfast is **Albemarle House** at 204 W. Queen Street, (919) 482-8204. This c. 1900 house is three blocks from the Albemarle Sound and is furnished with antiques and quilts. If you need to spread out, ask for the family suite. The owners serve a full breakfast and will be glad to give you sailing lessons or take you on a relaxing cruise.

Shopping

You'll find some antique shops along Route 17 and in Elizabeth City and Edenton. Outside Elizabeth City in Camden is the **Watermark Craft Co-op**, a must-see spot featuring the works of more than 700 craftspeople. It is on Highway 158 E. and is open daily from May through December. It closes on Sunday during winter months.

Downtown Elizabeth City has the **Pasquotank Arts Council Gallery** on Main Street featuring local arts and crafts. There also are a few antique stores.

In downtown Hertford, you'll find a traditional downtown with a hardware store, a pharmacy and other basic businesses. While downtown you can visit **The Wishing Well**, a craft shop. Stop in the **Hall of Fame Building** where you will find several antique stores as well as a shop run by the Perquimans County Art League.

Edenton has a gift shop in its visitors center on Broad Street as well as a few antiques stores near downtown.

North Carolina's Outer Banks

DAYTRIPS

A magical change will occur in your psyche as you sweep up onto the Wright Memorial Bridge and then coast down to the wonderland called the Outer Banks. We think it might have something to do with the calming vapors rising from the Currituck Sound. These strange and mesmerizing molecules will envelop all your hyper brain cells and numb them into a peaceful slumber that lasts as long as you stay on these fragile barrier islands. There's something special about the Outer Banks, with its laid-back attitude, long stretches of clean beaches and acres of protected flora, fauna and wildlife. To visit here is to shed the burdens of civilization without giving up any creature comforts or amenities. From accommodations to restaurants, shopping to historical sightseeing, this is a destination we always enjoy.

Getting There

From southside Hampton Roads, steer the car packed with beach chairs, sunscreen and coolers onto Interstate 64 E. Take the Battlefield Boulevard N. Exit (Va. Highway 168) and drive straight ahead to the Va. 168 Bypass to Nags Head. Don't worry if you miss the bypass, it connects back to Va. 168 on the other side of Chesapeake's Great Bridge area. Head straight on down Va. 168, which will turn into U.S. Highway 158 about 30 miles from the beach. (That's when those magic powers start taking over.) Aim for that mystical **Wright Memorial Bridge** and—bingo—you're in paradise. North Carolina's Outer Banks is only about 70 miles south of Hampton Roads, but depending on traffic, it can take you from 1½ hours to too long to tell to get there. But who cares? Summer weekends are especially crowded on the two-lane stretches of Va. 168, so plan your time accordingly.

Once you're on the Outer Banks you'll quickly find that you need to pay attention to the numbered milepost markers along the main road. You'll find locals using them as references when giving you directions.

Unless you're a regular on the Outer Banks, your first stop should be the **Aycock Brown Welcome Center** at the 2-mile post in Kitty Hawk. It is run by the Dare County Tourist Bureau and offers lots of brochures and free advice. The center is open from 9 AM to 5 PM daily off-season with longer hours in summer. Call (252) 261-4644. On Colington Road near milepost 8 the Outer Banks Chamber of Commerce Welcome Center also has a good stash of brochures, (252) 441-8144. Another place to stock up on information is the Dare County Tourist Bureau in Manteo at 704 S. Highway 64. Call (252) 473-2138 or (800) 446-6262. It is open from 8:30 AM to 5 PM weekdays and 10 AM to 4 PM on weekends and has a drive-up window for your convenience. The bureau also runs the Nags Head Visitor Center at Whalebone on Hwy 12, (252) 441-6644. It has some of the few restrooms available on this remote part of the island. The bureau also has a branch on Roanoke Island along Hwy. 64, (252) 473-6373. You'll find other visitor centers on Hatteras Island and Ocracoke Island.

Attractions

The beach.

Other attractions: It does rain occasionally on the Outer Banks, so here's where we would be forced to go if we couldn't splash in the Atlantic Ocean.

Use the 60-foot granite pylon on a mammoth dune, the **Wright Brothers Monument**, as a compass as you travel down the U.S. 158 Bypass road towards Kill Devil Hills. If you pretend it's December 17, 1903, you might just witness Wilbur Wright launch the world's first motorized flying machine off this dune and stay airborne for a full 12 seconds. This is where aeronautical history was birthed, and you can visit the re-created airstrip and rustic camp where Wilbur and brother Orville put the Outer Banks on the map here at the Wright Brothers National Memorial, (252) 441-7430. If you're here in June, you'll find yourself in the midst of modern examples of that original flying machine as they buzz through the air in the annual Wright Brothers Fly In and Airshow. There is a small entry fee at the National Park Service-run historic site, but it's well-worth it for all ages.

You'll see the next popular attraction even before you reach milepost 12 on Route 158 Bypass in Nags Head. It's the famous **Jockey's Ridge State Park**, (252) 441-7132, a sand dune that's a mile long, 12,000 feet wide and rising to 140 feet above sea level. It is 140 acres of playground for the physically fit, where you can hike to the top to catch spectacular views of the Atlantic Ocean on one side, the Roanoke Sound on the other. Kite-flying is a primo activity, and you can purchase some of the zaniest kites at Kitty Hawk Kites right at the foot of Jockey's Ridge at a little shopping center called the Kitty Hawk Connection. The center is also where those with a death-wish can sign the release form that will give them the stomach-churning pleasure of hang-gliding, monitored by experienced instructors. You have to make a reservation for the thrill of it all, so call (252) 441-4124 if you dare.

For a more down-to-earth experience with nature, why not try out the **Manteo Bike Path** that starts just past Pirate's Cove and ends up by the William B. Umstead Bridge over Croatan Sound. This winding ribbon of smooth black asphalt, connected by patches of sidewalk and wooden bridges, runs north of U.S. Highway 64 and weaves its way past the Fort Raleigh National Historical Site, the Elizabethan Gardens, businesses and homes on Roanoke Island. While you're at it, venture into downtown Manteo, where you'll find a quaint waterfront area with shops and restaurants. The path is a leisurely way to pedal, safe from traffic and an equally pleasant pathway for in-line skaters and joggers too.

If you have children, they'll have fun while also learning something about the country's first English settlement at **Roanoke Island Festival Park**. This state-run museum near Manteo features an 8,500-square-foot exhibition hall that opened in 1998. The museum highlights evolution of Roanoke Island and the Outer Banks from the 16th century, (252) 475-1500. Docked outside the museum is the *Elizabeth II*, a replica of the ship that brought the first settlers in 1585. The museum and ship are open year round. This is a good place to head if it is raining. Admission costs $8, $5 for children older than 6.

Another rainy day option is the **North Carolina Aquarium** on Roanoke Island, (252) 473-3493. Admission is free. For evening entertainment

Wheelwrights craft wheels for vehicles used at Colonial Williamsburg.

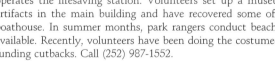

Photo: Colonial Williamsburg Foundation

take in *The Lost Colony* on Roanoke Island, (252) 473-3414, (800) 488-5012. This is the country's longest running outdoor drama. It relates the trials and tribulations of the first English settlement in North America. Tickets cost $16 for adults and $8 for children under 12. Ask about family night deals when you call for reservations.

Traveling south on N.C. Highway 12 towards Hatteras, you'll come to the quiet little town of Rodanthe. Here is the **Chicamacomico Life Saving Station**, restored to the glory it enjoyed back when it guarded the northern coast of Hatteras for 70 years. It was established by the U.S. Government in 1874. Today, the nonprofit Chicamacomico Historical Association oversees and operates the lifesaving station. Volunteers set up a museum of area lifesaving awards and artifacts in the main building and have recovered some of the lifesaving equipment for the boathouse. In summer months, park rangers conduct beach apparatus drills when funding is available. Recently, volunteers have been doing the costumed re-enactments because of federal funding cutbacks. Call (252) 987-1552.

Restaurants

Practically every restaurant on the Outer Banks offers three distinctive courses: seafood, seafood and seafood. We can almost guarantee that you will not be disappointed with any of these courses, and all you must choose is the atmosphere in which you want to join the clean-plate club. Like all Insiders, we have our favorites, and these are the places we highly recommend.

In the heat of the beach action is a quirky little place called **Awful Arthur's** that sits right across from the Avalon Fishing Pier at milepost 6 on the Beach Road in Kill Devil Hills, (252) 441-5955. If you don't have a brimming platter of their Alaskan crab legs washed down with Bass Ale straight from the tap, you might as well not even bother to come to the Outer Banks. It's casual, it's crowded and it's a good place to dive into the world of steamed seafood to slather with full-strength melted butter. If you pass on dessert, use those dollars to buy an Awful Arthur's T-shirt.

Point your car north towards the village of Duck and wheel into **Blue Point Bar and Grill**, (252) 261-8090, in the Waterfront Shops that dangle over the Currituck Sound. The 1940s-style diner will serve you unusual seafood dishes in the nouvelle cuisine manner, along with some sinful desserts whipped up fresh daily. Thanks to great food and articles in Southern Living and Gourmet, this place is packed seven days a week for both lunch and dinner. If you're claustrophobic, you might make a beeline for the outdoor dining deck. It's almost a necessity to call ahead for reservations at this more-than-popular little spot. Or try **Ocean Boulevard**, (252) 261-2546, at milepost 3 on the Beach Road in Kitty Hawk, an excellent venue by the same winning team. You'll find a superb wine list and an eclectic, creative menu.

A real insider's place in **John's Drive-In** on Hwy. 12 in Kitty Hawk, (252) 261-2916. This tiny drive-in has outrageous milk shakes and fruit and ice cream concoctions. Be sure to order the fish sandwich featuring whatever was caught that morning. Plan to get everything to go or head for the picnic tables outside since there is no inside seating.

If you're suffering sushi-withdrawal, check out **Tortuga's Lie Shellfish Bar and Grille** at milepost 11 on the Beach Road in Nags Head. Wednesday night is sushi night here, and, judging from the juggling to get a table, it's a sure sign of a global culinary invasion in this notoriously seafood town. Every night it's island-style cuisine, Bass Ale on tap and lots of locals. Give 'em a jingle at (252) 441-RAWW.

Several of our other favorites are **Penguin Isle**, (252) 441-2637, and **Owens Restaurant**, (252) 441-7309, in Nags Head; **Rundown Cafe**, (252) 255-0026, in Kitty Hawk; **Full Moon Café**, (252) 473-MOON and **Tranquil House Inn**, (252) 473-1587, in Manteo; and **Chilli Pepper's**, (252) 441-8081, in Kill Devil Hills. For the ultimate burger-and-shake lunch, hit the **Dairy Mart**, (252) 441-6730, in Nags Head or **Big Al's Soda Fountain & Grill** in Manteo, (252) 473-5570. The premier breakfast spot on the Outer Banks is **Sam and Omie's**, (252) 441-7366, in Nags Head. Order the country ham or eggs Benedict.

Shopping

One of the first signs that there is definitely a shopping experience in your Outer Banks future is **The Marketplace Shopping Center** you'll see on your left as you travel in on U.S. 158 towards the beach. There's an immaculate **Food Lion** for all the nibbles and cold drinks you'll require, along with some nifty shops including an excellent coffee shop called **Southern Bean**. There's also a cinema here showing first-run favorites.

Farther north in Corolla, you should visit the **Corolla Light Village Shops** and the **TimBuck II Shopping Center** for all kinds of clothing, book and gift shops. There's also a surf shop here.

Duck Village, south of Corolla and north of the main Outer Banks strip, is a shopper's heaven, with a plethora of small shops with gimcracks to fine art and clothing you'll not likely find anywhere else. You can weave in and out of one darling shopping plaza to another, like **Scarborough Faire** with the **Island Bookstore** and neighboring **Scarborough Lane Shoppes** with **Island Gear** clothing shop. Whip into the **Duck Waterfront Shops** for bargains at **Barree Station** and **Catalogue Outlet** and handcrafted fashions at **Donna's Designs**. A last must-stop is **The Lucky Duck** in Wee Winks Square. You'll not be able to resist the urge to touch every little thing in the place, including home accessories, cards, toys and games.

In Kitty Hawk, a trip to **Islander Flags** gets you a great souvenir to fly from your home. A trip to **Wave Riding Vehicles**, the Outer Banks' largest surf shop, is mandatory for all teens and pre-teens. In Kill Devil Hills, you'll find **The Dare Centre**, anchored by a Belks department store with all the fine clothing, cosmetics and shoes you might want.

You'll also find **Kmart** and **Wal-Mart** where, despite our conflicting feelings over seeing this type of commercialism entering the Outer Banks scene, you can find everything you might even think you need while on vacation. In Nags Head, **Glenn Eure's Ghost Fleet Gallery** is a fascinating art gallery where, if you're lucky, you'll find the gracious owners, Glenn and Pat, on hand to tell you all about the featured works. If you must have your mall-fix, there's the **Outer Banks Mall** with **Seamark Foods**, **Vintage Wave 70s store** and **Collector's Galley** with all kinds of collectibles. **Tanger Outlet Mall** is a must-see on the shopping circuit with everything for home and family at discount prices. **Pfaltzgraff Collector's Center**, **London Fog**, Bugle Boy and **Rack Room Shoes** are all here, among many others.

And, don't forget Manteo on Roanoke Island for shopping—or for a great break from the beach scene. Our absolutely favorite stop in this small town is **Manteo Booksellers**, one of the best book stores we have ever seen. You'll want to browse here all day. When you're finished here, spend the rest of the afternoon ambling around town and exploring shops like **My Secret Garden** with its home accessories and **Wanchese Pottery** where local potters are at work.

Don't leave Manteo without visiting the famous **Christmas Shop** on U.S. 64. Its rooms are filled with tinkling lights, ornaments and gifts of every description. Right next door is the **Weeping Radish**, where authentic German beer is brewed right on the premises. If there is a heaven after a hard day of shopping, it's sipping this nectar of the gods then indulging in a little something German.

Accommodations

Since the Outer Banks is a little farther-flung, we'll include accommodations options for you here. You do realize, we hope, that to try to pick out just a few of the worthy accommodations on the Outer Banks is almost as hard as picking out a restaurant. But, being the Insiders that we are, here goes.

Our top nod goes to a bed and breakfast in Manteo called the **White Doe Inn**. For beauty, pampering and peace, you can't find a better choice. Call for reservations at (252) 473-9851, (800) 473-6091. Other favorites in Manteo are the **Roanoke Island Inn**, situated on the waterfront, (252) 473-5511, (877) 473-5511 and **Tranquil House Inn**, also on the waterfront, (800) 458-7069 or (252) 473-1404. We also enjoy **Scarborough House Inn**, a Manteo bed and breakfast built to look like a classic seaside cottage, (252) 473-3849. In Nags Head, two of our favorites are the **Surf Side Motel**, (252) 441-2105, (800) 552-7873 and the **First Colony Inn**, (252) 441-2343, (800) 368-9390. In Kitty Hawk the **3 Seasons Bed & Breakfast** is the place for pampering, (252) 261-4791, (800) 847-3373. **Duck's Sanderling Inn Resort** is 12 acres of oceanside excellence, (252) 261-4111, (800) 701-4111. If you're on a tight budget check into the **Outer Banks International Hostel** in Kitty Hawk, (252) 261-2294.

INSIDERS' TIP

Smithfield's St. Lukes Church was built in 1632 and has been called "the most precious building in America."

For More Information

There are so many other fascinating places to wander on the Outer Banks that to discover every one you will need the *Insiders' Guide to North Carolina's Outer Banks*. In it you can get a full rundown on Manteo, Hatteras Island, Ocracoke Island, Oregon Inlet and Corolla, along with so many other wonderful hidden treasures just waiting for you to uncover.

Another resource is the **Dare County Tourist Bureau**. Call (800) 446-6262.

The Eastern Shore

The remote peninsula between the Chesapeake Bay and Atlantic Ocean is one of Virginia's best-kept secrets. "God's country" is what one person we know affectionately calls the Eastern Shore.

The 70-mile-long shore is the southernmost part of the Delmarva Peninsula that encompasses parts of Delaware, Maryland and Virginia. Physically it is connected to the Commonwealth of Virginia only by the Chesapeake Bay Bridge-Tunnel that links Virginia Beach and Cape Charles. But historically the Eastern Shore has been an important part of Virginia since it was settled in the early 1600s. Before that time Native Americans were the inhabitants, and their influence remains in the names of such locales as Nassawadox and Pungoteague.

In 1608 an expedition led by Jamestown Island's Capt. John Smith mapped much of what is now the Eastern Shore and its Chesapeake Bay and Atlantic Ocean islands. In 1614 the Jamestown government bartered with Native American residents and took possession of these lands. The English first settled here six years later at what was called Accomack Plantation, which in 1634 became one of the eight original Virginia counties.

In 1663 the region split into the two counties it retains today. Accomack and Northampton counties are home to 45,700 residents who live in rural areas or small towns. The largest town is Chincoteague with about 3,500 residents. Most towns have only 500 citizens or less. Many parts of the shore, particularly the Atlantic Ocean barrier islands, remain undisturbed wildlife havens thanks to more than three decades of preservation effort by The Nature Conservancy. The Virginia Coast Reserve, a Nature Conservancy subsidiary, owns 45,000 acres of the Eastern Shore, including 14 of the 18 barrier islands in the Atlantic Ocean. The Virginia Coast Reserve is the largest single landowner in the shore's two counties.

Both of the Eastern Shore's counties are agricultural centers renowned for growing Irish potatoes, Hayman sweet potatoes, azaleas and tomatoes. The Shore's 118,000 acres of croplands make this one of the most agriculturally productive parts of Virginia, and in the summer hundreds of migrant farm workers come to the Shore to pick the bounty. The Shore's abundant seafood harvest includes cherrystone clams and flounder.

There are numerous attractions throughout the Shore, but the most prominent are the Chincoteague National Wildlife Refuge and the Assateague Island National Seashore. Both are on Assateague Island, a barrier island that harbors wild horses and deer and is a bird-lover's paradise. The Eastern Shore has many other draws besides Assateague Island—outstanding hunting and fishing, historic homes and even a NASA museum. Many visitors come to chow down on fresh clams and crabs, unwind at country inns and just get away from it all. Summer is when beach-bound tourists flock to the Eastern Shore, but don't rule out the other seasons. Even in winter the Shore has its own special beauty, and generally mild weather lets you enjoy everything except swimming and sunbathing.

When driving on the Eastern Shore, at least occasionally steer off U.S. Highway 13, the Shore's boring main drag. On back roads you'll discover quaint fishing villages and historic towns with white clapboard homes. Because there is so much to see and do on the Eastern Shore, try to stay several days and soak up the local flavor. For a real treat, work in a trip to the Eastern Shore's Tangier Island in the Chesapeake Bay.

Tourist Information

There are three main sources of tourism information on the Eastern Shore. Virginia's Eastern Shore Tourism Commission, U.S. 13, Melfa, (757) 787-2460, produces a comprehensive travel guide for the entire region. You can request information by writing the commission at Box 460, Melfa, Virginia 23410. The commission shares quarters and a phone number with the Eastern Shore of Virginia Chamber of Commerce. The office is south of Melfa on U.S. 13. Stop by on weekdays from 8:30 AM to 5 PM, and during the same time on weekends and holidays from May through October. The Chincoteague Chamber of Commerce, 6733 Maddox Boulevard, Chincoteague, (757) 336-6161, promotes its island community and neighboring Assateague Island. The chamber has an office near the entrance to Assateague that is stocked with brochures. It is open Monday through Saturday from 9 AM to 4:30 PM. From mid-June through September the chamber also operates on Sundays from 12:30 to 4:30 PM. You can request information in advance by calling or writing P.O. Box 258, Chincoteague 23336. The Commonwealth of Virginia runs the New Church Welcome Center on U.S. 13 in New Church, (757) 824-5000, near the Maryland line. Besides providing information about the Eastern Shore, the office also includes brochures about attractions throughout Virginia. The center is open daily from 8:30 AM to 5 PM. You'll also find a Virginia Welcome Center that can clue you into attractions in the region and throughout the state.

Getting There

There's only one way to drive to the Eastern Shore from Virginia—up U.S. 13 and over the Chesapeake Bay Bridge-Tunnel, which consists of three bridges and two tunnels. You get on it in Virginia Beach off Northampton Boulevard. The toll is $10 each way, but don't sweat it, and consider the trip part of your adventure. Be sure to keep your lights on for safety—and turn them off later if it's daytime. Drive carefully since there's no room for error on the bridge-tunnel. In 1997, after several accidents, bridge officials outlawed passing on the bridge. Also known as the Lucius J. Kellam Jr. Bridge-Tunnel, this 23-mile structure divides the Chesapeake Bay from the body of water known as Hampton Roads. It was completed in 1964 after three and a half years of rigorous construction. The American Society of Civil Engineers was awed enough to name the Bay bridge-tunnel the outstanding engineering achievement of the year. It is the longest bridge-tunnel in existence and is one of the Seven Wonders of the Modern World. At their lowest points, the two tunnels dip 90 feet under the water.

In 1999 four years of construction produced a second set of bridges that merge into the roadway's two tunnels. This $250 million expansion project was designed to keep pace with bridge-tunnel traffic that is swelling by 7 percent a year.

When traveling along the bridge-tunnel you can take a break and fish from a 625-foot fishing pier along the way. Or just stop and admire the Chesapeake Bay from the overlook on the man-made Thimble Shoal Island about 3 miles out in the Bay. The rest stop includes a restaurant, a gift shop, restrooms and some interesting bridge-tunnel trivia to test your knowledge. For bridge-tunnel information call (757) 331-2960.

When you exit the bridge-tunnel, you will start your Eastern Shore adventure in a wildlife refuge that is home to deer and other creatures. Tune your radio to 1610 AM to hear recorded messages about the Eastern Shore of Virginia National Wildlife Refuge you are driving through. Once you're on the Eastern Shore, U.S. 13 leads you up the middle of the peninsula and into Maryland. Although this is the quickest route, it speeds you right by some of the most scenic parts of the Eastern Shore. Even though you're on a peninsula between the Chesapeake Bay and

Atlantic Ocean, you'll never see water unless you get off the main highway. Except for a few stately manor houses along U.S. 13 you'll mostly pass fireworks stands, small homes and an occasional McDonald's or gas station. Pull off U.S. 13 toward towns such as Cape Charles, Wachapreague, Accomac, Onley and Parksley, and you'll be treated to charming downtowns, fishing villages and restored houses several centuries old.

Pick up a copy of the free "Scenic Roads in Virginia" map published by the Virginia Department of Transportation and you'll see an easy way to take in the local scenery. Just over the bridge-tunnel at Kiptopeke you can veer onto Va. Route 600, which parallels U.S. 13. It will end at Va. Route 180 and give you the choice of going to the left toward Pungoteague or right toward Wachapreague. Either way will steer you onto other backroads that lead to Accomac or Onancock. Both are picturesque towns, and from either one you can quickly get back on U.S. 13. The scenic route is marked in green on the map.

Even without directions and a map, don't hesitate to venture off the main highway. The Eastern Shore is so flat and narrow that you can't get too lost. And if you do, your jaunt is likely to take you past creeks and notable architecture. You'll have no trouble finding a helpful resident to guide you back on course. Some travelers who frequently zip up U.S. 13 on their way to Maryland and points beyond always drive at least part of the trip on back roads.

To guide you on your Eastern Shore adventure, buy a copy of Off 13 - The Eastern Shore of Virginia Guidebook. Kirk Mariner, a minister and Eastern Shore native, first wrote this excellent book in 1987 and has updated it several times. The book provides insight into the approximately 40 communities that make up the Shore and is an excellent guide for steering you off U.S. 13.

In Chincoteague (pronounced shin-co-teague), there's only one way onto the island—down Va. Route 175 and over a causeway that takes you right to Main Street. Turn left and then right on Maddox Boulevard and you'll head right toward the bridge to Assateague Island. Most of the island's businesses are on these two streets. If you happen to ask directions of a local who tells you to get on Beach Road, remember that it is really Maddox Boulevard. The Beach Road name has been retired but many locals still give directions using the old moniker for Maddox Boulevard.

Attractions and Tours

The sister islands of Chincoteague and Assateague are the hands-down winners as the Eastern Shore's major attractions, with pristine beaches, wild horses and a variety of restaurants and accommodations. On Assateague, Mother Nature is chief planner, and you'll find no beachfront condos to spoil the view. Each year more than 1.5 million visitors come to these sister islands. Some vacation here because of the beach; others come to go bird-watching or to escape city life. Many visitors are drawn by the idyllic island lifestyle painted by author Marguerite Henry, who wrote the popular Misty of Chincoteague series starting in 1947.

Assateague Island

Assateague, an uninhabited barrier island with a 37-mile beach, is in both Virginia and Maryland and is adjacent to densely inhabited Chincoteague Island. All of Assateague is in the public domain as either the Chincoteague National Wildlife Refuge or the Assateague Island National Seashore. The U.S. Fish and Wildlife Service established the wildlife refuge in 1943 as a wintering area for migratory birds, and today it is home to more than 250 species. The refuge is on the Virginia end of Assateague. Also on the Virginia side of the island is Assateague Island National Seashore, managed by the National Park Service. The island's undeveloped seashore is the only place on the Eastern Shore to plunge into the Atlantic Ocean. Most of the other shoreline has marsh grasses and barrier islands separating the mainland from the ocean. Most of these uninhabited islands are owned by The Nature Conservancy, and some can be explored if you have access to a boat. On the Maryland side of Assateague is a state park that has the only camping spots on the island.

Admission onto Assateague from Virginia costs $4 a carload for a seven-day pass. Another option is a $12 pass that provides unlimited access for a year. You can get to Assateague by driving over a short causeway from Chincoteague. Once on the island you can hike, swim, picnic and bird-watch. There's no charge to walk or ride your bike onto Assateague by using the path that runs by the main road. It's about 3 miles to the beach.

There are numerous trails on the island, so be adventurous and tromp along marsh paths to look for waterfowl or hike the quarter-mile to the island's distinctive red-and-white 1833 lighthouse. Most of the island is accessible only by foot or bike. Just watch out for posted areas where birds nest. Bring along your binoculars and camera. On one visit we spotted deer, herons, pelicans, ducks, swans, geese and the wild horses that are Assateague's most famous inhabitants. Legend has it that the horses are descendants of mustangs who swam ashore when a Spanish ship wrecked offshore in the 16th century. They are the stars of the July pony swim, penning and auction that has benefited the Chincoteague Volunteer Fire Department since 1925. Each year as many as 50,000 people come to see the wild horses up close at this event. Two national visitors centers on the Virginia side of the island provide maps, information and occasional guided walks and talks.

Visitors Centers

Chincoteague National Wildlife Refuge Visitor Center
Assateague Island
• (757) 336-6122

This U.S. Fish and Wildlife Service visitor center is the first place to stop for information after entering Assateague Island. To get there take the first left on the island. During winter the center usually closes on Thursday. Otherwise it is open daily from 9 AM to 4 PM. Admission is free once you've paid to get on the island. Here you can pick up brochures, buy birding books, ask questions or watch a video about the island. Children will enjoy the touch table where they can get their hands on oyster shells, horse skulls and antlers found on the island. In warmer months interpreters give talks about the island during special programs.

Tom's Cove Visitor Center
Assateague Island
• (757) 336-6577

This visitors center is run by the National Park Service. If you remain on the island and follow the signs for the beach you'll find it. In the off-season, hours are usually 9 AM to 4 PM daily, but in the summer months they're 8 AM to 6 PM. Like the other visitors center, admission is free once you've paid to be on the island. Inside is an aquarium, displays that focus on the wildlife on Assateague, well-informed staff members and a small shop with books about the island. In the summer there are programs that range from bird walks to surf-fishing demonstrations.

Excursions

There are several private companies providing educational tours and programs that focus on the beauty and wildlife of Assateague Island. Signing up for one of these excursions gives you a new perspective on wildlife in this remote region.

Assateague Adventures
6273 Maddox Blvd., Chincoteague
• (757) 336-6565, (757) 336-6144, (800) 221-7490

Group lectures and tours on the ecology and traditions of Chincoteague and Assateague islands are the specialty of this company, which is affiliated with The Mariner Motel (see our Accommodations section). Topics range from decoy carving to wildlife photography. Participants can opt for package programs that come with lodging at the motel. Packages are offered only to groups, and prices vary.

Assateague Island Tours
Assateague Island
• (757) 336-6154, (757) 336-6798

Take a 14.5-mile trip through the Chincoteague National Wildlife Refuge. The trip lasts 90 minutes as narrators focus on the history of the area as well as what's going on today and the likely future. You're likely to spot some wild horses as you travel on a tour bus from the Chincoteague Wildlife Refuge Visitors Center. Trips are made daily in April, May and September. During summers there are two tours a day. The cost is $7 for adults, $3.50 for children. New in 1997 were boat tours around the island for $15 a person. Reservations are a must for the boat trip. Unless it's peak season, you don't need them for the bus tour. You can make reservations by phone or at the visitors center, which is on Assateague Island, (757) 336-6154 or (757) 336-3700. Call for exact departure times.

Captain Barry's Back Bay Cruises
Landmark Plaza, Chincoteague
• (757) 336-6508

This cruise company provides a variety of options for visitors who yearn to get out on the water. You can take bird-watching expeditions, trips that include crabbing and clamming or romantic evening cruises. Costs range from $15 to $30 a person depending on the type of cruise. Boats depart daily from late spring through early fall from Landmark Plaza at the end of Main Street.

Chincoteague View
Curtis Merritt Harbor, S. Main St., Chincoteague
• **(757) 336-3409, (757) 336-6861**

Take your choice of a one-hour cruise along Assateague Channel for $10, a two-hour cruise that also goes into the ocean for $15 or a charter-fishing trip for $30. Passengers also can book a tailor-made cruise that takes them to a remote beach known mostly to natives and accessible only by boat. Boats go out daily from spring through mid-November.

Island Cruises Inc. of Chincoteague
7058 Maddox Blvd., Chincoteague
• **(757) 336-5593, (757) 336-5511**

From spring through fall this company shows off local scenery with guided boat tours on The Osprey. The boat leaves from the Town Dock twice daily from June through August. Trips last 90 minutes and cost $10 per person. Reservations can be made by calling ahead or stopping by the cruise office, which is in the Refuge Motor Inn (see our Accommodations section).

Chincoteague Island

Chincoteague bills itself as Virginia's only resort island. One regular we know who vacations here at least once a year says Chincoteague has "a special spirit" that keeps drawing her back. The Norfolk resident particularly likes to rendezvous here with relatives from New York since the island is a convenient meeting spot for the entire family. Traditionally Chincoteague was a fishing community renowned for its oysters. It's only 7 miles long and 1.5 miles wide and is considered the gateway to uninhabited Assateague.

Chincoteague is a charming island loaded with motels, gift and craft shops, bed and breakfast inns and seafood restaurants. Main Street is a fun place to wander with its shops selling decoys, T-shirts and crafts. If you have a *Misty of Chincoteague* fan in your family, walk by Miss Molly's Inn at 4141 Main Street in Chincoteague. This is where author Marguer-

ite Henry lived while writing the first Misty book. You can also check in for a night's stay at the inn. In the summer of 1997 a Misty of Chincoteague statue was installed in town to pay tribute to its most famous former resident.

There are two interesting museums and an aquarium in Chincoteague plus a NASA center right outside town These are good places to work into your itinerary when you're ready for a break from the beach or when rain puts a damper on your outdoor plans.

Island Aquarium
6160 Main St., Chincoteague
• **(757) 336-6508**

A new diversion on the Eastern Shore in 1997 was an aquarium affiliated with Captain Barry's Back Bay Cruises. It's located in Landmark Plaza. Visitors can peruse a touch tank, string-ray tank, a marsh exhibit and other aquatic displays. The aquarium is open from 9 AM to 1 PM and from 5 to 10 PM daily from April through October. On rainy days, it stays open all day. Admission costs $3, $2 for children.

The Oyster and Maritime Museum
7125 Maddox Blvd.
• **(757) 336-6117**

Since 1965 this museum has celebrated Chincoteague's heritage by focusing on its longstanding oyster industry. The museum, which expanded in 1996, includes displays of oyster tools and shells. The museum is open April through November from 10 AM to 5 PM Monday through Saturday. On Sundays it is open from noon to 4 PM. Admission costs $2, $1 for children.

Refuge Waterfowl Museum
7059 Maddox Blvd.
• **(757) 336-5800**

Artistic duck decoys are the stars of this museum. The waterfowl museum highlights the history of decoy carving and includes information on all kinds of birds. It is open from 10 AM to 5 PM daily from April through mid-October. Admission costs $2.50, $1.50 for children.

NASA/Wallops Visitor Center
Va. Rt. 175
• **(757) 824-1344, (757) 824-2298**

This NASA center is 5 miles outside Chincoteague. It is a high-tech museum that highlights the U.S. space program, particularly the balloon and rocket experiments carried out across the road at the Wallops Flight Facility.

Wallops is affiliated with NASA's Goddard Space Flight Center. Displays include space suits, a moon rock and rocket-launching films. Admission is free. The visitors center is open Thursday through Monday from 10 AM to 4 PM from March through June and from September through November. In July and August the center opens seven days a week from 10 AM to 4 PM. The center closes from December through February.

Other Shore Attractions

Once you leave Assateague and Chincoteague, you'll find the rest of the Eastern Shore's attractions scattered throughout its length. Travelers who love to wander will have no trouble amusing themselves viewing historic houses and other bits and pieces of the Shore's heritage. While driving around the Eastern Shore, be sure to admire its unique historic architecture. There are more than 400 buildings that date from before 1865. The Eastern Shore has its own indigenous architecture— the big house/little house/colonnade/kitchen style that was common by the end of the 1700s. These houses evolved when someone built a home, added on another part and then another until you had an incredibly long house with varying roof lines (see our close-up in this chapter).

Heading south from Chincoteague on U.S. 13, take time to check out Parksley. This is a nicely restored Victorian town that grew up along a once-vibrant rail line. You can still get a sense of the railroad's importance in the Eastern Shore Railway Museum. A new addition to town's tourism offerings is the Accomack Northampton Antique Car Museum, which is affiliated with the train museum.

Eastern Shore Railway Museum
235 Main St., Parksley
• (757) 665-RAIL
Train buffs will have fun in this downtown Parksley museum, which opened in 1989. In 1996 it moved from the tiny train depot it had occupied to larger quarters across the road. The new location lets the museum better display its 3,000 artifacts that showcase the old New York, Philadelphia and Norfolk line that once ran through town. Tours are available of the 1906 depot that used to house the museum. Outside it are several train cars, including a 1927 observation car and a 1933 lounge car. The museum is open from 10 AM to 4 PM Tues-

day through Saturday. On Sundays it is open from 1 to 4 PM. It closes on Monday. Admission costs $1 for adults. Children 12 and younger visit for free.

Affiliated with the Railway Museum is the Worcester Accomack Northampton Daycoach (W.A.N.D.), which hooks up the antique train cars several times a year and hauls passengers from Parksley to other Eastern Shore towns. For information call (757) 665-6271 or (800) 852-0335.

Accomack Northampton
Antique Car Museum
235 Main St., Parksley
• (757) 665-7245
The museum opened in 1996 in a room attached to the Eastern Shore Railway Museum. It shows off about 10 vintage cars, including a 1951 Rolls-Royce, a 1927 Ford and two Model Ts. Admission is $1 for adults. Children 12 and younger get in free. The museum is open the same hours as the train museum - from 10 AM to 4 PM Tuesday through Saturday and on Sunday from 1 to 4 PM.

Villages

For a dose of history stop by Accomac and walk through the downtown area, where you'll see from the outside a 1784 Debtor's Prison and more restored Colonial architecture than anywhere in Virginia except Colonial Williamsburg. Onancock is another picture-perfect waterfront village with enough historic structures to warrant a walking tour. The Eastern Shore Tourism Commission and town merchants have free maps of Onancock available.

The many restored homes include one you can visit: Kerr Place, 787-8012. This Federal mansion is on Market Street, the town's main road. It was built in 1799 and is owned by the Eastern Shore of Virginia Historical Society, which opens the house to the public Tuesday through Saturday from 10 AM to 4 PM from March through December. It costs $3 to tour Kerr Place (pronounced "Car" Place). Also in Onancock is Hopkins & Brothers Store at the end of Market Street on Onancock Creek, (757) 787-4478. This is one of the oldest general stores still operating on the East Coast and is on the National Register of Historic Places. Merchandise includes dry goods as well as arts and crafts. The store, which shuts down some in the winter, also has a restaurant that serves seafood and steaks. In summer a boat ferries passengers from the store's dock to Tangier Island. (See our write-up on Tangier Island in this chapter).

In Locustville you can see the exterior of Locustville Academy, the Shore's only surviving school of higher education from the 1800s. Although it's usually closed, you can arrange to go inside by calling (757) 787-7480. In Willis Wharf visitors can call in advance and arrange to spend the day on a typical farm. Since 1993 longtime farmers Phil and Barbara Custis have welcomed city slickers to their sprawling Custis Farms near Willis Wharf. Visits include a hayride, lunch and the chance to observe the Custises cultivating potatoes, planting azaleas or doing other seasonal work. Call ahead at (757) 442-4121 or (800) 428-6361 to arrange group tours and get directions to the farm.

In Wachapreague, overlooking Atlantic Ocean barrier islands, visitors can pass the time watching the fishing fleets come in or arrange their own fishing trip by calling Wachapreague Marina at 787-2105. History and genealogy buffs will enjoy Eastville, where the downtown courthouse holds the oldest continuous court records in America dating from 1632. Cape Charles is a Victorian town created as a railroad terminus along the Chesapeake Bay. The town's main road ends right at the Bay where you'll find a gazebo, pier overlooking the water and walkways over the dunes. The center of town features several streets of vintage houses, many of which are undergoing restoration.

A walking-tour map available from the Eastern Shore Tourism Commission or the Cape Charles Museum and Visitors Center will guide you along the town's attractive residential streets. The museum and visitors center opened in 1996 on Va. Route 184 just before you get to town. It's housed in an old power plant and welcomes visitors during warmer months on Saturdays from noon to 5 PM and Sundays from 2 to 5 PM or by appointment, (757) 331-1008. The museum, which closes in winter, features photos of old Cape Charles and other displays relating to the town.

While you're in Cape Charles stop by Charmar's Antiques at 211 Mason Avenue, on the main downtown street, and ask to visit the country store museum next door, (757) 331-1488. Both are owned by Charles and Margaret Carlson, who are happy to show off their collection. The informal museum is open only by request but is worth asking about if you love Americana. Inside are hundreds of typical general store items, and none are for sale. You'll find a well-worn butcher block, brass cash reg-

isters and shelves lined with hundreds of patent medicine bottles. The Carlsons charge no fees to show off their collection, but there is a box on the counter where you can leave donations.

Natural Areas

Much of the Eastern Shore's attraction is its isolation and untamed lands. To get a feel for this remote area visit some of the natural areas open to the general public. These don't draw the big crowds like Assateague Island, but they are fascinating places to wander. At the southern end of the Eastern Shore just before the bridge-tunnel are Kiptopeke State Park and the Eastern Shore of Virginia National Wildlife Refuge. Both are just off U.S. 13 and are among the best locations on the East Coast for bird watching.

Eastern Shore of Virginia National Wildlife Refuge
U.S. Hwy. 13, Kiptopeke
• (757) 331-2760

The 725-acre wildlife refuge, which is adjacent to the Chesapeake Bay Bridge-Tunnel, is a major rest stop for migrating birds. Birding is at its best here from September through May. The refuge is open from dawn to dusk daily, and admission is free. In 1996 the refuge introduced its renovated and enlarged visitors center. It's equipped with $300,000 in electronic equipment, including videos and hands-on exhibits. Old favorites include a sandbox stocked with pelicans' bills, whale bones, shells and other beach objects. One popular spot is the huge viewing window overlooking a salt pond. It's equipped with binoculars, telescopes and birding guides to test your knowledge of the nearly 300 bird species that have been spotted at the refuge. There's also a short educational film and a display of duck decoys. Outside is a walking trail that leads through a maritime forest of loblolly pine, shrub thickets and holly. While the refuge opens a half-hour before dawn and closes a half-hour after dusk, the visitors center has more limited hours. From March through December it is open from 9 AM to 4 PM daily. Winter hours are 10 AM to 2 PM Friday through Sunday.

Kiptopeke State Park
3540 Kiptopeke Rd., Cape Charles
• (757) 331-2267

Kiptopeke State Park, which opened in 1992 at an old ferry stop, is one of Virginia's newest state parks. Its 375 acres border on the Chesapeake Bay and include areas for swimming, picnicking and camping. There also is a boat ramp, a fishing pier and a 1.5-mile hiking trail. Naturalists frequently lead programs in the summer that range from crabbing to campfire talks. The water here is shallow and the sand is white along the half-mile beach, making this an ideal family swimming spot. Lifeguards are on duty during the summer. Fishing is excellent at the park, thanks to the nine surplus World War II concrete ships sunk 1,500 feet offshore. The park is open from 8 AM to dusk daily with free admission. During the winter the campgrounds are closed but the rest of the park remains open. While here you may find volunteers banding birds for population studies. Since 1963 they have tagged more than 225,000 migratory birds. The park also has a hawk observatory where volunteers have observed more than 12 species of birds of prey.

INSIDERS' TIP

It's a free call from Hampton Roads to Cape Charles. However, you'll need to dial 1 and the 757 area code to reach the rest of the Eastern Shore.

Tangier Island

One of the most interesting parts of the Eastern Shore is Tangier Island—the most remote spot in Virginia. The island sits in the Chesapeake Bay, and you can get there by commercial boat from Onancock, Reedville (in Virginia's Northern Neck area) or Crisfield, Maryland.

Constant erosion has reduced this island in the Chesapeake Bay to only a mile wide and three miles long. Although it is part of Accomack County on the Eastern Shore, the island is 14 miles west of the Eastern Shore and 17 miles east of Reedville in the Northern Neck of Virginia.

Legend has it that Capt. John Smith discovered Tangier Island in 1608 and that Indians traded the island in 1666 to John West for two overcoats. The first permanent settler, John Crockett, arrived in 1686 with his sons and their families. By the 19th century there were 100 residents—half of them Crocketts. The island was used primarily to graze livestock.

During the Revolutionary War the British found Tangier Island a perfect base for raiding American ships. Pirates also found it a great hideaway. After the war, watermen began settling here. From 1808 through 1858 up to 10,000

people swelled the island each summer for Methodist camp meetings. The British again occupied the island during the War of 1812.

Since 1866 Tangier's residents—many of them still named Crockett—have depended on the Chesapeake Bay for their livelihood, with crabs being the primary catch. The island boasts that it is the soft-shell crab capital of the world, and when you arrive by boat you'll spot the soft-shell crab "farms" along the shore.

The island itself is the main draw. What you'll find is a tightly knit fishing community with fewer than 800 residents, many of them related. The island is no more than 7 feet above sea level with a small beach. The terrain is flat, with 80 percent of it covered with marsh, wetlands and water. In the summer you won't find much shade or many cool breezes so bring along a hat and sunscreen. Tangier residents are clustered in three communities known as "ridges," connected by roads that are little more than paths. Most people get around by foot, bicycle or motorized golf carts. Besides houses the island has one school, a post office and two grocery stores.

Except for the tourism trade, crabbing and clamming are the ways most families earn their livings. Residents are descended from generations of hardy watermen. Their isolation gives them a distinct accent that still rings with the Elizabethan tones of their forebears.

Most people stay only a couple of hours on the island, which gives enough time to grab a seafood lunch and stroll around. Tour guides wait for visitors at the dock and will give you a spin through the island on golf carts for about $2 a person. If you want to spend the night, there are three small guest houses. See this chapter's Accommodations section for details.

Getting There

You have several choices for arriving on Tangier Island. If you have your own boat, you can sail from Onancock, Saxis or Crisfield, Maryland, on the Eastern Shore. From the western shore of Virginia, you can leave from Reedville. At Tangier, you can dock at Parks' Marina, (757) 891-2567. For a quick trip to Tangier Island from the Eastern Shore, you can charter a plane. Call Chesapeake Aviation Inc.

Big House/Little House/ Colonnade/Kitchen style

Drive around the Eastern Shore, and you're bound to see examples of its distinctive vernacular architecture—the big house/little house/colonnade/kitchen style. These practical homes originated on the Shore in the 1600s and are still being built today.

In a typical 17th- or 18th-century scenario, a farming family would build a small wooden house with a detached kitchen. Later they might enclose the space between the house and kitchen with a colonnade or porch. As their family and fortune grew, they would attach a bigger house to the little house. The result was a long dwelling with a series of varying roof lines.

"If you are adding onto a structure, this is the easiest way to do it," says architectural historian L. Floyd Nock III, who lives in a historic house in Onancock. The little house portion of his residence was built around 1810. The big house was added in 1830. The original colonnade and kitchen were replaced in 1985 giving Nock's home a 175-year time span from start to finish.

"It is a very livable house," says Nock, who owns Shore Restorations and Designs. "We live in one end. When we have company, we can open up the other end."

Typical Shore houses in the vernacular style were only one room deep to take advantage of summer breezes. They used native woods for construction - pine for flooring, cedar and cypress for shingles, and cypress or pine for siding. The exteriors typically were whitewashed.

No one knows exactly how many big house/little house/colonnade kitchen-style houses there are scattered throughout the Shore, but there are dozens used today as private residences. There also are houses built in a variation on the traditional theme. At Holly Brook Plantation on U.S. 13 near Eastville, the colonnade comes between the big house and the little house. The original part of Holly Brook dates

Holly Brook Plantation is one of the Shore's longest houses.

Photo: Eastern Shore Tourism Commission

from the early 1700s. The Association for Preservation of Virginia Antiquities owns the house and leases it privately.

At The Haven, a private residence on Back Street in downtown Accomac, there is no colonnade. The Haven actually has six sections and is as long as half a football field. Its earliest part dates to 1794. The Haven and Holly Brook are two of the longest houses on the Shore.

The best way to see the houses is to buy a copy of Off 13 - The Eastern Shore of Virginia Guidebook by Kirk Mariner. This handy book gives specific directions for traveling the backroads and details the historic houses you'll see along the way. If you want to spend the night in a traditional big house/little house/colonnade/kitchen-style house, you can choose from Bayview or Wynne Tref. Both these bed and breakfast homes are in the country. Bayview is near Belle Haven, (757) 442-6963 or (800) 442-6966. Wynne Tref, a big house/little house variation, is near Locustville, (757) 787-2356. (See the bed and breakfasts listings in this chapter). Holly Brook also takes guests by special arrangement, (757) 768-7195.

in Melfa at (757) 787-2901. Commercial boats ferry visitors from three locations: Onancock, Reedville and Crisfield, Maryland. On the way over narrators clue you in on details about the Chesapeake Bay and life on Tangier Island. The trip over is a pleasant one, with sea gulls or geese flying overhead and fishermen at work in the Bay. Contact the following commercial boats for rides over.

Tangier and Onancock Cruises
Mailboat Dock, Tangier Island
• **(757) 787-8220**

The island-based Captain Eulice picks up passengers in Onancock on the mainland. It leaves from Onancock Wharf right by Hopkins & Brothers Store, which is at the end of Market Street on the waterfront. Tangier and Onancock Cruises operates the 90-passenger boat from June 1 through September 15 every day but Sunday. The boat leaves at 10 AM and arrives at Tangier one and a half hours later. The return trip starts at 1:30 PM, bringing you back to Onancock by 3 PM. Round-trip tickets cost $18, half-price for children between 6 and 12 years old. Preschoolers ride free. For information call (757) 891-2240. Although reservations aren't required for individuals, call in advance if it's peak tourist season.

The cruise company also offers a no-frills trip from Crisfield, Maryland—about a 50-minute drive past Onancock. You can hitch a ride on the mail

boat that leaves Crisfield Monday through Saturday at 12:30 PM. It heads back to the mainland from Tangier at 8 AM the next day (except for Sunday). The mail boat plies the waters year round. The cost is $10 each way. Don't expect any official narration except for your conversation with the captain, a Tangier native. If you take the mail boat, plan to spend the night on the island since it won't return to the mainland until the next morning.

Tangier Island Cruises
1001 W. Main St., Crisfield, Md.
• **(410) 968-2238**

The Steven Thomas, a 300-passenger boat, leaves daily May 15 through October from City Dock on Main Street. The boat departs at 12:30 PM and arrives at Tangier at 1:45 PM. You'll have a few hours to wander around before heading back at 4 PM. You'll dock in Crisfield at 5:15 PM. The cost is $20 for adults, with anyone younger than 12 riding for free. Reservations are recommended for groups of 20 or more. Call for reservations or information.

Tangier & Rappahannock Cruises Inc.
Va. Rt. 656, Reedville
• **(804) 453-2628**

From the western shore of Virginia, the Chesapeake Breeze ferries passengers from May through October 15. It starts out running on weekends and ends with the same schedule. From mid-May through early

INSIDERS' TIP

One tradition of longtime Chincoteague vacationers is winding up the day with ice cream. Popular spots are Muller's at 4034 Main Street, (757) 336-5894; Mr. Whippy at 4121 Main Street, (757) 336-6313; and Island Creamery Ice Cream at 6243 Maddox Boulevard, (757) 336-6236.

October it sails daily. The boat leaves from outside Reedville, a Victorian fishing village, at 10 AM and returns about 3:30 PM. The trips takes one hour and 45 minutes. The cost is $18.50 for adults. Children between 4 and 13 ride for $9.25, and those younger than 4 ride for free. Reservations are a must.

Accommodations and Restaurants

Chesapeake House
$ • Main St., Tangier Island
• (757) 891-233120

Comfortable rooms, full breakfasts and a family-style seafood dinner are designed for Tangier Island visitors. Prices are downright cheap. The dining room is also open to the public for dinner. This longtime-favorite inn is open April through October.

Shirley's Bay View Inn
$ • West Ridge Rd., Tangier Island
• (757) 891-2396

This Tangier Island bed and breakfast is in one of the island's oldest homes. The house was built in 1806 and has six guest rooms with shared baths. Guests enjoy full breakfasts. The hosts will pick you up at the boat dock in a golf cart. The inn is open year round.

Sunset Inn
$ • West Ridge Rd., Tangier Island
• (757) 891-2535

The sunsets are spectacular from this beachfront home on Tangier Island. Guests have a choice of rooms in the main house or cabins outside. The inn serves full breakfasts and is open year round.

Recreation

The great outdoors beckon on the Eastern Shore. The Eastern Shore's tidal marshes attract about 300 species of waterfowl and shorebirds. This East Coast flyway for migrating birds is one of the finest areas in the country for bird watching. In fact, the United Nations has named the Virginia Coast Reserve along the Eastern Shore as one of the few remaining Biosphere Reserves left in the world. In spring and fall the Shore boasts some of the world's highest bird counts.

Some of the best birding on the shore is in the public domain. For starters try Kiptopeke State Park, the Eastern Shore of Virginia National Wildlife Refuge or Assateague Island. For other suggestions on where to spy special birds, buy a copy of Curtis Badger's Birdwatcher's Guide to Virginia's Eastern Shore. Virginia's Eastern Shore Tourism Commission offers a free pamphlet that's a guide to the types of birds that frequent the Eastern Shore. Inside is a list for you to check off the birds you encounter.

Hunters enjoy seasons for deer, dove, duck and 12 other animals. Saltwater fishermen can go bayside or seaside for their catch. Their prime season stretches from May through November and includes everything from sea bass to shark and red drum. There are many charter boats and head boats that take you out with a crew that grew up fishing off the Shore. You also will find small boat rentals. Wachapreague, the flounder capital of the world, has the greatest number of charter boats. However, Cape Charles, Chincoteague and other coastal towns also have rental boats available. Virginia's Eastern Shore Tourism Commission can provide listings of charter boats. The commission also publishes a helpful hunting and fishing guide.

The flat, scenic Eastern Shore is perfect for bicycling, and within the last several years cycling tours have gained a following on the Shore. Eastern Shore Escapes, which is affiliated with The Nature Conservancy, arranges weekend bicycle outings that include stays in bed and breakfasts on the Shore. Other package tours revolve around birding and kayaking. For details call (757) 442-9412 or (888) VA-SHORE or write the organization at Box 395, Belle Haven, 23306. If you want to plan your own outing, call Citizens for a Better Eastern Shore, (757) 678-7157, and order a copy of the Between the Waters guide. You can write for a copy at P.O. Box 882, Eastville 23347.

Annual Events

No matter what time of year you visit the Eastern Shore, there's bound to be some type of celebration going on. Folks on the Shore can always find an excuse to get together for fun and good food. Throughout the year, the various communities hold numerous fund-raisers, events and festivities, focusing on island culture, wildlife and, of course, seafood.

The Shore's abundance of native seafood and homegrown produce means you'll need to put off any thoughts of dieting until you're safely back home. Check with the Eastern Shore of Virginia Chamber of Commerce, (757) 787-2560, or Chincoteague Chamber of Commerce, (757) 336-6161, for exact dates of annual events. If your visit coincides with a festival or carnival, be sure to stop by for some of the best seafood you'll ever eat. These small-town festivals and carnivals let you run elbows with locals and help you see first hand the pride they take in their communities.

You're forewarned that some of the most popular events require advance planning. While you can just roll into town for the Parksley Spring Festival or Railroad Days in Exmore, don't expect to do that for Chincoteague's July Pony Swim. This event is known worldwide thanks to the popular *Misty of Chincoteague* books. Each year huge crowds of families jockey for space on the compact island to see the

Please note that we do not include specific route addresses for the following events - you won't need them. Eastern Shore towns are compact and easy to negotiate and often don't have marked road names. Simply look around for the throngs of festival-goers, and you'll know you're in the right place.

March/April

Easter Decoy and Art Festival
Chincoteague
Chincoteague High School
• (757) 336-6161

Handcarved decoys are featured along with other crafts at this event that is always held on Easter weekend. It is sponsored by the Chincoteague Chamber of Commerce.

Spring Craft Show
Chincoteague
• (757) 336-6117,
(757) 336-5606

The Oyster and Maritime Museum sponsors this one-day show and sale in early April at Chincoteague High School. It features a variety of handmade craft items.

Indulge! It's all-you-can-eat oyster feast at the Chincoteague Island Oyster Festival in October.

Photo: Courtesy of Chincoteague Chamber of Commerce

Wachapreague
Spring Flounder
Tournament
Wachapreague
• (757) 787-2105

Saltwater anglers compete during the last two weeks in April to see who can haul in the mightiest flounder. The tournament is sponsored by the Wachapreague Hotel. Entry costs $30 a person. More than $2,000 in cash and prizes is up for grabs.

horses. You'd better have hotel, bed and breakfast or campground reservations well in advance. During pony penning time most Chincoteague establishments require you to stay an entire week.

Advance tickets are required for the May Seafood Festival and the October Harvest Fest as well as the Chincoteague Oyster Festival scheduled the same month. These are all-you-can-eat affairs known for the quality of their seafood. They are sponsored by the local chambers of commerce and have loyal followings of people who drive to the shore from other parts of Virginia just to eat. In fact, some outsiders join the local chambers just to have first crack at buying tickets since they sell out far in advance.

Historic Home and Garden Tour
Various Eastern Shore locations
• (757) 787-7161, (757) 678-7889

This is part of a statewide home and garden tour. The Eastern Shore's tour is always on the fourth Saturday of April. Each year different historic homes throughout the region are open for visitation for the day. It's worth a drive over just to see them. Tickets for the entire tour cost $15. A box lunch is usually sold at a church along the tour route.

May

Seafood Festival
Tom's Cove Campground, Chincoteague
• (757) 787-2460

This is one of the Eastern Shore's most popular annual events, and the $30 tickets usually sell out in advance. Virginia politicians and people who live hundreds of miles away drive over to sample some of the best seafood around. (Hint: don't miss the bags of steamed little neck clams. They're heavenly.) The festival, which started in 1968, is always on the first Wednesday in May. The festival is sponsored by the Eastern Shore of Virginia Chamber of Commerce.

International Migratory Bird Celebration
Chincoteague
• (757) 336-6122

The Chincoteague National Wildlife Ref-

Wild ponies graze on Assateague Island. The history of the wild ponies fascinates visitors from around the world.

Photo: Courtesy of Chincoteague Chamber of Commerce

uge is the setting for a weekend of workshops, nature walks and other activities geared toward bird watchers. This free mid-May event drew 7,000 visitors the first time it was held in 1996 and the numbers continue to grow.

Railroad Days
Exmore
• (757) 442-4546

The Exmore Railroad Museum Society

sponsors this free, one-day event that includes a parade, bake sale and small-town celebration in downtown Exmore.

June

Parksley Spring Festival
Parksley
• (757) 665-6161

The Parksley Merchants Association flings out the welcome mat for a free downtown celebration that includes music, food booths, a display of antique cars and even helicopter rides.

Chincoteague Power Boat Regatta
Chincoteague
• (757) 336-6161

Inboard speed boats take to the water during weekend races and displays sanctioned by the American Power Boat Association. This event started in 1996. Chincoteague is one of 60 national sites for the power boat regattas. There is no charge to watch the action.

Onancock Fireman's Carnival
Onancock
• (757) 787-7778

Carnival rides and games draw residents to this fund-raiser for the town's volunteer fire department. The carnival usually runs from mid-June to early July. Admission is free, and the only cost is for rides and food.

July

July 4 Celebrations
Various locations
• (757) 787-2460

Fireworks and other fun typically take place in the towns of Accomac, Cape Charles and Chincoteague on the evening of July 4. There's no charge to watch the excitement.

Eastern Shore Release Tournament
Wachapreague
• (757) 787-1125, (757) 442-3704

Since 1981 the Eastern Shore Marlin Club has sponsored this weekend fishing competition that sends anglers out to the Atlantic Ocean in search of the most fish, which they then release into the water. The entry fee is $50 a person. Trophies are awarded.

Wachapreague Fireman's Carnival
Wachapreague
• (757) 787-7818

A carnival sets up in town starting in mid-July and runs through early August. The event helps raise funds for the town's volunteer fire department. Admission is free, though rides and food cost extra.

Onancock Regatta Weekend
Onancock
• (757) 787-3363

Expect everything from an art show to a regatta and marine music during this weekend event sponsored by the Town of Onancock.

Deborah Blueberry and Craft Festival
Chincoteague
• (757) 336-3478

Blueberries are the star of this 10-year-old Chincoteague festival, which also features craftspeople showing their wares. Expect to eat blueberries prepared every way imaginable at this one-day event.

Chincoteague Pony Swim and Auction
Chincoteague
• (757) 336-6161

This is by far the most popular event on the Eastern Shore. Each year an estimated 50,000 visitors come to view Assateague's wild horses. The event started in 1925 and benefits the Chincoteague Volunteer Fire Company. On the last Wednesday in July "saltwater cowboys" round up horses and make them swim to Chincoteague where they are auctioned the next day. A carnival with rides is held the week of the festival as well as the week preceding it. Check in advance with the Chincoteague Chamber of Commerce for a brochure of events and advice on logistics, such as accommodations and where to park. The only cost is for rides and food.

August

Wachapreague Fish Fry
Wachapreague
• (757) 787-7824

Delicately battered fish and all the trimmings are on the menu at this annual event that benefits the Eastern Shore Association for Retarded Children. The cost for dinner is $6.

Chic Charter Club Tuna Tournament
Wachapreague
• (757) 787-2105

Female anglers concentrate on bringing in big tuna during this one-day tournament in mid-August. There is a $40 entry fee, and trophies are awarded.

September

Chincoteague Decoy Carvers Association Show
Chincoteague Fire House, Chincoteague
• (757) 336-6161

Local duck decoy carvers display their talents at this annual Labor Day weekend show. You'll find decoys in all price ranges.

Eastern Shore Fall Marlin Release Tournament
Wachapreague
• (757) 787-2105

Marlins are the fish of choice during this one-day tournament in early September. Once landed the fish are sent back to the ocean so they can grow even bigger for next year's action. The entry fee costs $20 a boat. Various prizes are awarded.

Wachapreague Fall Flounder Tournament
Wachapreague
• (757) 787-2105

For nine days in mid-September saltwater anglers take to the water in search of the biggest flounder. The tournament is sponsored by the Wachapreague Hotel. More than $2,000 in prizes are up for grabs. The entry fee is $30 per person.

Cape Charles Days
Downtown Cape Charles
• (757) 331-2304

Food, bands and other fun bring out enthusiastic local residents to celebrate their town's heritage during this free festival that's held on the beach.

Annual Autumn Lawn Sale
Onley
• (757) 787-2460

This giant sale at Nandua High School proves that one's person's junk is another person's treasure. Local residents set up booths at this annual mid-September event, which started in 1974. It is sponsored by the Virginia Tech Alumni Association.

October

Harvest Festival
Sunset Beach Inn, U.S. 13, Kiptopeke
• **(757) 787-8687**

A variety of Eastern Shore foods are showcased on the first Wednesday in October. This wildly popular festival is sponsored by the Eastern Shore of Virginia Chamber of Commerce. The food ranges from crab cakes to sweet potato biscuits. Advance $30 tickets are a must.

Eastern Shore Birding Festival
Sunset Beach Inn, Kiptopeke
• **(757) 787-8687**

Although this Columbus Day weekend event is headquartered at the Sunset Beach Inn in Kiptopeke, activities take place throughout the Eastern Shore. Many of them are at Kiptopeke State Park in nearby Cape Charles. A weekend of talks, nature walks and other events focus on the variety of birds migrating through the shore during the fall. Advanced tickets are recommended for this event, which started in 1992. Tickets cost $6 a day or $10 for both days. Children's tickets are half-price.

Chincoteague Island Oyster Festival
Maddox Family Campground, Chincoteague
• **(757) 336-6161**

Since 1972 Chincoteague cooks have prided themselves on this all-you-can-eat event held on the Saturday of Columbus Day weekend. Oysters are prepared any way you can imagine. Tickets cost $25 and sell out quickly. The festival is sponsored by the Chincoteague Chamber of Commerce.

Willis Wharf Homecoming and Waterman's Festival
Willis Wharf
• **(757) 442-9472**

Town residents show off their heritage with demonstrations using crab pots and fishing nets. Food and crafts are also on the agenda at this Saturday event sponsored by the Willis Wharf Festival Committee. The festival started in 1994.

Parksley Fall Festival Parksley
• **(757) 665-6161**

Crafts, food and music bring out local residents to this town celebration sponsored by the Parksley Merchant's Association. The free, one-day festival usually includes a display of antique cars.

Schooner Feast
Cape Charles
• **(757) 331-2304**

After the Great Chesapeake Bay Schooner Race, which ends in Norfolk, boats and their crews return to Cape Charles for a rest. That leads to a celebration at the downtown harbor

Soft wet sand, foamy waves washing ashore, and a bright sunny day on the Eastern Shore provide entertainment for beachcombers of all ages.

that includes bands and seafood. The one-day event is sponsored by the Cape Charles-Northampton County Chamber of Commerce. The cost is $15 a person, which includes lots of food.

November

November Antique Show
Belle Haven
• (757) 442-5768

A variety of antique dealers set up shop for a weekend sale that benefits the Northampton Accomack Memorial Hospital. This annual sale has been going strong since 1954.

Assateague Island Waterfowl Week
Assateague
• (757) 336-6122

During the last week in November, bird watchers can drive or hike along seven miles of Assateague Island roads that normally are closed to the public. Along the way they will see flocks of migrating snow geese. The week includes numerous workshops, films and lectures dealing with migrating birds, which are at their peak on the Eastern Shore during this time. The waterfowl week is sponsored by the Chincoteague National Wildlife Refuge. The only cost is the $4-per-carload charge required to get on the island.

Deborah Waterfowl Show
Chincoteague
• (757) 336-3478

This event coincides with Assateague Island Waterfowl Week and is on the last weekend in November. It is in Chincoteague and features the works of local decoy carvers as well as wildlife artists. The annual show has been held since 1986.

December

Cape Charles Holiday Sampler
Cape Charles
• (757) 331-2304

Get a feel for life in this small town by buying a ticket to this one-day annual event. Your $25 ticket includes a progressive dinner as well as house tours. You'll need to register in advance. The event is sponsored by the Cape Charles-Northampton County Chamber of Commerce.

Victorian Home Tour
Parksley
• (757) 665-6271

Check out some of Parksley's restored Victorian homes during this one-day tour in early December. Call ahead for details and ticket information.

Restaurants

As you can guess, seafood is the cuisine of choice on the Eastern Shore. You won't find it any fresher so take advantage of it and eat your fill of steamed clams, soft-shell crabs and flounder. You'll find most restaurants moderately priced and requiring only casual attire.

Price Code

The dollar sign with each restaurant entry estimates the likely cost of entrees for two, excluding alcoholic beverages, dessert, tax or tip.

$	Less than $20
$$	$20 to $35
$$$	$36 to $50

AJ's on the Creek
$$ • 6585 Maddox Blvd., Chincoteague
• (757) 336-5888

AJ's serves seafood, hand-cut steaks, pasta and veal in one of the shore's most elegant atmospheres. Standouts include the crab cakes and crab imperial. The restaurant serves dinner daily and lunch every day but Sunday.

Armando's
$$ • 10 North St., Onancock
• (757) 787-8044

Ever since it opened in 1988 in downtown Onancock Armando's has been the trendiest place to dine on the Shore. Its Argentine owner specializes in homemade pasta, seafood and divine desserts. He typically changes the menu each spring. Armando's is open Tuesday through Sunday for dinner. Reservations are recommended on weekends.

Beachway Restaurant
$$ • 6455 Maddox Blvd. Chincoteague
• (757) 336-5590

The Beachway gives seafood a different twist by serving it in crepes or bouillabaisse.

The Beachway has a reputation for luscious desserts. Stop by for breakfast, lunch or dinner.

Big Bill's Captain's Deck Restaurant
$$ • U.S. Rt. 13, Nassawadox
• (757) 442-7060

Seafood is king here. If you're really hungry, go for the "Moby" platter with crab imperial, oysters, scallops, clam strips, shrimp and trout. If you're on the Shore to fish, bring your cleaned catch and have it cooked and served to you with vegetables and side dishes for about $6. Breakfast, lunch and dinner are server daily.

Bill's Seafood Restaurant
$$ • 4040 Main St. Chincoteague
• (757) 336-5831

Bill's is renowned for jumbo flounder "so big it hangs off the plate," according to one devotee. Bill's has been in business for more than 30 years along Chincoteague's main drag and was serving fresh seafood even before then. Crab cakes and other fish are on the menu. You can start your day early at Bill's with its 5 AM opening time. The French toast is worth getting up for in the morning. The restaurant serves breakfast, lunch and dinner daily from spring through late fall. It typically closes from Thanksgiving through Palm Sunday.

Bizzotto's Gallery-Caffee
$$ • 41 Market St., Onancock
(757) 787-3103

The artwork is as enticing as the food at this trendy new café in downtown Onancock. It's open for lunch and dinner and has a variety of intriguing salads, sandwiches and other dishes. Besides being a great cook, the owner creates leather handbags for sale along with other crafts and artwork.

Chincoteague Inn
$$ • 6262 Marlin St., Chincoteague
• (757) 336-6110

This venerable seafood restaurant has a terrific waterfront location. Crab cakes keep customers coming back time after time, but you'll usually find swordfish, tuna, drumfish and other delicacies from the sea on the menu. Lunch is served outside on the deck, which is also the location for P.T. Pelican's Bar. The main dining room is open in the evenings. The restaurant is open daily from Easter through Columbus Day. It typically closes during the winter.

Don's Seafood Restaurant
$$ • 4113 Main St., Chincoteague
• (757) 336-5715

You'll find no filler in Don's special crab cakes—just pure, succulent crab meat lightly bound together. Shrimp, flounder and prime rib are other delights at this restaurant that's been a favorite of locals and tourists for at least 20 years. Be sure to check out the daily specials. Don's is open every day for breakfast, lunch and dinner in spring through fall. It usually closes during some of the winter.

Eastville Manor
$$ • 6058 Willow Oak Rd., Eastville
• (757) 768-7378

It didn't take long for word of Eastville Manor's excellent cuisine to filter over the bridge-tunnel to Hampton Roads. Soon residents of Norfolk and Virginia Beach were plunking down $20 in bridge tolls to go and try this restaurant. Many of them have become repeat customers. The restaurant opened in 1996 in an 1850s home. Its hallmarks are generous servings of seafood and beef topped with interesting sauces. Desserts are worth making room for after the meal. The Manor serves lunch Tuesday through Friday and dinner Tuesday through Saturday. Reservations are recommended. The restaurant closes for a few weeks in winter. When calling be sure to ask for directions. The restaurant is a few miles off U.S. 13.

Edward's Seafood
$$ • U.S. Hwy. 13 Onley
• (757) 787-2224

The locals love this place, and you will too. For most of the year this is strictly a wholesale crab distributor. But from June through September Edward's is transformed into a restaurant with all-the-crabs-you-can-devour dinners. Corn on the cob and hush puppies are the perfect side dishes. You'll know the restaurant is open when you see it highlighted on a sign outside. It typically operates Thursday through Sunday for dinner.

E.L. Willis & Co.
$$ • Willis Wharf Rd., Willis Wharf
• (757) 442-4225

This casual restaurant is housed in a former general store that dates to 1840. Local seafood stars on the menu, which also includes steaks, homemade desserts and soups. In warmer months you can dine on the screened-in front porch. Lunch is served every day but Sunday.

Dinner is available only on Friday and Saturday.

Etta's Family Restaurant
$$ • 7452 East Side Dr. Chincoteague
• (757) 336-5644

For some regular Chincoteague visitors, no trip is complete without a meal at Etta's. Open April through October, Etta's seafood keeps vacationers coming back for more. Although crab cakes and crab imperial are the top sellers, Etta's steaks also are popular. The restaurant is in a prime location overlooking the Assateague Channel and its lighthouse. In summer Etta's opens daily for lunch and dinner. In the off-season the restaurant closes on Tuesday and serves lunch only on weekends with dinner available at night.

Flounder's
$$ • 145 Market St., Onancock
• (757) 787-2233

Despite its name, Flounder's is known for having the best fried oysters around. The restaurant is a favorite with locals. It is owned by Linda Hurley, whose husband catches the oysters and whose mother fries them using an old family recipe. A chalkboard lists the daily specials. All are based on what the family catch is for the day. Flounders is open for lunch and dinner daily.

Formy's Barbecue
$ • U.S. Hwy. 13, Painter
• (757) 442-2426

This is one of our regular stops for excellent pork barbecue with cole slaw, baked beans and other fixings. The "que" is especially good fired up with Formy's secret sauce.

Garden and the Sea Inn
$$ • 4188 Nelson Rd., New Church
• (757) 824-0672, (800) 824-0672

Continental and regional cuisine are the standouts at this elegant country inn. Dinner menus are designed around seasonal local seafood and produce. The menu changes frequently. Reservations are recommended. The inn serves dinner in summer from Wednesday through Saturday although the days can vary. In the off-season dinner is offered on weekends. Be sure to call first for the current dining schedule.

Hopkins & Brothers Store
$$ • 2 Market St., Onancock
• (757) 787-3100

Seafood and steaks are the main fare of this waterfront restaurant inside a general store built in 1842. It was moved to its present location at Onancock's Wharf in 1966. Starting in early June the restaurant serves lunch daily and dinner from Wednesday through Saturday. The restaurant usually closes in the fall.

Island House
$$ • 17 Atlantic Ave., Wachapreague
• (757) 787-4242

Travel a few miles off the main highway to the Island House, whose new building was designed to resemble an old lifesaving station. The decor and view are great. Served inside the rustic interior are fresh seafood and Black Angus beef. The restaurant is open for breakfast, lunch and dinner daily. It is adjacent to the Wachapreague Motel and its marina.

Landmark Crab House
$$ • Landmark Plaza, 6160 Main St., Chincoteague
• (757) 336-5552

For fine dining, one of Chincoteague's best is this restaurant in a shopping center overlooking Chincoteague Bay. Seafood and steak are the standouts here. Outside is the Duck Bar where the view of the sunset is outstanding. While the Landmark serves only dinner daily from late March through October, its sister restaurant, the Shucking House Cafe, fills in the gap. During the months when the crab house is operating, the cafe serves breakfast and lunch in a casual atmosphere. During the off-season the cafe is also open for dinner on weekends, 336-5145. The two restaurants share the same building and kitchen.

Little Italy Restaurant and Pizza
$$ • 10237 Rogers Dr., Nassawadox
• (757) 442-7831

Italian native Franco Nocera brings authentic cuisine from his homeland to the Shore. Lasagna, eggplant dishes, fried calamari and pizza are the house specialties at this popular restaurant that opened in 1992. You'll also find calzone, stromboli and homemade tiramisu on

INSIDERS' TIP
Don't forget your camera—and plenty of film—when going on vacation. You'll want to record all the great fun!

the menu. The restaurant is just off U.S. 13 at the stoplight on the way to Nassawadox. It's one of our favorite places to eat on the Shore and is busy on weekend nights. Lunch also is served daily. The restaurant closes on Sunday.

LJ Street Sports Bar & Restaurant
$$ • 20250 Fairgrounds Rd., Onancock
• (757) 787-2144

Food and fun go hand in hand in this restaurant just outside Onancock. Besides steaks, ribs, seafood and sandwiches, you'll find pool, Ping Pong, electronic darts and a big-screen TV tuned to sporting events. The restaurant is open for lunch and dinner and has a band on weekend nights.

Maria's Family Restaurant
$$ • 6506 Maddox Blvd., Chincoteague
• (757) 336-5040

Whether you're hungry for breakfast or pizza, Maria's has it on the menu. This casual spot offers everything from seafood to excellent Italian dinners. It's open from breakfast to late-night dinners.

Market Street Inn
$$ • Market and North Sts., Onancock
• (757) 787-7626

Crab cakes are the top sellers at this downtown Onancock restaurant. Other Eastern Shore delicacies, such as flounder, are prepared to perfection. Try to save room for a slice of homemade apple or cherry pie. The Inn is open every day except Sunday for breakfast, lunch and dinner.

The Owl Restaurant
$ • U.S. Hwy. 13, Parksley
• (757) 665-5191

This restaurant specializes in country cooking and is renowned throughout the Eastern Shore for its homemade pies. It's been in business since 1947 and is a regular stop for one traveler we know. The Owl is connected to a 40-room motel and dishes up breakfast, lunch and dinner daily.

Peppers Deli
$ • 151 Market St., Onancock
• (757) 787-4357

The spotlight is on sandwiches at this casual eatery in downtown Onancock. Choose from classics such as corned beef or pastrami or sample the deli's 21 different specialty creations. You can also create your own signature sandwich from a wide variety of ingredients. Salads also are on the menu along with gour-

met dinner specials. Peppers serves lunch everyday but Sunday and dinner Thursday through Saturday.

Rebecca's Family Restaurant
$ • 7 Strawberry St., Cape Charles
• (757) 331-3879

Home cooking is at its best, and some locals name this as their favorite restaurant. Rebecca's is known for its oyster and clam fritters served with side dishes like baked corn and steamed tomatoes. Rebecca's is open in downtown Cape Charles for lunch and dinner, however, the restaurant closes on Tuesday nights.

Steamer's Seafood Restaurant
$$ • 6251 Maddox Blvd., Chincoteague
• (757) 336-5478

True to its name, Steamer's features freshly steamed crabs, clams and shrimp. Its specialties are all-you-can-eat crab and shrimp dinners. It adjoins the Island Creamery, which serves homemade ice cream and yogurt.

Sting Ray's Cape Center Restaurant
$$ • U.S. Hwy. 13, Cape Charles
• (757) 331-2505

This may look like a truck stop, but it offers a full menu of fresh crab, flounder and its famous, fiery Sting Ray Chili. Take note that the chili is only on the menu when owner Ray Haynie is there to properly spice it. This combination gas station/restaurant, dubbed "Chez Exxon" by the locals, is surprisingly elegant, with a menu that often includes lamb and chocolate torte. It recently garnered an article in Southern Living magazine. There's an extensive wine list from which to choose. Sting Ray's is also a popular breakfast and lunch spot.

Tammy and Johnny's
$ • U.S. Hwy. 13, Melfa
• (757) 787-1122

Throw health concerns to the wind and dig into some of the best fried chicken you'll ever find. Locals come from miles away to eat at this local drive-in. Other standouts include fried corn-puffs and sweet-potato fingers. Basic burgers and fries also are on the menu. Stop by for lunch or dinner daily.

The Trawler
$$ • U.S. Hwy. 13, Exmore
• (757) 442-2092

One of our favorite places to take a break along U.S. 13, The Trawler has excellent seafood and is famous for its she-crab soup and irresistible sweet potato biscuits. Several times a year The Trawler transforms itself into a dinner theater. The Trawler serves lunch and dinner daily.

The Village Restaurant and Lounge
$$ • 6576 Maddox Blvd., Chincoteague • (757) 336-5120

Dine by candlelight at this waterfront restaurant. Locals praise the Village for the quality—and quantity—of its local seafood. Be sure to try the signature Chincoteague oysters or the crab imperial. The Village is open for dinner daily.

Wolff's Sandwich Shoppe
$ • Va. Rt. 679, Atlantic • (757) 824-6466

Wolff's old-time charm is highlighted by Oscar the cockatiel. Sandwiches range from fresh-ground burgers to crab cakes and meaty subs. Wolff's also has clam strips and fish platters and serves both breakfast and lunch. This restaurant on the outskirts of Chincotegue is a popular hangout for nearby NASA workers.

Wright's Seafood Restaurant
$$ • Wright Rd., Atlantic • (757) 824-4012

Just a few miles outside Chincoteague, Wright's sits right on the edge of Watts Bay. Its large seafood selection runs from flounder to clams. Wright's popular all-you-can-eat specials team up steamed crabs with fried chicken, ribs or other entrees. Although Wright's is in the country there are big billboards to guide you. It's open for dinner every day but Monday. It also serves lunch on Sunday.

Accommodations

Whether you prefer family motels with a pool, country bed and breakfasts or exclusive inns, you'll find many options on the Eastern Shore. The majority are in Chincoteague, but accommodations are scattered all along the Shore. Some are in small towns; others in rural areas. In the past few years there has been a profusion of new bed and breakfast inns in restored historic homes, giving the Shore one of Virginia's largest concentrations of this quaint style of accommodation. Many are open year round; some only operate from spring through fall. All are antique-filled havens perfect for relaxing. If you're traveling with children, be sure to admit this fact right off the bat. Some bed and breakfasts and inns welcome only children older than age 10 or 12.

To help with your selection, the tourism commission has available a pamphlet called "Bed & Breakfasts of Virginia's Eastern Shore." If you need help mulling over all your options, contact Virginia's Eastern Shore Bed & Breakfast Association, (757) 331-4920. Its members are owners of the Shore's bed and breakfasts. If you specify what you're looking for, the association will make recommendations.

Price Code

The dollar sign with each entry indicates what it will cost for one night's lodging in a room for two people. Rates may go up in summer, particularly in the resort area of Chincoteague.

$	**less than $70**
$$	**$70 to $99**
$$$	**$100 and more**

Bed and Breakfast Inns

Ballard House Family Style Bed & Breakfast
$ • 12527 Ballard Dr., Willis Wharf • (757) 442-2206

The owners of this Victorian home welcome families. Children can explore Grandma Jo's attic filled with toys and books. They can crab off a wharf, play on a tree swing and walk along a nature path. Guests also can watch movies on cable TV or a VCR and sing together around a piano. They enjoy full breakfasts, afternoon tea and a midnight snack. The cookie jar is always filled and waiting. There are four guest rooms, two with private baths. Pets are accepted. The Ballard House is accessible to handicapped guests.

Bayview Waterfront B&B
$$ • 35350 Copes Dr., Belle Haven • (757) 442-6963, (800) 442-6966

If you're fascinated by country living and Eastern Shore architecture, consider this bed and breakfast. Its main house was built in the early 1800s and has been added on in the big house/little house/colonnade/kitchen-style. Bay View sits on the banks of the Occohannock Creek in view of the Chesapeake Bay. It is in the country near Exmore and Belle Haven. The innkeepers have had the house in their family for several generations. There are three guest rooms, one with a private bath. Amenities include a swimming pool, a tennis court, a dock for crabbing and 140 acres of woods for hiking as well as full breakfasts. Children are welcome.

Burton House
$-$$ • 11 Brooklyn St., Wachapreague
• (757) 787-4560

The owners of this bed and breakfast also run the adjacent Hart's Harbor House. This restored home, c. 1883, and its sister house are the only bed and breakfasts in Wachapreague, a fishing village that bills itself as "Little City by the Sea." Both overlook the marshes leading to the Atlantic Ocean. The Burton House provides seven guest rooms, six with private half-baths and one with a full bath. The inn serves full breakfasts and has bicycles available. Cabins are available for rent. There's also a small-boat marina on site.

Cape Charles House
$$-$$$ • 645 Tazewell Ave., Cape Charles
• (757) 331-4920

Opened as a bed and breakfast in 1993, this restored Colonial revival home is in the heart of Cape Charles near the Chesapeake Bay. Guests are treated to gourmet breakfasts, afternoon tea, wine and cheese as well as rooms with private baths.

Channel Bass Inn
$$-$$$ • 6228 Church St., Chincoteague
• (757) 336-6148, (800) 221-5620

This elegant inn is run by Barbara and David Wiedenheft, also owners of Miss Molly's Inn. It is a longtime favorite in Chincoteague. Traditional English afternoon tea and gourmet breakfasts are served in the dining room. The tea room is open to the public in the afternoons. The Channel Bass is a great romantic getaway. The five spacious bedrooms are elegantly decorated and have private baths.

Chesapeake Charm
$-$$ • 202 Madison Ave., Cape Charles
• (757) 331-2676, (800) 546-9215

This 1921 Victorian house has three guest rooms with private baths. The home is in downtown Cape Charles two blocks from the Chesapeake Bay beach. Full breakfasts are served.

Colonial Manor Inn
$-$$ • 84 Market St., Onancock
• (757) 787-3521

Built in 1882, this inn has welcomed guests since 1936, longer than any other Eastern Shore establishment. It has nine guest rooms, five with private baths. New owners have refurbished the inn and started serving full breakfasts. The inn is on two acres along the main street of historic Onancock. Children are welcome.

Creekside B&B
$$ • 24221 Finney's Wharf Rd., Onancock
• (757) 787-4414

This late-19th-century home has great water views. It's in the country three miles from Onancock and is surrounded by gardens. There are two guest rooms with private baths. Guests wake up to a full breakfast.

The Garden and the Sea Inn
$$-$$$ • 4188 Nelson Rd., New Church
• (757) 824-0672, (800) 824-0672

This elegant country inn opened in 1989. It was built in 1802 as Bloxom's Tavern and is 15 minutes from Chincoteague. There are five guest rooms with private baths, and some have whirlpools. Guests enjoy complimentary beverages, hearty continental breakfasts and afternoon tea. The elegant dining room, which is open to the public for dinner, features exceptional cuisine using regional foods. The inn typically closes during winter.

The Gladstone House
$-$$ • 12108 Lincoln Ave., Exmore
• (757) 442-4614 (800) BNB-GUEST

Get away from it all at this three-story brick Georgian-style home that started welcoming guests in 1994. Two guest rooms feature private baths. Amenities include four-course breakfasts plus coffee served in the guest rooms.

Hart's Harbor House B&B
$-$$ • 9 Brooklyn St., Wachapreague
• (757) 787-4848

Owned and operated by the same folks who bring you the Burton House (see previous entry), this c. 1870 home has been lovingly restored. It is furnished with antiques and overlooks barrier islands and thousands of acres of salt marsh. The inn offers three spacious rooms, each with a private bath. Cabins are also for rent. Full breakfasts are served, and bicycles are available. You can dock your boat at the owners' marina.

The Inn at Poplar Corner
$$-$$$ • 4248 Main St., Chincoteague
• (757) 336-6115

With its sweeping porches, this new inn blends in with its Victorian neighborhood despite the fact that contractors just put the finishing touches on it in the spring of 1996. The inn has four guest rooms with private baths and whirlpools. Guests are treated to full breakfasts. The hosts cheerfully loan bicycles and beach chairs. The owners also run the adjacent Watson House.

Island Manor House
$–$$$ • 4160 Main St., Chincoteague
• (757) 336-5436, (800) 852-1505

This home in the heart of Chincoteague was built before the Civil War by two men who later married sisters. To accommodate both families they split the Federal-style house in half and moved the front part next door. The restoration that created the Island Manor House several years ago reunited the two houses with an airy garden room. There are eight guest rooms, six with private baths. Full breakfasts and afternoon tea are served.

The Main Street House
$–$$ • 4356 Main St., Chincoteague
• (757) 336-6030,
(800) 491-2027

This Victorian home is right on Chincoteague Channel. Its screened-in porch offers spectacular sunset views, and there are two guest rooms. The owner is a former wildlife refuge manager with lots of information to share. Breakfast is continental-plus with heartier fare on weekends.

Martha's Inn
$–$$ • 12224 Lincoln Ave., Exmore
• (757) 442-4641, (800) 99-MARTHA

Built in 1936 by the owner's parents, this stately Georgian-style home has three guest rooms, one with a private bath. The three-story inn features an unusual circular staircase. Guests enjoy full country breakfasts. Outside are 3 acres of grounds.

Miss Molly's Inn (1886)
$–$$$ • 4141 Main St.,
Chincoteague
• (757) 336-6686,
(800) 221-5620

This bed and breakfast is where Marguerite Henry stayed while writing *Misty of Chincoteague*, which was published in 1947. Miss Molly, the daughter of J.T. Rowely who built the house in 1886, lived here until the age of 84. The Victorian house is in the heart of Chincoteague and overlooks Chincoteague

Bay. Guests enjoy full breakfasts and afternoon tea in the gazebo. The inn is known for its scones. There are seven guest rooms, five with private baths.

The Muller's Waterfront Bed & Breakfast
$ • Mosher Ln., Quinby
• (757) 422-4435

Get away from it all and enjoy roaming 14 acres along Upshur Bay and the surrounding marsh. Or bring your boat along and head out to the Atlantic Ocean from a nearby marina. Owners Bob and Ellen Muller joined the Eastern Shore's bed and breakfast lineup in 1996. They have five guest rooms with private baths in two country homes. In the morning they serve a family-style full breakfast.

Nottingham Ridge
$–$$$ • 28184 Nottingham Ridge Ln., Cape Charles
• (757) 331-1010

With 100 acres bordering the Chesapeake Bay, this Colonial-style home outside Cape Charles has its own beach. The four guest rooms have private baths. Breakfast is served on the porch overlooking the Bay, and wine and cheese are offered in the evenings. Sunsets here are spectacular, and you'll find a long stretch of pristine beach to stroll. This property has been in the same family for more than 300 years and is owned by a relative of neighboring Picketts Harbor Bed and Breakfast.

Picketts Harbor Bed and Breakfast
$–$$ • 28288 Nottingham Ridge Ln., Cape Charles
• (757) 331-2212

This bed and breakfast outside Cape Charles has a private Chesapeake Bay beach that stretches for 27 acres. Guests are greeted in the morning with full country breakfasts. There are six guest rooms, three with private baths. The owner's family has possessed this property since the early 1600s and is related to the proprietor of the neighboring Nottingham Ridge.

Pungoteague Junction Bed and Breakfast
$ • 30230 Bobtown Rd., Pungoteague
• (757) 442-3581

This 1869 house with a

INSIDERS' TIP
Chincoteague's famous July Wild Pony Swim and Auction started in 1925 after two fires devastated most of the town. The Chincoteague Volunteer Fire Company dreamed up the pony events to help pay for a new fire truck. Today money from the annual July event still benefits the Chincoteague Volunteer Fire Department.

wraparound porch has two guest rooms. The hosts serve full breakfasts and offer dinners upon request. Children are welcome and will find toys waiting for them.

Sea Gate Bed and Breakfast
$$ • 9 Tazewell Ave., Cape Charles
• (757) 331-2206

Built in 1912, this home is within walking distance of the Chesapeake Bay beach in historic Cape Charles. The bed and breakfast offers porches for relaxing, bikes for touring the town, full breakfasts and afternoon tea. Two guest rooms share full, private baths. The other two have private half-baths.

76 Market Street Bed and Breakfast
$$ • 76 Market St., Onancock
• (757) 787-7600

This restored Victorian home is in Onancock's historic residential district and is an easy stroll from the harbor. You'll wake in the morning to a full breakfast. The house features three guest rooms with private baths.

The Spinning Wheel
Bed and Breakfast
$$ • 31 North St., Onancock
• (757) 787-7311

This restored 1890s folk Victorian home is just off the main street of historic Onancock. Among its antique furnishings are several spinning wheels that give the inn its name. Five guest rooms each have private baths. Guests can have their full breakfasts served in bed or the dining room. Access to a private club allows guests to play golf and tennis, and the inn has bicycles available for exploring the town.

The Watson House
$-$$$ • 4240 Main St., Chincoteague
• (757) 336-1564, (800) 336-6787

This Victorian home in the heart of Chincoteague has six guest rooms with private baths and serves full breakfasts in the dining room or on the veranda. The inn offers afternoon tea and equips guests with free bicycles and beach chairs. The owners also own the Inn at Poplar Corner next door to the Watson House.

Wilson-Lee House
$$-$$$ • 403 Tazewell Ave., Cape Charles
• (757) 331-1954

After an extensive restoration, this bed and breakfast opened in 1996. It is in downtown Cape Charles in an elegant home built in 1906. There are six guest rooms with full baths. Guests are treated to full breakfasts.

Wynne Tref
$ • 28168 Drummondtown Rd., Locustville
• (757) 787-2356

This is a traditional 18th-century Eastern Shore home a mile from the Atlantic Ocean. Its name means "White House" in Welsh. The house is a variation on the big house/little house/colonnade/kitchen style of architecture. There is one suite with a private bath. The hosts serve hearty continental breakfasts.

Year of the Horse Inn
$-$$$ • 3583 Main St., Chincoteague
• (757) 336-3221, (800) 680-0090

This Colonial-style inn was built in the 1940s and was Chincoteague's first bed and breakfast. It is right on Chincoteague Sound and has a 100-foot pier for crabbing or fishing and a deck overlooking the Intracoastal Waterway. Three guest rooms have balconies and all have private baths and beautiful views. One room has a kitchenette, and there is a two-bedroom apartment available. Guests are served a continental breakfast.

Motels

There are many nice motels to choose from on the Eastern Shore. You'll find a concentration of them in Chincoteague and others scattered up and down U.S. 13.

Anchor Inn Motel
$ • 3775 S. Main St., Chincoteague
• (757) 336-6313

Anchor Inn Motel has 45 rooms, some of them efficiency apartments. The motel has a boat harbor, launching ramp, fish cleaning and storage areas and a swimming pool. Rooms have refrigerators, and some are handicapped accessible.

Anchor Motel
$ • U.S. Hwy. 13, Nassawadox and Onley
• (757) 787-8000 (Onley), (757) 442-6363 (Nassawadox), (800) 442-5533

The Nassawadox motel has 41 rooms and the Captain's Deck restaurant. The Onley location has 32 rooms and four efficiency apartments. The Nassawadox motel is handicapped accessible and accepts pets.

Assateague Inn
$ • 6570 Coach Ln., Chincoteague
• (757) 336-3738

This motel's 26 rooms, most of them suites, overlook a peaceful saltwater marsh behind tall pine trees. Amenities include a pool, a picnic area and a spa.

Beach Road Motel
$ • 6151 Maddox Blvd., Chincoteague
• (757) 336-6562, (800) 699-6562

Start your morning at a leisurely pace at this motel where each room comes equipped with a refrigerator and coffee maker. There are 23 rooms with a cottage and an efficiency apartment also for rent. A swimming pool, grills and picnic tables help you plan outdoor fun.

Birchwood Motel
$ • 3650 Main St., Chincoteague
• (757) 336-6133, (800) 441-5147

In the heart of Chincoteague, this 41-room motel has a swimming pool, crabbing pier, picnic area and playground.

Cape Motel
$ • U.S. Hwy. 13, Cape Charles
• (757) 331-2461

There are 16 rooms at this hotel 6 miles from the bridge-tunnel. It has an outdoor swimming pool and a picnic area with grills.

Captain's Quarters
$ • U.S. Hwy. 13, Melfa
• (757) 787-4545

This motel has 21 rooms, some with kitchenettes. It is handicapped accessible and accepts pets.

Comfort Inn
$ • U.S. Hwy. 13, Onley
• (757) 787-7787

The Comfort Inn has 80 rooms, some of which are handicapped accessible. There is a swimming pool and meeting room.

Comfort Suites
$$ • 4195 Main St., Chincoteague
• (757) 336-3700

Spread out in one of the 60 family suites at Chincoteague's newest motel. All rooms have a kitchen and a balcony overlooking the waterfront. There is an indoor swimming pool, a whirlpool, fitness center and outside sundeck.

Days Inn
$ • U.S. Hwy. 13, Cape Charles
• (757) 331-1000, (800) 331-4000

This is one of the nearest motels to the Chesapeake Bay Bridge-Tunnel. It has 102 rooms, a restaurant, a lounge, a meeting room and a swimming pool. The motel accepts pets.

Driftwood Motor Lodge
$ • 7105 Maddox Blvd., Chincoteague
• (757) 336-6557, (800) 553-6117 ext. 11

At the causeway to Assateague Island, the Driftwood has 52 rooms with balconies and patios. Rooms have refrigerators. There is an outdoor swimming pool, and bikes are for rent. The motel has an elevator to upper-level rooms. Restaurants are within easy walking distance.

The **Chesapeake Breeze** *ferries passengers from Reedville to Tangier Island.*

Photo: Courtesy of Northern Neck Travel Council

Best Western Eastern Shore
$$ • U.S. Hwy. 13 Exmore
• (757) 442-REST

This motel opened in 1996 with 52 rooms, including a few suites with whirlpools. There is an outdoor pool and complimentary continental breakfast. This motel shares owners with the neighboring Trawler restaurant.

Hotel Wachapreague
$ • 17 Atlantic Ave., Wachapreague
• (757) 787-2105

This 26-room motel sits along the marsh that leads to the Atlantic Ocean. It is a popular spot for fishermen who like to get an early start at the marina across the road. Rooms come with a small refrigerator and coffee maker, and some have kitchenettes. Pets are welcome, and some rooms are handicapped accessible. The owners operate an adjacent restaurant, The Island House.

Island Belle Motor Lodge
$ • 7020 Maddox Blvd., Chincoteague
• (757) 336-3600, (800) 61-LODGE

The lodge is just beyond the causeway to Assateague Island. There are 50 rooms, including some that are handicapped accessible. All

rooms have refrigerators. There is an outdoor pool and a meeting room. The lobby has a display of more than 600 handbells.

Island Motor Inn
$-$$ • 4391 N. Main St., Chincoteague
• (757) 336-3141

All 60 rooms have a view of Chincoteague Bay and small refrigerators. There is one large suite. You'll find both a heated indoor pool and an outdoor pool plus a fitness center with a hot tub. Amenities include a meeting room, fishing and crabbing pier, deep-water docking and an elevator.

The Lighthouse Motel
$ • 4208 N. Main St., Chincoteague
• (757) 336-5091

There are 25 rooms, some with refrigerators and microwaves, at this motel. Wheelchair accessible facilities are available, as are an outdoor pool and a screened picnic area.

The Mariner Motel
$ • 6273 Maddox Blvd., Chincoteague
• (757) 336-6565, (800) 221-7490

Between downtown Chincoteague and

> **INSIDERS' TIP**
>
> If you're looking for a special souvenir to take home, check our Annual Events chapter for arts and crafts fairs scheduled during your visit. These events offer visitors a wide array of unique, made-in-Virginia creations and often come with a bonus: food, music, and other entertainment.

Docks are the parking lots along the Eastern Shore.

Assateague Island, the Mariner has 92 rooms, including four efficiency apartments. It has a meeting room, an outdoor pool, laundry facilities, refrigerators in some rooms. It is handicapped accessible. Outside are picnic tables and a pony.

Refuge Motor Inn
$–$$ • 7058 Maddox Blvd., Chincoteague
• (757) 336-5511, (800) 544-8469

This 72-room motel is near the causeway to Assateague Island. It has an indoor/outdoor swimming pool, a fitness center and a hot tub. The inn has two suites. Outside are several Chincoteague ponies. There are bicycles for rent, a playground, grills and picnic tables. Rooms have refrigerators and some are handicapped accessible. There is a meeting room, laundry facilities and a gift shop.

The Sea Hawk Motel
$ • 6250 Maddox Blvd., Chincoteague
• (757) 336-6527

The Sea Hawk has 28 rooms, some of them efficiency apartments, along with two cottages. Amenities include an outdoor pool, playground and picnic area.

Sea Shell Motel
$ • 3720 Willow St., Chincoteague
• (757) 336-6589

The 40-room motel has several efficiencies and apartments. All rooms have refrigerators. There is an outdoor pool and a screened kitchen and eating area. A play area has picnic tables and grills.

Sunrise Motor Inn
$ • 4491 Chicken City Rd., Chincoteague
• (757) 336-6671, (800) 673-5211

This motel is less than a mile from the entrance to the Chincoteague National Wildlife Refuge and the Assateague National Seashore. Amenities include an outdoor pool, a picnic area with grills and a playground. Complimentary tea and coffee are offered each morning.

Best Western Sunset Beach Resort
$ • U.S. Hwy. 13, Kiptopeke
• (757) 331-4786, (800) 899-4SUN

This 81-room motel is within shouting distance of the Chesapeake Bay Bridge-Tunnel. It has a restaurant, an outdoor swimming pool, a playground, a meeting room and one of the best-kept secrets on the Shore—a wonderful private beach right on the Chesapeake Bay. There are beach chairs and colorful umbrellas for guests to use.

Waterside Motor Inn
$–$$ • 3761 S. Main St., Chincoteague
• (757) 336-3434

Guests at this 45-room motel can use a private pier for crabbing or fishing. All rooms have waterfront balconies, small refrigerators and coffee makers. Some rooms have microwaves and VCRs, and some are handicapped accessible. There is an outdoor waterfront pool, tennis courts and an exercise room with a Jacuzzi. A conference and hospitality room is available, and the inn has its own marina.

Chincoteague House Rentals

If you really want to spread out and stay awhile, rent a house on Chincoteague Island. There are about 800 of them available. There are several rental companies on the island, each marketing their own lineup of houses. You'll find them offering waterfront properties as well as those with a water view and some that require a short walk or drive to get to the water.

Chincoteague Island Vacation Cottages
6282 Maddox Blvd.
• (757) 336-3720, (800) 457-6643

Choose from more than 130 homes and cottages in Chincoteague ranging from efficiency units to five-bedroom homes. You can rent by the week, weekend or mini-week, which is Monday through Friday. Weekly rates in summer run from $190 to $1,125.

Island Getaways
Landmark Plaza
• (757) 336-1236, (888) 757-0100

This company handles about 40 houses and townhouses. Choices include cozy, one-bedroom units as well as expansive four-bedroom houses. Rentals are by the weekend, week or mini-week. Weekly rental costs in summer range from $350 to $1,000.

Island Property Enterprises
4065 Main St.
• (757) 336-3456, (800) FINALLY

You'll find this rental office right at the bridge as you enter Chincoteague. It handles 125 properties and rents them by the weekend, week or mini-week. Weekly costs in summer range from $350 to $2,400 depending on whether you're renting a one-bedroom cottage or a four-bedroom waterfront home.

Seabreeze Rentals
6755 Maddox Blvd.
• (757) 336-5980, (800) 795-3931

You'll find everything from efficiency apartments to five-bedroom homes for rent at Seabreeze Rentals. This company handles 37 properties in Chincoteague. Rentals are by the weekend, week or mini-week. Weekly rentals cost from $470 to $1,300 in summer.

Camping

Camping enthusiasts will find several large campgrounds on the Eastern Shore that welcome tent campers as well as those arriving in recreational vehicles. Most campgrounds front the Chesapeake Bay or another body of water. They generally operate from March through the early winter. Costs of campsites depend on whether you're roughing it in a tent or living the life of luxury in a full-equipped camper requiring hookups.

Cherrystone Campground
Va. Rt. 680, Cheriton
• (757) 331-3063

This campground is right on the Chesapeake Bay a few miles off U.S. 13. It has 700 campsites shaded by pine trees. Costs range from $20 to $26 a day. The 300-acre campground includes four swimming pools, fishing and crabbing piers, miniature golf, playgrounds, camping cabins, a store, tennis and volleyball courts and a nature trail. During the summer guests can reserve a spot on a charter boat that ferries them out into the bay.

Inlet View
Va. Rt. 175,
Chincoteague
• (757) 336-5126

Choose from waterfront views or wooded sites at this 500-site campground that sprawls along the southern end of Chincoteague Island. Campsite costs range from $17 to $21 a day. Inlet View has an enviable location along the Atlantic Ocean as well as Chincoteague Channel. Amenities include a camp store, boat ramp, fishing pier, restaurant and laundry facilities. The owners added a new swimming pool in 1997. Children will like the campground's pony rides and go-cart track, and they also can go crabbing or clamming.

Kiptopeke State Park
3540 Kiptopeke Rd., Cape Charles
• (757) 331-2267

This is the Eastern Shore's only public campground, and it is right on the Chesapeake Bay just off U.S. 13 near the southern end of the shore. There are 142 campsites in the 375-acre park. Campsite costs range from $16 to $22 a day. Visitors can swim in the Chesapeake Bay or stroll along the half-mile beach. The beach has lifeguards in the summer. The park has some of the Shore's best fishing—especially around the sunken World War II surplus ships that are 1,500 feet from the shore. Naturalists lead interesting summer programs for all ages. There is a 1.5-mile nature trail and some of the best bird watching on the East Coast. Volunteers man a bird-banding station that tags migratory birds. There also is a hawk observatory in the park where volunteers have logged more than 200,000 birds of prey since 1977.

Maddox Family Campground
6742 Maddox Blvd., Chincoteague
• (757) 336-3111, (757) 336-6648

This campground offers the closest camping to Assateague Island and overlooks the Assateague Channel. It has 561 campsites, a swimming pool, camp store, recreation center and laundry facilities. The campground invites guests to play shuffleboard or horseshoes. They also can go crabbing or bird watching. Campsite costs range from $19 to $26.

Pine Grove
5253 Deep Hole Rd., Chincoteague
• (757) 336-5200

This 37-acre campground is nestled among pine trees and has six ponds that harbor 50 species of ducks, geese and other birds. The grounds include a swimming pool, laundry room, store and playground. The campground is perfect for birdwatchers and also allows crabbing from its pier. There is a nearby boat ramp for campers to use. Campsite costs range from $17 to $22.

Tom's Cove Camping
Park Ridge Rd. and Beebe Rd.,
Chincoteague
• (757) 336-6498

Tom's Cove is the biggest campground on the Eastern Shore. There are 914 campsites at

INSIDERS' TIP
Don't forget to carry some cash. Some very small shops and out-of-the-way places may not accept credit cards.

the campground, which looks across the Assateague Channel to Assateague Island. The campground has fishing piers, a boat ramp, laundry and a marina. Campsites cost from $21 to $29 a day.

Shopping

Like everything else on the Eastern Shore, stores are scattered throughout its 70-mile length, and most of them cater to residents' basic needs. You'll find the greatest concentration of gift shops in Chincoteague, where it is fun to park the car and wander in and out of Main Street boutiques.

Chincoteague Shops

Chincoteague Craft Corner
4044 Main St., Chincoteague
• **(757) 336-3319**
An array of handmade crafts, jewelry and gifts tempt shoppers at this store. Popular items include baskets and miniature lighthouses.

Decoys Decoys Decoys
4039 Main St., Chincoteague
• **(757) 336-1402**
Like its name says, this shop is filled with duck decoys made by 175 carvers, some of them local.

Main Street Pottery
3811 Main St., Chincoteague
• **(757) 336-1546**
Local potter Carol Myers showcases her wares in this shop and studio. Among her specialties are teapots and vases.

Marsha Carter Gifts
6351 Cropper St., Chincoteague
• **(757) 336-3404**
Handmade sweaters are among the offerings at this well-stocked gift shop that features a variety of handcrafted art, jewelry and clothing.

Landmark Plaza
6160 Main St., Chincoteague
• **no phone**
This is Chincoteague's only shopping center. It is on Main Street overlooking Chincoteague Bay and features a variety of gift shops and restaurants. Tenants include The Brant Christmas Shop, the Kite Koop, Bangles

jewelry store, Landmark Crab House and the Grubstake Restaurant.

Pony Tails Candy Shop
7011 Maddox Blvd., Chincoteague
• **(757) 336-6688**
This shop sells Chincoteague Island's most famous local product—Pony Tails saltwater taffy—as well as other delicacies. Visitors often get to see taffy and fudge being made in the candy factory.

Other Shore Shops

Chincoteague isn't the only place on the Shore to spend your hard-earned cash. Most Eastern Shore towns have traditional downtowns with hardware, grocery and other stores that serve residents' basic needs. Mingled in with them are some interesting antiques and gift shops.

Blue Crab Bay Co.
23368 Atlantic Dr., Melfa
• **(757) 787-3602, (800) 221-2722**
For an authentic taste of the Eastern Shore visit this specialty food company's retail store in the Accomac Airport Industrial Park just off route 13. Blue Crab has been in business since 1985 and ships its food products nationwide. Its booming mail-order business includes customers such as Macy's, Marshall Field's and Disney World. Blue Crab's retail store relocated in 1999 from downtown Onancock and is adjacent to tis warehouse and plant. Look for gift baskets, seasonings, canned clams, and other Eastern Shore delicacies.

Bluewater Trading Co.
U.S. Hwy. 13, New Church
• **(757) 824-3124**
A varied mix of primitives and Victorian furniture and collectibles are the mainstay of this antiques shop. It also has nautical antiques.

Charmar's Antiques
211 Mason St., Cape Charles
• **(757) 331-1488**
This well-stocked antique store is in downtown Cape Charles and is one of our favorites. It always has an intriguing blend of antiques and collectibles in all price ranges. You'll also find restored clocks. Be sure to ask the owners to let you peek at their private collection next door. It's in a building outfitted to look like an old-time general store.

Deadrise Enterprises Ltd.
5 North St., Onancock
• (757) 787-2077

There's an eclectic mix of antiques and finely handcrafted furniture in this shop, which opened in 1996. It is located in downtown Onancock.

Decoy Factory Gift Shop
U.S. Hwy. 13, New Church
• (757) 824-5621

The factory affiliated with this shop bills itself as "the world's largest maker of decoys." You can watch woodworkers carving native waterfowl, and you can purchase decoys.

Eastern Shore Pottery
U.S. Hwy. 13, Capeville
• (757) 331-4341

This store is filled with a mind-boggling array of pottery. You'll find salt-glazed pieces as well as Mexican, Southwestern and Indian works. Bird baths, fountains and other decorative items also are in stock.

The Lore of the Shore

Writers love the Eastern Shore. If you need proof, check out the hundreds of titles at The Book Bin in Onley that deal with the history and lore of the Shore. The bookstore is on U.S. 13 in Four Corners Plaza in Onley, (757) 787-7866. The following is a sampling of Eastern Shore books that will help you understand this special region. Most are in stock at The Book Bin or can be special ordered from any bookstore.

• *Birdwatcher's Guide to Virginia's Eastern Shore* by Curtis Badger. This guidebook gives directions to the best birding locations on the Shore.

• *Chadwick the Crab* by Priscilla Cummings. This children's book tells the story of a Chesapeake Bay blue crab that ends up in an aquarium. There are other Chadwick titles in the series.

• *Child of the Bay* by Anne Nock. This beautiful coffee-table book describes the writer's childhood in Onancock.

• *Crab's Hole* by Anne Hughes Janger. This narrative gives the author's memories of growing up on Tangier Island.

• *Eastern Shore Virginia 1607-1960* by Nora Miller Turman. This is the definitive history of the Shore.

• *Eastern Shore Wordbook* by A.K. Fisher. This fun book details the unique Eastern Shore dialect. You'll learn that a "tut" is a rabbit and that a "two to two" is 12 bushels of oysters. The sequel is Entertaining Words from the Eastern Shore.

• *Heron Hill* by George Reiger. This focus of this book is environmentally correct living on the Shore.

• *Misty of Chincoteague* by Marguerite Henry. This beloved 1947 children's book is a classic about the wild ponies that live on Assateague Island.

• *Off 13 - The Eastern Shore of Virginia* Guidebook by Kirk Mariner. This is the all-time, best-selling book about the Eastern Shore. It leads readers on specific jaunts along scenic backroads.

• *Tom Young's Skipjacks* by Effie Young Lewis. In this book the author reminisces about her father's work building boats for watermen.

Famous Artists Sculpture Factory
U.S. Hwy. 13, Hallwood
• (757) 824-0800

If you fancy Western art this factory shop offers the chance to own reproductions of famous sculptures by Frederic Remington and other well-known artists. Several local artists also display and sell their paintings here.

Four Corners Plaza
U.S. Hwy. 13, Onley
• no phone

This strip shopping center is in Four Corners outside Onley. This bustling area has the Eastern Shore's greatest concentration of stores, gas stations and fast-food restaurants. Four Corners Plaza is anchored by a Roses discount store and Bayshore Market grocery store. It also has a state-owned ABC store for liquor, Glick's of Four Corners women's clothing shop, China Chefs restaurant and the Book Bin, which is stocked with the Shore's biggest selection of regional books.

Gina's Uniques & Antiques
U.S. Hwy. 13, Temperanceville
• (757) 824-0096

Fine glassware, porcelain and Oriental rugs and carvings are the specialties of this antiques store at the northern end of the Shore.

The Painter Gallery
U.S. Hwy. 13, Painter
• (757) 442-9537

This gallery is in an old house and showcases a variety of fine arts with changing exhibits from various artists. The gallery also houses the studio of Dr. Joseph D. Adams, a noted poet and artist. The gallery frequently sponsors poetry readings and writers' workshops. It's open Wednesday through Saturday from mid-May through early August.

Shore Plaza
U.S. Hwy. 13, Exmore
• no phone

This is the Shore's newest shopping center designed to give some competition to longstanding Four Corners Plaza several miles down the road. Shore Plaza opened in 1995 and is anchored by Kmart and Food Lion. It also has a Dollar Tree store.

Turner Sculpture
U.S. Hwy. 13, Melfa
• (757) 787-2818

Artists William and David Turner cast bronze animal sculptures from their Eastern Shore studio. Their work is world-renowned and housed at such places as the Brookfield Zoo in Chicago and the Philadelphia Zoo. Prices in the shop range from $25 to $35,000. Browsers are welcome.

Real Estate

If your trip to the Eastern Shore has you longing to put down roots, check out the real estate offerings. City dwellers most likely will think they stepped back 20 years in real estate prices. Browse through any Eastern Shore real estate brochure, and low asking prices attached to snapshots of idyllic homes will make you ready to haul out your checkbook. Many fine houses sell for well below $100,000. In the case of sprawling acreages along the bay or ocean, however, the price tag can top $1 million—especially if a magnificent plantation home is on the property.

Whether you're looking to retire, buy a weekend cottage or settle down permanently, you'll find plenty of options. You can choose from property on the bayside, seaside, in small towns or in the country. You can settle on a historic house to fix up, buy land to build your dream home or find a new dwelling in perfect move-in condition. With more than 400 buildings dating from before 1865, the Shore has one of Virginia's largest concentrations of historic homes. You can still purchase the big house/little house/colonnade/kitchen-style homes typical of the late 1700s. Other period homes, such as those from the Victorian era, can be bought for a low enough price that one person we've heard of decided on a whim to buy and put her house on her credit card. Older houses tend to be less expensive than newer construction of similar square footage. You'll find both handyman's specials and beautifully restored homes among the older property.

Like anywhere else, when you're looking for a home or some land, location is the key. As

> **INSIDERS' TIP**
> On the Eastern Shore directions are based on two things–whether you're going bayside or seaside. Bayside is west toward the Chesapeake Bay. Seaside is east toward the Atlantic Ocean. Bayside is characterized by numerous creeks that lead to the Chesapeake Bay. Seaside is outlined by marshes and barrier islands that protect the Eastern Shore from harsh ocean waves.

you'd expect, waterfront locations carry a higher sales price than landlocked property. Property facing the Chesapeake Bay is more popular and more expensive than waterfront property on the Atlantic Ocean side of the Shore. This is because navigable creeks give direct access to the Bay. The seaside, with its wonderful views and spectacular sunrises, is bordered primarily by marshes and tidal flats. This makes boat access to the ocean possible only in high tide and a few deep-water areas.

Something new to ponder is the Bay Creek development, which is being built near Cape Charles. This the Eastern Shore's first planned community. Its 1,700 acres are anchored by two semi-private golf courses—one designed by Arnold Palmer and the other by Jack Nicklaus. The first course will come on line in 2001 with the other to follow in a year or two. Homes will range from the luxurious to compact duplexes perfect for retired golfers. Bay Creek has an unbeatable location—more than five miles of shoreline along the Chesapeake Bay and two creeks. For details call (757) 331-2200 or (800) 501-7141.

There are about 30 real estate companies

Vacationers enjoy the Eastern Shore's natural habitat at the Chincoteague National Wildlife Refuge.

Photo: Courtesy of Virginia Department of Economic Development

on the Shore. Although there is no multiple listing service, there is a strong Realtors' board. Most agents are tapped into what's available on the market and cheerfully share commissions with competitors who bring buyers.

Blue Heron Realty
U.S. Hwy. 13, Machipongo
• **(757) 678-5200**

Blue Heron is known for its expertise in waterfront property. While many listings are in a moderate price range, the company also handles large waterfront acreage with magnificent homes selling for around $1 million.

Century 21-Eastern Shore Properties Inc.
6759 Maddox Blvd., Chincoteague
• **(757) 336-3121**

Selling homes in Chincoteague is the main focus of this real estate company. However, it also handles residential and commercial property as far south as Accomac.

Coldwell Banker Harbour Realty
Accawmacke Office Center,
22639 Center Pkwy., Accomac
• **(757) 787-1305,**
(800) 989-5852

This real estate company covers the Eastern Shore with offices in four towns - Accomac, Chincoteague, Nassawadox and Onancock. However, the Accomac office is the headquarters office for the Eastern Shore. Listings include homes, commercial buildings, farms and building sites. Waterfront property is one of its specialties.

Crockett Realty
155 Market St.,
Onancock
• **(757) 787-2031**

This family-owned real estate company sells mostly residential property in addition to land and some commercial sites. It is particularly strong in the Onancock and Onley area.

Kirkwood Properties
U.S. Hwy. 13, Exmore
• **(757) 442-3224**

Developing waterfront property is the specialty of this company. It has both homesites and commercial building sites available. All offer spectacular views, and some are on deep water and perfect for boating.

Mason-Davis Co. Inc.
23279 Court House Ave., Accomac
• **(757) 787-1010, (800) 288-7037**

Waterfront property is in Mason-Davis' portfolio along with farmland, commercial buildings and vintage homes in scenic towns.

Parr Properties - United Country Real Estate
U.S. Hwy. 13, Cape Charles
• **(757) 331-3782**

Although this company sells all kinds of homes and land throughout the Eastern Shore, its bailiwick is waterfront property. Among its listings are lots on the site of the former Arlington Plantation, which is being developed as a housing community on the Chesapeake Bay.

Other Services

Medical Care

Shore Memorial Hospital
9507 Hospital Ave., Nassawadox
• **(757) 414-8000**

Founded in 1928, the 158-bed hospital is the third-largest employer on the Eastern Shore.

The hospital has the Eastern Shore of Virginia's only emergency department and a full range of medical services.

Education

Eastern Shore Community College
U.S. Hwy. 13, Melfa
• **(757) 787-5900**

This community college offers two-year degrees in such areas as electronics engineering and business technology. It also offers one-year certificates in such fields as automotive repair and drafting. In interactive televised courses via Old Dominion University's Teletechnet, students can earn bachelor's degrees in nursing or master's degrees in business. Other degrees also are available through the community college's long-distance learning programs. Students can complete two years of study at the community college and then transfer to a four-year institution to complete their degrees. The college serves around 1,600 students per year in credit and noncredit offerings.

INSIDERS' TIP

Local chambers of commerce are excellent sources for information on local businesses and events. Call the Eastern Shore of Virginia Chamber of Commerce at (757) 787-2560 or the Chincoteague Chamber of Commerce at (757) 336-6161.

Real Estate and Neighborhoods

What you're certain to discover when you enter the wonderful world of Hampton Roads real estate is the voracity of neighborhood spirit, a spirit that can reach the level of territorial supremacy previously attributed solely to the primitive tribes of Mongolia. City dwellers, oceanfront habitants and rural pioneers all claim their lifestyle to be the ultimate in residential superiority. This puts new homebuyers (and renters) in our market in a delightful quandary—What would you like in your backyard? The Atlantic Ocean or the Chesapeake Bay? A manicured golf course? How about acres with a stable, or maybe the urban hustle-bustle of late-night restaurants and cultural centers?

After you've answered that question, the next decision is style. New construction or resale, townhome, ranch, high-rise condo or Southern Colonial—pick your favorite and you're sure to find it at the right price. So right, in fact, that if you hail from the West Coast, New England or Washington, D.C., you'll be pleased to learn that the median price of homes and apartments in Hampton Roads averages close to half of what you're used to. Not only will you find a lot more house for your dollar, you'll also save loads of time in your work commute. No matter where you choose to live, 30 minutes in rush hour is about all the time it will take to get from your breakfast table to your desk.

There are a few general rules of real estate in Hampton Roads. First, the closer to water, the more expensive the property or the higher the rent. Because we've been blessed with not only the ocean and the Bay, but also zillions of rivers, tributaries, creeks, inlets and lakes, your chance to land a waterfront property is fairly good. The price of the property rises proportionately with the size of the body of water it overlooks. So a home on the Atlantic Ocean might carry a price tag of more than a million dollars; a cedar-shake contemporary on the Chesapeake Bay, around $500,000; and a resale rancher on a marshy creek might be had for around $250,000.

The second rule is that a resale home in an older, established neighborhood generally sells at a lower square-foot cost than a new construction home in a new, planned community.

The final rule is that you really should have a definite focus on the style, community lifestyle and price of the home you're looking for. Faced with the alternatives of restored period homes, slick condo high-rises, beachy cottages, tract houses, city townhomes and country farmettes, the best advice is to take a couple of days for a just-looking tour through our different communities and neighborhoods. Some families even choose to rent for a year, until they can get a better feel for where they want to live.

By contacting a relocation specialist with any of our major realty companies, you can be inundated with brochures, magazines, maps, city-by-city information and market details to confuse you even further. These relocation specialists are used to that confusion and are expert at helping point you in the direction of your new home-to-be. They're also fountains of information for rentals, day care, job referrals for spouses, school systems, recreational opportunities and anything else that will help your family settle in to your new community. (Of course, this guide will answer many of those questions too!)

While nothing can beat the advice and counsel of a well-informed Insider, there are a slew of homebuying magazines that can serve as a wish list in narrowing your search. *Home Search*, *Harmon Homes*, *Real Estate Digest* and *For Sale By Owner* are the leaders in resale properties and are available free at local grocery and convenience chains. For new-home construction, *New Home*, a quarterly publication of the Tidewater Builders Association, is the definitive volume for those interested in a brand-new home in a new community. Our local newspaper, *The Virginian-Pilot*, publishes *Real Estate Weekly* each Saturday. This tabloid-size edition is a wealth of information, covering both resale and new construction, along with weekly updates on area lenders' mortgage rates and helpful editorial content.

All in all, real estate is big business in Hampton Roads. Home to numerous regional headquarters and, of course, the world's largest military base, people are constantly packing the vans for moves in and out of our market. To serve them, nearly 4,000 Realtors are at work around the clock, shifting folks between neighborhoods and between cities, across town, across the country and even across the world. Because of the competition, any one of these go-getters you choose will more than likely bend over backwards to ensure your satisfaction. And whether your chosen Realtor hails from a small, independent firm or a nationally affiliated company such as ERA, Century 21, The Prudential or RE/MAX, you can trust each one knows the business and the market he or she represents. If you do need assistance in making that Realtor choice, contact the Tidewater Association of Realtors, serving area cities, (757) 473-9700, or the Portsmouth-Chesapeake Board of Realtors, serving just Portsmouth, Chesapeake, Suffolk and Franklin, (757) 465-0884.

Real Estate Companies

To make your initial search a bit quicker, we've compiled a sampling of the major real estate firms serving Hampton Roads.

GSH Real Estate
4560 South Blvd., Virginia Beach
• **(757) 490-6500, (800) 735-6474**
Another independent firm, GSH Real Estate has provided nearly 50 years of service to the community. Hundreds of sales associates strong, GSH offers resale and new construction sales, relocation services and property management, including resort rental properties. Each of its 10 sales offices has a book with color pictures of every VA/HUD property available; it's updated daily. The firm also offers escrow and title services. It is a member of The Dozen, a selective and prestigious group of independent Realtors across the country that meets annually to share new ideas and service innovations.

Leading Edge Realty
4772 Euclid Rd., Virginia Beach
• **(757) 671-3343, (800) 476-3343.**
The 50 or so new construction experts in this firm have made a name for themselves over the last decade or so, working out of satel-

lite offices in new construction sites across the Hampton Roads region.

Long & Foster
3181 Shore Dr., Virginia Beach
• **(757) 496-9400, (800) 841-0060**
The largest real estate company in Virginia is a relative newcomer to the Hampton Roads market, but its hometown agents are well-known and respected. Help for resale and new construction, along with relocation services, is available at any of the 11 Long & Foster offices.

The Prudential Decker Realty
1101 Laskin Rd., Virginia Beach
• **(757) 422-2200, (800) 296-0003**
Known for its representation of some of Virginia Beach's most exclusive properties, Prudential Decker Realty holds its own with the big boys, especially in higher-end sales. It is an especially friendly firm, with well-respected agents in four offices and an excellent reputation for resale and new construction sales as well as relocation services.

Realty Consultants
4664 South Blvd., Virginia Beach
• **(757) 499-5911, (800) 368-3622**
This firm specializes in new construction and resale and covers a wide geographic area from Northeastern North Carolina to

Williamsburg. It also has an office in Newport News.

RE/MAX
**Alliance, 4701 Columbus St.,
Virginia Beach**
• **(757) 456-2345**
**Associates, 101 N. Lynnhaven Rd.,
Virginia Beach**
• **(757) 498-7000**
**Central, 505 S. Independence Blvd.,
Virginia Beach**
• **(757) 490-7300**

The independently owned and operated offices of the RE/MAX network are known for their aggressive marketing of properties and the longevity of their experienced agents. Naturally, their relocation specialists are excellent, as are their resale and new construction agents.

Rose & Womble Realty Co.
4190 S. Plaza Trail, Virginia Beach
• **(757) 340-6655**

A merger in 1998 combined two strong local real estate companies. The Rose & Krueth Realty side of the company was known for marketing new construction. Womble Realty had made its mark selling homes in some of the region's most established neighborhoods. The combined company and its 13 offices draws from the heritage of both its predecessor firms.

Seibert Realty
**601 Sandbridge Rd.,
Virginia Beach**
• **(757) 426-6200**

This boutique agency specializes in the resort area of Sandbridge and handles rentals as well as sales and new construction.

William E. Wood & Associates
800 Newtown Rd., Virginia Beach
• **(757) 499-9663, (800) 446-8260**

This is the region's largest real estate company, with nearly 20 offices throughout the area. You'll find a William E. Wood & Associates sales office in practically every popular neighborhood in Hampton Roads. Boasting a sales force of hundreds, this began as, and remains, a locally owned-and-operated firm, with specialists in resale, new construction, relocation, commercial and bank-owned properties. The company also has a strong property management division that handles a variety of rental properties.

Century 21
16 independent offices
• **(800) 446-8137**

The 16 independently owned and operated Century 21 offices are at work in Hampton Roads, offering topnotch advice on resale, new construction, investment and property management services. Because of their national affiliation, any of this network of Century 21 offices can provide excellent relocation information for moving in or out of the area.

Coldwell Banker
**Helfant Realty Inc.,
3300 Virginia Beach Blvd., Virginia Beach**
• **(757) 463-1212**
**Gifford Realty, 1547 E. Little Creek Rd.,
Norfolk**
• **(757) 583-1000**
**Harbor Group Real Estate,
3210 Academy St., Portsmouth**
• **(757) 484-4400**
**Garman Real Estate,
636 Cedar Rd., Chesapeake**
• **(757) 436-5500**

All the Coldwell Banker affiliates in Hampton Roads were strong independent companies before changing banners. Joan Gifford's company excels in medium-priced housing and rental properties. Gifford, a past president of the Norfolk Division of the Hampton Roads Chamber of Commerce and a past director of the National Association of Realtors, is herself a real estate landmark in the community. Dorcas Helfant, who can lay claim to the honor of being the first woman to serve as president of The National Association of Realtors, has long been respected for her commitment to the advancement of integrity in the industry. Harbor Group claims Portsmouth as home and is a knowledgeable firm for home buyers in this Hampton Roads city. Garman Real Estate is tuned into the fast-growing Chesapeake market.

Judy Boone Realty
809 E. Ocean View Ave., Norfolk
• **(757) 587-2800, (800) 966-5839**
217 Battlefield Blvd., Chesapeake
• **(757) 546-9494**

This small firm started by working a territory few others saw as promising: Norfolk's Ocean View area. It did great things for this neighborhood, fostering some quality development of bayfront land and lending new credibility to what had been a declining neighborhood. Now this family-owned and managed company has expanded into Chesapeake.

Nancy Chandler Associates
701 W. 21st St., Norfolk
• (757) 623-2382
636 Cedar Rd., Chesapeake
• (757) 436-5500

If you're interested in Norfolk's West Side, this is a great company to hook up with. While listings cover the entire market (due to some long-term agents who have strong roots in the upper-end marketplace), the neighborhoods of Ghent, Larchmont and Lochaven are Chandler strongholds. This close-knit group of real estate professionals offers excellent service for resale, new construction (especially downtown townhomes), property management and relocation services. With its acquisition of the Coldwell Banker affiliate in Chesapeake several years ago, Chandler has expanded its scope of operations to take advantage of the flourishing Chesapeake marketplace.

Hampton Roads Neighborhoods

Remember that territorial thing we mentioned in the introduction to this chapter? It would be suicide to even attempt to pick and present the best places to live in Hampton Roads, given the diversity of lifestyle alternatives the region has to offer. All we can do is to give you a general lay-of-the-land, pointing out some of the most popular communities, new and established, and then you're on your own. The neighborhoods that we'll address specifically are those that have a distinctive flavor, either sophisticated urbanite or country chic, that sets them apart from the rest. Your final neighborhood decision will most probably be based on your family's requirements, such as school systems, proximity to the workplace and budget. Let's take the Insiders' armchair tour from one end of the region to the other.

Virginia Beach

The Gold Coast
There's only so much Atlantic Ocean shoreline, and if you want it in your backyard, be prepared to pay a pretty penny. There's no such

thing as a bad oceanfront address; anywhere from about 42nd Street—just north of the Cavalier Hotel—to about 88th Street—just south of Fort Story—will do. There is however, a platinum strip of classic beach cottages that have survived the buy-the-lot-tear-down-the-house syndrome that plagues so much of the oceanfront. It stretches from about 43rd to 50th streets and it's worth a tour, even if you aren't buying.

Croatan
The oceanfront at the other end of the beach, south of the resort area, Croatan has become very fashionable. The homes here are rarely understated—the weathered cottage look is out, monolithic contemporaries are in. Croatan is very expensive but worth it, say residents.

The North End
This moniker describes the residential area of the beach that stretches north from the resort area to the curve where the Atlantic Ocean meets the Chesapeake Bay. The North End is bisected by Atlantic Avenue. If you're headed north on Atlantic Avenue, homes on the right side of the road are oceanside; homes on the left are landside. As you probably expect, the former tend to be a lot more expensive than the latter, but no real estate this close to the ocean is cheap. Oceanside homes include those oceanfront properties we discussed earlier as well as many rentals. Lots of the old rental cottages have been snapped up by well-to-do locals, who put in real heat and new kitchens and never have to contend with traffic when they go to the beach again. On the landside, you'll find a little bit of everything: weathered cedar-shake next to soaring contemporary next to a two-unit condo. But somehow it all works. Locals walk, jog, skate and stroll along a feeder road that runs parallel to Atlantic Avenue and neighbors tend to know each other.

Bay Colony/Princess Anne Hills
There's one "I-could-live-there!" home after another in these premier inland neighborhoods that form the classiest part of the Beach's North End. Many of these sprawling mini-estates border on Crystal Lake and Linkhorn Bay, and their price tags float upwards accordingly. Home to many upper middle-management and corporate executives, entry into the life of the Beach's rich and famous will set you back no less than $200,000 for a pleasant starter home, a hairsbreadth past $2 million if you're on a roll. This is a very active real estate market,

Ghent, An Insiders' History

While there certainly is a lot that's new in Ghent, there's a whole lot more that's old. This popular community in Norfolk's West Side can boast almost more historical roots than anyplace else in the territory.

Though there's heated debate as to where the name Ghent actually originated, most agree it was to commemorate the Treaty of Ghent that formally ended the War of 1812 when it was signed in Belgium. Version one traces the name to Jasper Morgan, a plantation owner who gave his home the name in 1821. Version two gives all the credit to Commodore Drummond, who carried a copy of the Treaty of Ghent on his ship to Norfolk and so named his plantation in 1830.

Whoever started it all, little did they know what was to follow. In 1890, the publication Norfolk's Industrial Advantages reported that Ghent property was sold at $1,400 an acre, and no homes could be built there that cost less than $7,500—a mega-home in that time. John Graham accepted the challenge and erected Ghent's first home at 502 Pembroke Avenue, and by 1892 was paying welcome calls to neighbors Horace Hardy (442 Mowbray Arch), Richard Tunstall (530 Pembroke), Fergus Reid (502 Pembroke) and William H. White (434 Pembroke Avenue).

The majority of the streets in Ghent were named in honor of principals in the Ghent-Norfolk Company, a subcorporation of three syndicates formed abroad after the Civil War to develop Virginia's rich resources. Today you can stroll down Bossevain Avenue (after a Dutch banker), Stockley Gardens (after the same Dutch banker's birthplace in Northampton County) and Olney Road (for Richard Olney, who later became secretary of state for President Cleveland).

In the heart of Ghent Square, sits the Terminal on the Square that houses the Fred Huette Foundation, a horticultural society. The charming building first knew life more than a century ago as the Norfolk-Portsmouth ferry terminal concession

Norfolk's Historic Ghent district is home to many buildings of architectural significance.

Photo: Courtesy of Norfolk Convention and Visitors Bureau

building. While the terminal building itself was torn down in 1964, the concession building was taken apart, piece by piece, each one carefully numbered and matched to a diagram. In 1974, the Housing Authority took all the pieces out of the warehouse and set upon solving the most difficult jigsaw puzzle ever created—somewhere along the line, somebody lost the carefully diagrammed plans for the building's reconstruction. But here it is today, restored to better than its former glory and serving as a central landmark in this vibrant community.

Ghent also claims a few of our country's firsts in the wonderful world of food. Bosman & Lohman, liquidated in 1924, was the largest peanut company in the world in its earliest days and is credited with introducing commercially sold peanut butter to the United States. James G. Gill added a two-bag coffee roaster to his wholesale grocery store in 1902 and begat the Norfolk-based First Colony Coffee and Tea Company. Abe Doumar is said to have invented the very first ice cream cone, introduced at the St. Louis Fair in 1904. Abe created a machine to make the cones and kept it at Doumar's, the restaurant that bears his name, where it is still operational today.

however, with many old-timers fleeing to the carefree condominium lifestyle, so if this is the sort of lifestyle you crave go for it.

Shadowlawn

This unpretentious community is at the South End of Virginia Beach, tucked just far enough behind the resort area for some peace and quiet, but always just a bike ride away from the action. Home prices tend to be lower in Shadowlawn than in the North End, so the area attracts many young homeowners and renters who want that beachy lifestyle at an affordable price.

Cape Story/Cape Henry

These neighborhoods off Virginia Beach's Shore Drive skirt the nearby beachfront of the Chesapeake Bay. They also have the singular distinction of being adjacent to Seashore State Park—whose beautiful bike/walk trail cuts right through both neighborhoods. Cape Story used to have a slightly worn-around-the edges feel; today, many homes have been renovated and the neighborhood is getting pricier. Cape Henry Shores has always been pricey—mainly because about half of the homes are on the water.

The Great Neck Corridor

Just minutes from the ocean and close to business centers, the Great Neck corridor lays sole claim to the most affluent per-capita demographics in the city. While you can start in a condo you can move into for the $90s, count on higher-end single-family homes to set you back up to a million. Along Great Neck Road, you can turn into such coveted neighborhoods

as Broad Bay Point Greens (that owns one of the best golf courses around) to Wolfsnare Plantation or Alanton, and loads of small pockets of affluence in between. Waterfront naturally commands the highest price tag, and many of the secluded mini-mansions have been built to take advantage of the inlets of Lynnhaven and Linkhorn Bays. For single families in this prestigious area, have at least $170,000 in your back pocket.

The Little Neck Corridor

Let the chips keep falling. We're talking the highly desirable neighborhoods of Kings Grant, Middle Plantation and Little Neck Cove—all upper-middle-class magnets for those who feel comfy in a sprawling home with lots of lawn and, perhaps, a waterfront vista of the Lynnhaven Bay or Western Branch of the Lynnhaven River. While many Realtors urge that this is an excellent opportunity to snap up a waterfront property, better have your financial ducks in a row for the $250,000 plus bucks these beauties will demand.

Kempsville

Now we're talking suburban spread. The first real Virginia Beach suburb, the Kempsville area keeps getting larger and more popular, what with neighborhood additions such as Fairfield, Dunbarton and Indian Lakes, and with neighbor community Salem Woods a short hop down the road. A quick zip to the interstate, you're still a ways from the oceanfront, but you are in the belly of retail heaven with strip centers galore lined up with specialty stores to serve your every indulgence. All in all, the Kempsville area is a solid market.

Olde Towne Portsmouth historic district, one of five in the city, has the largest concentration of antique homes between Alexandria, Va., and Charleston, S.C.

Photo: Courtesy of Portsmouth Convention and Visitors Bureau

The Pembroke Corridor

Leave it to Virginia Beach to toss the old with the new and come up with a dish that suits everyone's taste. For older, established and very desirable addresses, you can check out Thoroughgood, the Haygood area and Lake Smith. Whip down to mucho affordable Aragona Village and then swing the pendulum to the newest star in Virginia Beach's crown, Church Point. All you need to create a new neighborhood today is 260 acres of prime real estate, then invite the region's premier builders and crayon out huge lots into pockets called The Mews ($200,000 and up), The Commons ($300,000 and up) and The Quays (up to $1 million). This really is one handsome private residential development, and worthy of a serious look by affluent buyers.

Chesapeake Beach

North of Church Point, and kissing the Chesapeake Bay, is the home to many beach-combers who prefer yards of sand, not grass. A weird architectural mix of high-tech condos, townhomes, old beach cottages and stark cedar contemporaries, both home styles and family backgrounds melt into one under the hot Hampton Roads sun. What residents share, regardless of their home's selling price ($75,000 to $200,000 plus), is their explicit love for the casual beach lifestyle. If you're a sand-in-your-shoes kind of person, this is one great place to hang your flag.

Green Run/Holland Road Corridor

Green Run, the first PUD (Planned Urban Development) in the area, has come by hard and tough times. Single-family homes, townhomes and condos share the cul-de-sacs and curved streets that were the master plan of GSH Real Estate's Oscar Ferebee in the 1960s. Today, new construction developments such as Parkside Green, Woods of Piney Grove, Holland Pines, Princess Anne Crossings and Landstown Meadows call new homebuyers farther down Holland Road and entice them more by offering solidly built, value-priced homes starting in the high $90s. While this particular area may seem way off the track for many urbanites, the area creeps right up to the Virginia Beach City Municipal Complex and is just a stone's throw from the connecting interstate system.

Cypress Point/Glenwood

The link that connects these neighborhoods is golf—beautifully manicured championship golf courses, all encroached by single-family homes and condos that beckon with their country-club, resort-feeling lifestyle. Both target families on the way up (and empty-nesters on the reverse downward spiral) and offer pockets of glamour to varying degrees. Many different builders have opted on prime home sites in these two popular neighborhoods, so plan on a full day to inspect the fully decorated model homes in each.

General Booth Corridor

The road that leads away from the beach at Rudee Inlet has seen a great deal of development in the past 20 years. The first neighborhood you pass is Croatan, but if you keep going south into what used to be the farmland of Virginia Beach, you'll find a little something for everyone. Big spenders can find ego-soothing digs in Lago Mar, while first-time buyers can check out Strawbridge. Ultimately, General Booth takes you all the way out to the Virginia Beach Municipal Center, where several affordable new neighborhoods are currently being developed in an area called Courthouse Estates. Out here, Virginia Beach has a much more rural, pick-your-own strawberries kind of feel, but the kids still ride skateboards.

Pungo

It sounds like country—and it is. A drive out here from the resort area will remind you why they used to advertise Virginia Beach as "the world's largest resort city." You'll find pumpkin patches and horse farms in Pungo, along with lots o' land and lots of classic old farmhouses that just need a little TLC. There also are new neighborhoods cropping up in former farmland. If you want the country life and a Virginia Beach address, this is your haven. The prices out here vary according to acreage; the houses themselves are usually reasonably priced for their size.

Sandbridge

Yet another oceanfront alternative, this neighborhood is far, far away from the madding crowd. Getting here is a bit of a trick—lots of Insiders have to get directions—but it's a beautiful drive along a curvy two-lane road covered with a canopy of green leaves in the summer. The Sandbridge beach has suffered some erosion during the harsh nor'easters we're prone to around here, but its natural beauty and beach-cottage simplicity continue to draw both buyers and renters alike. Homes on the water start at around $210,000, so living on the oceanfront is considerably less expensive here than it is elsewhere in Virginia Beach.

Norfolk

Freemason District/Ghent/ Ghent Square

This is where the Downtowners migrate and mingle. The Freemason district is as close

REAL ESTATE AND NEIGHBORHOODS

A beachfront property allows the benefit of beach activities during quiet times, like this couple taking a sunrise stroll.

Photo: Courtesy of Virginia Tourism Corporation

to city living as you'll find in the area, what with cobblestone streets and the Hampton Roads version of row houses. New affluence meets old money in the condominiums enveloping the area, such as Harborplace, the Tazewell complex, the Pier and Archer's Walk. New condominiums are going up along the water, and the neighborhood recently gained a new upscale apartment complex that demands some of the highest rents in the region.

Ghent and West Ghent are two other older, well-established neighborhoods, the former sprinkled liberally with spacious apartment buildings and rehabbed condominiums. West Ghent is where you'll find many of the grand old houses—three-story jobs that can accommodate young, professional families with kids and pets to spare.

For new construction with that old-timey feel, Ghent Square is the place, a planned urban development with a mix of traditionally styled townhomes and single-family residences. The 65-acre urban pocket features large expanses of brilliant green common areas, so while homes may be packed tight, a feeling of spaciousness pervades. It is definitely an address you'll be proud to claim.

Larchmont/Edgewater

Within walking distance of the sprawling Old Dominion University, these two back-to-back neighborhoods are where you'll find a congenial mix of professors, young business folk, students and, along the bordering Elizabeth and Lafayette rivers, corporate presidents. The older homes are shaded by huge, mature trees, and the quiet streets are usually packed with kids on in-line skates with moms and dads biking alongside. With homes priced from the upper-$100s, it's a great place to relocate if you want to find yourself surrounded by friendly, well-educated residents who take pride in maintaining the integrity of one of Norfolk's most coveted neighborhoods.

Lochaven/Meadowbrook/ North Shore Point

We'll be moving on up when we tour through these premier neighborhoods, home to gracious Colonials, Georgians and Cape Cods, many of which hug the banks of the Elizabeth and Lafayette Rivers.

Many of these superb residences are still

owned by the families who built them, and you'll pay at least $250,000 and up to even consider these addresses. What you get in return, however, is an exceptionally stable neigh-

Norfolk's Freemason neighborhood features cobblestone streets and row houses.

Photo: Courtesy of Norfolk Convention and Visitors Bureau

borhood, with a large, manicured lot and, if you're lucky, a backyard with a river view.

Talbot Park/Belvedere

These neighborhoods near Bon Secours DePaul Medical Center have Granby Street as their dividing line, with the more moderately priced Belvedere on the east. More and more young people are finding jewels in the rough in many of these older homes and choosing these neighborhoods over their Ghent sisters for convenience and value. Many of the Talbot Park residents claim the Elizabeth River as a neighbor; Belvedere's border ends on the ever-calm Lafayette River.

Lakewood/Lafayette Shores

Across the river from Granby Street you can get a glimpse of the docks that belong to the residents of Lakewood, a relatively small pocket of lovely and oh-so-exclusive Colonial and Tudor homes set among quiet, heavily treed streets. Across Willow Wood Drive is an executive community of exceptional custom homes called Lafayette Shores. This gated 66-acre community boasts the last remaining waterfront home sites available in the city, and many corporate leaders have snapped up the offer and built their dream homes.

Ocean View

Until a few years ago, the only things Ocean View could offer were the beauty of the Chesapeake Bay, rickety old beach cottages, colorful bars and a wild St. Paddy's Day parade. Today the View is trying hard to improve itself and the effort shows. Sparkling new condominium and single-family communities are taking advantage of the valuable, if previously neglected, real estate. Of particular note is Pinewell By The Bay, a newer community of huge single-family homes that rests on the bayfront. While prices for these Charleston-style homes average $250,000 and up, you'll get a lot more home for the dollar than any you could find on the oceanfront in Virginia Beach. For a less expensive investment with a built-in marina, Bay Point offers townhomes and condominiums starting in the $60s. At the end of Pretty Lake Avenue, Bay Point takes advantage of its magnificent views of both the Chesapeake Bay and Little Creek Inlet.

Portsmouth

Olde Towne

With the largest number of authentic Federal-style homes dating from the Colonial period between Charleston, South Carolina, and Alexandria, Virginia, Olde Towne residents share the spirit of renovation along with a sense of history. While prices average in the low $200s, these homes are less expensive than their Norfolk counterparts, even though they are only separated by a quick tunnel ride under the Elizabeth River. The 62-acre residential area supports its heritage with a passion, and a stroll down the clean, quiet rebricked streets illuminated by antique electrified gas lamps proves that no neighborhood can ever be too old to restore to its past glory.

Sterling Point/Green Acres

From the Elizabeth River, you can see the docks of the residents of Sterling Point, and the river's tributaries will take you to many Green Acres backyards. Both neighborhoods were developed in the 1950s and have that rancher-type feeling, but lots are large with many trees and the streets are remarkably litter-free. Green Acres borders on the Elizabeth Manor Country Club and hubs around Green Lake in its center. It's technically part of the Churchland area. Homes here hover around the $150,000 mark, with waterfront prices at $300,000.

Churchland

Where Portsmouth's up-and-comers call home, Churchland is almost like a small city unto itself, served by a flotilla of shopping strips, groceries and movie theaters. One of its neighborhoods, River Shore, is a neat-as-a-pin brick rancher community, blessed with heavily wooded lots. If you can snag a waterfront property here, you'll have a breathtaking view all the way to Newport News.

Along Carney Creek, a small western branch of the Elizabeth River, is Hatton Point, with fairly new homes that each have a distinctive personality. While most of the interior homes are ranches, some of those that border the water are truly magnificent. Home resale prices in both neighborhoods begin around $100,000.

For luxury condominium living, Churchland has Cypress Cove that offers residents their own boat slip on the Elizabeth River and Carney Creek. Credited with being the first condominium development in Portsmouth, prices average $140,000.

Just past Churchland on your way north, you'll run into Western Branch, an old-line neighborhood that's currently enjoying a spurt of new life and new construction. Of note is The Crossings, a brand-new community of single-family homes priced from the mid $100s.

INSIDERS' TIP
Always take time to stop at visitors centers or chamber of commerce offices when you're new in town or just visiting. The staff can point you in the direction of fun and may know of special events or have coupons for you to use.

If you're looking for a new home in an old-fashioned neighborhood, this might just be your ticket to the mortgage company.

Chesapeake

Chesapeake has a split personality. One face is that of old-line, deeply entrenched Chesapeake natives like those of the Great Bridge and Deep Creek areas. Flip the coin and you'll see the youthful expression of newly developed neighborhoods like River Walk and Greenbrier. Together they make for a city bulging at the waist from too many good meals of incoming industry, migrating families and the retailers who serve them.

Because homes in this awakening city are simply more affordable than their comparable counterparts in Virginia Beach, the call of the once-rural Chesapeake has reached deafening proportions, especially to builders who firmly believed that the outskirts of Virginia Beach was the true mecca. But throw in an acclaimed golf course, oversized homesites and developers who know how to squeeze a great home out of a tiny dollar, and you've got one of the hottest real estate markets in the region.

Greenbrier

Twenty years ago, a group of investors had the vision to turn what was once fertile farmland into one of the fastest-growing commercial and residential areas on the East Coast. Today, it's a community of 3,500 homes and growing, along with a championship golf course, gorgeous shopping mall, numerous spanking-new strip centers and hundreds of offices and industrial plants.

Just 15 minutes from Norfolk via the interstate, the Greenbrier corridor, especially along the golf course, offers single-family homes where young families can spread out and grow. One of the newest and last communities to be built here is Emerald Greens, with homes constructed by some of the area's premier builders. While prices are somewhat hefty, plan on $250,000-plus average, what you'll move into is scads of square footage with a backyard view

of a manicured fairway or green. For more streamlined condominium living, sneak a peak at The Country Club Collection by The Franciscus Company. Realistically priced from

Homes dating from the Colonial period, are popular in the Hampton Roads area.

Photo: Courtesy of Portsmouth Convention and Visitors Bureau

the $90s, this trio of condo complexes borders the golf course, and one of them is certain to meet your living standards.

River Walk

Another Chesapeake phenomenon, River Walk on the Elizabeth spans 300 acres between Great Bridge Boulevard and the Intracoastal Waterway. While it seems light years away, it's only 10 minutes from the business district in Downtown Norfolk. Here you'll find private enclaves of custom homes, such as Mystic Isle, Quiet Cove, Laurel Haven and Watch Island. Those seeking a more streamlined way of life will delight at the varied condominium alternatives, from Inlet Quay to Beacon Point to Creek Side, all set in heavily wooded sites. Condos start at around $120,000 with remaining custom homesites from $40,000 before the house. You can stop at River Walk's Information Center, 114 Marina Reach, to pick up some exquisite marketing propaganda and browse through their library of available home plans.

Great Bridge

The school system is superb, the people downright neighborly. This is Great Bridge, the

Holiday Home Tours

Historic houses are decked to the nines during the holidays, and the owners of some of them proudly put out the welcome mat during several traditional December home tours. This is a great way to get in the holiday mood while picking up decorating tips for your own abode.

Different houses are highlighted each year, and proceeds from tickets benefit a nonprofit organization. You'll find volunteers eager to share the history and details of each special home with you.

Tours are usually held during the first two weeks of December and are publicized in The Virginian-Pilot's Sunday "Home" section. They also are listed in Port Folio magazine's weekly events calendar.

If you plan a day of house touring be sure to wear comfortable shoes and leave the high heels at home to save wear and tear on hardwood floors—and your feet.

The following are some of the annual December tours:

Holly Homes Tour to benefit the Children's Hospital of The King's Daughters. Homes in either a Virginia Beach or Norfolk neighborhood are featured. While they usually are older homes, occasionally the tour features elaborate custom-built houses. Call (757) 668-7098.

Woman's Club of South Norfolk Christmas Open House Tour. This tour highlights this vintage Chesapeake neighborhood. Call (757) 545-2581.

Christmas in the Country Home Tour. Since 1962, the Cape Henry Woman's Club of Virginia Beach has showcased a historic home in early December. The annual event also includes an optional luncheon and craft and bake sale. Call (757) 481-6857 or (757) 428-2201.

Suffolk-Nansemond Historical Society Annual Candlelight Tour. This event celebrated its 23st anniversary in 1999. It features an evening tour of several older homes as well as entertainment, a gift shop and tea and dessert. Call (757) 539-1131 or (757) 539-6312.

Colonial Place-Riverview Holiday Homes Tour. The Colonial Place-Riverview Civic League sponsors this tour of Norfolk homes build in the early 20th century. Call (757) 627-1441.

Lafayette-Winona Civic League Holiday Open House. This tour of one of Norfolk's historic neighborhoods features turn-of-the-century homes. Proceeds benefit the Lafayette-Winona Historical Designation Association. Call (757) 627-1879.

Holiday Homes Chesapeake. Newer homes take center stage in this tour, which features a different Chesapeake neighborhood each year. If is sponsored by the Great Bridge woman's club. Call (757) 482-4642.

Olde Towne Candlelight Home tour. Vintage homes dating to 1800 are the stars of this tour of downtown Portsmouth residences. Live music is featured in some homes. The tour is sponsored by the Olde Towne Civic League.

Port Norfolk Tour. One of Portsmouth's turn-of-the-century neighborhoods showcases its homes, which include Victorian wonders as well as sturdy four-square styles. The tour is sponsored by the Port Norfolk Civic League and includes refreshments.

If you're in the mood for a road trip, here are some nearby holiday home tours:

Christmas Homes Tour sponsored by the Green Spring Garden Club of Williamsburg. Featured are several homes in near Colonial Williamsburg. In 1997 the garden club sponsored its 38th annual tour. Call (757) 220-0701 or (757) 564-8564.

Fort Monroe Historical Tour of Homes. This walking tour lets visitors into the

(Continued on next page)

grand residences built by the Army in the late-19th and early 20th centuries. The fort is just over the Hampton-Roads Bridge-Tunnel in Hampton's Phoebus area. Call (757) 874-8550.

Christmas in Smithfield. This two-day tour of elaborate late-19th century homes coincides with an antiques show and sale at Smithfield High School. Call (757) 357-6424.

Carrollton Christmas Homes Tour. The Friends of the Carrollton Public Library sponsors this tour of historic and contemporary houses. Carrollton is near Smithfield. Call (757) 238-2538.

Old-fashioned Christmas Home Tour of Parksley. This Eastern Shore town goes all out with carolers in Victorian attire and horse-drawn carriage rides for its annual tour of homes. Most were built in the early 20th century. Call (757) 665-4783 or (757) 665-6271.

Christmas in King William County. The Garden Club of the Middle Peninsula goes all out with tours of homes in small towns along a scenic route between Hampton Roads and Richmond. Call (804) 758-3250.

Christmas Tour of Homes in Currituck, North Carolina. The United Methodist Women of Pilmoor Methodist Church sponsor this tour of historic and contemporary homes. Call (919) 232-3391.

Christmas Candlelight Tour of Edenton, North Carolina. This two-day tour of grand, restored homes is sponsored by the Edenton Historical Commission. Call (800) 775-0111 or (919) 482-2637.

Cape Charles Holiday Sampler and Progressive Dinner Tour. Take your time looking at these early 20th-century homes decked out in their holiday

Holiday trimmings and historic surroundings bring a special Christmas feeling to the historic neighborhoods of the Hampton Roads.

Photo: Courtesy of Colonial Williamsburg Foundation

finery. This tour includes dinner and musical entertainment. Cape Charles in on the Eastern Shore just over the Chesapeake Bay Bridge Tunnel from Virginia Beach.

Christmas in Cockrell's Creek. This tour of homes is in Fleeton outside Reedville in Virginia's Northern Neck. It benefits the Reedville Fisherman's Museum and features homes dating from the early 20th century to more recent years. Call (804) 453-6529.

granddaddy of Chesapeake neighborhoods. Sprinkled with solid ranches and farmhouse Colonials, the many individual neighborhoods that make up this huge "city within a city" corridor are blessed with large, wooded lots and super out-in-the-country smells. But, if you're thinking "rural," you're wrong. Here's where

you'll find Chesapeake General Hospital, financial branches, food places of every description and shopping strips galore. If you're thinking of settling in a neighborhood that has a handle on mixing the old with the newfangled, Great Bridge is the place. In one direction you'll drive into the new communities of Forest Lakes,

Cheshire Forest and Cedarwood, all master-planned neighborhoods with varying levels of single-family custom homes. Do a U-turn and drive in another direction to Etheridge Manor, Country Mill, Mount Pleasant Heights and Brandermill offering exceptional, if architecturally similar, single-family homes at remarkably low prices, from the low $100s. If you want to start off big while still preserving your pocketbook, here's where to look.

Suffolk

Riverview

Most of the homes are old and large, the sort of red-brick Colonials that age with grace and style. This neighborhood is within the city limits of Suffolk proper, and home to generations of the town's elite. Entry is not so steep - in the $80-$90,000 range, but the prices head up from there to $750,000.

Lakeside

Many of the Colonial and ranch-style homes in this older neighborhood date from the 1920s and some are on Lake Kilby. Prices vary accordingly, anywhere from $80,000-$300,000.

Harbour View

This area of northern Suffolk has a whole lotta shakin' goin' on. The opening of the Monitor-Merrimac Bridge-Tunnel made the region easily accessible to the interstate and the Peninsula, and it has rapidly developed into a hot little bedroom community for workers in Newport News and Norfolk. It consists of all-new construction that starts in the highly affordable range of $80,000 but expect to pay much more for custom homes.

Utilities

Bell Atlantic Telephone, (757) 954-6222
Cox Communications, (757) 497-2011
Charter Cable TV, (757) 539-2312 or (757) 238-2232
Hampton Roads Sanitation District, (757) 460-2261
Southeastern Public Service Authority (Recycling), (757) 420-4700
TCI of Virginia, (757) 424-6660
Virginia Natural Gas, (757) 466-5550
Virginia Power, (757) 858-4670
Waterworks: Virginia Beach, (757) 427-3580; Norfolk, (757) 441-2334; Portsmouth, (757) 393-8524; Chesapeake, (757) 547-6352; Suffolk, (757) 925-6390.

INSIDERS' TIP

If you're a newcomer you may be welcomed by a Greetings 2 U representative. The local company calls on more than 400 homes a month to greet new residents. Hostesses come bearing friendly advice and a basket loaded with free samples from area businesses. Greetings 2 U visits newcomers in Chesapeake, Virginia Beach and Suffolk. To make sure the company knows you're here, call (757) 547-3850.

Retirement

The retirement market is a growing one for Virginia Beach, Norfolk and surrounding cities. Some older residents have lived here most of their lives, but many have come here in later years—lured by the Atlantic Ocean, the Chesapeake Bay, the moderate climate and reasonable taxes. Most older newcomers have relatives in the area or once passed through here during their military careers and decided to make it home.

In 1995, for the first time, Virginia ranked in the top 10 travel destination states for retirees. It's also become a popular place for them to settle down. For many retired people the Chesapeake Bay area with its mild climate and numerous attractions is the perfect place to put down roots.

More than 85,000 people age 65 and older live in the area. Lifestyle options for them are varied—from totally independent living to gracious retirement communities, assisted living and nursing home care. There also are many services and activities geared toward keeping older residents active and independent.

Senior Services

American Association of Retired Persons
• (800) 424-3410

AARP is the ultimate organization for anyone older than age 50. This national organization has several local chapters that provide information, services and activities for older adults. There are chapters in Virginia Beach, Norfolk, Portsmouth, Chesapeake and Suffolk. Since volunteer officers change positions frequently, it's best to call the national organization to get a current phone number of the people heading up the chapter that's closest to where you live.

AARP Senior Community Services Employment Program
201 Granby St., Norfolk
• 625-7001

This service sponsored by the American Association of Retired Persons helps find part-time jobs for local residents older than age 50 who need additional income to help meet their living expenses.

Elderhostel Inc.
7575 Federal St.,
Boston, MA 02110
• (617) 426-8056,
(617) 426-7788

Virginia Wesleyan College, Old Dominion University and Atlantic University are among the local participants in Elderhostel Inc. This highly regarded program provides the opportunity for people 60 and older to attend more than 1,900 colleges around the country for a week. They live on campus and enjoy classes that range from history to music appreciation. Prices are so reasonable that some people we know go Elderhostel-hopping for a few weeks and make that their vacation. While many people choose to come to our area for Elderhostel, Hampton Roads residents tend to head to colleges in other areas for a new experience. For a catalog call or write Elderhostel.

Ghent Venture
820 Colonial Ave., Norfolk
• (757) 640-8566

This popular Norfolk program provides fun, educational sessions for anyone age 50 and older. It started in 1982 and is sponsored by seven churches and one synagogue in the Ghent area of Norfolk. Sessions run for six weeks at First Presbyterian Church and regularly draw big crowds. Participants come between 10 AM to 2:30 PM on Thursdays to take a variety of free classes—from lapquilting and mah-jongg to foreign languages and money management. The program includes interesting book reviews and lectures. A hot lunch is available, or participants can brown-bag it. Call ahead for a course schedule and to find out when to sign up for the next session.

M.E. Cox Center for Elder Day Health Care
644 N. Lynnhaven Rd., Virginia Beach
• (757) 340-4388

This nonprofit center was founded in 1975 to provide daycare services for older Virginia Beach residents. It started in St. Nicholas Catholic Church and moved a few years ago to its own building next door. The center cares for about 45 people. The center provides weekday exercise programs, lunches, health monitoring and recreational activities for older adults who are unable to remain at home by themselves.

College Courses

State-supported institutions such as Old Dominion University, Norfolk State University and Tidewater Community College allow state residents older than 60 to take one course a semester for free. To do this you must have been a Virginia resident for at least a year and you must pay taxes in the state. You can sign up on the day the class starts and attend the session if it isn't full. For information contact the registrars' offices at the colleges. (See our chapter on Colleges and Universities.)

Senior Law Center
125 St. Paul's Blvd., Norfolk
• 627-3232

If you're an older adult with a limited income who needs legal assistance, this center may be able to help. It is run by Tidewater Legal Aid and provides legal advice for free or at reduced cost.

Senior Services of Southeastern Virginia
7 Koger Center, Ste. 100, Virginia Beach
• (757) 461-9481

If you're older than age 60, don't hesitate to learn about Senior Services, formerly the Southeastern Virginia Areawide Model Program Inc. This group was incorporated in 1968 as a nonprofit organization. In 1972 it was one of 10 national programs for the aging selected for a federal grant. A year later it became the region's official Area Agency on Aging. It is considered the region's ombudsman for older adults.

Senior Services' goal is to help older residents live independently so they can be involved in the community and enjoy their lives. The organization is an advocate for the elderly that unites the region's various providers of services for retired residents. Its staff can refer older adults and their families to organizations that can help with everything from activities to adult day care and in-home services. Senior Services itself offers case management for people needing assistance with daily living. It also has a service that provides aides, homemakers and other workers who can help someone remain in their home. When the time comes to move to assisted living or a nursing home, it acts as a referral source.

If you're older than 60, Senior Services will issue a photo identification card that will get you senior citizen discounts at numerous businesses. If you need transportation, Senior Services vans take you to doctor's appointments, geriatric day care and recreational programs. Rides must be arranged in advance.

This is a United Way agency and also provides weekday lunches to participants at area senior centers and delivers meals to homebound people. It offers job counseling, training and placement for people older than 55 and also helps them find volunteers opportunities.

Senior Centers

Virginia Beach Senior Programs
Various locations, Virginia Beach
• (757) 471-5884

While Virginia Beach does not have any free-standing senior centers, it does provide a variety of activities for older adults through its six recreation centers. These facilities are operated by Virginia Beach's Department of Parks and Recreation and draw rave reviews from retired residents we know. Activities for older adults range from water aerobics to bridge and crafts. You can call and get a quarterly schedule of

INSIDERS' TIP
If you're a Virginia resident older than age 60, you can take one free college class a semester at state-supported universities.

RETIREMENT

It's great to be retired when you get a Virginia Beach golf course all to yourself!

Photo: Courtesy of Virginia Fairways

activities. Senior Services serves hot lunches on weekdays for older adults at the recreation centers, which are spread throughout the city. (See our Recreation chapter for details.)

Norfolk Senior Center
924 W. 21st St., Norfolk
• (757) 625-5857.

This is one of the largest and busiest senior centers in the region. It is a nonprofit center run by its own board and opened 27 years ago in the Ghent area. The center has classes for ages 55 and older ranging from crafts to computers and ballroom dancing. It brings in a variety of speakers, runs a gift and thrift store, and operates two Norfolk adult daycare centers for those who cannot be home alone. A van takes center participants on shopping trips, to festivals and on other outings. The center also has a Senior Wellness Center that screens for medical problems. Senior Services of Southeastern Virginia provides lunch daily to the center's participants.

Ocean View Senior Center
600 E. Ocean View Ave., Norfolk
• (757) 441-1767

Bridge, bingo and ceramics are among the typical activities offered at this center, which is run by the Norfolk Department of Parks and Recreation. You'll find older adults keeping active with country line dancing lessons and tai chi classes. Senior Services of Southeastern Virginia serves hot lunches here on weekdays.

Portsmouth Senior Center
4040 Victory Blvd., Portsmouth
• (757) 465-2977

This center is directed by the city's Department of Parks and Recreation. It is housed in Tower Mall on Victory Boulevard. The center sponsors a variety of senior activities, including Chesapeake Bay cruises, parties and day trips. Daily activities range from bingo to music lessons and movies. A quarterly schedule of activities is available. Senior Services serves lunch on weekdays at the center.

Chesapeake Senior Center
1000 Outlaw St., Chesapeake
• (757) 382-2000

Fun outings, crafts, sewing, dancing and bridge keep older adults active and busy. Chesapeake's Parks and Recreation Department operates this center. Senior Services of Southeastern Virginia serves lunch here on weekdays.

Suffolk Senior Center
350 N. Main St., Suffolk
• (757) 925-6388

Suffolk's Parks and Recreation Department oversees this senior center that helps fill older adults' days with activities and programs. In addition to arts and crafts, the center sponsors occasional trips to area attractions. Senior Services serves lunch on weekdays.

Other Lunch Locations

Senior Services of Southeastern Virginia also brings hot lunches to two recreation centers in Norfolk that have large numbers of older adults who come there. They are Lambert's Point Recreation Center at 606 W. 29th Street, (757) 664-7500, and Southside Recreation Center, 925 S. Main Street, (757) 664-6450.

Community Service

If you have a few hours to spare, nonprofit groups will welcome you with open arms. Feel free to contact directly any organization that interests you. Two retired Virginia Beach people we know found their niche shelving books at the nearby library they frequent. A Norfolk widow puts her cooking talents to work whipping up meals for a soup kitchen operated by her church. There are several clearinghouse organizations around that can help you find just the right spot for your time and talents.

City of Norfolk Volunteer Program
City Hall Building, Room 100, Norfolk
• (757) 664-4487

Norfolk residents can find plenty of ways to serve their city, and many of them are within walking distance. This city-operated service matches volunteers with libraries, recreation centers and city offices that can use their time and skills.

Retired Senior Volunteer Program (RSVP)
Various locations

RSVP keeps tabs on volunteer opportunities for people 55 and older. It links willing volunteers with hospitals, schools, museums or other nonprofit places needing their services. In Norfolk call (757) 622-6666 or come by the Norfolk Senior Center at 924 W. 21st Street. In Portsmouth, call (757) 393-9333 or stop by 700 London Boulevard. In Suffolk, call (757) 539-6385 or come by 350 N. Main Street.

RETIREMENT

Service Corps of Retired Executives
200 Granby St., Norfolk
• (757) 441-3733

This national organization, which is better known as SCORE, uses retired executives to counsel fledgling business owners. The years of wisdom these volunteers share is free to the client. The SCORE office is in the region's Federal Building. It is one of the busiest SCORE offices in Virginia and typically serves 1,500 clients a year.

Senior Services of Southeastern Virginia Volunteer Services
7 Koger Center, Ste. 100, Norfolk
• (757) 461-9481

Senior Services' staff links nonprofit organizations in need of help with older adults who have time and energy to share. Another program coordinates volunteer opportunities that are augmented by a small stipend for low-income adults who are 60 and older. In this program, they provide friendship and respite care to homebound and disabled adults who have special needs.

Volunteer Hampton Roads
129 W. Virginia Beach Blvd., Norfolk
• (757) 624-2400

This is the region's major clearinghouse for volunteers of all ages. It publishes listings of volunteer opportunities with more than 500 area nonprofit organizations. Volunteer Hampton Roads has been around 40 years under various names. Its newsletter details volunteer needs as do occasional listings in *The Virginian-Pilot*. Call for a volunteer profile to be sent to you to complete so you can be matched with the perfect position.

Wellness Programs

If you're into fitness, check with area malls. Many mall walking groups meet regularly to stride through the climate-controlled environments. Some malls also sponsor occasional breakfasts and programs for their walkers. The YMCA and many area hospitals have programs geared toward older adults.

Bon Secours DePaul Medical Center
100 Kingley Ln., Norfolk
• (757) 889-5976

DePaul has the Gerontology Institute, which does assessments and peer counseling and has a resource center. DePaul's Classic Care Program offers health screenings, support

groups and help in filing insurance claims for members older than age 55. One popular program is Friday night dinner at the hospital. Meals are bargain-priced, and there is usually a piano player or other entertainment.

Eastern Virginia Medical School
700 W. Olney Rd., Norfolk
• (757) 446-7040

In 1996 EVMS created the Glennan Center for Geriatrics and added some internationally known geriatric researchers to its staff. Look for cutting-edge research into aging to come from this EVMS team, which specializes in medicine for all aging populations.

Old Dominion University
Hampton Blvd., and Bolling Ave., Norfolk
• (757) 683-3133

Old Dominion University runs a popular Elderfitness Program through its Wellness Institute. The focus is exercise and wellness programs designed strictly for older adults. Programs are held on the ODU campus.

Sentara Leigh Hospital
830 Kempsville Rd., Norfolk
• (757) 363-6610

Sentara Leigh Hospital operates the Sentara Select Plus program for Sentara Health System hospitals. The program includes free classes, health screenings, educational programs and social activities.

YMCA of South Hampton Roads
322 W. Bute St., Norfolk
• (757) 624-9622

The YMCA has Active Older Adult classes at its eight area YMCAs. Fitness classes include water aerobics, arthritis management sessions, low-impact aerobics, and strength and flexibility training.

Maryview Medical Center
3636 High St., Portsmouth
• (757) 398-2273

Maryview has a Senior Advantage Program that sponsors social events and helps older adults tackle insurance claims.

Chesapeake General Hospital
736 N. Butterfield Blvd., Chesapeake
• (757) 482-6143

Chesapeake General has a wellness program for older adults at its Lifestyle Fitness Center, (757) 482-6132. Health screenings, bowling leagues and Friday night dinners are part of the program. The Chesapeake hospital also has an

Older Adult Mental Health Program that includes inpatient and outpatient services.

Housing Options

Housing options range from total independence to varying degrees of assistance. Buying a single-family home, a condominium or townhouse certainly is an option. Throughout the region you'll find a variety of prices and neighborhoods that range from historic to brand new. (See our Real Estate chapter.) If you like a great view—and don't mind paying for the privilege—scout out some of the possibilities along the Chesapeake Bay, the Atlantic Ocean and the Elizabeth River.

Apartments are also worth considering. You'll find some that particularly appeal to older residents, including the Hague Towers and Pembroke Towers in Norfolk and many apartment buildings in the Wards Corner area of the city.

There also are numerous subsidized apart-

The ocean, the bay and the mild climate lure many retirees to this area.

Photo: Courtesy of City of Virginia Beach

ments that rent for reasonable fees. However, many of these require lengthy waits to get in and have strict guidelines on income levels. Among the apartments designed for people on limited incomes are John Knox Towers, Cromwell House and Stonebridge Manor in Norfolk and Chesapeake Crossing in Chesapeake.

If you prefer a retirement community that

lets you live independently but offers numerous amenities, right now there are only a few to choose from in South Hampton Roads. And, if you don't mind traveling a little farther, there are others in Williamsburg and Newport News.

Before settling on a retirement facility, take time to explore it and get to know residents and staff. Eat a meal or two to see if you like the food. Check out the recreational activities and learn what your options are should your health suddenly decline. If you are considering a continuing care community that charges a large entrance fee, make sure you know what is covered and what percentage is refundable if you decide to leave.

Atlantic Shores Retirement Community
1398 Gibraltar Ct., Virginia Beach
• **(757) 426-0000**

This upscale retirement community opened its first units in 1996 after several years of construction. The new community is on 200 acres near the Dam Neck Navy base. It is adjacent to Red Wing Lake Municipal Golf Course and is a mile from the Atlantic Ocean and its beaches. Atlantic Shores was developed by Rauch & Company of Chicago and Lifecare Services Corporation of Des Moines.

The completion of the first phase in 1997 gave Atlantic Shores both multiunit buildings and detached villas with garages. The complex has 340 units, many of them villas, as well as a clubhouse, a skilled nursing center, tennis courts and a swimming pool. Living in Atlantic Shores requires sizable enrollment fees. Since the project is a cooperative, buyers own equity in their units. They also pay monthly service fees.

First Colonial Inn
845 First Colonial Rd., Virginia Beach
• **(757) 428-2884**

If you're interested in an independent retirement community but don't want to pay an up-front fee, take a look at First Colonial Inn. It is strictly a rental community for retired people. The 185 apartments in this three-story building in the Hilltop area range in size from

RETIREMENT

studios to two-bedroom models. Besides independent living, First Colonial Inn has 21 personal-care apartments that provide assistance with bathing, dressing and medications.

First Colonial Inn is managed by Excel Retirement Communities of Fort Worth, Texas. Amenities include three meals a day in the dining room, twice-monthly maid service and laundering of linens and towels as well as transportation to nearby shopping centers, banks and doctors' offices. Most apartments include full-size kitchens. There are many recreational activities from which to choose.

Residents pay only a monthly rental that includes some meals. Apartments also come with kitchens. Some units are available immediately, while larger units sometimes require a wait of a few months.

Marian Manor
5345 Marian Ln., Virginia Beach
• (757) 456-5018

The Catholic Diocese of Richmond sponsors this retirement community just off Virginia Beach Boulevard. It has 16 apartments with kitchenettes for those who prefer independent living. Residents can still enjoy three meals a day in the Marian Manor dining room. There also are 85 studio apartments for people who need assisted living. These units are equipped with a refrigerator, and microwave ovens are allowed. Marian Manor is a rental community. Its amenities include a recreation center, transportation and a full roster of activities.

Also on the Marian Manor grounds is a 30-bed intermediate care facility. In 1998 Marian Manor opened a sister community on Princess Anne Road, Our Lady of Perpetual Help. Its 120 rooms will include assisted living, an Alzheimer's unit and a nursing home.

Westminster-Canterbury in Virginia Beach
3100 Shore Dr., Virginia Beach
• (757) 496-1100

Westminster-Canterbury is the hands-down winner for the best location of any area retirement community. It is built right on a beach overlooking the Chesapeake Bay and has 16 acres of grounds. This 14-story complex features 335 independent-living apartments and in 2000 is in the midst of a major expansion. It also has 50 assisted-living units as well as a healthcare center with 75 beds. Westminster-Canterbury opened in 1981 as a joint venture of the Presbytery of Eastern Virginia and the Episcopal Diocese of Southern Virginia.

It is open to any person age 65 or older who can live independently. Apartments range in size from studios to two-bedroom units. Most have full-size kitchens. The smallest studio apartments sometimes are available immediately. Expect to wait from one to five years for larger apartments—the bigger the apartment the longer the wait.

Amenities include one prepaid meal a day, weekly maid service, bed and bath linens, 24-hour security, an indoor swimming pool, a whirlpool, a steam room, gardening areas and a full roster of activities. As residents need more help, they can move to assisted living and a nursing home that are part of the facility.

Admission to Westminster-Canterbury requires paying a sizable entrance fee that guarantees lifetime occupancy in an apartment, the Assisted Living Center or Health Care Center. In addition, residents pay monthly fees. The amount of both the entrance fee and monthly fees depends on the size of the apartment. There is a limited amount of financial assistance available.

Continuing Care

There are more than 60 nursing homes in the area—far too many to discuss here. In the past couple of years there has been a boom in assisted-living facilities. These can bridge the gap between independent living and nursing-home care by providing gracious surroundings and supplemental help for older residents.

The staff of assisted-living facilities typically help with bathing and dressing, transportation to doctor's offices, dispensing medicine and recreation. All meals are served in the dining room, and residents are expected to dress in street clothes. Elegant common areas are brightened by chintz curtains and potted plants, while residents' rooms are personalized with furniture from home.

After spending months exploring this assisted-living option for an ailing parent, we can

INSIDERS' TIP

Make sure to find out beforehand if the adult-care home or nursing home you are looking into is licensed. The Department of Public Health and Human Services can tell you if the home is licensed and if any complaints have been registered against it.

RETIREMENT

forewarn you that you will be confused. Licensing varies from facility to facility, and you must be careful you're not comparing apples and oranges. It's crucial you know how ambulatory the resident must be. Some centers are licensed only for residents who walk independently or with a walker. Others will allow residents to be in wheelchairs. However, at some centers residents must get into wheelchairs by themselves. At other centers employees can assist them into wheelchairs.

Among the possibilities to consider are Brighton Gardens and Marian Manor Retirement Community in Virginia Beach; Ghent Arms, The Ballentine, Province Place of DePaul and Leigh Hall in Norfolk; and Georgian Manor in Chesapeake. All are privately owned except Marian Manor and Province Place, which are affiliated with a Catholic church, and Georgian Manor, which is owned by Chesapeake General Hospital. Sentara Healthcare has Sentara Villages in Virginia Beach, Norfolk and Chesapeake. The villages offer assisted living. Sentara also operates several nursing homes. Sentara provides a Senior Assessment Center to help determine what type assistance—from meal delivery to nursing home care—older residents need. It has an Alzheimer's unit in one of its nursing homes, (757) 463-0100. Sentara also

INSIDERS' TIP

Senior Services of Southeastern Virginia, (757) 461-9481 is the region's ultimate source for information geared toward older adults.

sponsors an adult daycare program. Call (757) 463-0600 for information.

Older adults recuperating from a broken bone, stroke or other medical problem will find the most intense rehabilitation program at Sentara Norfolk General where a program is run in conjunction with Eastern Virginia Medical School, (757) 668-3487. Norfolk's Lake Taylor Hospital, the region's only long-term care hospital, also has a physical and occupational therapy program, (757) 461-5001. Several nursing homes also provide rehabilitation services.

Numbers to Know

American Association of Retired Persons (AARP) - (800) 424-3410
Virginia Beach senior programs - (757) 471-5884
Norfolk Senior Center - (757) 625-5857
Portsmouth Senior Center - (757) 398-3777
Chesapeake Senior Center - (757) 382-2000
Suffolk Senior Center - (757) 925-6388
The Ghent Venture - (757) 640-8566
Ocean View Senior Center - (757) 441-1767
Senior Services of Southeastern Virginia - (757) 461-9481

RETIREMENT

Higher Education

LOOK FOR:
• Colleges and Universities
• Other Opportunities

Doctor. Lawyer. Executive chef. Name almost any career you are interested in, and chances are you'll find a degree in it offered somewhere in Hampton Roads. There are six major colleges and universities based in the five-city area. In addition, the region's large military population has attracted a number of out-of-area colleges that offer undergraduate and graduate degree programs here. And, if that's not enough, there are four other colleges on the Peninsula within easy driving distance—Christopher Newport University in Newport News, the College of William & Mary in Williamsburg, and Hampton University and Thomas Nelson Community College, both in Hampton.

If you're holding down a job and thinking of earning a degree on the side, you'll find that easy to do here. All colleges offer evening programs, and some also have early morning and weekend sessions that cater to working students. Locally, Old Dominion University is a pioneer in bringing classes to students at suburban education centers and through telecommunications.

In Hampton Roads there are also more than 50 private career colleges

Virginia Wesleyan College is the only private liberal arts college in the area.

Photo: Courtesy of Virginia Wesleyan College

and schools that train mechanics, computer technicians, cosmetologists, travel agents and chefs, to name a few of the possibilities.

For residents with a lifelong love of learning, reasonably priced adult education programs can teach them to tap dance, paint or become a tennis ace. Most of these fun classes are run by city parks and recreation departments. However, some are offered through the continuing education departments of area public schools. (See the Schools chapter for details.) Area colleges also schedule a wide range of noncredit courses for the community. Most programs publish quarterly guides listing class times and fees. Two of our favorite places to take classes are Norfolk Parks and Recreation Department's Lakewood Dance and Music Center, (757) 441-5833, and Old Dominion University, which always has a wide range of community and continuing education courses, 683-4247.

Colleges and Universities

Major colleges and universities based in the area that are accredited by the Southern Association of Colleges and Schools are:

Eastern Virginia Medical School
721 Fairfax Ave., Norfolk
• **(757) 446-5600**

Established in 1973, Eastern Virginia Medical School (EVMS) is one of only three medical schools in Virginia. The school is operated by the Medical College of Hampton Roads from a campus in Norfolk. However, its students and medical residents use 30 area hospitals and clinics as their training ground. From its first class of 24 medical students, the school has grown to an enrollment of about 600 students who come from Virginia as well as other states. Each year EVMS sponsors 20 residency programs, a psychology internship and fellowship programs that attract about 300 physicians. Besides the M.D. degree, EVMS grants doctoral degrees in clinical psychology and biomedical sciences through cooperative programs with area universities. It also offers art psychotherapy and physician assistant degree programs. EVMS offers a master's degree in public health in conjunction with Old Dominion University. In 2000 it opened a new library that serves both students and the public.

EVMS receives some state funding but depends heavily on support from area cities and private donations. In fact, the school got its start when area residents raised $17 million in the late 1960s and early 1970s to start the school. Having a medical school in Hampton Roads has brought a full range of sophisticated medical services—including heart transplants

INSIDERS' TIP
Virginia residents who are older than 60 can take classes for free at state-supported institutions such as Tidewater Community College and Old Dominion University.

and in-vitro fertilization—to the region. The school has also greatly increased the number of physicians working in the area.

EVMS is noted for its Jones Institute for Reproductive Medicine—the first in-vitro fertilization clinic in the United States. In 1981 the Institute helped produce the country's first in-vitro baby. Since then more than 1,600 in-vitro babies have been born with the Institute's help. It has the world's highest pregnancy rate among in-vitro programs and draws patients from across the country. The Institute has an international reputation for treating reproductive problems. In 1994 it gained international acclaim for its genetic engineering, which produced a healthy child for a Louisiana couple who were carriers of the deadly Tay-Sachs disease. In 2000 EVMS received a $25 million grant from the Bill and Melinda Gates Foundation to find ways to prevent the spread of sexually transmitted diseases.

Another major program of EVMS is the Diabetes Institutes, which has dedicated itself to finding a cure for diabetes as well as running treatment programs for area residents with diabetes. EVMS also operates the Center for Pediatric Research, the Virginia Prostate Center and the Glennan Center for Geriatrics.

Norfolk State University
240 Chapman Ave., Norfolk
• **(757) 683-8600**

Founded in 1935 as a division of Virginia Union University, Norfolk State (NSU) has grown into one of the country's five-largest historically black colleges. It has an enrollment of more than 8,100. Students come from throughout the United States and 35 foreign countries.

In 1944 NSU became part of the Virginia

college system and in 1979 gained university status. Today it has nine schools and 32 departments. NSU offers seven associate, 44 bachelor's, 14 master's degrees and one doctoral degree. Degree programs include education, nursing, journalism and social work. There are 15 intercollegiate sports, including football and basketball. In 1997 NSU's teams began competing in the National Collegiate Athletic Association's Division I.

NSU operates the Ronald I. Dozoretz National Institute for Minorities in Applied Sciences, which recruits top high school seniors across the country to study science. In the last few years NSU instituted a master's degree program in science and its first doctoral program, which is in social work.

NSU is renowned for its marching band and Army ROTC program. It has the country's second-largest female ROTC cadet enrollment, and its total ROTC enrollment is the largest in Virginia for a nonmilitary school.

Besides its 130-acre campus in Norfolk, NSU operates a satellite center in Portsmouth and a graduate center in Virginia Beach with Old Dominion University. The two universities recently built a joint mini-campus in Virginia Beach that serves 7,000 students.

Old Dominion University
5210 Hampton Blvd., Norfolk
• (757) 683-3000

Founded in 1930 in Norfolk as a branch of the College of William and Mary, Old Dominionn University (ODU) became independent in 1962. In 1970 the state-supported institution gained university status. It has an enrollment of more than 18,000. Students come from across the United States as well as 80 foreign countries. ODU offers 65 bachelor's, 64 master's and 21 doctoral degree programs. In 1996 ODU added weekend courses to make it easy for working students to attend class. Through its Career Advantage Program, a few years ago ODU became the first state-supported university in Virginia to make professional internships available to every student.

ODU is one of Virginia's top Ph.D. research institutions. Its proximity to NASA Langley Research Center in Hampton has helped it become the leader among Virginia universities in NASA research contracts. ODU is a partner in

the Continuous Electron Beam Accelerator Facility (CEBAF), a massive nuclear physics project that opened in Newport News in 1994. The university has expanded its physics faculty to meet its goal of having one of the country's premier physics programs.

ODU already is recognized worldwide for its Department of Oceanography, which offers two graduate degrees and includes the Center for Coastal Physical Oceanography. ODU's Applied Marine Research Laboratory conducts environmental studies for regulatory agencies and private organizations.

At ODU, degree programs include business, education, science and English. ODU recently added a master's degree in public health in conjunction with Eastern Virginia Medical School. There are 16 varsity sports, including basketball, sailing and soccer. In recent years both ODU's sailing and field hockey teams have been ranked No. 1 in the country. In 1997 its women's basketball team made it to the NCAA finals.

Besides its Norfolk campus on Hampton Boulevard, ODU operates the Old Dominion University Peninsula Center in Hampton. It is a partner in the ODU-NSU Virginia Beach Graduate Center. The two universities recently completed a mini-campus in Virginia Beach that they share. Many courses are offered at the satellite locations, which utilize both on-site instructors and teleconferencing. ODU widely uses telecommunications to beam courses to distant locations. ODU is the country's largest provider of distance learning classes.

Regent University
1000 Regent University Dr., Virginia Beach
• (757) 579-4000

Founded in 1977 as CBN University, this private graduate school gained a new name in 1990. Regent shares an 800-acre campus in Virginia Beach with The Christian Broadcasting Network. Its more than 1,600 students come from across the United States and 20 countries. They earn master's degrees in business, communication, counseling, education, government, law or divinity. Regent also offers doctorates in communication and leadership studies. The university is gaining a national reputation for its film degree offered through its communication school.

Regent is the only university in South Hampton Roads to offer a law degree. All its

Numerous supportive facilities in the Tidewater area offer college and university students rich resources in the areas of scientific, marine, historical and environmental studies.

Photo: Courtesy of Virginia Tourism Corporation

classes are taught from a Christian perspective. Regent also has a long-distance learning component that beams courses to faraway students via the miracle of modern telecommunications.

Tidewater Community College
428 Cedar Rd., Chesapeake
• **(757) 547-5100**
7000 College Dr., Portsmouth
• **(757) 484-2121**
1700 College Crescent, Virginia Beach
• **(757) 427-7100**
300 Granby St., Norfolk
• **(757) 683-9414**

Founded in 1968, Tidewater Community College provides training and higher education throughout the region. It has campuses in the Green Run area of Virginia Beach, the Churchland area of Portsmouth, the Great Bridge section of Chesapeake and downtown Norfolk. The Norfolk campus officially opened in 1997 and has some of the region's most technologically advanced classrooms. TCC had been teaching downtown classes for several years while its buildings were being completed. TCC also offers off-campus programs at area high schools, military bases and other locations.

With more than 18,000 students—the majority of them part-time—TCC is the second-largest community college in Virginia. TCC offers two-year associate degrees as well as occupational training in 90 different programs. In addition to academic courses in English, math and business, TCC offers training in such fields as truck driving, landscaping and welding. It recently added railroading and culinary arts to the programs at its Norfolk campus. Many TCC graduates transfer to four-year colleges; others launch right into their careers. The college recently has moved aggressively into computer and Internet training through continuing education courses that have attracted a loyal following. TCC operates a Visual Arts Center in downtown Portsmouth that trains art students and displays their works.

Virginia Wesleyan College
1584 Wesleyan Dr., Norfolk/Virginia Beach
• **(757) 455-3200**

Virginia Wesleyan, founded in 1966, straddles the Norfolk-Virginia Beach city line. It has a 300-acre campus and a student body of more than 1,300. Students come from 35 states and nine foreign countries. The private college is affiliated with the United Methodist Church and offers a liberal arts curriculum.

Virginia Wesleyan students can earn bachelor's degrees in 35 areas including business management, communication and physics. They can participate in varsity sports including basketball, baseball, soccer and tennis.

The college's adult studies program schedules classes early in the morning, at night and on weekends. It is aimed at working adults eager to return to college and earn a degree. To keep college within working students' budgets, tuition is half-price for evening classes. One popular offering is an alternative certification program for professionals who want to become teachers. Participants must have a degree in math, science, English, history or a foreign language. By taking three concentrated courses, student teaching for a semester and passing the national teacher's exam, they can be certified to teach.

Other Opportunities

Educational options abound in Hampton Roads. Here is a sampling of what is offered in the region:

A master's degree in transpersonal studies from Atlantic University. The private university is affiliated with the Virginia Beach-based Association for Research and Enlightenment and the Edgar Cayce Foundation. It also offers an independent studies program. Call (757) 428-3588.

Courses in law enforcement, data processing, English and business at the Suffolk branch of Paul D. Camp Community College. At this public college, associate's degrees are available in some fields with certificates offered in more technical fields. Call (757) 925-2283.

An associate's degree from ECPI College of Technology in Virginia Beach. The proprietary school offers training in such fields as computer programming, word processing and accounting. Call (757) 490-9090.

A two-year culinary arts degree from Rhode Island-based Johnson & Wales University. The University has a Norfolk branch of its College of Culinary Arts that trains chefs. It also offers a series of excellent one-night community classes for people who love to cook. Call (757) 853-3508.

Graduate courses at the Hampton Roads Graduate Center run jointly in Virginia Beach by the University of Virginia and Virginia Tech. Among the offerings are engineering degrees and teacher recertification. Call (757) 552-1890.

Schools

Whether you are searching for the right kindergarten or high school for your children, Hampton Roads has an abundance of choices. You'll find plenty of parents pleased with their cities' public schools as well as those loyal to private or parochial schools. The best part is that the region has a multifaceted educational system that easily fills students' needs and meets parents' demands—from special education to gifted programs and everything in between.

LOOK FOR:
• Public Schools
• Magnet Schools
• Private Schools
• Home Schooling

Public Schools

Each of the five cities in this area has its own public school system that operates independently.

Until the last decade Virginia was the only state in the country with appointed school board members. However, legislation gave localities the choice of electing the people who oversee education. Virginia Beach was the first area school district to opt for electing its school board. Now every other area city but Norfolk has shifted to letting the public decide who sits on the board. Norfolk remains a staunch supporter of a school board appointed by city council.

In Virginia the current emphasis is on the state-mandated Standards of Learning. This new program ensures that all students in Virginia learn the same material at the same grade level. Within a few years schools must have a certain percentage of students pass the Standards of Learning tests or lose accreditation. Passing most of the tests will become a requirement for high school graduation.

To enroll a student in a school district for the first time, you will need the child's Social Security number, a certified birth certificate, a completed physical examination form, an immunization record and a report card from the child's last school, if the child has attended one.

If you're enrolling in September, don't wait until the last minute to get this done. The pediatricians are swamped with parents needing medical forms completed. And, it's likely your child's old school doesn't have time to pull records and send them to you.

Kindergarten students must be 5 years old by September 30 to enroll. However, several districts let parents send students whose birthdays fall within a month or two after that cutoff. The exact date varies with the district, and in some districts parents must pay tuition to enroll a younger child. Kindergarten is not mandatory in Virginia, although we're hard-pressed to think of any parents who don't send their children to kindergarten.

Public schools throughout the region tend to draw students from nearby neighborhoods. Bus service is provided for students living too far to walk to school.

All public schools offer a wide range of academics, sports and extracurricular activities. Programs are provided for gifted and talented students and those with special educational needs. In the region, there are strong links with the business and military communities. Some organizations adopt entire schools and channel a lot of energy into improving them. Others occasionally provide lecturers and tutors.

Virginia Beach Public Schools

Virginia Beach has the largest public school district in the region and the second-largest in Virginia. The district is the 38th largest in the United States. It has more than 77,000 students and 6,500 teachers.

The school district operates 10 high schools, 14 middle schools, 53 elementary schools and seven specialized centers. Since the city's population boom in the mid- to late-1980s, the school district has worked to alleviate overcrowding by building new schools throughout the city. In 2000 a new high school is under construction and many schools are being renovated.

Kindergarten in Virginia Beach operates in two half-day shifts. Students are assigned to either morning or afternoon sessions. Students in 1st grade and beyond attend school all day.

For students with special needs, the school district offers several programs. Gifted 1st-graders can participate in school-based programs that challenge them. Those in grades 2 through 6 can attend the Old Donation Center, a select school for gifted students, or remain in their home school as part of the gifted resource program. Similarly, gifted middle school students may apply for admission to Kemps Landing Magnet Center or receive instruction through the gifted resource program in their home schools. In addition, programs are available for students with talent in visual arts and dance.

Individual schools also have other gifted programs as well as classes for special education students. Ocean lakes High School operates a magnet center for math and science. In addition, Princess Anne High School offers an International Baccalaureate diploma. In the program, juniors and seniors can take two years of advanced-level courses and complete 200 hours of extracurricular and community-service activities.

Students needing additional help are assisted by reading resource teachers and other remedial instruction. Some schools offer special instruction for students who speak English as a second language.

Virginia Beach's high schools offer both regular and advanced studies. Those in advanced studies take high-level classes in math, science and language. They also are required to complete more courses to graduate. Advanced placement classes are offered in art, biology, calculus, chemistry, computer science, English, foreign languages, physics and United States history. High schools offer instruction in French, German, Latin, Russian and Spanish.

Alternative schools include the Virginia Beach Central Academy, which offers a core curriculum and vocational courses, the Technical and Career Education Center, and the Center for Effective Learning.

Adults 17 and older can attend evening classes at the Open Campus High School to earn their high school diploma or GED certificate. They also can study at the Adult Learning Center, which has some basic courses as well as more recreational ones.

Virginia Beach numbers to note:
Superintendent's Office, (757) 427-4326
Office of Student Services, (757) 427-4791
Gifted /Talented Center, (757) 563-1255
Adult Learning Center, (757) 473-5091
Technical and Career Education Center, (757) 427-5300
Open Campus, (757) 473-5200
Recreational Classes, (757) 473-5091
Public Information, (757) 427-4320

Norfolk Public Schools

With about 38,000 students, Norfolk has the second-largest school district in the region. There are five high schools, eight middle schools and 35 elementary schools, some of which are undergoing renovation and expansion. The district has more than 2,700 teachers.

The Norfolk school district offers a number of special programs. More than 5,000 students participate in gifted courses. For students in kindergarten through the 5th grade, there is the Field Lighthouse Program. One day a week gifted students travel to Stuart Gifted School or

SCHOOLS

teachers from Stuart visit schools for specialized studies. The center is also where foreign-speaking children spend part of the day learning English.

Students in grades 7 through 12 can take honors classes in math, science, social studies, communication skills and foreign languages. Students in grades 6 through 12 who are eager for more learning can stay after school for the Arts & Sciences Extended Day Program. The curriculum includes computer science, future problem solving and architecture/engineering. Students whose interests lean toward high technology can get practical training at the NORSTAR Student Research Institute, which conducts space shuttle experiments and robotics projects.

The school district operates Chesterfield Academy, a science and technology magnet school for elementary students. Ruffner Middle School also is a magnet school. Older students leaning toward health careers can participate in the Medical School for Science and Health Professions through Eastern Virginia Medical School. In 2000 the first International Baccalaureate class graduated from Granby High School. The IB program offers students in grades 11 and 12 a chance to earn a year of college credits in science, math, English, foreign languages, history and the arts.

Norfolk Public Schools has many programs designed for special education students. The district runs St. Mary's Infant Home for severely disabled children. The school district has a program for disabled preschoolers. Students who are kindergarten age and older are mainstreamed, if possible, with the help of resource rooms.

Each summer about 500 talented middle-school students participate in Junior University held at Granby High School. Elementary students can participate in a five-week summer enrichment program. Talented high school musicians can perform through the Strolling Silver Strings ensemble.

Preparing children to learn is an important goal for the school district. It offers an extensive prekindergarten program and a full-day kindergarten. Norfolk also has Early Childhood Education Centers for 3-year-olds and their parents.

There are several specialized centers run by the school district. The Coronado School is for pregnant students. The Norfolk Technical Vocational Center helps students prepare for careers, while Tech Prep helps prepare students for the workplace or post-secondary education. The Madison Career Center provides vocational training as well as adult basic education and preparation for the GED.

In Norfolk, adult education courses, which run the gamut from quilting to computers, are administered by the city's parks and recreation department. The reasonably priced classes are scheduled year round at the city's recreation centers and are some of the better bargains in town.

Norfolk numbers to note:
Superintendent's Office, (757) 441-2107
Adult/Vocational Education, (757) 441-2957
Gifted Programs, (757) 441-2638
Special Education Services, (757) 441-2743
Recreational Classes, (757) 441-2149

Portsmouth Public Schools

There are nearly 18,000 students attending Portsmouth Public Schools. The district has three high schools, four middle schools and 19 elementary schools. More than 1,200 teachers work with these students.

Gifted and talented programs run from kindergarten through grade 12. Through the Spectrum Program for the Gifted and Talented, students can participate in a variety of programs.

Students in grades one and two are offered the Explorer program that supplements everyday studies. Once a week gifted and talented instructors also come to the schools for special programs. Grades 3 through 5 have the Search program, which takes students to one of the district's five gifted and talented labs for a full day of studies once a week. The Discover program takes middle school students to a bi-monthly session and supplements their program with workshops and seminars. High school students have both honors and advanced-placement labs.

The school district also operates a Montessori School at Park View Elementary, an earth and space school at Douglas Park Elementary, and an aerospace program at Hunt Middle School.

High school students can opt for the math science and aerospace technology program at Norcom High School, the visual and performing arts program at Churchland High School or the international studies program at Wilson High School.

The school district offers a variety of special education programs. Some are based in regular classrooms; others involve resource rooms or special education centers. Preschoolers and early elementary students can get special help at the DAC Center for Learning.

Among the school district's special centers are New Directions, which provides alternative programs for middle- and high-school students. The EXCEL Campus offers adults and older high school students the chance to earn their GED or to take computer and other helpful courses in the evenings.

Portsmouth numbers to note:
Superintendent's Office, (757) 393-8742
EXCEL Campus, (757) 465-2958
Special Education Program, (757) 393-8658
Vocational Education Program, (757) 393-8869
Gifted Programs, (757) 393-5059
Recreational Classes, (757) 393-8481
Public Information, (757) 393-8743

Chesapeake Public Schools

The Chesapeake Public School District gained acclaim in 1990 when it put a warranty on all its graduates. This guarantees that any employer can "return" a Chesapeake graduate to the school district if he or she fails to have mastery of basic skills.

Since Chesapeake has been one of the country's boom cities during the past few years, the influx of new residents has challenged the school district to expand. It is one of the fastest growing school districts in Virginia and keeps building new schools to keep pace with new housing subdivisions. The district operates six high schools, eight middle schools and 28 elementary schools. The district has nearly 37,000 students and more than 2,300 teachers.

Gifted and talented programs are available for those in grades kindergarten through 12. Younger students have in-school programs, while 5th and 6th graders go once a week to the

Field trips are particularly fun when the class goes to the Virginia Marine Science Museum.

Photo: Courtesy of Virginia Beach Department of Convention and Visitor Development

SCHOOLS

Laboratory School for the Gifted and Talented. There they do problem solving and learn more about math, science and computers. Middle school students can participate in gifted programs in most subject areas, while senior high students have advanced placement and honors courses.

Chesapeake's special education preschools serve children who are developmentally delayed. Special education students attend assigned schools. Those who can be mainstreamed are included in regular classes. Resource rooms and teaching assistance are available along with some self-contained classes. A preschool education program is designed to help children ages 2 to 5.

Among the school district's special centers are the Adult Education Center, which offers preparation for the GED as well as career-oriented classes for working adults. The Chesapeake Center for Science and Technology offers vocational courses training in such fields as engine repair and nursing; and the Alternative School for students whose discipline problems prevent them from attending their assigned high schools.

Chesapeake numbers to note:
Superintendent's Office, (757) 547-0165
Gifted Programs, (757) 494-7640
Vocational Education Programs, (757) 547-0153
Adult Education Program, (757) 482-5680
Special Education Programs, (757) 494-7664
Recreational Classes, (757) 547-6411
Public Information, (757) 547-1033

Suffolk Public Schools

Suffolk, which is experiencing rapid residential growth, has a burgeoning school population to go with it. From 1994 to 1998 the school census rose 16 percent to 11,200 students. There are more than 700 teachers in the district.

To make room for new students, the school district opened a new elementary school in 1996 to replace a smaller school. In 1997 another elementary school was expanded and renovated. In 1998 a new elementary school opened and renovations started on an older school. A new middle school will open in 2001. Plans call for adding a high school and elementary school as funding become available. Several others schools are to be renovated during the next few years. There currently are 11 elementary schools, three middle schools and two high schools in Suffolk.

Gifted and talented programs start in kindergarten for students who show exceptional potential. In the Kids Involved in New Directions (KIND) program, children in grades K through 1 attend enrichment classes. In the Student Trial Enrichment Program (STEP) students in grades 2 and 3 meet with specially trained teachers for additional learning programs.

INSIDERS' TIP
Norfolk Academy, founded in 1728, is Virginia's oldest independent secondary school. It is the 13th-oldest secondary educational institution in the country.

Gifted students in grades 4 through 8 can participate in the QUEST program, which is designed to develop independent learning skills, creative potential and high-level thinking skills. In high school, teachers can offer gifted students special units designed to challenge them. Through a dual-credit program, students can earn college credits at Paul D. Camp Community College by taking such advanced courses as calculus, biology, U.S. history, computer science and physics. Art and music classes involve elementary and middle-school students in creative programing.

The school district has programs for special education students ranging in age from 2 to 21. A Parent Resource Center helps parents and educators learn new ways to work with the disabled. Elementary and upper-level programs for more severely disabled and special education students are consolidated at several schools. As many students as possible are mainstreamed.

The school district operates the Pruden Center for Industry & Technology, which trains high school students during the day for careers in 19 areas, such as child care, culinary arts and welding. The Pruden Center is a joint project of the Suffolk School District and neighboring Isle of Wight County School District. At the same facility the two districts also operate the Center for Lifelong Learning, which coordinates adult basic education, GED preparation, continuing

SCHOOLS

education and corporate training programs. The school district also cosponsors a school for practical nurses at Obici Memorial Hospital.

Suffolk numbers to note:
Superintendent's Office, (757) 925-5500
Special Education Parent Resource Center, (757) 925-5579
Pruden Center for Industry & Technology, (757) 925-5590
Recreational Classes, (757) 925-6328
Public Information, (757) 925-5500

Magnet School

For high school students there is only one regional magnet school in south Hampton Roads—the Norfolk-based Governor's School for the Arts, (757) 451-4711. The school provides intense training in dance, music, theater, visual arts or other performing arts for about 300 public school students. The program is sponsored by the Virginia Department of Education and public schools in Chesapeake, Norfolk, Portsmouth, Suffolk, Virginia Beach and nearby Franklin, Isle of Wight County and Southampton County. The school, which started in 1987, is one of five regional magnet schools in the state and the only one focused on the arts. Graduates have gone on to such prestigious schools at Yale, Princeton and Juilliard.

Magnet school students take academic courses at their home high schools in the mornings. They then hop on buses and congregate in Norfolk for afternoon arts studies. Dancers, artists, singers, musicians and actors meet at various locations such as Old Dominion University and Norfolk State University. The school's theater department is in a renovated downtown Norfolk building.

Private Schools

Stroll through the region's neighborhoods on an early fall morning and you may wonder why clusters of students are gathered on different corners. Chances are they are waiting for buses headed for their various schools. Gathered in one block may be the public school students. A few streets away you may see the group waiting for buses from Norfolk Academy or Norfolk Collegiate School. Rounding the corner may be the parent driving the car pool for a private school with no bus system.

In these neighborhoods the mix of public and private school students is pretty even. And there's not a lot of rivalry between the students. In the afternoon you're likely to see a cross-section of the older children playing street hockey. Younger ones may gather for a game of soccer in someone's yard as their parents wind down by chatting with neighbors.

If you're interested in private or parochial schools, there are more than 50 to choose from. Some are only for primary school students; others accept children from preschool through graduation. You'll find both religious and secular schools as well as one for students with learning disabilities. Among the secular schools, private owners run some while independent boards run the others. There are schools with dozens of organized sports and extracurricular activities and others with just a few offerings.

Despite these differences all schools pride themselves on their small class size and emphasis on excellence. Upper-level schools all tend to have college-preparatory curriculums. Tracking down the right school for your child can be a time-consuming but rewarding process. The ideal is to start your search a year ahead of time, but when that's not possible you can jump start the process with a lot of legwork.

Your best resources are other parents who have been down the same road and settled on schools for their children. Grill as many of them as you can for their insight. Then call the schools and ask for information packets. After perusing them spend time in the schools talking to administrators, teachers and students. Be aware that admission policies vary greatly. Some schools have open admissions but others are very selective, and there may be competition for a limited number of slots.

Be sure to check into accreditation since it varies widely. Some schools have no accreditation.

Others are accredited by the selective Virginia Council for Private Education and the Virginia Association of Independent Schools. Schools with these designations are also recognized by the state Board of Education. Other schools are accredited by the Association of Christian Schools International, the Southern Association of Colleges and Schools, the Virginia Catholic Educational Association and the American Montessori Society.

To get you started on your school search, we have included a sampling of private schools that is by no means all-inclusive. Since tuition varies widely depending on grade level, call schools for specific information. Remember that transportation, before-school care and other special services cost extra. And, most schools charge an enrollment fee. When comparing schools, be sure you know exactly what the tuition covers. To avoid throwing your budget out of whack, find out if there are any additional mandatory funds or fees.

Some schools offer tuition discounts for families enrolling more than one student or for military families. A few have some aid available for financially strapped families.

Atlantic Shores Christian Schools
1861 Kempsville Rd., Virginia Beach
• (757) 479-1125
1219 N. Centerville Tnpk., Chesapeake
• (757) 479-9598

This Christian-centered school was organized in 1985 and has a preschool through high school program that includes a college-preparatory curriculum along with training in music and sports. There are two campuses—one in the Kempsville area for elementary students and an 18-acre complex a mile away for secondary students. Enrollment in the preschool and elementary program is 400 students; there are 270 secondary students. Besides Virginia Beach, students come from Chesapeake, Portsmouth, Suffolk and nearby parts of North Carolina. Extended care is available for grades K through 6, and there are both half-day and full-day kindergartens.

Baylake Pines Private School
2204 Treasure Island Rd., Virginia Beach
• (757) 464-4636

Started as a preschool in 1951, this school now also takes students through the 8th grade. It is at the entrance to the upscale Baylake Pines neighborhood but draws some of its 550 students from as far away as Norfolk and Chesapeake. The academically oriented school features a traditional curriculum grounded in phonics, reading, math and science and also promotes creativity. Students begin French lessons in kindergarten and science labs in 2nd grade. There are both all-day and half-day kindergartens.

Bayview Christian School
707 E. Bayview Blvd., Norfolk
• (757) 480-9154

This Christian school was founded in 1979 by Bayview Baptist Church and is adjacent to the church in the Ocean View area. The school's 125 students run the gamut from preschoolers to 5th graders. Although most are from Norfolk, many live in outlying cities and have parents working at the nearby Norfolk Navy Base. Before- and after-school care is available. For working parents there's also a summer program and childcare available on non-school days. The Bible and Christian teachings are integrated into all areas of study.

Cape Henry Collegiate School
1320 Mill Dam Rd., Virginia Beach
• (757) 481-2446

With more than 750 students, this is the largest private school in Virginia Beach. Cape Henry was started in 1924 and has a 30-acre campus. Its individualized learning programs are for preschoolers as well as high school seniors. Middle school and upper-school students are required to complete community service work. There are both half-day and full-day kindergartens. The upper school focuses heavily on college preparatory studies with some honors and advanced placement classes available. Younger students also have some accelerated classes. The Academic Enrichment Program helps students who may have trouble maintaining the academic pace. There is before- and after-school care for younger students and an all-day summer program. Buses bring students from Virginia Beach and parts of Norfolk and Chesapeake.

Catholic High School
4552 Princess Anne Rd., Virginia Beach
• (757) 467-2881

The only Catholic high school in south Hampton Roads opened in 1994 on a 16-acre site. It has a long history, however, since the new school replaced the 44-year-old Norfolk Catholic High. The school has an enrollment of 450 in grades 9 through 12 and concentrates on a college-preparatory curriculum in a

Catholic environment. Community service is emphasized, and graduates must complete at least 80 hours of volunteer work.

Chesapeake Bay Academy
715 Baker Rd., Virginia Beach
• **(757) 497-6200**

The academy has a specialized curriculum for students with learning disabilities, attention deficit disorders and other learning needs. The school was organized in 1989 and uses an individualized, multisensory approach for students in kindergarten through 12th grade. Its student body averages about 60 students who come from as far away as Williamsburg. This is the only area school to concentrate on bright students with special academic needs. The school has one teacher for every five students. Its goal is to get students on track academically so they can move on to other schools. In 2000 the academy will move into a new building constructed just for the school.

Christ The King School
3401 Tidewater Dr., Norfolk
• **(757) 625-4951**

For more than 40 years, Christ The King School has provided a well-rounded education with a solid grounding in religion. The school, which has 275 students, has a preschool program, a full-day kindergarten and students attending through 8th grade. Students can study band, drama, art and journalism along with the core curriculum.

Court Street Academy
447 Court St., Portsmouth
• **(757) 393-2312**

Founded in 1966, this academy offers a traditional curriculum for preschool through 8th grade. For the academy's 170 students, the emphasis is on the mastery of basic skills. The kindergarten program lasts a full day. Before- and after-school care is available. Although the school is in Court Street Baptist Church, it is not directly affiliated with the church. Transportation is available for students in Portsmouth and parts of Chesapeake and Suffolk.

First Baptist Christian School
237 N. Main St., Suffolk
• **(757) 925-0274**

Started as a kindergarten more than 25 years ago, the school is affiliated with First Baptist Church. It has more than 100 students in preschool through 6th grade. Most come from Suffolk. The school provides a Christian-based education and has both half-day and full-day

kindergarten programs. There is before- and after-school care, and vans will take children to and from public school.

Ghent Montessori School
610 Mowbray Arch, Norfolk
• **(757) 622-8174**

Founded in 1978 this school is housed in a building designed for the Montessori approach, which lets children move freely around their rooms working on a variety of projects. Students can start as young as age 2. The school goes through 6th grade. Enrollment is about 150, and students come from throughout the region. Classes combine several ages of students so younger ones can observe older ones, who get a chance to teach what they've learned. To appreciate the Montessori style, parents are encouraged to enroll children before they are 4 years old. On occasion, upper level slots go to students not previously in Montessori studies. Full-day and extended day programs are available.

Greenbrier Christian Academy
311 Kempsville Rd., Chesapeake
• **(757) 547-9595**

This academy was founded in 1982 and goes from kindergarten through high school. It is situated in the fast-growing Greenbrier area on a 20-acre campus and draws its 750 students from Chesapeake, Suffolk, Portsmouth and Virginia Beach. Greenbrier has a full-day kindergarten and before- and after-school care available for younger students. Integrated with the school's basic curriculum are Bible studies.

Hebrew Academy of Tidewater
1244 Thompkins Ln., Virginia Beach
• **(757) 424-4327**

The academy, which opened in 1955, offers a general and Judaic education for students in preschool through 8th grade. Its 240 students come from throughout the region, including the Peninsula. Besides emphasizing a core curriculum of science, math and language, students take daily classes in Hebrew, the Torah and Jewish history, laws and customs. The school has a program for students with learning difficulties. Kindergarten is a full-day program. Transportation and before- and after-school care are available.

Holy Trinity School
154 W. Government Ave., Norfolk
• **(757) 583-1873**

This school in the Ocean View area was founded in 1934 and has 180 students. It provides a Christian education for students in kindergarten through 8th grade and has both before- and after-school care available.

Nansemond-Suffolk Academy
3373 Pruden Blvd., Suffolk
• (757) 539-8789

Founded in 1966 for grades 1 through 7, the academy added an upper school in 1970 and now educates preschoolers through high school seniors. The academy is on a 50-acre campus and has an enrollment of about 1,120. Most students come from Suffolk, but the academy also attracts students from Portsmouth, Chesapeake and nearby counties. The academy stresses a college-preparatory curriculum, offers honors and advanced placement courses in high school and sponsors several athletic teams. Extended care is available for younger students. Transportation is also available.

Norfolk Academy
1585 Wesleyan Dr., Norfolk
• (757) 461-6236

With a founding date of 1728 and an enrollment of about 1,200, this is the region's oldest, largest and most prestigious private school. Students can enroll in 1st grade and stay until they graduate. Liberal arts and college preparatory work are stressed as well as community service and independent study. In the upper school there are advanced placement courses. There are about 40 extracurricular activities, an emphasis on fine arts and dozens of athletic teams. Norfolk Academy produces many National Merit Scholars. Buses bring students from Norfolk, Virginia Beach, Chesapeake and Portsmouth. Before- and after-school care is available for grades 1 through 6. The academy also operates the Summer Bridge program for high-achieving middle school students in public school who come from low-income families. The students study at the academy in the summer and return to their public schools in the fall.

Norfolk Christian Schools
255 Thole St., Norfolk
• (757) 423-5770
7000 Granby St., Norfolk
• (757) 423-5812
5045 Indian River Rd., Virginia Beach
• (757) 467-2904

From their start as a grammar school in 1952, these schools have grown into two campuses in Norfolk as well as a Virginia Beach affiliate. The schools are evangelical and non-denominational and go from preschool through high school. About 700 students from throughout the region attend the schools. There are both half- and full-day kindergartens. Special programs are available for students with learning disabilities and those who need accelerated studies. The upper and lower Norfolk schools are about a block apart. In 2000 lower school students moved into a new school building. Transportation is available. The school runs a prekindergarten program in Virginia Beach at Virginia Beach Alliance Church, 5045 Indian River Road, 495-3944.

> **INSIDERS' TIP**
> Most private schools have excellent summer programs that combine learning with fun and help children fill idle hours.

Norfolk Collegiate School
5429 Tidewater Dr., Norfolk
• (757) 625-0471
7336 Granby St., Norfolk
• (757) 480-2885

Founded in 1948 as a kindergarten, Norfolk Collegiate has grown into a complete school system with academic programs that take students through high school. There are two campuses with about 700 students who come from throughout the region. A new lower school opened on nine acres on Tidewater Drive in 1999. The middle and upper schools are on 5 acres on Granby Street. Kindergarten is a full-day program. The school stresses a college-preparatory curriculum, and advanced studies are offered to high school students. Transportation is available.

Parkdale Private School
321 Virginian Dr., Norfolk
• (757) 583-5989

Although this school only goes through 2nd grade, we're partial to it since one of our children attended preschool here. Parkdale started in 1957 as a preschool and kindergarten and has about 175 students. Its proximity to Norfolk Naval Base draws students from throughout the region. There is before- and after-school care for students as old as 14 and transportation for them to and from nearby public schools.

Portsmouth Catholic Elementary School
2301 Oregon Ave., Portsmouth
• (757) 488-6744

Since 1970, this school has provided a Catholic education. Its 235 students range from preschoolers through 8th graders. The school has a prekindergarten program as well as a full-day kindergarten and both before- and after-school care.

Portsmouth Christian School
3214 Elliott Ave., Portsmouth
• **(757) 393-0725**

Biltmore Baptist Church started this school in 1965 as a church ministry. It added a grade a year until it built up a Christian program for kindergarten through 12th grade. Enrollment is about 700, and students come mostly from Portsmouth, Chesapeake and Suffolk. There are both half-day and full-day kindergartens and some extended care.

Ryan Academy
844 Jerome Ave.,
Norfolk
• **(757) 583-RYAN**

Ryan Academy started in 1988 on the site of a former private school that dated back to the 1950s. Its 100 students include kindergartners through high school seniors. The academy also has a program for students with learning difficulties. It has an all-day kindergarten. Transportation is available.

Star of the Sea Catholic School
311 Arctic Crescent, Virginia Beach
• **(757) 428-8400**

Founded in 1958 and affiliated with St. Mary's Star of the Sea Catholic Church, this school has nearly 300 students who come primarily from Virginia Beach. It emphasizes a Catholic education for students in preschool through 8th grade. There is a full-day kindergarten.

St. Pius X School
7800 Halprin Dr., Norfolk
• **(757) 588-6171**

Established in 1956, this parochial school is for kindergarten through grade 8. Enrollment is about 500. The school has both half-day and full-day kindergarten and after-school care available.

Stonebridge Schools
4225 Portsmouth Blvd., Chesapeake
• **(757) 488-7586**

Stonebridge was founded in 1980 to offer a Christian, nondenominational, college-prepa-

ratory curriculum. Its 300 students come primarily from Chesapeake, Portsmouth, Suffolk and Virginia Beach. There are two campuses. The lower school is on Portsmouth Boulevard in the Western Branch area; the middle and high schools are in Faith Baptist Church on Jolliff Road. There are half-day kindergarten classes for 4-year-olds and a full-day program for 5-year-olds. Extended care is available, and transportation is an option for students in Virginia Beach and the Great Bridge area of Chesapeake.

Trinity Lutheran School
6001 Granby St., Norfolk
• **(757) 489-2732**

The school has programs for 155 students, preschoolers through 5th grade. It was established in 1945 and offers a Christian education. It has both half-day and full-day kindergartens as well as before- and after-school care.

Virginia Beach Country Day School
2100 Harbor Ln., Virginia Beach
• **(757) 481-0111**

Started in 1975, the school offers classes for preschool through 5th grade. It has a 4-acre campus and an enrollment of about 100. Students come primarily from Virginia Beach and Chesapeake. There are both half- and full-day kindergartens. Extended care is available, and there is a summer program. Transportation is available.

Virginia Beach Friends School
1537 Laskin Rd., Virginia Beach
• **(757) 428-7534**

Organized in 1955, this is Virginia's only Quaker school. It promotes the values of community, equality, harmony and simplicity. The school has an 11-acre campus and is for preschool through 12th grade. There are 155 students who come from throughout the region. Before- and after-school care is offered. There are both half-day and full-day kindergartens.

The Williams School
419 Colonial Ave., Norfolk
• **(757) 627-1383**

Housed in a historic home in the residential Ghent area, this school was founded in 1927. It has nearly 150 students in kindergarten through 8th grade, with most coming from Norfolk and

INSIDERS' TIP

If you are a student, make sure to travel with your student ID. Many venues offer a student discount when you show your card.

SCHOOLS

Portsmouth. The school prides itself on its environment, which nurtures individuals while giving them a solid grounding in basic studies.

Home Schooling

For personal or religious reasons, some area families choose to educate their children at home. Families who opt for home schooling can affiliate with the Oak Tree School in Chesapeake—an umbrella organization for home schoolers. For a reasonable annual tuition, the school does testing and maintains student records. It offers diplomas, training for parents, counseling and a student identification card. Students completing 12th grade earn a diploma from the school, which is in New Life Chris-

tian Fellowship Church at 1101 Volvo Parkway. Every three months Oak Tree sponsors a public meeting for parents and anyone else interested in home schooling. Call (757) 547-0101. Norfolk Christian Schools also has a program that lets home-schooled students participate in some classes and activities, (757) 423-5770). Home School Plus provides classes one day a week at Ingleside Baptist Church in Norfolk. Classes are geared for home-school students. Call (757) 466-3477.

The Home Educators Association of Virginia has information to help guide home-schooling parents. Call (540) 635-9322 or write the association at Box 1810, Front Royal, VA 22630-1810.

Childcare

LOOK FOR:
- Extended Care
- Day Camps
- Preschools
- Nannies
- Babysitting

If you're from out of state, you may be surprised to see how loosely some daycare providers are regulated in Virginia. The Commonwealth is one of only three states that completely exempts a caregiver from regulation if she or he keeps no more than five unrelated children in the home. In addition, the caregiver may also tend to any children in the immediate family plus others who come only before and after school. Virginia also does not regulate church-sponsored daycare centers.

That's not to say you won't find some excellent family daycare homes or church centers. It just means parents must do their homework, ask a zillion questions and trust their instincts when checking out potential providers. Once you select a caregiver, be constantly on the lookout for potential problems. From experience, we know childcare can work smoothly one day and fall apart the next. Try to keep an option in the back of your mind, and be ready to move swiftly if your instincts say you need to make a switch.

When it comes to childcare, your best sources of information are other parents. Hunt them down and ask for suggestions on who to call. Be sure to jot down the names of any providers they recommend avoiding.

There are numerous licensed childcare centers in the area that meet state standards on staffing, curriculum, safety and nutrition. To find out about them contact the **Virginia Social Services Department**. Its Eastern Regional Office is in Virginia Beach. Call (757) 491-3990.

Another good resource is the **Child Care Resource and Referral Center** of The Planning Council at 150 W. Plume Street in Norfolk. This regional nonprofit organization has its own Childcare Assurance Program (CCAP) that involves on-site inspections of family daycare homes. For a nominal fee, parents can receive a listing of CCAP- and state-approved providers. Before paying, however, check to see if your employer has arranged to provide information to workers for free. Call (757) 627-3993.

In the region, about 70 daycare centers and 400 home providers belong to **Places and Programs for Children** at 620 London Boulevard in Portsmouth. This nonprofit group was formed in 1974 to upgrade regional childcare. It offers ongoing training to childcare providers and conducts inspections to make sure homes and centers meet standards for health, safety and nutrition. The organization also runs several highly respected childcare centers. Call (757) 397-2981.

Only about 10 area childcare centers and preschools are certified by the **National Association for the Education of Young Children**. The association has standards that are stricter than the state's. For a listing of area members call (800) 424-2460.

Military families can help solve their childcare dilemmas by calling the **Navy Family Service Center**. The Norfolk-based center is on Hampton Boulevard near Norfolk Naval Base. The Family Service staff can steer you toward childcare centers affiliated with area bases. You also can find out about military-approved providers who can accept only military or Department of Defense dependents. Call (757) 444-6289.

Some parents have had luck locating good childcare through the classified section of *The Virginian-Pilot*. So many family daycare providers advertise here that there is a separate Babysitting/ Childcare section in the classifieds (category 5085).

For suggestions on childcare centers pick up a copy of *Tidewater Parent*, a monthly tabloid newspaper. This free, locally produced newspaper is loaded with ads from caregivers. And, it frequently runs helpful articles on childcare. You can usually grab a copy at grocery stores, childcare centers, consignment stores and just about anywhere else parents gather. For more information call (757) 363-7085.

Parents whose children have developmental disabilities may want to contact **Child Development Resources**. The nonprofit organization is headquartered in Williamsburg but serves children and their families throughout the region. Call (757) 565-0303.

Extended Care

For before- and after-school care, try the **YMCA** of South Hampton Roads. It offers on-site service in many public elementary schools and some middle schools. Besides supervised recreation, children get snacks and homework assistance while their parents receive peace of mind. Fees average about $50 a week. The YMCA also runs well-respected summer camp programs in area cities for school-age children that suits many working parents' schedules. Camp starts right at the end of school and offers 11 weeks of swimming, crafts and other activities. Call (757) 456-YMCA in Virginia Beach, (757) 622-YMCA in Norfolk, (757) 398-5511 in Portsmouth, (757) 547-YMCA in Chesapeake, and (757) 934-YMCA in Suffolk.

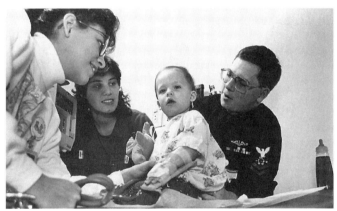

Finding quality healthcare for children is made easier in Hampton Roads by the presence of Children's Hospital of The Kings Daughters.

Photo: Courtesy of Children's Hospital of The Kings Daughters

In Norfolk the **YWCA** of South Hampton Roads provides extended care from September through May in several schools. Fees are based on income. Call (757) 625-4248.

You'll also find before- and after-school care at many private schools (see the Schools chapter). Some private schools also have fun summer programs that make life easier for parents whose work continues year round. Cape Henry Collegiate School, Norfolk Academy, Norfolk Christian School and Norfolk Collegiate School are among those with elaborate summer offerings.

Day Camps

Savvy parents start exploring the summer day-camp option no later than early March since programs fill up quickly. One of the most popular ways to fill long summer weeks for elementary students is with the Zoo Camp run by the Virginia Zoo in Norfolk. There are six one-week sessions. Younger students stay a half-day while those in 2nd grade and above can participate in full-day programs. Campers explore such topics as endangered species and animal care. Call (757) 626-0803.

Also gaining a following are marine camps sponsored by the **Virginia Marine Science Museum** in Virginia Beach. These are designed for students ages 8 through 16, who get lots of hands-on fun during one-week camps. For information call (757) 437-4949. **The Norfolk**

Botanical Garden sponsors several weeklong day camps that let young botanists learn about plants while having fun exploring the Garden's vast acreage. Call (757) 441-5830.

Old Dominion University is home base for several excellent summer camps for students. The most popular ones are marine science camps for students ages 6 through 19. Children love the fact that they must dress to get wet on field trips to collect marine organisms. For information call (757) 683-5100. For many local children, the highlight of the summer is attending sailing camp at ODU, whose sailing team is frequently top rated in the country. For information call (757) 683-3372. ODU also offers camps in music, (757) 683-4075; arts, (757) 683-4423; various sports, (757) 683-3375; and science, (757) 683-5101. To register for any of the camps call (757) 683-4247.

There are three terrific choices for the artistically inclined. The **Contemporary Arts Center of Virginia** in Virginia Beach runs one-week camps that last either a half-day or a full day. Most classes are for ages 6 to 12, but there usually is one session for preschoolers. Typical courses range from photography to painting to cartooning. Call (757) 425-0000. The **d'Art Center** in Norfolk also runs art camps for children ages 6 through 10. During one-week sessions students focus on specific activities such as painting or working with clay. Call (757) 625-4211. For elementary students, The **Chrysler Museum** sponsors half-day sessions that blend museum tours with hands-on creativity. Call (757) 664-6200.

Another possibility for summer camp is the **Jewish Community Center** in Norfolk whose Shalom Children's Center runs two four-week camps for ages 2 through 13. Older children can choose from drama and sports camps while younger ones explore activities ranging from art to swimming. Call (757) 489-1371. Most of the larger private schools also operate summer camp programs that are open to all children. Both Norfolk Academy and Norfolk Collegiate run continual camp programs featuring everything from sports to computers and art, (757) 461-6236 or (757) 480-1495.

To help explore all the summer options, the *Tidewater Parent* publication sponsors a free summer camp trade show each February and runs a listing of camps in its February issue. For details call (757) 363-7085.

Preschools

As far as preschools go, there are many excellent choices. Again, your best bet in finding the one that is right for you is to talk to other parents. Look around your neighborhood—or the area near your office—to see what schools are nearby. Many preschools are in churches. Others operate independently. Numerous private schools for older children also have a preschool program (again, check our Schools chapter).

Although a few preschools stick to the traditional half-day program, most have melted under pressure from two-career parents and added extended-day options. Some preschools also have summer fun days or camps that go beyond the September to June school year.

Even at preschools with half-day programs, working parents may be able to find another parent to keep their child after hours. There are caregivers who have built their businesses caring for children after preschool ends at noon. Ask the schools for recommendations and try to hook up with other parents for carpooling.

Once you've come up with a list of preschool possibilities, call for brochures and tuition schedules. Then take your time visiting the schools and getting to know the teachers and directors. You may want to go without children at first so you can concentrate on asking key questions. Once you narrow down your list, take your child and spend some time soaking up the surroundings. If you're like us, you and your child may go to the same schools two or three times before making a final decision.

For some of the most popular preschools, the wait to get in can be long. Start your search as early as you can—at least a year ahead of time is not unreasonable. Be aware that some locals register their children at birth for a couple of the most prestigious preschools. Of course, there are plenty of newcomers who have lucked into a slot when a family suddenly moved from the area. So don't give up hope.

Hint: among the preschools with the longest waiting lists are the Child Study Center run by Old Dominion University in Norfolk, (757) 683-4117; the Stratford Preschool in Virginia Beach, (757) 460-0659; and the First Presbyterian Church Preschool in Norfolk, (757) 625-0667.

Nannies

Finding in-home childcare is a definite possibility. If you place a classified ad in the Help Wanted section of *The Virginian-Pilot*, you'd better have a telephone answering machine. The one time we tried it, the calls easily topped 100, and only a few of those sounded like anyone we'd want to hire.

Although there are parents who have found excellent caregivers through the classifieds, many prefer to use a service to do the screening. There are several active services in the area.

We've had good personal experience with **AuPairCare**. It is headquartered in San Francisco and provides European nannies ages 18 to 25. The au pairs, both young women and men, work an average of 45 hours a week, live with families as family members and can stay in this country 13 months. Since AuPairCare is the largest au pair provider in the area, it has several local counselors to work with families and au pairs. The weekly cost averages just more than $200 for any number of children. Call (800) 4AUPAIR.

Babysitting

If you're new to the neighborhood, right now is the time to start cultivating that teenager or college student down the street as a babysitter. There seems to be a dearth of people in that age group, and finding reliable babysitters can be a ruthless business. In fact, don't be shocked if that friendly neighbor who welcomed you with brownies refuses to reveal the name of her sitter.

We've had great success hiring workers at our childcare center for occasional babysitting. But since we once called a dozen teens before snaring a sitter for a fairly impromptu Saturday night outing, we try to keep a long list of good prospects. Soon, you too may be asking any responsible teen or college student whether he or she babysits. Once we spot a likely prospect, we start grooming them for potential duty by getting them acquainted with our family. The going rate is about $3 an hour for teenage babysitters. If you're hiring a young babysitter, make sure he or she has completed the American Red Cross' babysitting course that is offered to students 11 and older.

One regional resource is Old Dominion University's excellent **Child Study Center**. If you mail a written notice of what type help you're looking for (regular, occasional, weekend), it will be posted on a bulletin board in the center. Be sure to specify where you live. Send information to Child Study Center, ODU, 45th Street and Hampton Boulevard, Norfolk 23519. You also can tack notices in Webb Center, ODU's student center, as well as at other local colleges.

Since 1949, **Baby Sitters of Tidewater Inc.** has rescued countless newcomers from babysitting dilemmas. Many of them now rely on the service for all their babysitting needs. The business has passed from its founder, Emma Johnson, to her daughter-in-law, Clarice Johnson. This is a word-of-mouth service that hires mainly retired teachers, nurses and grandmothers. You can book a sitter for a day, evening, weekend or while you go on vacation.

For one or two siblings, Baby Sitters of Tidewater charges $5.50 an hour with a required minimum of four hours. There also is a $7 transportation fee if you live within 30 miles of the sitter. It costs $9 an hour for children from two families. Although there are many sitters on call, try to reserve your sitter several days in advance. Call (757) 489-1622 during the day.

Many churches, especially those with preschools, have **Mother's Morning Out** programs. This is usually a drop-in service for toddlers that lasts only a couple of hours one or two mornings a week. These programs can be a great sanity saver for stay-at-home moms, and they provide valuable peer interaction for children.

For sick children, **Sentara Home Care Services** will send a nursing assistant to tend to your children at home as long as their fevers are less than 101 degrees. This is a definite option for working parents whose children face a lengthy recuperation at home. Children should be registered in advance of illness. The home-care service is at 8 Koger Executive Center in Virginia Beach. Fees are $10.50 an hour between 7 AM and 3 PM on weekdays and slightly more at other times. A minimum of four hours is required. Call (757) 461-5649.

Healthcare

Every day, thousands of commuters on their way to and from the Norfolk Naval Base pass a small park on Hampton Boulevard. It's not much to look at, just a grassy lot with a bench. But no matter what the season, the ground always blooms with yellow flowers.

The Girl Scouts plant those flowers, in remembrance of the yellow-fever epidemic that devastated Norfolk in 1855. During that time, the park served as a mass burial site for the victims of that disease. Today, it is a poignant reminder of how far medical care has progressed in our region. Just blocks away from the park stands a thriving medical center, home to Eastern Virginia Medical School, Sentara Norfolk General Hospital and Children's Hospital of The King's Daughters. Few of the residents who fell ill or cared for the sick in 1855 could have imagined the medical procedures that would someday be performed at these and other Hampton Roads facilities.

Today, patients travel from all over the world to receive medical care in Hampton Roads. Among their destinations is The Jones Institute for Reproductive Medicine at Eastern Virginia Medical School, which performed the country's first in vitro fertilization and has helped thousands of people become parents. Children with debilitating facial or genitourinary defects find help at Children's Hospital of The King's Daughters, where expert pediatric surgical teams give them the chance of a normal childhood. Women who have lost one or both breasts to cancer travel to Sentara Norfolk General and Sentara Leigh Hospitals, where plastic and reconstructive surgeons have developed techniques that use the patient's own tissue to reconstruct the breast. And men who require complex genitourinary reconstructive surgery find the nation's top surgeons in that specialty in Norfolk as well.

The region also attracts national acclaim with special programs that put our experts on the road. Operation Smile International has donated reconstructive surgery to tens of thousands of indigent children in developing countries. Begun by local surgeon Dr. Bill Magee and his wife, Kathy, in 1983, Operation Smile puts together teams of volunteer surgeons, physicians, nurses, dentists, social workers, psychologists, speech therapists and other medical professionals, who travel to Africa, South America, Vietnam, the Philippines, and other countries. Operation Smile volunteers have performed life-changing operations on thousands of children who would otherwise face permanent disfigurement from problems such as cleft palates and lips, burn scars and club feet. When not in the operating room, Operation Smile volunteers provide educational support and training to healthcare professionals in these struggling countries.

Physicians For Peace is a similar organization. Formed in 1987, it sends teams of U.S. physicians and healthcare specialists to war-torn areas of the Middle East to further their mission of "international friendships and peace through medicine." Several years ago when Israel and the PLO signed a peace agreement in Washington, D.C., Norfolk urologist Dr. Charles Horton, president of Physicians for Peace, was invited to observe the proceedings.

While we're proud of these international contributions, we're also grateful to have good medical care in our own backyards. Quality medical care means that families don't have to travel outside the region to receive expert or specialized treatment. And an active medical community provides more than 50,000 jobs, which is especially important now that the community is adjusting to military downsizing.

Of course, the medical community in Hampton Roads—like medical communities across the nation—is also adjusting to changing market forces. In recent years, local healthcare facilities have been adapting to the new environment of managed care, which puts less emphasis on hospitalization and more emphasis on quality outpatient care. Hospitals' inpatient populations are growing smaller and more seriously ill while outpatient services and preventative care burgeon. That means more inpatient rooms need to be equipped for intensive care, while other areas of hospitals need to be made user-friendly for outpatients. To accommodate these changes, many of our medical facilities have updated their physical plants over the past several years. For instance, in 1999 Portsmouth Naval Hospital finished a $330 million expansion that replaced the aging hospital with a new, 464-bed facility.

Such changes have been facilitated by the growth of healthcare networks, which not only own hospitals, but also may operate nursing homes, health maintenance organizations and physician practices. The largest of these in Hampton Roads is Sentara Healthcare, which has brought six hospitals as well as several urgent-care centers, nursing homes, assisted-living facilities and diagnostic centers under its umbrella. Sentara also provides health coverage to the citizens of the area, mainly through two large health maintenance organizations—Sentara Health Plan and Optima Health Plan.

In 1998 Sentara took over Tidewater Health Care, one of the region's largest health networks. The merger gave Sentara control of Virginia Beach General Hospital as well as a nursing home, urgent-care centers, and an ambulatory surgery center. Also in the deal were two health maintenance organizations—Priority Health Plan and Health First.

Another major player in the healthcare field is Maryland-based Bon Secours health System. In 1996 Bon Secours took over DePaul Medical Center of Norfolk. It also owns Maryview Medical Center in Portsmouth and Mary Immaculate Hospital in Newport News.

The last network to mention is FHC/TPI Health Systems. Its parent company is First Hospital Corporation of Norfolk, which is the largest mental health care company in the country. This company provides the lion's share of inpatient treatment in our area. Its managed-care division, Options Mental Health, also provides contract services for Medicaid and military families across the country.

While such growth should swell the pride of any newcomer to our area, knowledge of our outstanding emergency and trauma-care network will likewise comfort any short-term visitor. Sentara Norfolk General operates a Level I trauma center and burn/trauma unit, along with the Nightingale air ambulance helicopter. It is joined by several Level II emergency rooms throughout the region. Numerous urgent-care centers provide both minor emergency care and primary care for residents and visitors. A list of local healthcare facilities follows.

Hospitals and Medical Centers

Virginia Beach

Sentara Bayside Hospital
800 Independence Blvd., Virginia Beach
• **(757) 363-6100**

This 158-bed acute-care facility, part of the Sentara network, specializes in outpatient diagnostic and surgical services. The hospital recently added a new wing that houses all outpatient services, an expanded emergency room, additional surgical suites and a critical-care unit. The hospital has also established Virginia Beach's first surgical residency training program

with Eastern Virginia Graduate School of Medicine. Among its inpatient services are a birthing center, a six-bed Children's Unit and the region's first Recovery Care Center, which allows family-assisted care for patients undergoing minor medical procedures.

Sentara Virginia Beach General Hospital
1060 First Colonial Rd., Virginia Beach
• **(757) 481-8000**

SVBGH is a 274-bed acute-care hospital providing a comprehensive array of services, including five "Centers of Excellence"—cardiology, women's and infants' health, cancer, orthopedics and neuroscience. In addition, SVBGH offers certain sophisticated tertiary services such as a Level II Trauma Center, open-heart surgery, a neonatal intensive-care unit and the Tidewater Perinatal Center for high-risk pregnancies.

Special services offered by SVBGH include The Coastal Cancer Center, which is affiliated with the Cancer Center at the University of Virginia, The Cardiac Fitness Center, The Heart Institute, The Diabetes Treatment Center and a Sleep Disorders Center. SVBGH also offers Maternal/Child Health Education classes including Lamaze, breast-feeding and newborn-care classes in addition to health screening and support groups. In 1998, the hospital joined the Sentara Healthcare Network.

Norfolk

Bon Secours DePaul Medical Center
150 Kingsley Ln., Norfolk
• **(757) 889-5000**

A 366-bed, acute-care facility, DePaul was founded in 1855 and is affiliated with Bon Secours Health System, which also owns Maryview Medical Center in Portsmouth.

DePaul's "Centers of Excellence" include The Cancer Center, which has been selected by the American College of Surgeons as a teaching hospital cancer program. The Center for Birth, offers single-room maternity care. The Diabetes Center, houses the inpatient component of the Diabetes Institutes of Eastern Virginia Medical School. The Gerontology Institute, which is designed for the senior community; and The Hearing and Balance Center, a joint program with EVMS that treats those with hearing and balance disorders. In 2000 DePaul opened an assisted living community next door to the hospital.

Children's Hospital of The Kings Daughters
601 Children's Ln., Norfolk
• **(757) 668-7000**

Built in 1961, CHKD is Virginia's only free-standing, full-service pediatric hospital. Home to the EVMS Department of Pediatrics, the hospital serves as a regional referral center for a variety of pediatric subspecialties. These include cancer, neonatal medicine, infectious diseases, orthopedics, and craniofacial and urological reconstructive surgery. CHKD operates the region's only pediatric emergency room and kidney dialysis center.

The hospital is licensed for 186 beds and has a 38-bed neonatal intensive-care unit and a 12-bed transitional-care unit for ventilator-dependent children. CHKD also has more than 50 outpatient programs, providing ongoing care for children with disorders such as asthma, sickle cell anemia, lead poisoning and cystic fibrosis. A neuro-developmental center assists children with developmental disorders and rehabilitation needs through a combination of disciplines, including neurology, psychology and speech pathology.

A unique facility dedicated to the children of Hampton Roads, CHKD enjoys loyal support from the community. The hospital was founded more than 100 years ago as a visiting nurse service for indigent children by the Norfolk City Union of The King's Daughters. That charitable organization remains dedicated to the hospital today, raising funds through special events and increasing community awareness of the hospital.

Associated with the hospital are the Barry Robinson Center for emotionally disturbed and learning disabled children. The Discovery Care Centers provide daycare centers near several high-employment areas in the region. Children's Home Health provides private duty nursing and durable medical equipment to children who can be cared for at home.

Lake Taylor Hospital
1309 Kempsville Rd., Norfolk
• **(757) 461-5001**

A 332-bed, long-term care/chronic-disease hospital, Lake Taylor is governed by the Hospital Authority of Norfolk and managed by Riverside Health System. The hospital, which is more than 100 years old, is the only one in the state that offers chronic-disease care including AIDS treatment.

Included in the facility is a 104-bed wing providing intensive recuperative care for patients with long-term chronic diseases and a 228-bed nursing facility for long-term residents who require either skilled or custodial care.

Sentara Leigh Hospital
830 Kempsville Rd., Norfolk
• **(757) 466-6000**

This 250-bed acute-care hospital with all private rooms is centrally located to serve residents of Virginia Beach, Norfolk, and Chesapeake. The hospital is known for its Institute of Video Surgery, offering state-of-the-art techniques for general, urological, gynecological and orthopedic surgeries. Its Orthopedic Specialty Center serves the majority of the area's joint-replacement patients, and its recently expanded Family Maternity Suite has 16 suites for labor, delivery, postpartum and recovery. The hospital also includes an Ambulatory Surgical Center, a hospital-based Breast Center, mobile mammography and mobile diagnostic units, a Rehab Specialty Center, cardiac diagnostic services and breast and reconstructive surgery.

Sentara Norfolk General Hospital
600 Gresham Dr., Norfolk
• (757) 628-3000

This 644-bed tertiary-care facility complements the services provided by two other acute-care hospitals in the Southside Sentara network. SNGH, located on a large medical complex that includes Eastern Virginia Medical School and Children's Hospital of The King's Daughters, is known regionally and nationally for many of its programs. The hospital's Heart Pavilion has been recognized by MetraHealth as a nationwide Center of Excellence for cardiac surgery, cardiac catheterization, angioplasty and electrophysiology services. The hospital is part of perinatal-care network coordinated with EVMS and CHKD. It also provides the region's only Level I Trauma Center and air ambulance. The hub of the Sentara Cancer Institute, which offers new resources and treatments to residents of eastern Virginia and northeastern North Carolina, is at SNGH. Other specialty services include microsurgery, the Comprehensive Epilepsy Program, a Sleep Disorders Clinic and transplantation services.

Portsmouth

Maryview Medical Center
3636 High St., Portsmouth
• (757) 398-2200

Part of the Bon Secours Health Systems Inc., Maryview is a 267-bed, general hospital that offers a variety of technologically advanced diagnostic inpatient and outpatient services. Its special services include many centers, including a maternity center, the Martha W. Davis Cancer Center, the Plastic Surgery Center and the Eye Center. Expansion and renovation projects have added ambulatory surgery operating rooms, an intensive-care unit, and an expanded emergency department. Maryview also operates two freestanding urgent-care facilities called Maryview MedCare Centers, located at 3105 Western Branch Boulevard, (757) 484-5002, and at 4700 George Washington Parkway, (757) 487-9200. An inpatient psychiatric hospital, Maryview Psychiatric is in the same campus.

Portsmouth Naval Hospital
Foot of Effingham St., Portsmouth
• (757) 953-7986

The oldest naval hospital in the United States and the second-largest naval hospital in the country, the 500-bed Portsmouth Naval Hospital offers superlative healthcare to the military community, including active duty and their dependents, and retirees. A new $154 million hospital provides all types of inpatient and outpatient care.

Chesapeake

Chesapeake General Hospital
736 N. Battlefield Blvd., Chesapeake
• (757) 547-8121

Chesapeake General is a 260-bed regional healthcare resource serving southeastern Virginia and northeastern North Carolina. In 2000 Chesapeake General started a $22 million expansion and renovation that will increase outpatient services and the number of birthing rooms.

The 500-plus members of the medical staff offer services in 34 medical subspecialties. The hospital's newest addition, the Cancer Treatment Center, offers state-of-the-art radiation therapy and provides patients with access to a full realm of cancer services from diagnosis to support groups.

Diagnostic capabilities include cardiac catheterization, computerized tomography and MRI, mammography, EEG and peripheral vascular laboratory services. A fully-staffed rehabilitation services department offers inpatient and outpatient physical, occupational and speech therapy. Nursing units include

> **INSIDERS' TIP**
> Hampton Roads is home to the country's oldest and second-largest naval hospital, which is in Portsmouth. Portsmouth Naval Hospital offers healthcare to the region's military population, including active duty members and their dependents and retirees. Many healthcare practitioners who receive advanced training through the military at PNH set up private practices in the area after their retirement from the military. In this way, the military strengthens the quality of medical care offered to the civilian population as well.

subspecialties in orthopedics, cardiac care, women's health, pediatrics, oncology and geropsychiatry.

The Birthplace, the hospital's obstetrical unit, features nine Labor, Delivery, Recovery, LDR rooms, two operating rooms and three triage beds. The Mother-Baby Care Unit offers 22 private postpartum rooms and nursing care for both mom and baby.

The hospital operates the Lifestyle Fitness Center, which offers cardiopulmonary rehabilitation, diabetes education, health screenings, fitness evaluations, exercise programs, nutritional counseling and wellness activities for older adults. Similar programs are also available at the Family Health & Wellness Center in the Deep Creek section of the city.

Additional services include ComfortCare Home Health Service, The Women's Health Center, Georgian Manor Assisted Living Facility and Health Care on Call, (757) 640-5555 ext. 5700, a telephone service that provides information on hundreds of health-related topics.

Suffolk

Obici Hospital
1900 N. Main St., Suffolk
• (757) 934-4000

A 222-bed medical center, Obici offers diagnostic and acute-care services, including neuro-ophthalmology, cardiac catheterization, cardiac rehabilitation, comprehensive radiology services, MRI, mobile lithotripsy, rehabilitation medicine, an outpatient surgery center and a 24-hour emergency department. The hospital also operates a Cancer Center, a Psychiatric Care Center, a Women's Health Center, and subspecialist physician outreach practices in Smithfield and Gates County, N.C. A three-year registered nursing school and one-year LPN school are affiliated with the hospital.

In 2002 the old Obici Hospital will close when a new $85 million hospital is completed. The new Obici Hospital will

have 133 beds and an enhanced focus on outpatient care.

Psychiatric Hospitals

Virginia Beach

Virginia Beach Psychiatric Center
1100 First Colonial Rd., Virginia Beach
• (757) 496-6000

This FHC/TPI Health Systems facility specializes in adult inpatient psychiatric treatment, including detoxification and rehabilitation from chemical dependency, crisis stabilization and

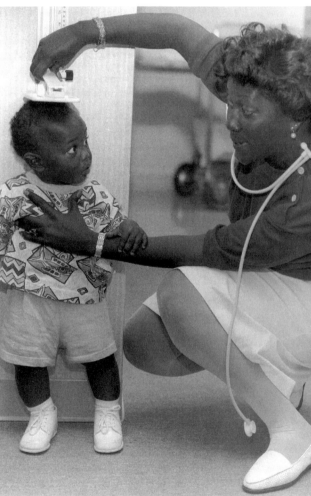

Norfolk is home to the state's only freestanding pediatric hospital, Children's Hospital of The Kings Daughters.

Photo: Courtesy of Children's Hospital of The Kings Daughters dual diagnosis treatments. Partial hospitalization and assisted-living services are also offered here.

Norfolk

Norfolk Psychiatric Center
860 Kempsville Rd., Norfolk
• **(757) 461-4565**
This FHC/TPI Health Systems facility offers crisis stabilization and inpatient psychiatric treatment to children, adolescents and adults.

Portsmouth

Maryview Medical Center
36 High St., Portsmouth
• **(757) 398-2200**
This 54-bed facility is adjacent to Maryview Hospital and provides psychiatric and chemical dependency treatment for adults and adolescents. Along with a Women's Treatment Program and a Pain Management Program that includes the Headache Institute, the facility offers the innovative "Turning Point" program for patients in the early to middle stages of chemical dependency.

Medical School

Eastern Virginia Medical School
Fairfax Ave., Olney Rd. and
Mowbray Arch, Norfolk
• **(757) 624-2273**
One of three medical schools in the state of Virginia, Eastern Virginia Medical School (EVMS) was founded in 1973 by community leaders who believed that a medical school would improve the quality of patient care in the region. In two decades, their enthusiasm has been validated. In addition to attracting a roster of top-notch subspecialists who teach, treat patients from the community and do research at the school, EVMS has trained thousands of physicians, many of whom have remained in the area to practice.

EVMS has earned national prominence with the Jones Institute for Reproductive Medicine. The Jones Institute was the first in vitro fertilization clinic founded in the United States, and in 1981 it successfully sponsored the United States' first in vitro birth. In 1993 researchers at the Institute used genetic engineering to help a Louisiana couple carrying the deadly Tay-

Sachs gene produce a healthy child. In 1995 the Jones Institute started clinical trials to screen embryos for Down's Syndrome during the in vitro fertilization process.

The Jones Institute also conducts important research on contraceptives. The Contraceptive Research and Development program (CONRAD) was established in 1986 with a $28 million grant from the U.S. Agency for International Development—at the time the largest grant ever issued by a government agency to a single institution for biomedical research. Since then, EVMS has received additional grants to continue the CONRAD program, most recently a $45 million grant to study new ways to prevent HIV transmission.

Other prominent research/treatment programs at EVMS include: the Diabetes Institute, the Sleep Disorders Center, the Center for Communications Disorders, the Head and Neck Tumor Biology Program and the Gerontology Institute. Although these are specialized programs, EVMS is also well-known for its focus on primary care. One-third of the school's graduates become family doctors, internists and general pediatricians.

EVMS and Children's Hospital of The King's Daughters are partners in The Center for Pediatric Research, which studies the special health needs of children. Among its projects is a study of the role of human milk in infant nutrition and health, funded by the National Institute of Health.

Unlike most medical schools, EVMS has no single teaching hospital or university partnership. Although its primary teaching hospitals are Sentara Norfolk General and Children's Hospital of The King's Daughters, EVMS has affiliations with 20 healthcare facilities in Hampton Roads. Its physicians provide clinical care all over the region.

Emergency Services

Call 911 for emergency assistance. If a crisis requires ambulance service in Hampton Roads, you can be assured of attention from the best in the business. Every member of our ambulance crews has had at least 125 hours of training and has been certified by the state of Virginia as an Emergency Medical Technician. Even more training can be claimed by cardiac technicians and paramedics.

Because speed of response is critical in emergency situations, you might find a fire truck wheeling up to your door. Not to worry. All Hampton Roads firefighters have been extensively trained as first responders, and if they are the closest emergency vehicle to your given address, they will be first on the scene.

If your situation does not warrant calling out our emergency angels, you will most likely find a freestanding acute-care facility or hospital emergency room close to where you are. Regardless of where you go, or who you might need to call, we advise that you take not only personal identification, such as a driver's license and medical insurance card, but a list of current prescription medicines and respective dosages for any examining physician.

INSIDERS' TIP

Virginia Beach is the largest city in the country to rely on all-volunteer rescue squads for citizens' emergency service. The city's 11 volunteer squads save taxpayers an estimated $11 million a year while providing quality medical care and transportation to hospitals.

Physician Matchmakers

If you are new to the area, asking co-workers or neighbors about the physicians and dentists of choice is an excellent way to find a new doctor. If you would like more information, however, there are several referral services that can also help you select a physician. Most referral services operated by local hospitals or health systems have information on physicians who admit patients to their facilities. These services can help you find a doctor who is close to your home or office, and tell you who accepts your insurance, where the physicians went to school and which hospitals they admit patients to. Feel free to call any of the following for no-charge, no-obligation information:

Virginia Beach Medical Society, (757) 481-4516

Norfolk Academy of Medicine, (757) 466-8883

Portsmouth Academy Medicine, (757) 398-4100

Sentara Hospitals Physician Referral Service, (800) SENTARA

Physician Finder, Maryview Hospital, (757) 398-2131

Health Care Connection, Chesapeake General, (757) 547-7800

Tidewater Dental Society, (757) 627-8534

Tidewater Optometric Society, (757) 490-4015

Children's Health Line, CHKD pediatric referral service, (757) 668-7500.

MedMatch Obici Hospital, (757) 934-4999

Health Departments

Virginia Beach, 3432 Virginia Beach Boulevard, (757) 431-3500

Norfolk, 830 S. Hampton Blvd., (757) 683-2700

Portsmouth, 800 Crawford Parkway, (757) 393-8585

Chesapeake, 748 Battlefield Boulevard, (757) 382-8600

Suffolk, 1217 N. Main Street, (757) 686-4901

Crisis and Emergency Numbers

Police, Fire or Medical Emergencies, 911
Battered Women's Hotlines: Virginia Beach, (757) 430-2120; Norfolk, (757) 625-5570; Portsmouth, (757) 393-9449; Eastern Shore, (757) 787-1329
Child Abuse Center of Hampton Roads, (757) 622-7478
Poison Control Center, (800) 552-633
Red Cross Language Bank Translators, (757) 446-7760, (757) 446-7756
Response - Sexual Assault Support Group, (757) 622-4300
Tidewater AIDS Crisis Task Force, (757) 626-1027
United Way of South Hampton Roads, (757) 853-8500
United Way Help Line, (757) 625-4543
Virginia Family Violence Hotline, (800) 838-8238

Media

There are two sides to the media story in Hampton Roads. If you're the viewer, listener or reader, you're lucky. We've got lots of excellent choices here, and every single radio station, television channel and print publication is constantly striving to improve its relationship with you, its demographic darling. If you work in this industry, however, you'd better learn to swim with the sharks. Hampton Roads is a fiercely competitive, volatile media market.

LOOK FOR:
• **Publications**
• **Radio**
• **Television**

Consider our radio market alone—more stations than most markets twice our size. Flip on the tube and you'll find not only the big three, but also more than 50 cable channels fighting for your attention. The print category is dominated by our venerable daily newspaper, *The Virginian-Pilot*. In addition to our morning paper, we also have scores of weekly and monthly specialty publications that cover everything from parenting to partying, marine life to metaphysics, home buying to higher consciousness.

Of course, everybody vies for the same advertising dollar, and such a competitive market makes as well as reports on the news. In 1997, *The Virginian-Pilot*, Cox Communications, and WVEC-TV 13 joined forces to form a new TV station called Local News on Cable, or LNC. The station reports the local news 24 hours a day with its own anchors and features occasional on-air spots with local newspaper journalists.

LNC was developed in part to respond to the region's unorthodox work schedule. Many workers in the region report to military or federal government offices long before sunrise and finish their days around 3 PM. So be assured that program directors and producers are looking for ways to reach you around the clock. And whether it's a helicopter traffic report at six in the morning or a radio talk show at midnight, plugging into Hampton Roads' diversified media will help you sound just like a native in no time.

Publications

From the plethora of publications that come from our market from week to week, you can be sure that if you're thirsty for knowledge, you'll not have any farther to go than your local grocery store's pickup rack to take a big drink. Here are the major "pubs" that appear with continuity, offering different spins on their respective themes and keeping all of us abreast of the newest, latest, hottest and most controversial subjects in the community.

Of special note to those who, because of disabilities, cannot see or hold printed material, Hampton Roads Voice is a free reading service heard on public radio station WHRV 89.5 FM. The 24-hour service is supplemented by programming from Touch Network based in New York and provides daily readings of local, regional and national newspapers, special publications, monthly magazines and periodicals. Special equipment is needed to receive the closed-circuit programming, and there is a waiting list. For more information call (757) 489-9476 or (757) 881-9476.

The Virginian-Pilot
150 W. Brambleton Ave., Norfolk
• **(757) 446-2000**

Owned by Norfolk-based media giant Landmark Communications,

The *Pilot* is the only daily game in town for both news lovers and advertisers. The paper covers all of South Hampton Roads and has a North Carolina section that covers the northeastern portion of the state. With the largest circulation of any daily newspaper in Virginia (around 202,000), *The Virginian-Pilot* has a long tradition of excellence and even a few Pulitzers to its credit.

"The paper," as we Insiders fondly refer to it carries an easily digestible mix of in-depth articles, news blips and brief stories. Its well-tuned business, sports and entertainment sections make our daily perusal of the paper very productive.

The *Pilot* offers several special-interest supplements—community-oriented tabloids for each of the five Southside cities, a weekly "Green Sheet" that contains the TV listings and a special section for teens each Friday. Anyone house hunting must have the latest copy of Saturday's Real Estate Weekly for the latest on-the-market reports as well as updated mortgage information from local lenders. Community tabloids that focus on the news in a smaller spectrum include *The Beacon* in Virginia Beach, *The Compass* in Norfolk, *Currents* in Portsmouth, *The Clipper* in Chesapeake and *The Sun* in Suffolk.

Suffolk News-Herald
130 S. Saratoga St., Suffolk
• **(757) 539-3437**

A small general-interest daily newspaper, the *News-Herald* features local happenings along with major international news of the day. Its circulation is approximately 6,000 copies. It's available at racks throughout Suffolk or by subscription.

Port Folio
5700 Thurston Dr., Virginia Beach
• **(757) 363-2400**

Don't let the fact that it's a free weekly fool you. This is the information bible for people who want to know where to go and what to do. Along with timely cover stories that highlight (or expose) a local personality, trend or event, *Port Folio* offers a wealth of info about where to dine, to party and to meet the person of your dreams. Make sure you check out the first edition of every month. Inside is "Home," a voyeur's peek in-

side some of the most gracious and glamorous homes in the area. There are also weekly columns on arts and musical events and timely reviews and news from the restaurant scene. All in all, it's a slick piece of work that never fails to come up with topical, fascinating tales about what's going on in Hampton Roads.

Byerly Publications
1024 Battlefield Blvd., Chesapeake
• **(757) 547-4571**

Byerly has long been known for its commitment to the important little things in life, like what's going on next door. Cover to cover, these are decisively hometown papers—and a must for newcomers who want to get a full, positive picture of their new community. The weekly Byerly community publications include: *The Chesapeake Post*, published each Wednesday; *The Portsmouth Times*, published each Thursday; and *The Virginia Beach Sun*, published each Wednesday.

Real Estate Magazines

Even if you've snagged the best realtor in town, there are a number of real estate publications to help you focus before jumping in the car for the major open-house assault. All are free and multiplying at a rack at the grocery or drug store nearest you. They include: *Home Search*, *Harmon Homes*, *Real Estate Digest*, *For Sale By Owner* and the *Tidewater Builders Associations' New Homes and Apartment Guides*.

Tidewater Parent
5700 Thurston Ave., Virginia Beach
• **(757) 363-2400**

Anyone living with a person who's less than 3 feet tall should tuck a copy of this publication in the diaper bag. Published monthly, it is the definitive guide to child-rearing in Hampton Roads, with articles aimed at education, constructive play and mommy-relief.

Radio

Every market has its own favorite radio personalities that fans love, and love to hate. We're no different. WCMS's Joe Hoppel is our answer to Mr. Country-Western, Mike Arlo is Mr. Classic Rock at WAFX, and Eric Worden is the wake-up call of choice for baby

INSIDERS' TIP
New to the area? Real estate publications are free, easy to find at grocery and convenience stores, and usually represent a large segment of available properties.

MEDIA

boomers who still want to be cool every morning at 93.7 "The Coast."

Anyone looking for alternative radio will love the fact that we have two public radio stations—siblings WHRO and WHRV. WHRO is where you'll find mostly classical music. WHRV is where to tune for *Prairie Home Companion, Car Talk,* and other fun and informative fare, including an excellent locally produced talk radio show called *Hear/Say*, which airs every weekday at noon.

The programming listed here for each station is current as of this writing, but stations jockeying for higher ratings have been known to change formats overnight.

Adult Contemporary
WPTE 94.9 FM
WWDE 101.3 FM
WJQI 1600 AM

Christian/Gospel
WYFI 99.7 FM
WKGM 940 AM
WPMH 1010 AM (Inspirational)
WTJZ 1270 AM (Gospel Contemporary)
WPCE 1400 AM
WLQM 101.7 FM/1250 AM

Classical
WFOS 88.7 FM (and
Big Band)
WHRO 90.3 FM

Country
WGH 97.3 FM
WVES 99.3 FM
WCMS 100.5 FM
WLQM 101.7 FM
WCMS 1050 AM
WLQM 1250 AM

Easy Listening
WXEZ 94.1 FM

Jazz
WHOV 88.1 FM
WHRV 89.5 FM (Folk, NPR)
WNSB 91.1 FM (NSU student station)
WJCD 105.3 FM

National Public Radio
WHRV 89.5 FM
WHRO 90.3 FM

News/Talk/Sports
WVNS 670 AM

WNIS 790 AM
WTAR 790 AM
ESPN Radio 1310 (All sports)
WVAB 1550 AM (Business and news)

Oldies
WVKL 95.7 FM
WSVY 107.7 FM
WFOG 92.9 FM

Rock - Classic and Modern
WKOC 93.7 FM (Modern)
WROX 96.1 FM (Modern)
WNOR 98.7 FM/1230 AM (Classic and modern)
WAFX 106.9 FM (Classic)

Top-40
WNVZ 104.5 FM

Urban Contemporary
WMYK 92.1 FM
WOWI 102.9 FM

Television

Along with enough channels to make your VCR groan, Hampton Roads is home to the Christian Broadcast Network (CBN). CBN is a worldwide network of Christian stations, most famous for its popular 700 Club, produced at state-of-the-art facilities in Virginia Beach. If you'd like to watch a live taping of the show and take a free tour of the studios, just call (757) 424-7777 for ticket availability.

MEDIA

Television Stations

WTVZ Channel 2 (Fox)
WTKR Channel 3 (CBS)
LNC Channel 4 (Local News on Cable)
WAVY Channel 10 (NBC)
WVEC Channel 13 (ABC)
WHRO Channel 15 (PBS)
WGNT Channel 27 (UPN)

Cable TV

More than 50 channels zip right into your

home when you're cable connected, ranging from MTV to good old CNN and A&E. HBO, Showtime and Cinemax are popular premium add-ons, and pay-per-view is slowly establishing a following, especially for sports freaks who are denied access to ultimate showdowns in regular programming. Several cable companies operate in Hampton Roads. Contact the one that services your city for specific rates and installation fees.

Cox Communications, Virginia Beach, Norfolk, Portsmouth, (757) 497-2011

Insight Cablevision, Isle of Wight, Smithfield, Southampton County, (757) 572-2328

Charter Cable TV, Suffolk, (757) 539-2312

The Military

The minute you arrive in Hampton Roads you are likely to know this is a military community. But in case you're not observant, here are some clues:

If you flew in, chances are good that you spotted at least a few Navy uniforms on the plane.

If you're driving into downtown Norfolk or Portsmouth, you'll see gray-hulled Navy battleships docked at ship repair yards. A hodgepodge of shipyard cranes stand at attention, ready to lower supplies to shipyard workers.

Cross the Hampton Roads Bridge-Tunnel from Hampton to Norfolk and you can glimpse ships anchored at Norfolk Naval Base.

Look skyward when you hear air traffic in Virginia Beach and you'll probably spot a trail from an F-14 Tomcat, F-18 Hornet or other fighter plane based at Oceana Naval Air Station.

Arrive here by private boat, and you'll glide past miles of shipyards and Navy bases that hug the shoreline.

With this visual introduction, it won't take long to learn that Norfolk Naval Base is the largest Navy base in the world. Team it up with all the other branches of the Armed Forces located here—Army, Marine Corps, Air Force and Coast Guard—and you have the United States' largest concentration of military might.

Throughout the entire region there are nearly 110,000 military personnel with more than 82,000 of them attached to the Navy. There also are 40,000 civilian Department of Defense workers and more than 50,000 military retirees. Hampton Roads is home to seven of the country's largest military installations. The area's 20 shipyards rely heavily on military business and are the United States' biggest concentration of repair yards. The region is homeport to 68 percent of the 194 ships assigned to the Atlantic Fleet. It also is home base for 49 aircraft squadrons.

Norfolk is headquarters for the North Atlantic Treaty Organization command that oversees the Atlantic area. Attached to the NATO command are military officers from the 16 member nations who come here to live and work.

In 1999 the Department of Defense spent more than $8.6 billion in the region, making the military the backbone of the economy. Virginia typically ranks at least third in the country in Department of Defense spending, with the bulk of allocations going to Hampton Roads and Northern Virginia. On a per-capita basis, Virginia is frequently first in defense expenditures.

The region's history is intertwined with that of the Revolutionary War, World War I, World War II and every other major war or conflict (see the History chapter). During Operation Desert Storm in 1990 and 1991, more than 40,000 military personnel shipped out to the Persian Gulf and stifled the local economy. Before the battle groups left, ship

LOOK FOR:
• Norfolk
• Virginia Beach
• Portsmouth
• Peninsula Bases
• Help for Newcomers

repair yards, ship chandlers and other local companies worked around the clock to gear up for war. When the war heroes returned in 1991, they were greeted by thunderous celebrations not seen here since the end of World War II.

In recent years when the federal Base Realignment and Closure Commission scrutinized all aspects of the military, Hampton Roads officials united to preserve the region's military might. Hampton Roads made it through relatively unscathed and lost only a few operations. In fact, Hampton Roads was one of the few areas in the country to gain installations and personnel shifted from other bases. Oceana Naval Air Station in Virginia Beach had one of the biggest coups when it became the lone site of the Navy's F-14 Tomcat training. By 2000, the base had added more than 8,200 new personnel and their families and was being considered for even more aircraft squadrons. As a result of base closures in other areas the Coast Guard moved about 1,000 workers to commands in Portsmouth and Norfolk.

Local optimists believe the region will continue to benefit as obscure bases in other parts of the country are consolidated into larger operations, such as the ones we have here. The Hampton Roads Planning District Commission study gives some credence to that idea by showing that in 1971 less than 3.9 percent of the United States' armed forces were stationed in Hampton Roads. Today that percentage is more than 5 percent.

In 1993 the region fortified its military presence when Norfolk become the training center for all joint military operations. This makes Norfolk second in prominence only to the Pentagon.

The military gives Hampton Roads a unique flavor. Your neighbors will be people who have lived all over the world. However, they may move away within a few years to new duty stations. The comings and goings of large battle groups affect everything from rush-hour traffic to business at area malls.

If you're interested in seeing the military bases, the most accessible ones are Norfolk Naval Base, Little Creek Naval Amphibious Base, Oceana Naval Air Station and Fort Story. You can generally drive onto these bases during the daytime with nothing more than a valid drivers' license and your current vehicle registration papers. Guided tours of the Norfolk Naval Base are available daily. On weekends there are always ships open for touring there and at the Little Creek Naval Amphibious Base. Fort Story in Virginia Beach also is open to the public daily. There are two historic attractions on the Army post—the Old Cape Henry Lighthouse and First Landing Cross—as well as a public beach. Check out our Attractions chapter for specific information on visiting area military bases.

The following are the region's major military installations.

Virginia Beach

Camp Pendleton State Military Reservation
1096 S. Birdneck Rd., Virginia Beach
• (757) 441-5140

Camp Pendleton is used mainly as an air defense artillery range. It is on the south end of the Virginia Beach oceanfront and is the Virginia National Guard's summer training camp. Its 120 buildings can hold 1,700 troops.

Fleet Combat Training Center - Dam Neck
General Booth Blvd. and Dam Neck Rd., Virginia Beach
• (757) 453-6542

This 1,170-acre oceanfront base has one of the best beaches in the area. Its real purpose, however, is to train young recruits or boot camp survivors. It has a curriculum of more than 100 courses offered to about 15,000 sailors a year.

Fort Story
Shore Dr. and Atlantic Ave., Virginia Beach
• (757) 422-7755

This Virginia Beach Army base is on a beautiful site where the Chesapeake Bay meets the Atlantic Ocean at Cape Henry. It was created in 1917 and has 1,451 acres that include a great beach that's open to the public on weekends. The base is an installation of the U.S. Army Transportation Center at Fort Eustis in Newport News. Fort Story's military and civilian workers primarily maintain amphibious craft.

Little Creek Naval Amphibious Base
Shore Dr., Virginia Beach and Norfolk
• (757) 464-7923

This is the major base for the amphibious forces of the United States Atlantic Fleet, including the elite Navy SEALS. The base is in both Virginia Beach and Norfolk. See the Norfolk section above.

Oceana Naval Air Station
Oceana Blvd., Virginia Beach
• **(757) 433-3131**

This is the home to the Navy's East Coast squadrons of F-14 Tomcats and F-18 Hornets. Within the past few years the base gained 15 new squadrons and more than 8,000 personnel and their families as bases in other parts of the country closed. This nearly doubled the personnel working on the 5,000-acre base in Virginia Beach. This master jet base has a plane land or take off every two minutes, making the airspace around Oceana very busy.

Norfolk

Armed Forces Staff College
7800 Hampton Blvd., Norfolk
• **(757) 444-5431**

The college is part of the National Defense University, which started in 1946. Its Norfolk campus prepares mid-career officers for joint and combined staffs duty during quarterly sessions a year. Each session has about 200 students who come for three months of intense study.

Little Creek Naval Amphibious Base
Shore Dr., Norfolk and Virginia Beach
• **(757) 464-7923**

This is the major base for the amphibious forces of the United States Atlantic Fleet, including the elite Navy SEALS. The base, which is in both Virginia Beach and Norfolk, is home to about 30 ships. It is on 2,120 acres next to the Chesapeake Bay and is the East Coast base for the Landing Craft Air Cushion craft (LCAC).

Norfolk Naval Base
Hampton Blvd. at Taussig Blvd., Norfolk
• **(757) 444-7955**

This sprawling complex is in the Sewells Point area of Norfolk. It got its start in 1917 when the United States government purchased 474 acres of the old Jamestown Exposition site for a Navy base. Another 300 acres were soon added by filling in adjacent waterways, and the base has expanded from there to nearly 5,000 acres and more than 2,600 buildings. There are more than 65,000 military and civilian employees working on what is the largest Navy base in the world.

The base's naval station is homeport for about 100 ships. During the year there are about 5,000 arrivals and departures from the station's 15 piers. Nearby is a submarine base that has 25 subs homeported there. The Naval Air Sta-

tion is home to more than 30 aircraft squadrons. With an aircraft taking off or landing every three minutes, this is one of the world's busiest airports.

The Navy Public Works Center supports numerous shore activities while the Fleet Industrial Supply Center keeps ships throughout the world stocked with more than 600,000 different items.

Major commands on the base include the Atlantic Division of the Naval Facilities Engineering Command (LANTDIV), the Training Command of the U.S. Atlantic Fleet (TRACOM) and the Fleet Training Center (FTC).

Just down the road from the base are a Marine Base and the headquarters for the Commander-in-Chief Atlantic Fleet (CINCLANT), which commands more than 132,000 personnel. The command supplies and services more than 180 ships and 1,179 aircraft.

Adjacent to the Atlantic Fleet headquarters is that of NATO's Supreme Allied Commander Atlantic (SACLANT). This command watches over ships and personnel in 12 million square miles of Atlantic Ocean—from the North Pole to the Tropic of Cancer and from North America to Europe and Africa. Next to the Atlantic Fleet headquarters is U.S. Atlantic Command (USACOM), whose major function is to train forces from various branches of the Armed Force as joint units so they can work together during times of war.

U.S. Army Corps of Engineers
803 Front St., Norfolk
• **(757) 441-7500**

The Corps of Engineers' Norfolk District headquarters oversees several field offices around the state. The corps is responsible for dredging waterways and issuing permits for construction in wetland and coastal areas. The office has about 300 employees, most of them civilians.

Portsmouth

Coast Guard Atlantic Command
431 Crawford St., Portsmouth
• **(757) 398-6272**

This command was formed in 1996 and absorbed and expanded the duties of the Fifth Coast Guard District, which was long headquartered in the city. The command coordinates lifesaving efforts along the East Coast from Canada to the Caribbean and to the Great Lakes. The Coast Guard's Maintenance and

Logistics Command Atlantic is based in downtown Norfolk. Various Coast Guard installations employ more than 1,000 military and civilian workers in the area.

Norfolk Naval Shipyard
Effingham St., Portsmouth
• (757) 396-9550

The 230-year-old naval shipyard is the

Navy submarines and ships intrigue visitors to Norfolk Naval Base.

Photo: Courtesy of United States Navy

country's oldest. It occupies a 5-mile stretch along the Southern Branch of the Elizabeth River in Portsmouth and has more than 200 buildings. The yard has the country's oldest dry dock, which opened in 1833. This is a high-security facility employing about 7,200 workers who repair and improve everything from missile systems to berthing compartments on Navy ships.

Portsmouth Naval Hospital
620 John Paul Jones Cir., Portsmouth
• (757) 953-7986

This is the oldest Navy hospital in the United States, and it is the second-largest one in the country. It's also one of the busiest, with 1.8 million outpatient visits a year. The hospital's first patients were admitted in 1830. The 363-bed hospital has a full range of services and operates several clinics. In 1999 the hospital wrapped up a $330 million renovation and construction project that included a new 464-bed hospital.

Chesapeake

Naval Security Group Activity Northwest
1320 Northwest Blvd., Chesapeake
• (757) 421-8227

This activity operates on 4,500 acres in Chesapeake. It is a high-security intelligence with more than 1,400 employees. The base monitors top-secret communications from around the world. Both Navy and Coast Guard personnel work here.

Peninsula Bases

Across the Hampton Roads Bridge-Tunnel are several other major bases that are included in the region's military complex. They are the Yorktown Naval Weapons Station in Yorktown, Langley Air Force Base in Hampton, Fort Eustis in Newport News and Fort Monroe in Hampton. Both Fort Eustis and Fort Monroe are Army bases. Newport News also has Newport News Shipbuilding, a private company that makes nuclear-powered aircraft carriers and submarines. With nearly 20,000 employees, the shipyard is one of the state's largest private employers.

Help for Newcomers

The best source of information for new military families is the Navy Family Services Center. It has a wealth of information on the area and services for Navy and Marine Corp members and their families. The center has a Relocation Assistance Unit that dispenses welcome packets and other information. If you get here ahead of your household goods, you can rent cookware, cribs, cots and other necessities.

Navy Family Services also has tips on childcare, jobs for spouses, counseling and many other services. The center is at 8910 Hampton Boulevard in Norfolk. Call (757) 444-2102 or

(800) FSC-LINE. To reach the center's 24-hour hotline, call (757) 444-NAVY.

If you arrive here by flying into Norfolk International Airport, look for the Airport Information Booth. There usually is a Navy representative stationed there to answer questions and help you get moving in the right direction.

The Navy Welcome Center and Housing Office is in Norfolk just off Hampton Boulevard near the Norfolk Naval Base. The office is at 7924 14th Street near the Navy Lodge. It's hard to see from the main road so call (757) 444-2850 for directions.

To help get oriented read some of the free weekly or biweekly newspapers geared toward the military. They are available on base, in shopping centers and in other public areas. The *Flagship*, published by local media giant Landmark Communications, is the official Navy publication. It is published every Thursday. Other military-related papers are *Soundings*, the *Jet Observer*, the *Gator* and *The Wheel*. Each Wednesday, *The Virginian-Pilot* includes a military page as part of its "Metro" section.

Worship

There are more than 500 churches and synagogues in the Hampton Roads area—enough to fill nine pages of listings in the Yellow Pages. Worship options range from established mainline churches that are centuries old to nondenominational congregations started only a few years ago.

In recent years area churches and synagogues have seen a resurgence of young families coming back to the religion they abandoned during their teenage and college years. Many churches have been quick to respond to the needs of these younger members. Potluck family dinners, parenting classes, strong youth programs and free babysitting during

Freemason Street Baptist Church is renowned for its Gothic Revival architecture.

Photo: Courtesy of Freemason Street Baptist Church

committee meetings are just a few of the inducements that help keep the 30-something crowd hooked on religion.

Hampton Roads' religious heritage is more than 350 years old. In 1637 the Colonial government established the Elizabeth River Parish of the Anglican church. The parish's first church was built in 1641 at what is now Norfolk Naval Base and was called "Ye Chappell of Ease."

A 1637 entry in the records of Lower Norfolk County, which yielded Virginia Beach and other area cities, ordered that a "penance of the church" be carried out by a local resident. At the time church services in the county were held in private homes, but in 1639 Lynnhaven Parish church was built in what is now Virginia Beach.

Until the Revolutionary War began in 1776, the Anglican religion was the only one officially recognized in British-controlled Virginia. However, Rev. Frances Makemie introduced the Presbyterian religion to Norfolk while living here between 1684 and 1692. In Norfolk, First Presbyterian Church on Colonial Avenue traces its roots to The Church on the Elizabeth River, which was founded before 1678.

Today there is still an Anglican church in Newport News. But there are also dozens of other religions represented here—from African Methodist Episcopal Zion to United Pentecostal. Besides the basic Baptist, Catholic, Episcopal, Jewish, Lutheran, Methodist, Presbyterian and Unitarian churches, there are numerous nondenominational churches. The region also has congregations affiliated with the Friends, Greek Orthodox, Mennonite and Muslim religions. Jewish synagogues include Conservative, Messianic, Orthodox and Reformed congregations. Temple Beth El on the outskirts of Suffolk dates from the early 1900s and is noted for having a congregation composed of African-American Jews.

Congregations range greatly in size. Some have fewer than 50 members while others have rolls numbering in the thousands. Among the largest are First Baptist Church of Norfolk, Atlantic Shores Baptist Church and the Rock Church. All are in the Kempsville area of Virginia Beach and Norfolk. First Baptist has more than 6,000 members and relocated to the suburbs from downtown Norfolk in 1970. Already cramped for space, it is building a second church on 45 acres in Chesapeake. Atlantic Shores is an independent Baptist church with more than 5,000 members. Rock Church is nondenominational with more than 3,000 members. One of the fastest-growing congregations is Calvary Revival Church of Norfolk more than 3,000 members.

One major influence on the area's religion is the locally based Christian Broadcasting Network. CBN's world headquarters, located in Virginia Beach, includes studios that broadcast worldwide the 700 Club TV talk show hosted by Rev. M.G. "Pat" Robertson, CBN's founder. Robertson's home is on the Georgian-style CBN campus along with Regent University, and the Founders Inn and Conference Center. Although CBN isn't affiliated with any one religion, it has hundreds of employees and many followers in the region who lean toward fundamentalist churches. Therefore, there are many churches in the populous Kempsville area near CBN.

If you're a newcomer, finding the right church involves visiting various ones to see what suits your needs. Get recommendations from friends and neighbors and scout out your neighborhood to see what churches are nearby. Then take your time attending services and classes and getting to know the members.

You can learn more about area churches by reading The Virginian-Pilot's Saturday religion page. Besides discussing topics of current interest, it includes listings of upcoming special programs and services at area churches. For recommendations on specific churches, contact the following offices of religious organizations:

Baha'i Faith, (757) 491-9721
Catholic Diocese of Richmond, (804) 588-2941
Church of Jesus Christ of Latter Day Saints, (757) 488-2239
Episcopal Diocese of Southern Virginia, (757) 423-8287
Lutheran Council of Tidewater, (757) 623-0155
Norfolk Baptist Association, (757) 463-6525
Presbytery of Eastern Virginia, (757) 397-7063
United Jewish Federation of Tidewater, (757) 671-1600
United Methodist Church, Norfolk District, (757) 473-1592

WORSHIP

Index

INDEX